BY PENELOPE LEACH

*The First Six Months: Getting Together With Your Baby* (1987)

*Your Growing Child: From Babyhood Through Adolescence* (1984)

*Your Baby & Child: From Birth to Age Five* (1978)

*Babyhood* (1974, 1983)

# YOUR BABY & CHILD

# YOUR BABY & CHILD

## *From Birth to Age Five*

NEW EDITION, REVISED AND ENLARGED

# PENELOPE LEACH

Photographs by Camilla Jessel

*$18—*

*Alfred A. Knopf  New York 1993*

THIS IS A BORZOI BOOK PUBLISHED BY ALFRED A. KNOPF, INC.

**Library of Congress Cataloguing in Publication Data**
Leach, Penelope.
  Your baby & child from birth to age five / Penelope Leach;
  photography by Camilla Jessel.—2nd ed.
  p.  cm.
  Previously published in London in 1977 under title: Baby and child.
  Includes index.
  ISBN 0-394-57951-8
  ISBN 0-679-72425-7 (pbk.)
  1. Infants—Care.   2. Child care.   3. Child development.
  I. Leach, Penelope.   Baby and child.   II. Title.   III. Title: Your
  baby and child from birth to age five.
  RJ61.L4   1989
  649'.122—dc 19    89-1873 CIP

Hardcover Published September 20, 1979
Paperback Published November 30, 1980
New Edition, Revised and Expanded, Published September 1989
Seventh Paperback Printing, June 1993
Third Hardcover Printing, June 1993

YOUR BABY & CHILD was edited and designed by Dorling Kindersley Limited, London.
Editorial Director: Christopher Davis
Project Editor: Sybil del Strother
Art Director: Bridget Morley
Art Editors: Neville Graham, Nick Harris
Assistant Editors: Lionel Bender, Elisabeth Fenwick
Designers: Dick Boddy, Stuart Jackman, Debbie MacKinnon
Artists: David Ashby, Helen Cowcher, Claire Davies, Douglas Hall, Nick Hall,
Sarah Kensington, Andrew Macdonald, Kevin Molloy, Coral Mula, Charles Pickard,
Andrew Popkiewicz, Ann Savage, Roger Twinn, Kathy Wyatt.
Camilla Jessel wishes to thank all those who allowed their children to
be photographed and also the Save the Children Fund for permission to reprint
the photographs on pp. 269, 420, 438, and 439. Photographs on pp. 19, 197, 351,
352, 417, 437 and 440 reproduced by kind permission of Penelope Leach.

The publisher would like to thank Dr. Judith Gardner and
Dr. Alia Antoon for their special assistance in preparing the first
and the revised American editions of this book.

Set in Monophoto Apollo by Vision Typesetting, Manchester, England.
Printed and bound by R.R. Donnelley & Sons, Harrisonburg, Virginia.
Manufactured in the United States of America.

*To all the children of the Maze.
Past, present and future*

A book of this kind relies on ideas and information from so many sources that it is impossible to thank each person individually. I gratefully acknowledge my debt to research workers worldwide, to supportive colleagues and to the parents and children who have shared bits of their lives with me over the years. I am especially grateful to those who gave me the feedback on the first edition which has guided this new one.

My own education in parenthood began in my close extended family, went on through the births and upbringing of our own children and still goes on now in a household spanning three and a half generations. Special thanks to my husband, Gerald, to my mother, Elisabeth Ayrton, and my sister, Prue Hopkins. Thanks also to my younger sister, Freja Gregory, for producing Alexander. He gave Melissa and Matthew the experience of babies most adolescents lack, and has kept my hand in!

I owe a renewed debt of thanks to Camilla Jessel, whose new photographs match the magic of the old, and to Christopher Davis and his colleagues at Dorling Kindersley who have done so much to make this new edition of the book possible.

Finally I should like to thank Sybil del Strother, who worked on the first edition as an assistant editor, then used it while she had her own family, and has returned to this edition as the ideal editor.

PENELOPE LEACH

# Contents

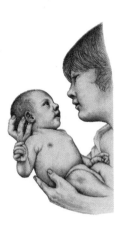

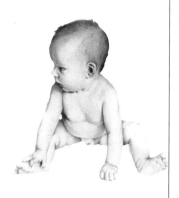

# Introduction

"Your Baby and Child" is written from your baby or child's point of view because, however fashion in child-rearing may shift and alter, that viewpoint is both the most important and the most neglected.

This book looks at what is happening within your child – let's say a boy – from the moment of birth until the time when you launch him into the wider world of school. It looks at the tasks of development with which he is involved, the kinds of thought of which he is capable and the extremes of emotion which carry him along. Babies and children live minute by minute, hour by hour and day by day, and it is those small units of time which will concern you most in your twenty-four-hour caring. But everything he does during those detailed days reflects what he is, what he has been and what he will become. The more you can understand him and recognize his present position on the developmental map that directs him towards being a person, the more interesting you will find him. The more interesting he is to you, the more attention he will get from you, and the more attention he gets, the more he will give you back.

So taking the baby's point of view does not mean neglecting yours, the parents', viewpoint. Your interests and his are identical. You are all on the same side; the side that wants to be happy, to have fun. If you make happiness for him he will make happiness for you. If he is unhappy, you will find yourselves unhappy as well, however much you want or intend to keep your feelings separate from his. I am on the same side, too. So although this is a book, it will not suggest that you do things "by the book" but rather that you do them, always, "by the baby."

Rearing a child "by the book" – by any set of rules or pre-determined ideas – can work well if the rules you choose to follow fit the baby you happen to have. But even a minor misfit between the two can cause misery. You can see it in something as simple and taken-for-granted as the "proper" way to keep a newborn clean. Bathed each day according to the rules, some babies will enjoy themselves, adding pleasure for themselves and a glow of accomplishment for you to the desired state of cleanliness. But some will loudly proclaim their intense fear of the whole business of nakedness and water. However "correctly" you bathe such a baby, the panic-stricken yells will make your hands tremble and your stomach churn. You are doing what the book says but not what your baby needs. If you listen to your baby, the central figure in what you are trying to do, you will abandon the bath and use a washcloth. Then both of you can stay happy.

*Through your love,
the newborn,
wrapped in mystery
unfolds . . .*

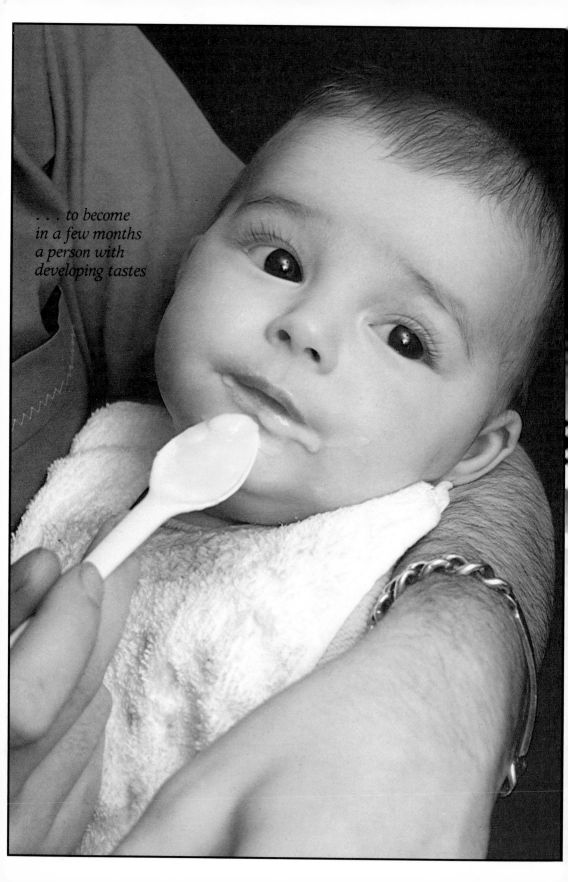

*. . . to become
in a few months
a person with
developing tastes*

*. . . and then a toddler,
venturing out from beneath
your sheltering wing*

*. . . and eventually a child who, secure in your love,
can discover the pleasures of other children.*

This kind of sensitively concentrated attention to your own real-life child who is a person-in-the-making is the essence of love. Loving a baby in this way is the best investment that there is. It pays dividends from the very beginning and it goes on paying them for all the years that there are. He is, after all, a brand new human being. You are, after all, his makers and his founders. As you watch and listen to him, think about and adjust yourselves to him, you are laying the foundations of a new member of your own race and of a friendship that can last forever. You are going to know this person better than you will ever know anybody else. Nobody else in the world including your partner, however devoted, is ever going to love you as much as your baby will in these first years if you will let him. You are into a relationship which is unique and which can therefore be uniquely rewarding.

Loving a baby or child is a circular business, a kind of feedback loop. The more you give, the more you get, and the more you get, the more you feel like giving. . . . It starts in the very first weeks. You chat to your baby as you handle him and one day you notice that he is listening. Because you can see him listening you talk to him more. Because you talk more he listens more and cries less. One magical day he connects the sound he has been hearing with your face and, miraculously, he smiles at you. Less crying and more smiling from him mean that you feel like giving him even more of the talk that so charmingly pleases him. You have created between you a beneficial circle, each giving pleasure to the other.

It goes on like that too. A crawling baby tries to follow you every time you leave the room. If his determination to come too makes you increasingly determined to leave him behind, each trivial journey to the front door or the washing line will end in miserable tears from him and claustrophobic irritation for you. But if you will accept his feelings and willingly wait for him and help him stay with you, he will pay you back in contented charm and turn the chore you had to do into a game you both enjoy. Later still your pre-school child will chatter endlessly to you. If you half-listen and half-reply the whole conversation will seem, and become, tediously meaningless for both of you. But if you *really* listen and *really* answer, he will talk more and what he says will make more sense. Because he talks and says more, you will feel increasingly inclined to listen and to answer. Communication will flourish between you. So this whole book is orientated towards you and your child as a unit of mutual pleasure giving. Fun for him is fun for you. Fun for you creates more for him and the more fun you all have the fewer will be your problems.

I have written the book in this way because experience with my own children and with the children of many families who let me share their relationships with each other as part of my research constantly reminds me that pleasure is the *point* of having children. We have them (usually) because we want them and we cope (somehow) because we love them and enjoy them loving us. That must always have been so. Why else did our distant ancestors, lacking our contraceptive choices but unburdened by our respect for human life, not expose all their babies as soon as they discovered what a nuisance they were? Yet now we assume – often wrongly – that every permanent couple will want children, but we refuse to take the business of loving them, of *minding about them*, seriously. We are in danger of taking away all the joy, leaving only guilt and hard work in its place. There are women feeling guilty about enjoying home-based life with a baby when they "ought to be doing something more worthwhile" and women who do not enjoy home-based life who feel guilty at working outside their homes "because my children need me. . . ." There are even women who, having fought to "have their cake and eat it too" feel guilty because they are managing to work and care yet feel that they do neither "properly." Fathers fare no better. For every chauvinistic male who still believes that "babies are women's work," another wants to share his child's life and upbringing and cannot do so because, whatever its professed ideals, society still puts work before people. And even when the social practicalities of life run smoothly, there are couples everywhere castigating themselves for not being "really *good* parents." Few could describe those parents but they are certainly mythical. We have edged parents into a no-win situation: an emotional trap.

Children do not need superhuman, perfect parents. They have always managed with good enough parents: the parents they happened to have.

This book is meant both to help you find the courage to guard yourself against unnecessary guilt and to find positive courses of action which will truly benefit your child where your self-reproach will not. Guilt is the most destructive of all emotions. It mourns what has been while playing no part in what may be, now or in the future. Whatever you are doing, however you are coping, if you listen to your child and to your own feelings, there will be something you can actually *do* to make things right. If your new one cries and cries whenever he is put in his crib, guilty soul-searching about your "mishandling" will get none of you anywhere. Stop. Listen to him. Consider the state that his crying has got you into. There is no joy here. Where is he happy? On your back? Then put him there. Carrying him may not suit you very well right this minute but it will suit you far better than that incessant hurting noise. Only when peace is restored to you all will you have the chance calmly to consider more permanent solutions. If your three-year-old panics when you put out her bedroom light, stop. Listen to her; listen to your own feelings. There is no luxurious rest for her or well-earned adult peace for you. Put the light on again and let both of you be content. It does not matter whether she "ought" to be scared of the dark; it only matters, to everyone present, that she *is*.

Bringing up a child in this flexible, thoughtful way takes time and effort. It involves extremely hard work as well as great rewards. But what worthwhile and creative job does not? Bringing up a child is one of the most creative, most worthwhile and most undervalued of all jobs. You are working to make a new person, helped to be as you believe a person should be.

But every creative person is also a craftsman. He learns the tools of his art just as a tradesman learns the tools of his. You can learn this craft too. Once you have accepted the principle of striving for everyone's intertwined happiness in all your dealings with your child, you will be able to see that there are easy and difficult, effective and ineffective, ways of doing almost everything that needs to be done. So a large part of this book is devoted to helping you to find the ways that work for you. Some of them came to me directly from my own mother; some of them were learned the hard way on my own children; most of them come to me from the thousands of other parents who let me watch them coping. . . . Daily life with a baby or small child is made up of hundreds of minutes of minutiae. The more smoothly those minutes roll by, the more easily his hair gets washed, his meal gets prepared or he is settled to sleep, the more time and emotional energy you will have for enjoying yourself and him. So no detail is too trivial to think about. You can make up a crib in many different ways but the way that keeps your baby warm but not too hot, snug but not restricted, comfortable in his particular sleeping position, is the way that is best for you. You can store playthings in many different ways, but the way that makes light of the cleaning up while keeping the room tidy enough for you and the toys available enough for him is the best.

I am not laying down rules because there are none. I am not telling you what to do because I can't know what *you* should do. I am passing on to you a complex and, to me, entrancing folklore of childcare which, once upon a time, you might have received through your own extended family. I hope that you enjoy it. I hope that it will help you to enjoy watching your baby turn into a person, and to enjoy looking after him and helping the process along. If it can play a part in helping you to make your child happy and therefore in making yourselves happy, help you to revel in your child as your child revels in you, it will have done its job.

The baby for whom you are reading this book may not be your first. Second babies are supposed to be "easy" but you may find the first months of this second round dauntingly difficult, especially if your first child has taken up most of your time and energy for the last couple of years. If she needed so much from you, how can this one possibly manage with less? And if everything you give him has to be taken from her, how can you bear it? You know that your toddler must be helped to accept the new baby (see p. 277) but in advance of the birth you may bitterly resent him on her behalf. She is a person whom you know and love; he is a stranger. After the birth your feelings may swing just as immoderately the other way. You know that your toddler is bound to be jealous but on your new baby's behalf you are a tigress. You hurt her feelings by being over-protective and then you hate yourself.

Caring for babies and small children demonstrates Parkinson's law in reverse: somehow, time and energy expand to meet the demands made upon them. You *will* do as well by the new baby as by the first *and* you will not seriously deprive either in the process. It is not because second babies are easier; it is because their whole situation is quite different.

First babies have the unenviable task of turning people into parents. You had to learn all the practical, craft aspects of parenting. You had to learn how to change a really dirty diaper without having to change all your clothes as well; you had to learn to manage a breast or bottle with one hand so as to hold the telephone with the other and you had to discover how wide your doorways were before you could stop being afraid of banging her head on the frames. Although the new baby may seem amazingly small and fragile for a few hours, you actually know all that. The skills stay with you, like riding a bike.

First babies take up every moment of your time because when you aren't caring for them you are waiting for them to wake up and cry. This time around you know that your baby will cry when he needs you and, far from dithering about until he does, you will be snatching every moment to spend with your toddler. Your days will be fuller and you may miss the cat-naps, but they seemed full enough last time and you certainly felt tired.

Your first baby really *needed* your undivided attention because she didn't just have to demand one-to-one attention, she had to orientate you towards childcare and teach you not to *try* to write your novel in the daytime and only to invite the kind of friend who would pretend it was the baby she had come to visit. Your second baby will find your attention fully on tap (although he may have to claim it from his sister) and he will find much more to entertain him because she is there.

You wouldn't have left her to sit in her high chair for a minute after she finished her lunch, but he stays there, absorbed in watching her fingerpaint with yogurt and then watching you clean it up. You always took her straight out for a walk after her afternoon nap but he will get taken out and about on her affairs and try out the sandbox and the big swings at a much earlier age. Staying at home for an afternoon (because she has a cold) may be a change for him rather than an unfair deprivation. As for her, your beloved first-born: it may be tough on her for a while, but she has had all your attention to compensate her for being the one you learned on and she may well enjoy having you house-bound by a new baby even before she can begin to enjoy him. And one day, with any luck, she'll do that too.

Meeting the needs of twin (or more) babies at the same time is far more difficult to begin with than meeting the needs of two of different ages, though it may be easier in a few months' time. The basic problem is the sheer incompetence of human newborns — especially their inability to support their own heads or turn their bodies to reach a nipple. Picking a new baby up, carrying him so that he feels secure and holding him so that he can suck and breathe at the same time takes two hands. If you have two babies at the same time you really need an extra pair of arms to go with them. A second parent is ideal but if that is impossible do try to think of somebody else. She does not have to be deeply involved or take terrifying responsibility — it's only *arms* you are short of — but she does need to be with you, whenever nobody else is, for at least the first few weeks.

Twin babies share a womb, parents, most of each other's company and almost all the major landmarks of childhood from birthdays to starting school. Neither they nor anybody else is going to forget their twinness and their difference from one-at-a-time children. Try to make sure that their individuality does not get lost in their duality. You will find it easier to bias your own behavior toward treating them as two singles rather than a pair if you remember that being fair does not mean treating them both alike but taking equal trouble to meet the needs of each. You may have difficulty with other people, though.

To anyone but the parents a baby is a baby is a baby. If you had had one, your family and friends would not have needed to study him closely in order to recognize him as the Andrew of your birth announcement. Try to help them make the effort involved in knowing which is Andrew and which is Angus, otherwise people will lazily refer to them as "the twins," and when you come into the room with a single bundle they will not know who they are greeting. Non-identical twins may or may not look alike. They are just brothers or sisters or one of each, after all. Even identical twins probably will not look alike in their earliest months because of differences in birthweight and birth experience. The more you can force people to realize that they are not the same, the more readily they will see them as separate children and the easier it will be for you to bring them up to know themselves as unique individuals.

The book is organized by approximate age-stages in a child's life, starting with what birth may mean to a baby and ending at around the fifth birthday. Although the timing of developments varies from child to child, their sequence is the same for all human beings. So whether or not your child is the age I suggest for the Older Baby or the Pre-School Child, you will be ready for each new section when your child has completed most of the developments of the one before.

This is a big book. But children, being people, are a big subject. In the main text I hope that you will find your child and yourself in every usual circumstance. Less usual ones, like illnesses and accidents, have their own A–Z at the back of the book, where there is also a section of extra ideas for play. You will find references in the text to these sections written like this: Ref/FEVER. There is a separate index, so whenever you want information on a particular topic, look it up by name and hope that the name you think of is one of the names for that topic that occurred to me too!

The book is addressed directly to "you." I mean that word to apply to both parents when both are involved or to either one when he or she must cope alone. But I mean it also to apply to anyone who cares, deeply and continuously, over a long period, for any small new person. "You" may be a grandparent or a caregiver. Babies don't care about blood relationships, they only care about caring.

"You" is a bisexual word, so carers can be people irrespective of sex. Not so babies. Short of dehumanizing both sexes as "it," English insists that an individual child is either male or female. We cannot escape the problem with apparently neutral words like "baby" because as soon as possessive pronouns are needed, sentences like "the baby needs his/her bottle . . ." begin to litter the page. So even though this book is about the development, handling, feelings, thoughts and activities of all normal babies, the narrative baby has to be either "he" or "she." I have chosen to use "he" because even today it is easier for most parents to accept that pronoun as applying to either sex. Where gender specifically affects a child's nature or needs, you will find a boy or a girl specified. Where the text does not separate the sexes out, what is said applies equally to both: to your child, from the moment of birth to the comparative independence of school.

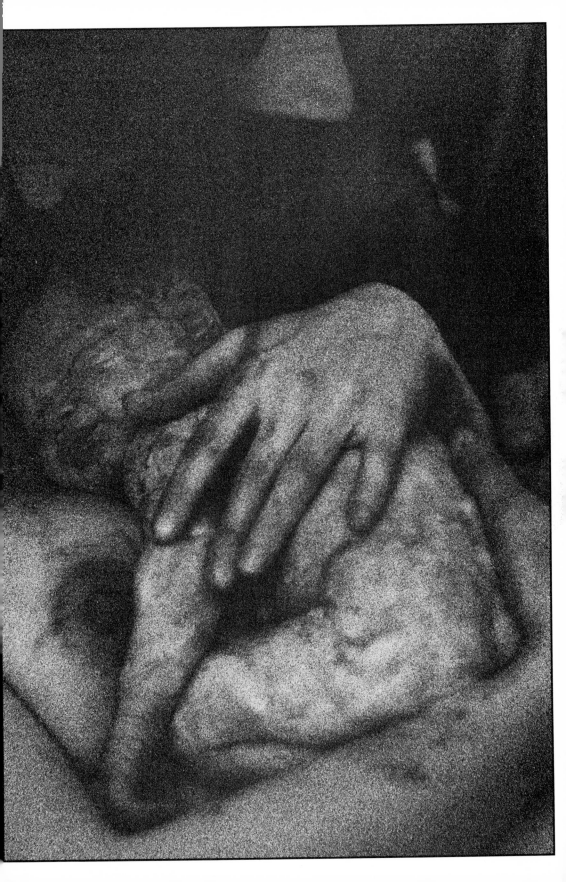

# Birth

It takes three to make a birthday. Most mothers and a still increasing number of fathers remember the birth of their first child as the most important experience of their lives. But the person for whom this day is truly vital is neither of you two but the third person: the baby.

The baby is closely confined in a warm dark prison of exquisite, neutral comfort. Everything around him is of the same texture and at the same temperature as himself. Greasy vernix coats his skin; amniotic fluid fills the spaces between his body and the walls of the womb; there is no friction, no sensation, no change. His eyes are ready but there is nothing for him to see. He has no need to breathe or to digest food, so he feels no sensations from within himself. He can sense sound and movement, but muffled by his insulated liquid environment. He is sealed off from the world, untouched and untouchable.

But the baby is outgrowing his seed-bed. Soon your womb which has nurtured him must reject him. Soon his body must start functioning for itself while his dormant senses receive the full shock of stimulation from the outside world. He must prepare for birth.

His exit from your womb will be down a tight elastic passageway formed by the opened cervix and the vagina. The space available is limited by the space between your pelvic bones. There is enough room but there is none to spare. Just as a stake goes more easily into earth if its leading end is sharpened, so the baby will get through most easily if he enters the passageway with his smallest part opening the way. His head has a smaller diameter than his hip girdle so, in a normal birth, he will settle in a head down position. To help him further if the way is very tight, his skull has membrane-covered spaces called fontanelles between the bones. Under heavy pressure these spaces allow his head to compress a little, narrowing itself still further. The compression works best if the baby's head enters the birth canal facing towards your backbone. So his final position in readiness for birth will usually be head down and back to front.

As the time for birth approaches and his position is settled, baby and womb drop down together in your abdomen so that his head is engaged in the basin-shaped bones of your pelvis, through the still closed cervix. Now he is held still and quiet. His movements will no longer kick the bar of soap off your belly in the bath. You can breathe more easily too, with a little more room between the top of your loaded womb and your diaphragm.

When labor begins, even the best prepared parents tend to be taken by surprise. It is not that the beginning of the process is difficult to recognize; it is that even the most careful words cannot describe the overwhelmingly physical nature of the birth process nor prepare you for the extraordinary feeling of having your body taken over by forces which are outside your conscious control. We are brought up to control and manage our bodies' functions, waiting for lavatories and privacy, holding back coughs and yawns, fending off sleep in public. . . . But childbirth cannot be controlled in this sense. Once labor begins, your baby is going to get himself born with or without your conscious cooperation. The contractions will go on at their appointed rate and strength until the birth canal is fully open. The muscles of your womb will push the baby down that canal and go on pushing until he emerges. You cannot call a time-out, decide to make a phone call or wait for the doctor, change your mind about having the baby at all. . . . There is no way out of the experience except through it, because it is not really your experience at all but the baby's. Your body is the child's instrument of birth.

You cannot see your baby turned, forced and molded by the muscular contractions which you feel as labor pains. You cannot watch his slow progress down the birth canal, forced by your body's convulsive and irresistible pushing. You cannot know whether he feels pain and fear. But that baby is the point of the whole labor process. It is his safe arrival with which your body is concerned. He, not you, is the star of the show. It may help you as you labor if you can think of him while your body strives to produce him. It will certainly help him if you can consider his likely feelings from the moment that he emerges.

Giving birth is an experience which often threatens to be overwhelming. Your body has a demanding job to do and it will do it, but your mind and your emotions can protest violently at being taken over. If they do, you will tense up to each contraction instead of softening to it; you will fight your body's control instead of going along with it. The results can be painful and distressing. Prenatal training helps enormously by taking the mystery out of labor and teaching you how to help it along rather than hampering it. But an involved partner, who has trained with you and will see you right through the birth, makes all the difference. Although he is totally involved emotionally, he is unaffected physically. With him to watch over you, abandoning your normal self to the birth process feels safer. He has the same knowledge that you have been given so, if the physical sensations should threaten to overwhelm you, he can remind you to do as you have been taught. If accumulated minor discomforts, like backache and a dry mouth, should bother you, he has the time to offer the backrub or the wet sponge that will relieve them. As labor progresses, drawing you deeper and deeper into the vortex of birth, he may become the most important person in the room to you. Nurses and doctors come and go doing whatever is physically necessary, but he is there for you to hold on to emotionally. When the world becomes a blur of strange effort, his is the face you can still see clearly; his words are the ones you can still understand. By the time the baby emerges, even the most reluctantly participant father will be sure of his vital role in the whole affair. Yours will be a truly mutual baby from the very beginning.

Although more and more couples are taking mutual involvement for granted, and although fathers are now being welcomed by almost all hospitals, there will always be some fathers *and* mothers who do not want it that way. A father who cannot face witnessing a difficult birth or whose partner prefers to manage alone can ensure that she feels adequately supported if he can only bring himself to talk with her about the experience afterwards.

You, the new mother, have been through a tremendous experience; a major physical and emotional crisis. You will almost certainly find that you need to re-live it; to talk about it detail by detail, work it out, understand it, think about your feelings. There may be practical details which confuse you and which need sorting through before you can stop thinking about them: How did it manage to get dark without you noticing? How long was it between your going into the delivery room and the baby's arrival? Emotional details may feel important too: Did the nurses think you had done well? Did they understand why you were upset about this, that or the other? Is everyone proud of you and can you feel proud of yourself? Until the birth experience has been talked through, it will not slip comfortably away to the back of your mind, leaving you free to give yourself wholeheartedly to mothering the baby you have produced. It is the women who can find no one to talk to or who are too shaken by the birth experience to make themselves talk who tend to find themselves brooding over it. The birth becomes something they do not want to think about but cannot clear from their thoughts. Clearing your mind for mothering is vital because your baby needs you. His experience has been far more shattering than yours. Because we cannot know exactly what he feels during birth we tend to behave as if he felt nothing. We concentrate on his safety, leaving consideration of his comfort or happiness for later. But with highly developed birth technologies, there is no reason why a baby should not be safe *and* comfortable. We must learn to look at his birth with his likely feelings in mind.

Brutally forced through a tight passage from a soft, quiet, warm, dark haven into a world of light and noise and texture, every bit of the baby's nervous system reacts with shock. It is the shock of birth that stimulates him to make the fearful effort to breathe for himself. The placenta, which fed his circulation oxygen from your bloodstream, has finished its work, but the blood still pulsing in the umbilical cord buys him a little time. He must breathe, but if he can make this vital transition for himself we can avoid the old brutalities of slapped bottoms: we can wait on him gently and perhaps discover the beauty of a first breath without crying.

If he is to breathe easily, his nose and mouth must be clear of amniotic fluid and mucus. But if he can clear them himself, we need not torment him with tubes. We are so used to routine suction for new babies that we still sometimes forget how those tubes must feel to him.

Safely breathing, the baby needs time to rest and to discover that even though the womb has ejected him, there is still comfort in his world. Your belly, soft and slack now, forms an ideal cradle. On it, he can be almost as comfortable as he was in it. There he can rest.

But he cannot rest unless his surroundings are toned down. The staff needed those glaring lights for a safe delivery, but once the baby is safely delivered they can be turned down lest they hurt his eyes. He has never seen light before.

The birth attendants needed to talk and to move around during the delivery. But there is nothing now that cannot wait. The room is hushed lest sudden noises frighten him. All sounds have been muffled until now.

If all is dim and quiet, warm and peaceful, the baby will relax after his traumatic journey. His breathing will steady. His crumpled face will smooth itself out and his eyes will open. His head will lift a little and his limbs will move against your skin. Put very gently to your bare breast, he may suck, discover a new form of human togetherness and feel a little less separated. These are his first contacts with his new world: let him make them without distress. These are his first moments of life; let him have them in peace.

The baby must be weighed. But why must he be weighed now? His weight will not change in half an hour. He must be washed. But why now? The vernix that has protected his skin for months is not harming it just because he has been born. He must be dressed. But why now? Your warmth, a soft wrapping and the heat of the delivery room are all he needs. He must have drops in his eyes, a dressing on the cord stump, a physical examination, a crib to lie in. You must be washed and changed, moved to a bed, given a drink, settled to sleep. All these things must indeed be done, but none of them need be done right now. The baby is born. He is living independently. The time for high-powered technology and efficient nursing is over. It is time for a pause of warm and peaceful intimacy among the three of you.

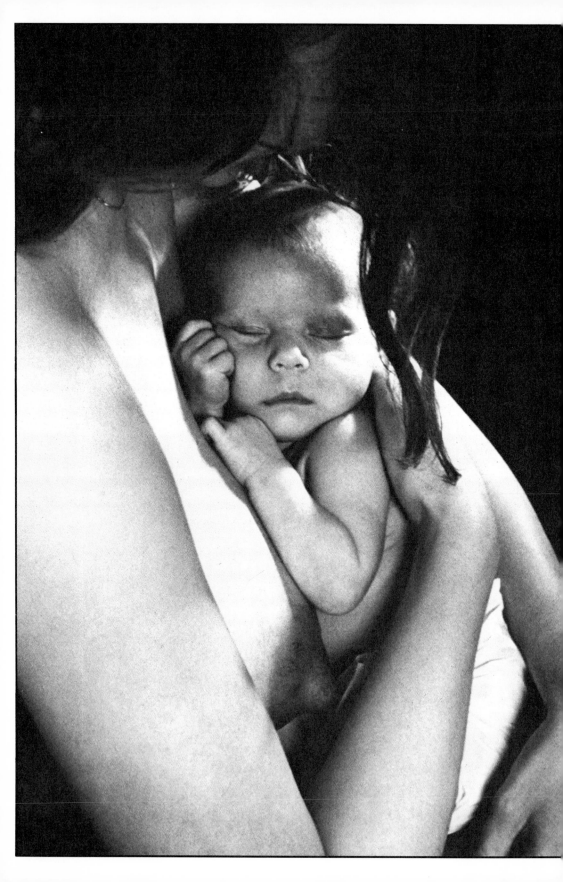

# THE NEWBORN

## *The first days of life*

Birth feels like the climax to long months of waiting, but it is not really a climax at all. You were not waiting to give birth, you were waiting to have a baby. Your labor has produced that baby and there is no rest between the amazing business of becoming parents and the job of being them. Don't expect too much of yourselves during these first, peculiar days. All three of you have a tremendous amount of adapting to do. The feelings and behavior of today have very little to do with next month because by then all three of you will have changed. Your baby will have settled into life outside the womb, and you will both have settled into parenthood.

Most couples remember this as an intensely emotional and confusing time. Everything is felt too much: stitches and pleasure, responsibility and pride, selfishness and selflessness. You are still desperately tired. Your hormone balance is disturbed, your milk is not fully in, your cervix not yet closed, your body striving for equilibrium. Your partner has no direct physical effects but he has an emotional tightrope to walk. He has to concede to you the prime role as the one who labored yet he has to make you feel that this is the child of you both, that he too is deeply involved. If he pays too much attention to the baby, he risks making you feel that you are no longer his central person. If he concentrates on you he risks the charge that he does not care for his newborn. Many men remark wryly that during these first days after birth there is no way that they can get it right.

As for the baby: what he has to cope with is without parallel in human experience. While he was inside you, your body took care of his. It provided his food and his oxygen, took away his waste products, kept him warmly cushioned and protected, held the world at bay. Now that he is separated from you, his body must take care of itself. He must suck and swallow food and water, digest it and excrete its wastes. He must use energy from that food to keep his body functions running, to keep himself warm and to go on growing. He must breathe to get oxygen and keep his air passages clear with coughs and sneezes. While accepting all these new duties he must also cope with a positive bombardment of stimuli as the world rushes in on him. Suddenly there is air on his skin, there is warmth and coolness, there are textures, movements and restrictions. There is light and darkness and there are things to see, coming into focus and blurring out again. There is hunger and emptiness, sucking, fullness and burping. There are sounds and smells and tastes. Everything is new. Everything is different. All is bewilderment.

Your newborn baby's behavior is a series of reactions to what he perceives as random stimuli. He has instincts and reflexes and working senses but he has no knowledge and no experience. He does not know that he is himself, that the object he sees moving in front of his face is his own hand or that it remains part of him when it has vanished to lie beside him on the blanket. He does not know that you are people either. He is programmed to pay attention to you, to look at your faces and listen to your voices. He is programmed to suck when you offer him a nipple. He is programmed for survival but he knows nothing.

While he remains a newborn, rather than a baby who has settled into life outside the womb, his behavior will be random and unpredictable. He may cry for food every half hour for six hours and then sleep without any for another six hours. This morning's "hunger" does not predict this afternoon's because his hunger has no pattern or shape as yet. His digestion has not settled; hunger signals have not taken on a clear and recognizable form for him. He simply reacts to momentary feelings. His sleep is similarly formless; ten-minute snatches through the night and a five-hour stretch in the day tell you nothing about how he will sleep tomorrow. He may cry, too, for no reason that you can discover and stop as suddenly and inexplicably as he began. His crying has few definite patterns of cause and effect because, apart from physical pain, he has not yet discovered how to differentiate between pleasure and displeasure.

When you start looking after this small, new human being, you lack that first essential for watchful care: baselines. The baby is brand new. However much you know about babies in general, neither you nor anyone else knows anything about this one in particular. You do not know how he looks and behaves when he is well and happy so it is difficult for you to know when he is ill or miserable. You do not know how much he "usually" cries because he has not been around for long enough for anything to be usual. So there is no easy way of knowing whether this crying suggests that anything is amiss. You do not know how much he usually eats or sleeps so you cannot judge whether today's feeding or sleeping is adequate or excessive. Yet his wellbeing is in your hands. Even without baselines of usual behavior against which to judge, you have to make continual assessments and

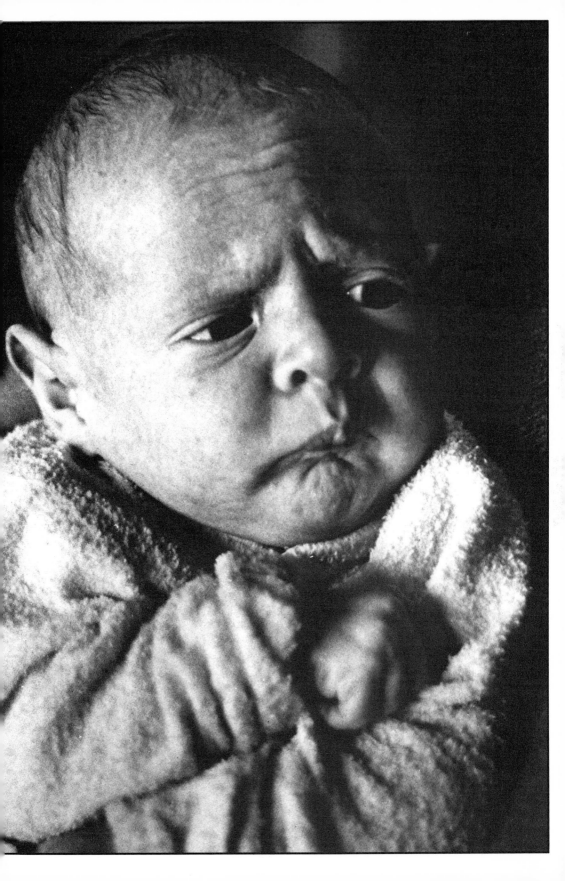

adjustments while you learn your baby and he learns life. There is a lot of learning for all of you. It may take only a week after his birth for you to feel secure in your caring and for him to feel secure in his world. But it may take a month. It has taken some eighty pages of this book to lay down the basic essentials and they are the hardest working pages the book contains. Once you and he have learned them, established your baselines, got to know each other, everything will suddenly seem much easier and smoother for all of you. You will be dealing with a baby person rather than a newborn. The next section and all the sections after that are incomparably easier.

During these first days, don't torment yourselves if you do not feel anything for the baby that you can recognize as love. When parents first meet a baby, seconds after birth, recognition can reverberate between them so that all the waiting and the wanting culminate not just in *a* baby but in *this* baby, who seems to come out of the mother's womb and into her arms and heart in a single move. People call this "bonding" and it has been so idealized in recent years that parents to whom it does not happen sometimes fear a basic lack in their relationship with their babies from the very beginning. Remember that "bonding" has not been emphasized as an exhortation to *parents* but to delivery-room staff, who should not get between the post-natal threesome for a bustle of routine care until there have been time and opportunity for them all to greet each other. That opportunity is important but instant bonding is not. If it did not happen to you remember that previous generations of women seldom held their new babies until they had been washed and weighed and dressed, and that many mothers were anesthetized at the time of delivery so that their first meeting with their babies had to wait until they were awake and aware. There was no failure of love between these women and their babies, and it is absurd to think that your relationship with your baby might falter or fail because no lightning-bolt bonded you together on the delivery table.

Love will come but it may take time. However you define the word it must have something to do with interaction between people who know each other, who like what they know and want to know more. If there is love, there must be a sharing, a giving and taking of affection and support. A brand new baby is neither lovable nor loving. He is not truly lovable because he has not yet got himself into predictable, knowable shape nor had time to produce the characteristics which will make it clear for evermore that he is a unique person. You may love him on sight because he is your baby; the fulfilment, perhaps, of a plan or a dream; but you cannot instantly love him as one person loves another; he is not fully a person until he is settled. He is not loving because he does not yet know of his own existence, let alone yours. He will learn to love you with a determined and unshakeable passion unequalled in human relationships. But it will take time.

The mixed feelings you have toward your baby now are neither a guide for the present nor a warning for the future. The overwhelming tenderness that sweeps over you as you cradle his heavy, downy head can give way in a moment to furious irritation at his crying. Your pride in being a parent can be swamped in claustrophobia as you realize that you are committed to him forever and will never again be free to be an entirely separate individual person.

If you can let it, your body will start loving the baby for you even before he is properly a person. Whatever your mind and the deeply entrenched habits of your previous life may be telling you, your body is ready and waiting for him. Your skin thrills to his. His small frame fits perfectly against your belly, breast and shoulder. That hard, hot head is there for your cheek to rub and your thumb molds itself to the startling grip of those small, bony fingers.

Reveling in the baby physically speeds up the time when he can join in this essential business of loving. He will not lie passively, leaving it to you to make all the advances. If you will have him close, he will make advances to you, too. He has a built-in interest in you because you are essential to his survival. He will see to it that love comes.

Your body's commands and your baby's physical reactions are your best guide to handling him in these very first days. Child-rearing plans and policies are no use to you yet. Plans and policies can only be judged by the consistent responses they evoke and nothing you can work out will get consistency from an unsettled newborn.

The baby needs to be handled so that his new life seems as little different as possible from life in your womb. His needs are simple, repetitive and immediate. He needs food and water in the combined form of milk; he needs warmth and comfort from cuddling arms and soft wrappings in a small, safe bed; he needs just enough cleanliness to keep his skin from getting sore and he needs protection. That is all he needs. The baths and changing mats, powders and lotions, brushes and bootees that tempt you in every baby shop will be fun for you to buy and nice for him later. But for now he is a bundle and he should be a bundle. Wrap him warmly, hold him closely, handle him slowly, feed him when he is hungry, talk to him when he looks at you, wash him when he is dirty and give him peaceful time to come to terms with life. Unless he is actually ill and under medical care, there is absolutely nothing which it is your duty to do to him if it makes him jump or cry. Peaceful contentment means that you have got it right. Distress means that you have got it wrong. Let his reactions guide you.

If you can manage this, the baby will gradually come to realize what he needs and to realize that he gets what he needs when he needs it. By the time he is a settled, knowable, lovable small person, he will know the world to be a good place to be alive in. And that, after all, is the best start you can possibly give him.

# Birthweight

After the sex, your baby's weight is usually the first thing you are told about him or her. Babies come in a large variety of shapes and sizes, so why does it matter to everybody exactly what this one weighs? Because the birthweight, whatever it may be, is your baby's own personal starting point for growth.

*Average babies*  The average birthweight for babies is just over 7lbs (3.2kg). But that average conceals many variations. Boys are usually a little heavier than girls; first babies are usually rather lighter than their younger brothers and sisters, while on the whole large parents have large babies and small parents have smaller ones. So your baby can be exactly the right size for him without being average.

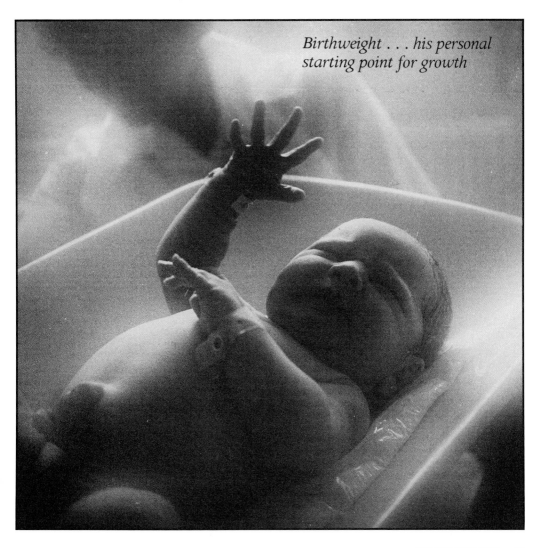

*Birthweight . . . his personal starting point for growth*

*Heavy babies*     If you give birth to a 10lb (4.5kg) baby, you will be rightly proud of yourself for having delivered him. And he will probably look more beautiful and seem more mature than most of the other newborn babies in the nursery as he will be well covered with fat. Don't be too disconcerted, though, if the hospital staff keep a special eye on him for a few days. A very few exceptionally heavy babies are the result of the mother having diabetes or pre-diabetes. It is important for the staff to be sure that this particular one is just a well-grown baby whom nature meant to be large, rather than a baby whose metabolism has been disturbed in the womb and whose exceptional weight comes from excess water which has been retained in his body after birth.

*Lighter babies*     If your baby is below average birthweight but weighs more than $5\frac{1}{2}$lbs (2.5kg), he will be treated like an average birthweight baby except that he will probably be encouraged to feed more often. The chances are that you are smaller than average too and that this is a healthy baby who is meant to be small.

    If the baby weighs $5-5\frac{1}{2}$lbs (2.2–2.5 kg), he well probably be put in an isolette, however healthy and lively he seems to be. This is because some babies who are born weighing less than $5-5\frac{1}{2}$lbs (2.2–2.5kg) have trouble with breathing, with keeping warm and with sucking. So to play safe, *all* babies who are under this weight are started off with special care. Look upon it as a precaution only. Don't jump to the conclusion that there is something wrong with him. If there are no problems, he will probably be allowed to come out of the isolette and be returned to a crib by your bed within a few hours.

    Small babies used to be kept in the hospital until they had regained their birthweights or until they had tipped the scales at a particular weight. Nowadays the decision to let you take your baby home is more likely to be based on how he is managing his new way of life and, above all, on how quickly he settles to feeding.

    If your baby is born weighing less than 5lbs (2.2kg) then he probably is lighter than nature meant him to be. The lighter he is the more special the care he will need. The particular kind of care will depend partly on whether he is light because he is premature or because he is small-for-dates.

*Premature babies*     Most very small babies are small for the simple reason that they have been born prematurely – before the completion of the usual 40 weeks in the womb. Missing time in the womb means that the baby has missed out on some growing time. It also means that he has missed out on some getting-ready-for-independent-life time. The more weeks inside the womb he has missed, the more difficulties he is likely to face. A baby born after 36–38 weeks gestation will probably only need to have things made very easy for him, by being kept in an isolette with extra warmth, extra oxygen and tiny feeds of a very easily digested mixture at frequent intervals. A "younger" baby may need more help than that. He may need to have some of the responsibilities of independent life taken right off him for a while. He may be fed, for example, by a tube passed down his nose into his stomach because he is not yet able to suck or swallow for himself.

*Small-for-dates babies* Small-for-dates or dismature babies have not grown as much as they are expected to during their time in the womb. They may have spent the full 40 weeks in the womb but still be very small at birth. Or they may have been born prematurely but be even smaller at birth than they ought to be after that period of gestation.

The immediate treatment given to a small-for-dates baby will be similar to that given to a premature one, but the hospital staff will be anxious to find out just how long he did spend growing in the womb and therefore just how small-for-dates he really is. They will probably question you closely about the exact dates of your last menstrual period before the pregnancy began and check back on any ultrasound scans. After all, you might have made a mistake. If your baby was born weighing 4lbs (1.8kg) after 40 weeks in the womb, then he really is small-for-dates, but if your calculations were one cycle wrong, and the baby has actually only been growing for 36 weeks, he is premature.

A baby who really is small-for-dates has usually been short of nourishment in the womb. The placenta may have been inadequate or you may have had problems with your health which prevented the baby from getting all he needed for optimal growth. The more the hospital staff can discover about the reasons for your baby's small size, the more they can do to help him catch himself up.

*Isolettes* An isolette or incubator is the nearest equivalent we have to an artificial womb. The baby has emerged from inside you so he can no longer rely on your body to operate his. The isolette acts as a half-way house between total physical dependence and being a completely independent physical entity. If he is managing reasonably well immediately after delivery, it may be used only to give him steady warmth, peaceful isolation, controled humidity and perhaps a little extra oxygen. If he is having problems, it can be used to help him with the functioning of almost all his body systems. Whether it is used to give your baby a great deal of help or only a little, the isolette is a very safe place for him to be. As long as he remains in it, he will be under constant supervision by specially trained nursing staff. Specialist doctors will keep a careful eye on his progress, while the highly sophisticated machinery of the isolette itself will record any changes in his condition, and set off warning signals whenever he needs attention.

But, even though you know that an isolette is the best place for your new baby just now, having him in there will probably make you utterly desolate. After that long pregnancy and those hours of labor there is no baby to hold. Instead of being in your arms or by your bed the baby lies looking strange and other-worldly in a machine that would look at home in a space laboratory.

Your whole being is keyed up for physical contact with the new baby, but the process which started with conception, ran through pregnancy and birth and should have culminated in a baby to hold, has been interrupted. Your body yearns for the baby. A week to wait may not seem long to others but seems like eternity to you as you lean, weeping, against the isolette. It may help you if you can remember that hormonal upheaval is making you feel every-thing extra acutely. Your body's turmoil will settle over the next day or two and you will feel more able to face what must be faced.

*Accept the isolette as your friend because your baby needs it. This machine-womb is not as good as yours, but it is safer for him than the outside world while he catches himself up.*

The period while your baby is in an isolette is going to be a difficult one for you, but there is quite a lot that you can do to make it easier:

**Talk to the nurse or the pediatrician.** Tell them that you want to know everything there is to know about your baby's condition. Once you understand exactly what problems he is having and the purpose of any tubes or gadgets which are attached to him, he will stop seeming like the hospital's baby and start seeming more like yours to take care of.

**Make it clear that you want to be with the baby** as much as possible. If the isolette is in the nursery on your maternity floor, you will probably be allowed to go in whenever you like. If the isolette is in a "special care" unit separate from the maternity floor but in the same hospital, the nurse will arrange a wheelchair for you until you are fit to walk.

If your baby has had to be transferred to another hospital because the one you are in does not have the facilities he needs, it may be possible for you to go too. If not, you should still be allowed to visit as soon as you are well enough to travel.

**Explain that you want to help.** Unless your baby is very fragile indeed and being stimulated as little as possible, you will be encouraged to touch him through the glove-holes of the isolette. Soon you will be able to help with his physical care, perhaps by changing his diaper inside the isolette. If he is in reasonably good shape you may even be allowed to take him out and hold him for a minute or two.

Perhaps the most important thing you can do to help the baby, yourself and the hospital is to get your breast milk supply going. Very small babies really need to have breast milk as soon as they are ready for any milk at all. Often the milk is given by tube or dropper until the baby is strong enough to suck for himself. Even if your baby is not ready for milk yet, he will need to be breast-fed when he is stronger. You can get the supply established while you are waiting for him.

The hospital staff will show you how to use a breast pump to express your milk. This is much quicker and easier than expressing by hand (see p. 58). If your milk is not needed for your own baby immediately, the staff will probably ask if they may have it for the "milk bank" which is kept for premature or sick babies.

If you have to go home leaving the baby still in special care, you may be able to spend your days in the hospital and express your milk for him there. Even if you cannot be at the hospital *every* day, it will still be worthwhile expressing your milk. Only by continuing to empty your breasts can you be sure of having a good supply for him when he joins you at home (see p. 53).

**Look on this time as an extra bit of pregnancy.** Once you are over the shock and disappointment of not having your baby with you immediately, you may be able to look on the waiting-time as a sort of hiatus between the birth and starting to be a mother.

Although his birthday is the day he was born, just as it is for any other child, try to get used to the idea that his real starting point will be the day the hospital declares him large and fit enough to come home. If he was born after only 34 weeks inside you and you compare him to full-term babies who were born in the same week, he will always seem to be behind them in development. He has a lot of catching up to do.

*The "blues"* "Baby blues" or "fourth-day blues" are not an inevitable part of the post-natal days, but they are very common. If your baby has to be in an isolette away from you, or has even the mildest problem – such as jaundice (Ref/JAUNDICE) – that will probably be the focus for your misery.

But even if you had an easy delivery, have a beautiful, healthy baby and cannot think of any reason for being miserable, you can suddenly find yourself in floods of tears. Don't let those tears frighten you. And don't decide that *because* you are crying you *must* be unhappy. Tears of this sort spring partly from physical and emotional anti-climax after the birth, and from hormonal chaos as your body struggles to adapt to not being pregnant any more and to making milk. If you can calmly let them flow – even weep luxuriously into your partner's neck – they will probably stop as suddenly as they began.

*Going home*    Going home may be more of an effort and less of a thrill than you expected. However eager you were to leave the hospital it can seem like a haven of safety once you are out on your own. Your body is tired after labor and the stress of pregnancy. Your hormones are working overtime. With all that physical upheaval, you are also up against the emotional turmoil of introducing a new person into your life and your family. Depression, with its dragging tiredness and pointless tears, may take the shine off these first days at home.

But however peculiar you feel now, your new self, new family and new responsibilities will seem quite ordinary and easy in a few weeks. Try to be patient and gentle with yourself. Lean, heavily, on your partner or anyone else who offers support. Let them look after you while you look after the baby. In the meantime don't try to accomplish anything practical. This is a time for people and their feelings. Talk out your own and your partner's; play out your toddler's, and keep that baby close.

*Post-natal*    Post-natal depression is not at all the same as the temporary mood-
*depression*    swings of the first days after birth. It can overwhelm you at any stage in your baby's first months and last for a long time. Depression is a real illness. Any major upheaval can touch it off: a bereavement or divorce, moving or a job change. In the end people almost always recover on their own. But when the upheaval is a birth, there's a baby to think about. Your baby needs your loving care and if you're depressed you cannot give it.

Depression drains everything of joy and color, saps your self-confidence and energy and turns you in upon yourself. Even if you can find the drive to meet your baby's physical needs, depression will deny you your pleasure in him and therefore deprive him of being your joy as well as your responsibility. So, if you should suffer from post-natal depression, you will need medical, practical and emotional help, and quickly.

The question is: will you get it? If you are feeling utterly worthless, you probably will not feel worthy of your doctor's time. If putting on your clothes takes superhuman effort, telling somebody how you are feeling will probably be beyond you. Partners, grandmothers and friends should all be alert to the possibility of post-natal depression so that the second time they find themselves saying "do pull yourself together" they bite it back and suggest help instead. And if a mother cannot find the energy to seek help for herself, somebody must do it for her. Community health services and family doctors all respond sympathetically.

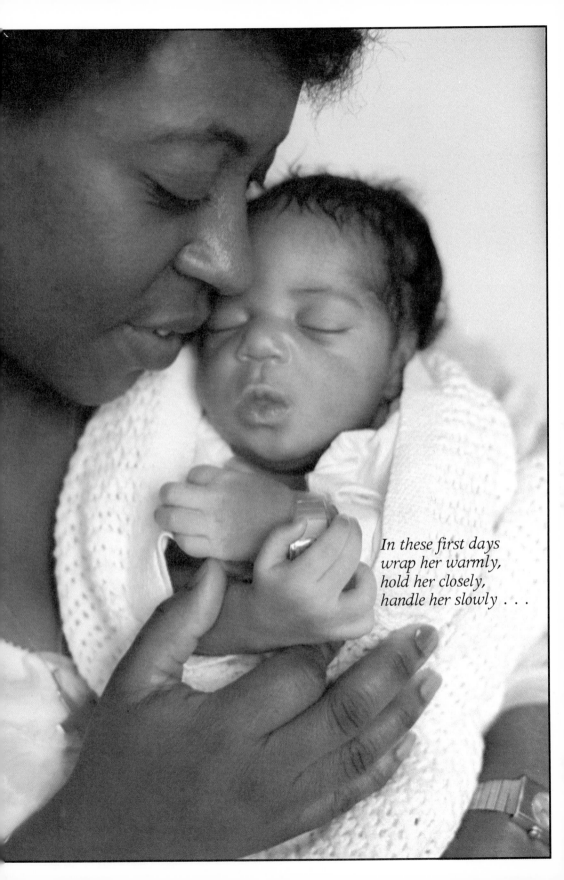

*In these first days
wrap her warmly,
hold her closely,
handle her slowly . . .*

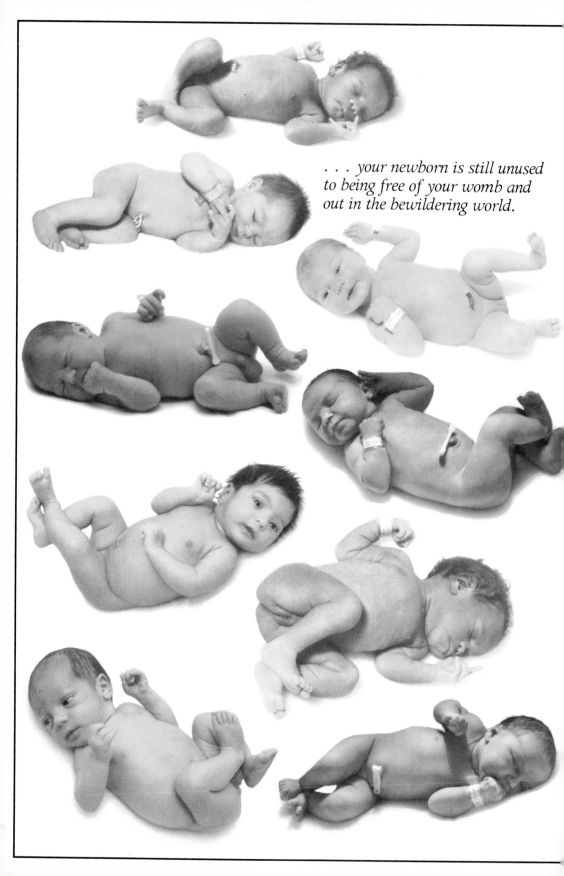

*. . . your newborn is still unused to being free of your womb and out in the bewildering world.*

# Newborn peculiarities

A newborn baby's physiology is not the same as that of an older baby, a child or an adult. It takes time for this new body to settle into life outside the womb and to become fully efficient. During this settling period the baby may display all kinds of color changes, spots, blotches, swellings and secretions. Many of them look very peculiar. Most of them would indeed be peculiar if they occurred in an older person, but are normal, or at least insignificant, when they occur in the first two weeks of life. Hospital staff take these newborn peculiarities for granted and, because they know that they are nothing to worry about, often forget to warn parents about them. The result can be unnecessary panic just when you need all the peace you can get.

The following list describes some of the commonest of these phenomena and tells you why they happen and what they mean. If you need direct reassurance or if you are not sure that what you see matches what is described on the list, consult your doctor. Above all, do remember that these things are normal or unimportant only in a *newborn* baby. If you notice one of them after your baby is two to three weeks old you should certainly ask your doctor for advice.

## Skin

**Bluish hands and/or feet.** *These mean that the baby's circulation is not yet efficient at getting the blood around to the extremities, especially after a long period asleep and still. They turn pink again when the baby is moved.*

**Half red, half pale.** *The blood pools in the lower half of the baby's body so that the lower half is red and the upper half pale. Again this is caused by immaturity of the circulation. The color difference will go when you turn the baby over.*

**Blue patches.** *Called "Mongolian blue spots," these are just temporary accumulations of pigment under the skin. They are more usual in babies of African or Mongolian descent but can also be seen in babies of Mediterranean descent or in any baby whose skin is going to be fairly dark. They are nothing to do with Mongolism (despite the name) nor are they anything to do with bruising or with blood disorders.*

**Spots.** *New babies get many kinds of spots. The kind that parents often worry about are red spots with yellowish centers. They are called*

*"Neo-natal urticaria." These spots form because the baby's skin and its pores do not yet work efficiently. The spots need no treatment, are not infected (although they look as if they are) and they vanish after the first couple of weeks.*

**Birthmarks.** *There are many kinds of birthmark; only a doctor can say whether the mark that worries you is a birthmark and if so whether it is the kind that will vanish on its own or not. But remember that red marks on the skin often arise from pressure during the birth. This kind will vanish within a few days.*

**Peeling.** *Most babies' skin peels a little in the first few days. It is usually most noticeable on palms and soles.*

**Scurf on the scalp, cradlecap.** *This is as normal as skin peeling elsewhere; it is nothing to do with "dandruff" and does not suggest lack of hygiene. A really thick cap-shaped layer is called "cradlecap." If it upsets you, your doctor may suggest an ointment or oil.*

## Hair

Any amount of hair on the head, from almost none to a luxuriant growth, is normal. Babies born late, after extra time in the womb, may have a great deal of rather coarse hair. Whatever it is like at birth, most of the newborn hair will fall out and be replaced. The color of the new hair may be quite different.

**Body hair.** *In the womb babies are covered with a fine fuzz of hair. Some, especially premature babies, still have traces, usually across the shoulder blades and down the spine. It will rub off in the first week or two.*

## Head

**Oddities of shape.** *These are almost always due to pressure during birth and will right themselves over a few months. The head may become slightly flattened if the baby is always put to sleep on one particular side. It is worth making sure that new babies are put on alternate sides, at least until they learn to roll themselves over.*

**Fontanelles.** *These are the soft areas where the bones of the skull have not yet fused together. The most noticeable lies towards the back of the top of the baby's head. Fontanelles are covered by an extremely tough membrane and there is no danger whatsoever of damaging them with normal handling.*
*In a baby without much hair, a pulse may be seen beating under the fontanelle. This is perfectly normal. If the fontanelle ever appears sunken, so that there is a visible "dip" in the baby's head, it is a sign of dehydration*

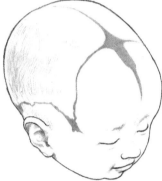

*(usually due to very hot weather or a fever). The baby should be offered diluted fruit juice or water at once.*
*If the fontanelle should ever appear to be tight and tense and to bulge outwards, the baby should see a doctor urgently as it could be a sign of illness.*

## Eyes

**Swollen, puffy or red-streaked eyes.** *These are often noticed soon after birth and result from pressure during it. Swelling and inflammation subside over a few days. Any recurrence of trouble with the eyes, once newborn problems have resolved, should be promptly reported to the doctor.*

**Yellowish discharge and/or crusting on lids and lashes.** *This is the result of a very common mild infection known as "sticky eye." It is not serious but the baby should be seen by the doctor who will recommend drops or a solution for bathing the eyes.*

**Squinting.** *Many babies whose eyes are perfectly normal have a squinting appearance in the early days of life. If you look at your baby closely you will probably find that it is the marked folds of skin at the inner corners of the eyes which make you think they are squinting. These folds of skin are perfectly normal and become less and less noticeable during the baby's first few weeks.*
*Until the baby has strengthened and*

learned to control the muscles around the eyes, it is quite usual for there to be difficulty in holding both eyes in line with each other so that they can both focus steadily on the same object. As your baby looks at your face, you may suddenly notice that one eye has "wandered" out of focus. A "wandering eye" almost always rights itself by the time the baby is six months old. But point it out to the doctor at your next visit so that a check can be made on its progress. A true squint means that the baby's eyes never both focus together on the same object. Rather than moving together and then one wandering off, the eyes are permanently out of alignment with each other. If you are the first to notice that your baby has a "fixed squint" you should report it at once to the doctor. Early treatment is both essential and highly successful (Ref/EYES).

### Ears

**Discharge.** *While it is normal for a baby's ears to produce wax, it is never normal for them to produce any other kind of discharge. If you are not sure that the substance you see coming from the ear is wax, consult your doctor. If it is wax, he will be only too pleased to reassure you. If by any chance it is pus, treatment is urgent.*

**Protruding ears.** *If you think that your baby's ears stick out too much, it is worth making sure that you smooth back the one your baby is just going to lie on. A good long nap each day with* the ear bent forward under the head will not improve matters. Otherwise you can only wait for the ears to become less noticeable as your baby's head assumes a more mature shape and as more hair grows.

### Mouth

**"Tongue tie."** *The tongue of a new baby is anchored along a much greater proportion of its length than is the tongue of an older person. In some babies the anchoring fold of skin is so long that the baby has almost no tongue which is free and mobile. In the past such babies were thought to be "tongue tied." It was believed that unless the anchoring skin was cut so that the tongue was free, the baby would not be able to suck properly or to learn to talk. Now we know that a true "tongue tie" — one which will not right itself with normal growth — is exceedingly rare. Most of the growth of a baby's tongue during the first year of life is in the tip so that by the first birthday the tongue is fully mobile. In the meantime its close anchorage has no effect on sucking, eating or speech.*

**White tongue.** *While they are being fed only on milk, babies often have tongues which are white all over. This is absolutely normal. Infection or illness produces patches of white on an otherwise pink tongue.*

**Blisters on the upper lip.** *These are called "sucking blisters" because the baby makes them himself with his suction. They can occur at any time while the baby is purely milk-fed. They may vanish between feedings. They are unimportant.*

### Breasts

*Swollen breasts are perfectly normal for babies of both sexes in the first three to five days after birth. They are caused by hormones flooding through the mother just before the birth. The hormones are intended for her but they sometimes get to the baby, too. The* swollen breasts may even have a tiny quantity of milk in them. They should be left strictly alone as any attempt to squeeze milk out might introduce infection. The swelling will die down in a few days as the baby's body rids itself of the hormones.

### Abdomen

**Umbilical hernia.** *A small swelling close to the navel, which sticks out more when the baby cries, cannot actually be called "normal," but is very usual indeed. It is caused by a slight weakness of the muscles in the wall of the abdomen, which allows the contents to bulge forward. Most such hernias right themselves completely by one year and most doctors believe that they heal more quickly if they are not strapped up. Very few ever require surgery.*

**Cord stump.** *Your doctor will check the cord stump and make sure that your baby's navel heals cleanly. If you should see any redness or discharge, report it immediately.*

## Sex organs

The genitals of both boys and girls are larger, in proportion to the rest of their bodies, at birth than at any other time before puberty. During the first few days after birth they may look even larger than normal because hormones from the mother have crossed the placenta, entered the baby's bloodstream and caused temporary extra swelling. The scrotum or the vulva may also look red and inflamed. All in all the baby's sexual parts may look conspicuous and peculiar. But don't worry. The doctor or midwife who delivered the baby will have checked that all is normal. The inflammation and swelling will rapidly subside during the baby's settling period and he or she will soon "grow into" those apparently over-large organs.

**Undescended testicles.** A boy's testicles develop in the abdomen. They descend into the scrotum just before a full-term birth. If the doctor cannot feel them during his examination of the newborn, it may be that they are "retractile": he can "milk" them down into the scrotum but they can still go up again into the abdomen. Provided that they can be "milked" down, they will certainly descend on their own. An undescended testicle is one which cannot be persuaded into the scrotum and does not lodge there of its own accord by the time a premature baby reaches his expected date of birth. If you cannot feel your son's testes in the scrotum, mention it to the doctor who checks him at around six weeks of age.

**Tight foreskin (phimosis).** The penis and the foreskin develop from a single bud in the fetus. They are still fused at birth and they only gradually become separate during the first few years of the boy's life. A tight foreskin is therefore a problem which a new baby cannot have. You cannot retract his foreskin because it is not made to retract at this age. You cannot wash underneath it because it is only meant to be cleaned from outside in babyhood. Circumcision (surgical removal of the foreskin) is medically advisable in only a minute proportion of babies. When it becomes necessary it is usually because attempts have been made to retract the foreskin forcibly before it was ready to retract of its own accord (Ref/ CIRCUMCISION).

## Elimination and secretions

**Meconium.** This is a greenish black sticky substance which fills babies' intestines in the womb and has to be evacuated before ordinary digestion can take place. Almost all babies pass meconium in the first 24 hours. If a baby is born at home, the nurse must be told if none is passed by the second day. Failure to pass meconium might mean that there is an obstruction in the bowel.

**Blood in stools.** Very occasionally blood is noticed in the stools in the first day or two. It is usually blood from the mother, swallowed during the delivery. Keep the diaper to show to the doctor or nurse.

**Reddish urine.** Very early urine often contains a substance called "urates" which looks red on the diaper. As it looks like blood you may prefer to keep the diaper to show the nurse.

**Frequent urine.** Once the urine flow is established the baby may pass water as often as 30 times in the 24 hours. This is entirely normal. On the other hand a baby who stays dry for 4–6 hours at this stage should be seen by the nurse or a doctor. It is just possible that there is some obstruction to the flow of urine.

**Vaginal bleeding.** A small amount of vaginal bleeding is common in girls at any time in the first week of life. It is due to maternal estrogens passing into the baby just before birth.

**Vaginal discharge.** A clear or whitish discharge from the vagina is also quite normal. It will stop in a very few days.

**Nasal discharge.** Many babies accumulate enough mucus in the nose to cause sniffles or some visible "runniness." This does not mean that the baby has a cold or other infection.

**Tears.** Most babies cry without tears until they are 4–6 weeks old. A few shed tears from the beginning. It does not matter either way.

**Sweating.** Most babies sweat a great deal around the head and neck. This has no importance unless the baby shows other signs of being feverish or unwell. It is a good reason, though, for rinsing the head and hair frequently as the sweat may irritate the skin in the folds of the neck.

**Vomiting.** Spitting up a little milk after feedings is normal. (For a full discussion see p. 69).

# Feeding

Only you can decide whether to breast- or bottle-feed. It is your body and your baby. Nobody has the right to pressure you either way or to criticize you whatever you decide. Breast milk is *physically* better for babies because it is the milk that nature intended for them. It even adjusts itself during a feeding – so that the baby first gets "foremilk," which he can gulp down to satisfy his thirst and desire to suck, and then the richer "hindmilk," which satisfies his appetite. But modern baby formula can be very nearly as good. Breast-feeding brings the two of you as close as it is possible for a mother and baby to get, but you can make close, warm physical contact by using a bottle, too. So don't listen to partisan arguments. Instead, think about yourself, the baby and your whole family unit:

*Breast or bottle?*  **What are your feelings now?** If you are looking forward to the physical relationship your baby will want to have with you, you will probably enjoy breast-feeding. There is an obvious, natural connection between the baby's hungry, seeking mouth and your full breasts. It feels very right and very pleasurable too.

But if you find the whole idea embarrassing, you may not enjoy actually *doing* it. If you don't enjoy it, then it will not work very smoothly. Both you and the baby may be happier using a bottle. And if you have a partner who is against you breast-feeding – perhaps because he feels that your breasts are private to your adult sexual relationship with him – his lack of support may make it very difficult for you. Although it has to be your decision, you will need to try and bring him around to your way of thinking in advance.

**What kind of life do you plan after the birth?** If you mean to stay at home and make the baby's care your priority for a few months, either way of feeding will suit you. But at the *very* beginning you may need more extra help if you are breast-feeding than if you are bottle-feeding. Getting your supply of milk tuned in to your baby's demands for it can be time-consuming and tiring and, since stress and fatigue really can reduce your breast milk, you will need to be able to relax and rest.

Once the baby is a month or so old and breast-feeding has become second nature to both of you, it will give you far more freedom to get out and about with the baby. So if you have visits or vacations planned, or if you like to be able to go out and do things on the spur of the moment, breast-feeding will tie you down less than bottle-feeding, with all its preparation and paraphernalia.

If you plan to go back to work within a few weeks of the birth, bottle-feeding may seem an easier option and may indeed prove to be so. But it will still be worth your while to get the baby established on the breast. A new baby is extremely portable; you might be able to take him with you to the job at least for a couple of months. And even if you want to be able to leave the baby with your partner or a caretaker, you may prove to be somebody who can express breast milk so easily that you might as well leave bottles of breast milk as bottles of formula. This also applies to partners or grandparents being able to feed the baby, for their own pleasure or to relieve you of some night feedings. If you have a copious milk supply and can easily express in the evening what the baby will need during the night, you can take turns with somebody else without bothering with formula.

**Are you still uncertain which you want to do?** Keeping your options open while you make up your mind means starting off with breast-feeding. You can always wean a baby gently from the breast to a bottle but you cannot switch from formula to breast milk because, if the baby has not been sucking regularly from your breasts, they will not be making milk.

*Advantages of starting your baby at the breast*

The baby's sucking will get your milk supply established so that you have the option to go on breast-feeding or to change over to a bottle if breast-feeding does not work out for you.

While the baby is establishing your milk supply he will be getting the colostrum which breasts produce first of all. Colostrum gives the baby water and sugar (which he could also get in the form of "sugar-water" from a bottle if he was not to be breast-fed) but it also gives him just the right amount of protein and minerals *plus* many important antibodies from you that will protect his health while he is building up his own immune system. There is no artificial equivalent of colostrum, which is why even a few *days* at the breast give babies a head start.

If your baby should have any health difficulties in the newborn period – mild jaundice, for example – he will really *need* to be fed on human milk rather than formula. Babies whose mothers decide in advance against breast-feeding are often given breast milk from the hospital milk bank if they are unwell.

Early feedings – perhaps complete with "after-pains" (see p. 53) – speed up the return of your womb to normal, even if you do not go on breast-feeding long enough for your figure to benefit from feeding your baby the extra fat you laid down in pregnancy!

## First feedings

Newborn babies don't need much food in the first three or four days of life. Breast-fed babies get colostrum. Bottle-fed babies may be given sugar-water first; when they are offered milk, the water part of that milk is what they need most. They probably will not take much, anyway. As we shall see, feeding is something babies have to learn.

Because they take little food, babies usually lose weight for four or five days before they start to gain. It is quite usual to lose 8oz (225g) over five days and then gain it back over the next five. A baby's weight at ten days is therefore expected to be roughly the same as it was at birth.

When a newborn baby is thirsty or hungry he feels uncomfortable so he cries. But at this early stage he does not cry *to be fed*. He does not know that his discomfort comes from hunger; that sucking will bring him food or that food will make him feel better. He has to discover that sucking = food = comfort.

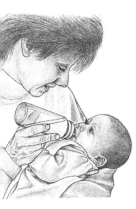

Some babies are so ready to suck that this vital learning takes place quickly and easily. They may have been practicing sucking their fingers in the womb (we know that some babies do) and once they are born they suck anything that comes their way. Of course, when such a baby is offered the breast or a bottle he sucks that too. Sucking gives him milk. Milk makes him feel good. The feeding lesson is learned.

Other babies are not at all like this. They cry piteously with hunger-pain but when their mothers try to put a nipple in their mouths they yell around it. Even a taste of colostrum or milk does not stop the crying. The connection between that taste and comfort has not been made yet. With a baby like this early attempts at feeding can be a struggle.

However, whether yours is a "sucky baby" or not, you can be quite sure that he has been born with a set of sucking reflexes. If you use these reflexes, instead of trying to force a nipple into his yelling mouth, he will suck. Once he has sucked a few times and discovered the food-comfort, all will be well.

## Evoking the sucking reflex

A baby who is hungry turns his head *toward* a gentle touch or stroke on the cheek. So if you are holding him in the crook of your left arm, ready to feed him from your left breast or from a bottle held in your right hand, stroke his right cheek, or let your breast do so, and he will turn his head in toward you.

As he turns his head his lips will purse. Both these maneuvers are reactions to your touch on his cheek, but once he has made them he is ready for a further cue: the touch of nipple, finger or anything suckable on his pursed lips. As soon as he feels it he will latch on and begin to suck. It sounds very simple and it is. But it is easy to give contradictory cues, by touching *both* cheeks, for example; to give them in the wrong order, by touching his lips first; or to spoil the timing, by not being ready with a nipple for that pursed mouth. Above all, it is easy to be too active. You cannot force him to suck. Give him the cues and trust him.

## The right circumstances for first feedings

If a baby's sucking reflexes are respected and used in his very first feeding experiences he will quickly learn the lesson sucking = milk = comfort. But it helps him to learn and it helps him to get enthusiastic about the whole feeding business if the feedings are kept comfortable and peaceful. It is not always easy to arrange life for your baby exactly as you would like it, especially in a busy hospital, but these are some of the things you should try to avoid:

**Don't try to feed a baby who is really upset and screaming.** He will not suck well. He is overwhelmed by his feelings. He cannot respond to your invitations to suck himself better. In a hospital this can be a problem. The staff may want your breast-fed baby to wait for his feeding because they want you to get an amount of rest – especially at night. The bottle-fed babies on the floor may be fed on a schedule, with nurses making up all their feedings at certain hours. If you are breast-feeding make it clear to the night staff that you do want to be woken up whenever your baby is hungry. If you are bottle-feeding insist on an extra bottle if he seems really hungry at the "wrong" times. If, despite all your efforts, he has been kept waiting and is upset, then he needs comforting by close wrapping, rocking or walking before you attempt to persuade him to suck.

**Don't let noise and movement distract your baby from sucking.** If you are at home, try feeding him quite alone at least for a few days. If you are in the hospital, bend down over him so that your face is directly above his. If you can get him to focus on you, other things will be less distracting. Wherever you are, keep up a gentle stream of talk. Your voice will block out the other sounds.

**Don't try to force a sleepy baby to stay awake.** In the very first days many babies are too sleepy to suck for long. It does not matter if he goes to sleep after a few sucks. He will wake again when he needs a few more (see p. 67). But it *does* matter if he is bounced and jolted and has his feet flicked in misguided attempts to make him take the "proper" amount. Feeding should be gentle bliss.

You want the baby to discover that sucking brings milk and that milk feels good, so it is important that the sucking should be properly rewarded. In breast-feeding a somewhat pendulous breast (especially one that is not yet full of milk but only has some colostrum in it) can block the baby's nose when he tries to suck so that instead of reward he gets a panic because he cannot breathe. The answer is to adjust his position or use the fingers of your free hand to depress the breast a little just above the areola so that his nose is kept clear (see p. 56).

In bottle-feeding the baby may be offered a nipple with too small a hole. Instead of an easy reward for his sucking he has to work for every sip and in these early days he may easily give up. If you up-end the bottle, milk should drip out of the nipple at a rate of several drops per *second*. If it is slower than that, ask for a larger holed nipple if you are in the hospital, or enlarge the hole with a red-hot needle if you are at home.

## Breast-feeding

Getting started with breast-feeding is not always easy. Just as many babies need to be tactfully shown how to use their sucking reflexes, so many breasts have to be gradually persuaded into easy performance of the function for which they are designed. Many first-time mothers find the first few days worrying, strange and uncomfortable; as a result some abandon the attempt to breast-feed within a week of the birth. Don't give up before you have given yourself a chance to experience the glorious time ahead when these early problems are over and the milk is there, like magic, whenever the baby wants it. Because they know, from experience, that this happy state is coming, second-time mothers who have breast-fed before hardly ever let early difficulties put them off. They know that once the milk supply is fully established, breast-feeding will be worthwhile.

If you have small breasts, don't let glimpses of more lavishly endowed women, feeding their babies in the hospital, make you feel inadequate. The size of your breasts has no relevance to their ability to produce an abundant supply of milk. Milk is produced in deeply buried glands, not in the surrounding fatty tissue.

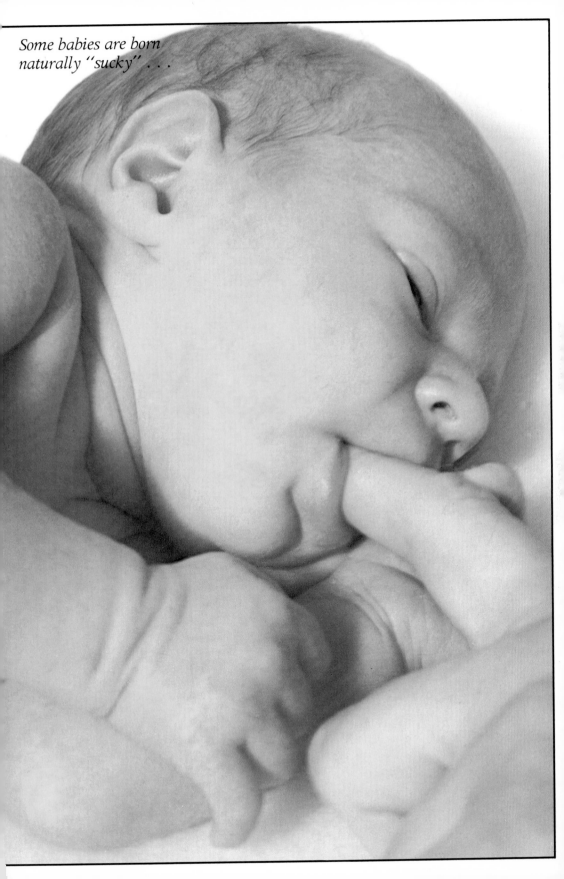

*Some babies are born naturally "sucky"...*

. . . others need to be helped. The baby
has reflexes which tell him what to do
if you give him the cues . . .

. . . a gentle touch on his cheek from breast
or finger, and he will turn in toward you

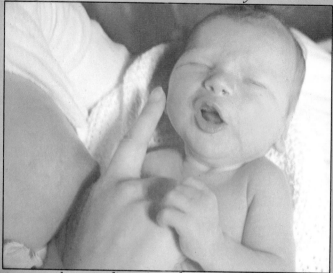

. . . mouth open, lips pursed,
the right moment is now

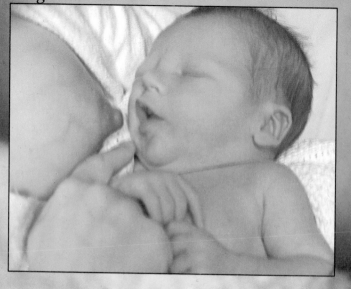

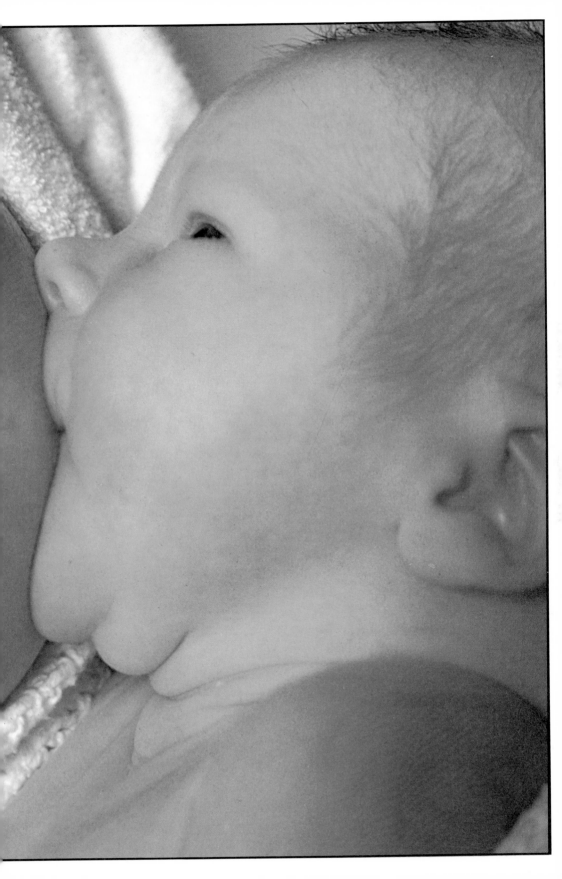

*. . . sucking gives him milk*
*. . . milk makes him feel good . . .*
*the feeding lesson is learned.*

Don't be surprised or disheartened if the whole feeding business is a struggle as long as you remain in the hospital. A busy maternity floor is not the best place to combine learning yourself with teaching your baby. The availability of expert help seems comforting but may not be of very much practical use. Helping someone persuade a new baby on to the breast is rather like helping her tie a necktie. You can do it yourself or let her do it; two of you together make a muddle. You will probably work things out better when you and the baby can be alone together in your home surroundings, with everything under your own contol and the privacy you need to experiment without feeling a fool.

It will probably be three to five days after the birth before your real milk comes in. When it does, don't decide that it is no good because it looks bluish and watery compared with thick yellowy colostrum, or the creamy-looking formula given to the baby in the next bassinet. Breast milk is *meant* to look like that. It is perfect.

Your baby should be put to the breast regularly during these first days, both to get that vital colostrum and to practice feeding while your breasts are still soft. Without practice in the whole business of sucking, the newborn will find your larger, harder, milk-filled breasts more difficult to cope with.

When the milk does come in there are various minor, short-lived but uncomfortable problems which may arise:

*Engorgement*   After the birth, tremendous hormonal activity in your body instigates milk production. Often the milk "comes in" overnight so that your breasts suddenly become large and tightly swollen both with milk and an increased supply of blood. Sometimes the chemical messages the breasts receive are over-emphatic and the breasts become engorged: rigidly hard, hot and painful with even the areolae around the nipples distended.

Breasts in this state are always uncomfortable and may be extremely painful. Fortunately the hormonal imbalance will settle down within a day or two. Your breasts will never again be so large, tight or uncomfortable, even when you are producing three times as much milk for a larger and hungrier baby.

The cure for engorgement is to get rid of some of the excess milk. You will not be able to do this at once by suckling the baby because he will not be able to get hold of the swollen areola. You must first soften the breasts a little, by bathing them repeatedly with hot water, and then very gently express some milk by the method described on page 58.

If your baby does not take enough milk at intervals frequent enough to keep you comfortable, you will get some relief from very cold washcloths or wrapped ice-cubes laid on the breasts. A simple over-the-counter pain-reliever will help, too.

*Sore nipples*   Soreness from unaccustomed use is much rarer than people used to think. Unless you are red-headed or very blonde, with pale skin and very pink nipples, you should be able to avoid soreness without limiting your baby's luxurious sucking time.

**Avoid washing nipples with soap** in late pregnancy or while breast-feeding. They have built-in lubrication from tiny glands around the areola ("Montgomery's tubercles") which you don't want to remove. It is more effective than any cream you might use to replace it, and more hygienic, too.

**Don't massage and scrub nipples to harden them.** They are made for the job of breast-feeding and you don't want them tough, you want them flexible and elastic.

**Try to let them air-dry after feedings,** speeding up the process with warm air from a hair dryer if you are rushed.

**Keep plastic-backed breast pads for special occasions.** Once they are damp they will keep your nipples damp and soggy. Ordinary pads are better; frequently changed bras are better still. You can often stop leakage by pressing the center of the nipple firmly *in* with the end of your finger.

**Never pull a sucking baby off the nipple.** Wait until he pauses for breath or break the suction by inserting a gentle finger in the corner of his mouth (see p. 57).

**Make sure your baby never sucks on the *nipple*;** his jaws must squeeze the areola with the nipple itself drawn right to the back of his mouth.

**At the first sign of soreness, adjust your position** so that a different part of the nipple takes the main stress (see p. 55).

*Cracked nipples*   If a sudden, thin, sharp pain darts through your nipple as the baby latches on, and continues as long as he sucks, there may be a tiny crack in the nipple. A cracked nipple must be rested and reported to your doctor who will probably give you some cream to put on it to aid healing and prevent infection. Healing will only take a day or two, but during this time the baby must be fed only from the other breast. You can gently express the milk from the affected side (see p. 58).

*Hard, sore lumps in the breast*   Very occasionally one of the tiny tubes which carry the milk from glands to nipple gets blocked. Milk gathers above the blockage and cannot escape. You will be able to feel a small, hard, painful lump.
   Bathe the breast repeatedly with hot water and massage it gently, then feed the baby. If the lumpiness and pain subside, you have helped the milk duct to clear itself. If they do not, see your doctor the same day. The lump could be due to an abscess forming rather than to a simple blockage.

*Breast abscesses*   These are usually the result of infection getting into the breast through an untreated crack in the nipple. One area of the breast will be hard, red and painfully throbbing. You may have some fever and feel unwell. It is important to see your doctor on that same day, although you can safely continue to feed the baby from the affected breast while you wait.
   If a breast abscess is treated in the early stages (usually with antibiotics), you will be able to go on feeding the baby normally throughout the treatment period and you need have little pain. If the abscess is neglected you may have to confine the baby to the other breast for many days and it may be memorably painful.

*After-pains and the "let down" reflex*

Your baby is helped to get the milk from your breasts by the draft or "let down" reflex. Sucking, hunger cries, or the baby's mere presence when your breasts are full, release the hormone oxytocin into your blood. This makes the muscle fibers around your milk glands contract, forcing their milk down into the milk ducts. Oxytocin also makes the muscles of your womb contract and some women feel the contractions as mild colicky pains. They stop being noticeable after two or three days.

Sometimes the draft reflex makes the second breast leak milk while the baby sucks from the first, or it makes both breasts leak when they are overfull or when the sight or sound of any young baby reminds your body of your own (see pp. 55 and 56).

*Supply and demand*

How much milk have you got? How often should the baby have it? In breast-feeding these two questions go together because your breasts will make as much milk as your baby sucks from you. The more he takes the more you will make. The more often he takes it the quicker you will make more. This is why a mother can make exactly the right amount of milk for a 6lb (2.7kg) baby *or* exactly the right amount of milk for twins who weigh 13lbs (5.9kg) between them. This is why she can make enough for the baby in his second week of life and also in his twenty-second week. . . .

Breast-feeding is a natural supply and demand system. It therefore depends on the baby being allowed to behave naturally. The system often fails if he is kept to an unnaturally rigid schedule. The natural system works like this:

The breasts make milk and the baby drinks it. As the breasts are emptied, so they at once start to make more milk. If the baby had his fill at that first feeding, he will be satisfied for some time – perhaps for as much as three hours – so the breasts will only make about that same amount of milk again. But if he did not get quite enough at that first feeding, he will be hungry quite soon. He will want to suck again. If he is allowed to, he will empty the breasts yet again and they will be stimulated to make more milk.

The more often he empties the breasts, the more milk they will make. Eventually, perhaps after a day, perhaps after a week, the breasts will be making so much milk that the baby will stop being hungry so often. He will only empty the breasts every three or four hours, so they will slow their production down to that level.

**Let the baby suck as often as he is hungry.** For a few days he may want to be put to the breast 10, 12 or even more times in the 24 hours. As long as your nipples do not get sore or cracked (see pp. 51 and 52) and as long as you use these almost non-stop feedings as periods of rest, it does not matter how often you suckle him.

**Give both breasts at each feeding** and start him on each alternately so that each breast gets its fair share of stimulation from his hungriest sucking.

**Don't rigidly limit the baby's sucking time.** The composition of the milk changes as he sucks with thirst-quenching foremilk first and then the more concentrated hindmilk. Two minutes on each breast may give him as much to drink as he can hold without giving him all the calories he needs. You could try, for example, five minutes on the first side and as long as he wants on the other.

**Don't offer a bottle instead of the breast,** even if he sucked so recently that you are sure there cannot yet be any more milk for him. There will always be a little, and preventing him from taking it will make your breasts fill up more slowly.

**Don't offer a bottle as well as the breast** because his demands are so frequent that you feel he must have more. Frequent sucking will sustain him and cue your breasts to make more milk.

*Expressing milk*

At the beginning, the baby's demands may be very variable, because he is not very settled or efficient at sucking. It is worth expressing any milk that he leaves, so that your breasts make plenty for the next feeding when he may be hungrier.

Don't try to express until no milk comes out. As you drain the breast, it makes more milk, so you will never completely empty it. Stop when the milk only appears in drops (see method p. 58).

*If you are worried about your milk supply*

Don't give up until you have checked all the following points:

**Are you letting the baby suck whenever he likes?** It doesn't matter to him if he has to suck very often to keep himself satisfied. That's the way he puts right any temporary shortage of milk.

**What makes you think you haven't enough?** Frequent crying just means frequent feeding; the only real signs of milk-scarcity are failure to gain weight – and that means *any* weight, not just gaining 3oz (85g) this week instead of the "recommended" 8oz (225g) – and, more immediately, having dry diapers after two or three hours, or not producing at least eight really wet ones in 24 hours.

**Does your worry relate to extra work?** A temporary shortage when you first come home from the hospital or first start coping with your household and perhaps your toddler, as well as the baby, is very common. You need more help and more rest.

**Are visitors or older children getting in the way?** In the early days the let down reflex (see p. 53) can be inhibited by other people so that the baby cannot get the milk that is there for him.

**Are you uncertain of the quality of your milk?** Don't be. Breast milk is *always* perfect. If your breast-fed baby has spots or indigestion, they would *certainly* be as bad and would probably be worse if he was bottle-fed.

**Have you started taking contraceptive pills?** These hormones can reduce the supply of breast milk. You are right to use contraception from the first time you make love after having the baby, because breast-feeding is *not* an adequate protection against pregnancy even if your periods have not started again, but you need an alternative method (Ref/FAMILY PLANNING).

**Are you in touch with a breast-feeding counselor?** Your doctor may give you excellent advice and support but an experienced breast-feeding mother from a post-natal support group, like the ones run by the LaLeche League, may be able to give you the kind of one-to-one, ever-available support which can make all the difference.

## Starting breast-feeding

You and your baby will soon take breast-feeding pleasurably for granted, but while you are getting used to it, mutual comfort is important. Clothes that open down the front, for example, make it easier to bare your breasts than "fishing" down the neck of a sweater; they give the baby a good sucking position, too. A controlled milk flow, a comfortable chair, plenty of time and all the privacy you personally want will all help you both to enjoy yourselves.

### Feeding position

*Cradle the baby in the crook of your arm so that her well-supported head is above the level of her stomach. If you hold her flat, the air she takes with the milk will not be able to rise to the top of her stomach for easy burping. Leave her outside hand free – she will soon enjoy stroking the breast as part of actively feeding rather than passively being fed. Turn her whole body toward you but don't hold her head.*

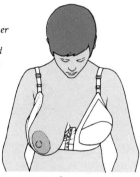

### Nursing bras

*These open in front and have a separate flap for each breast, which means that you can release one breast at a time. Wearing a nursing bra also helps to reduce milk leakage.*

## Comfort during feedings

It is important that you are comfortable during feedings and able to relax completely. The ideal nursing chair is low enough for you to sit with your feet flat on the floor, upright enough to support your back all the way up, and armless so that you do not bump the baby's head. If you feed lying down, use plenty of pillows to support your full weight. Don't try to lean on your elbow – it will ache.

### Avoiding backache

*Pillows support your arm and the weight of the baby on it . . .*

*or pillows support the baby so that your arm takes no weight.*

*You will get backache if you try to put your baby's mouth to your nipple by leaning over to her or by lifting her up to you.*

*So, sit forward with a pillow supporting your back and cross your legs so that your raised knee brings the baby within reach.*

*Alternatively, sit back so that the chair supports you all the way up your spine. Put a pillow on your lap and lie the baby on that.*

## Putting the baby to the breast

The whole technique of breast-feeding will soon become obvious to you because it is based on making the baby comfortable and you will be able to see when she is not! After a few days she will need little encouragement or stimulation of her sucking reflexes because she will have learned the sucking = food = pleasure sequence by experience. But starting off right is important, and it remains important to avoid making her feel smothered, choked or forced.

**Helping her to suck**

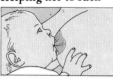

*If your baby takes only your nipple into her mouth she will get no milk. Her suction and the compression of her lips will actually close the openings. Her attempts are very likely to make your nipples sore.*

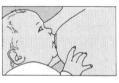

*Milk will flow out of the openings in your nipple when she uses her jaws to press rhythmically around the base of the areola, while simultaneously exerting suction. Help her to take the nipple and the areola right into her mouth. When she is sucking, her lips should be sealed around the meeting edge of the areola and the skin of your breast.*

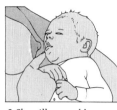

*2 She will respond by turning inward toward the breast. After a few days the touch of your bare breast against her cheek will be enough to evoke this response.*

*3 As she turns inward, her lips will purse. If the nipple touches them now . . .*

**Sucking reflexes**
*1 When you are ready to give the breast, prepare the baby to take it by gently stroking the cheek nearest to you.*

*4 . . . she will take it and settle to nursing.*

## Giving her breathing space

Your baby has to breathe through her nose while she is sucking. A feeling of smothering will panic her and might even put her off breast-feeding. If your breast obstructs her nostrils, try changing her position, or depress the breast gently just above the areola to give her a "breathing hole" without breaking her suction.

## Reducing the flow

Sometimes the "let down" reflex works too well for a new baby. As soon as she starts to suck, milk pours out, making her gulp and choke. You can slow up the flow by putting your middle and forefinger on either side of the areola, just above the baby's lips, and pressing gently upward. Remove them when her sucking rhythm steadies.

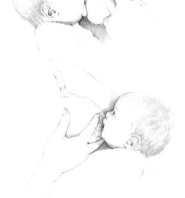

## Breast care

Don't wash the natural lubricant off your nipples with soap, or dry them forcibly after feedings. Warm water-splashing and air-drying should keep your nipples comfortable. Start each feeding at the breast she ended up with last time. Each breast will then get the stimulation of her hungriest sucking at alternate feedings.

Don't try to remove the baby from your breast by pulling against her suction. She exerts a tremendous pull and it will hurt your nipple. Wait, if you can, until she stops for a rest. If not, break the suction by slipping your forefinger down between the areola and her lips.

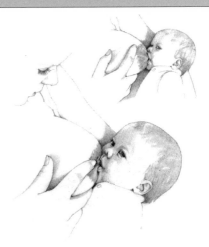

### "Which breast first at this feeding?"

*The baby is having the left breast first this time, but will you remember which to offer first at the next feed?*

*If you are liable to forget, use a code: tuck a tissue into your bra on the side she sucked first.*

*Next time start her on the breast with no tissue. Easy to remember: the waiting breast will leak into its tissue.*

## Looking after your nipples

Nipples vary in their sensitivity. You may find that to avoid soreness, you have to look after yours throughout the breast-feeding period; but if you take trouble during the early weeks, they may adapt sufficiently to look after themselves thereafter.
Preventing your nipples getting sore is rather like preventing your baby getting diaper rash. Like her bottom, your nipples are exposed to continual friction, which can make them dry and flaky, and to continual damp, which can make them soggy. The combination of damp and friction can make for chapping. Some suggestions for avoiding these discomforts are shown below.

**Air-drying**

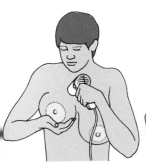

*Let both nipples dry in the air after feedings. A hair dryer will speed things up.*

*Keep leaking nipples dry with squares of disposable diapers or breast shields. Avoid waterproofed pads which exclude air.*

*When you wash, use plain water without soap. Don't rub nipples dry; blot the water off gently.*

*If you should get cracked nipples, consult your doctor for ointment.*

BREAST-FEEDING   **57**

## Expressing

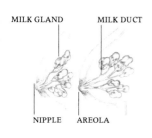

MILK GLAND     MILK DUCT

NIPPLE     AREOLA

**How to express**

Milk is produced by glands distributed through the breast tissue. It gathers in minute sacs (the alveoli) and travels down milk ducts which widen into ampullae, placed inside the areola. There the milk stays until the sucking baby presses the areola between her gums to squirt it from the ampullae through the openings in the nipple. At the same time her suction draws further milk down the ducts and calls the draft reflex into play.

When you want to express – to get milk out without the baby's help –

you have to replace her stimulation by using gentle massage to start the milk moving down the ducts and pressure on the areola to move it from the ampullae through the nipple. If you are ridding yourself of unwanted milk or ensuring emptied breasts, express into the washbasin or wherever you please. But if the baby is to drink the milk, use a sterile jug and refrigerate it. Don't go on trying to express until the breast is empty. That time is never. Stop when the milk comes in drops instead of jets.

**Breast pumps**
*If you find it difficult to express by hand, a breast pump may help. Electric pumps can be rented. Some mothers find the suction uncomfortably strong.*

1 *Support the breast in one palm and use the other to stroke repeatedly downward as far as the areola. Work evenly all round the breast.*

2 *Now support the breast in your right palm. Place your thumb about halfway up the breast . . .*

3 *. . . and run it firmly down.*

4 *As your thumb reaches the edge of the areola, press in and up and milk will squirt from the untouched nipple.*

5 *Don't squeeze the nipple; you will close the ducts. Squeeze the edge of the areola up and in so the nipple stands out.*

## Expressing from overfull breasts

*The breast in front is full, ready for sucking; the one behind is overfull; the baby cannot grasp the engorged areola so she cannot suck.*

Breasts which become overfull usually leak out the milk they cannot hold. Sometimes they become engorged with blood so that the swelling of the breast actually prevents milk escaping. Engorged breasts are painful. The normal massage technique of expression is impossible. So, bathe the breasts in water as hot as they can comfortably bear. Soaking in the bath is the easiest way, otherwise keep applying washcloths. The breasts may spontaneously leak milk after a few minutes. If not, apply alternate gentle pressure with your fingers above the areola and more washcloths until milk comes.

*Breast-feeding brings
you and your baby as
close as you can be . . .*

*. . . but a baby can revel in bottle-feeding too.*

# Bottle-feeding

We have no real alternative to the breast-fed baby's colostrum, so while the bottle-fed baby may start life with one or two drinks of sugared water, formula will be offered by the second day. This is much sooner than a breast-fed baby would find milk, so your baby may take very little. The water content is needed much more than the food content, so don't worry.

If your baby does take all the milk offered, weight gain may start from birth instead of after a few days' weight loss. Although early weight loss often worries parents, don't be too enthusiastic about every ounce your baby gains; bottle-fed babies can get too fat.

*Choosing a formula*

Cow's milk is ideal for calves but it is not the natural food for babies. It contains too little sugar and the wrong kind of fat. Its protein makes indigestibly solid curds in the baby's stomach and it contains more minerals – especially sodium – than human milk. Babies under six months should not be fed on any kind of unmodified cow's milk or on goat's milk either, so ignore liquid, dried or evaporated milk from dairies, supermarkets or health food stores. Bottle-fed babies need a breast milk substitute, or formula.

Modern formulas are based on cow's milk but are more or less extensively adapted to bring the made-up food as close as possible to breast milk.

Even the recommended formulas do vary, though. Most now include the right amount of all the necessary vitamins. They are available with or without supplementary iron. Make your choice in consultation with your doctor. And seek your doctor's advice about whether to give your baby the normally recommended multivitamin drops in addition to the particular formula you have chosen.

Formulas vary in their convenience as well as their constituents. In powdered form most mix easily when they are simply shaken up in the bottle with the required amount of cooled boiled water. Some of the formulas are available as liquid concentrate, rather like ordinary evaporated milk. The 8oz (225g) or 32oz (900g) cans are heavy to carry and must be refrigerated after opening but the formula is easy to measure and mix in cans. The milk can be kept in the opened can provided it is refrigerated, but any that is left after 24 hours should be thrown away.

If neither the weight of your shopping nor storage-space is a problem, some formulas are available in convenient ready-to-drink form. And for the ultimate in labor-saving, though at a considerable cost, you can buy ready-to-drink formula sealed into pre-sterilized disposable bottles.

*Preparing bottle-feedings*

You cannot safely take a happy-go-lucky approach to preparing bottles, especially while your baby is very young. Hygiene is important if he is to stay well, and correct preparation of the formula is important to proper nourishment.

*Hygiene*

There are bacteria everywhere. We all carry them on our hands and our clothes. We breathe them, eat them and excrete them. Most of them are harmless. Very few types will make us ill unless we take in such a large number all at one time that our bodies' defenses are overwhelmed.

A new baby, especially one who is not breast-fed, has few defenses against common germs. It takes time for him to build up immunity to them. In an ordinarily clean home, he will cope with the germs that he sucks off his hands or breathes in the living room. But when he is feeding it is different. Milk, especially milk which is around room temperature, is an ideal *breeding ground* for germs. So while he might pick up a few off his own fingers and deal with them perfectly well, he will pick up an enormous, and possibly overwhelming number from a bottle which has been left standing around in a warm room. Gastroenteritis is still one of the most common reasons for young babies being admitted to the hospital. To keep the baby's milk as free from bacteria as possible:

**Wash your hands** before handling the milk or equipment, especially after using the lavatory or handling pets or their food. If you use liquid concentrate, keep a special can-opener for those cans and sterilize the top with boiling water before you puncture it.

**Use a sterile formula** and keep the packet closed or the can tightly covered and refrigerated once it has been opened.

**Sterilize everything you use in measuring, mixing or storing** the made-up milk. That means measuring spoons, mixing jars and the water in the food itself.

**Sterilize bottles, nipples and nipple covers.** Provided that you put a sterile nipple cover over the sterilized nipple on your ready-filled bottle, that nipple will still be sterile and safe when you take the cover off to feed the baby.

Bacteria which escape your precautions (by landing on the sterile nipple as you put it on the bottle, for example) cannot multiply dangerously while the milk is boiling hot or while it is icy cold. It is the in-between temperatures that help them to flourish. To minimize the chances of bacteria breeding:

**Cool the made-up milk quickly,** preferably by putting it in the refrigerator while it is still hot.

**Keep it cold until the baby wants it.** Don't put a bottle to warm in advance of him waking up, or keep it warm for him if he drops off to sleep for more than a few minutes in mid-feeding. *Never* put warm milk in a thermos or electric bottle warmer.

**Throw away any milk the baby leaves.** Don't try to save that half bottle for next time and don't pour the now unsterile remains back into your jar of sterilized formula in the refrigerator.

*Making up the formula*   When you combine milk powder or liquid concentrate with boiled water, you are constructing food and most of your baby's drink. If you do it in exactly the proportions the manufacturer suggests in the mixing instructions, you will end up with a food that is as close to the composition of breast milk as it is possible to get with that particular formula. The baby will get the right amount of nourishment and the right amount of water.

Research workers have found that a great many bottles are not made up accurately. It is largely this inaccuracy which makes bottle-feeding unsatisfactory for many babies. *Follow the manufacturer's instructions exactly.* Making a bottle is not like preparing instant coffee. You cannot make it better by putting in just a little extra powder, or more thirst quenching by adding extra water. If you add too much powder, the milk will be too strong. The baby will get too much protein, too much fat, too many minerals, and not enough water. He will get fat because you are giving him too many calories, and thirsty because you are giving him too much salt. Because he is thirsty, he will cry, and because he cries you will give him another bottle. If that bottle is too strong, too, he will be even more thirsty. So it will go on. The result can be a baby who cries a lot, does not seem terribly well or happy, puts on a lot of weight, and seems to need a lot of feeding.

Don't be afraid to offer extra drinks of plain, boiled water, but don't add anything to make formula "nicer" or "more satisfying."

**Never guess at quantities.** Measure milk powder accurately by filling the scoop provided and slicing off the surplus at scoop level with a knife. Wiping the surplus off on the edge of the can or smoothing it off with a spoon will not be accurate; you will almost certainly end up with a somewhat packed or heaped scoop. Shaking off the surplus may leave you with either too much or too little powder.

Measure liquid concentrate accurately by pouring it either directly into the bottle or into a marked-off measuring cup and then holding it up to your eye level to read off the marked ounces. If you check the level with your eye above it, you will think there is less milk than there really is.

Measure the water accurately by boiling it (to sterilize it) *first*, and pouring it into your bottle or measuring cup when it has cooled. If you measure the water first and then boil it, some of it will be lost in evaporation.

If you really do make up your baby's bottles *exactly* as the manufacturer recommends, and as long as you resist the temptation to add a spoonful of cereal in the vain hope of a better night, you can treat the resulting milk exactly as if it was breast milk. The baby can have as much as he eagerly drinks, as often as he is hungry, and leave what he does not want. You don't need to carry your scientific accuracy in *making* the milk on into *feeding* it!

# Starting bottle-feeding

Your baby's bottle, nipples and the equipment used to prepare the milk need scrupulous attention to prevent a build-up of bacteria. The amount of equipment you buy depends on which type of formula you use and on how you organize your sterilizing. The bottles and accessories below give some idea of the available choice.

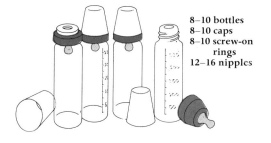

8–10 bottles
8–10 caps
8–10 screw-on
 rings
12–16 nipples

or, if using disposable bottles,
6–8 bottle
 holders,
 rings and caps
1 roll of
 disposable
 bottles

## Easy sterilizing

You can sterilize everything by keeping it totally submerged in fully boiling water for at least ten minutes. Make sure bottles are full of water, nipples etc. trapped under a cup: equipment which floats may not be fully safe.

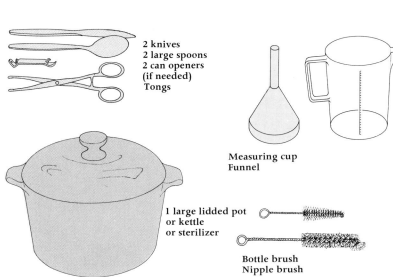

2 knives
2 large spoons
2 can openers
(if needed)
Tongs

Measuring cup
Funnel

1 large lidded pot
or kettle
or sterilizer

Bottle brush
Nipple brush

## Once a day...

Wash everything with hot water, detergent and bottle brush.

Turn nipples inside out; rub with salt if slimy but rinse very well. Force water through holes to be sure no milk is left there.

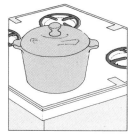

Put all your washed bottles, nipples, spoons, jars etc. into a container. Make sure everything is covered with water. Boil, covered, for ten minutes. Remove equipment with sterile tongs.

After a feeding, rinse bottle and nipple and leave by the sink ready for your daily wash-up and sterilize session. If using disposable bottles, treat nipples, caps, rings etc. in the same way.

N.B. Glass bottles can be sterilized in a dishwasher with a sterilizing cycle.

## Preparing bottle-feedings

Formula must be made up accurately if the bottle is to contain the right number of calories. Use only the scoop provided for milk powder and level off with a knife to avoid overfull measures. Sterilize water by boiling *before* measuring as some will evaporate. If you want to make up feedings for 24 hours, you can store them in a sterile jar in the refrigerator, or fill sterile bottles and refrigerate those.

## Making up powdered formula

Boil water and let it cool to hand-heat. Wash your hands.

Pour water into sterile jar. Check correct quantity by holding at eye level.

Add required number of scoops of milk powder, levelling each with knife.

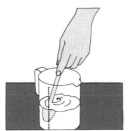

Stir the mixture thoroughly with the sterile spoon.

**Either** cover jar and refrigerate . . .

### If you have no refrigerator . . .

*Each bottle must be made as needed; it is not safe to leave prepared bottles standing at room temperature. Choose a powdered formula that will mix when shaken in the bottle. Put warm boiled water in bottle; check quantity at eye level. Add correct number of carefully levelled scoops of powder. Screw on nipple and nipple cover. Shake well.*

. . . **or** fill sterile bottles from the jar, putting more in each than the baby will drink.

Taking care not to touch the tops, screw nipples upside down on the bottles. Cover with their sterile caps.

Put in refrigerator.

## Making up a liquid formula

Wash top of can. Sterilize by pouring boiling water over it. Punch two holes with sterilized opener.

Pour ready-to-feed formula into sterile bottles. Pour correct quantity of concentrate, checking by holding at eye level.

For the concentrate, add the correct amount of cooled boiled water.

Cap bottles. Refrigerate and use within 24 hours. Cover and refrigerate remaining concentrate.

## Giving the bottle

Being physically close to you during feedings is just as important to the bottle-fed baby as to the breast-fed one. Always give her the bottle while she is cradled in your arms: resist any temptation to prop it for her so that she can feed herself. Choose a chair that supports your back while your feet are flat on the floor. Have a table nearby to hold the bottle in its warmer. Support the baby's head well above the level of her stomach, and support your cradling arm too or it will ache.

### Testing temperature and flow

*Cold milk is not harmful but most babies prefer it warm. Stand it in a jar of hot water for a few minutes. Then shake the bottle and uncap it; put the nipple upright and test the milk's temperature on the inside of your wrist. It should feel just warm. Milk should come out at several drops per second. Enlarge a too-small hole with a red-hot needle.*

### Tilting the bottle

*Make sure the baby gets the bulbous tip of the nipple well back in her mouth. Always keep the nipple full of milk.*

### Sucking reflexes

*1 Make sure that you are settled and ready before you alert the baby to the bottle.*

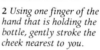

*2 Using one finger of the hand that is holding the bottle, gently stroke the cheek nearest to you.*

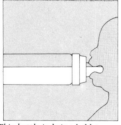

*This bottle is being held too flat, the nipple is only half full of milk and the baby will suck in air with her feeding.*

*As the baby sucks, she removes both milk and the air from the unfilled space in the bottle. If no air can get back in, a vacuum will form. The nipple will go flat and the baby will not be able to get any more milk. To prevent or cure this, pull gently against her suction so that the vacuum is momentarily released and you see air bubbling back in. Hold the bottle firmly all the time so that the baby*

*3 She will turn her head toward your touch, pursing her mouth as she does so.*

*4 At the touch of the nipple on her pursed lips she will take it deeply into her mouth and settle to sucking.*

*can pull against it with her suction. If you hold it too loosely, her efforts will move the bottle around instead of pulling milk out.*

## Carrying bottles with you

Never carry warm formula. It is a dangerously ideal breeding ground for bacteria. Carry the baby's milk icy cold from the refrigerator. Keep it that way by putting the sterile sealed bottles in an insulated picnic box (safe for up to 8 hours) or by burying them in ice cubes in a plastic bag (safe for around 4 hours). Warm the bottles as you need them by standing them in hot water from a thermos for a few minutes.

Wide-necked flasks will take a bottle direct; narrow-necked ones mean carrying a jar as well. If you are going to need more bottles than you can safely keep cold, measure milk powder (*not* liquid) into empty sterile bottles and seal. Mix with boiled water from a thermos as you need each one. Always carry at least one more feeding than you think you will need during the trip. This will help in case of breakdowns or delays.

## Supply and demand for the bottle-fed baby

How much and how often should bottle-fed babies be fed? They do best if they are treated exactly as if they were breast-fed. Milk should be offered whenever the baby seems to be hungry and the feeding should only be stopped when eager sucking ceases. Don't try to push him to take *more* than he really wants, though. If he were breast-fed, you could not see how much he'd left. If you stick to these principles in the very early weeks, you will never have to worry about whether to feed "on schedule" because the baby's own schedule will gradually evolve out of his digestive pattern.

A new baby is used to having his food needs continually replenished by transfusion feeding in the womb. Now they must be met by digestion of food from a stomach that starts full and gradually empties. While he gets used to this change he may demand food at irregular and frequent intervals. If he cries only an hour after drinking 3oz (85ml) of formula, you may ask yourself whether he can possibly be hungry again already. The answer is that although his stomach cannot yet be empty, he feels a need to have his food topped off.

If you offer him a bottle whenever he seems hungry, he will only take the amount he needs. If he drinks it all, you can assume he needed it. If he takes a little, the comfort of sucking and of your care will make him feel better. If he drinks none, what have you lost? One bottle of formula.

If you meet these irregular demands willingly, they will stop by themselves in a few weeks. It takes rather longer for a baby to digest formula than breast milk – around three to four hours. True hunger signals are tied in to the near-completion of the digestive process. Once his digestion is working more maturely and he has got used to this new kind of hunger, he will neither feel nor express distress until he *has* digested the last meal so his demands will fall into the same pattern as a conventional schedule.

Exactly the same process of maturing and settling into a feeding pattern will take place if you keep your baby to a strict four-hour schedule from the beginning. Offered feedings only at 6am, 10am, 2pm, 6pm and 10pm, he will eventually expect food at these intervals. The difference is that these early weeks will be miserable for you all. The baby will wake and cry. If you do not feed him because it "isn't time" you will try every other method of comforting him, which will be hard work. Because what he really wants is food, and because he will get hungrier and hungrier while you are working away at other methods of comfort, nothing you do will really soothe him. By the end of the session you will be feeling that unhappy mixture of guilt and anger and helpless despair. To crown it all, when the clock does at last say the "right time" and you give him a feeding, he will probably not suck well or take enough milk to keep him happy until the next scheduled meal. All that crying will have tired him and filled his stomach with air. He will probably fall into exhausted sleep after an ounce or two and wake up again an hour later to repeat the whole performance.

So don't fall into the trap of thinking that if you feed your baby whenever he seems hungry he will get into the habit of demanding food frequently. He does not wake from habit, he wakes from hunger. When he is mature enough not to be hungry so often he will not wake up and cry.

# Burping, bubbling, or bringing up air

There is always air in your baby's stomach. He swallows some while crying or just breathing as well as when he feeds. If you feed with the baby in a fairly upright position, the heavier milk will find its way to the bottom of the stomach and the lighter air will gather at the top. When the stomach is uncomfortably distended with milk and air the baby will burp some of the air out.

*Burping midway through feedings*

Some babies swallow so much air that their stomachs get uncomfortably distended before they have had enough milk. They need a half-time burp to make room for the rest of the feeding. A breast-fed baby who needs to burp will probably do so when he is shifted across from the first breast to the second. A bottle-fed baby will stop sucking. If you hold him upright for a moment, he will burp and then return to his feeding.

There is no need to remove the nipple from the mouth of a baby who is sucking happily, just in case he has too much air in his stomach. If he is still sucking, he is not uncomfortably full and should be left to suck in peace.

*Burping after feedings*

All your baby needs is the opportunity. Hold him upright against your shoulder; rub his back or pat it gently, and see what happens. If he has not burped after three minutes, he does not need to.

Don't feel that you must not put him in his crib until he has burped. He may not have taken in much air this time. If he needs to burp later, he will do so, with or without your help.

A sitting up position is often recommended for burping. Be sure that while he is sitting forward with his chin supported in your hand, his stomach is not folded so that it is difficult for the air to rise above the milk level and escape. Don't try to force air out of him; force will certainly bring milk with it.

If your baby is one of the few who really seems uncomfortable until he has burped, but is slow to do so, he may manage better if you put him to sleep lying on his stomach rather than on his side. In this position he can burp if he needs to, and if he brings milk up with the air (see opposite), there is no risk of him choking on it.

---

## Burping

Burping is an overrated problem. Your baby will get air in her stomach. Milk, which is heavier than air, will fall below it if you hold her upright, so she will usually burp the air out. But if she does not, don't waste time thumping her. Her stomach may not be uncomfortably distended this time; she may burp later in her crib; either way it does not matter.

*The best burping position: the baby is stretched out straight and upright. Rubbing or patting her back may help.*

*A burp in this position will almost certainly bring milk with it as air cannot rise above the milk level.*

*In this position the baby's stomach is folded, making it difficult for air to rise above the milk level and escape.*

*Spitting up milk*     Almost all babies sometimes bring up some milk along with the air. Usually the quantity is very small, although it may look a lot because it is mixed with saliva and spread all over your shoulder! If you are worried, spill $\frac{1}{4}$oz (5ml) on purpose to give you a standard of comparison. If it really *is* a lot, there are several possible reasons for it:

The baby may have sucked more than he could comfortably hold. He is sensibly bringing back the overflow.

You may have fed him in too flat a position, preventing the air from rising above the milk. Try holding him more upright.

You may have bounced him about, mixing the air with the milk, or banged him on the back before the air had reached the top of the stomach. Handle him gently immediately after feedings.

You may have delayed his feeding while he cried, or you may have made him cry mid-feeding by trying to make him burp when he wanted to suck. The crying will have put a lot of extra air into his stomach, followed by the rest of his milk.

You may not have tilted the bottle sufficiently to ensure that the entrance to the nipple was always covered with milk. The baby will have had sucks of pure air between sucks of milk and it will all be mixed up together in his stomach.

The hole in the nipple may have been too small so that the baby had to suck very hard and swallowed air with each mouthful of milk. Check that when you hold the bottle upside down, milk drips out at several drops per second. (Don't check with water; because it is thinner it comes out faster than milk.)

Some babies spit up a great deal, bringing back milk at every feeding – sometimes more than once. They may reduce your clothes to ruins and you to despair but *they do themselves no harm.* Check with your doctor if you are worried, but unless your baby is failing to soak his diaper (*without* being given extra drinks of water) or to gain weight, you can be sure he is not losing more from his feedings than he can spare.

*Vomiting*     If a baby brings up milk some time after feeding, it will be curdled because digestive juices will already have been working on it. If an hour or more has passed since the feeding, it may smell nasty. The baby may only have had some air trapped inside the stomach which has now come up bringing the partly digested milk with it, or there may be a digestive disturbance or it may signal the beginning of an illness.

If the baby seems unwell and especially if there is any fever or any sign of diarrhea, consult your doctor or clinic. If the baby seems perfectly well let hunger guide feedings as usual and just keep an eye open for any symptoms.

*Projectile vomiting*     This is quite different either from hiccuping milk up with some air or from ordinary vomiting. The baby spurts milk out toward the end of a feeding with such force that it may hit the floor or a wall as much as three or four feet away.

A baby who does this regularly probably has a condition called "pyloric stenosis." This is a fault in the muscles of the stomach outlet. It is much more usual in boys than in girls and is easily and permanently corrected by a small operation (Ref/VOMITING).

# Food and growth

New babies need as much breast milk or properly made formula as they willingly drink and the offer of some cooled boiled water a couple of times each day. They do not need anything else until they are at *least* three months old (see p. 128).

Once the birthweight has been regained at around ten days old (see p. 44) the baby will gain weight at around 1oz (28g) per day. Of course there will be day-to-day variations, but he will average 6–8oz (170–225g) each week.

Many parents find it difficult to leave it entirely to the baby to decide how much milk to take. They feel a great need to know exactly what he "ought" to have so that they can be sure he is having enough. But feeding a baby is not an exact science because babies vary just as much as older people in their food needs. A baby with a slow, efficient metabolism will have plenty of energy and grow well on fewer calories than a baby who burns his food up faster and less completely.

Most adults are bad at adjusting their food intake to suit their individual metabolisms. Our eating is mixed up with habit, social customs and pure greed. But a small baby's adjustment is almost always perfect, at least until we confuse it for him by introducing solid foods. Whatever quantities your baby takes, you can be quite sure that they are right for him provided he is offered as much as he wants whenever he wants it; he is contented most of the time and becoming more contented as he gets older and more settled; he is active whenever he is awake and becoming more so with age and he gains weight steadily at somewhere near that expected 6–8oz (170–225g) each week.

If your baby is bottle-fed you may want to know approximately how much milk he is likely to want – if only so that you can organize your shopping. It is usually reckoned that babies should have about 3oz (85ml) of milk for each pound of their bodyweight *offered* to them during an average 24-hour period. That means around 21oz (595ml) for a 7lb (3.2kg) baby and around 27oz (765ml) for a 9lb (4.1kg) baby. But don't let those figures affect your feeding. The baby can have more if he wants it and will often take less. Remember that if he were breast-fed you would not know how much he'd had.

*Expected weight gain*  If you find yourself worrying about your baby's weight gain or you want a scientific way of supporting your own observations of his or her abundant good health, you need to understand the importance of the rate of weight gain we expect and therefore of your baby's *expected* or *ideal* weight.

Your baby's birthweight is his personal starting point for growth. Whatever that birthweight was, he will grow roughly the same amount and at approximately the same rate as all other babies. His overall growth follows a pre-set trajectory rather like a rocket which, once launched, follows a pre-determined pattern. You fuel his growth with proper food and adequate care and as long as you do so the upward growth curve will be steady. If illness, starvation, serious neglect or emotional disturbance should lead his weight gain to dip downward off that expected curve, he will need an extra boost of food-energy to put him back on course. If over-concentrated bottles or concealed cereals should lead his weight gain to peak upward off his personal curve, he will need the milk reduced to its proper composition so that he can get back on course.

So a baby needs to be fed, always, according to his expected weight. If he has gained much less than average, feeding him as if he had gained normally will give him the chance to gain fast for a while. If he has gained very fast, feeding him as if he had not will give him the chance to slow his rate of gain for a while. Of course if he is being fed on demand, with neither restriction nor forcing, he will see to this for himself. But if his food is limited by a scanty breast milk supply or strict scheduling, or if it is pushed on him by an over-strong formula or too-early solids, he may not be able to make the adjustment for himself. Assuming that the weight the scales tell you that he *is* equals the weight he is *meant to be* could lead you into a vicious circle of misfeeding. Let's look at how this might happen in practice.

Imagine that your baby was born weighing 7lb (3.2kg) but was ill after birth, lost more weight than average and now, in his third week, is being bottle-fed and weighs 6lbs (2.7kg). If you accepted that 6lbs (2.7kg) actual weight as normal for him you might assume that six times 3oz (85ml) would meet his needs in each 24 hours, offer him that much, be pleased when he drank it all and then horrified to find that he was not gaining weight. The point is that that baby's *expected* weight is not 6lbs (2.7kg) but around 8lbs (3.6kg) so that 18oz (510ml) of milk could not possibly be enough. He needs to be offered around 24oz (680ml) and to be allowed to drink as much of it as he wants.

*Calculating your baby's expected weight*

| Calculation | Example baby's expected weight | |
| --- | --- | --- |
| *Start with the birthweight* | *Birthweight* | *7lbs* |
| *Subtract 1oz per day for days 1–5* | *Weight at 5 days* | *6lbs 11oz* |
| *Add 1oz per day for days 6–10* | *Weight at 10 days* | *7lbs* |
| *Add 1oz per day or 6–8oz per week from 10 days to 3 months* | *Weight at 30 days* | *8lbs 4oz* |
| | *Weight at 2 months* | *10lbs 2oz* |
| | *Weight at 3 months* | *12lbs* |

*Height or length matter, too*

Weight gain is not the only way to assess a baby's growth. Children are not meant to get fatter and fatter but bigger overall. Getting taller (or longer) matters, too. Your baby's length will change much more slowly than the weight and it is far more difficult to measure accurately, but whatever your baby's length at birth, approximately $\frac{3}{4}$in (2cm) will be gained each month or just over 2in (5cm) in three months.

Just as there is an expected *weight* for a baby of any age, related to birthweight, so there is an expected *length* at any age, related to birth-length. A complete record of your baby's growth means charting both measurements together (Ref/GROWTH). You will find that if all is going well, the two will rise in a consistent relationship to each other.

Changes and
exceptions to
normal growth
patterns Having said all this, babies do not continue to grow at the same rate
as each other forever. We interfere with the regularity of growth
by overfeeding or underfeeding, or introducing solid foods early or
late. Life interferes too, making one child subject to many
infections and another resistant to them. Eventually the child's
own hormones interfere: the pre-puberty growth spurt takes place
at different times and rates in different people. But for most babies
the pattern shown on the growth charts on pages 510 to 513 will be
the norm for at least the first year and often for the first three years.

The most common exceptions are premature babies (see p. 32).
They may be very slow to get started with feeding and therefore
with growing. They may do no more than hold their low position,
relative to average babies, for a long time.

Small-for-dates babies (see p. 33) may make startling growth
during their early weeks, especially if they were partly starved in
the womb. With excellent care such babies may change position
from the very bottom of the lowest section of the chart to
somewhere near the top of that "small baby" section.

Babies who are ill immediately after birth or in their first weeks
may fail to start gaining weight or may actually lose some. Again
excellent care may lead to a spurt of "catch up growth" so that the
baby's personal growth curve shifts upwards and then settles
down on the new, higher trajectory.

Babies who are bottle-fed from birth may lose no weight in the
first days. They may even gain very fast from the beginning,
especially if the formula is made too strong or they are encouraged
to take a set amount. An even greater rise in such a baby's weight
curve may be seen if solid foods are added early to the full quota of
over-concentrated milk. It is in a case like this that the importance
of recording length as well as weight becomes clear: a baby who is
gaining weight faster than nature intended will not gain length to
match it. The disparity is your cue that your child is getting obese
rather than simply growing large.

*"Average" is
easier* Society is geared to average babies. If your baby was not of average
birthweight you need to be aware of it and allow for the difference.
Baby clothes which are sized by age may mislead you. A stretch
suit for "birth to three months" means 7–12lbs (3.2–5.5kg) and
length to match. It will not last your ten pounder for long. Over-
the-counter medicines still occasionally advise dosage by age
rather than weight and that can be extremely misleading. A small
baby needs less of any medicine than a larger one.

Above all, don't be taken in by the various "sayings" about
weight gain which you may hear quoted as gospel truth. This one,
for example: "A baby should double his birthweight by six months
and triple it by a year." Well, should yours? If you look at the chart
on page 510 you will see that the average birthweight boy in the
middle will indeed double his birthweight in six months and triple
it in a year, but the small baby at the bottom will almost double his
in *three* months and triple it in six. If he gained "by the saying," he
would be half starved. As for the big baby at the top, while his
birthweight may indeed double by six months it will be nowhere
near tripled by a year. If he gained "by the saying," he would be
grossly fat.

# Keeping your baby warm

Warmth is important to new babies. If their environment is kept warm, they do not have to use any energy in warming themselves and they also tend to be relaxed and contented. If their environment gets cool, they have to use energy on heat-production instead of using it for the activities of living and growing. They tend to be fretful and restless, too. If they are allowed to get cold, there is a possibility of dangerous chilling (see below).

*Ideal warmth*  All human beings make heat for their bodies in the same way. When we need more warmth, our metabolic rate goes up, with a faster heart beat and quicker breathing. We use up some of our food-calories to release energy in the form of heat. This process of heat-production is efficient in a baby from the moment of birth, but unlike older people the new baby is not very good at *conserving* the heat that he makes. Instead of getting warm and staying warm, he loses heat as fast as he makes it. He has to go on and on using energy to make warmth until extra heat provided from outside relieves him of the necessity.

Experiments have shown that a *naked* newborn baby does not stop using energy to make warmth until the temperature immediately around his body reaches about 85°F (29°C). While this is too hot for an ordinary family room, it is a reasonable temperature to aim at in a room where you bathe a brand new baby. The rest of the time you can ensure that the air around his body stays at this ideal temperature simply by dressing him. Three light layers of clothing (such as a tee-shirt and diaper, a stretch suit and a blanket) will keep the air inside the bundle warm enough with room temperatures around 68°F (20°C).

*Cooler temperatures*  A baby's ability to conserve his own warmth improves with age and weight. His ability to spare some energy for heat-production improves too. A baby who was premature and now weighs only around 6lbs (2.7kg) should definitely be kept indoors at a steady temperature and should only be undressed in really warm places. On the other hand, a three-month-old baby weighing around 12lbs (5.5kg) will have begun to be able to conserve warmth and can well afford to use some energy on keeping himself warm for at least some of the time.

Between those extremes, commonsense precautions will keep your baby warm enough to be both safe and contented. Exposure to very cool temperatures should be kept brief. A short trip in his carriage with the air temperature in the 50s will not hurt him. The insulation of his wrappings will conserve his warmth for some of the time, and making his own heat for the rest of it will not drain him of energy. A whole morning in the carriage in the yard is a different matter. Why should he be forced to work at keeping warm for so long when he could get just as much fresh air beside an open window?

Don't let him cool right off while he is deeply asleep. As long as he is awake or merely dozing, his heat-producing mechanism will "switch on" as soon as it is needed and prevent him from getting chilled. But if his sleep is so deep that the cold does not disturb him, the mechanism will not come into play and he could go straight from sleep into a chilled state (see below). If your house cools off markedly during the night, you must make sure that his room is separately heated at least for a few weeks.

*Signs of chilling* A baby who is managing to keep himself warm but would be happier if outside conditions relieved him of the task will be restless. His breathing will be faster than usual and he may cry. While his hands and feet may feel cool, his chest and stomach, under his clothes, will still feel normally warm. As soon as you take him to a warmer place (especially out of a cool breeze), he will become calmer and more relaxed.

A baby who is losing the battle to stay warm and is in danger of becoming chilled behaves quite differently. He is very quiet and still. He will not cry until he is beginning to get warm and can therefore spare the energy which crying takes. His hands and feet will feel cold and even the skin of his chest under his clothes will feel cool to your hand. Do not simply add more wrappings. He is already cold and is showing you that he cannot make more heat for himself at the moment. Extra wrappings will insulate the coldness in. He needs to get warmer first – perhaps by being taken into a warm room and given a warm feeding or by being cuddled under a wrap or blanket. After that, extra wrappings will insulate in the warmth that he needs.

If such a baby were given no help in getting warm or was left asleep with his heat-producing mechanism not working, he could slip into the next stage of chilling which is called the "neo-natal cold syndrome." This is very rare but it is dangerous. Vital bodily functions run so slowly that the baby is lethargic, floppy, difficult to wake up and unable to suck. His hands and feet look swollen and bright pink. His skin is very cold to touch. A baby in this condition needs urgent medical attention as he will have to be re-warmed slowly and with great care.

*Getting too hot* Hot weather seldom bothers babies as long as they have plenty to drink so that they sweat freely, and loose light clothes so that the sweat can evaporate and cool them. When it's really hot, banish plastic pants, which prevent evaporation, and use a sun-canopy instead of the stroller hood, which traps warm air around the baby. If he is irritable and his skin is dry, sponge him with warm water and fan him. Overheating is more often caused by clothes than high air temperatures, though. Don't leave your baby to sleep in a carry nest or even in a snow suit; once you have brought him inside, you must take off outdoor clothes, however reluctant you are to disturb him. And don't overdress him in a warm room. He doesn't need wrappings *and* blankets *and* a quilt. . . .

*Direct heat* Direct heat is a hazard to small babies. Until the friction of clothes and exposure to air, wind and sun have toughened it, the baby's skin is very fragile. Guard it from obvious threats like sunburn and hot water bottles, and from less expected ones too. Don't leave him on a rug close to the fire, a light bulb or a radiator.

# Everyday care

## Handling your baby

New babies have an instinctive fear of being dropped which shows whenever their heavy heads are allowed to flop or their uncontroled limbs dangle in space. They can neither support their own heads nor control their own muscles and they are only relaxed and happy when someone does it for them. In a crib or carriage the mattress provides support; in someone's arms the adult body supports the baby's, but being picked up or put down introduces a potentially alarming moment when one kind of support is removed before the other is established.

The answer is to give new babies a moment with *both* kinds of support before either is removed. If you are picking your baby up, arrange your hands and arms under and around him while the mattress is still supporting the weight. Don't even begin to lift until the baby has felt the new security your hands are providing. When you put the baby

down, reverse the process: keep your supporting hands in place as you put him down so that the baby has time to register the security of the mattress before you remove them.

Arranging your hands and arms takes practice before it becomes an unthinking skill. But you will not go far wrong if you think of new babies as badly wrapped parcels. If you pick them up around the middle, both ends will flop. If you concentrate on supporting their heads, their legs will dangle. You have to gather them together so that you can move them in a compact bundle. Above all, do make sure that your baby is aware of what you are going to do before you do it, that you move slowly and that you keep to a minimum the distances through empty space which he must travel. If, for example, you are picking your baby up from a porta-crib on the floor, kneel down to take the baby into your arms. Don't stand up until he is nestled against you.

## Picking up and putting down

Give the baby a few moments supported by your hands and the mattress before you take one of them away. Never pick her up without alerting her to your presence by talking to her and touching her. Would you like to be swooped into the air by an invisible giant?

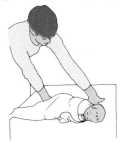

*Put your left hand under her neck and your right hand under her bottom. Spread the fingers to support her head and thighs.*

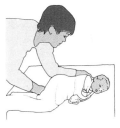

*Lean down so that your left wrist and forearm follow her spine right down to her waist level.*

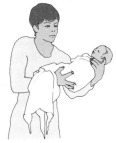

*Lift slowly. Your arms support her in the same position as the mattress.*

*Your arms are in the right position to put her to your shoulder without any more jouncing around.*

*You can even free your right hand by shifting your left elbow around to brace her against you.*

*To put her down, lower her slowly until her head and back are on your left hand and arm on the mattress.*

*Lower her bottom and when it too is supported, gently slide your hands from beneath her.*

EVERYDAY CARE  75

# Dressing and undressing

Dressing and undressing upset many babies. They fear the feeling of air on bare skin and dislike being pulled around. So keep nakedness to a minimum and try to pull the clothes rather than the limbs. At the beginning you will probably feel that you do not have enough hands to support that wobbly neck *and* hold the whole baby steady *and* pull the clothes on or off.

Use a firm surface, such as a bed or changing table, and lie the baby on that while you deal with the bottom half. This is much easier than doing it on your lap because it keeps the baby properly supported and both your hands free.

It is the top half that causes problems, and here the type of clothes you use will help or hinder you (see below). Take the baby on your lap and cross your knees so that the upper one supports the lower back. That leaves a hand for the head and another for clothes.

## Undressing

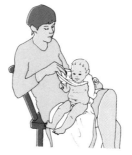

*Settle him on a blanket on your lap with your legs crossed, your left arm around him, and his head against your bosom.*

*Lift the top garment to shoulder level, concertina each sleeve with your left hand and lift it off his arm with your right.*

*Now shift your left arm so that the wrist supports his neck and he sits with his head just clear of your bosom.*

*Stretch the neck of the garment wide open, using your right hand and the thumb of your left.*

*Lift it cleanly over his head without scraping his nose or ears or jerking his head back.*

*Wrap him immediately in the blanket he is sitting on and cuddle him against you.*

## Clothing

Try to buy clothes that will be easy for both of you. If everything the baby wears fastens down the front, for example, you will not have to turn him over to do up the back.

If all long sleeves are raglan type, you will be able to use your hand to guide the baby's through, instead of trying to push that soft little fist through a tight sleeve by itself.

If none of the clothes has ribbons or strings to tie, you will not find them in a knot just when you are in a hurry, and you will not find them chewed or wrapped around the baby's neck either.

If most of the clothes are made of stretch materials, the whole business will be far easier.

## Dressing

*Settle him as for undressing. Use your right hand and the thumb of your left to stretch neck of garment.*

*Pop it over his head, keeping it open so that it goes on without scraping his nose or ears.*

*To pull on each sleeve, first put your left hand up the sleeve in reverse and grasp his hand.*

*Then, with your right hand, pull the sleeve over his arm rather than his arm through the sleeve.*

## Cleanliness

Babies do not need to be kept nearly as clean as most of us keep them. It is adults who like them to smell of baby powder. The chief purpose in washing a new baby is to remove from the skin anything which might irritate and make it sore. The skin would take care of itself if it did not get drenched with urine, smeared with feces, splashed with sticky milk and lightly speckled with dust.

Most mothers will be taught by the hospital staff, to bathe their new babies every single day. If you want to carry on with this, a reasonably easy method is given on p. 145. But if, like many mothers, you find that the bath is something that neither you nor the baby can enjoy just yet, you don't have to do it. You can make your baby perfectly clean by "topping and tailing," and what is more you can do it without frightening him or putting yourself through the horrors of trying to hold a slippery screaming mite safely with shaking hands in a bath full of water. . . .

The topping and tailing method of washing a new baby concentrates on cleaning thoroughly the bits that really need it: the eyes, nose and ears, the face, hands and bottom. It keeps undressing (and therefore re-dressing) to a diaper-changing minimum, and it can all be done without picking the baby up.

Notice that the method does not include any interference with any *inside* part of the body. It does not include poking bits of cotton balls up the nose, cleaning out the ears with "Q-tips," or pulling back the foreskin of a little boy (Ref/CIRCUMCISION). All of a baby's orifices are lined with mucous membranes which are designed to bring out any dirt. The slight flow of mucus from the nose will carry dirt out with it; wax will work its way out of the ears and within reach of your cotton balls in its own good time; tears bathe the eyes continually and far more efficiently than you can. So concentrate on wiping away what appears on the outside. Don't go hunting up the nostrils or into the ears with twists of cotton balls; if you do, you may actually push back the dirt. It is a good principle never to interfere with any part not visible from the outside.

Always use warm boiled water and a separate cotton ball for each eye and wipe from the inner to the outer corners. This will avoid the risk of spreading any minor infection from one eye to the other.

## Topping and tailing

Put the baby on a towel on a bed or changing table. Gather together a bowl of warm *boiled* water – this is for his eyes – another of ordinary warm water, cotton balls, washcloths, a soft towel, clean diapers and any cream, powder, etc.

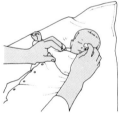
*Wipe each eye with its own cotton ball and boiled water. Wipe always from inner corner outward.*

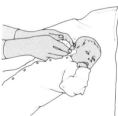
*With another cotton ball, wipe around ears and neck to get rid of dried sweat which might cause soreness.*

*Use a further cotton ball to clean around his mouth and chin creases to remove dried milk and dribble.*

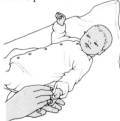
*Use a clean washcloth dampened in warm water to wipe his hands, checking for any sharp fingernails (see p. 143).*

*Now take off his diaper. If he is merely wet, wipe him with a damp washcloth.*

*If he is soiled, get the worst off with the diaper, then use soap on one washcloth and rinse it off carefully with another.*

*Dry every skinfold, not forgetting the crease between his buttocks; apply cream if you like, powder if you must!*

### Diapers

Disposable diapers are available in a vast range of sizes, shapes and qualities. You can often find Rolls Royce diapers at Ford prices among supermarket own–brands, so look for features rather than best-known name:

**Absorbency** need not go with bulk. Slim-line diapers with an inner layer are more absorbent than thicker ones.

**A one-way lining** next to the baby's skin keeps the bottom dry when the diaper is wet.

**An adjustable waist** is essential for a reasonable fit.

### Using disposables

Disposables are bulky to carry home. Once you have found a kind you like, look into bulk-order schemes which deliver to your door. If you can store enough to meet minimum order requirements, you may get a price reduction as well. Don't buy too many in the newborn size, though; work out what you are likely to need at about eight diapers per day to begin with and a weight gain of around 1oz (30g) a day.

"Disposable" means "throwaway"; it does *not* mean "flush away"! You'll also be more popular with neighbors and garbage disposal people if you put diapers in plastic bags before getting rid of them.

### Using washable diapers

Some parents still swear by washable diapers. If you are already equipped to launder and dry them, they will cost less money in the long run although they'll cost a lot more work than disposables. A diaper service may be the answer. The service provides a container with plastic liners. Each week it collects soiled diapers and drops off a supply of clean diapers.

Choose between shaped and rectangular, velcro-fastening or diaper-pins. You will also need one-way liners, and plastic pants.

### Changing diapers

Whatever kind of diapers you use, changing your baby is going to punctuate your life for a long time. It's worth organizing "changing stations" to make the whole business quick and easy.

**A changing table is easier than your lap** because it leaves both your hands free and saves your clothes, too. You don't need an elaborate piece of baby furniture; a plastic changing mat on an ordinary chest, table or trolley will do. Try to place your mat at a height that saves you from backache. If a sofa is the obvious piece of furniture, kneel on the floor rather than stand bent double.

**Keep everything you need gathered within reach.** Once you've put the baby on that mat, you can't leave him while you search for wipes or cotton balls.

**Babies who are only wet don't need washing** at every diaper change. Baby lotion or oil on cotton balls or wipes are quite enough between regular baths or topping and tailing sessions. Don't use soap if your baby's bottom tends to get sore; wash, when you must, with plain water.

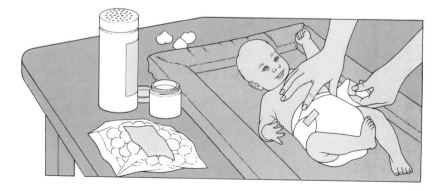

# Excreting

**"Changing" stools**  Once the baby's bowel is cleared of meconium (see p. 42), and milk feeding – whether from the breast or from a bottle – has begun, "changing" stools will be passed. As the name suggests, their rather peculiar character is due to the changeover from transfusion feeding in the womb to ordinary digestion.

Changing stools are usually greeny-brown, semi-fluid and frequent. But sometimes they are bright green, full of curds and mucus and violently expelled. If they look like this, don't automatically assume that the baby has violent diarrhea. Peculiar-looking stools are a feature of these early days.

If the stools really worry you, take the baby to the doctor, with one of the soiled diapers in a sealed plastic bag, so that he can check that there is no infective diarrhea (gastroenteritis). If the baby is being breast-fed, gastroenteritis is extremely unlikely. If feeding is by bottle, it is a possibility, but it is still a remote one if the baby seems contented and sucks well.

It may be three weeks or even more before your baby settles to passing normal or "settled" stools.

**"Settled" stools**  A baby who is having only breast milk and extra water will *probably* pass orangey-yellow stools with the consistency of mustard and only a mild sour-milk smell. But he may sometimes pass stools that are greenish, full of mucus or otherwise peculiar without being in any way unwell. Try not to take too much interest in his diapers: concentrate on his general wellbeing.

He may have so many movements each day that you never change a diaper that is not soiled as well as wet. On the other hand, he may have only one movement every three, four or even seven days. Both extremes and everything in between them are absolutely normal. And it is normal for him to swing from one to the other.

A breast-fed baby's food is always perfect for him. A bottle-fed baby's food may not be. If the formula you have chosen is not right for him, then you may get your first clue from your baby's stools. Don't switch back and forth between formulas without medical advice, though.

Bottle-fed babies usually pass stools which are more solid and formed than those of the breast-fed baby, because formula leaves more residue than breast milk. They are a pale brown color and smell more like ordinary stools. They are usually less frequent than the stools of a breast-fed baby.

**Constipation**  If a bottle-fed baby goes for a day or two without passing a stool and then passes a hard one which causes obvious discomfort, he is constipated. Lack of fluid is a common cause; offer extra drinks of water. If the stools remain hard, the remedy is to adjust the amount of sugar he has. Sugar loosens the stools by fermenting in the intestine and hurrying the passage of waste. A little sweetened diluted fruit juice as a mid-morning or mid-afternoon drink will probably lead to comfortably soft stools.

*Diarrhea*  If a bottle-fed baby suddenly starts to have diarrhea he should see the doctor in case he has got gastroenteritis. If he is vomiting as well, goes off feedings and/or seems feverish or ill, then the appointment should be made as an emergency. Gastroenteritis can be extremely dangerous to babies, especially to very young ones. The immediate danger is loss of fluid from the body due to the diarrhea and exacerbated by any vomiting (Ref/DEHYDRATION). The baby should be offered as much cooled boiled water as he will drink.

But most loose stools will be found to be due to diet not to infection. Too much sugar can cause diarrhea, just as extra sugar corrects constipation. Are you adding cereal to the bottles instead of giving the formula exactly as the manufacturer recommends? Are you giving the baby lots of fruit juice? Or giving him drinks of sugar water or a pacifier dipped in something sweet?

Too much fat can also cause loose stools. If your baby is not digesting the particular fats in his formula, the stools will smell very nasty. Once again, take the baby and a soiled diaper to the doctor. If he feels that the fat in the milk is not agreeing with the baby, he may recommend that you change to a different formula. Don't switch formulas before you consult your doctor.

*Color changes*  Even before you introduce any solid foods, some "extras" can cause quite alarming color changes in the stools. Grape juice, for example, may turn the stools reddish or purple. Various over-the-counter medicines will color the stools, while if the doctor has prescribed iron for the baby, the stools may be blackish.

*Urine*  It does not matter if the baby wets himself very often; it may matter if he wets himself infrequently.

A new baby who is dry after a couple of hours needs watching. His body may be using up more fluid than usual because he is starting a fever. Or he may need more than usual because it is a hot day or because he is wearing a very warm blanket. Give him plenty of extra drinks of water or juice, and see if he is still dry after another two hours. If he is (and he almost certainly will not be), phone your doctor. The baby just might have an obstruction.

Too little fluid, especially when the weather is hot or when he has fever, can make the urine extra strong and concentrated. If it is really strong, it may stain the diaper yellow and redden the baby's skin. Once again, he needs more to drink.

If the urine goes on being very strong, even though the baby is drinking plenty, and especially if it begins to have a nasty fishy smell, then you should take him to the doctor. It is possible he has a urinary infection.

Of course if you think there is blood in your baby's urine, you will make an immediate appointment with the doctor. But pause to think for a moment. If your baby is a girl and the redness you can see is blood, it may be coming from the vagina rather than from the bladder. Vaginal bleeding is quite normal during the first few days of life (see p. 42), and on a wet diaper can easily look as if it is part of the urine. Equally, the redness on the diaper may not be blood at all if, for example, it follows the baby's first drink of diluted grape juice.

# Sleeping

New babies sleep exactly the amount that their personal physiology tells them to sleep. There is nothing that you can do to make your baby sleep more than this amount and nothing that the baby can do to sleep less. Unless he is ill, in pain, or extremely uncomfortable he will do his sleeping wherever he finds himself and under almost any circumstances. So your power over his actual hours of sleep is very limited. By making him comfortable you can ensure that he sleeps as much as he wants to, but you cannot put him to sleep. On the other hand, if you are somewhere where you cannot make him very comfortable – in a bus, for example – you need not worry about him being kept awake. If he stays awake, it is because he does not need to sleep.

*Separating sleep from wakefulness*

At the very beginning of life the baby often drifts so gradually from being awake to being asleep that it is difficult to tell which state he is in at any given moment. He may start a feeding wide awake and ravenous, suck himself into a blissful trance so that only his occasional bursts of sucking tell you that he is still at least a little awake, and then drift into sleep so deep that nothing you do will wake him.

This kind of drifting does not matter at all from his point of view. He is simply doing what he needs to do when he needs to do it. But from your point of view it is a good idea to help him gradually to make a more complete difference between being awake and being asleep. It will be much easier for you to organize your life later on if you know that the baby is either awake (and therefore bound to need some attention and company), or asleep (and therefore unlikely to need anything at all for a while). Babies who do learn early to be either fully awake or fully asleep are likely to be the ones who sleep for reasonably long periods at night, too.

So, rather than letting him drift and doze on somebody's lap, it is a good idea to start from the very beginning to "put him to bed" when he needs to sleep and to "get him up" when he is awake. If he is always put into his carriage or crib when he is really sleepy, he will soon come to associate those places with being asleep. If he is always taken into whatever company is available when he is awake, he will make that association too.

*Disturbances to sleep*

A sleeping baby need not mean a hushed household. Ordinary sounds and activities will not disturb him at this early age. But if everybody creeps about and talks in whispers while he is asleep, there may come a time when he cannot sleep unless they do. It is therefore important to let him sleep through whatever sound level is normal for your household so that he does not come to expect a quietness that will make all your lives a misery.

At this stage he will be disturbed most often by internal stimuli. Hunger will disturb him; being cold may disturb him if he is not in a very deep sleep; pain will wake him and so may passing a bowel movement or burping. Sometimes the jerks and twitches of his body as it relaxes toward deep sleep will disturb him too.

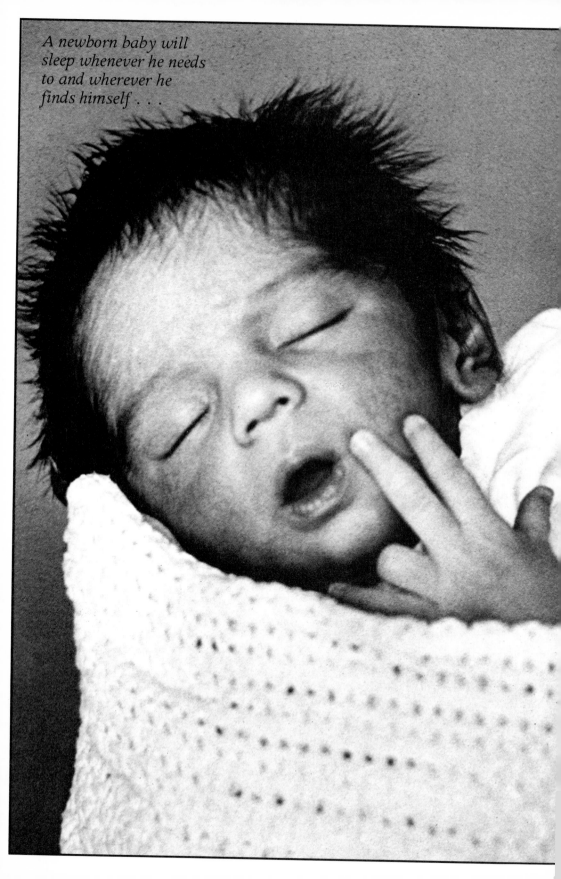

*A newborn baby will sleep whenever he needs to and wherever he finds himself . . .*

Of course, outside stimuli can disturb the baby, but when they do it will usually be because they change very suddenly. He may drop off to sleep quite happily with the television set on, but wake when it is switched off. A toddler playing around the room will not keep him awake but one coming in may wake him.

*Helping your baby to separate night from day*

Although human beings are mainly diurnal creatures, sleeping by night and active by day, babies do not seem to have a clear and inbuilt mechanism instructing them accordingly. They start off sleeping and waking randomly through the 24 hours. It takes time and sensible handling to persuade them to do most of their sleeping at night and most of their being awake in the daytime. The majority learn to adopt this pattern fairly rapidly, if not as rapidly as their exhausted parents would choose!

You can speed up the process by making a clear difference between going to bed for the night and ordinary daytime naps, from the beginning. "Topping and tailing" him and changing him into nightclothes can be part of this. Giving the suppertime feeding in his room can be part of it, too. Above all, put him down to sleep in the crib and the room that he is going to use all night, rather than putting him in his stroller somewhere else in the house as you might during the day.

**Take extra trouble to make the baby comfortable.** If you are merely putting him to bed for a daytime nap, it may not matter very much to you if a burp wakes him a little while later. When it is night, try to ensure that he has finished with burping and that nothing that you can foresee is going to disturb him.

**Wrap the baby up securely** (see p. 89). In the daytime it does not matter if his own movements bring him fully awake as soon as his sleep lightens. At night you want him so securely wrapped that he will not wake even during the normal periods of light sleep which intersperse heavy slumber.

**Darken the room sufficiently** to make it seem different from daytime, and to ensure that when he opens his eyes (as all babies do from time to time during the night) his attention is not caught by anything brightly lit or clearly visible. But leave a dim (15 watt) light on so that you can attend to him during the night without switching on more lights.

**Make sure the room is warm** and that it stays warm. Getting chilly will wake him if it happens when he is in light sleep, and can be risky if it happens while he is in deep sleep (see p. 73).

**Keep night feedings as sleepy and as brief as possible.** The baby is bound to wake up because he cannot yet get through the night without food and drink, but the less completely he awakens, the better. Make sure, before you leave him, that everything you will need during the night is gathered together. You don't want to have to carry him around while you search for a dry diaper.

When he cries, go to him immediately so that he has no time to get into a wakeful misery. Don't play and talk while you feed him; concentrate on soothing cuddles instead. Daytime feedings are social playtimes, but night feedings are for sustenance only.

Lack of sleep, more especially, *broken* sleep is the very worst part of parenting for many people. It is not just new babies who wake because they have to be fed; *all* babies wake from time to time and most of them insist on adult company and comfort when they do. You can cross your fingers for the kind of baby who sleeps all night, every night, from six weeks of age, but don't hold your breath. There are a great many parents who have not managed to share a single unbroken period of seven hours sleep by the time their child is three. . . .

There are two very different approaches to this problem-area and it is worth trying to decide which will suit you, so that you start out as you mean to go on. The first approach is a basic acceptance of this small new person not just into your life but into your nightlife and your bed. A "family bed" will not stop your baby from waking up and it will not save you from night feedings in the first weeks. But if he is sharing your bed with you, your baby's awakenings and his feeding will disturb you far less than they will if you have to go to him. And, because he is where he best likes to be – close against you – he will go back to sleep far more quickly and easily. Sharing beds is not dangerous. You will not smother the baby yourself and your pillows can easily be kept out of his way.

Babies who sleep in "family beds" from early on often wake much less than other babies as they get older. As they get older still, they may wake but find it unnecessary to wake you. After all a toddler who is with you in bed does not need to cry for a cuddle because he is already having it or can just snuggle up.

But "family beds" do have snags and it's sensible to foresee them if you can. Once you start having your baby in bed with you, or at least once he has had a few months of this way of sleeping, you are very unlikely to be able to persuade him, without a long and miserable fight, that a separate crib in a separate room is nicer. And however much you enjoy sharing a bed with your six-week-old baby, you may find that you change your mind later on. A baby or toddler in your bed does cut down your privacy, and being with him by night as well as by day can make you as an individual feel totally submerged.

The second approach welcomes the baby into your life but determinedly excludes him from your nightlife and your bed. It means doing everything you can to help him sleep happily alone. It means going to him whenever he cries for you but never taking him in with you or letting him come to you when he is older. It leaves you much freer when he sleeps well but it may condemn you to endless visits to his cribside when his teeth are bothering him or he has bad dreams and, later still, it may mean returning him to his bed night after night.

Nobody can make this choice for you. You may not be able to make it either: even once you have decided on the second approach, a bad week may find you taking your baby into bed with you at 3am after all because nothing seems to matter except being allowed to get your head down. Try to be aware of the choice and think about it, though. Your worst option is an attempt to compromise, sometimes letting him sleep with you and sometimes trying to insist that he stay alone.

If you plan to aim for separate beds, there are a few steps which you can take to maximize your own sleeping hours even during these early weeks of night-feeding:

**Wake the baby for a late-night feeding at your bedtime.** If you wait for him to wake, you will be losing sleeping time. If you go to sleep for an hour and then he wakes, you've been disturbed an unnecessary time. It will not hurt him to be fed before he knows he is hungry.

**Think of your own small-hours comfort.** If you are bottle-feeding, leaving the bottle ready in the refrigerator and a thermos filled with hot water to warm it will cut down your work. If a hot drink helps you get back to sleep, leave that ready in a thermos, too. If cold feet keep you awake after feedings, you could think about an electric blanket. . . .

**Feed the baby as soon as crying begins.** If you "leave him to cry," he may indeed cry himself back to sleep, if he was not very hungry. But he will keep you awake while he is crying and then wake again, *extremely* hungry, just as you have gotten back to sleep yourself. If you "make him wait a bit," he will keep you awake with his crying and when you finally feed him he may be too tired and upset to take a full feeding. He will wake you again sooner than he might have done if you had fed him promptly. If you "give him sugar water," the sucking and thirst-quenching may put him back to sleep. But once again the peace will not last; his stomach will soon remind him that you fooled him.

**Discipline yourself to sleep the moment the baby is settled.** It is easy to lie awake wondering if he is going to need another burp or another ounce. If he does need you, he will soon let you know. If he does not, waiting for him to cry will lose you yet another piece of sleeping time.

**Move the baby out of your room as soon as possible.** His small snifflings and movements at your bedside may disturb you more than you realize. If they mean that you peep into the crib every half hour you may actually disturb him. Of course you *must* be sure that you will hear even the smallest cry, but you will get far more rest if you cannot hear anything quieter and less urgent than that.

**Decide whether one or both parents are going to cope.** Although the very early night feedings seem part of the excitement of having a baby and you may both want to be involved, there is a long stint of too little sleep ahead of you. There is not really much point in both of you waking for every feeding unless doing it together makes it all much quicker. Breast-feeding mothers usually decide that a snack and a chat is not enough compensation for having a husband who is exhausted too. Most of them prefer to manage alone and perhaps get paid back with afternoon naps on the weekends. Bottle-feeding parents sometimes work out a sharing system, with one parent doing one night and the other the next. But for many couples even that does not really work because the mother finds that she wakes up anyway. If she cannot get back to sleep until she knows the baby is settled again, she might as well give the feeding herself.

# Crying and comforting

Parents often wish that their babies never cried at all. But without any crying you could neither be sure of meeting your baby's needs nor ever relax and think about other things. Crying is babies' way of communicating and they have different cries for communicating different information (see p. 149). Babies cry when they need something and it is because you know that yours will do so that you can assume, under all normal circumstances, that a baby who is not crying needs nothing. It would take serious illness, severe chilling, or smothering, to make a baby suffer in silence.

Babies never cry for nothing. The statement that they cry "to exercise their lungs" is nonsense. Their lungs get all the exercise they need in breathing. A baby cries for a reason; he needs something. If you can find out what it is that he needs, and provide it, the crying will stop. Usually the need is simple. Hunger. Feed him and he stops crying. But sometimes the baby cannot be satisfied so easily. The parents offer everything they can think of but the crying goes on and on.

A baby who cries and cannot be comforted is extremely difficult to cope with calmly. The sound churns his parents up emotionally. He seems to reject all their efforts to help him. They feel useless, frustrated and, eventually, angry. If the crying and the ineffectual attempts to comfort go on for long, it begins to seem to the parents that the baby *will not* stop crying. They lose sight of the fact that he *cannot* stop until he has been understood. The parents get more and more tense. Because they are tense they handle the crying baby less calmly and he therefore cries more. Some bouts of crying which have no other obvious cause may even be set off by some tension or unhappiness in the parents which the baby senses through their handling, their facial expressions or their voices.

The causes and the "cures" for crying that are outlined here are designed to answer those frantic questions which come into the mind of almost every parent at some time: "What is the *matter* with him?"; "What can I *do*?" Somewhere in this chapter there is something that will comfort (or at least explain) your baby.

## Causes and cures of crying

*Hunger*   Hunger is the most common cause of crying in a young baby and the easiest to deal with. Research studies have shown that if the baby is hungry, only milk will stop the crying. The baby may suck sweetened water, fruit juice or a pacifier, but he will start to cry again after a few seconds. His need can only be met by food going into his stomach. Just sucking, or even sucking combined with a pleasant taste, will have no effect.

*Pain*   Pain certainly causes crying from the first minutes of life, but it is often difficult to be sure whether a crying baby is distressed by pain or by something else. For example, he may stop crying when he is picked up, and immediately pass gas from one end or the other. Can we assume that the gas was causing pain? It may have been giving him "bellyache"; it may have been making his stomach feel uncomfortably distended or it may have had nothing to do with the crying, being passed merely by chance when he was picked up (see p. 68).

Certain kinds of pain cause a very clear reaction: the baby will probably cry heartbreakingly if his bottle or his bath is even a few degrees too warm. He will not appreciate being pricked with a safety pin either. But minor knocks and bangs may pass unnoticed in these early weeks, especially if it is the baby's hands or feet which are affected. The myelin sheathing of some nerves is not completed for months after birth, so the baby is less sensitive to some kinds of pain than is an older child.

*Over-stimulation, shock and fear*

Too much of any kind of stimulation will cause crying. Loud sudden noises, unexpectedly bright lights, sharp or bitter tastes, cold hands, hot face cloths, too much laughter, tickling, bouncing or hugging can all overcome the new baby.

Sudden happenings, particularly if they involve a sense of being about to fall or be dropped, tend to cause shock and real fear. As well as cry, the baby may tremble and pale.

If there is a minor accident, such as a bang on the head while being carried through a doorway, the baby's crying is as likely to be due to the shock of the bang as to actual pain.

*Mistiming*

The amount of any kind of stimulation that is "too much" depends on the baby's mood and state. What he enjoys when he is awake, content and well-fed may make him cry when he is sleepy, irritable or hungry. For example, physical games which he enjoys when he is feeling sociable will reduce him to despair if they are used to "cheer him along" when he is not. Tired, sad babies need cuddles, not play. Hungry ones need food.

Mistiming feedings will obviously cause crying from hunger, but mistiming the rate at which the baby gets the milk can cause trouble too. If you offer food too slowly – by having the hole in the nipple too small or by taking him off the breast or bottle to burp – the distress of his hunger breaks through the relief of feeding, so that the baby who was crying because he was hungry stays hungry because he is crying too much to suck.

Bathing or changing a baby who is very hungry will cause crying, both because it delays the arrival of food and because being handled when he needs a feeding tends to irritate him. He should not be bathed immediately after a feeding as a great deal of jouncing around is likely to make him bring up milk, so choose a wakeful period for baths, or wake him to be bathed before he has woken himself from hunger. Diaper changing after feedings does not matter if it is gently done. But if the baby is one who needs to burp at half-time, or drops off to sleep and needs waking up, you can change him in mid-feeding.

Getting from a sleepy state to sound slumber is often difficult for small babies. Try not to make it more difficult by changing his surroundings when he is just geting drowsy. If you must push him to the store in his stroller, start the expedition before he begins to drop off so that he can go to sleep to smooth motion, or wait until he is sound asleep and then start.

*Being undressed*  Many parents assume that it is their own clumsiness and inexperience which make babies cry when their clothes are taken off. Although skill certainly helps by making the process as quick and smooth as possible, many babies cry literally for the loss of their clothes. What often happens is that the baby gets increasingly tense as his outer garments are removed and finally howls when the garment next to his skin – vest or undershirt – is taken off. This reaction has nothing to do with being cold: it can happen however high the temperature of the room or the undressing hands. The baby misses the contact between the fabric and his bare skin. He does not like the feeling of his skin exposed to the air.

He will stop crying as soon as he is dressed again. But he can usually be kept completely calm while he is naked if a piece of textured material (a towel, a diaper or a light blanket) is laid across his chest and stomach.

*Cold*  As we have seen (see p. 74), feeling chilly will cause crying if the baby is awake or almost awake at the time. Much of the crying that goes on when babies are first put to sleep outside in their strollers is due to feeling cold air, especially a cool breeze. It is not a dangerous kind of cold – the crying reaction will keep the baby making heat for himself – but he does not like it. The crying will stop as soon as he is brought into a warm room.

*Jerks and twitches*  Most new babies jerk and twitch when they are in that drowsy state of near-sleep. A few are startled awake over and over again by their own movements. They cry, drowse, jerk and cry again, unable to get themselves past the twitchy state and into deep sleep.

Efficient wrapping up or swaddling (see opposite) will always deal with this kind of crying.

*Lack of physical contact*  Babies who cry until they are picked up, stay cheerful while they are being held and then cry again when they are put down are usually crying because they are uncomfortable without physical contact. This kind of crying for lack of "contact comfort" is often misunderstood. Parents are told that the baby is crying "because he wants you to pick him up." The implication is that he is making an unreasonable demand on you and that if you "give in" you will start "bad habits." In fact, the reverse is true. The baby is not making unreasonable demands, you are. He is not crying to make you pick him up but because you put him down in the first place and deprived him of contact comfort. It is natural and instinctive for a small baby to be most easily content when he is being held by somebody. In many parts of the world (and not only in "primitive" societies either) babies are held and carried almost all the time. Grandmothers and older sisters take turns when mothers must be free, but most chores are carried out with the baby slung on the mother's back.

Picking the baby up and cuddling him will almost always stop the crying. If it does not, then holding him against your shoulder, so that his stomach and chest are pressed against your breast, will. If whimpers still break through the contact comfort, walk with the baby in this position; the rocking movement will soothe him and peace will descend.

You probably cannot hold and walk your baby for hours on end, even if there are two of you to take turns and you use a sling or carrier. But you can deal with most of your baby's need for contact comfort by wrapping him up in such a way that the wrapping itself gives him the same feeling of warmth and security that he gets when he is held close in your arms against your body.

Wrapping your baby up is rather like old-fashioned swaddling except that it is not intended to "keep his back straight" or any nonsense of that kind. It is intended simply to give him tactile comfort, by surrounding him with a warm, soft, gentle holding layer of material which prevents his own little jerky movements from disturbing him.

Efficient wrapping is magically soothing to most babies. Wrapping which is too loose may have the opposite effect. Your aim is to encase the baby completely so that his limbs are gently held in their preferred position and so that, when he moves, he moves as one complete bundle rather than feeling himself moving within the blanket. If you use the method outlined here, you need not worry about getting the wrapping too tight. It is held in position only by the baby's own weight, and this is not enough to hold it tighter

## Wrapping up

Wrapping your baby up is the most effective of all ways of giving overall physical contact with a warm, soft surface. Once wrapped, the baby will also stay warmer than with ordinary covering. Stray drafts will not easily penetrate the parcel. Although wrapping is most often used to promote sleep, it will also help your baby to feel securely held when being carried around.

*Lie the baby on a soft, light receiving or thermal blanket.*

*Take one side up, level with the back of the head.*

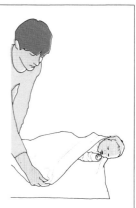
*Bring it down diagonally over the shoulder; elbow held, hand free. Tuck the end under the baby's knees.*

*Take the other side up with as much tension as you can without shifting the baby.*

*Fold this side straight down.*

*Lift the baby a little to secure the end beneath the body.*

*The result: a secure bundle; warm, relaxed, ready for sleep.*

than is comfortable. The ideal wrapping material is light and slightly stretchy so that it molds itself a little to the baby and "gives" with him. A receiving or small thermal blanket will do in winter. In hot weather a flannelette crib sheet will be comfortably warm to feel without being too hot to wear. In extremely hot weather a baby who enjoys the comfort of being wrapped but is too hot will be happy if a soft gauze material is used.

The baby's natural position is with his arms bent at the elbow and his legs flexed. Wrap him like this, making no attempt to straighten him out before you start. Above all, leave his hands where he can suck them if he wants and is able to do so.

Babies vary widely in the length of time they continue relaxing best when wrapped up. Let your baby be the judge: when he wants to rid himself of the wrappings he will begin to kick and struggle to get them undone.

You can also keep crying for contact comfort to a minimum by making sure that all the surfaces the baby lies on are warm and soft. Plastic laminates and sheets may make life easier for you but they are horrible for him. So cover all plastic mattresses, mats, etc., with a textured fabric such as terrycloth. Even a cloth diaper spread under him will make a difference.

*If all else fails . . .* If you have looked for all these causes and tried all these "cures" and your baby still cries, inexplicably, maddeningly, there are a few other techniques you can try. But "try" is the operative word. There may be nothing you can do but your best; you may all have to live through a difficult few weeks.

*Rhythm* A baby who cannot relax can be helped to do so by a variety of constant rhythmical stimuli. These seem to work by blocking out whatever internal or external discomforts were bothering him. You apply a soothing blanket of overall stimulation which wipes everything else out for the baby. It will not work if there is a simple cause for the crying which you have failed to discover. Hunger, for example, will break through everything. But it will work if the trouble is some kind of general and diffuse irritability or a tenseness which is preventing a tired baby relaxing into sleep.

**Rhythmical sounds.** You can buy a recording of a mother's heartbeat, as heard by a baby in the womb. It can be very effective. Soft rhythmical music on the radio or stereo works almost as well but make sure that it does not stop before the baby is properly asleep. If it does, the change in stimulation will wake him.

The burring sound of a fan or heater works excellently. So does the sound of a car engine. Most babies sleep peacefully in cars while they are running but tend to wake again the moment the engine is switched off, so a desperate drive around the block in the small hours may not really solve your crying problem!

**Rhythmical movements.** Rocking a baby is universally effective in stopping crying and inducing sleep. Parents who find that it does not work are almost certainly rocking too slowly. Research has shown that the effective rate is at least 60 rocks per minute through a travel of about three inches. Such a rate is difficult to achieve by hand, even if you have a rocking cradle. There are various automatic rocking gadgets available, but you may find it easier to walk with the baby. Time yourself and you will find that a walk around the room rocks him at just about this rate. It seems likely that the soothing effect of this rate of rocking comes directly from his experiences in the womb, when you walked about with him inside you.

You can provide this kind of rocking and lots of contact comfort while leaving yourself free to get on with at least a few other things, if you carry the baby on your chest. There are a variety of commercial carriers available, but for soothing crying babies a simple sling made out of a small crib sheet is probably as good as a bought model. A stiff carrier puts a barrier between his body and yours. A sling holds him warmly against you.

*Sucking*  Sucking will not stop a hungry baby crying unless it brings him food, but it will almost always soothe a baby who is not hungry.

**Pacifiers.** There are pros and cons to the use of pacifiers (see p. 150). Reasonably contented babies can manage perfectly well without them and it is better that they should do so. But they can certainly help babies who are often miserable and difficult to comfort in any other way. The furious howling mouth latches on to the pacifier and all that energy goes into sucking instead of crying. Gradually the rhythm of the sucking becomes gentler. Eventually the baby goes to sleep. Even while he sleeps, having the pacifier in his mouth protects him against a fresh bout of crying: whenever something begins to disturb him, he sucks instead of waking.

If you decide that your baby does need a pacifier, do guard against the habit of popping it into his mouth whenever he cries. Try first to find out what he needs, and provide it. His pacifier should be used only when you have tried everything else.

**Thumbs and fingers.** Some babies find and suck these before they are born and use them efficiently for comfort sucking from the first day of life. Others cannot find their own hands without help until they are several weeks old (see p. 157). If a lot of crying that is difficult to "cure" is worrying you and you do not like the idea of a pacifier, you might compromise by helping the baby's hand to his mouth to see whether he can quiet himself by sucking it.

*Extra warmth*  As we have seen (see p. 74), wakeful babies tend to be fretful if they are having to warm themselves, and flourish when air temperatures around them are high, provided they are lightly dressed. If your baby is crying and you cannot persuade him to stop, you can use *extra* warmth to calm him down and help him to relax. Although the warmth will not cure whatever discomfort is making him cry, he will react to the discomfort less if you can keep the temperature at around 75°F (24°C) until the episode is over.

A baby who is often miserable and difficult to comfort will give you and himself more peace if you take trouble about warmth right through the newborn period. Wrap him carefully when you carry him. Don't put him outside in his stroller on chilly days or take him for trips in a cold car until he has grown up a bit. Keep his own room and any other rooms he regularly uses as near 75°F (24°C) as you can manage until he sems happier and more settled.

# Colic?

There is one quite common kind of crying which you will not find in the previous pages. It usually begins something like this: your three- to four-week-old baby seems to cry more, and more distressingly, in the evening than at any other time. As he becomes more settled, so that his daytime crying lessens and he becomes easier to comfort, the evening crying builds in regularity and intensity until he is having regular screaming fits every late afternoon or early evening.

Somewhere around this time you probably take your baby to the doctor. You want to know why he is having these regular and uncontrollable screaming fits and why you do not seem able to comfort him. What is the matter with him?

Your doctor will examine the baby and talk to you. He will assure himself (and you) that the baby is healthy and thriving and that there is no physical reason, such as pain or indigestion, to account for his apparent distress. By the end of the interview you will know that nothing is seriously the matter with your baby but you may still be no closer to understanding why he screams or how to live with it.

The answer is probably "colic" (or "evening colic" or "three-month colic"). If your doctor does not use these terms to you it is probably because the terms are extremely unscientific. "Colic" sounds like the name for an illness needing diagnosis and treatment, potentially serious. But "colic" is not an illness; only a very distressing pattern of newborn behavior with no known cause, no treatment and absolutely no ill-effects except on parents' nerves. The term is used here because your nerves matter and even an unscientific name may help you through the two or three bad months ahead if your baby does have "colic." You are the ones who are going to have to see your normally cheerful baby beside himself with screaming every evening. You are the ones who are going to have to try everything you can think of to help and accept the fact that, although every one of those things helps for a little, nothing but time ends each episode.

Don't be too ready to believe that your baby really does have "colic" though. If you jump to that conclusion when he cries in the evening for the third day in a row, you may miss some much more obvious and easily dealt with kind of distress. The chart opposite may help you to identify the syndrome.

*Living with "colic"*

There is very little you can do for a baby suffering from "colic." Your helplessness, together with the fact that the dreadful bouts of screaming occur at the time of day when you are most tired and in need of peaceful time together, makes colic one of the most difficult things for new parents to cope with.

Try to accept the fact that the cause is unknown. If you continually search for a cause, you will only confuse every other aspect of your babycare by changing feedings, feeding techniques and routines, all to no avail. "Colic" has been variously put down to overfeeding, underfeeding, too rich, strong or weak feedings, milk which was too hot or too cold, milk which flowed too fast or too slowly, allergies, hernias, appendicitis, gall bladder trouble, gas and nervous exhaustion in the mother! All these contradictory explanations share one decisive fallacy: if any one of them was the cause of "colic," why should the trouble occur after one and only one feeding in the 24 hours? However you feed your baby, you do not do it in a particular way at 6pm. If the baby had a physical problem, it would not reveal itself only at this time of day. If maternal fatigue was a cause, rather than a result, of "colic," the trouble would not occur when father took a turn with the bottle....

So instead of worrying about *why*, worrying in case you are doing something wrong, worrying in case the baby is ill, try for a mood of constructive resignation. You are faced with a bad few weeks. Although you cannot cure the baby's attacks, you cannot leave him to suffer them alone, either. He will need all your time and attention while they last, so concentrate on organizing life so as to free yourself to cope with the least possible stress. And remember: however awful the "colic" may be, it will not harm your baby, neither will it last for any longer than twelve weeks at the very most.

| Your baby may have "colic" if: | Your baby does not have "colic" if: |
| --- | --- |
| *She cannot settle after her late-afternoon or early-evening feeding but starts screaming as soon as she has finished, or drops off to sleep but wakes screaming within half an hour.* | *He cannot settle after his late-afternoon or early-evening feeding but cries and grumbles on and off for quite a long time before going finally to sleep. Grumbling can mean a lot of things but it never means "colic."* |
| *She does not just cry, she screams, drawing her legs up to her belly and seeming beside herself.* | *His crying is ordinary crying even if it is hard crying. Drawing his legs up to his belly is not a sign of "colic" — babies always do that when they are crying hard.* |
| *Everything you do seems to help for a minute. She will suck your nipple or a pacifier so that you think you have found the answer but then the screaming starts again. A belch stops the screaming — but it starts again. Being rocked interrupts the screaming — but only for a few seconds. Having her tummy rubbed produces miraculous silence — but it does not last.* | *Anything you do brings the crying spell to an end within half an hour of its beginning. If a feeding or a pacifier does the trick, the baby was hungry or needed to suck; either way he is not having "colic." If a burp enables him to sleep, he had gas rather than "colic," and if cuddling or rocking or rubbing soothes him, he was lonely or too tense to go to sleep.* |
| *When you interrupt the dreadful screaming, the baby remains shaky and sobbing until it starts again.* | *When you interrupt the crying, he is calm at least until you try to stop comforting him and put him back to bed.* |
| *The whole episode goes on for at least an hour and perhaps for three or four hours but is then over and done with for the day.* | *The episode ends inside half an hour and the baby then sleeps or stays happy for at least 15 minutes before he cries again. He may be having a bad day, but he is not having "colic."* |
| *A similar pattern repeats itself every day at about the same time and is never seen at any other point in the 24 hours.* | *Occasional screaming spells take place at any time of the day or night. They may be hard to bear but they are not "colic."* |

# *Adjusting to your baby's behavior*

Some babies are much more difficult to look after happily than others. You cannot choose your baby's temperament any more than you could have chosen his or her sex. You may have the "kind" of baby you find easy to understand, sympathize with and handle, or a "kind" of baby who needs handling that does not come at all naturally to you.

All healthy newborn babies have many characteristics and behaviors in common. But each one of them is also a unique individual who has already had a unique set of experiences in the womb, during birth and immediately after it. All these things play a part in how the new baby settles in to life; how he reacts to you and to the world. You also are unique individuals with years of complex experiences behind you. All this will play a part in what you expect your baby to be like, in how you react to him.

If your expectations match the reality of your baby and the ways of handling that come "naturally" to you happen to suit that baby, the interaction between you will be comparatively smooth and easy from the beginning. But if these things do not match, you and the baby will have to do much more adjusting to each other. Suppose, for example, that this is your second baby and that your first was a child who was basically calm and placid and thrived on lots of stimulation and rough and tumble play. You will probably start off by handling the new baby as you handled the first; if his reactions are similar all will be well. But if he happens to be a particularly sensitive and jumpy baby, who is terrified by anything fiercer than a gentle cuddle, your interaction will not be easy at all. Both of you will have to learn. His behavior will affect your handling, teaching you to be more gentle; your handling will affect his behavior, teaching him to be more relaxed.

At this very early age you have to try to combine handling your baby in ways which suit him *now*, allowing for the fact that some of his most extreme behaviors may be reactions to pre-natal and birth experiences and may therefore change radically when he has settled down. You have to accept him for what he is today but leave it open to him to be something quite different next month or next year. A mother whose natural behavior is outgoing and energetic but whose baby is jumpy may make tremendous efforts to adjust her handling to suit her son. Having done so, she may get so used to thinking of the baby as "nervy" or "highly strung" that she goes on treating him extra carefully long after the baby has grown out of his newborn jumpiness and become ready for more robust handling. If the mother's mind is closed to the possibility of her baby changing, she may quite forget to offer him noisy toys and rough and tumble play at six months and she may try too hard to protect him from bumps and falls when he learns to walk at around a year. The little boy may have to fight for his independence during the toddler stage.

So whatever your baby is like now, handle him in the ways which seem to keep him happy and calm. But while you react sensitively to his present needs, try not to let labels stick. You will affect him and he will affect you; what kind of person will eventually come out of the interaction between you, nobody can know. That is part of the excitement of rearing a new human being.

## Uncuddly babies

Whatever their other characteristics, most small babies revel in warm, close physical contact with adults. When a "cuddly" baby is feeling miserable, jumpy or extra-wakeful, you will often find the answer in holding and hugging, stroking and singing or jiggling and dancing. And when you cannot do any of those things you may be able to give him a similar safe security by wrapping him up or carrying him in a sling.

*Typical behavior:* Uncuddly babies seem to reject, even to resent, the physical constriction of enfolding arms or blankets. They do not want to drop their heavy heads confidingly on to adult shoulders or to tuck their feet snugly into adult curves. Far from relaxing them, restriction makes them furious.

*Living with it:* Uncuddly babies usually revel in a different kind of contact. They are physically active (and often rather confident) babies who are quick to enjoy free kicking and other physical adventures. In the meantime they prefer eye contact to cuddling contact. If your baby hurts your feelings by trying to escape your holding arms, try putting him on a bed or rug and sitting over him so that he can study your face. He wants to look at you and he may start smiling and "talking" to you rather early. If you long to stroke the creases in his pudgy wrists and kiss the dimples in the small of his back, do it while he is in his infant seat or on his changing mat. He will not only accept your sensual pleasure in him, he will also be delighted if you will play with his fingers, bicycle his legs and blow raspberries against his tummy.

"Cuddly" babies need eye and voice as well as body contact. "Uncuddly" babies need holding as well as looking and listening. Over a few months your baby will come to enjoy every kind of contact you offer him. But in these very first weeks, recognizing his bias toward one or the other may ease your life – and his.

## Miserable babies

Just as there are adults who always look on the black side of everything, so there are babies who are inclined to the miseries. Babies who are miserable usually take a long time to settle happily into patterns of being soundly and comfortably asleep, awake and ravenous, full, awake and happy and then asleep again. They behave as if little bits of all those states stayed jumbled up together, keeping their behavior unpredictable and preventing them from settling down to enjoy life.

*Typical behavior:* The baby is tired and fretful but he cannot relax enough to go to sleep. He whimpers and dozes his way through the afternoon and then he is irritably hungry but not joyful about sucking. He is probably slow and difficult to feed. When the feeding is over he is awake but not very sociable. He soon gets tired of being held; does not seem to take much notice of being talked to but is not pleased to be returned to his crib. He probably wakes often in the night.

A baby like this may gain weight more slowly than most and be slow to start smiling or playing with his hands (see p. 157). Often he even looks unhappy. He is the opposite of all those smiling babies in the babyfood advertisements.

*Living with it:* A baby you cannot make happy is very depressing. Like the baby who cries without apparent reason (see p. 86), he will tend to make you feel inadequate as a parent. If his miseries go on for very long, you will probably feel put-upon too. You will be lavishing love and care on a baby who seems to give nothing in return. While these feelings about a miserable baby are very natural, it is important to try to keep them at bay. Don't let yourself feel that his unhappiness is a criticism of you. It is life outside the womb that your baby does not like very much, not you. You must stay on his side or you will not be able to offer the warm, gentle, patient attention which will, eventually, help him to feel happier. Work to get him to look at you, listen to you, smile at you. If you can only get him to the stage where he responds, the worst of his miseries will be over.

As well as loving the baby whether you get any response or not, try all the suggestions for crying babies on pp. 86–91 and check especially that you are trying the following:

**Keep the baby indoors in a very warm room,** but not overheated by too many clothes. See if that makes him more relaxed. If it does, you could keep him in for a month – he can get plenty of fresh air with a window opened at the top.

**See that the baby gets plenty of milk,** as much as he will willingly take whenever he seems to want it.

**See if the baby sleeps more easily when carefully wrapped** (see p. 89). There is no harm in wrapping him for every sleep-time until he starts to kick the wrappings off.

**See if the baby is happier with a great deal of contact comfort.** If he likes being carried around, use a sling so that you can carry him on your back most of the time he is awake for a few weeks.

**Don't introduce new aspects of life** until he seems much happier with what he is already experiencing. Don't, for example, try a new baby hammock or a first car ride or even a first drink of fruit juice until he has stopped being so miserable.

*Jumpy babies*  All newborns are startled by loud noises, turn away from bright lights and throw up their arms and cry if they feel they are going to be dropped. Jumpy babies take this kind of behavior to extremes. They may startle and cry, tremble and pale at quite low grade stimuli. They seem to be frightened of almost everything, and perhaps they are. Perhaps it is life outside the safe, warm, dark haven of the womb which frightens them.

*Typical behavior:* The baby overreacts to every kind of stimulation, whether it comes from inside him or from outside. Hunger takes him rapidly into a frenzy of desperate crying. His own jerks and twitches stop him relaxing into sleep. Picking him up makes him tense; putting him down makes him jump. Any change in his surroundings, however slight it may be, alerts and may alarm him. With this kind of baby even a telephone ringing in the next room may be enough to make him jump.

*Living with it:* The baby is not going to learn not to be frightened by being frightened. His nervous system is not going to become better able to accept minor shocks by being shocked. He is going to become calmer only by a combination of maturing and gentle handling that lets him find less and less in daily life to upset him.

Caring for a jumpy baby can be a real challenge. If you see it as such, it can even be enjoyable. You set yourself to get through each day, or each bit of a day, without ever doing anything or letting anything happen which startles the baby or makes him cry. Your aim is to keep the stimulation which the baby receives below his tolerance level while he matures enough to be able to accept more stimulation happily.

**Never hurry when you are handling the baby.** When you pick him up, for example, he needs due warning so that his muscles can adjust to the change of position. When you carry him he needs you to move slowly and smoothly, supporting his head so that it does not wobble and never letting him feel insecurely held.

**Keep handling to a minimum.** For example, a jumpy baby will certainly hate being bathed and should be simply "topped and tailed" until he is calmer. He will probably hate bumpy stroller rides and wide open spaces, too. Let him move only from crib or stroller to lap and back again for a few weeks.

**Cut down on physical stimulation by careful wrapping.** Changes of position and being moved from one place to another will be far less worrying for him if he is properly wrapped up (see p. 89). The wrappings will provide a protective cocoon between him and the outside world.

**Make sure that everyone who handles the baby is quiet and gentle.** You want him to discover that the world and the people in it are safe. A jolly uncle with good intentions and a loud laugh can frighten a jumpy baby in a way that makes him want to retreat even more from his new world. Protect him; he has plenty of time for learning to make social contacts.

*Sleepy babies*  Babies who seem to have an almost unlimited capacity for sleep probably feel just as unready for life outside the womb as do miserable or jumpy babies. But they react to it quite differently: instead of protesting or recoiling they avoid life by staying asleep.

*Typical behavior:* The baby is "no trouble." He makes almost no demands and probably has to be woken up for most of his feedings. It is often difficult to persuade him to stay awake for long enough to suck very much at a time and once he has sucked himself back to sleep he may be unwakeable. He does not seem to care very much about his surroundings or routines. He seldom cries for long but he seldom seems particularly happy either. He is playing a sleepy, neutral game.

*Living with it:* Although the baby's lack of responsiveness may disappoint you, this is a comparatively easy "type" of baby to cope with. While he is so sleepy, you can be regaining your strength and collecting your wits in readiness for the active motherhood which will come when the baby matures a little.

**Make sure that the baby wakes up enough to eat.** Occasionally an exceptionally sleepy baby who is being fed on demand fails to gain as much weight as he should because he does not demand as much food as his body needs. If you have to wake him for feedings, then of course there is no harm in waking him to suit your convenience, but make sure that you do so at least every four hours. Add in a couple of extra feedings if his sleepiness means that he only sucks for five minutes at a time.

The baby may be perfectly willing to sleep through a 12-hour night from the beginning. Don't let him. That is too many hours without water, quite apart from the food itself. Wake him at your bedtime and first thing in the morning and bless the fact that he probably will not wake you in the small hours!

**Don't take the baby's sleepy isolation for granted.** In other words, don't let his willingness to be shut away in his crib for hours lead you to *expect* him to behave like that. Give him lots of opportunities for sociable cuddles and talk. Try to get him interested in looking at things and being talked to. If he is fast asleep on your lap after two minutes, it is fair enough to put him back to bed, but try again to play with him at the next feeding. You want him to realize, gradually, that being awake is fun.

## Wakeful babies

Babies vary in the amount of sleep they need, right from the beginning of their lives. Most babies will sleep for something like 16 hours in the 24 to start with. Very sleepy ones may sleep for 22 hours in every 24. A really wakeful baby may never sleep for more than 12 hours and may seldom do that sleeping in stretches of more than two hours at a time.

*Typical behavior:* The baby is not especially miserable or especially jumpy. There is nothing "keeping him awake," he just does not sleep for the number of hours we expect of very small babies. He will have a feeding and drop off to sleep immediately. But an hour or two later he is awake again, not because he is ready for more food but just because he has stopped being asleep. Because he spends so much time awake he will probably show more interest in the things around him at an earlier age than most babies. His development in every area may be rapid because he is spending so much more time looking, listening and learning.

*Living with it:* This is not the kind of baby you can care for in short concentrated bursts of time and then ignore in between. He makes himself felt almost all day and often for a good deal of the night, too. How you react to him will probably depend at least partly on how much else you have to do. A jealous older child, for example, will suffer much more from a very wakeful baby than from one who naps in a corner for much of the toddler's day. The main trouble with a wakeful baby is that he is spending a lot of hours awake at an age when it is difficult to find entertainment for him. He cannot

handle toys yet; he is not ready for physical play or even for being propped up. Start by reminding yourself that he would sleep if he needed to; try to accept his wakefulness, and don't feel that he "ought" to be asleep. If you try to make him behave as other babies do, you will waste a lot of time tucking him away for naps he does not want, and you will make him miserable too because he will be bored and lonely.

**Find different ways of keeping the baby company.** Perhaps his stroller could come into the kitchen? If so, you can park it close beside you and get into the habit of stopping for quick chats as you move around. If he has a bassinet that lifts off its stand, he could lie in that beside you while you are reading or watching television.

**Find easy ways of carrying your baby.** Although you obviously cannot carry him around all the time, being carried is perfect entertainment for a wakeful newborn. A sling inside the house might let you do simple housework with the baby on your back. A canvas carrier will let you take him around the stores and other interesting places instead of leaving him, bored, in his stroller. (Don't use a crib-sheet sling outdoors with a new baby; it will not be warm enough for him.)

**Arrange different places where the baby can lie on the floor.** A spare carriage mattress or changing mat to carry from room to room is useful. He will get less bored if he has lots of changes of scene.

**Give the baby interesting things to look at.** This will help him entertain himself. Hang things from the stroller hood or above the crib, and change them often so that he always has something new to look at. Make or buy a mobile or two, so that he can watch something that moves. (For further suggestions, see p. 170).

**Be prepared to treat your baby like a somewhat older one.** He will be packing a lot of learning into all those hours awake, so you need to keep an eye on his development and be sure that you offer new kinds of entertainment as soon as he shows that he is ready for them. The next section (see p. 149–87) should help.

# Using his body

There is much to learn about looking after very new babies and, because they have not yet settled down, caring for them is a very demanding job. It is easy to get so involved in daily care that you find yourself treating your child like a very precious kind of object rather than a developing person, a new human being.

But your baby is human and your baby is developing – every moment of the day. Don't let night feedings and wet diapers take up so much of your attention that you miss the fascinating changes that are taking place, the signs of your baby beginning to grow up.

*Postures and head control*

Newborns are very scrunched-up looking creatures. Whatever position you put your baby in, he will curl himself inward with his body taking up its position in relation to his head. This is because at this stage of life his head is so large and heavy in relation to the rest of him that it acts as an anchor and a pivot.

Until the rest of him grows a little so that his head becomes relatively lighter, and until he can get some control over the muscles of his neck, the baby's voluntary movements will be restricted. At the beginning he can lift that head a little and he will always turn it to avoid smothering, but movements of his limbs are restricted by his curled position, while the fact that his head is always turned to one side prevents him from seeing things which are directly above him.

A baby's muscle control starts from the top and moves gradually downward (see p. 152). When you hold him against your shoulder in the first hours after birth, he rests his head against you. If you do not support his neck for him, that head will simply flop. Within a week he can force those neck muscles to lift the head away for a second or two. A few days later he practices head control so continually that when you hold him it feels as if he were deliberately bumping his head against you: effort-flop-effort-flop, again and again. By three to four weeks he can balance his head for several seconds provided you keep absolutely still. But he still needs your supporting hand whenever you carry him and especially when you lift him or put him down.

*Reflex physical activities*

During the first week of life, this baby, whose muscles are still so incompetent even in balancing his head, exhibits some remarkably mature-looking behaviors which sometimes fool parents into believing that they have produced an infant who will crawl or even walk at a few weeks of age! But these are not voluntary or controled movements. They are simply reflexes which will die out over a few days and then be re-learned months later as new accomplishments at the appropriate stage of development.

*False crawling*

If you put him on his stomach, the baby's naturally curled-up position leads him to flex legs and arms so that he looks as if he were about to crawl off. He may even "scrabble" so that he wrinkles his crib sheet. The position will be unlearned when the baby becomes able to uncurl himself and lie flat (see p. 153).

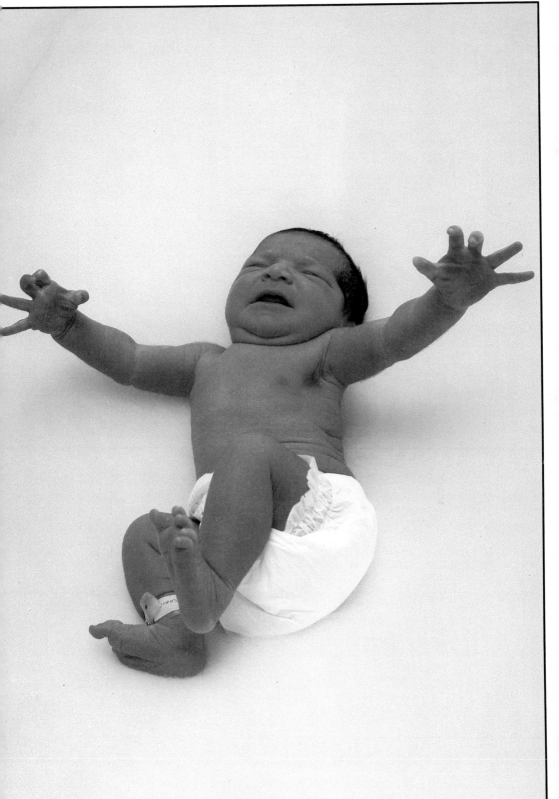

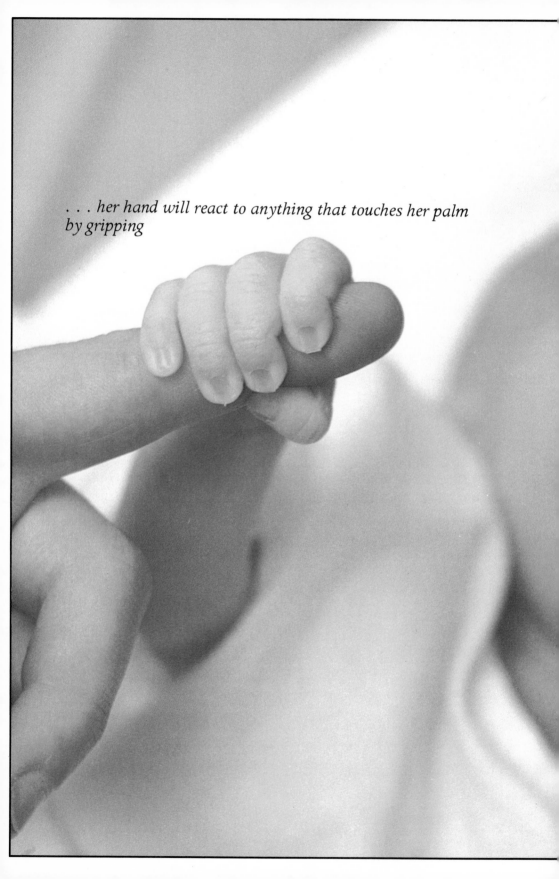

*. . . her hand will react to anything that touches her palm by gripping*

*. . . in the first hours
this reflex hand grip
is powerful enough to
support the baby's weight . . .
but the strength will go
from it overnight*

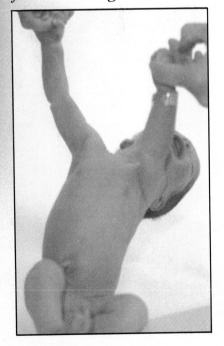

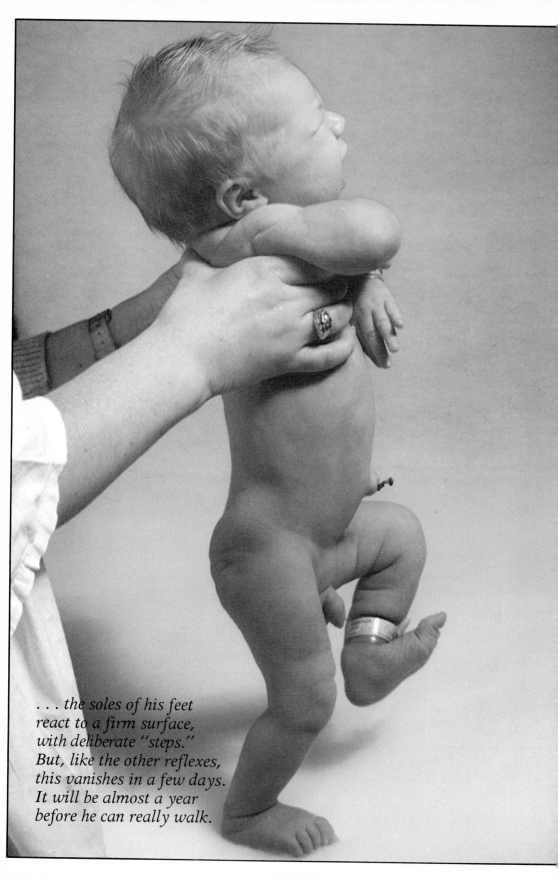

. . . the soles of his feet
react to a firm surface,
with deliberate "steps."
But, like the other reflexes,
this vanishes in a few days.
It will be almost a year
before he can really walk.

*False walking*    If you hold the baby upright with his feet just touching a firm surface, he will take quite deliberate "steps," placing one foot after another while you support his weight. Once again he will quickly unlearn this. By the time he is a week old he will simply sag if you hold him upright.

*False clinging*    In the first days of life a baby's hand grip is incredibly strong. In theory, you could hang him up by his hands and he would cling on tightly enough not to fall. But don't try it. The ability passes between one day and the next. You might choose the next for your experiment!

But although the baby's extraordinary strength of grip passes off, some degree of reflex hand grip remains. If you put your finger or a rattle into his closed fist, his hand will grip itself around it. When you try to remove it, his fist will close even more tightly in a reflex attempt to hang on. This reaction to the feel of a grippable object in his palm will remain through all the weeks that must pass before the baby is ready to learn to take hold of objects on purpose. So hanging on with his hands is not something which, like crawling or walking, he has to unlearn and then learn all over again. In this instance the reflex action eventually gives way to deliberate action.

The reflex response which leads a baby to hang on to whatever he finds in his hands may be left over from pre-history when our ape-like ancestors' children kept themselves safe by clinging to their mothers. Today's human babies cannot cling on to an adult's clothes with their hands, arms and legs, as baby monkeys cling to their mother's belly fur. Yet they seem to want to. They are happiest and most relaxed when they are carried in a face-to-face position, legs straddling your belly, arms around your neck. When they are not being carried, being closely wrapped up, or even having a piece of warm textured material laid across their chests and stomachs as if they were pressed against a warm mother, usually calms the fretful and pleases the calm.

*A reminder to be careful . . .*    If your baby, who would like to cling to you, feels that he is about to be dropped, he produces a violent and obviously distressed reflex which is called the "Moro response." If you jerk him while you are holding his hands, you will see his arms snatch up at yours and his legs curve convulsively upward as if seeking a body around which to clasp themselves. If you put him down carelessly, so that your hands start to release him before he feels the firm security of the mattress, he will throw out both his arms and legs and then flex them violently; his head will jerk back because the reflex movements have upset his head control; he will probably cry out in fear.

Like other reflexes, the Moro response has lost its direct usefulness to the baby because, unlike his furry ancestors, he does not have the muscle power to save himself from a fall by holding on. But the response is still a useful one. Every time your baby reacts in this violently startled way you will know that you have handled him too roughly, too unexpectedly or without taking enough care to support his heavy head. Moro responses are a hint to parents to take more care.

# Using his senses

Each of your baby's five senses is in working order from the moment of birth. A baby does not have to learn to see, to hear, to sense touch through the skin, or even to smell or taste. The equipment for all these activities is in-built. What is lacking is experience: knowledge of what things look or sound like; how different things feel or smell or taste. All five senses are bombarded with stimuli as soon as the baby comes out of the womb. Learning through the senses goes on from that moment.

Finding out exactly *what* a new baby senses is exceedingly difficult because he cannot tell us what he is feeling. Research workers have to find ways of measuring the baby's responses without his direct cooperation. Often we cannot say more than that babies respond with pleasure to certain kinds of sensory stimulation and with distress to others. The sense of touch is an instance in point. We know that babies react with calm pleasure to warm, soft, firm pressure, especially up the front surface of their bodies. We know that they react by gripping to the feel of an object in their fists; we know that they react with sucking reflexes to a stroking touch on the cheek. But we do not know exactly what they feel or what difference they sense when their skins are tickled with a feather or stroked with sandpaper.

*Smelling and tasting*

We assume that newborn babies have a sense of smell because we know they have a sense of taste and the two are intimately linked. But experiments in smell-differentiation would be impossible. Offered bad eggs and daffodils, babies can neither tell or show you whether they can distinguish between them nor which they "prefer." They have to go on breathing even if each breath brings an odor they find noxious. They are not yet able to hold their breath on purpose.

Taste is easier to test. Bitter, acid or sour tastes make the baby screw up his face, turn his head away and/or cry. He can also differentiate accurately between plain, slightly sweetened and very sweet water. We know this because while he will suck a bottle containing any one of these, he will suck longer and harder as the sweetness increases. No wonder it is so difficult to control the sugar-intake of older children!

*Hearing and making sounds*

Your baby's only deliberate sounds during these early days are crying. It may seem to you that all the crying sounds the same, but in fact there is a repertory of different cries which represent different states of feeling. Whether or not you feel you can recognize, by ear, the difference between one kind of cry and another, you will almost certainly find yourself reacting differently to each. When the types of cry are analyzed by sound spectrograph you can actually see the differences between them, differences of tone, of duration and of rhythm (see p. 149).

A baby's pain cry has a particular intensity and rhythm. Instinct will tell you to take the stairs three at a time. You will find that you are thinking of nothing but getting to the baby – fast.

A hunger cry is quite different. It has particular patterns of sound and pause which are the same for all babies but quite different from any of your baby's other cries. If you are breast-feeding, that particular cry may start the "let down" reflex so that your milk starts to flow even as you get up to go to the baby. If you are bottle-feeding, the cry probably directs you to the kitchen to start warming the bottle. In this case, however, although you will have no doubt at all that the baby needs you, you will not have the sense of urgency that comes with the pain cry.

Fear sounds different again. The fear cry is a sound of pure desolation and is highly infectious. By the time you reach your baby your own pulse will be racing and adrenalin will be flooding through your body, readying it to fight any danger to protect him.

By the time he is around four weeks old, your baby will begin to make other sounds besides crying. He will make small gurgly googly noises when he is relaxed after a feeding and little tense whimpery sounds when he is building up toward hunger cries. He is moving toward the next stage in communication – cooing.

*Listening*  Babies can hear from the moment of birth. They can sense and differentiate sound vibrations while they are still in the womb and they react with soothed pleasure after birth to recordings of heartbeat sounds, which they have lived with before it.

Loud, sudden sounds will make your baby jump. The sharper the sound the more extreme will be his reaction. Thunder rolling around the house will not bother him nearly as much as a plate smashing on a hard floor. Just as clearly as he dislikes these sounds, the baby enjoys (or at least is soothed and relaxed by) repetitive rhythmical sounds. He will enjoy music, but he will enjoy the rhythmical pounding of a drum or the steady whirr of your vacuum cleaner just as much – as far as we can tell.

But while the baby clearly *hears* all these sounds, the ones to which he *listens*, with obvious concentration, are the sounds of people talking. He has a built-in interest in voices and in voice-like sounds. Because they come from the caretakers without whom he cannot survive, he is programmed to pay attention to them.

Unless you are on the look-out for it, you may not notice how much your baby enjoys your voice during these first weeks. At this stage his looking and listening systems are still separate. He listens without looking for the source of the sound he hears, so he often listens to your voice without looking at you. But if you watch him carefully, you will see his reactions to your loving prattle. If he is crying, he will often stop as you approach the crib, talking. He does not need to see you or to feel your touch first. If he is lying still when you begin to speak to him, he will start to move excitedly. If he is kicking, he will stop and freeze to attention, concentrating on your voice.

It will be a long time before the baby can understand your words but from the first days of his life he will react to the tones he hears in your voice. When you talk softly and caressingly he reacts with pleasure, but if you speak sharply to an older child while handling the baby, he will probably cry, while if something should make you cry out in fear while you are holding him, he will be instantly panic-stricken.

**Looking**    Babies can see, clearly and with discrimination, from the moment of birth. If your baby seems to spend a lot of waking time gazing blankly into space or looking toward a brightly lit window or blowing curtain, this is not because babies are incapable of seeing anything more detailed, but because you do not put anything else within easy visual range.

A new baby *can* focus his eyes so as to see things clearly when they are at different distances. He can, but he seldom does because, until his eye-muscles strengthen, it is very difficult for him. The easy focusing distance for a new baby is about 8–10in (20–25cm) from the bridge of the nose. At that precise distance he can see clearly but objects which are further away are blurred. If he lies in his crib with nothing within his focal distance to look at, he will look across the room at whatever he can perceive through the distance-blur. Brightness and movement (as every near-sighted person knows) are the two things that will be visible to him.

If, armed with this information, you deliberately put things close enough to your baby's eyes for him to see them clearly, he will "choose" to pay attention to much more subtle stimuli than brightness or movement. You can test his "choices" for yourself by holding pairs of objects where he can look at them. He will look at a simple circular red rattle if there is nothing else close enough for him to see, but if you add a sheet of paper with a complicated black and white pattern on it he will turn his attention to that instead. He will look at a simple cube, but add a more complex shape such as a tea strainer and he will look at that. He is programmed to give his attention to complex patterns and shapes because he must learn a complex visual world.

His fixed-focal distance is not a matter of random chance. On the contrary, it is exactly the distance which separates his face from yours when you hold and talk to him or when you are breast-feeding. Just as voices are the most important things for him to listen to, so faces are the most important things for him to look at and he is innately programmed to study them intently whenever he can. It may even be that the blurring out of more distant objects is developmentally useful to him as it helps him to concentrate on those vital faces undistracted by other things.

New babies do not know that people are people so your baby cannot know, when he studies your face, that what he is looking at is *you*. He simply gives his full visual attention to any face or to anything he sees which is face-like. His criteria of "face-like" have been studied in detail. If an object or a picture has a hairline, eyes, a mouth and a chin-line, the baby will react to it as a face. If you watch his eyes you will see that he starts at the top, scans that hairline, moves his gaze slowly down to the chin-line and then back to the eyes. Once he is looking the stimulus in the eye, he will go on for much longer than he will look at anything else.

While it is interesting to try out this reaction by showing your baby a simple sketch of a face, or a balloon with a face drawn on it, looking at real faces is much more valuable to him. When he has learned enough about faces you will get your reward for patiently giving him yours to study. One day soon that intent scanning will end as usual at your eyes but it will culminate in his first true social gesture to the outside world. It will end with his first smile.

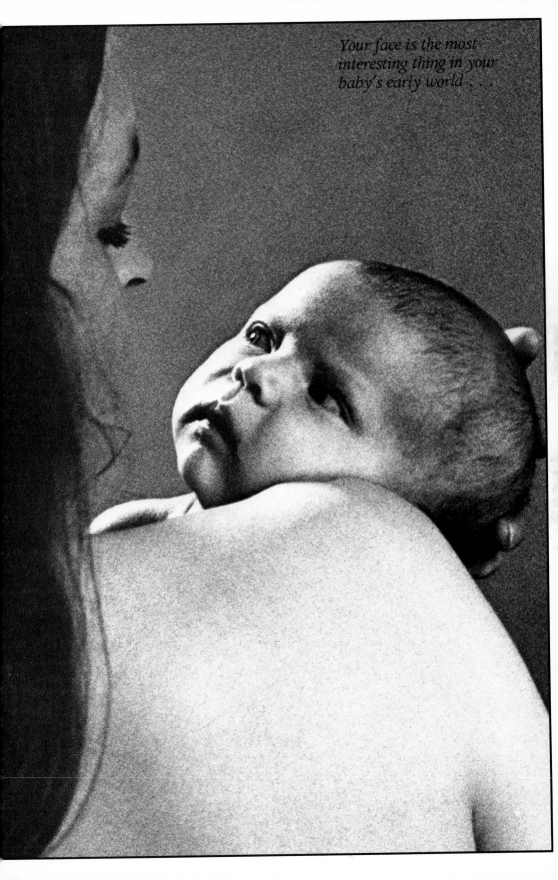

*Your face is the most interesting thing in your baby's early world . . .*

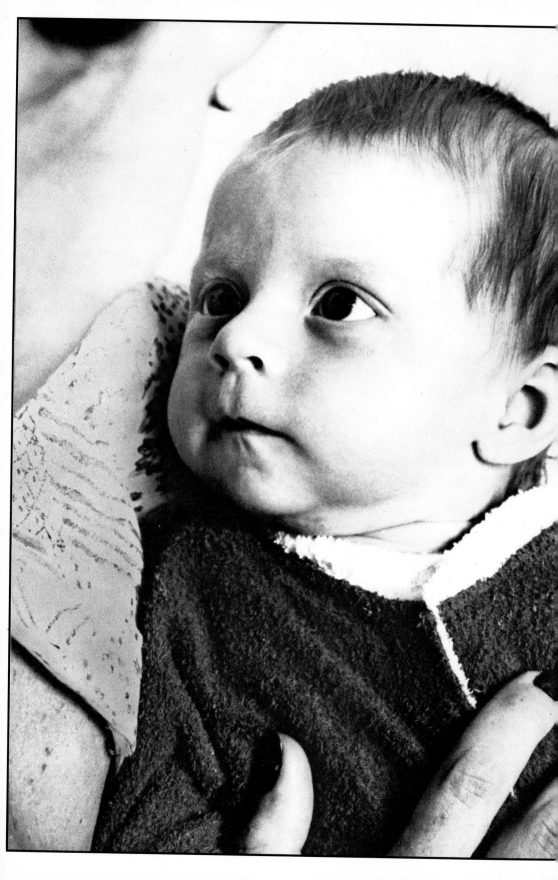

# THE SETTLED BABY

## *The first six months*

One day you will find that you have stopped regarding your baby as a totally unpredictable and therefore rather alarming novelty and have begun instead to think of him as a person with tastes, preferences and characteristics of his own. When that happens you will know that he has moved on from being a "newborn" and has gotten himself settled into life. Nobody can date that moment except you. An easy birth, close satisfactory contact immediately after it, and a good fit between his needs and your expectations will all tend to bring it forward. Postnatal depression, feeding difficulties, or a baby who needs handling in a way that does not come naturally to you will all tend to keep it back. But whether he is settled at two weeks or at two months, that moment will come.

A settled baby is a manageable proposition. He may be a little devil, but he is a little devil you know. You can tell how he likes to be handled even if it is not the way you would choose to handle him. You know what to expect from him even if it is the worst. You know what frightens him even if it is almost everything. Above all, you can tell when he is happy, however seldom that may be, and when he is miserable, even if that is almost always. So once your baby is settled you know what you are up against. Instead of trying to survive from hour to hour, get through another day, avoid thinking about another week, you can begin to work and plan for reasonable compromises between his needs and those of everyone else.

The baby will make it clear that his prime need is for people, in the shape of you, his constant caretakers. Your love for him may still be problematic, but the dawn of his attachment to you is a matter of sheer necessity. If he is to survive, he has to attach himself to you and ensure that you take care of him. As these first few weeks pass, his interest in people becomes increasingly obvious. Your face fascinates him. Every time it comes within his short focusing range he studies it intently from hairline to mouth, finishing by gazing into your eyes. He listens intently to your voice, kicking a little when he hears it, or freezing into immobility as he tries to locate its source. Soon he will turn his eyes and his head to see who is talking. If you pick him up, he stops crying. If you will cuddle and walk him, he remains content. Whatever else he likes or needs, he clearly likes and needs you. You can begin to have some confidence in yourselves as the parents of this new human being.

But in case these settled responses to your devoted care are not enough to keep you caring, the baby has a trump card still to play. Somewhere between four and eight weeks he is going to smile at you. One day, when he is studying your face in his intent and serious way, he scans down to your mouth and back to your eyes as usual. But as he gazes, his face slowly begins to flower into the small miracle of a wide toothless grin that totally transforms it. For most parents, that's it. He is the most beautiful baby in the world even if his head *is* still crooked, and the most lovable baby in the world however often he wakes in the night. Few adults can resist a baby's new smiling. Even the most reluctantly dutiful visitors have been known to sneak back to the cribside to try for one more smile, all for themselves. . . .

When the baby smiles it looks like love, but he cannot truly love you yet because he does not know one person from another. His early smiles are an insurance policy against neglect and for pleasant social attention. The more he smiles and gurgles and waves his fists at people, the more they will smile and talk to him. The more attention people pay him, the more he will respond. He will tie them ever closer with his throat-catching grins and his heart-rendingly quivery lower lip. His responses create a self-sustaining circle, his smiles leading to your smiles and yours to more from him.

There is no harm in assuming that these enchanting early smiles are meant for you personally. They soon will be. It is through pleasant social interaction with adults, who find him rewarding and therefore pay him attention, that the baby moves on from being interested in people in general to being able to recognize and attach himself to particular ones. By the time he is around three months old it will be clear that he knows you. He will not smile at you and whimper at strangers. He still smiles at everyone. But he saves his best signs of favor, the smiliest smiles, for you. He becomes both increasingly sociable and increasingly fussy about whom he will socialize with. He is ready to form a passionate and exclusive emotional tie with somebody and you are elected.

Under what we still think of as "normal family circumstances" most babies select their mothers for this first love. But it is not the blood-tie which gives you the privilege. The privilege has to be earned. You earn it not so much by *being* his mother as by *mothering* him. And mothering does not just mean taking physical care of him. The love he is forming is not cupboard-love, based on the pleasures of feeding. He will fall for people who mother him emotionally, talking to him,

*One day, when he is studying your face,*
*his face will slowly begin to flower . . .*

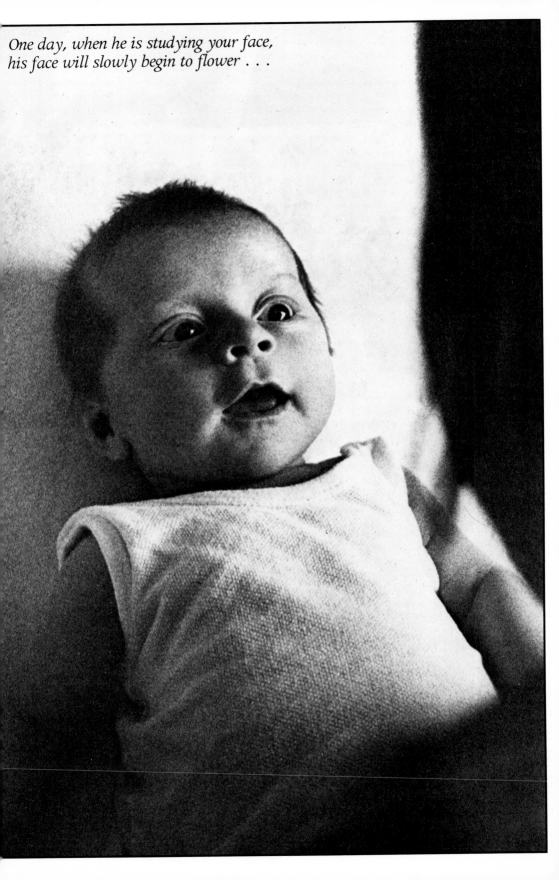

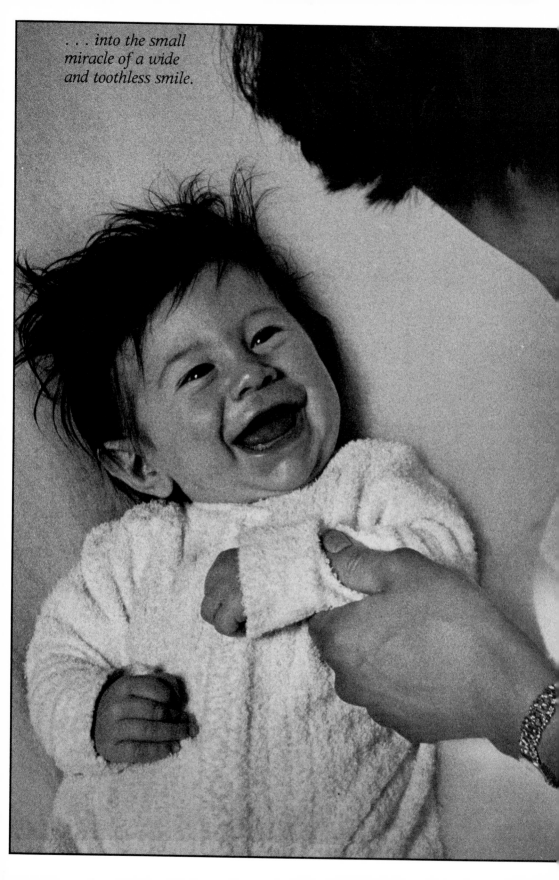

*. . . into the small
miracle of a wide
and toothless smile.*

cuddling him, smiling and playing. If you had to share his total care with one other person and you handed over all the physical tasks, using your limited time for loving, you would keep your prime role in the baby's life. But if you used your time for his physical needs and left the other person to be his companion, it would be the companionable adult to whom he became most closely attached. He needs someone to come when he needs help or company, someone who notices when he smiles and smiles back, who hears when he "talks," listens and replies. Somebody who plays with him and shows him things, brings little bits of the world for him to see. These are the things which really matter to three-month-old babies. These are the things which make for love.

Every baby needs at least one special person to attach himself to. It is through this first love relationship that he will learn about people and about the world. It is through it that he will experience emotions and learn to cope with them. And it is through this baby-love that he will become capable of more grown-up kinds of love; capable, one far-distant day, of giving to his own children the same kind of devotion he asks for himself now. Babies who never have a special person, receiving adequate physical care but little emotional response, or being looked after by a succession of caretakers, often do not develop as fast or as far as their innate drive and their potential for personality allow. But provided he does have at least one special person, your baby can make other people special too. His capacity for love is not rationed any more than yours is. The reverse is true. Love creates love.

Even today few fathers are in a position to receive their baby's very first attachment because mundane matters like jobs prevent them from being ever-present, always-responsive people. But a father who can accept, support and encourage the unique relationship between his partner and his child will find that there is a unique relationship waiting for him too. It comes a little later and it is built on the first, but it is just as vital to the child.

If the two of you are fortunate enough to be able to share your baby's care, the baby will respond equally (though differently since you are different people) to each of you and his emotional life will be both richer and safer for not being vested in one person alone. If you want, or need, to share your time between the baby and an outside job, you need not lose out on the relationship provided that the baby remains – and feels that he is – your primary concern. He need not lose out provided that your part-time replacement is a genuinely loving, mothering figure (see p. 273).

At four or five months, a father who cannot be the person who is always there and continually involved in the baby's routine care may find himself especially valuable. When he does come home, or stays home because it is a weekend, his face, his talk and his play strike the baby as fresh and interesting. Because he has not spent the day trying to fit a sufficiency of chores and sanity-preserving adult activities around the baby's needs, he may be able to offer more of the social contact the baby craves. As the baby grows up enough to remember and anticipate pleasure, a father can concentrate on building his own, peculiarly fatherly, relationship with his child. Instead of competing for the special mother-relationship, he can create his own and may find himself with a prime place in his baby's affections.

Many women passionately enjoy this stage of motherhood. The baby flatters you with his special attentions, making you feel special, beloved, irreplaceable. He needs you for everything. He must have adequate physical care but he must have emotional and intellectual care too: play, toys, help and opportunity to practice each tiny new ability. Whatever the baby becomes able to do, he needs and will want to do it; it is up to you to make it possible for him. Yet, with all this needing, his hour-by-hour care is comparatively easy. He is no longer irrational and incomprehensible as he was when he was newborn, yet he is not awake most of the day and into everything as he will be once he can crawl in the second half of the year. You still get daytime periods of peace and privacy and you can still put the baby on the floor and know that he will be safely there when you next look.

But some women hate it. Instead of taking pleasure in being so much enjoyed and needed, they feel shut in and consumed by the baby's dependence. They yearn for at least a little time when the baby needs nothing practical and nothing emotional either. The continual effort of identifying with his feelings, noticing his needs and padding his journey through the passing days makes them feel drained. Once you begin to feel like this, practical care seems easy compared with coping with his loneliness or boredom.

Understanding your own importance is both the prevention and the cure. All the vital developments of these months are waiting inside your baby. He has a built-in drive to practice every aspect of being human, from making sounds, using his hands or rolling over, to eating real food or roaring with laughter. But each aspect is also in your hands. You can help him develop and learn or you can hinder him by holding yourself aloof. You can keep him happy and busy and learning fast or discontented, bored and not learning as fast as he could.

If you do help him, you and the whole family will gain because the baby will be cheerful and easy and a pleasure to have around – most of the time. If you refuse to help him, trying to ration your attention, everyone will suffer and you will suffer most of all. The baby will be difficult, fretful and no pleasure to anyone. You will be unhappy because, however much you may resent the fact, your pleasure and his are tied together. If you please him, his happiness will please you and make it easier for you to go on. If you leave him miserable, his misery will depress you and make it more difficult. You may resent his crying, resent the fact that he needs you – again. But ignoring the crying not only condemns him to cry, it also condemns you to listen to his crying. So when you try to meet his needs, tune in to him, treat him as he asks to be treated; you do not only do it for him, you do it for yourselves, too. Like it or not, you are a family now. You sink or swim together.

# Feeding and growing

By the time your baby is around two weeks old, he will have learned about feeding either at the breast or from a bottle. Those first confusing days, when neither of you knew quite what you were doing, are over.

The baby wants to eat. He wants you to feed him because he cannot feed himself. You want to feed him because you know that he must eat if he is to grow and be healthy. So you and your baby are both on the same side. To worry or to fight over feeding is a waste of both your energies and a waste of fun for you both.

The fun part is important. If you watch the baby at the beginning of a feeding you can see that he is hungry and that the feeling of the milk going down inside him is lessening the hunger pain. You can see that he is enjoying being held and cuddled while he sucks. And you can see that the actual sucking is important to him too. After three or four gulping minutes he settles into a perfect rhythm; a burst of sucks and then a breath and a rest and another burst of sucking. Soon an expression of blissful satisfaction spreads across his face. The rhythm slows a little; the pauses get longer, the bursts of sucking shorter. Now he is drunk with milk and pleasure, almost asleep. Just giving the odd suck now and again to remind himself that the milk is still there for him.

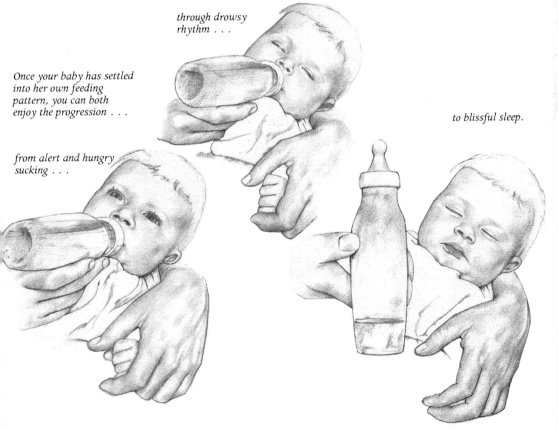

*through drowsy rhythm . . .*

*Once your baby has settled into her own feeding pattern, you can both enjoy the progression . . .*

*to blissful sleep.*

*from alert and hungry sucking . . .*

It all sounds easy. And for some parents with some babies it is easy. But for others it is not. The baby may go on with the unsettled and unsettling behavior which is typical of the newborn period for longer than you expect. This is especially likely if he was a premature baby of if he had any particular difficulties immediately after birth. He may produce some new and puzzling behavior over feeding, or you may be so anxious to do right by him that you cannot believe it is meant to be as straightforward as it seems.

If your baby is reasonably contented most of the time, is gaining weight steadily and is getting increasingly active when he is awake, you can be sure that there is nothing the matter with his feeding from *his* point of view.

If he does not seem to be thriving in this easy, cheerful way, you will, of course, consult your doctor. But consider first the possibility that he is simply not getting enough to eat at the times when he is hungry.

*Growth*  As we have seen (see p. 70), babies gain something like 1oz (28g) each day from the time they are ten days old until they are around three months. But after the first quarter year, the rate of growth slows down a little. In the second three months your baby will gain around 5–6oz (140–170g) each week, and around $2\frac{1}{2}$in (6cm) overall. As we stressed before, *regularity* of gain is more important than amount. A baby whose weight gain, week by week, has been neatly following the shape of the curves on the average growth chart (Ref/GROWTH) but who suddenly slows right down so that the curve flattens off, may be being underfed. However, if the baby has always gained more slowly than most babies, so that the curve has always been flatter than average, you may just have a baby who is meant to gain rather slowly.

## Breast-feeding

*Underfeeding*  Underfeeding in a breast-fed baby can creep up on you very gradually in a way which is unfairly difficult to spot. What often happens is this: having got breast-feeding started, your milk supply is plentiful during the first two or three weeks while you are getting plenty of rest and not (we hope) worrying too much about the rest of your household. The baby settles down to some kind of feeding pattern (although it is as likely to be two-hourly as four-hourly!) and you rightly assume that demand and supply are dovetailing nicely.

But eventually you have to step back into running your household again. Many mothers embark on a spurt of activity instead of getting back into the rhythm gradually. Whether it happens when the baby is two weeks old or four weeks old, suddenly taking up all your old activities *plus* caring for the new baby is bound to make you very tired.

Getting tired and harassed tends to reduce the milk supply. And meanwhile the baby is growing. He needs more milk this week than he did last, so if your fatigue means that there is less available, he is bound to be hungry. His hunger is easy to cope with: you just let him suck more often. But one of the reasons you are tired and harassed is that he needs such frequent feeding. The more other things you want or need to do the harder it becomes to let the baby suck whenever he wants to.

This kind of situation is not easy to spot. The baby's behavior may not tell you very much because discontent and crying, a tendency to wake only two hours after his last feeding and a demand for two feedings in every night, are not *new* behaviors. They seem like his unsettled behavior in the newborn period, so you may not realize that he would be settling by now if he were not hungry. The behavior of your own breasts may also mislead you. You probably wake each morning with more milk than you know what to do with and in urgent need of a clean nightgown! So how can your baby be short of milk?

The answer is that your supply is copious when you have been resting, but gets less and less adequate as your busy day wears on. If you think carefully back over the past few days you will probably recognize a pattern of your baby being content for reasonable periods between each feeding you give him – from, say, 4am to 4pm – but getting less and less contented from 4pm until you have had your first good sleep of the night. In busy households your milk will often be at its lowest for the baby's early evening feeding because it follows that chaotic couple of hours during which older children need picking up from school, the house needs tidying and supper must be cooked.

What to do depends on how much you want to go on breast-feeding. If you do want to, then the baby has to be given the chance to make more milk for himself, just as he did at the very beginning when you were getting breast-feeding going (see p. 53). The milk is stimulated by his sucking. The more often he sucks, the more milk you will make. When his frequent sucking has built up the supply until it meets his needs, he will suck less often. It is a beautifully simple system and it really does work. But remember that it will take at least two weeks to make a real difference to the baby. He will need the first week to stimulate you to make the extra milk he needs. It is only in the second week that you can expect to get a nice surprise from the scales and to find yourself caring for a calmer and more contented baby.

## Keeping up the milk supply

Once you have got your milk supply up to the level where it meets your baby's needs, you will want to make sure that it remains ample. As well as offering him the breast whenever he seems to be hungry, a few other things will help you both:

**More rest for you, especially toward the end of the day.** This is important. Discipline yourself to rest for a while each afternoon, however difficult it may be to make arrangements for older children or to resist the waiting chores.

**Expressing any milk left over from feedings** early in the day when you have got plenty. The baby probably cannot drink all that is available to him then, but if you empty the breasts for him they will produce more at the next feeding.

**Taking the time and trouble to drink when you are thirsty.** The baby will be taking more than a pint of fluid from you. While it will not help your milk supply to flood yourself with fluid, it does help to make sure that you really drink what you need. If there's no time for tea or coffee, at least take a drink of water.

**Taking the time and trouble to eat properly.** As long as your diet is adequate the quality of your milk will be fine. Your body meets your baby's needs first, now, just as it did while you were pregnant. But if that diet is only *just* adequate, the fact that the baby's milk is using up a lot of calories, protein and vitamins may leave you short. And that will make you you feel tired and droopy: less able to cope with the demands being made on you.

*Some things will not help . . .*

**Worrying.** We do not entirely understand *how* worry and anxiety affect physical functions such as breast-feeding, but there is no doubt that they do. Many mothers see this most clearly if they try to feed the baby in circumstances which are too public for them to feel relaxed: the breast is full, the baby sucks, but tension prevents the "let down" reflex, so the milk does not flow in response to the stimulation of the sucking. As farmers say when dealing with a nervy cow, "you have to gentle her or she won't let it down." You have to try to "gentle" yourself, relax, go easy on yourself.

**Trying to keep the baby to a schedule,** even if it is one which he seemed to have settled on for himself a week or so ago. Your breasts must have the stimulation of extra sucking if you want them to produce extra milk.

**Giving the baby a bottle-feeding as well.** If you give him a bottle he will be less hungry; he will not therefore instruct your breasts to make the full amount of milk he needs. The time for complementary bottles is after you have decided that you cannot or do not want to bother to produce more milk.

**Leaving a baby-sitter to give occasional bottles of formula.** Breasts which are left full of milk for several hours receive the signal "you have made more than is needed; make less." Once your supply is consistently adequate you will be able to use a bottle occasionally, but while you are trying to increase your supply it is better to take the baby with you when you go out or to leave expressed breast milk for him if you want to go alone.

**Patent medicines which claim to increase breast milk.** Like "tonics" and medicines which claim to increase your sexual vigor, most of these are merely multivitamins and magic. They probably will not do you any harm but unless your diet is very deficient in vitamins they will not do you any good either.

**Birth control pills.** It is known that many decrease the milk supply. Discuss an alternative method of contraception with your doctor or family planning clinic (Ref/FAMILY PLANNING). If the pill is the contraceptive you prefer, you will certainly be able to start it again when your baby is four to five months old. If you have breast-fed successfully for that length of time, the whole supply–demand situation will be perfectly adjusted and will override the slight lessening caused by the pill. Furthermore you will probably have started your baby on some extra foods by that time so that he will no longer be dependent on you for every single calorie he requires.

If you can dedicate two weeks to trying to increase your breast milk and your baby's contentment, you will almost certainly succeed. Almost every healthy woman can produce enough milk for her baby, irrespective of his size and hunger, *but not all of these can do so while doing much else.* Some women are happy to treat breast-feeding as an almost full-time activity for a few weeks; abandon all idea of "feeding times" or "sleeping through the night" and just concentrate on the baby. Other women don't want to or simply cannot. If you have a toddler or older child, already a little saddened by your absence for the birth and your new distraction from her, you may feel that being available to play with her, to take her out and to care for her as you used to do is just as important as breast-feeding. If there is nobody who can take care of your household and you, lying about most of the day while the baby cuddles and sucks and dozes may mean no food in the house, no clean clothes for anybody and loneliness for you. And if your nipples tend to get sore and the house is closing in on you, you may just feel that you've given breast-feeding your best shot and that's enough. Just as the original decision to breast-feed was necessarily yours, so the decision to carry on with exclusive breast-feeding whatever the cost must be yours too.

Do make a positive decision, though. You can ensure that your baby gets plenty of milk while reducing your time-commitment to breast-feeding by giving him complementary bottles of formula. But once you start regular complementary bottles there is a very high chance that the amount of milk he takes from the bottle will gradually increase, that the amount of breast milk you make will therefore gradually decrease and that within a couple of months you will be feeding him entirely from the bottle. It will not matter to the baby but be sure, before you begin, that it will not matter horribly to you.

*Complementary bottles*

Choose and prepare a bottle formula just as you would for a bottle-fed baby (see p. 61). Feed the baby from the breast as usual, but at the end of each feeding, when he has taken all he can from both breasts, offer him a bottle of the prepared formula. The amount of formula he drinks will be roughly the amount he still needs after taking all your breast milk. It may be nothing at some feedings, quite a lot at others.

If he is only willing to drink any formula after certain feedings of the day (it will probably be the late afternoon and evening ones when your milk supply is at its lowest), you need only offer bottles at those feedings.

It may be several days before the baby will accept the bottle. Babies who have settled to breast-feeding do not usually take easily to an artificial nipple. If yours refuses to drink any formula at all, you may not be clear if he is refusing it because he is already getting enough from the breast or because he dislikes the new method. The only way to be sure is to persist in offering the formula for at least five days. If he is hungry, the baby will have given in and accepted it within that time. If he has not accepted it, he is probably not hungry. Check on his weight gain, though.

**Complementary bottles tend to reduce breast milk.** Once the baby accepts the bottle and takes all the extra he needs from it, he will be hungry less often than before. Your breasts will receive less stimulation because he will suck less often, so it will be difficult for you to maintain, much less increase, your supply.

**They tend to reduce your motivation to breast-feed.** Even if your baby is only taking a few ounces per day from a bottle, you still have the expense of buying and the trouble of sterilizing feeding equipment and of preparing formulas. You may soon feel that you are getting the worst of both worlds and might as well let breast-feeding tail off.

**They tend to reduce the baby's motivation to breast-feed.** Even if he is reluctant to begin with, a baby who has learned that milk comes out of bottles as well as breasts is likely to get "lazy" about breast-feeding – especially about bothering with that last half ounce which takes considerable sucking effort. As soon as the breast milk stops flowing freely he looks around for the bottle.

In theory you can breast-feed and give complementary bottles as necessary right through to weaning time. Some mothers actually do this. They are usually the ones who very much enjoy breast-feeding and are therefore prepared to take double trouble in order to go on. However, most mothers find that starting on complementary bottles means a gradual end to breast-feeding and a switch to full bottle-feeding.

You cannot overfeed a breast-fed baby unless you give something else as well as milk.

A hungry baby who has a mother with a copious milk supply and is not a very active type may get fatter than the baby next door who is also breast-fed. Don't compare them. He will not get too fat for himself unless you start adding solid foods before he needs them, or giving him too many sweet drinks (see p. 125).

## Bottle-feeding

Underfeeding is rare in bottle-fed babies but it can happen. A baby who cries a great deal, seems generally discontented with life and is gaining weight slowly, is probably not getting enough to eat. Check the following points:

**You may be working out your baby's needs too rigidly.** Although it is true that his body will require about 3oz (85ml) of formula for each pound of his "expected" weight (see p. 70), this does not mean that you should prepare exactly that number of ounces, divide it equally between the number of bottles he takes, and then wait for him to drain each one.

If you do this you are not allowing for the fact that, like anyone else, he will be hungrier at some times than at others. Suppose that his "requirement" is 30oz (850ml) of milk per day and you divide this into five bottles of 6oz (170ml) each. If he drains the first two, leaves 2oz (57ml) in each of the next two and then drains the fifth, he will have had 4oz (115ml) less than he is likely to need during the 24 hours. Regularly emptied bottles are a reproach, not a cause

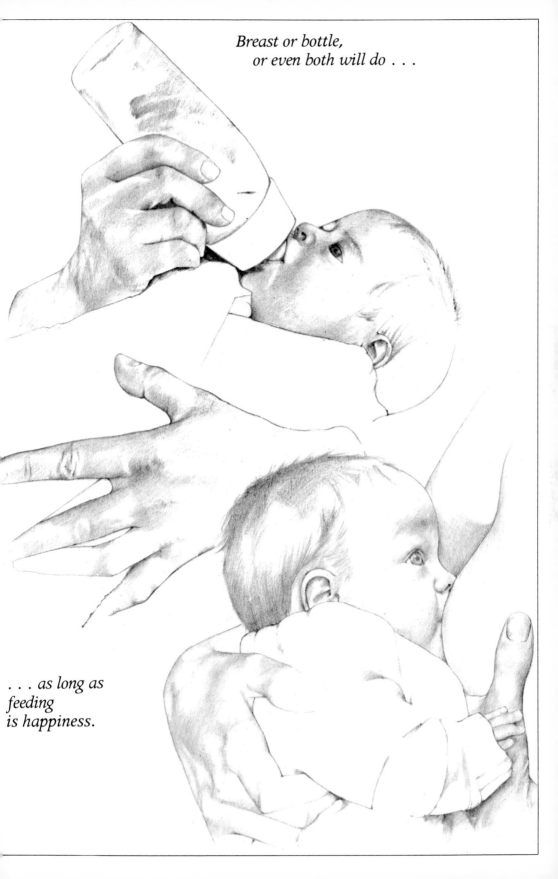

*Breast or bottle,
or even both will do . . .*

*. . . as long as
feeding
is happiness.*

for congratulation. If the bottle is emptied, how can you be sure that the baby would not have liked a little more?

Use your calculations of his requirements as a rough guide only. Put at least 2oz (57ml) more than you think he will drink into each bottle. Only in this way can you be sure of giving him the chance to drink all he wants and to compensate for a small breakfast by having a huge lunch.

**You may be scheduling feedings too strictly.** The baby's digestion will take around three hours to deal with a full feeding, so most of the time he will not demand food much more often than this. But his appetite will vary; he will not always take a full feeding. If you do not allow him to make up for a small breakfast by having a mid-morning snack, but make him wait until the next "proper" mealtime, he may not then be able to hold enough extra milk to make up. Suppose that he only drinks 3oz (85ml) of milk at breakfast time instead of the usual 6oz (170ml). A couple of hours later he will be hungry. If you make him wait until lunch time he will not be able to drink the usual 6oz (170ml) *plus* the 3oz (85ml) he missed earlier. His stomach simply will not hold 9oz (255ml) of milk. Repeated day after day this kind of situation can lead to a great deal of fretfulness as well as to low weight gain.

**You may be using a nipple with too small a hole.** A baby who is really hungry will work hard and patiently to get milk however slowly it flows. But once he has had 2 to 3oz (57 to 85ml) the acute hunger pains stop. Then the effort becomes too much; the feeding is taking a long time; the baby gives up and goes to sleep.

He will wake again in a couple of hours and demand more food, but if the same thing happens repeatedly you may find that you have a baby who demands frequent feedings, never takes much of any of them and does not gain much weight.

So make sure that the milk drips rapidly out of the nipple when you turn it upside down. The baby should be able to get at least half the feeding during the first five minutes of sucking.

**You may be dealing with an exceptionally sleepy baby** (see p. 97). This will right itself in a few weeks as he grows up enough to be more alert. In the meantime don't rely on him telling you he needs food. Watch the clock, wake him for feedings at reasonable intervals and use the things that will interest him most – your face and voice – to keep him awake while he sucks. If he drops off despite your efforts, don't try to pour milk into his sleeping mouth; you cannot force him to feed. He will not starve if you feed him little and often while you wait for him to grow up a bit.

*Overfeeding* Many bottle-fed babies gain weight rapidly from birth and are fat by the time they are six weeks old. The risk of obesity is one of the reasons for preferring breast to bottle-feeding.

Unfortunately it is not a risk that many people take seriously because a fat baby looks cuddly and sweet. But it is not good for him to be fat now and some experts believe that if you let him get fat during the early months he will be more liable to obesity later in life. A fat child may be laughed at; a fat teenager may suffer agonies of self-consciousness, while a fat adult is extra liable to many

*While steady weight gain is important, fat does not mean fit.*

illnesses and may go through misery trying to keep his weight down. So don't let yourself envy the parents of roly-poly babies: you want fitness not fatness.

Bottle-fed babies do not get too fat from being allowed to drink as much properly-made formula as they want, whenever they want it. They get fat either because the formula is not made up accurately or because they are given extra foods or sweet drinks as well. Remember that unless your doctor specifically recommends it (which he might if your baby is exceptionally large) he should not have "solids" until he is at least four months old (see p. 128). Remember, too, that when he does have solids they should never be concealed in his bottle, but should be given separately, from a spoon, so that he can take all his milk, if he wants it, without having a lot of extra hidden calories forced down.

**Make those bottles up accurately.** Extra milk powder or concentrate means a bottle containing the usual number of ounces but more than the usual number of calories.

**Remember that a baby can be thirsty without being hungry.** A drink of water will break the vicious circle of formula-thirst-crying-more formula-more thirst-more crying.

**Remember that vitamin C fruit drinks contain a lot of fructose** even if they "contain no added sugar." That natural fruit sugar means calories. Modern babymilks usually contain adequate vitamin C so that your baby does not *need* these drinks at all, especially since he can take extra vitamin C in multi-vitamin drops. If you want him to have fruit drinks for pleasure, stick to once a day and make sure they are well-diluted.

## Fretting for food when weight gain is normal

Although there are many reasons for fretfulness which have nothing to do with food, the way a baby is fed can cause discontent even if the weight gain is normal.

**This fully-fed baby may be hungry.** That sounds like a contradiction but it is not. His normal weight gain shows that his body is receiving enough food for its needs every 24 hours. But that does not mean that there cannot be many times during any 24-hour period when he feels hungry enough to be miserable. Think of a child at boarding school. He is fed a carefully planned diet which keeps him growing at an appropriate rate. Yet he complains that he is always starving. Why? Because that careful diet is doled out to him at pre-determined times and in pre-set quantities; he is fed according to his overall *needs* but not according to his immediate *appetite*. If you jettison all your ideas about "proper" feeding times and feed the baby when he is hungry, he will probably drink exactly the same number of ounces as before and gain the same number too. But he may do it with half the number of crying jags.

**This fully-fed baby may be thirsty.** If the baby is allowed to feed whenever he is hungry, is gaining weight normally, but still seems very fretful, it may be his water intake that needs adjusting. Milk is food and drink in one. There is no way a baby who is thirsty but not hungry can get the water without the food. Breast-fed babies are better off in this respect because, as we have seen, breast milk contains less sodium than most formulas and sodium can be thirst-making. Furthermore, the first milk a baby takes from a reasonably full breast (the foremilk) is more thirst-quenching than the richer hindmilk which follows. A minute or two at the breast may solve your thirsty breast-fed baby's problem, but even then he may need extra water in hot weather or when he is feverish.

Any baby who cries for the breast or a bottle, sucks eagerly for a few seconds and then stops and cries again should be offered a couple of ounces of water which has been boiled and cooled.

Apart from this, babies should be offered the chance of at least two extra drinks of boiled water every day. There is no harm in offering water much more often than this. If he is not thirsty, he will not drink it.

## Night feeding

Most bottle-fed babies will go on needing six feedings in the 24 hours until they are at least six weeks old. Many will need five feedings until they are somewhere around four months. If you are breast-feeding, you may not differentiate between a "feeding" and a "quick suck" so these numbers may seem irrelevant. But as long as your baby has six feedings, you are bound to have to wake up once during your normal sleeping hours. If you are clever though, you need seldom wake twice. And once the baby is content with only five feedings a day you should be able to get a solid stretch of six or seven hours sleep almost every night.

Being woken, night after night, is a tremendous strain; more of a strain than doctors or nurses, friends or relations often realize. It is not the hours of sleep lost which make you so tired. Most of those can probably be made up by going to bed earlier or having an afternoon nap on a weekend. The exhaustion comes from the continual disturbance of your sleep *patterns*. Being woken, even for a few minutes, two or three times every night for weeks on end can make you feel like sleepwalkers.

*Juggling feeding times so that you get more sleep*

Maximum rest for you as well as contentment for the baby depend on your managing to take a flexible approach to his night-time hunger. Keeping him waiting for feedings or trying to enforce a schedule will doom you to unnecessary weeks of broken nights.

The secret of juggling night feedings to suit you all is to stop yourself thinking in disciplinary terms. Don't let yourself believe that doing without a sixth feeding is "good" of the baby; virtue does not come into it. Nor should you feel that feeding him before his is ravenous, or giving him a few extra sucks by way of a snack, is "spoiling." It is simply good sense.

If you can genuinely accept this, you will realize that you can usually anticipate and prevent a demand for food which is going to come up at a totally uncivilized hour. You do it by waking the baby up and feeding him instead of waiting for him to wake you. Why fall exhausted into bed at midnight, knowing that the baby will want food at around 2am *and* around 6am, when you can wake him just before you go to sleep and thus ensure that he will only disturb you at around 4am?

### Organizing better nights

This is how one set of parents juggled their baby's night feedings so that they only had to wake once instead of twice. Once the baby only needed five feedings they fitted neatly around an unbroken 6-hour sleep.

*The baby was fed around 9:30pm. She then woke between 1 and 2am and again at about 5am. Her remaining feedings came at conventional times: roughly 9:30am, 1:30pm and 5:30pm. Her exhausted parents decided that something must be done. . . .*

NIGHT FEEDINGS
DAY FEEDINGS
CRYING TIMES
PARENTS' SLEEP

*They fed her as usual at 9:30pm but did not wait to be woken in the small hours: they woke and fed her just before they settled to sleep at around midnight. After a few nights the baby took to waking them only once — around 4am.*

*When it was clear that she needed only five feedings per day they opted for an earlier bedtime. They woke her sooner each night until her midnight and 9:30pm feedings merged into one 10pm feeding. They had almost six hours sleep before she woke around 4am.*

*If a late bedtime and no small-hours feeding had suited them better, they could have pushed her 6pm feeding forward toward 7pm; left her until 11pm or midnight, and then got six hours' sleep before a comparatively civilized 6am.*

---

*Going through the night without being fed*

Very few real (as opposed to baby-book) babies abandon their sixth feeding at six weeks, and not all cooperate in having their fifth feeding "juggled" for their parents' convenience by three or four months. If yours is one of the babies who seems to need more feedings by night than by day and who is still waking you constantly when he "ought" not to be waking you at all, you may well find that your patience and good sense are being eroded by sheer exhaustion. Try to hang on to them. Your baby wakes (usually) because he is hungry. Because he is hungry he cries. A feeding will stop him crying immediately but nothing else will stop him for any useful length of time. So don't feel under any moral pressure to resist feeding him. Don't decide that staving him off for half an hour with a drink of sweetened water means that you have won a disciplinary battle. Your baby will sleep through the night when he is ready to do so. In the meantime any method of *forcing* him to go without a feeding will only make him unhappy and lose you even more sleep.

**Leaving the baby to cry** is a common but nonsensical prescription. If he is not hungry, then some other need is being communicated and he should have immediate attention. If he is hungry, food is the right, quick and easy answer.

The longer you leave a hungry baby to cry the more hungry and tired he will get. When you finally give in, the tiredness may mean that he takes only a small feeding before sleep overcomes him; he will wake again all the sooner.

If you refuse to give in and you leave the baby to scream for an hour or more, he may go back to sleep because he is exhausted. But you will still have gained nothing. Half an hour's nap will revive him and his now ferocious hunger. You will have been kept awake through the first crying bout and now you are awake again. . . .

These miserable fights are totally useless. You cannot teach your baby not to wake up in the night. He cannot wake himself up on purpose any more than you can so he cannot "learn" to stay asleep on purpose either.

**Giving drinks that are not food** may put your baby back to sleep for a few minutes if he was only a little bit hungry. But the sweetened water or juice and the sucking only give him a few calories, a temporary feeling of fullness and a warm cuddle. It will not take him more than half an hour to discover that his tummy is still empty; he will wake you again just as you have sunk back into heavy sleep.

If your baby wakes, crying, so soon after a feeding that you cannot believe he is ready for more milk, by all means offer a drink of water. He may simply be thirsty. Under all other circumstances it will be just as quick and infinitely more effective to give him what he is actually asking for: food.

**Giving an extra-large feeding in the evening** will not help unless you were actually underfeeding him before (see p. 122).

Babyfood manufacturers sometimes try to cash in on parents' need for more sleep with advertising copy which says "for a peaceful night for your baby *and* you, give . . . ." But a baby's appetite and digestion do not work like an engine; you cannot make him go for longer without a refill by forcing in extra fuel. If he is already taking a full feeding in the evening, it will consist of as much as he wants and, by definition, he will not want any more. If you force extra calories into him, by putting cereals into his bottle, for example, he will still digest it at the normal rate. The extra will affect his figure but it will not affect his sleep.

## Mixed feeding

Breast milk or formula is a complete food and drink except that some breast-fed babies may need a little extra iron by the time they are four months old. In theory your child could go on living on milk alone forever but in practice a milk-only diet would not work out very well.

Although the foodstuffs in milk are complete they are very diluted: milk contains far more water than anything else. As the baby gets heavier he needs more calories so he drinks more milk. Eventually he reaches a point where he is drinking all the milk that his stomach can hold at every feeding, yet four or five 7 to 8oz (200 to 225ml) stomachfuls per day do not give him quite as many calories as his body requires. Since he literally cannot hold any more milk on each occasion, the only way he could get more food would be to feed more frequently. If you had nothing but milk available for him, you would find that he began to demand back the night feedings he had just abandoned and to demand the bottle or breast at more and more frequent intervals through the day. Fortunately you do have something else available: solid foods which are far more concentrated sources of calories than milk. Tiny quantities of a solid food give the baby the extra calories he needs without stretching his milk-distended tummy much further.

There are social reasons too for offering your baby solid foods. You are trying to bring up a human being and human beings eat "real" food. He needs to get used to a wide variety of tastes and textures; he needs to learn that good food can come from a plate as well as a breast or bottle. Until he has learned these things he cannot join you, happily, at your family meal-table.

Once a baby is ready for solid foods, do give them all from a spoon rather than adding any to his bottle. Feeding your baby a bottle which has a spoonful of cereal mixed into it is forced feeding – it means that he cannot get his accustomed quantity of milk (and that means water, too) without getting the added cereal as well. It deprives him of any chance of saying "no" to the cereal without saying "no" to the milk. If you are ever tempted to add *anything* to your baby's bottle remember that breast-feeding is nutritionally ideal and you can't spoon cereals into breasts . . . .

*When to start*  While there are no hard and fast rules that apply to all babies, no baby should start solid foods before he is four months old without special medical reasons. After this age, your baby's weight, hunger and feeding pattern will cue you when to start.

Your aim should be to spot the time when he is coming near to the limits of milk-only feeding so that you introduce him to the brand new experience of minute tastes of solid foods before he really needs their food value. If he is over four months and bottle-fed, you can estimate this time quite accurately enough if you consider the baby's milk consumption, the number of feedings he is having and his weight.

**Milk consumption.** If your baby is taking 7oz (200ml) at most feedings, you can assume that he is near the limits imposed by the capacity of the stomach. To get more food there would have to be more meals rather than larger ones.

**Number of feedings.** If 7oz (200ml) is all he can take at a meal, then seven times the number of feedings he has each day will tell you how many ounces of milk he could take. If he has five feedings, then he could drink as much as 35oz (1 litre). If he only has four feedings, then he will not manage more than 28oz (800ml).

**Weight.** Your baby's daily needs are likely to be around 3oz (85ml) of milk for every pound that he weighs (see p. 70). So consider whether the maximum number of ounces he could take in his chosen number of feedings adds up to somewhere near this figure. For example, a 10lb (4.5kg) baby is likely to need 30oz (850ml) of milk per day. Five feedings (maximum 35oz; 1000ml) is still plenty, but four feedings (maximum 28oz; 800ml) would be barely enough.

If the baby is breast-fed, so that you do not know exactly how much he drinks, you can use his weight combined with his demands for food to tell you when to introduce solids. If he weighs as much as 12lbs (5.5kg), he cannot be getting enough for his needs in less than five feedings each day. A baby's refusal to lengthen the interval between feedings and/or a sudden demand for an extra, sixth, feeding, will tell you that he needs something more than milk.

An average birthweight baby who has gained weight at the normal rate will probably pass 12lbs (5.5kg) in his fourth month. Since this is also about the age when he will be ready to go for longer intervals between feedings, this may be a sensible time to start solids. A very large baby may reach 12lbs (5.5kg), and therefore his stomach's limits on five feedings per day, earlier than this. Consult your doctor about whether milk on demand is still enough. A very small baby will not reach 12lbs (5.5kg) until he is much older, but he should probably start tastes of solid foods by his fifth month. If you leave the new experience until he is much older than this, he may find the new tastes and feeding methods hard to accept. If he is entirely breast-fed he might also begin to need more iron than he gets from breast milk.

*First solid foods are extras*  These early tastes of solid foods are intended more for education than for nutrition. You start offering them while your baby is still getting enough from his milk alone to cover the possibility of his needing a tiny bit extra and to get him used to them. They are extra, and they are not meant to change his diet or to replace any part of it. The beginning of mixed feeding is not the beginning of weaning.

**Keep the quantity of solids down and the quantity of milk up.** Don't let advertising by babyfood manufacturers convince you that your baby should match increasing quantities of solid foods to decreasing quantities of milk. Instead, feed very small quantities of solid foods and the usual amount of milk, increasing the solids only if the baby wants more as well as the milk.

**Never force solid foods on the baby.** Offer tastes and let him decide whether he wants them or not.

**Offer a wide variety of flavors.** Find out, by experiment, what the baby likes and what he does not. Even at this early stage he will have definite preferences which you should respect.

*What solid foods should the baby have?*  Most of the baby's diet will consist of milk for weeks yet. Even when he does begin to reduce his milk intake because he positively wants more solid foods, the milk that he goes on drinking will provide almost all the protein, minerals and vitamins he needs. His first solid foods are needed only for their calories – their fuel – and there are calories in every kind of food. So it does not matter which particular foods you choose to give him, provided that they are of a semi-liquid texture, that the baby likes the taste and that the food does not give him indigestion. He will get no more benefit from a "high protein" cereal than from an ordinary one. He does not need the extra protein, only the calories which are in both.

*Cereals*  Cereals are the traditional first solid foods. They are marketed specially prepared for babies and they only need mixing with formula for a bottle-fed baby or with water or expressed breast milk for a breast-fed one.

Cereals have the advantage of being rich in iron which is important to breast-fed babies. They also have a bland milky taste which is sufficiently like the baby's accustomed food to make them acceptable. On the other hand most babies refuse cereals unless they are sweetened, and once you add sugar, even a tiny portion of cereal will add a lot of calories to the day's diet. So try unsweetened cereal, but if your baby refuses, keep quantities of sugar very small indeed. A single teaspoon of the dry cereal mixed with three teaspoons of milk and a quarter teaspoon of sugar will be plenty.

*Strained fruits*

Many babies prefer strained fruits to cereals. While the taste of fruit is more surprising to him than the taste of cereal it is also more interesting and pleasurable. If being given fruit makes him enthusiastic about these early lessons in eating, give it to him. The more he enjoys solid foods now, the more easily he will accept them later on when they become important in his diet.

*Strained vegetables*

These are another excellent first choice if your baby likes them. If he enjoys the taste as it is, fine. If he refuses, convention will probably help you resist the temptation to sweeten them! Carrots, which are naturally sweet, are often preferred to other vegetables.

Once your baby happily accepts one or two solid foods it is good for him to be offered a wide variety. You can buy special babyfoods for him or put tiny portions of your own cooking through a blender or food-grinder (see p. 137). If you want him to like your cooking, make sure he has some home-cooked foods from the beginning. If he gets very used to the bland sameness of commercially prepared babyfoods, he may later reject the stronger and more definite tastes of your foods. Fresh stewed apple, for example, is nothing like "apple dessert."

*Home-prepared foods*

Since you do not have to worry, at this early stage, about feeding your baby a "balanced diet" of solid foods, you can simply put a tiny portion of any bland food which you have available through a food-grinder. A teaspoon of mashed potato mixed to a semi-fluid texture with milk or gravy would be excellent. So would carrots or other bland vegetables similarly treated. Any fruit except strawberries (which occasionally cause an allergic reaction), or very seedy ones like raspberries, will be good for him if they are stewed and pureed. They can be made less strong tasting by being mixed with milk or yogurt.

*Commercially prepared foods*

Cans and jars are an extravagant way to feed a baby at this early stage. He will only need one or two teaspoons of food at a time, yet the jars hold three or more tablespoons. You cannot use the remainder up over several meals because the foods will not stay safe for more than 24 hours after opening, even in a refrigerator, and you do not want to offer the same food three times running.

Dehydrated foods can be used as gradually as you like. Buy several different kinds, both sweet and savory, so that your baby can explore variety. You can also ring the changes by occasionally mixing the food with fresh stock (not made from a salty cube) or water instead of milk.

*Feeding your baby's first solids*

There is no hurry; go slowly. Learning to eat solid foods is a big task for your baby. Up to now he has connected being hungry with sucking for milk. Now he has to learn that hunger can be satisfied by foods other than milk and that these foods can be taken in ways other than sucking. To begin with he will not understand what you are trying to do when you put a spoon to his mouth. He will not know that what you are offering is something that will quell his hunger so he will have no reason to cooperate. If he is hungry, he will want his bottle or the breast. If you upset or frustrate him, by trying to force food into his mouth when he is rejecting it, you may put him off the whole business.

**Cash in on his curiosity and interest.** If you wait until four or five months before introducing any solid foods your baby will probably already be interested in the way you eat and in the foods that he can see other people enjoying. If he is sitting on your lap while you eat lunch and he is watching every mouthful you take, give him a taste (of something suitable!) off your finger. Sharing in the pleasures of family eating is the very best way to introduce him to the whole idea of food-that-is-not-milk.

**Use his ability to play with his hands.** At this age a baby will not get much nourishment out of finger-foods but he will very much enjoy them. Being allowed to clutch and suck at a crust makes up for passive spoon-feeding, and the fact that the baby puts the food to his own mouth makes it more likely that he will find the strange taste and texture interesting rather than infuriating. Watch him every moment though. If a crumbly piece breaks off in his mouth you will need to fish it out before he chokes.

**Time the meal.** Don't try to teach him about solid foods at meals for which your baby is always frantic. The early morning feeding, for example, is not usually a good one to begin with. He is barely awake but he is ravenous. Let him suck in peace.

*Spoonfeeding*

Your baby has no reason to suppose she is going to enjoy her first solid foods. You have to help her. She has to discover that the tastes are pleasant and she has to learn to get the food far enough back in her mouth for swallowing. Only after that will she discover that the food copes with hunger!
Don't force her. Let her suck the food off for herself; stop the meal if the taste makes her cry, or when her closed lips say "enough."

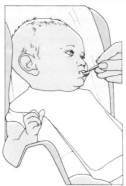
*Hold a tiny spoon to the baby's lips and let her suck off the contents. She will get enough to taste. If she likes it she will go on. . . .*

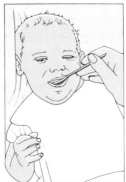
*If you put too much food on the spoon and put it too far back in the baby's mouth, you are forcing her to swallow; she may gag and she has no chance to "say" whether she likes it.*

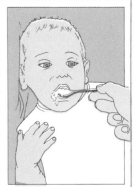
*If you put the food on the front of the baby's tongue, it will simply dribble out again. She cannot get it far enough back to taste or swallow. You will both be frustrated.*

Whatever time of day you select for introducing solids, don't try to give spoon foods to your baby while he is desperate to suck. If you do, he will yell with hunger and frustration around every spoonful. On the other hand, don't wait to offer them until he is full of milk. He will be too sleepy and lethargic to bother. A sandwich system can often work best: a few minutes sucking to allay the worst of his hunger and assure him that the breast or bottle is still safely there for him; then the offer of some solid food; and then as much more milk as he wants.

**Feeding the meal.** Taking food without sucking is very difficult for babies until they get the hang of it. If you put the food on his tongue, he does not know how to get it far enough back in his mouth to swallow. It will simply dribble out again. If you dump it at the back of his mouth, he may gag and will probably then reject spoonfeeding, sometimes for weeks. The technique that usually works best is to use a tiny spoon – an old-fashioned demitasse spoon is ideal – and to hold it just between the baby's lips so that he can suck the contents off. If he sucks at it, he will get some of it far enough back in his mouth to swallow. If he likes the taste, he may become positively enthusiastic.

**Knowing when to stop.** If you use this method of spoonfeeding, he will be able to "tell" you when he does not want any more: he will turn his head away from the spoon or close his lips instead of sucking. But if you put food right into his mouth, you will not be able to tell when he has finished. Dribbling the food out, gagging, crying may all be signals to stop, but they may also be the result of bad feeding technique or a baby who is not very good at eating yet.

*Digesting early solids*

Most babies over four months can digest a wide range of foods easily. Conventions about "suitable" foods have little factual basis. A British mother might not consider avocado suitable because in Britain it is a luxury food. Yet in California or Israel avocados are commonplace and are often fed to babies.

It is important not to add salt to the baby's food because extra salt can stress immature kidneys. It is sensible to avoid spices and exotic seasonings as these may burn the baby's mouth or even inflame his stomach, and it is essential to avoid coffee, tea and alcohol which are all drugs. Otherwise, he can try any food which the rest of the family usually eats. But try it out *slowly*. Introduce any food which is new to him on its own and as a single teaspoonful the first couple of times. If it should disagree with him you will then know exactly which food to avoid for a few weeks.

Remember that he cannot chew yet. If you feed him lumps he will have to swallow them as lumps. He will not like doing so and he may choke. So strain, grind or liquidize his early meals. If you use a blender it will not get rid of seeds or tough skins. His digestion will not deal well with these things at first, so you will also have to strain foods which contain them.

Too much sugar or too much fat can upset the baby's digestion. He has been accustomed to that perfectly balanced milk diet and he will need time to adjust to sugary chocolate pudding or butter with his vegetables. Even once he can digest animal fats and sugar, keep them low for the sake of his future health and eating habits.

*Allergies*    If yours is a family which suffers from allergic disorders like asthma or hay fever, consult with your doctor before you start mixed feeding. If the baby has already shown signs of being prone to allergy – if he has eczema, for example – he may advise you not even to try possible culprits like egg-white or strawberries at this early stage. Otherwise don't worry. An allergic reaction to a tiny quantity of food is unlikely to be violent. Just withhold that food until he is older (Ref/ALLERGIC CHILDREN).

*Juggling feeding*    By around five months most babies are ready to begin to adapt to
*times once your*    family mealtimes, however many "snacks" they have from the
*baby is having*    breast or bottle in between. Your baby still won't last from supper
*solids*    to breakfast time, though, so that stretch of time can be broken either by a late night breast- or bottle-feeding or by an early morning one, whichever you prefer. If your household wakes early and you like to go early to bed, you will probably prefer the early morning. If you like to sleep in but always go to bed late anyway, a late evening bottle- or breast-feeding may suit you better.

Three common feeding patterns for this age group, each suiting a differently organized household, are given below:

| Feeding pattern | Comments |
| --- | --- |
| **Early waking baby in early rising household.** *The baby has a milk feeding between 5am and 6am and then sleeps again. The morning rush is over when the baby next needs attention: breakfast at 9–10am. She has lunch rather late, between 1:30 and 2pm and, with the help of a drink of juice, lasts until supper which is served with the rest of the family at around 7pm.* | *The whole pattern is dependent on the baby having that early morning feeding. If she begins to sleep later in the mornings, she must either be woken for it or have her feeding pattern altered, as below.* |
| **Later waking baby in family that stays up late.** *The baby wakes and has breakfast with the rest of the family at around 8am. He has lunch at about 12:30pm and then an early supper served specially – at about 5pm. He wakes or is woken for a milk feeding at the parents' bedtime.* | *This pattern gives the father more opportunity to be with the baby as he will see him at breakfast and at his late night feeding. It gives the mother more peace in the evening as the baby can be put to bed before the adult evening meal, but it also gives her more of a rush in the morning if she has to cope with the baby's breakfast at the same time as everyone else's.* *The pattern is dependent on that late night feeding. If he is allowed to sleep through without it, the baby will not last until breakfast time.* |
| **The middle road.** *The baby wakes at around 7am. She is happy to accept breakfast at once, in which case her lunch will come early and she will have a late-evening milk feeding.* *But she is equally happy to be given milk alone when she wakes and then to have a late breakfast, lunch and supper.* | *This pattern need not be fixed one way or the other. You can probably keep it flexible from day to day as long as you are willing to give the baby something extra to keep her going. She might need an instantly available snack while she waits for breakfast on "early" days, and something between lunch and supper on "late" days.* |

## Turning first solids into meals

By five to six months babies who have enjoyed their first tastes of solid foods will be learning that food from a spoon can satisfy hunger. Although sucking milk will go on being vitally important for many months, they will have learned to look forward to solids as well. Such babies are ready to begin, very gradually, to eat more spoon and finger-foods and to rely less on the breast or bottle.

The "sandwich" system makes it easy to recognize this stage. You prepare the baby's solid food and then settle down to feed him from the breast or bottle. Recognizing his dish, he will begin to hurry that first sucking in order to get to the dish sooner. If he likes what is in it, he may eat it all and then want only a token amount of milk to finish up with.

Once he begins to behave like this you can offer rather more solid foods (perhaps three teaspoons instead of one) and be prepared to abandon the "sandwich" system when he shows, by gesture, that he wants to start a meal with his solids or that, having sucked and then eaten, he does not want any more milk. He is *beginning* to wean himself by very gradually shifting his allegiance from milk to "real" food. But he is doing it because he wants to, not because anything is being forced on him. It is important to let him set the pace. There may be days or even weeks when he reverts to wanting only milk and there may be certain feedings in each day when he continues to need two sucking sessions. If you let him lead, you can be sure that he will take the milk/food combination that he wants and that what he takes will also be what he needs.

Eventually he will probably arrive at a pattern. First thing in the morning he will almost certainly need to suck before he can eat. If this first meal is his fourth milk-only feeding, being given now rather than in the late evening, he will obviously have only milk. But if the meal is breakfast, let him suck as much as he wants and then have his solid food afterwards.

At lunch time he will probably be eager for his solids and he may be generally less interested in sucking at this time of day. Offer him the breast or bottle after his meal, but once he shows you he is uninterested, offer a drink from a cup instead.

At suppertime he may need a suck first, to calm him down after his bath and playtime. Then he will be ready to eat his solid food before having a long peaceful suck (perhaps in his own room) to ready him for bed.

If he still has a milk feeding to come in the late evening, this will obviously be a time just for simple, sleepy sucking.

During this in-between stage your baby is learning to manage with fewer but larger meals than he has been accustomed to. He will learn fast and happily if you keep the whole business of eating pleasurable for him. Often he will need a snack to keep him going. Instead of an extra milk feeding he will sometimes enjoy something hard and edible to hold and chew. The more practice he gets in managing finger-foods the sooner he will get some actual nutrition as well as enjoyment out of them. He will want to play with his solid foods, too, and the more you encourage him to dabble with his fingers and mess with a spoon the sooner he will learn to feed himself. All in all, happy meals at this age mean lots of mess, so it is a good idea to get organized and equipped for it.

# Starting solid foods

As soon as your baby begins to take a real interest in solid foods, it is time to get organized so that meals are quick and easy for you and comfortable for him. This is no longer a tiny baby to be held on your lap to suck a tiny portion of puree off a spoon. This is a person who is going to eat with gusto. Your baby still needs to be held and closely cuddled while sucking, but the rest of the time a chair will be more comfortable and will leave you freer to help him and get things you have forgotten! There is going to be a fantastic mess too, so instead of trying to prevent it, organize things so it does not bother you. There is a lot of baby-feeding equipment on the market, but here are some types to guide you. Choose carefully – this equipment is going to be around for more than a year.

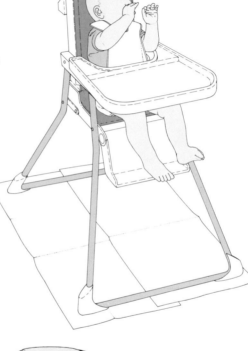

### High chair
*There are many high chairs available. Spread newspaper underneath at mealtimes. A plastic sheet looks more elegant but needs washing instead of just throwing away. You are now all set for maximum fun and minimum mess. . . .*

### Bibs
*The ideal bib. Its stiff plastic cannot smother. It has no strings to tangle, and spills are caught in the pocket, not in the lap. It's available also in disposable form.*

*Terrycloth or fabric bibs look pretty but need constant laundering.*

*Thin plastic bibs are best avoided – the strings tangle and the baby might smother.*

### Baby seat
*Easy to adjust for the youngest baby, and with its own clip-on tray, this seat is ideal for early meals.*

### Dishes
*In this dish you can serve two things separately, while the warm water compartment keeps food warm. It has a suction cup on the bottom so the baby cannot turn it over. Ordinary plastic dishes will do, of course, but they are all too good as hats. . . .*

### Cups
*A training cup is easy to hold, easy to drink from, and will not spill. The worst it can do is drip. . . .*

*This mug makes it easy for the baby to get the angle right, but it is weighted and heavy to handle.*

*A mug without a lid? Then it must be for pouring. . . .*

## Helping your baby to eat

Try to think of yourself as helping the baby to eat rather than feeding her. Once she sits up to meals she will certainly want to join in with her hands as well as her mouth. Let her dabble and smear, dip her fingers in the dish and suck them and try to find out what a spoon is for. It is messy but it is vitally important. The more she feels that what she eats is under her own control rather than simply being ladled into her, the more she will enjoy the whole eating-game. The more she enjoys it now, the less trouble you are likely to have later with fads and food refusal. And lots of practice now means that she will be able to feed herself completely independently at an early age.

So try not to boss her. Skin washes, her bib protects clothes, and paper protects the floor; let her dig in and enjoy herself.

*Don't discourage any method of getting food from plate to mouth. Enthusiasm is what matters.*

*Let her have her own spoon; only by playing with it can she learn to use it.*

*When she knows what it is for but cannot get a load to her mouth, fill yours and swap it for her empty one.*

## Finger-foods

Foods that are meant for fingers are good for morale; they make eating easy and fun. Hard foods are good for the baby's jaws, too, while a finger-snack can bridge the gap until the next proper meal is ready.

*Begin with a raw carrot, an apple slice or a cooked smooth chop-bone: just like a toy, but nicer-tasting than plastic.*

*With practice she learns that she can get food from a crust or zwieback. They will keep her busy and quell her most urgent hunger.*

*Later she will feed herself with cut up finger-foods: much nicer than spoonfuls of lumpy food. Pat her on the back if she gags.*

## Preparing food

At this age all but finger-foods will have to be smoothly pureed. Most babies prefer the texture of heavy cream; a stiffer, mashed-potato texture tends to make them gag. Try to avoid anything which may disgust your baby. A piece of gristle can upset eating for weeks.

Some foods simply need reducing to semi-liquid texture. You can use a blender and adjust the final puree with extra stock, milk or water. Seedy, stringy or very rough-textured foods, like raspberries, cabbage or minced meat, need straining too. A grinder will both liquidize and strain.

Plates, dishes and spoons do not need sterilizing but should be drip-dried (if not machine-washed). Kitchen towels are bacteria-traps. Training cups can trap drops of milk in the spout; wash them carefully and sterilize at least once a day.

Don't open canned foods with the opener you use for cat food! And scald the top of the can with boiling water first. Don't prepare foods with unwashed hands or on a surface you have used for raw meat. Cover cooked food and cool it quickly. If you must serve leftovers, reheat them to full boiling point so that the food is re-sterilized.

# Sleeping

While newborn babies often drift randomly in and out of sleep, sometimes spending long periods suspended between the two states, settled babies are much more definite about the difference between the two. Once asleep you can be fairly sure that they will not wake up again for a while; once awake you can be equally certain that they will not go to sleep again until they have been fed. At three or four weeks of age sleeping and feeding still go hand in hand. Left to follow their own inclinations babies wake up because they are hungry and go to sleep because they are full. Their waking time is therefore concentrated around feedings – the physical care given before them and the affectionate attention given after them.

*Wakeful periods*  By around six weeks, the relationship between feeding and sleeping begins to slacken a little. The baby will still be inclined to go to sleep when he is fully fed, but he will not always sleep until he is ravenously hungry again. He may begin to wake up, sometimes, just because he has had enough sleep for the moment.

Most babies adopt one particular time of day for being wakeful. A common one is the second part of the afternoon. The baby sleeps after breakfast through most of the morning. He has his lunchtime feeding and sleeps again, but this time he does not sleep right through until hunger wakens him. He naps for a couple of hours and then wakes anyway. Many mothers encourage this pattern because it is a convenient time to pay social attention to the baby. He could have his daily drink of fruit juice when he wakes up, and then a stroller ride to the store or a period of free kicking on the floor with no diapers and plenty of your attention. An hour or two of this and the baby will be very ready for his bath and the next feeding. The physical exercise and the play will have tired him. He will probably sleep well until his late evening feeding.

Of course some babies adopt different and less convenient times of day for being awake. If your baby tends to nap for only an hour or so after breakfast and then stays awake all morning and sleeps all afternoon you can probably alter the pattern by juggling the feeding times. An extra "snack" feeding when he wakes in the middle of the morning may well put him back to sleep again. If you then let him sleep on until a later lunch, he will, over a few days, shift toward being awake in the afternoon.

By the time the baby reaches three to four months he is likely to have two or even three wakeful periods in the day. As before, a good feeding makes him inclined to sleep. But as he gets older his naps get progressively shorter.

*Sleeping difficulties*  In this age-group any difficulties are yours, not the baby's. He will sleep as much as he needs to sleep; he is still not capable of keeping himself awake and he is no more capable than you are of waking himself up on purpose. You need never add worry about whether he can be getting enough sleep to worry about the fact that you certainly are not!

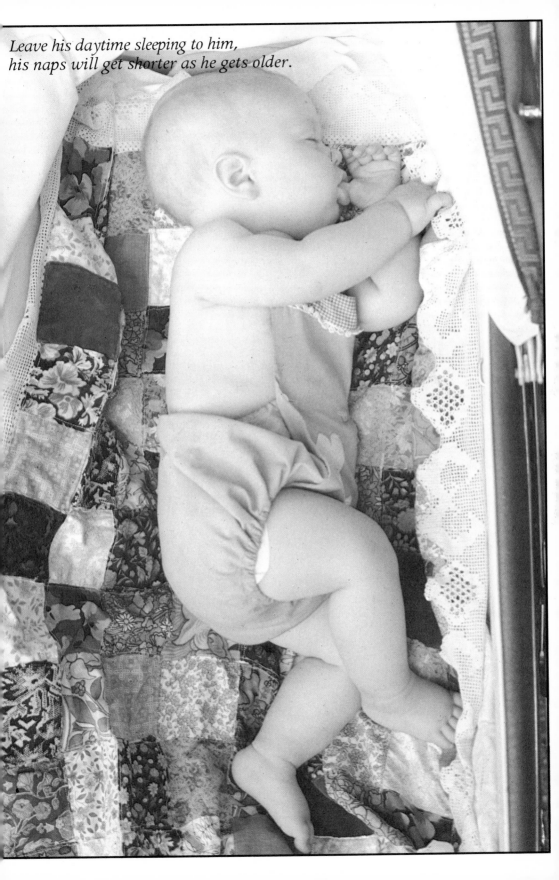

*Leave his daytime sleeping to him,*
*his naps will get shorter as he gets older.*

*Night-time sleep*   If your baby does not sleep soundly for reasonable periods at night, it is worth checking back to page 83. He may not yet have made a complete difference between night behavior and day behavior and you may need to help him become a diurnal creature.

Check for sources of outside disturbance too. If he still shares your bedroom, your own sounds and movements may be stimulating him to full wakefulness whenever his sleep lightens. And frequent peeps into the crib may be making matters worse. Energetic kicking which dislodges wrappings and covers may mean that he gets cold and uncomfortable. A baby bag, shaped like a dressing gown with the bottom closed, will help him to feel both safe and warm. If you start using one now, you may save yourself serious problems later on when he gets to the climbing out of bed stage (see p. 313).

A lot of evening wakefulness can be the result of "colic" (see p. 92) which has got him accustomed to spending those particular hours awake. If he did have "colic" but it is now over, get him up when he wakes, give him a good cuddle and then put him down again. With no discomfort to keep him awake he will soon drop off. If the evening fretting has nothing to do with "colic" and the baby is fully breast-fed, check that your milk supply is adequate for his early suppertime feeding. He might just need a snack.

Remember that as he gets older your baby needs to spend more and more time awake. If he sleeps practically all day, he is bound to choose the evening or night for wakefulness. You may need to adjust the pattern of his day.

Waking at an ungodly hour of the morning usually simply means that the baby has had enough sleep, even if you haven't. While he still has five feedings per day his early morning feeding will probably buy you another couple of hours' peace. Once it is clear that he only needs four feedings per day you will have to choose between peaceful baby-free evenings or a later start to your morning. You will not be able to have both (see p. 134).

*Daytime sleep*   In the very early weeks you may well find it almost impossible to relax or get on with anything other than babycare while your baby is awake. Only when he goes to sleep can the rest of life start up again. If he does not go to sleep, or if he keeps waking up, you will probably feel that you have accomplished nothing all day. This kind of feeling is very natural while you are coping with a new and unsettled baby but it is important to get yourself over it as quickly as you can. It is only for a very few weeks that being asleep remains the baby's usual state, with being awake as the exception. He is a human being and very soon being awake will be his usual daytime state with sleep – in the form of separate naps – the exception. You have to teach yourself to accept and enjoy the baby as a wakeful member of the family. Once you can get over the phase of saving everything you need to do until he is next asleep, you will find that there are ways of doing almost everything you have to do while keeping him pleasant company. Once you have accepted that he is a person, to whom you can chat while peeling potatoes, babycare and at least the domestic aspects of your life will join up. You will find that you have learned to do two (or three or four) things at once while enjoying all of them.

While your baby's eating and sleeping are still interconnected you will probably find that he usually sucks himself to sleep. He stays at the breast, or goes on with his bottle until the nipple finally falls from his mouth. Even though you may hold him up in case he needs to burp, he does not surface again but is slipped into his basket or his crib already soundly off. That's a lovely, luxurious experience for your baby and it's nice for you too because, knowing that he is already sleeping, you can at once turn your attention to other people or things.

But just as it is important to think ahead about the way you want to handle nightwaking (see p. 84) so it is important to think about this way of getting from wakefulness to sleep. A baby who drops off while he is feeding, or while you are cuddling and patting him to get up gas, is not *going* to sleep, you are *putting him to sleep*. And while you may enjoy doing that now, you will not enjoy doing it for the next two or three years.

A lot of later sleeping difficulties are at least partly caused by older babies relying on being put to sleep. And it's easy to see why. You nurse your baby until he is completely unconscious of his surroundings. Then you slip him into his bed and leave him. That's fine until he next wakes, but when he does wake (and remember everybody does wake from time to time) everything has changed. The last thing he remembers is being in your arms; now he finds himself alone in bed. Of course he is not going to snuggle himself down and close his eyes again. He is going to cry. "What's happened? Where are you?" When you come to him he wants you to pick him up again and put him back to sleep in that same way. He may only be able to drop off in your arms; he may even need to be put to the breast again so that he can drop off while sucking. He goes back to sleep and once again you slip him into his crib. Next time he wakes the whole pattern repeats. There are a great many families with babies of a year or more who are still breast- or bottle-fed two or three times in every night because there is no other way in which they can get back to sleep after a normal awakening.

Letting your baby suck himself to sleep, and putting him into his bed already asleep, isn't something that you can, or would want to, avoid altogether. But it is sensible to make sure that he doesn't *always* go to sleep that way. Get him relaxed and sleepy in your arms, but make sure that he is actually aware of being put into his crib; that he gets the chance to experience its comfort and your departure and to drift into sleep just because sleep overcomes him. If you much prefer putting him to sleep in the night, you could make a point of putting him down awake for daytime naps when it does not matter so much if you have to go back to him. But eventually it is a good idea if he usually goes to sleep on his own at bedtime too. If you settle him down and he doesn't drift off but starts to cry, of course you will go straight back to him. If necessary you go back to him several times, until sleep does overtake him. If that seems a lot of trouble compared with just nursing him until he is asleep, think of the future. Once he is weaned and able to roll over to make himself comfortable, you want him to be able to surface in the night and drop off again, just as you do yourself. If he has never discovered how to go off to sleep without you he will have to call for help every single time he wakes up.

# Excreting

New babies' digestions gradually settle down with the rest of them. Once this has happened you will be able to recognize the type and frequency of stool which is normal for your baby. A baby who is fed only on breast milk is most unlikely to suffer any digestive disturbance, to get diarrhea or to become constipated. Don't be concerned if there are sometimes several stools per day and then there are days without one. Frequency does not matter either way. Even a week without a stool does not mean constipation if the final product is soft and easily-passed.

Cow's milk formula leaves a baby with more waste to dispose of, so bottle-fed babies will produce larger, firmer stools and will usually pass them one to four times per day. As we have seen (see p. 79), gastroenteritis is a real and serious possibility in a bottle-fed baby, so a *sudden* attack of diarrhea, with unusually frequent and watery stools, means a same-day trip to see the doctor. Take one of the soiled diapers with you. If the baby also seems ill, with fever and/or vomiting, get to a doctor quickly.

Stools that loosen gradually over several days are more likely to be due to diet than infection. Take a baby who seems off-color to the doctor, otherwise consider sugar intake. Perhaps you have been giving extra fruit juice or sweetened water to drink. If you give nothing but accurately-made formula and plain boiled water for a few days, the stools will probably return to normal. You can then re-introduce fruit juice if you wish, but make sure it is even more diluted than usual.

Bottle-fed babies can suffer from constipation. If a baby's body requires extra water (due to hot weather, or fever, for example), it will extract every possible drop from the food waste and the stool will be dry, hard and difficult to pass. Plenty of extra drinks of plain water will help, but if uncomfortably hard stools continue, diluted fruit juice once or twice a day may be the solution.

**When you start mixed feeding** Whether your baby is breast- or bottle-fed, the stools will change when you introduce solid foods. Color changes or particles of undigested food simply mean that the baby's digestion is not yet breaking down the new substances completely. If you go on with tiny quantities it will soon adapt. A stool which contains obvious mucus as well as undigested food means either that the baby cannot yet digest that particular food, or that it was given in a form which contained too much roughage. Withhold that food for two or three weeks and then re-introduce it in an even smaller quantity and more finely sieved.

**Regular movements** Filling the stomach sets off a reflex which shifts waste down the intestine into the rectum. Once your baby feeds regularly, regular movements may be passed during or immediately after feedings. Don't be tempted to try to "catch" these in a potty. The few soiled diapers you might avoid could not possibly be worth the discomfort to your baby or your inevitable irritation when you "miss" (see pp. 219 and 315).

# Everyday care

## Handling your baby

Tiny babies feel insecure and frightened when they are unbundled. That is why changing their clothes and bathing them and generally mucking them about needs to be kept to a hygienic minimum. But gradually, as babies get confidence in their own bodies, all that changes. You can see the change in what they do when you are not handling them. At the beginning your baby chose to lie all scrunched up as if still in your womb. And the baby liked to be closely wrapped with the whole skin surface in contact with something warm and soft. During the second and third months the baby straightens out. Arms and legs move. Wrappings are fought off. Now the baby is ready to enjoy physical freedom, and to enjoy being handled and bathed.

## Cleanliness

"Topping and tailing" is still the easy way to keep your baby clean enough for comfort between baths. But physical activity is increasing; if your changing mat is high up, don't take your hand off her.

Your baby handles many objects and sucks her hands, so wash them twice a day by rubbing between your soapy ones. The baby will like the feeling but will not like soap in either eyes or mouth. . . .

Short fingernails are hygienic and will stop her gouging her face during hand play. Use tiny, blunt-ended scissors. If the baby's wriggling makes nailcutting seem impossible, try doing it while she is asleep.

Sticky milk or spilled solids left on the face will make it sore. Wash with plain water or use baby lotion or oil if the skin is dry or chapped. Your baby's head needs wiping over to get

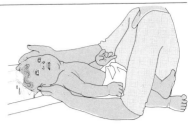

rid of city dust or dried sweat. If it is matted with food, shampoo the hair, with non-sting shampoo. Hold the baby along your arm and damp hair with a washcloth. Lather once, then rinse with a washcloth repeatedly dipped in clear water.

The baby's bottom needs careful washing as traces of urine and feces will make the skin sore. But the genitals need no special attention in either sex. Don't try to pull back a boy's foreskin or wash between a girl's labia. Hidden parts look after themselves, better than we can.

## Diaper rash

Diaper rash can mean anything from slight redness and heat to severe inflammation with sores or pustules. One can lead to the other. Skin gets chapped by friction and damp or irritated by traces of detergent left in diapers. Acid urine stings and makes it worse. Bacteria, or fungal infections like thrush from stools, then infect the sore skin.

To prevent it: take care in sterilizing and rinsing washable diapers; and keep the baby's bottom as dry as possible with frequent changing, discretion in the use of plastic pants and as much time as possible with no diaper on at all. If her bottom tends to get sore, wash urine off whenever you change her, and coat it with a silicone-based barrier cream, or with diaper rash ointment.

If diaper rash does develop, consult your doctor if there are actual sores or yellow spots. Otherwise keep her lying on rather than in a diaper for as much of the day as you can. Banish plastic pants. Change her the moment she is wet or soiled and clean her with oil or vaseline rather than water and soap. Don't use protective creams until the rash is better as these keep air off the skin. Be patient: the baby is bound to be irritable – her bottom is sore.

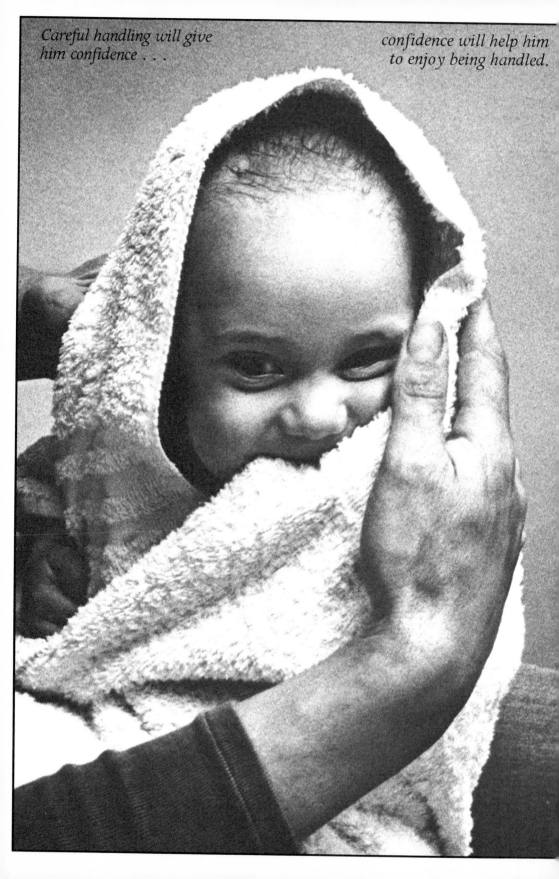

*Careful handling will give him confidence . . .*

*confidence will help him to enjoy being handled.*

**Bathing**

If your baby has uncurled his body and begun to kick, he is probably ready to enjoy being bathed. Instead of lying tensely in the water, on the edge of panicked crying, he feels the water floating his body and it makes him feel light and free and powerful. Because the water supports some of his weight, he can do his best and hardest kicking with its help. You will need a waterproof apron!

Although you can manage without one, a baby bath – on its own stand or put on a firm table or in the big bath – makes bathing much easier. A small portable bath means that you can choose both a warm room and a height that doesn't give you backache. If you have no small bath, a fixed basin or sink will do but watch out for fixed taps. It is easy to bang the baby on them or scald him with a drip from the hot one.

By around three months, a bath may be one of your baby's favorite games. If so, do allow plenty of time and let him revel. Bathing before his evening feeding is often better than in the morning. A long glorious splash leaves him beautifully exercised and relaxed, ready for supper and bed.

*Collect everything you need. Undress the baby on a towel on your lap. If he is soiled, get the worst off with the diaper, then wrap him in the towel while you test the water, 85–90° F (29–30° C), or warm to your elbow is right.*

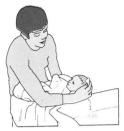

*Rinse his hair and wash his face while he lies on your lap still snugly wrapped. . . .*

*Unwrap and hold him with the fingers and wrist of the left hand supporting his head, the right hand supporting his bottom and thighs.*

*Lower him into the water and hold him while he gets used to it. When he has relaxed you can withdraw your right hand.*

*With his head supported on your left wrist and your fingers grasping his left upper arm, your right hand is free to wash and play.*

*To lift him out, keep the same grip with your left hand and put your right under his bottom, grasping his left thigh. He's slippery.*

*Wrap him in the towel, pulling it up around his head. Pat him dry, and check that his creases are dry before you re-dress him.*

**Going in the big bath**

Somewhere between three and six months, babies and their thrashing limbs will get too big for any form of small bath and you will have to transfer to the adult one. Be tactful about it. Your baby may find the vast expanse of water and the towering walls frightening at first. If the baby does seem worried, try putting the usual small bath inside the big but empty one for a few days so that the baby can get used to the look of it.

Holding your baby securely is more of a problem at floor level. Don't try to bend down to it; kneel on the floor with everything you need beside you. A rubber mat or old bath towel in the bottom of the bath will stop the baby slipping away from you and make him feel more secure too. Keep the water shallow. If it is deep he will float and if it is more than 4–5in (10–13cm) deep it will cover his face if he should slip from your grasp. Be sure that the hot tap is properly turned off before you put him in.

Remember that the bath is wide. Unless you grasp the baby's shoulder with your fingers as well as supporting the head on your wrist, he could roll over and get his face in the water.

## Doubtful babies

If your baby is doubtful about bathing – not really afraid but not quite happy either – there are a number of things you can do which will probably help him to relax and enjoy it. If you have taken trouble over all the following points and the baby still seems unhappy, you should treat him as a frightened baby (see below).

| Do | Don't |
| --- | --- |
| *Get the room really warm so that she does not get tense and shivery as you undress her. A temperature as high as 75°F (24°C) is ideal if you can manage it.* | *Bathe her in a room which is actually cool. If the temperature must be below 65°F (18°C), abandon the bath for today.* |
| *Make the water pleasantly warm to your wrist or elbow (don't test it with your hand which is probably accustomed to really hot washing-up water). Run the cold water in first and then warm it from the hot tap.* | *Use water that feels cooler than your wrist or elbow – it will feel chilly to her skin – or risk putting her into water which is too hot – it will give her a shock.* |
| *Put her in the water as soon as you have undressed her. Soap her by using your free hand, wearing a soap mitt if you find this helpful.* | *Soap her on your lap first and only put her in the water to rinse. She will feel uncomfortably chilly while being soaped and worryingly slippery while being lifted into the water.* |
| *Let her splash herself – and you.* | *Splash her.* |
| *Avoid getting soap in her eyes. If you do, sponge it out with a damp facecloth.* | *Try to get soap out of her eyes by splashing water in them.* |
| *Give firm support with your hand to her neck and the back of her head, as shown on p. 145.* | *Hold her under her shoulder blades. She will feel as if her head might go back and under the water.* |
| *Make sure that you lift her straight out of the water and into a really large, soft, warm towel. Pat her dry through it and give her time to adapt to being out of the water before you open the wrapping towel to check that her skin folds are dry.* | *Let her feel cold even for a second while you reach for a towel or try to wrap her in one that is damp or too small. Rub her dry, or leave her naked while you dry her skin folds.* |

## Frightened babies

Some babies take a long time to learn that a bath can be fun. Babies who still dislike being undressed and put to kick on a big surface probably will not enjoy being bathed either. Stick to topping and tailing them while they grow up a bit.

Even a baby who enjoys free kicking may dislike being bathed. No baby will get over a fear by being frightened. Don't bathe a frightened baby. Don't even sit beside the bath to wash him. Wrap in a big towel on a bed or changing mat and wash the baby bit by bit instead. This gets the baby just as clean and accustomed to feeling wet all over.

If you resist the temptation to try a bath for at least a month, even the most frightened baby will have

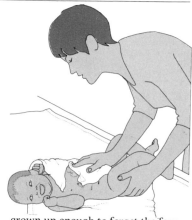

grown up enough to forget the fear. Then, with infinite care and tact, you can try again. You may well find that you now have a water baby.

# Teething

The fact that a baby is in the process of cutting a tooth is too often used to explain fretful or irritable behavior or even illness. A baby who cries a lot and is difficult to keep cheerful is very hard to bear, as we have seen. Deciding there's a physical cause for crying may make it easier to stay patient with the baby, but at this age putting it down to teething is neither accurate nor safe.

**Teething seldom causes trouble in babies under four months.** Since the first tooth will not be cut until five to six months, irritability in a three-month-old baby is most unlikely to be due to that future event.

When a tooth is nearly due it is still most unlikely to cause anything more notable than a slightly inflamed gum, a bit of dribbling and a lot of chewing. The first teeth are cut very easily. It is the first molars, cut at around a year, which can announce their arrival with real pain.

**Believing that your baby's behavior is due to teething may lead you to neglect real illness.** A few babies each year reach the hospital in a serious condition because parents assumed that signs which were really symptoms of illness were only due to teething and therefore did not call their doctor in time.

**Teething cannot cause fever, diarrhea, vomiting, loss of appetite, convulsions or "fits."** So if your baby seems ill, consult your doctor irrespective of the state of his coming teeth. If the baby seems well, all you need do is wipe the dribble off his chin so that the continual wetness does not make it sore and give hard zweibacks or teething rings if he seems to want to bite a lot.

**Try to avoid using teething gels** on the baby's gums. Most of them contain quite powerful drugs. Just rubbing the gums with your finger will probably help just as much. If your baby seems really uncomfortable, try some of the ideas on page 326.

Babies cut their teeth in a particular order and roughly at certain ages. But there is a wide variation in those average ages. A baby who cuts teeth earlier than average is not brighter or more forward than the baby who cuts them later. The actual age at which they appear has no importance – except that once your baby has a tooth you will never again see that particular toothless grin!

## Teeth and chewing

First teeth are not chewing teeth, they are biting-off teeth. A baby cuts the front teeth first, and does not chew with those any more than an adult does.

Babies start chewing with their gums and perfect the technique long before they acquire teeth at the back of the mouth to help them. So don't assume that a baby with one solitary front tooth cannot chew. He can and must.

Babies start teaching themselves to chew as soon as they can get their hands and the toys that they hold into their mouths (see p. 158). It is important that they should be given *foods* to chew soon after this, and certainly before six months.

Babies who are fed entirely on semi-liquid foods until they have some chewing teeth at around a year often refuse to chew food at all. They have gotten so used to slops that really solid food revolts them and makes them gag. If your baby is given hard foods to suck at the four-to-five-month stage when objects are being explored by mouthing, he or she will take much more easily to family meals later on. Chewing hard foods is good for the baby's developing jaw, too. It makes it less likely that orthodontic treatment (braces and so forth) will be needed later on. Feeding themselves, with their own hands, long before they can feed themselves with a spoon, also gives babies a good start toward feeling enthusiastic and independent about eating. So as soon as toys go in your baby's mouth, give him hard foods to put in too. Peeled pieces of apple are good; so are hard baked crusts, sugar-free zwieback or raw scrubbed carrots.

But your baby should never have any of these things when lying down – he might choke or poke an eye with the carrot. And once babies cut a tooth or two you need to be extra watchful even when they have these foods while sitting in their chairs. New teeth are sharp. Your baby might grate a tiny piece off that apple and choke on it. If you are there, a quick pat between the shoulder blades will help him cough it out of the windpipe.

*Teeth and weaning*  Your baby's first tooth will be visible as a small, pale bump under the gum for days before it emerges. When its point breaks through, it will be sharp. You may be tempted to regard it as a signal to speed up weaning. But there is no need to worry about the possibility of the baby biting your nipple. This first tooth, and the second one which will follow it two or three weeks later, is a bottom tooth. The baby has no matching top tooth against which to pincer anything. It will be months yet before he can bite you.

## First teeth

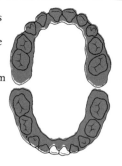

After months of toothless grins, your baby's teeth will begin to emerge. The first one, cut somewhere near the six-month birthday, will be a bottom front tooth, and the one next to it will follow. Early teething does not mean that your baby is advanced, nor does late teething mean that he is backward. Babies reveal their teeth in a particular order, but at widely varying ages.

# Crying and comforting

Some babies cry more than others. Even once they are "settled" there are babies who seem more inclined to the miseries, more jumpy or just generally less contented than other babies.

But there are changes during the second and third months which make even "difficult" babies easier to live with and love. Your baby may still *begin* to cry many times every day, but he will no longer go on and on despite all your efforts at comfort – unless, of course, you are coping with "colic" (see p. 92). Pick the baby up for a cuddle and a chat and the crying will stop. If he is in pain or acutely hungry, it may start again. But usually he will stay calm just as long as you will go on cuddling.

So instead of those dreadful times in the newborn period when you felt like the most useless parents in the world, you will now know that you are magic. Maybe you wish the baby did not need your magic quite so often, but at least it is better to feel useful. The crying becomes more comprehensible, too. The baby still uses that basic hunger cry. He still lets out that pain cry which makes your heart thud. But he adds a "grumbly" cry, a sort of whimpery, fretful, almost whiny sound. And he uses that one first on most occasions. He is not saying "disaster!" or "I'm starving!" just "I don't seem to be quite happy just now." Soon afterward he adds an "anger" cry, quite unlike any of the others. It is an indignant roar: "Come back!" it seems to say, or "I want it!" or "Don't!"

Maybe you could not describe all these different cries in words. But you will know them apart when you hear them. When he starts to grumble, you know that he is *getting* hungry or *getting* bored. You know it is time to do something for him and it is easier to think what to do because you are not overwhelmed by the urgency of a full-throated roar. So at least you can begin to understand his crying better, and you can always stop it, at least for the moment. But what can you do to make him *start* crying less often?

## Typical cries

The baby's repertoire of cries grows. Presented visually from a sound spectrograph you can see the differences in volume, pitch and rhythm in three typical ones. More important, you will soon be able to distinguish the cries when you hear them and know what it is he needs.

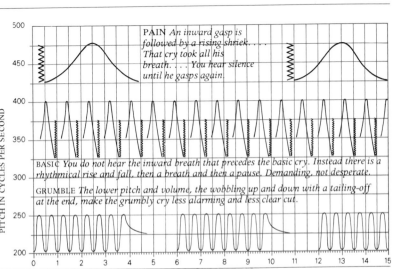

PAIN *An inward gasp is followed by a rising shriek. . . . That cry took all his breath. . . . You hear silence until he gasps again.*

BASIC *You do not hear the inward breath that precedes the basic cry. Instead there is a rhythmical rise and fall, then a breath and then a pause. Demanding, not desperate.*

GRUMBLE *The lower pitch and volume, the wobbling up and down with a tailing-off at the end, make the grumbly cry less alarming and less clear cut.*

PITCH IN CYCLES PER SECOND

TIME IN SECONDS

# Causes and cures of crying

All the causes and cures of crying that were suggested for the newborn baby (see p. 86) may still apply to this older one. But there are some new aspects to consider now, too.

*Sucky babies*  Some babies are better soothed by sucking than by anything else and it may be difficult to distinguish the need to suck from the need to feed. If a breast- or bottle-fed baby is fed "on demand" but needs extra comfort sucking, he may already be able to suck his own hands. Encourage him by helping his fist to his mouth a few times and by making sure you do not wrap his arms so that he cannot reach that precious thumb. If he is going to suck *something*, his own hands are much the best: always available and far more hygienic than anything you can provide. Thumb sucking usually comes later, though. Most babies cannot yet get their hands to their mouths or get satisfactory suction on a tiny digit.

*Pacifiers*  If your baby cannot or will not suck his fingers, you could give a pacifier. It is rare for books to suggest pacifiers, but there is no doubt that they can make a miraculous difference to a few miserable or jumpy babies. Let us look at some pros and cons:

| Advantages | Disadvantages |
| --- | --- |
| If the baby takes to it, the pacifier will soothe him to sleep, or soothe him after a fright. | Once he is used to it he may not be able to do without it. He may want it for years. Can you stand the look of it? |
| If he sleeps with a pacifier in his mouth, disturbances will make him start sucking again (thus soothing himself) rather than waking him right up. | If the pacifier falls out of his mouth in the night, he may wake and cry for it. He will not be able to find it for himself so he will always need your help in going back to sleep (see p. 141). |
| A pacifier *will* probably *mean* that he will not take to sucking his thumb. | If he often has a pacifier in his mouth, it will prevent him from putting toys, etc., in his mouth, which he must do in order to explore them properly (see p. 159). |
| | Unless you are very fussy about sterilizing them, pacifiers are unhygienic. |
| | Unless you are very careful, you will find yourself shoving the pacifier in his mouth every time he is unhappy, instead of trying to find out what is the matter. |

On balance it is probably better to try to do without a pacifier altogether, but if your baby is *really* miserable, you could try giving one for a few months, at bedtime only. Peaceful evenings and nights may raise the morale of the whole family. If the baby is a happier person by around six months, you could try taking it away altogether before the baby is old enough to remember it or miss it for long. It is at the crawling and toddling stages that pacifiers seem most unaesthetic, unhygienic and limiting to a child's explorations. Whatever you decide about pacifiers, *don't* compromise with a small bottle filled with sweet drinks. These are the shortest road to rotted first teeth; there is also a risk of your baby sucking and gagging while asleep. If you want to give your baby a drink, give it in a bottle on your lap.

*Wakeful babies who are bored* A lot of your baby's crying may be due to you expecting him to sleep more often and for longer periods than he needs. He may be a baby who needs much less sleep than average – remember that some three- and four-month-old babies never sleep for more than 12 hours in the 24. Or you may not yet be able to get on with life when he is around, so that you keep trying to tuck him away.

If he is a very active baby (and many wakeful ones are), the physical restrictions of wrappings and covers will frustrate him. When he must be alone in his crib or stroller, try leaving him free to kick. If the weather is cold, a baby bag will keep him warm without restricting him too much.

Even with freedom to move around, he will get very bored if he spends a lot of time alone but awake. Interesting things to look at, swipe at and eventually touch will do a great deal to keep him happy (see pp. 170–71). If he has always slept on his stomach, try putting him on his back with his stroller under a tree or near your dancing laundry or with lots of interesting objects hung close over his crib and changed frequently.

Even interesting objects are no replacement for people. If your baby spends a lot of time awake but alone, he is probably crying because he is lonely. After all a baby who is *asleep* in the yard does not know that he is alone; a baby who is awake is alone and conscious of it. If you take him into the family circle whenever he is awake, the excess crying may stop overnight. You are fascinating to your baby and so is everything that you do. When you are doing simple jobs around the house or yard, he will enjoy being part of you and your activities from the vantage point of a carrier on your back. When you cannot carry him, there are lots of other ways to arrange for him to feel part of your activities, now that he is old enough to be propped up. Try to get in the habit of telling him what you are doing.

He can be propped in his carriage with a cushion under the mattress and the carriage parked close to you. He can sit in his infant seat close to the sink or the dining table or wherever you are working. No matter how tedious the chores you are doing, they will not bore him. You may be fed up with peeling potatoes but he has never met a potato before; introduce him.

When he is tired of being propped, a rug on the floor is an ideal playground unless your home is full of dogs and toddlers. He will not watch television but he will be happy to watch you doing yoga or vacuuming. But perhaps the best of all solutions for older wakeful babies is a baby bouncer. A canvas seat harness attached by elastic cords to a door frame or ceiling hook gives him a perfect all-around view of the world and, at the touch of his toes on the floor, a delightful freedom to dance and twirl and jump. . . . Baby bouncers make miserable babies happier and happy ones happier still. As soon as your baby can manage to hold his head and upper back straight he can begin to learn his world from this entrancing new angle.

# Using his body

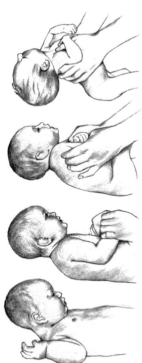

*At birth a baby's head is simply too heavy, but by 6 weeks he can hold it for a second while by 3 months he brings it with him if you pull him up. By 6 months he is trying to get up by himself. . . .*

As we have seen (see p. 100), babies are born with very little control over their limbs or their bodies and with their postures dominated by their over-heavy heads. Muscle control starts from the top; babies learn to support their heads on those wobbly neck muscles. It moves downward in an orderly and unvarying sequence. By the middle of the first year the baby can hold the back muscles steady enough to sit up. By the end of the year he is fighting for control of the leg muscles so as to stand upright.

All babies follow the same pattern of physical development but each one goes down that path at his own particular rate. Like runners they set off together and follow the same track, but some spurt along one stretch and stand still at another, while others jog steadily all the way. So perfectly normal babies may be weeks ahead of, or behind, equally normal babies of the same age, yet they will all be learning their new physical skills in the same order. A baby may learn to sit alone early or late. But yours will certainly learn to sit before standing.

Because the rate at which a child moves on from one accomplishment to the next is so variable, children continually shift their positions relative to each other. For example, your niece may learn to sit alone weeks earlier than your daughter, but having got herself to sitting position she may not go on to crawl for a couple of months. Meanwhile your daughter "catches up" by learning to sit and then, instead of pausing, goes straight on to crawl within a week of first sitting.

So while milestones like learning to roll over, sit up, crawl, stand and walk are quite a useful guide to *what* you can expect your child to do next, they are not at all a useful guide to *when* the next development will take place. If milestones are used to compare different children, they can make mothers feel competitive and can lead to quite unwarranted jealousy and heartbreak. Your baby is not better or worse than your neighbor's child because he learns to manage something sooner or later than he. Your baby is an individual person taking his own time along the developmental track. Comparing this person with anyone else is as foolish as comparing an apple with an orange. *Your baby is unique.*

### Head control

By six weeks most babies will have got their necks sufficiently under control to be able to balance their heads upright as long as whoever is holding them keeps still.

If you walk around carrying the baby, or bend down while you are holding him, his head will still flop. He needs your hand at the back of his neck as he is lifted and put down, or whenever you tip him even a little off center.

Over the next six weeks or so those neck muscles get firmer and his control moves gradually down to include his shoulders. He is growing and putting on weight, too, so his head is getting lighter in relation to the rest of him. By the time he is three months old his control of his head will be complete. Your supporting hand will be needed only when you pick him up or move him unexpectedly.

*Postures*  As the baby's head control improves, so all his postures – the physical positions that he adopts spontaneously – change too. He gradually uncurls from that newborn position (see p. 100). He learns to lie flat on his back with the back of his head on the mattress and both arms and legs free. On his stomach he learns to stretch his legs out from underneath him, and to turn his head to either side instead of keeping it always turned in one preferred direction. Held at your shoulder he keeps himself upright instead of curling himself in to rest his head in the hollow of your neck. If you pull him gently to sitting position by his hands, he learns to bring his head with him instead of letting it drop backward or resting his chin on his chest.

These small and gradual physical developments are vitally important. The baby's postures and muscle control affect both the things he can do himself and the use he can make of the world around him. Curled in fetal position, his head always turned to one side, he could see nothing above his crib. Now, when he lies flat he has a clear view above him and one that he can enlarge by turning his head. Now he can enjoy toys, mobiles and faces hung there for his delight. Now, too, his limbs are freed. He will begin to discover the joys of physical activity.

*Uncurled and kicking, the three-month baby discovers the joys of vigorous play.*

*Kicking*  Most babies will have "uncurled" by the time they are three months old. Once your baby has reached this stage, he will begin to look as if he is happy in his body, and having fun learning to use it.

Now, if he is awake he is moving. As he lies on his back, he kicks, moving one leg after another in a smooth bicycling action, quite different from the jerky little movements he made earlier. His arms wave too. We shall see later that his hands, moving in and out of view, become his most important "toys" (see p. 157).

As he lies on his stomach, he practices a new kind of head control. He bobs his head up off the mattress, rather as he bobbed it off your shoulder a few weeks earlier. Soon he learns to hold this head up position for a few seconds. Once he can do that, he learns to take some weight on his forearms too, so that not only his head but also his shoulders come clear off the mattress.

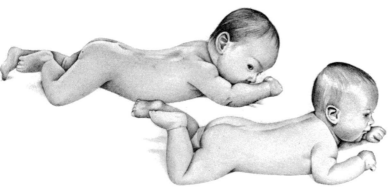

*Once he can lift his head off the mattress it will not be long before he discovers how to get his shoulders off too by taking his weight on his forearms.*

*Rolling*　Even at nine or ten weeks, babies are so physically active that if you put them down to sleep on their sides, they will roll themselves on to the broader base of their backs. There is no point in putting your baby on one side once this has begun. The days when the baby's sleeping position was entirely up to you are over.

By three months, the baby will have learned a much more difficult trick – and one which leads to many a bump on the head. He has learned to roll from his back on to his side. That changing table which seemed so safe and convenient may become a danger between one diaper change and the next.

Think what a lot of entertainment and independence these tiny physical developments give the baby. He can exercise himself; watch his feet and his hands; roll enough to shift position and change his view of the room; lift his head so that he can see something different.

But think, too, how little it takes to spoil all this for him. Restrictive clothes or blankets will stop him kicking; a crumpled sheet will stop him rolling; a bare white wall will take away his pleasure in being able to look around. If he is to get the most out of his own development, he needs your help.

*The beginnings of learning to sit up*　Once your baby can hold his head steady as you carry him gently around, and hold it clear of the mattress when he lies on his tummy, his muscle control will move downward to his upper back. If you pull him gently to sitting position, he will not curl right over so that his head almost touches the floor, as he did earlier; he will hold up his head and shoulders, so that only the middle of his back and his hips are still saggy.

Between three and four months, being pulled to sitting may become one of your baby's favorite games: you only have to take his hands for him to try to pull *himself* up, using your hands as handles. Even without adult hands he will try to sit up by this stage. Lying on his back, resting after an energetic kicking bout, he

*At 3 months he can manage his head and shoulders; it is his back that is still saggy. It will be a few more weeks before the sag is confined to hip level.*

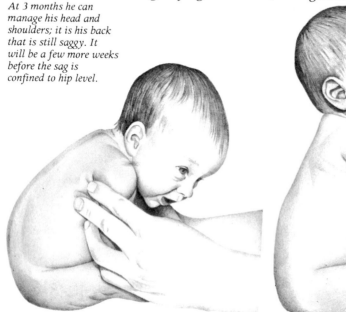
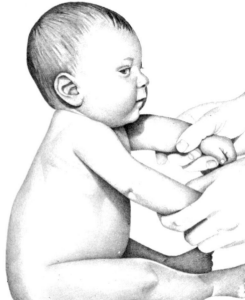

## Propping

Propping is good for babies. It brings them into the family circle and gives them a view of everything that is going on. There is no truth in the old myth that being propped up can strain your baby's back. But if she is to be comfortable, she needs to be propped carefully, with a firm straight slope from her bottom to her head.

*Upholstered furniture is not the best place for propping. The baby's bottom has slipped, her back is bent and her head pushed forward.*

*A pillow under the baby is also inadequate, but put under the mattress it makes just the right slope for comfort and a good view.*

*Best of all, an adaptable chair like this will keep her comfortably propped anywhere.*

will lift his head clear of the floor. A month later he can lift both his head and his shoulders and may get an amazing glimpse of his own feet as he does so!

All this means that the baby now needs to spend at least some of his waking time propped up. Propping him up brings him into the family; he can see what is going on; people catch his eye as they pass, pause for a smile and a chat; propping him makes him more of a person and less of a "thing."

But it needs care. Propped in the corner of a sofa or armchair, he gradually slips down, his back bends more and more and his head is pushed forward. He cannot wriggle back to get comfortable again, either. He can be made comfortable in his stroller, if pillows are put *under* the mattress so that he leans against a firm smooth slope, and he may enjoy a fabric "bouncing chair" at the very beginning. But much the best solution is a baby chair which can be adjusted from a nearly reclining position to a nearly upright one. A chair like this lets the baby tell you how upright he is ready to sit. If you strap him into the chair set at around its halfway mark when he is about two months old, he will relax comfortably in it. After a few days or weeks you will see him craning his head and shoulders forward from the backrest as he tries to sit more upright. If you then notch the chair up one more hole, the process will be repeated. Choose a seat that is light, portable and stable, and use it so that the baby can be close to you and watch what you are doing. It is ideal for early mixed feedings too. Later on, by buying the stand and tray that go with it, you can turn it into a high chair and use it right through toddlerhood (see p. 136).

By five or six months, the baby's muscle control will have moved downward again. Now his back will be under control although his hips still sag. When you pull him to sitting he may provide all the muscle power himself, only needing your hands for balance. When you prop him he may only need support at the bottom of his spine, sitting in his carriage, for example, with a pillow wedged under his bottom. By the time he reaches his half birthday, you may be able to sit him on the floor and take your hands away for a second. There will only be the problem of balance left for him to solve before he sits alone.

## The beginnings of learning to crawl

Once babies have learned to hold their heads up and take their weight on their forearms as they lie on their tummies, it does not take them long to learn to pull their legs up under them and get their bottoms in the air. By four or five months, many babies have learned that they can get more purchase on the mattress or floor if they pull their legs right up and push with their feet rather than their knees. At about the same time they may learn to lift their shoulders by pushing up with their hands rather than their elbows. Now the baby has both ends organized for crawling but he still cannot put the two together so as to be on hands and knees.

Often babies try so hard to put these two positions together that they look as if they are see-sawing: head-down-bottom-up and then bottom-down-head-up. A real crawl, moving along deliberately with his tummy right off the floor, is very unusual before six months. But a see-sawing baby often covers quite a lot of ground; enough ground to go off the edge of the bed or over the top of that flight of stairs. . . . Your baby is not fully mobile yet, but it is nevertheless high time for commonsense safety precautions.

Some babies cut out these preliminaries to crawling because they dislike being put to lie on their tummies at all. They are usually babies who are especially interested in looking at things and in interacting with people. They object to having their view of the world restricted, so they fight to roll over on to their backs again, and may even succeed before they are six months old.

A baby who reacts like this will stop objecting to lying on his tummy as soon as he can get there of his own free will by rolling over from his back. He will probably manage this soon after he has perfected rolling in the other direction. There is no reason to suppose that his refusal to practice crawling preliminaries will make him late in successful crawling. He will probably just leave *trying* to crawl later than most babies but manage to perfect the process and get moving rather faster.

## The beginnings of learning to stand

Standing is a later accomplishment than sitting or crawling. Muscle control moves downward. Babies cannot control their legs until they have acquired control over their backs and hips.

But practice starts early. Held in "standing" position on your lap, your three-month baby sags pathetically; but he soon begins to take a tiny proportion of his own weight by pushing down with his toes while he practices straightening his knees. By four to five months the knee-straightening has become rhythmical so that it feels as if he were "jumping." Once he reaches this stage he will probably refuse to *sit* on your lap at all: he will turn himself inward, fasten his fists in your clothes and fight to get himself upright. Standing gives him warm contact with your body, a chance to gaze into your face and a delightful view of the world over your shoulder, that moves as he "jumps."

By the time he is six months old you may have decided that he is a gymnast in the making who is convinced that you are a trampoline. . . .

*Bottom down, head up and head down, bottom up: the see-sawing baby will soon put the two positions together.*

# Seeing and understanding

As we have seen (see p. 108), newborn babies have a built-in interest in looking at faces and at complicated shapes and patterns. Babies are born interested in people because people must care for them. They are born interested in complicated-looking objects because they must learn to manage a complex world.

During these months your baby will begin to understand things he or she sees. The baby will learn to know one thing from another and *do something* about each, adding action to looking.

*Finding you*
In his first days, your baby will study any face or any object or picture with the hairline-eyes-mouth pattern which makes it seem like a face. But he quickly learns to distinguish real faces from phoney ones. When his smiling starts, by around six weeks, he smiles at you, your neighbor or a face-sketch. But by eight weeks, you or your neighbor will get faster, wider smiles.

By three months, the baby not only knows real faces from fake ones, he also begins to know one face from another – especially the familiar from the strange. He still smiles and "talks" to that smiling, talking neighbor but he smiles more readily at you.

By four months he knows you and he infinitely prefers you. He is not alarmed by strangers – that stage may come later – but he is restrained with them whereas he is free, confident and joyous with you. Before he reaches six months, the signs of his emotional attachment to you as individual people are flatteringly clear. On your lap he behaves as if your body belonged to him; he explores your face, sucks your nose, puts his fingers in your mouth. . . . Handed to the stranger he is polite but decorous. When you hold out your arms to take him back, he comes to you with grins and crows of delight. He has understood that those people he keeps on seeing are his special people. He forces you to accept the role by singling you out for charming attention.

*Finding hands*
It takes a baby longer to find his hands than to find you. Your face is deliberately put within his focal range many times each day, but his hands are usually out of sight and out of mind until he himself can do something that leads to their discovery.

As long as they are continually fisted, the baby is not ready for his hands. Only when they are open during most of his waking time is he ready to have things put in them, to start finding them.

A six-week-old baby finds his hands by touch. He grasps one with the other; pulls them; opens and shuts the fingers. But even at eight weeks, when those hands are sometimes open, he does not know that they are a part of him. He uses one hand to play with the other as if it were an object. He does not bring his hands up to look at them. If, at eight weeks or so, a rattle is put into the baby's hand, he will grasp it and finger it just as he does his own "other" hand. But because he now waves his arms freely, as he lies flat on his back, he is likely to make that rattle sound. When it sounds, he follows the noise with his eyes and sees, for the first time, his own hands and the rattle in them. For the next two or three weeks, toys that are easy to grasp, light enough to be safe and make some sound when they are waved around are of real importance. They direct the baby's eyes and attention to what his hands are doing. They help him to establish the relationship between himself and his hands; the relationship between what those hands do (wave around) and what happens (the noise).

By ten to twelve weeks the baby does not need the sound any more, though he may still enjoy it. He has truly found his hands by now, by eye as well as by touch. He knows where they are and plays with them constantly, watching them all the time. He lies for minutes on end, bringing his hands together; spreading them apart so that they go out of sight; bringing them back again; pulling the fingers . . . he is as concentrated as a five-year-old watching television.

Once the baby's hands are under this much control, at around three months, he will explore them with his mouth as well as his eyes and the other hand. One finger goes into his mouth; it is taken out again; inspected, put back in the mouth with a thumb for company, looked at again and so on.

Now that his hands go in and out of his mouth, so will everything else. His mouth has become part of his exploring equipment. He will not fully understand an object unless he *does*

*Hands are the three-month-old baby's very best toys. They come and go, they move, they feel nice, taste nice and are always available. This is the most vital stage in learning the fine manual skills which make a human baby so different from any other creature. . . .*

put it in his mouth. If you are worried about hygiene, you must find the baby toys which are suitable for sucking as well as for holding and looking at. Trying to stop him putting things in his mouth is wasted effort and wrong too. It is better to spend the time and energy on washing his toys from time to time.

Because the baby's mouth is part of his exploring equipment, it is obviously a pity if it is continually occupied by a pacifier. Very sad and fretful babies, who really need their pacifiers almost all the time, probably are not ready for much play with their hands yet. But most babies can now have their comfort-sucking saved for bedtime, or especially stressful times, so that their mouths as well as their hands can take part in playtime.

*Starting to use hands*

As we have seen, babies start out by using their hands and their eyes separately. They finger a toy without looking at it and they look at a toy without touching it. As long as looking and touching stay separated, the baby is passive: only looking, unable to do anything about what is seen. To become an active participant in life, the baby has to put these two things together and learn to reach out and touch and take the things that he sees.

Getting hold of things is a very complicated business. You have to see something, want it, estimate how far away it is, and then use complicated movements of the arm to get your hand to it. Even then you have to make fine adjustments of that hand in order to get hold of the object. Learning to do this is called learning "hand-eye coordination" – learning to put what the hands do together with what the eyes see. The development of hand-eye coordination in the first half of this vital year is as important as the development of crawling and walking is in the second half. What is more, this coordination of hand and eye remains important right through life. The child who is good with a ball or a hammer is one whose hand-eye coordination is well developed. The competent driver will be well coordinated too.

*Encouraging hand-eye coordination*

You cannot *teach* a baby to coordinate hands and eyes: babies cannot start learning until they have grown up enough to be ready. As soon as they are ready, they will start learning.

But once the learning does start, you can help it along. Research has shown that babies brought up in old-fashioned residential nurseries, with few toys, not much adult attention and hours and hours spent in their cribs with nothing to do, are very slow in learning to reach out and grab things. The minute those babies are given attention and interesting things to look at and to handle, their hand-eye coordination develops much faster. So obviously it is important that babies *do* have this kind of stimulation.

Even babies reared by the most conscientious parents sometimes get less help with this kind of "play" than they could use. It is not that the parents do not *want* to give the baby everything he can use, it is because the stages of development of hand-eye coordination are not very obvious. If you do not know what stage your baby has reached, you cannot tell what he will enjoy using. So let us look at the order in which babies do learn these skills, the ages when most of them manage each stage, and the particular things that parents can do to help the whole process along.

# Using hand and eye together

*0–8 weeks*  The baby's curled up position and "nearsightedness" mean that he does not see much except when he is picked up or something is deliberately shown to him at about 8in (20cm) from his nose. If this is done, he will focus his eyes on the object and indicate his interest in it with his body. If he was lying still, he will start to wriggle; if he was kicking, he will "freeze to attention." If the toy is moved slowly, still within his limited focal range, he will follow it with his eyes. If it is moved too fast or taken too far away for him to see it clearly, he will lose interest at once. The minute he loses sight of the toy he has forgotten that it ever existed.

**What you can do to help.** Until the baby opens his hands (at about 8 weeks) and begins to play with them, he does not actually *need* toys to play with. But practice in focusing his eyes on things is good for him. Remember that his best focusing distance is 8–10in (20–25cm), and that your faces are the most interesting objects in the world to him.

*2–2½ months*  The baby is beginning to uncurl his body, to open his fists and to watch his own hands when they happen to come into view. He is still very nearsighted, but he is much quicker to focus his eyes on things that are shown to him. He is better at following a moving object with his eyes, and will probably turn his head, too, to keep it in view for longer.

**What you can do to help.** Those open hands are asking to have things put in them. Toys (such as many kinds of rattle) which make a sound as they are moved are very useful. The sound will attract the baby's attention to what his hands are doing, and will speed up the moment when he makes that vital connection between what his eyes see and what his hands do.

*2½–3 months*  Most babies now watch their hands while they play with them. The baby who does this is connecting seeing with doing. If you watch carefully, you will soon see that when you show him an object he does not only look at it and try to keep it within view, he also tries to do something about it. Usually what he does is to take a vague swipe at the object with whichever hand is nearest to it. He may also look from his hand to the object and back again.

**What you can do to help.** The baby needs practice in controlling his hands and in estimating, by eye, the distance between them and the object he wants. He also needs as much experience as possible of his own power and control over objects. He needs games which give him the message "I see that, I do this, and something happens." Things to swipe at are superb toys at this stage. A woolly ball can be hung from a string above his crib, so that the ball is about 10in (25cm) above his face. He will hit at it and sometimes his hand will connect so that it swings. The same kind of thing hung from a twig when his stroller is outside will keep him even happier. His successful swipes will make the twigs move as well as the ball. A light rattle, hung up in the same way, makes a change – the baby will discover that his swiping makes a satisfying noise as well as producing movement.

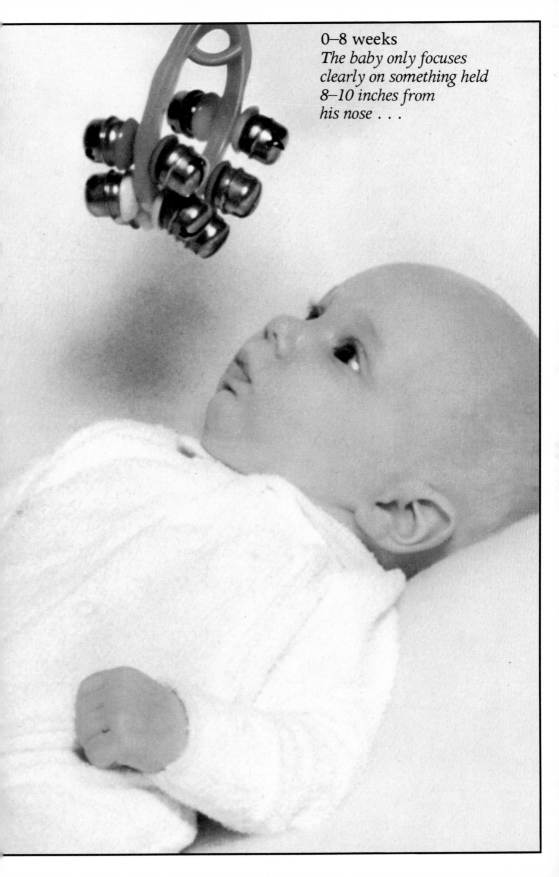

0–8 weeks
*The baby only focuses
clearly on something held
8–10 inches from
his nose . . .*

**2–2½ months**

*The baby is now quicker to focus and can follow a moving object with his eyes . . .*

*. . . he follows it from side to side*

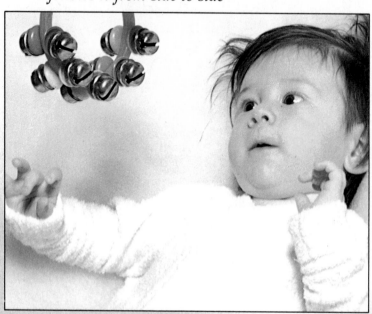

*. . . and up and down too*

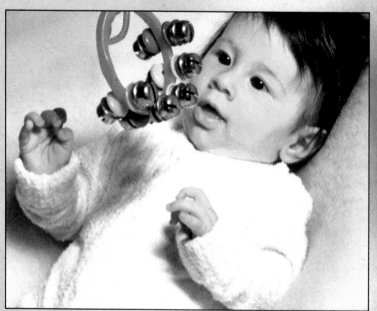

*. . . the sound a rattle makes when put into his hands will help him to connect what his eyes are seeing with what his hands are doing.*

**2½–3 months**
*Soon he will try to do something about
the object you show him. His first
deliberate action will probably be
to swipe at it . . .*

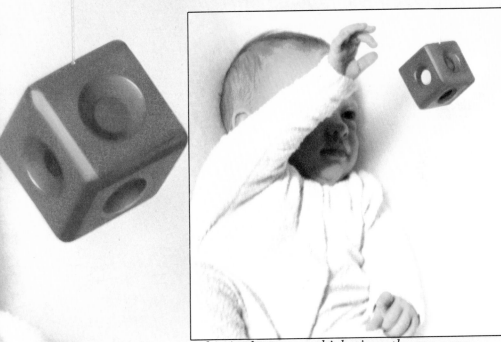

*. . . this is the game which gives the message —
"I see that, I do this, and something happens. . . ."*

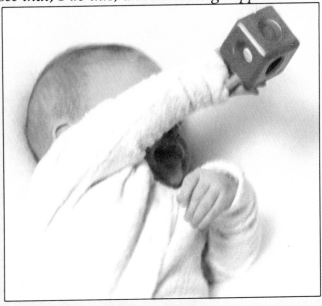

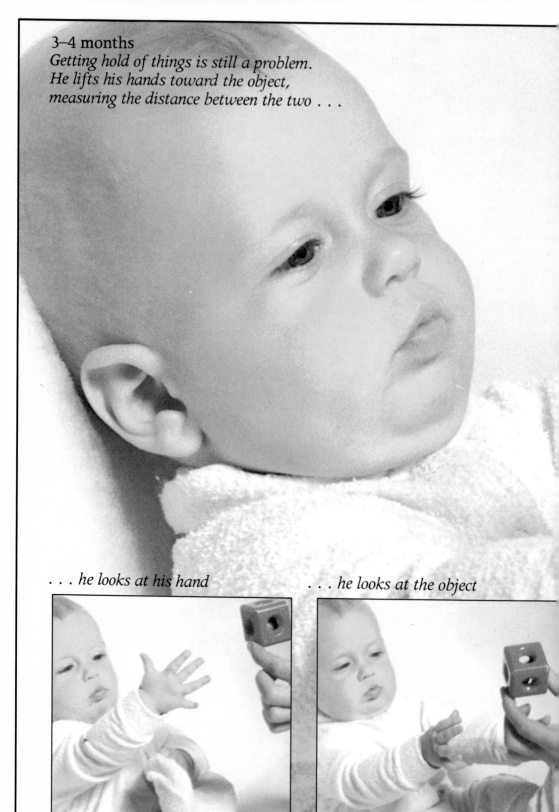

**3–4 months**
*Getting hold of things is still a problem.*
*He lifts his hands toward the object,*
*measuring the distance between the two . . .*

*. . . he looks at his hand*

*. . . he looks at the object*

*. . . and only then can he bring them together.*

**4–6 months**
*By her half birthday she can focus on an object at almost any distance and lift her arm and hand straight to it. She can get hold of things too, even adjusting her hand to suit the size.*

*3–4 months*    The baby may still swipe at things, but most typically he looks at an object, looks at his own nearest hand, lifts the hand toward it, "measures" the distance by eye again and then goes on repeating this until he actually manages to touch the toy. He does not manage to get hold of it, though. He almost always misjudges and closes his hand before it gets there.

**What you can do to help.** Swinging objects are not suitable now: the baby is no longer happy just to hit things, he wants to touch them. If they swing away, he will be very frustrated. The ideal toy, while he is alone, is a "crib gym" fixed across his crib or carriage within his eye-line and within easy reach of his hands. There are "stabiles" which fix on, too. Left with these the baby will spend long periods getting his hands to within touching distance.

Adults who hold toys out to babies at this stage often spoil their practice by mistake. The glancing backward and forward from toy to hand to toy takes so long that the adult gets sorry for the baby and puts it in his hand. Have patience. Don't help him until he has actually touched the object he wants. *Then* he needs to have it put in his hand so that his pleasure in having touched the toy can be increased by having actually *got* it.

This kind of careful, slow reaching out is easiest for the baby if he is in sitting position, so that his body is supported and his hands and arms are free to move. He will enjoy having toys on the tray of his chair, now. He will also like touching things as he sits on your lap – wearing beads or a medallion around your neck is a good way to keep him happy on a bus or at an adult gathering.

*4–6 months*    The baby can now focus on objects at almost any distance, and follow them with his eyes in any direction. Gradually he stops needing to look backward and forward between the object he wants and his own hand. He knows where his hand is. He only needs to keep his eyes on the object. By six months, he will lift his arm and hand straight to the thing he wants. During this period he also learns to get hold of what he touches. He will keep his hand open until it makes contact, and then close it around the toy. Or he will go for a large object with both arms open, and succeed in clutching it to himself.

**What you can do to help.** The more interesting things the baby is given to look at and to reach out for, the more quickly he will learn to reach straight out without looking at his hand and to get hold of the thing he is touching. He needs (and enjoys) lots of practice. But be careful about the objects you allow within his range: once he *can* get hold of things he will, and everything he gets hold of will go into his mouth – cigarettes and scissors as well as rattles and zweibacks.

# Toys for hand and eye

There are plenty of toys available which will give your baby good practice in using her hands and eyes together. But at this stage she needs constant variety rather than well-made toys that will last. A bit of improvisation with ordinary household objects will give her extra fun and learning while saving you money and storage space.

## Things for looking at

Until she can touch, your baby learns by looking. She will soon know all about the string of plastic ducks across her carriage or the mobile hung low over her crib. Here are two variations that are easy to set up.

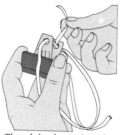

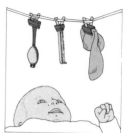

*Buy 1 yd (1m) of ½in (12mm) wide elastic and 6–8 bulldog clips.*

*Thread the elastic through the rings on the clips, taking a turn around each so that they stay evenly spaced out.*

*Stretch the elastic tightly across the elbow hinges of the carriage hood or the top bars of the crib, and tie it.*

*Now clip up objects of various shapes and colors; a sock, sieve, ball, tassel, rag doll . . . change them often.*

*Put a small hook in the ceiling above her crib, and attach a long string to it for lots of different "mobiles."*

*Anything light will move in the air currents. Try various balloons, foil plates, paper streamers or toy windmills.*

*A coathanger on that string is the basis for a more elaborate mobile. It will do for Christmas decorations.*

*If you don't want to make a hole in the ceiling, an old-fashioned hat stand by the crib is a good substitute.*

## Toys for trying to touch

Soon your baby will try to touch the things she looks at. Objects that are in range must be safe to handle as well as firmly attached in case she makes a lucky grab and pulls one off.

**Stabile**

*A crib stabile like this is safe and interesting, especially if you add some extra objects.*

**Crib arm**
*With or without a musical box attached, a crib arm like this gives you the choice between its own rotating mobile and any number of interesting objects.*

## Toys for swiping

Her first successful touching will be swiping. Just swiping is fun but you can help her discover that her actions have results by choosing objects and places carefully.

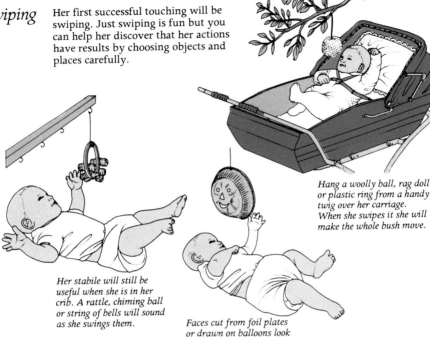

Hang a woolly ball, rag doll or plastic ring from a handy twig over her carriage. When she swipes it she will make the whole bush move.

*Her stabile will still be useful when she is in her crib. A rattle, chiming ball or string of bells will sound as she swings them.*

*Faces cut from foil plates or drawn on balloons look different as she moves them.*

## Toys for getting hold of

Practiced swiping leads to grabbing. This will happen mostly when she is sitting up, but she can practice in her crib if you provide an appropriate toy. It needs to be secure, her stabile is not strong enough.

### Crib gym

*You can buy a "crib gym" to stretch across her crib. Its own safe-to-handle objects will take her weight even if she uses them to try to pull herself up.*

*You can use ribbon to tie a changing selection of objects for her to grab. Keep the ribbons short, though. They must be strong enough to take her weight, and that means that they could be dangerous if she got entangled in them.*

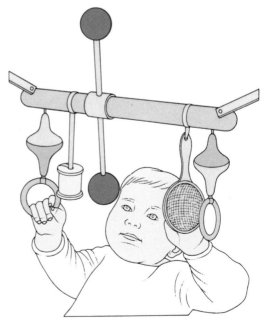

# Hearing and making sounds

By the time babies are around four or five weeks old they will be beginning to link up their listening with their looking. One day your baby lies on a changing mat gazing absently toward the ceiling while listening intently to your pleasant chat. The next day the baby listens just as intently, but stops gazing at the ceiling, beginning instead to search visually for the source of your voice.

If you watch carefully at this stage you may see your baby's first social smile. This first one is not produced as a reaction to your smiling face or even to your smiling *talking* face. The baby smiles to your voice alone. Once your talking face is discovered, the baby will smile to the sound *and* the sight. Only two or three weeks later still will your smiling face, without that vital voice, be enough to evoke smiles.

During the second month, the baby begins to react to a wider variety of sounds than before. A crash will still make him jump, music will still soothe him, but sounds in the neutral middle range become important too. His reaction to any particular sound will usually depend on the mood and state he is in when it begins. If you switch on the vacuum cleaner while he is feeling grumbly and on the verge of crying, the sound will act as the last straw; he will cry. But if you switch that same vacuum on when he is feeling happy and playful, it will probably make him smile and kick. It is as if these medium-range sounds act as a general stimulus, making the baby feel more strongly whatever it was he was feeling before the sound began. Only voices seem to please him consistenly, whatever the circumstances and whatever his mood.

*First deliberate sounds*

Because a baby has a built-in interest in listening to people's voices, it is not surprising that his own first deliberate sounds usually happen in a social situation – while he is being held and played with by an adult. He will have made a few sounds that were not crying from soon after birth, but those contented gurgles after feedings and little whimpers before crying are not deliberate sounds. They are the result of his physical state. A full stomach, a totally relaxed throat and a half-open mouth lead to "contented" gurgles. A tense throat and faster breathing lead to whimpering.

By around six weeks, a baby responds to being smiled at and talked to by smiling and kicking and general signs of pleasure. By around two months, he adds some sounds of his own to his smiling. He grins and kicks, watching your face and producing small explosions of liquid sound. A couple of weeks later, he has sorted out smiling from talking. Now, if you smile, he smiles back. If you talk, he talks back.

Babies who are talked to a great deal are talkative. Babies who are usually cared for in silence, are not handled much at all or are usually handled while you carry on a conversation over your shoulder with an older child talk much less. Of course, babies do not *only* talk when they are talked to. They also talk when they are on their own in their cribs or strollers. But on the whole the more social talking a baby experiences, the more of this "practice talking" he will do when he is alone, too.

These early vocalizations are not "talk" in the sense that the baby is trying to say something specific, but they are "talk" in the sense that he is deliberately trying to join in communication with you. He is using his voice as a means of interacting with you. You say something to the baby, he says something back and then pauses, as if waiting for your reply. When you say something more, he waits until you stop and then makes some more noises. His social intentions are made even clearer by the fact that only a *voice* makes him behave like this. Other sounds have no effect. Some research workers experimented by following each sound made by babies with the tinkling of a little bell. That did not make any of them "answer," nor did it affect how much the babies talked overall. Your baby "answers" because *somebody is talking to him*, not just because he *hears a sound*.

Even when the baby is alone, his sound-making has a conversational rhythm. You will hear him make a sound and then pause, as if he were listening to the sound he had just made. Then he makes it again and pauses again. This kind of "practice," combined with playing with his hands, is often a baby's best solitary entertainment at this age. In fact babies who talk a lot (both to adults and to themselves) are likely to be more contented when alone than less chatty babies. This is yet another reason why babies who are given plenty of attention by adults tend to be more contented and less demanding than babies whose parents ration the attention they give for fear of spoiling (see p. 185).

*Babbling*  The second three months of a baby's life typically produce a positive spate of what is technically called "babbling." He has reached a stage of overall development which makes life very stimulating and exciting for him. As he kicks and rolls, plays with his hands, swipes at objects and triumphantly touches them, he celebrates and comments with streams of talk. He will still talk most of all when you talk to him, but he will seldom stay silent for long even if he is occupying himself alone.

At three to four months most of the baby's sounds are open vowels. He says "Aaah" and 'Oooh." This stage is often called "cooing" and the name is accurate: he sounds very like a dove.

The first consonants which he adds to his cooing are P, B and M. These turn his cooing sounds into noises which sound much more like words. The one parents usually notice most is "Maaaa." Unwary mothers assume that their babies are trying to name them. They may even worry because the baby says "Maaa" but does not say "Daaa." In fact this is nothing whatsoever to do with naming or not naming anybody. The baby says "Maaa" because the M sound comes first in his speech development. He does not say "Daaa" because the D sound is always learned later.

Learning to make more and more complicated babble-sounds by going through these stages in sound-making is built in to a baby's development. He will babble more fluently if he is talked to a great deal but he will babble to some extent even if he is badly neglected or hears no sounds from outside because he is deaf. You cannot assume that the hearing of a baby under six months is normal just because he babbles and makes sounds. Deafness will not show itself in his voice until the second half of his first year. You can only spot hearing-loss early by watching the baby's reaction (or lack of reaction) to sounds from outside himself. If he never turns his head to look for the source of your voice and does not jump when you drop a saucepan just behind him, consult your doctor however much he talks.

*Listening*   By the time your baby is four or five months old, being talked to will not only make him talk more, it will also help to speed up the rate at which he learns to make more and more complex sounds. Whenever you speak to him he will listen intently, watching your face. When you leave a space in the flow of words he will answer you. When he is alone he will practice running through his repertoire of sounds.

Many parents assume, all through the language-learning period, that their children learn to talk by copying. They simplify the things they say to their children and they emphasize particular words, thinking that they are making the job of imitation easier. But, as we shall see (see p. 252), babies do not learn to speak by imitation and attempts to make them respond parrot-fashion are both ineffectual and valueless. When you talk to your baby you provide something much more important than a model to copy: you provide him with pleasurable social stimulation to make every sound that he already can make and to achieve new ones.

Babbling sounds are identical for all human babies, whatever their nationality and whatever the language or accent used in talking to them. Because the sounds are universal, they naturally include noises which sound like attempts at words, but words in whose language? If listening parents speak English, they select the English-sounding noises, label them attempts at words and dismiss the rest as "mere babble." Italian parents pick the Italian-sounding noises, Japanese parents select the Japanese sounds. . . . But in truth your baby is not trying out words in any particular language; he is not trying for words at all. He is just babbling. His sounds will not become different from those of his foreign friends until he starts to make real words at about a year.

Although the listening baby is not trying to imitate you he is learning your voice. Just as he learns, during this age period, to distinguish familiar people from strangers by looking at them (see p. 157), so he learns to distinguish them by listening, too. By the time he is six months old he will show you, by his excitement, that he has heard a friend talking in the front hall. If you go into his room talking, he will begin to smile even before he has disentangled himself from the bedding enough to look at you. But if a stranger should go in and talk to him, the face he lifts from his crib will be a watchful and suspicious one.

*Helping your*   The ease, fluency and complexity with which your baby babbles
*baby to "talk"*   now is closely related to the ease and speed with which he will learn to use real language later on. His talkativeness now is at least partly dependent on stimulation from the adults around him, and his talkativeness later will dictate his readiness for many kinds of

learning. Making sure a baby gets the talk which will stimulate him is therefore a very major parental responsibility.

Talking to babies is easier for some people than for others. Natural talkers chat to anyone who is around and if the person who happens to be around is the baby, he gets the benefit. Some adults have a real sense of babies being people from their earliest weeks. To them, it would be as rude to ignore an idle baby as it would be to ignore a grown-up friend. But other people are naturally quiet and do not talk very much even to each other. Talking to a baby who cannot even answer in words may make them feel silly – as if they were talking out loud to themselves. A natural, easy chattiness is a good quality to look for in a caregiver, especially if it isn't one you have yourself!

It is no good trying to force yourself to behave in a way that feels unnatural to you. You cannot just decide to turn yourself into a talkative person. But you can deliberately set up a few situations which help you to talk to your baby; if you do, you may find that his responsiveness to your conversation inspires you to talk to him more and more.

**Show your baby a picture book,** point to and name the things in it and tell him, just as you would tell a three-year-old, what they are doing. He will enjoy the pictures and the talk even without understanding them, and he's entitled to a library card right now.

**Tell the baby what you are doing whenever you are handling him.** As you undress him, tell him which garments you are taking off which parts of his body. As you bathe him, tell him which part you are soaping or what you are reaching out for. As you give him a meal, tell him what is in it and what is coming next.

**Ask questions.** He will not answer you in words but he may do so in expressions, intonations and gestures: "Is that nice?" "Where's it gone?" "Is it too cold?". . . .

**Talk naturally, without over-simplifying what you say.** At this stage it is your fluent, interesting-sounding talk that he needs to stimulate him. If you try to keep your words simple, the pace slow and the subject matter comprehensible, you will sound stilted and unnatural. Your baby will respond just as gleefully to your comments on the latest political developments or the price of cheese as he will to a carefully chosen sentence about the family dog. If baby talk comes naturally to you, use it. If it is false to you, don't use it. It does not matter, at this stage, either way.

**Make a point of having some play-talk time alone with your baby.** This is especially important if chatting to him in front of other people makes you feel silly, or if you have an older child around who also needs lots of conversation and is infinitely better at making sure that she gets it!

**Most important of all, listen to the baby** and try to answer him, in words, every time he makes noises at you. He does not want a running commentary or monologue from you every moment of the day, he wants conversation. If you are not a person who finds it easy to start many conversations yourself, you can at least discipline yourself to reply whenever he tries to start one.

# Playing and learning

Play is more than "just fun" to babies. Play is learning and practicing what they have learned. It is finding things out and exploring what they find. It is anything that stimulates them to use their bodies and their senses and to develop their thinking and their intelligence. So while play must be fun (or the baby will not go on with it), not all play has to be *deliberate* fun. Your baby will get some play value out of every single ordinarily pleasant thing you do with him or her, from changing a diaper to feeding a meal.

But when you do play deliberately with your baby you are doing a very important job: you are teaching him. The toys you offer him are as valuable to him now as educational equipment will be when he is a five-year-old. The games you play with him are as important as the project his teacher will work on with him when he goes to nursery school. Although the baby would probably like you to play with him almost whenever he is awake, the time that you can devote to deliberate play is almost certainly limited. So it is worth making sure that it is spent in offering him the most appropriate, and therefore interesting and enjoyable, experiences you can possibly think up.

*Making the most of play time*

**Adjust kinds of play to your baby's moods.** Like everybody else he enjoys different things when he is in different moods. When he is feeling tough and good, he enjoys rough and tumble play. It makes him triumph in his body and, gradually, in his own control and power over it. But when he is feeling tired or unwell, the same games frighten and upset him. He does not feel controled and powerful now; he feels manhandled.

When he is feeling quiet and affectionate, he revels in being cuddled and crooned to. But when he is feeling restless and energetic, the same games make him feel imprisoned.

When he is tired or hungry or miserable, no game is any good. He does not want your play, he wants bed or food or comfort.

**When you are being a playmate, adjust your timing to the baby's.** His reactions are much slower than yours, especially when the play that you are offering stretches new abilities to their limits. If he is to take his full share in the "game," you must train yourself to play at his pace. If you speak to him, for example, wait five seconds for him to answer and then get impatient and say something else, you have done him out of his turn. Wait. It may take him fifteen seconds to find his answering sound.

If you hold out a toy for him to take, wait while he starts the painstaking process of reaching out for it, but then lose your patience and put it into his hand after all, you have done him out of his part. Wait. Give him time to get his hand there; time to succeed in the play-task you have set him.

If you smile down at him for a few seconds, blow him a kiss and then turn away, you have left him yet again with no part in the game. He was probably going to smile back at you but you did not give him time. Now he is smiling, puzzled, at your back.

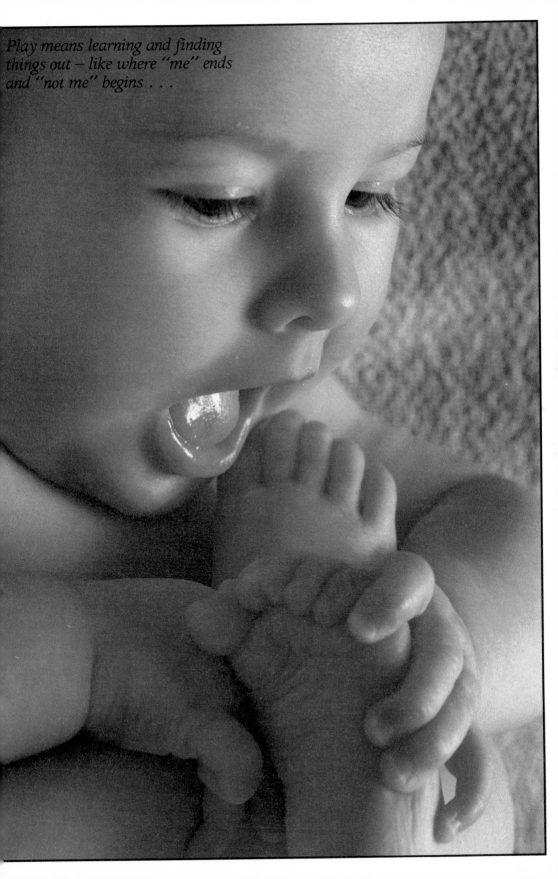

*Play means learning and finding things out — like where "me" ends and "not me" begins . . .*

*Play means using all the senses — like hearing a message and feeling it too . . .*

*Play means endless investigation*
*– of the way things feel*
*and the way they move . . .*

*Play means pleasure . . .*

*Some like it rough . . .*

*some like it gentle . . .*

*. . . most like a bit of each.*

**Adjust your games to your baby's temperament.** There is a "right" intensity of stimulation for every baby – enough to interest him and make him notice, but not enough to overwhelm him and make him withdraw. The swinging-in-the-air game that makes one five-month-old baby crow with delight will really frighten another. The gentle lullaby that makes one smile and try to sing will pass unnoticed by another. You know your own baby best; the more alert you can be to his reactions, the more easily you will be able to get your play just right for him.

Does he hate loud noises? Then don't give him a metal spoon to bang on that saucepan, give him a plastic spatula instead. Don't give him a rubber duck with a loud squeak either, put sticky tape over the squeaker hole until he has gotten acquainted with it.

Is he physically timid? Then don't play "Bumpin' up and down in my little red wagon," bouncing him on your knee. Play "This little piggy went to market" instead, playing with his toes.

Is he physically very active? Then don't confine him in his chair with a rattle, put him on the floor instead and help him to "bicycle" his legs and learn to roll over.

**Provide the "right" amount of novelty.** Between about three and six months, babies are most alert to and interested in things which are familiar enough to be manageable to them but yet slightly novel. Entirely familiar objects bore them – they have found out all they can about them, there are no more discoveries to be made. What your baby will like best is another rattle, rather like the last one but a bit bigger, perhaps, and a different color. A piece of paper like the one he had yesterday, but tissue this time so that it feels different and makes a new kind of rustle. A music box like the first one but with a new tune; a mobile as before but with different shapes; a long balloon instead of a round one, or a plastic bottle instead of that plastic jar. . . .

**Give your baby the chance to play naked.** By two to three months most babies take a tremendous pleasure in being naked, in striking contrast to their fear of nakedness earlier on (see p. 88). Naked playtimes have everything to recommend them. The baby has the chance to discover and practice new physical skills, unhampered by clothes and coverings, and he has the chance to "find" all the parts of himself that are usually hidden from view and from touch under diapers and shirts. He also experiences a complete change in the texture of his world, as air or sunlight finger his skin while he rolls and chortles. Physical play and cuddles with you take on a new dimension, too. You will probably find his bare dimpled back irresistible.

But he needs to be warm and he needs to be safe. The center of a double bed with a towel spread over it is an ideal playground – at least until he learns to roll right over. A rug on the grass under a tree is an idyllic place for him to play when the weather is warm.

*Playthings* Throughout this age period, beloved adults are your baby's best playthings. Your body is his gymnastic equipment; your muscles supplement his so that with you he can do a thousand things he cannot yet do alone. Your face and voice together are entrancing to him; the things that you do and the things that you use all fascinate him. If you will give him your attention, your affection and your help, you give him the best kind of play there is.

But gradually the baby needs and wants to learn about his world and the things as well as the people that are in it. He needs objects. Toys for this age-group are designed to be safe, colorful and easy for the baby to hold. The better ones are also intended to provide him with a wide variety of experiences of different shapes, weights and textures. So there is a lot to be said for buying rattles and rings, cuddly toys and mobiles, squeaky toys and balls.

But these bought toys alone will not be enough for the baby at this stage. Whatever you give him to play with, he will do very little with it. His main interest in objects is in getting hold of them; looking at them, feeling them and exploring them with his mouth. Once he has thoroughly examined an object in this way he is ready for a different one. To buy enough toys to satisfy his insatiable curiosity about different objects you would have to be a millionaire with unlimited storage space. The answer lies in lending him a carefully chosen range of ordinary household objects to supplement his own possessions.

From your baby's point of view almost every drawer and cupboard is full of playthings...

...and the supermarket is a toy store...

Sharing your things with him — as long as they're safe — makes chores into fun for both of you.

*Everyday objects for play*

All objects are new to new babies so they will enjoy anything you are prepared to lend. It does not matter what the object is *for* as your baby will not be able to make it work. Color, shape, weight, sound and feel are what matter. The suggestions on page 183 include items available in almost every home: you can probably add many more (see p. 534).

**Caution.** Your baby will suck and bite at everything. Things that are safe when whole can become dangerous when broken; yogurt cups, for example, are sharp once they have cracked. Play needs careful supervision; "toys" need regular inspection. The baby will learn to take things apart; make sure the contents of a home-made "rattle" cannot be swallowed or cause gagging. The baby will drop things; avoid anything heavy enough to hurt. Sucking sometimes means swallowing; watch out for poisons such as newsprint or a drop of cleaning fluid in a plastic bottle.

*Helping your baby to explore objects*

During these months your baby will become very efficient at reaching out to touch objects but will still have trouble in picking them up. It is only in the second half of the year that he will learn to use his fingers and thumbs separately and develop a fine pincer-grasp. In the meantime he will find it easiest to get hold of things if he can use a two-handed approach, trapping the toy he wants between his wrists and then scooping it up with his palms. This kind of play is easiest for him if he is firmly supported in sitting position with both arms free and the object on a table or tray in front of him. Your lap as you sit up to table is an ideal support. Failing that he needs to be put into his infant seat or high chair with its own table.

At this stage he can only attend to one object at a time, and he certainly cannot choose between several. A trayful of toys will only confuse him. He plays best if you put one or two objects on his table and replace them with others when he has clearly become bored with the first lot.

If the baby is playing with one of your kitchen toys and you want it back, offering another object is the only way you can get it without a fuss. He cannot yet release it on purpose and he will bitterly resent having it removed by force. So make use of his inability to do two things at the same time – offer him a spoon and he will drop the saucepan you are waiting for.

# Loving and spoiling

Loving and playing, putting yourself in your baby's place, thinking about needs and moods, noticing every gesture and sound all add up to a lot of attention. Should your baby have so much? Will he or she not get spoiled?

Older children and adults who are selfish, thinking only of their own gratification and giving no thought to other people's needs, are spoilers of everyone's pleasure. When a four-year-old hurtfully rejects a present which was the best her grandma could afford, or bawls for a third ice cream with her second still melting in her fist, watching adults agree that she is "spoiled rotten." So horrid is the prospect of being responsible for a spoiled child that many parents start trying to prevent it almost from the moment of their baby's birth. "She must learn that she isn't the only fish in the sea," they declare. "Life is tough and he'd better get used to it" and even "Mommy only likes *good* little girls. . . ."

But these phrases, echoing down the years from our own childhoods and applied without much thought to our new children, have no sense or meaning in the life of a baby. In order to become spoiled (or indeed to become the opposite, a paragon of unselfishness and thought for others), a child has to be able to *want* things as well as to *need* them. He has to be able to see himself as a being who is separate from everyone else. He has to appreciate other people's rights as well as his own and he has to be able to plan to assert his own over theirs. A baby can do none of these things. He feels a need and he expresses it. He is not intellectually capable of working out involved plans and ideas like "If I make enough fuss will he . . .?"; "They let me do . . . yesterday and I want to do it again today so I'll. . . ." So when I say that babies cannot be spoiled, I am not saying that they are naturally "good." I am saying that *they are not grown up or clever enough to be spoiled*.

Meeting a baby's needs is a tough job at times. Every baby has phases when because his needs are changing he has to express a lot. Understand the new needs so that you quickly meet – or even anticipate – them and he will stop needing to express them so loudly or so often. But if you begin to worry about spoiling, or if you let other people suggest that your baby is getting spoiled, you may not set yourself to understanding and meeting those needs but to resisting them. Friends and relations who tell you that your baby is "canny," that "he's twisting you round his finger" and that he *ought not* to "demand" so much attention, can damage not only your confidence and morale but even your relationship with your baby. You probably won't be able to change their attitudes so try to become so confident of your own that theirs cannot hurt you. And don't let yourself in for sharing your baby's care with a sitter or a nanny with "those who ask don't get" attitudes.

When a baby naps for an hour although you'd expected three hours' peace, the easy answer is to get him up and help him play. The fear-of-spoiling answer is the direct opposite: "I'd meant to pick you up at 2pm but now you're crying for me at midday I'll jolly well see that you wait until 2:15 because you've got to learn. . . ." What could a baby learn from this? What message could your disciplinary behavior convey to him? "Don't bother to call me because I will not come until I am ready."? "Don't tell me when you are unhappy because I am not interested."? "The more you tell me what you need the less likely I am to give it to you."? "I will only do things for you if you do not ask."? In this situation everybody loses.

**The baby loses** because his needs are not met, or they are met only after so much delay that he loses his vital confidence that they *will be* met. He becomes anxious; quicker to cry and fuss and slower to accept comfort. Where earlier he might have been happy to play alone in his crib when he woke, now the experience of being left has taught him to associate the crib with loneliness and boredom. Soon he starts to cry the moment he opens his eyes.

**You lose** because the less you meet the baby's needs the more demanding he becomes. As your determination to resist him hardens, so his natural demands turn into anxious ones. You get caught in a vicious circle which is actually creating the thing you sought to avoid: an unreasonably demanding and whiny baby.

**The rest of the family loses** because resentful parents and an anxiously demanding baby are not much fun to live with.

If you are already feeling "put upon" and over-burdened by the job of caring for your baby, it is difficult to believe that offering even more will make things easier for both of you. If you are run off your feet while rationing your attention, you probably feel that, without rationing, the baby's demands would simply exceed the time and energy you have available. But it is not so. Bringing up a baby is undeniably hard work, but parents who always meet their baby's demands fully and without unnecessary delay have *less* work, *less* drudgery and *less* stress.

An actual example may prove the point most easily. The chart opposite describes a single night in the lives of two mothers of three-month-old babies. Mother A believes that she can and should save time and energy by rationing her attention to her baby. Mother B is not haunted by the spoiling specter; she finds it easiest just to do for her baby whatever the baby seems to want.

Whichever mother you are inclined to agree with, you will see that in this real situation Mother A was clearly the loser. She spent more of her night awake and she spent the time less pleasantly too. By keeping her baby waiting for his feeding Mother A induced a long period of frustrated and miserable crying so that when she finally went to her baby he could not be pleased to see her. He was much too upset to greet her with a rewarding smile. Even when she offered him the feeding, he was too distressed to settle to it with pleasure, so Mother A did not get the satisfaction of watching him luxuriate under her ministrations. Giving the feeding was tiresome and frustrating for her; it took much longer than it would have taken had he been calm, and once he had sucked a couple of ounces, exhaustion and indigestion overtook him. Because he had not managed a full feeding, Mother A faced the possibility that he would wake again in a couple of hours. . . .

| Time is 3am. Both babies wake and cry. | Mother A *(who worries about spoiling)* | Mother B *(who is not concerned about spoiling)* |
|---|---|---|
| | *Wakes; listens; checks time; finds baby has only slept 3 hrs since last feeding. Puts head under pillow and tries to go back to sleep. Cannot sleep through noise. Gets up after 20 mins, feeling cross and disgruntled.* | *Wakes. Listens to make sure crying persists, gets up sleepy but resigned.* |
| **Time awake before reaching baby** | **22 mins** | **2 mins** |
| | *Baby is in lather of misery. Too upset to smile at mother. Sobs shakily as she prepares to feed him. Cannot settle easily to feeding. Needs frequent burping as has swallowed so much air in crying. Takes 30 mins to get through 3oz (85ml) of milk.* | *Baby stops crying as mother enters room. Smiles at her as she is lifted. Settles at once to lusty sucking. Needs burping in the middle of feeding. Takes 20 mins over full feeding.* |
| **Feeding time** | **30 mins** | **20 mins** |
| | *Still needs more burping and has to be re-settled twice before he finally drops off.* | *Sucks self to sleep at end of feeding. Burps as she is lifted back into her crib, then goes instantly to sleep.* |
| **Time to resettle baby** | **15 mins** | **2 mins** |
| **Time from first being woken** | *Mother is free to get back into bed and go to sleep herself.* | *Mother is free to get back into bed and go to sleep herself.* |
| | **1 hr 7 mins** | **24 mins** |

Nobody *likes* giving night feedings, but where Mother B could go back to sleep feeling she had done a satisfactory job pleasantly, Mother A was bound to feel that Babies are Hell and Night feedings a Torment. When the 5am summons racketed through the house she was all set to start another day feeling resentfully at odds with her baby.

Even if you feel that this proves the point where meeting your baby's *physical* needs is at issue, you may still feel that you should resist his demands when "he doesn't really *need* anything, he just wants attention." But your baby is not yet old enough to want anything that is not also a need. Attention from adults *is* a real need; just as real as his physical needs. Without food or warmth he will die; without social attention from adults he will not be able to become a full human being.

Your baby needs loving adults not only to provide for his bodily needs but for comfort and reassurance. He needs you, or whoever stands in for you, to interpret the world for him, to demonstrate and help him practice all the thousands of skills he must acquire. He needs you to do for him all the things which neither his brain nor his muscles can yet manage. He needs you to be his special person; to talk to him and to love him so that he too can learn to be a special individual person who can talk and who can love.

Be glad and honored that your baby needs you so much. He is probably the only person in the world who will love you 100 percent without criticism or reservation. Enjoy his company; he is probably the only person in the world who always wants to be with you and would never prefer anyone else. Make him feel good and let him make you feel good, too. You have everything to gain and nothing to lose.

# THE OLDER BABY

## *From six months to one year*

In this half of his first year your baby will be ready to use the control over his body for which he has worked so hard. He will sit alone, crawl about, and get hold of anything that is left within his reach. He will discover fascinating things to do with those objects, too. He will find a wastepaper basket and empty it, find a book and scrumple it, find the TV and switch it on and off, find the cat's food and eat it. . . . He will no longer have to be content with the places you put him and the things that you bring him. He will need constant vigilance. But it is not only for safety reasons that he will need continual attention; he needs it for emotional reasons, too. There is nothing more devoted than a six-month-old baby who has been allowed to attach himself to his mother and father – except that same baby, three months later!

Getting more and more attached to their "special" people is a feature of this half year for all babies. But who those "special" people are is as variable as families themselves. As we have seen a baby's primary attachment is usually to whoever shares most of his waking time with him (see p. 112). For most babies that is the natural mother. For a few it is the father. For some it may be an adoptive, substitute or foster mother, whether related to him or not. If the baby has only one really "special" person – if a mother is caring for him full-time and on her own, for example – the attachment which develops may be especially intense and, while it may be deeply satisfying to both of them, it will also be rather precarious. Babies really *need* their "special" people and the most devoted can have an accident or become seriously ill. . . .

Babies do not have a fixed quota of love to give, so having more than one person who is "special" to him does not deprive a baby's mother of anything. If she is the one who cares for him most of the time, even if she also works while he is cared for by somebody else, she will probably remain his most basic person however much he loves and thrives with his other caretaker. The same applies, of course, to families where both parents are present and involved. If the mother is the constant companion and playmate, she will probably be the baby's primary person but, provided the father is a loving and regular part of his life, he will be "special" too and, if the mother should become boring by comparison, the allegiance of the one-year-old may change. If the father takes charge of the baby's care while the mother comes and goes, these first relationships will probably be the other way around. And if two involved but busy parents share with a loving caretaker as well, the baby's emotional life will only be enriched.

However many devoted, fun people your baby becomes attached to, he will almost certainly select one – let's assume it is you and that you are his mother – for his first (and arguably his most important) love affair. The baby has learned to know and love you better than anyone else and now he wants you all the time and all to himself. He does not want to share you or to have you give your time and attention to anyone or anything else. His ideal would be your continual presence and constant attention. He feels passionately for you physically. He will sit on you, play with you, stroke and pull you, pop food (and worse) in your mouth, behaving as if your body belonged to him.

The possessive demands of a lover are delightful if you love him or her but irritating if you do not. In the same way, the physical and emotional relationship which babies in this age-group demand of their mothers tends to please and flatter those who have enjoyed motherhood so far. But it can be too much for those who are already finding their babies over-demanding, and who fear, as the clinginess increases, that they may be getting spoiled. Such a mother may find her baby's physical demonstrativeness positively embarrassing. Taught, all her life, to keep her own feelings under control, neither displaying nor giving way to them, she is faced with a baby who is simply demanding to be cuddled and kissed, patted and stroked. He holds out his arms for more, laughing with glee when he is tickled, sucking his mother's nose if it comes within range and purring like a sensuous kitten when it is time for a bath or a new diaper.

If you can persuade yourself to accept and be proud of your own prime importance to your baby, you may find that you can revel with him in the relationship. Look at yourself through your baby's eyes and you will see yourself as good and warm and loving; worthy of all this devotion and with plenty of your own to offer. If you can, you should. The baby is practicing loving for life. The more he can love, now, and feel himself loved back, the more generous with, and accepting of, all kinds of love he will be, right through his life. He will find it easy to respond to the emotional needs of your grandchildren when his turn comes for parenthood. You will help yourself, too. Finding your baby irresistibly delicious will help you, more than anything else, to ride comfortably through the hardworking and sometimes stressful months ahead.

At six or seven months all the signs of your baby's devotion are positive ones. He is nice to everybody but he is nicest of all to you. His swiftest, widest grins, his longest "conversations," his earliest laughter and very first "songs" are all saved for you. But soon you will see a negative side to all this joy. If he so much likes to have you with him, it is natural that he should come to dislike having you leave him. He will probably reach a point, at around eight months, when he tries to keep you in sight every moment of his waking day; when he cannot, he will be uneasy, tearful or even panic-stricken.

Psychologists call this reaction "separation anxiety," but whether or not you see anything worthy of such a name in your baby depends both on his physical development and on his exact home circumstances. If he can already crawl when the uneasiness first strikes him, he will keep you in sight simply by crawling after you wherever you go. If you happen to spend your days in an open, single-story space, he may hardly ever have to watch you vanishing. But if he gets anxious about you before he gets mobile, he will be in quite a different situation. He cannot follow you so he will keep an eagle eye on you instead, starting to whimper whenever you move from his immediate vicinity.

On a good day at home you probably will not find it difficult to help your baby keep you in sight. You arrange life so that you can do your things while he does his close by. You get into the habit of chatting to him while you work, commenting on his activities without interrupting your own. When you must leave the room, you either wait for him to follow or you scoop him up and take him with you to the front door or to the clothes line. . . . But on another day and in another mood you may find yourself resenting his minute-by-minute dependence. You are being loved more than you can stand. Once irritation begins to grow inside you, his behavior feeds it with each successive half hour. You leave the room and he howls. You come back, comfort him and start to iron. He rolls and crawls beneath your feet, almost pulling the iron on to himself by its cord. A friend comes for coffee and, determined not to lose your attention completely, the baby insists on sitting on your lap, using all his new sounds to join, or interrupt, the conversation. To crown it all, when your friend leaves you go to the bathroom, only to find your little burden thundering piteously on the door. . . . Every mother has days like that sometimes. But they are no fun. You can keep them as few as possible if you look at the baby's feelings from his, rather than your, point of view.

To you, it seems totally unnecessary for the baby to cry just because you have gone to the clothes line. But when the baby loses sight of you, he *minds*. You are the center of his world; the mirror in which he sees himself and everything else; his manager, who copes with him and helps him cope with other things. When you go away from him *you* know where you are going and how short a time you will be gone, but as far as *he* is concerned, you might be gone forever. Out of sight is still

191

out of mind. He registers your absence but cannot yet hold an image of you in his mind so as to wait calmly, and look forward confidently, to your return. Over the next few months he will discover "object constancy": learn that things (and people) do not cease to exist just because they go out of sight and hearing. And, from continual experience, he will learn that wherever you have gone you will always return. But right now he only knows that you have vanished and that he feels bereft.

If you try to override his feelings, ignoring his cries, prying off his clinging arms or shutting him in a playpen to stop him following, he will get more and more anxious. The more anxious he feels the more determinedly he will cling to you. If you try stealth, sneaking out of the room when he is busily occupied, he will occupy himself less and less because he will keep an ever-closer eye on your movements. Once you can accept that his feelings are real and, in terms of his stage of thought-development, reasonable, separation anxiety becomes much easier to live with. Take him around the house with you whenever you can and let him follow when he is able. When you must leave him, find a phrase that you always use to signal your departure, such as "bye-bye for now." This will give him fair warning, so that he does not feel deserted or betrayed. Another phrase – a "here I am again" – can mark a definite ending to the separation, something that he will gradually come to recognize and expect after any parting.

Learning to understand these things is a necessary condition for calm separation but it is not necessarily sufficient. Understanding that you still exist and will come back does not mean that your baby has to like you to go: in many ways he resents the discovery that you and he are separate people; resents your *ability* to leave him. You may not be able to prevent him minding, prevent him from tearing you apart by crying and holding up his arms to you as you leave for work; but by nine months or so you can prevent it *harming* him by making sure that you leave him with someone else to whom he is also attached. He needs another "special" person whom he can use as his "completing half" until you come back. He cannot manage alone. He cannot manage with a stranger or even with an acquaintance whom he has seen only in the street. But he can and will manage with someone else with whom he has a real, loving relationship and within minutes of your departure he will climb out of his sea of despair and on to her life-raft. So when you ask yourself "is it all right for me to leave him?" (for the evening or four mornings each week), ask yourself how well he knows your substitute and how they feel about each other. Your absence is a negative but it can be balanced by a presence which is positive.

Toward the end of this first year your baby may seem to add anxiety about contact with people he does not know to his anxiety about being apart from you. Usually the two kinds of fear are mixed together because the occasions when you notice that he is extremely shy with strangers are the ones when you want to detach him from yourself.

Perhaps you want to hand him to an admirer who asks for a cuddle; perhaps the nurse tries to undress him for examination or a stranger stops to play with him as he sits in his stroller in the library whose shelves are absorbing all your attention.

Usually it is not the strangers themselves who distress your baby; it is what they *do*. He is happy to smile and talk to people he does not know provided they behave discreetly and keep their distance. Unfortunately many adults do not think of babies as real human beings and therefore do not respect their human dignity and extend to them the same kind of courtesy they automatically accord to older people. Some adults are shyer than others but even the least shy would be disconcerted if a stranger rushed up in the street and kissed and hugged him or her. We like to know people before we accept close approaches and physical affection from them; babies feel the same, and deserve protecting from those who try to treat them like pets.

If the baby is allowed to peep over your shoulder at the people in stores and buses, to play peek-a-boo with visitors around your legs and to go voluntarily toward them when curiosity overcomes shyness, he is far more likely to feel like making friends with people who are at present strangers. Letting him make the social running now will produce a toddler who is confident and interested in new people.

Anxieties over being away from you and being with people who are neither you nor known friends are real fears. Like other fears they will die down most quickly in babies who are given least cause to feel them. At present your baby is too newly in love with you to take you for granted. But if you can ride him through this period of intense and potentially anxious attachment on a wave of securely returned and protective adoration, he will come to take your love and your safety for granted in the end. Only when he has had a full measure of you will he be ready for other adults and for other children. Only a ground-base of confidence in his home relationships will make him free and ready to turn his attention outward as he gets older.

# Feeding and growing

Just as babies' ideal rate of weight gain slows down in their second three months from about 6–8oz (170–227g) per week to around 4–5oz (114–142g) per week, so it now slows down even further. From around six months to the first birthday a weekly gain of 2–3oz (57–85g) with an overall height increase of 3–4in (8–10cm) is perfectly adequate.

Although the general shape of the growth curve of all babies will follow the "average" curves given on the charts (Ref/GROWTH) you can expect more wiggles in the record that you keep for your own baby. Illness may mean no weight gain at all for a couple of weeks. A high gain will then catch the baby up. Once you have really embarked on solid feeding, food preferences will make the weight gain more variable too. If your baby gets a passion for some very nourishing cheese dish and eats it for supper every night for a week, more weight will be gained than during the week when the preferred food was vegetable soup.

Unless you or your doctor are worried about the baby's weight gain or general health, there is no longer any point in weekly weighing. Monthly is ample.

*Types of milk*  At around six months you can begin to introduce ordinary cow's milk into your baby's diet. If he is breast-fed you can use store-bought milk instead of your own to mix with cereals or to offer from a cup. If he is bottle-fed you may want to consider abandoning his formula. Don't be in a hurry, though. That specially modified formula with its added vitamins and iron still has a lot to offer. You may want to go on with it until the baby is nearer to a year old and on a full mixed diet.

If you do give your baby regular cow's milk, it *must* be pasteurized or sterilized and you must be able to refrigerate it. Never be tempted by milk "straight from the cow." You cannot be sure of the health of the animal or the hygiene of the milking arrangements. In an emergency, boil the baby's milk but, if you know you are going somewhere where safe supplies will be uncertain, keep using that formula.

Don't give up formula if your baby is slow to take to solid foods or has digestive or allergic problems (Ref/ALLERGIC CHILDREN). On ordinary cow's milk and little else, he could go short of iron.

If the rest of the family uses skimmed or low-fat milk, you will need to buy whole milk specially for the baby. He needs the calories you are trying to avoid and the fat-soluble vitamins you can do without. If you are continuing to buy a special milk for him, you may feel that it might as well be formula, especially if you are already using a ready-mixed formula which involves no extra trouble.

Do remember that as long as your baby drinks any kind of milk from a bottle his feeding equipment must be sterilized. By six months you can give up sterilizing feeding dishes and so forth but bottles of milk are different. The nipples can easily trap traces of milk and warm milk is the ideal breeding ground for bacteria.

# Weaning

As long as your baby has at least four feedings every day, and drinks 6–8oz (170–227ml) from a bottle or takes a full breast-feeding at each one, he will still be getting most of the food he needs from milk alone. You can assume that around 30oz (852ml) of milk each day give him most of the calories and all of the protein he needs. So his solid foods are only necessary to fill the gap between the calories in his milk and the calories his appetite demands.

Soon after six months most babies will be ready to abandon their fourth feeding – whether they have been having it early in the morning or late at night – and to settle down to a regular pattern of three meals per day with, or without, some snacks in between. Dropping a feeding at once does your baby out of 6–8oz (170–227ml) of milk each day and puts his need for solid foods up.

A gradual start to weaning is likely to reduce his milk intake too. Although your baby will probably be perfectly content to abandon sucking at lunchtime and have a drink of milk from a cup instead, he will not get through as many ounces by this new drinking method. Determined efforts to wean him away from sucking altogether will undoubtedly cut his milk consumption right down, so you need to go at weaning very gently, making due allowance for the fact that if your baby can no longer have his milk by sucking breast or bottle he may well refuse to have it at all.

*Weaning breast-fed babies*

Breast-fed babies can go on having all their milk from their mothers until they are ready to have all of it from a cup. Although you can use bottles for expressed breast milk or for water or juice, a lot of breast-fed babies never have bottles at all.

Only you and your baby can decide on the right time to start weaning. A few babies get bored with breast-feeding and take to a cup even before their mothers feel ready to start stopping. A few mothers see no reason to wean their babies at all. They go on breast-feeding until the baby is a toddler who is using the breast entirely for comfort. As long as it feels right to you and your baby either extreme or anything in between is fine.

Whenever you decide to start weaning your baby from the breast, do allow time to do it gradually. Suddenly refusing to let a baby suck from the breast can make him feel that you are refusing *yourself*. And suddenly giving up breast-feeding can give you days of physical discomfort. Take it slowly and both your baby and your breasts will usually adapt without problems.

If, for example, you cut out his lunchtime breast-feeding in favor of milk from a cup, your breasts will get less stimulation. Although you may feel uncomfortably full in the middle of the day on the first few occasions, your breasts will adjust and make less milk within two or three days. If you also offer your baby milk from a cup as well as solid food at his other meals, and then let him suck as much as he wants at the end of the meal, he will gradually take less and less from the breast so that you will make less. Over a few weeks he will probably reach a point where he is taking only a token few sucks in the morning and a small "comfort feeding" at his bedtime. That night-time session will be the last to be given up, but, as long as they do not rely on breast-feeding for going to sleep (see p. 141), many babies will abandon it of their own accord by the time they are a year old.

If you do not want to go on being even partly committed to breast-feeding for this long you will probably be wise to introduce a bottle after all. Although most six-month-old babies can be adequately nourished by solid foods and whatever milk they will drink from a cup, they may badly miss sucking for comfort, especially at bedtime.

## Weaning bottle-fed babies

Some parents take a very easy-going attitude to bottles and are happy to see them used as comfort-objects and usefully non-spill cups well into the pre-school period. Other parents regard bottles as a necessary evil and can hardly wait until their babies are capable of eating from spoons and drinking from cups. There are advantages and disadvantages both to leaving it to the baby and to positive weaning. You do need to decide quite soon, though, what your attitudes are. Letting your baby do what he likes with his bottle through this half year, and then suddenly deciding that he must give it up altogether, is likely to cause him a lot of trouble and distress.

**If you leave it to the baby** he may get more and more attached to his bottle, not as a source of food and drink but as a source of sucking-comfort. While it's good for him to have that comfort, he will become more and more able to think of it, and demand it, at odd times of day and at night. Will you mind seeing him toddling around with it in his mouth? Will you be able to say "no" for the sake of his teeth if he screams for a bottle to suck whenever he wakes in the night?

**If you wean your baby as soon as he drinks from a cup** he may miss that sucking-comfort. Will you mind if he takes to sucking his thumb? Cutting out the bedtime bottle can usher in problems over settling for the night while refusing to give any milk from a bottle can lead to the baby refusing to take any milk at all from a cup. Is getting rid of bottles important enough to you to compensate for coping with that kind of difficulty?

## A compromise weaning policy

If you start weaning your baby at around six months old and take about six months over gradually reducing dependence on the bottle, you will almost certainly find that you can get the best of both extremes. Take the process in very gradual stages:

**Introduce a cup at 4–5 months** and gradually get your baby accustomed to the idea that milk, pleasant-tasting fruit juices and water can all come out of this as well as out of a bottle. By six months the baby will probably be willing to take all extra drinks from a cup so that juice and water no longer come from a bottle.

**Abandon the lunchtime bottle** in favor of solid foods, with milk from a cup, soon after six months or as soon as he eats spoonfuls rather than only tastes.

**Abandon the late night bottle (or early morning one)** as soon as the baby shows you, by sleeping right through the night, that three main meals a day is now enough. When the baby needs

*Food and bliss in one.*
*Don't hurry to wean your baby*
*from "her" beloved breast . . .*

*. . . but when your baby is ready for other foods, fingers are the natural tools for eating. Make it easy with cubes and slices . . .*

. . . *it doesn't matter how the food gets there*

. . . *as long as it does, and he enjoys it*

. . . spoons are fun too — fun to wave, to bang,
to bite, and fun to eat off — sometimes.

something between meals, offer drinks from a cup together with hard finger-foods (see p. 137) as snacks to bridge the gap.

If all goes smoothly, the baby will now only be having two bottles per day: one after the solid part of breakfast and the other after the solid part of supper, before bedtime.

**Let the baby go on with these two bottles as long as they are drunk sitting on your lap.** Somewhere around the first birthday the baby's drive to move around the room and to be independent will become so strong that he will hate sitting still. This is where you can practice a bit of parent-upmanship: if you *never*, even *once*, let the baby discover that a bottle can be taken around the room on crawling adventures, he will eventually want to move about more than to suck. Your baby's feelings will not be hurt because the bottle will be right there if it is wanted, but sucking will gradually be given up in favor of activity.

**Treat the bottle as if it were the breast.** Once this point has been reached, don't be trapped into letting the baby carry the bottle off "just this once." If you do – perhaps because you are visiting friends and you want them to see your relationship with the baby at its smoothest – he is bound to demand to carry it off again the next night and the one after.

**Don't use the bottle for anything other than milk.** If you suddenly decide to give juice, or water from the bottle again – perhaps because it is the easiest way to carry it on a picnic – the baby is almost certain to fuss next time a drink is given from a cup.

**Buy the baby a cup with a lid and a spout.** Few babies can manage an ordinary cup without any help before they are a year old. Even babies who can drink from them before this will spill as they put the cup down. But managing alone is important to your baby. The changeover from bottle to cup is likely to be greeted with far more enthusiasm if you do not have to insist on holding it. A spouted training cup will only drip milk if the baby up-ends it and it will not actually spill even when it is dropped. Furthermore, drinking from the spout is a compromise between ordinary drinking and sucking and it is therefore a less abrupt change for the baby.

## Solid foods

*Quantities and qualities of solid foods*

The average six-month-old baby needs about 800 calories every day. There are 280 calories in every pint of ordinary cow's milk, so as long as he is drinking, say, four 8oz (227ml) bottles each day he will be getting just over 575 calories from his milk alone. He will only need about 200 calories from solid foods. Two cans or jars of commercially prepared babyfood, or one of these and one helping of baby cereal will provide that amount of energy. If you expect him to eat three two-course meals a day while drinking this much milk he is bound to get either fat or fussy or both.

As weaning progresses, your baby will drink less milk and therefore need more solid food to fill the calorie gap and give him energy for activity and growth. As long as he drinks one pint of milk every day he will continue to get plenty of first class protein, ample calcium and plenty of vitamins of the "B" group. He will not get enough iron or enough vitamin A, D or C. So if he is a baby who eats almost anything you offer, it is sensible to make sure that his meals are rich in these particular nutrients. If (like most babies) his food choices are limited and idiosyncratic, remember that a small helping of fortified baby cereal will give him the iron he needs, while daily multi-vitamin drops will make certain that he gets enough vitamins.

You do not have to try to persuade him to eat expensive high protein foods like meat and fish if he does not like them or you prefer not to serve them. His milk takes care of his protein requirements. There is no point, either, in going out of your way to buy the commercially prepared foods that use "high protein" as an advertising point. He cannot use protein over and above his body's needs. Give him whatever he likes of what you want to serve.

If your baby refuses milk altogether for a while – perhaps because you have taken away his bottle and he resents being offered milk from a cup – he will need meals which offer him some of all the main food groups: protein foods like meat, fish or soy products; carbohydrate foods like cereals, breads and pastas; dairy products like cheese and yogurt and of course vitamin-rich and delicious vegetables and fruits. Family-type meals, in fact, but in an easy to eat form and in tiny quantities. You will probably find that milk plays quite a large part in your baby's meals even if he never drinks it. A lot gets "lost" in cooking for a baby. It takes at least 2oz (57ml) to mix a helping of baby cereal to the texture most prefer, for example; 1oz (28ml) to cream a small potato, soft-scramble an egg or make pudding to go with his fruit.

## *What solid foods should your baby have?*

As we saw in a previous chapter (see p. 133), ideas of which particular foods are suitable or unsuitable for babies vary dramatically from country to country. If few British babies like spaghetti with tomato sauce it is because they are seldom offered it until they are toddlers and have become accustomed to "British food." An Italian baby will have been given pasta dishes since weaning began. He will probably loathe mashed potatoes instead.

There are very few foods which you normally serve to your family which the baby should not have. As long as you avoid much salt, extra sugar, lots of butter and cream, hot spices, alcohol, coffee and tea, the baby can try anything you are cooking. You will soon find out whether he likes it and whether his digestion copes with it or not. But stick to the policies outlined earlier (see p. 133) of introducing new foods one at a time and in tiny amounts. If there is a digestive upset you will know what has caused it. If the baby is allergic to the food the reaction will be slight.

A lot of parents feed babies between six and eighteen months on almost nothing but commercially prepared babyfoods. A few take pride in avoiding them altogether. Both extremes are a pity: as in most dietary matters your baby will do best with a mixture.

Don't scorn prepared baby *cereals*. Rich in vitamins, fortified with iron and using valuable milk in the mixing, they are far more nourishing than the dry breakfast cereals served to older people and they are only "fattening" if you add a lot of sugar. They make an excellent breakfast for a baby or toddler who enjoys them.

Commercially prepared jars, cans and packets of babyfood can also make a valuable contribution to your child's diet as well as saving you a great deal of time. Most are extremely careful to use top-quality ingredients and to keep less desirable constituents, such as sugar and animal fats, at a low level. A commercially prepared "dinner" will be as nutritious as food you cook yourself when you are taking trouble and will often be more nutritious than the meal you prepare yourself using supermarket short-cuts and convenience foods.

But try not to deprive your growing baby of the variety and fun of home-cooked foods. That valuable "dinner' is the same today as it was last week; the meal you cook yourself will never be exactly the same twice over because even if you use the same recipe, your ingredients will vary. Even at this early age a baby can enjoy the flavor of tomatoes that have just come into season or of a gravy that is especially good. And he will soon welcome a crispy cheese topping or crunchy grated carrot instead of that inevitable purée . . . .

|  | Home-prepared foods | Commercially prepared foods |
|---|---|---|
| *Convenience for you* | *Can be a nuisance to prepare for the baby alone, although are no trouble if you are cooking for others and can adapt the meal.* | *Are never any trouble to prepare.* |
|  | *Awkward to carry hygienically or to find in strange places.* | *Easy to carry with you and serve anywhere.* |
| *Food value* | *Variable. Freshly cooked and quickly served food will be excellent; leftovers may not be as good.* | *Always the same, although different varieties have unexpected differences, in calories, etc.* |
| *Adaptability* | *Can be adapted to suit your baby's individual appetite, taste and digestion. Can also be served in different ways to make a change in appearance or texture. Different kinds of food can be served separately so that the baby can discover what food he likes and dislikes and choose what to eat and what to leave.* | *Cannot be adapted at all. A meal is a meal, with everything mixed together so that a fat baby must have all the carbohydrate if he is to have the meat; a bored baby must see a dish that always looks the same, and a baby of taste cannot separate peas from carrots.* |
|  | *Familiar foods can be made suitable for finger-feeding as the baby gets older, with cubed or grated, rather than pureed, vegetables, cheeses, etc.* | *Finger-feeding is impossible. "Chunky" varieties made for older babies are often disliked.* |
|  | *Foods can be selected to fit with dietary convictions, such as vegetarianism, or restrictions due to allergies or intolerances.* | *Although some vegetarian meals and some "gluten free" and other special meals are available, the range is too limited for constant sole use.* |
| *Preparation for family meals* | *Excellent; the baby will become accustomed to various tastes and textures and eventually see that he is eating the same as you.* | *Not good. All tend to be bland, so that "apple variety" is no preparation for the tartness of fresh stewed apple. The baby may become so used to consistently smooth textures that food that needs chewing is rejected. His food does not even look like yours.* |

A mixture of home-prepared and commercially prepared foods will probably suit you best. Your baby could share family meals whenever you are cooking something which he likes and which it is easy to make suitable for him – by withholding seasonings until his portion has been served, and by straining or liquidizing.

When the main dish of a family meal consists of something he dislikes, which disagrees with him or which you consider unsuitable, it could be replaced with an egg, some cheese or a can or jar of commercially prepared babyfood; he could still share the accompanying vegetables.

When only the baby is to have a cooked meal, serving commercially prepared food will save you time and be better for him than a meal made up of leftovers. While fresh fruits are ideal for his sweet courses, using cans or jars of fruit will save you stewing tiny portions, while other sweet varieties can be used to make a second course for him when other members of the family are not having one.

When you are going out, commercially prepared foods make it easy to give him a meal which is adequate both nutritionally and from the point of view of hygiene.

## Self-feeding

Problems over a baby's eating often dominate the lives of whole families for months on end, as we shall see (see p. 296). You can do a great deal to avoid them by cultivating a relaxed and accepting attitude now. Ideally your baby should feel that eating is something pleasurable which he himself does because *he wants and enjoys the food*. Try to avoid making him feel that eating is a duty and something which is done to him because *you want him to have the food*.

At six to eight months, your baby is bound to be fairly passive during eating, because he has to be fed: he cannot yet manage to feed himself. But being fed is an uncomfortable business. Try exchanging a few spoonfuls with your partner and you will find that the food never comes at exactly the rate or in exactly the combinations you would have chosen and that the whole business makes you feel extraordinarily helpless. Keep the months when your baby must put up with this to a minimum by encouraging him to take part in the process himself and by handing it over completely to him as soon as he can get the food from plate to mouth by any means he chooses and no matter how much mess results.

**Give your baby a spoon** as soon as he will take one from you, even if he merely bites and waves it. Let him do what he likes with the spoon – by around eight months he will sometimes manage to dip and lick it. A few weeks later he will actually eat off it – sometimes. In the meantime use a second spoon yourself and be prepared to swap your loaded one for his empty one so that he can fill his mouth while you refill the spoon.

**Positively encourage your baby to eat with his fingers.** If you let him dabble in his food and then suck his fists at six months, he will soon learn to do it on purpose. You will be able to slow down your spoon-work to let him get as much food for himself as he can.

*A spoon for
messy fun . . .*

*. . . soon becomes
an efficient tool
for eating.*

**Give your baby some easy finger-foods.** While dipping and sucking are fun, picking up cubes of bread and butter or diced cooked carrots or pinches of grated cheese is much more satisfactory. At six months these finger-foods will keep him actively involved in his meal while you feed him the mushy food. By nine months to a year he will hardly need any mushy food at all. He will eat with his fingers and sometimes with a spoon, and you will only need to help him get the last of his ice cream or gravy.

**Don't impose your ideas of suitable combinations.** If he wants to dip cheese in chocolate pudding or stir bread into his jelly, why should you care? Every society has its own conventions about what goes with what. He will adopt yours in the end.

**Don't try to make your baby eat anything without eagerness.** Many foods are good for him but none are irreplaceable or worth the dangers of persuasion or force. When he has had enough food it is actually better for him to stop eating, so don't keep him sitting there hoping he will eat a bit more.

**Don't make the baby eat different courses in their "proper" order.** If you will not produce his sweet course until he has eaten the main course, he will often miss the pudding altogether because the thought of it will not encourage him to finish meat that he does not want. Later on, when he understands what you are doing, it will only make him want the forbidden course more.

**Expect a mess and arrange to cope with it.** A really efficient bib (perhaps the kind with an ever-open pocket at the bottom to catch his dribbles and misses) will keep his clothes clean. A thick layer of newspaper under his chair will catch the rest and can simply be thrown away afterwards. If you simply cannot feed him in a public place without finding yourself holding his hands out of the way while you pop neat spoonfuls in his mouth, feed him in private. Trying to make him eat tidily is the best possible way of putting him off the whole business.

*If you think your baby eats too little*

Beware! You are almost certainly wrong because babies are designed for survival and will not, under any circumstances, starve themselves if they are offered milk and manageable solid foods. Worrying about the amount your child eats may create problems for all of you later on (see p. 297), so cultivate the habit of trusting the baby to know how much is enough. If this trust eludes you:

**Look at the baby's growth.** If the upward curve on his weight and length chart is steady, he is getting enough to eat.

**Look at the baby's energy and vitality.** If he is lively and active, he is not going short of food.

**Consider the baby's milk intake** and remind yourself that milk is food. He may be drinking almost everything he needs.

If you are still tempted to push food at him, have him checked by your doctor and discuss his charted growth. Even if she can see at a glance that your baby is well-nourished, she will be happy to give you the time necessary for reassurance. She will know how important it is for you to relax about your baby's eating before he enters toddlerhood.

# Sleeping

Just as parents often expect babies to eat more than they need, thus starting feeding problems, so they often expect them to sleep more than they need, thus inventing sleeping problems.

Babies' need for sleep varies widely. Your baby's need in the second half of this first year will probably be consistent with the first. A baby who has always slept comparatively long hours will continue to do so. One who has always been comparatively wakeful will continue this pattern. But, overall, the number of hours per day which the baby spends sleeping will drop. Although it is often said that babies in this age-group will, and "should," sleep for 14–16 hours out of every 24, research has shown that the average number of hours slept is around 13 and the range around that average runs from as few as 9 to as many as 18 per day.

Although there is still some connection between the baby's eating and his sleeping, so that a good meal still makes him inclined to feel sleepy, the connection is not nearly as strong as it was. He will not necessarily fall asleep after each meal; intriguing activities may be enough to keep him interested and awake. His pattern of sleep during this half year is likely to consist of a 10–12 hour night, which may or may not be broken by brief awakenings, and two separate "naps" during the day, which may be anything from twenty minutes to three hours long.

Until around six months the baby will still fall asleep when he needs to. Nothing except acute hunger, illness or pain will keep him awake. So if you put him comfortably to bed at night and settle him for naps during the day, you can assume that he will sleep if he needs to and that if he does not sleep, he does not need to.

Between six and nine months this changes. The baby becomes able to keep himself awake, or to be kept awake, by excitement, tension or a reluctance to release himself from the world, or from you, by falling asleep. It is by this stage that it becomes vital for your baby to know how to go to sleep alone (see p. 141). If he still relies on you to put him to sleep, difficulties are inevitable.

*Difficulty over going to sleep*  This is one of the most common and most disruptive of all child-rearing problems. You will be lucky if you do not suffer from it to some extent with at least one of your children, so do not add to your misery when it first strikes, by assuming that everybody else's child goes to bed like an angel, and that your child's behavior is your fault.

Trouble when the baby is put to bed at night becomes common at around nine months, the first age at which children are able to keep themselves awake on purpose. After this time you cannot assume that your baby will sleep if he is tired and that if he does not sleep he is not tired. The reverse can be true. The baby can get over-tired; if this happens he becomes so strung up and tense that he cannot relax enough to go to sleep.

The first signs of trouble sometimes follow an obvious upset. For example, research has shown that many babies who have been admitted to the hospital, even for a few days, have trouble settling to sleep once they return home. But the disturbance that starts night-time trouble need not be a traumatic one. A vacation away from home can break the baby's routines so that problems begin when the family returns home. A new room can disturb him in the same way; even a rearrangement of the furniture in his old room can leave him feeling disoriented and unable to drop easily into sleep. So since bedtime trouble is a great deal easier to prevent than it is to cure, it is worth being extra careful about introducing major changes into your baby's surroundings during this age period. Even the most glorious vacation may in the end cause more trouble than it was worth.

It is more usual, though, for trouble over going to sleep at night to start gradually without any obvious cause. The basic factor that lies beneath it is your baby's passionate attachment to you. If he allows himself to go to sleep, he allows himself to go away from you altogether. Rather than do this he will scream and cry when you leave him; greet your return with delight and scream again as soon as you leave. If you sit with him, he will lie quietly; but as soon as you move toward the door, he will snap fully awake again. His ability to keep himself awake will certainly outlast your patience. After all he has nothing else to do all evening; you have plenty.

*Preventing difficulty over going to sleep*

The answer lies in making it possible for your baby to release you gradually at night. Your aim is to narrow the gap, for the baby, between the state of being awake and with you and the state of being asleep and without you. If he is suddenly carried away from the warm, bright living room, full of the pleasant and familiar sounds of people, up three flights of stairs to a cool, dim, silent room on the top floor, put to bed and then left to listen to your footsteps receding, he is likely to panic. Exactly what he thinks we cannot know, but his sobs seem to say "you are going, you are gone, I have lost you, I am alone forever. . . ."

Reorganizing his bedtime routine and his sleeping arrangements may enable you to soften this situation for him. If he is bathed, taken down to the family for supper, played with by an adult for a few minutes, and then taken to a nearby room with the lights on, the door open and all those family sounds still audible, he will feel far less cut off. If, instead of instantly going right away, you spend the next ten minutes or so tidying away dirty clothes, readying things for the next morning and generally puttering around near his open door, he can settle himself and begin to drift toward sleep in the comfortable knowledge of your presence. But eventually you have to leave. If you have managed to prevent your child feeling panic-stricken and bereft by your departure, these are months during which he will develop ways of giving *himself* security and comfort. He will use these to help himself cope with being without you.

*Comfort habits*

A baby's comfort habits are under his own control in a way which the comfort which he gets from other people is not. He cannot force you to stay with him or to go on cuddling him; the amount of comfort you will give him is up to you. But he can rely on as much comfort as he wants if it comes from himself.

This is both the strength and the weakness of all comfort habits.

They are good for the baby because they give him an independent and autonomous source of security; make him more able to rely on himself and leave him less at the mercy of the adult world. But they can be bad for the baby if he relies on them so much that he cuts himself off from the kinds of comfort which do come from other people. In general, then, a baby who uses a comfort habit to keep himself calm and relaxed while his mother leaves him to fall asleep at night is doing himself nothing but good. But a baby who often uses that comfort habit during the day, when a parent or beloved caretaker is present and the world of toys, play and exploration is open to him, is showing signs that all is not well. Of course an occasional incident need not worry you. His desire to rock in a corner instead of playing, today, probably means nothing more than that he is particularly tired or is feeling unwell. But if this kind of behavior were usual for him it could mean that he needed to give himself a lot of comforting because he was not getting enough from anyone else. At the furthest extreme, a child who is totally withdrawn into a world of rhythmic rocking is usually showing us that he cannot manage or get satisfaction from the world of people and activity.

**Sucking** is the most basic of all comfort habits. Your baby may have been sucking his fingers, thumb or a pacifier for months. But now the sucking takes on a new significance for him. He may be able to let you leave him calmly provided he is sucking, but not otherwise. As you leave, he sucks harder. He sucks instead of crying; uses the comfort of the sucking instead of the comfort of you. Sucking is so basic that your baby may combine it, now, with other forms of comfort.

**Cuddlies.** Dignified by psychologists with the name of "transitional comfort objects," these are soft things, ranging from gauze diapers through old crib blankets to more conventional soft toys, which many children adopt with passion at about this time and use either with, or instead of, sucking. A baby's cuddly takes on a very real emotional importance for him. It is his familiar; the thing that spells safety and security, wards off evil and promises your return. He may simply hold and finger it or he may use it in all kinds of elaborate ways. A scarf, for example, may be wound around his head with one end looped across his face so that he can suck his thumb through it.

If your baby has adopted something in this way it will be his most important possession; the thing that must not be forgotten when you go on vacation or left behind if he has to go to the hospital. You probably will not even be able to wash it as often as you would like. Hygiene will lead to protests because you have ruined its precious familiar smell! Parents with foresight will quickly realize that, with years of use ahead of it, the child's cuddly had better be duplicated in case of disaster. If it is something simple like a gauze diaper, you can put two or three away for emergencies. If it is a soft toy, it would be wise to buy a second and put that somewhere safe. If it is a piece of blanket or rag, you may be able to cut it in half without the baby noticing and keep the second half against the dreadful day when the first falls to pieces or gets thrown away. Such a "second" will not entirely prevent misery, because the new object will not look or feel or smell quite the same as the one that has shared your baby's crib for months or years. But it will be very much better than nothing.

**Rituals.** These are comfort habits which your baby will build with your help. They are really part of making the process of releasing you a gradual one. A baby who is building bedtime rituals will insist that you do exactly the same thing tonight as you did last night; tomorrow he will want the same again. The only "risk" is that once the two of you have begun to formalize his going-to-bed routines in this way, he may build the ritual up until a routine that took three minutes each night when he was nine months old takes thirty-five minutes when he is three!

Your personal rituals will depend on your own routines, but a very normal bedtime process might go something like this: you carry the baby into his room and around it so that he can say "goodnight" to three favorite pictures. Then you hold him up to get two soft toys off the shelf. Next, baby and toys are put into the crib, each gets a kiss in turn and the baby gets an extra one. You then cover him up, turn down the lights, kiss him one more time, sing a lullaby, spin his mobile and leave, adjusting the door to an exact six inches open.

If your baby does take to a ritual of this kind, he will come to expect every bit of it every night. Boring for you perhaps, but infinitely better than enduring anxious screams. Do make sure that anyone who is ever going to put your baby to bed knows the details of his chosen ritual. His grandmother cannot be expected to cope successfully while you have an evening out if she is not equipped with the same tools for peace that you use yourself.

**Rhythmical movements.** When your baby was very small you probably walked with him, rocked him and patted him whenever he needed comforting. Whatever was causing his distress he found rhythmical physical activity soothing. Most older babies still find physical rhythm soothing and many find ways in which they can provide it for themselves.

Obviously harmless rhythmical comfort habits include stroking or pulling that cuddly or twisting a lock of hair. A noisy nuisance, but nothing worse, is rocking on hands and knees so that the crib whizzes all over the floor. Slightly more worrying is the kind of rocking in which the baby bangs his head on the end of the crib with each rock.

**Head banging.** If you notice that your baby is head banging every evening you need to find out whether it is the rhythmical sound and the rhythmical jar that he finds satisfying or whether he is actually causing himself pain on purpose. The easiest way to find out is to fix several sheets of cardboard to the head of the crib. Don't use a crib-bumper or other soft padding because you will deprive him of the noise. He can still thud against cardboard but he cannot actually hurt himself.

If your cardboard-padding is acceptable, don't worry about head banging in the crib. But if the baby cannot settle as he usually does or transfers his head banging to the unpadded side-bars, ask yourselves why he wants or needs to hurt himself.

*Twiddling his ear . . .*

*. . . sucking his fingers*

*. . . he finds his own ways of comforting himself when you are not there.*

Is he angry with somebody and turning that anger in on himself? Is somebody or something frustrating him beyond easy bearing? If the head banging only built up when his father went away on a trip or when he changed caretakers, his father's return or being given the chance to get used to the new person more slowly may deal with the whole matter. If you can't think of anything obvious, just giving the baby lots of extra individual attention and lots of chances to play aggressive banging games with you may relieve his inside tension.

If, instead of lessening, the head banging spreads from evenings in the crib to daytime in any old place and your baby or toddler begins to bruise himself deliberately against the walls or furniture, consult your doctor. Don't let anyone put you off by telling you "don't worry, lots of children do it." Not many do and they need to be helped to be happier.

**Masturbation.** If pinned diapers and sleeping suits don't foil them, some baby boys make a rhythmical comfort habit out of pulling their penises. Some baby girls adopt a version of rocking which rhythmically rubs their vulvae against the crib mattress or bars. Even if you easily accept that it is natural and right for all babies to explore the parts that are usually covered with diapers whenever those diapers are taken off, finding your baby rocking away, red-faced, panting and obviously excited, may shock you.

Try not to be shocked and if you are, try not to let it show. Masturbation will do your child no harm, now or later, and discovering its pleasures early does not suggest that a baby is "over-sexed." All babies have sexual feelings (even though most adults prefer to believe otherwise) and sooner or later they all discover that rubbing their genitals feels good. The only possible harm in the situation is the harm you, or another loved adult, could do by over-reacting. If your baby is happily playing with himself alone in his crib, leave him be.

*If bedtime still upsets your baby . . .*

Sometimes, despite all your attempts to make it easy for your child to let you go, with plenty of encouragement of comfort habits and lots of cooperation in making gentle rituals, a baby does still become really upset about going to bed. Pulled between a crying baby and your burning meal it is easy to lose sight of your long-term goals and react to the immediate stress in ways which are likely to ensure months of trouble. It is worth thinking out the whole matter during a calm daytime moment.

What you want is to have your baby settle happily into bed and drift contentedly off to sleep on his own leaving you free to concentrate on other things. That means that tearing yourself away leaving him to howl cannot be the right answer, even if you are capable of doing it. He is *not* settling happily, and being abandoned will certainly increase his feeling that it is not safe to let you go out of the room in case you never come back. But staying with him, or bringing him back downstairs, is not a long-term answer either. You are not getting your adult evening-peace and far from beginning to discover that it is safe to be on his own, the baby is finding that you agree with him that it is intolerable.

The long-term answer may involve a lot of short-term effort while you convince your baby that it *is* safe to let you go because you always *will* come back, but that it isn't any use demanding to get up again because you will not let him. You give him what he *needs* – reassurance – but you will not necessarily give him what he *wants* – more playtime.

**Try to keep the pre-bedtime hour affectionate and enjoyable.** A squabble over supper or a jealous tussle for father's attention will be enough to increase his uncertainty about how much he loves and is loved, and therefore how safe it is to let you leave him. This is not the time of day for sudden discipline.

**Always make sure that the baby knows bedtime is coming up,** by following the same evening routine of, for example, bath, play, supper, bed.

**Keep to going-to-bed rituals, or even invent some for your baby.** Getting a teddy bear settled into bed, for example, can be a good lead in to getting him settled too.

**If, after all this, your baby cries when you leave, go back.** Reassure him that you are still close by; kiss him again and leave. You may have to repeat this over and over again, but it is the only sure way eventually to convince him both that you *will* come and that you *will not* get him up.

**If repeated visits are necessary, try using your voice alone.** It may be enough reassurance for the baby if you simply call pleasantly to him. If so, you can at least keep him calm while simultaneously cooking supper and saving your own legs.

*Waking in the night*  Although babies can, and often do, sleep solidly for a 12-hour period, some wake frequently, even if only briefly. This kind of waking used to be called a "bad habit": babies were ignored when they woke or even scolded or smacked for awakening, the argument being that this would "break the habit." But the baby cannot wake himself on purpose. If something disturbs him before he has had enough sleep, or he comes awake during one of the "light sleep" periods everybody has every night, leaving him to cry is not going to prevent the same thing (or something different) from awakening him the next night. "He will soon learn not to do it," people say. But how can your baby learn not to do something which is outside his conscious control?

The baby is at an age and stage where his daytime care is extremely demanding. A continuance of disturbed nights can be very exhausting for you. So if something external (see p. 214) is disturbing him, it will be worth almost any amount of trouble to prevent it. If the cause is internal (see p. 214), so that you cannot actually stop the waking up, it may help, now that feeding is not part of the night waking pattern, if you decide between you to take responsibility for the baby on alternate nights. The "off-duty" partner may still be awakened by the baby but at least she need not get out of bed.

*Outside disturbances*
Some of the night waking of this age group is due to the baby being woken up by external events. He no longer sleeps as deeply as he did when he was younger. You cannot necessarily assume that once he is asleep, almost nothing will wake him.

Noises which blur into the general level of background noise during the day can become disturbingly sharp in the comparative silence of the night. Heavy traffic on the road outside his room, low flying aircraft or trains on a nearby line may all disturb him.

He may also sense comings and goings around him even if they are not very noisy. Admiring visitors peeping into his room may wake him. If he shares your room, your movements, your whispered conversations and your sleeping noises may all tend to disturb him, too.

Getting cold will make him more likely to wake up. A very cool room is much less dangerous to him than it was when he was younger because he will not pass straight from deep sleep into a chilled state, but if he kicks his covers off and begins to cool, he will also begin to wake. If nothing happens to warm him again, he will wake right up and cry.

A very sore bottom, due to diaper rash, sometimes means a lot of night waking because the urine stings his skin whenever he wets himself. Toward the end of the year he may have some bad nights because of teething pain with his first molars (see p. 326). You can't prevent a first awakening of this kind, but an appropriate dose of a children's acetaminophen liquid may help for the rest of the night.

**Reorganize the baby's sleeping arrangements** so that noises are less likely to disturb him. If the room he is in is the only one available, you could double-glaze its windows. Even heavy curtains help.

**Don't let visitors go into your baby's bedroom** and don't go in yourself unless you have reason to believe he needs you. Leave his door ajar so you can take a reassuring peep from a distance.

**Make sure the baby stays snugly warm.** A baby bag or sleeper suit will keep his own warmth insulated in even if he does kick off the blankets. More overnight heating in his room may be needed too.

**Protect a sore bottom** with a thick coating of a silicone-based protective cream at night and by using a diaper with a stay-dry lining.

*Internal disturbances*
Unfortunately most of the night-crying in this age group is due to disturbances that come from within the baby. Whenever his sleep lightens he may come to consciousness. If he finds himself awake but perfectly happy he will drop off again without telling you about it, provided he does not depend on action from you to *put* him to sleep. But if he finds himself awake and anxious or afraid, he will cry for you.

Some kind of nightmare, or nightfright, is common. Of course there is no way that we can know what form it takes because the baby cannot tell us, but he wakes, usually, with a sudden terrified scream. He appears afraid, is completely reassured the moment one of his parents appears, and often goes back to sleep even as he is comforted. The baby may repeat this behavior several times each night and every night for months. The pattern seems to be most common in those babies whose parents are afraid of spoiling them and therefore do not pick them up readily when they cry by day. It is almost as if the subconscious part of the baby's mind is making up at night for too little loving attention by day; making sure, during sleeping hours, of a love he feels uncertain of when he is awake. If your baby seems to be falling into this pattern try to put yourself into his place and see whether he might feel that he has to fight for your affectionate attention.

**Slow up on anything that seems to be putting a strain on the baby.** If you are trying to wean him from his bottle, for example (see p. 196), you may be going faster than he can easily bear. A return to some sucking could bring you more peace.

**Make sure that bedtime is relaxed and enjoyable.** Going to sleep feeling warmly loved and protected may help him to stay comfortably asleep all night.

*If a pattern of waking is set . . .* If your baby starts waking and crying several times each night so that you begin to feel like zombies, taking him into bed with you the first time he wakes may bring peace for the rest of the night. Do *try* not to do it out of sheer desperation and against your own intentions, though (see p. 84). If he shares a family bed during a few weeks or months of nightmares, it isn't likely that he will happily sleep apart from you just because they end. If you are determined not to take the baby into your bed, go to him immediately when he cries. The disturbance will cease as soon as he sees you, hears your voice or feels your stroking hand. With practice you can give this kind of instant comfort half asleep and roll straight back into bed.

*Waking early in the morning* The baby does not know what time it is. He wakes because he has had enough sleep. Once you have finally abandoned the idea of an early-morning bottle or breast-feeding it is not very likely that you will be able to persuade him to go back to sleep again.

   If he cries or shouts for you there is no point in trying to ignore him. You will have to go in the end so you might as well go at once. But you need not let him get up and start his day.

**Make sure the baby has light to see by and toys to play with.** If his room is dark in the early morning, leave a low-watt light on. Put a selection of toys in or beside his crib and he may occupy himself, at least for a while.

**Be prepared to make the baby comfortable** by changing his diaper, removing his sleeping bag and offering him a drink. Ten minutes spent in this way may earn you another hour in bed.

**Consider offering the baby the company of an older child** if you have one. If the older child sleeps with the baby or is allowed to go to him when he wakes in the morning, they may entertain each other beautifully. There are no grown-ups around to create jealousy; the baby is safely imprisoned in his crib so he cannot pull hair or steal toys; he has nobody to appeal to except the older child

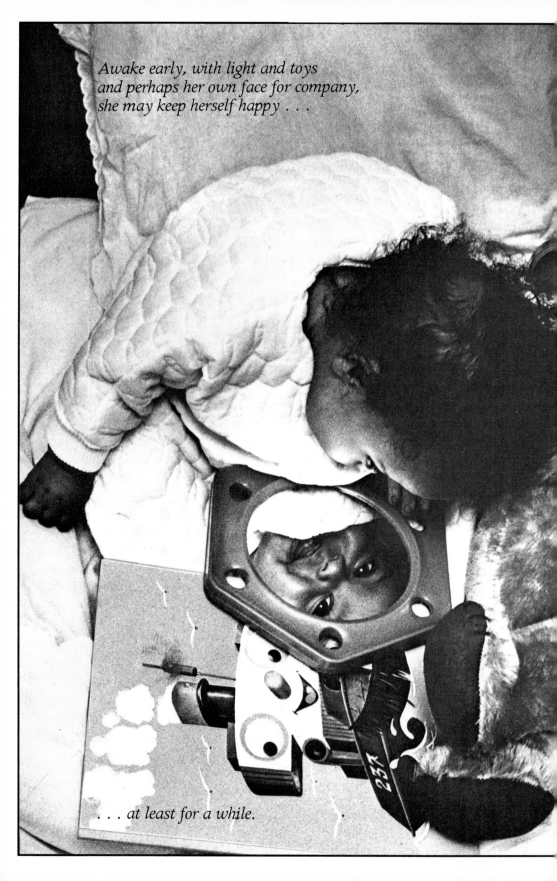

*Awake early, with light and toys
and perhaps her own face for company,
she may keep herself happy . . .*

*. . . at least for a while.*

so he offers all the charm he normally reserves for adults. These early-morning play sessions sometimes create and often cement a close and affectionate relationship.

Wakeful babies and daytime sleep

As we saw earlier, babies who need much less daytime sleep than the average are harder work for their parents to look after, but get considerable advantages because of the extra hours they spend in looking, learning and interacting with adults.

Even if your baby only sleeps for twenty minutes on two occasions during each day, he may well be happy to spend much longer than this comfortably settled in his crib or stroller with toys to play with and interesting things to look at (see p. 170). So don't be too quick to decide that because he does not actually sleep during each nap, he should not be put down to rest at all.

**Stick to the routine of a morning and an afternoon rest.** Ignore a brief protest on being left – any sensible well-attached baby is bound to announce that he would prefer you to stay with him. If after a couple of minutes he is happily playing or talking and looking at things, leave him. He may be enjoying a rest from his demanding life just as you are enjoying a rest from him.

**Go to the baby quickly when he gets bored and grumbles.** If you leave him he is bound to begin to feel that his crib is a prison. He will not go happily into it next time.

A wakeful baby is living a much fuller life than one who sleeps for several hours each day. You will have to find ways of getting on with your life while sharing it with your baby, rather than dividing it into periods of babycare and adult activity. The chapters beginning on pp. 259 and 266 should help you. So too should the thought that your baby is probably intelligent (most very wakeful babies are) and, with plenty of waking time spent with you, will probably turn into an extremely sociable and competent toddler.

# *Excreting*

Once solid foods and/or cow's milk are added to breast milk or formula, the baby's digestion has to cope with food that moves more slowly through the intestines and contains more waste. The result is less frequent and bulkier stools which look and smell more like those of an older person.

*Constipation*    Babies vary in the frequency with which their bodies need to evacuate waste. A daily movement is not a prescription for, or a sign of, good health. Your baby is only constipated if, when a movement is finally passed, it is dry and hard enough to make its passage difficult or painful.

If your baby does have hard movements, offer lots of extra drinks. Fruit juice or vegetable juice is good as the small amount of extra sugar has a mildly laxative effect.

**Don't give any form of laxative** without instructions from your doctor. They are practically never needed and it is a great mistake to try to override the body's natural rhythms.

**Never use soap sticks or suppositories** unless you have specific instructions from a doctor. The baby's bowels will open when they need to. It is not your job to control them.

*Diarrhea*    As we saw in an earlier chapter, new foods may prove difficult for a baby to digest at first. Undigested particles are a signal to go slow with that particular food. A lot of mucus usually means that the food was too coarse and needs straining.

A sudden increase in his intake of sugar or fat can also cause very loose stools, but on its own this will not make him ill. If, in addition to loose stools, he seems unwell, goes off his food, runs a fever and/or vomits, you should take him to your doctor on the same day. He may have gastroenteritis. While this is not quite such a serious threat in this age group as to younger babies, the loss of fluid can still rapidly make them exceedingly ill. So get medical help quickly and, while you are waiting for it, offer him as much cool boiled water as he will drink. At this time, contrary to all other times, a minute quantity of extra salt will be good for him. A quarter of a teaspoon dissolved in each pint of water you offer him will help his body retain the vital fluid (Ref/DEHYDRATION).

Sensible precautions will help you avoid gastroenteritis. The hygiene "rules" are just the same as for younger babies (see p. 62) but in addition:

**Don't stop sterilizing bottles, nipples, etc.** just because he now drinks ordinary milk. Add his training cup to the sterilizer; that spout can trap bacteria-breeding drops.

**Don't use the family milk carton** it if has been standing around the kitchen. Keep his milk covered and refrigerated.

**Don't carry warm milk in a thermos.** Carry it cold and warm it when it is needed.

**Don't buy dairy products from a store with no refrigerator.**
Cream doughnuts, milkshakes, etc., are not safe unless kept cold.

**Don't buy ice cream for the baby from ice cream vans.** The ice cream itself is cold enough to be safe but the scoops and spillage may be contaminated. A wrapped water ice pop is far safer.

*Potty training*  Late in the first year most babies have learned to sit up by themselves and some have adopted quite regular times of day for passing bowel movements. Some parents decide that they might as well sit their baby on a potty at these times. They call this "toilet training" but it is important to realize that there is no *training* in it at all. The baby is simply being put in the right place at the right time for the movement to be caught in a potty instead of a diaper. The baby can neither understand nor cooperate.

True toilet training means helping a child to recognize his own full bowel or bladder and then to do something about it – like telling his mother or going to find his potty. He cannot begin to be trained until he can recognize his own "need to go." Most children do not even realize when they *have* soiled or wet themselves until they are at least a year old; very few are capable of anticipating their own needs until well into the second year.

Catching a baby's movements in a potty may seem harmless even if it is not doing anything toward eventual toilet training. But it is a mistake. If you start doing it when he is seven months old he probably will not object: the potty will seem no odder to him than some of the other places that you sit him down. But two months later he is likely to hate it. He has learned to crawl; he does not want to sit still anywhere for a minute longer than he need, and sitting on a potty seems to him the most pointless kind of sitting of all. When you sit him in his chair he gets a meal; when you sit him in his stroller he gets a walk; when you sit him on his potty he gets nothing – except the movement which he was going to have anyway. So if you go along with his wishes, the potty that you introduce early will be abandoned again within a very few weeks. If you do not go along with his wishes, but insist that he sit on that potty, you run a real risk of starting a battle long before your child is physically ready to learn to use it properly.

There are other reasons for avoiding early "training" too. A little frivolous arithmetic will show that however successful you might be at catching your baby's movements, you will not save yourself any time and effort by doing so. Research has shown that no matter when you begin to introduce a baby to a potty, he will, on average, became reliably clean and dry by the middle of his third year. Suppose that you start putting him on a potty at six months, six times per day: you will have done so 4380 times before you reach your objective – a fully "trained" child. You will have had to undress and redress him on each occasion and you will have failed to catch the movement a good many times too so that there will still have been soiled diapers to deal with. If you leave out this "catching" stage altogether and start proper toilet training at, say, twenty months you will only have to pot your baby about 2000 times for the same effect. Since changing him is quicker than potting him, you have everything to gain by waiting from your own point of view as well as his. Don't buy a potty at all this year.

# Everyday care

## Now that your baby is older . . .

As babies get older they spend more and more time on the floor. Once they can crawl they get exceedingly dirty. Washing them is by no means as easy as with the younger age group who kept (more or less) still.

You will need to develop techniques for washing the face of a person who sucks the washcloth whenever it comes near and for changing diapers while toes are being chewed. It is not easy but if your sense of humor stays intact, it can be fun.

Your baby's skin will have toughened up by now so you need not be so careful about patting dry instead of rubbing, or using unscented soap. Your child will enjoy a good rub. In fact he or she will probably enjoy being handled and physically fussed over altogether. If you want to try out trendy clothes or the latest babycare gadgets, now is the time. . . .

## Bathing

An evening bath is probably a "must" now. In the morning she only needs her bottom cleaned and her face and hands sponged, but by the evening she will be grubby from top to toe. Your baby will probably love being bathed. But it is a backbreaking job for you. Don't try to lean down to her, kneel on the floor so you are at her level. At six months she will try to do gymnastics all around the bath, making tidal waves and turning in your hands like a dolphin. Later she will struggle to sit up, her uncertain balance making a dowsing all too likely. By about eight months it may be easier to keep her safe in the bath if you put her into it in sitting position and hold her there. Keep hold of her every moment – she is slippery and so is the bath.

Kneel by the bath with an arm around her shoulders, holding her arm. Steady her with your other hand on her thigh.

Choose a moment when she is well-balanced to grab for what you need with the hand from her thigh. Have everything on the floor.

She will enjoy floating and pouring toys. Help her with that same hand. Don't remove the one that is around her.

Watch out for the soap; if it is within reach she will grab for it. Nasty to eat and painful if she then rubs her eyes. . . .

A shiny tap will attract her attention too. If it is hot, wrap it in a washcloth, in case she wriggles near it even as you hold her.

At 9 or 10 months she may try to pull herself out of your grasp and stand up. Don't let her. The bath is too slippery to be safe.

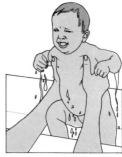
To lift her out, hold her firmly under both armpits. She is heavy, slippery and probably protesting. . . .

Don't try to stand up with her until you have dried her on the floor.

220    SIX MONTHS TO ONE YEAR

## Making bathtime happy and safe

| Do | Don't |
|---|---|
| Collect everything you might need before you begin, and put it all where you can reach with one hand. | Even turn around to reach for something once she is in the water. It does not take her even one second to slide her head under. |
| Put a good warm bath mat beside the bath and plan to kneel on it with your things. | Try to bathe her from standing position, even from sitting on a stool; you can only hold her at her level. |
| Run all the water before you put her in. Wrap a washcloth around the hot tap if it still feels very hot to touch. | Risk even a trickle of extra hot water while she is in the bath; she could get a kicking toe under it. |
| Let her sit up if she wants to, keeping one arm around her. Keep your other hand free for washing and playing. | Let her practice her independent sitting balance in the water; a tumble could put her off her bath for months. |
| Give her suitable things to play with in the water. | Make bathing a question of washing and no fun. |
| Bathe toddlers or older children separately just for these few months when the baby is nearly sitting or just sitting but not yet able to cope safely with the slippery surface. | Have a child in the water with her; a by-accident-on-purpose push or splash is all too easy. Don't even have another in the room if you can arrange occupation elsewhere. The baby needs your full attention. |

## Frightened babies

As at earlier ages the immediate answer to bathing a baby who is frightened is *don't*. Wash her as best you can away from the bathroom. At the same time use her new mobility and her desire to explore to get her gradually used to thinking of water as fun. Sit her on a big towel on the floor beside a washing-up bowl. Help her to splash and call her attention to the ripples. Once she will put her hands in she will probably play. Give her a cup and a duck, and encourage "water play" at the end of every sponge bath. As soon as she has accepted that water is fun, she will probably enjoy putting her feet in and splashing, so spread newspaper under the bowl.

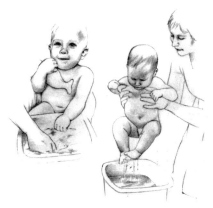

Once she enjoys splashing she needs a larger container. Her old baby bath is ideal. Don't put her in yet. She will soon try herself. . . .

When she tries to crawl in you will have dealt with the worst of her fear. A couple of hip-baths and you can . . .

. . . transfer the full baby bath from the floor to the empty big tub, and let her crawl in there too.

After a few nights of a bath in a bath she will happily accept the same three inches of water run directly into the tub.

## Hairwashing

Whatever they feel about baths many babies develop an acute dislike of having their hair washed at around eight to nine months. This often remains a problem right through early childhood so it is worth doing what you can to get it right from the beginning.

The baby is usually afraid of getting *water* in her eyes. Don't make the mistake of thinking that she is crying because there is soap in her eyes and that splashing water in her face will make it better. Water was probably the trouble in the first place; if you add more and more she will think you are deliberately tormenting her. If it is clear that she is afraid of

having water poured on her head, do not try to show her, by force, that there is nothing to be afraid of. If you try to wash or rinse her hair while she screams and struggles, you are bound to get water if not soap in her eyes. Her worst fears will be confirmed.

If a struggle has begun, give up. The baby's short memory is still on your side. Don't try to shampoo her hair again for at least a month. In the meantime sponge bits of food out of her hair and brush it with a soft damp brush to stop it looking lank and greasy. When you do try to shampoo again there are a few tricks you might find useful:

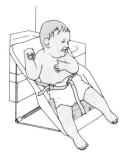
*Sit her backwards on to the basin so that she cannot even see any water. Use her chair on a chair, or sit her on your lap.*

*Have the basin full of warm water, wet her hair by wiping over it with a wet washcloth.*

*Pour non-sting shampoo into your hand and rub it over her head. She will not be frightened: all she feels is your familiar hand.*

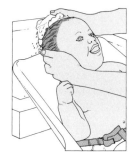
*Rinse her hair by dipping the washcloth repeatedly into the basin. She need never feel water pouring or dripping on her.*

## If the baby is still frightened

There are a few other tricks you can try, although none of them is a sure prescription for peace. It may be a matter of finding what your child dislikes least. Don't wash her hair in the bath. If you do, she will be aware of a great deal of water all around her, and her dislike of hairwashing will probably spill over into a dislike of being bathed at all.

**Eye infections**
If an eye infection ever requires treatment, ask your doctor for ointment, not drops. Most babies loathe having drops put in their eyes. Such treatment may start hairwashing troubles all over again.

*Lots of water play will help her to get used to putting water on her own face. A hand-shower is a good toy for this if the thermostat is safely accurate . . .*

*A rather small big brother can be a good example. Even if he is not keen himself he may put up with it to help reassure the baby, whose fears he can well understand.*

*A headband, bought or made by cutting the crown from a shower cap, stops water crossing her hairline. Swimming goggles keep it out of her eyes. Once she believes you, the problem may be solved.*

## Diaper rash

The general toughening up of the baby's skin usually means that diaper rash is less of a problem than it was earlier in her life. But for some babies new maturity brings new problems. . . .

## Protecting the baby's bottom at night

Sleeping through the night can lead to a sore bottom. The baby probably now goes for eight to twelve hours without a change of diaper and during that time she passes a great deal of urine.

Good quality night-time disposable diapers with a one-way layer next to the baby's skin and a built-in plastic backing may keep her both dry and comfortable. But elasticized legs may keep air away from her bottom so that it gets steamy and sore. You may have to settle for less efficient waterproofing in order to allow some air circulation.

As babies get bigger and wetter, some parents decide to use cloth diapers at night even if they are devoted to disposables the rest of the time. You can add a one-way liner for all-night comfort but you will need to choose the plastic pants with care.

If she wears plastic pants, which efficiently keep moisture off her clothes and bedding, air is unable to circulate around her sodden skin. Her bottom is kept warm, wet and airless all night and is likely to get sore. If she does not wear plastic pants, her clothes and bedding will get wet which means that she will get cold and uncomfortable and you will have a heavy laundry load.

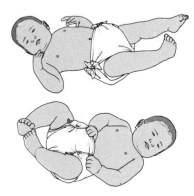

Tie-on plastic pants have just the right balance of efficiency and air circulation. They will not keep her bed perfectly dry but they will allow some evaporation. If you use snap-pants, leave the bottom snaps undone so the elastic legs are not pulled perfectly tight.

## Protecting the baby's bottom by day

As we have seen (p. 182), it is very good for babies to play with no diapers on, or no clothes at all if the weather is hot enough. But once your baby can sit alone, and especially once she starts to roll over and crawl, her bottom will get rubbed against the carpet or the lawn and the friction will tend to make her skin sore. In the same way, sand on a beach may feel lovely at the time, but the grit will rub those soft creases. Once this has happened, urine and feces are much more likely to sting and set up diaper rash. You may find that a pair of soft cotton underpants gives her most of the freedom of nakedness while protecting her skin.

Her bottom is less accustomed to sunlight than the rest of her. She will enjoy crawling around naked in the sunshine with her bottom up in the

air, but 20 minutes of this will be enough to produce a burned bottom. Once again, use soft cotton pants to protect her. If her bottom does get burned a silicone-based cream will keep urine off it.

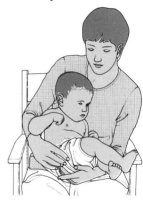

## Cleanliness and hygiene

Once your baby can get around a room alone, picking things up to explore them by mouth as well as by hand, it is important to distinguish between cleanliness and hygiene. Cleanliness is anathema to an exploring baby who cannot learn and have fun while staying clean. But hygiene is vital to health. You will get the balance between the two about right if you are exceedingly fussy about food and excreta but not very fussy about the cleanliness of anything else.

## Protecting your baby from bacteria

Good hygiene is a matter of protecting your baby from an overdose of harmful bacteria. There are bacteria everywhere but very few of them are harmful and the body's defenses can cope adequately even with the harmful ones provided it gets them in small amounts. A potentially dangerous build-up of bacteria is only likely to be present on an object which provides them with a breeding ground.

An object is *safe* when it is dry and free from food, even if it is dusty or generally grubby. The piece of paper your baby extracts from the waste-paper basket may not look *clean*, but it will not be a breeding ground for dangerous bacteria.

An object is *unsafe* when it has been in contact with food (especially milk) and then left at room temperature. The tiny piece of cheesecake you dropped yesterday may still look quite edible, but it is likely to be teeming with bacteria. The rate at which they multiply is enormously fast.

If your kitchen hygiene is good, with adequate sterilization, refrigeration and care about keeping cooked foods covered and cold *or* hot but never warm, you need not take any extra care about the rest of your house. Normal cleanliness is enough. There are, however, one or two traps for the unwary:

Bacteria regard excreted food as food, so lavatory hygiene and hand-washing are important. We all excrete bacteria in our feces and even an invisible trace of fecal material will provide a bacterial breeding ground. So wash your hands after attending to your own or the baby's toilet needs, and wash the baby's if he has been exploring while you changed a diaper. Be scrupulous, too, about mopping up any "accidents" or cleaning up after a baby who has burped up some milk.

Bacteria regard animal food or excretions as food, so if you have pets as well as a baby, keep their food dishes out of reach and deal immediately and thoroughly with any animal "accident." Don't let the baby finger the dog or cat all over and then suck his hands: most animals keep themselves scrupulously clean, but some do not. When your baby is crawling in parks or gardens, you will obviously have to watch out for animal excreta.

## Keeping poisons out of reach

Don't let concern about bacteria blind you to the much more likely hazard of poisonous substances. A full ashtray will not give your baby gastroenteritis but if he eats cigarette butts he will be exceedingly ill. That bottle of sherry will not give him gastroenteritis either but the alcohol could kill him. It is not the grubbiness of that box that need worry you but the possibility that its paint contains lead. . . .

# Teething

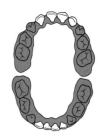

Teeth usually appear fast and furiously during this half year. A first lower incisor, cut at around six months, is closely followed by its next door neighbor. At around seven months most babies produce a top incisor and by eight months all four of these top front teeth are often through. By nine to ten months the remaining two lower incisors appear so that babies have achieved a row of four top and four bottom teeth. There is usually a pause before the first molars. Some babies produce one of these by the first birthday, others not until a month or so after it. Few babies suffer anything but the most fleeting and trivial discomfort while cutting their front teeth. Their sharp, flat shape helps them to come through easily, more easily than the larger, broader molars which are to come. Make sure that your baby has plenty of things to bite. Fingers and toys are fine, but any hard (reasonably clean) smooth object will both help and provide an interesting change. Once the baby has two or three teeth, chewing on a variety of objects will also help to "file down" their exceedingly sharp points.

*Teeth and weaning*

As we said in a previous chapter (see p. 147), these first teeth are not chewing teeth and their appearance should not therefore speed up the process of weaning. But occasionally once a baby has a pair of bottom teeth and two or more top ones, he will try to chew the nipple of his bottle or to nip your nipple. Don't decide that he is forcing you to wean him. As long as the nipple is well back in his mouth in the proper position for sucking (see p. 66), he cannot bite: the position of his jaws prevents it. Biting is therefore only a problem when he has temporarily stopped sucking and is playing instead. Remove the nipple from his mouth with a firm "no"; give it back if he wants to suck some more, but don't let him play with it in the front of his mouth. Many breast-fed babies actually learn not to bite after a week of this handling.

*Looking after your baby's teeth*

Once he has two or more teeth side by side, try to make sure that bits of his finger-foods do not get caught between them and stay in his mouth for hours. If you can see a piece of carrot or a shred of apple, remove it. Encourage him to like plain water to drink. As long as he is getting all the vitamin C he needs, plain water is better for his teeth than endless sweet drinks and it helps to rinse milk and other foods out of his mouth too.

Start brushing his teeth with a soft toothbrush and a fluoride toothpaste. You want your baby to accept this as routine from the earliest possible moment. Even if brushing accomplishes little, the fluoride will help to keep his tooth-enamel healthy.

As well as looking after the teeth that he now has, you should be thinking about the strength and health of his second teeth. Calcium and vitamin D are especially important for them. If you live in an area where the drinking water contains little fluoride, your dentist may advise giving the baby extra, in the form of tablets dissolved in his drinking water.

# Crying and comforting

Most babies cry much less in the second half of this year than they did earlier in their lives. They cope more robustly with the hurly burly of ordinary daily life. The sudden loud noises and quick movements which used to make them startle and cry often now make them laugh. When things do displease them they will often express worry or alarm with facial expressions and whimpery sounds, only embarking on full-fledged crying if nobody comes and offers reassurance.

But although babies tend to cry less readily and less often than before, there are various aspects of their development in this half year which will lead to considerable crying if they are not understood. Learning to understand them in your baby is important because they are all developments which will continue into toddlerhood. Sensitive handling, which is well-tuned to your son's or daughter's needs and emotions now, will certainly make life easier for all of you later on.

*Crying from fear*  When your baby was younger he may have given the impression of being afraid of a great many things. Now he is much more confident about life in general but he is likely to develop intense fears about one or two particular things. He may, for example, be quite unworried by most loud noises, but appear terrified by the sound of the vacuum cleaner. He may enjoy every kind of rough and tumble play but intensely dislike having clothes pulled on or off over his head. He may love his bath and everything to do with water, but then panic if he sees the dirty water running away out of the drain.

Fears of this kind often seem completely irrational. You may be quite unable to see why the vacuum cleaner's sound should worry him when the noise of the washing machine does not. But irrational or not, the baby's fears have to be accepted and respected. It may help if you think about some of your own irrational anxieties. We all have them. Why, for example, do you mind spiders when you are not afraid of flies?

The best way to handle these quirky fears is by avoidance whenever possible. Use the vacuum cleaner during the baby's nap times or while he is in his stroller in another room. Don't empty his bathwater until he is well out of the way; avoid buying clothes with tight necks and no fastenings. The less you frighten your baby the faster his fear will die down. You will only make it more intense if you try to force him to face it.

*Crying at the unexpected*  During these months your baby is beginning to build up a lot of expectations about people and about his daily life. He is also making patterns in his mind; learning routines, rhythms and rituals. When these strong, new expectations are contradicted he is afraid. For example, the baby has learned that when he has been awake for a little while in the morning, either his mother or his father will come to greet him and get him up. If a total stranger were to walk in instead of the familiar parent, his expectations would be shattered and he would cry in fear. Yet that same stranger walking into the house to join the family for a meal might well get brilliant smiles. It is not the stranger the baby minds but the unexpected context in which she appears. In a similar way the baby has built up expectations about feeding from a bottle. If he is accustomed to milk which is warm and you suddenly feed him milk which is icy cold he will probably cry from the shock. It is not that he dislikes cold milk, it is just that it is not what he was expecting.

Experiences which are totally new to the baby may affect him in the same way as experiences which contradict his expectations. His very first ride on a swing, his very first taste of ice cream, or his very first meeting with a horse may all make him cry. They are all experiences which are potentially enjoyable but he needs time to get used to them.

Supporting your baby through unexpected or novel experiences is an important skill. As he gets older his horizons will broaden. It is novel experiences which will gradually make the fabric of his life richer. Even at six months you will probably find that you can warn him, by word, touch and gesture, when something unexpected or new is coming up. You can foresee the things that may be going to alarm him and turn his attention to your own calm presence so that he receives the experience with and through you. If he has that first swing sitting on your lap, with your interested reassuring voice telling him about this new sensation and your familiar arms holding him steady, he will probably enjoy it from the beginning.

## Crying from helplessness

Babies have strong emotions but very little power. As far as we know, their loves and hates, their wishes and wants are as strong as ours, but because they are still physically incompetent and unable to use language, there is much less that they can do about them. A lot of your baby's crying is in place of action. He cries because a situation has arisen in which he can do nothing to help himself. His crying is a signal to you to take action for him.

You go out of the room. The baby wants to go with you. He cannot follow, either because he is not yet mobile or because he is trapped in his stroller or his playpen. He cannot ask you to take him with you. So he cries. Another time he is playing happily in his crib when the toy which he was enjoying drops through the bars. He cannot get it for himself. He cannot call to you to pick it up for him. So he cries. Out on a walk, a friend of yours whom the baby does not know stops to chat. She holds out her arms to the baby saying "You'll come to me for a cuddle won't you, darling?" The baby feels your arms starting to hold him out. He cannot tell you not to, or answer the stranger's rhetorical question with words; he can only cry his "no!"

If you are sensitive to cues from your baby that are more subtle than crying he will not need to cry so often. If, for example, you make a point of indicating to him that you are intending to leave the room, he can hold up his arms to ask you to take him too. If you are half-listening to his contented play in his crib, his dismayed silence will alert you to the dropped toy. He will not then need to cry. At the same time the growing independence that mobility gives him will help to counteract his feelings of helplessness. The crawling stage may be exhausting for you but it often brings great relief to your baby. At last he can go where he wishes and get what he needs – at least within the limits of the freedom that you are prepared to allow him.

*Crying from anger and frustration*

Crying from helplessness usually diminishes as mobility increases in the first year. But crying from frustration and anger tends to build up in its place. By your baby's first birthday these emotions may lie behind most of the crying that takes place in any single day.

The crawling, exploring baby gets himself into continual trouble. He has to be constantly checked both for the sake of his own safety and the safety of other people's possessions. Removing

*She cannot understand why you keep interfering . . .*

him from the refrigerator door eight times in ten minutes may drive you mad but it drives him mad too. He wants to open that door and he is months away from understanding why he may not, or even from remembering that you will not let him. The more he grows up and discovers things he wants to explore and do, the angrier it will make him when he is prevented from doing them, either by you or by his own incompetence.

It is not always possible or desirable to prevent this kind of crying. You have to frustrate the baby when his intentions are unsafe or destructive. And he must attempt difficult and frustrating tasks if he is to learn. So a certain amount of angry, frustrated crying is inevitable. But a baby who feels continually beset by restricting adults or continually defeated by his own immaturity will not forge ahead in his development. There is a balance to be struck between too much frustration and too little.

When you must frustrate the baby, because what he wants to do is dangerous or damaging, you can make use of the fact that "out of sight is out of mind" and will be so for months to come. There is no need to have a long drawn out tussle about that refrigerator. Take the baby right out of the room or put a childproof fastening on the door and, after a brief burst of anger, he will forget the whole issue. Fortunately he is still infinitely distractible.

When the baby frustrates himself, it is for you to judge whether he can learn by the situation he has got himself into or whether he can only fight himself into a fury of frustrated crying. If he is struggling to get the lid off the toy box and there is a good chance that he will succeed, leave him to it. The success will be worth the effort. But if you can see that he is not going to be able to manage alone, help him. You will not offend his dignity by interfering. Managing alone is not yet important to him for its own sake. He just wants that lid off, no matter how.

Just as some very young babies cry more readily and more persistently than others, so older babies vary too. Some seem to have a far greater tolerance of frustration than others; a setback that makes one howl leaves the next still smiling. Parents cannot do very much about these innate differences so there is no point in worrying about them. If you stay tuned in to your baby and handle him in the way his cues to you suggest, you are doing the best you can. Don't decide, even during this half year, that your baby's temperament is set for life. He may be a real trier later on even if he is easily frustrated now. On the other hand, being placid now may not stop him taking life hard later on.

But even though some of these kinds of crying are bound to occur and some babies do cry more readily than others, the overall amount that your baby cries is some kind of index of how contented he is with life. If nothing ever seems to go right for him for more than five minutes at a time, it is worth sitting down and thinking about what it is that most often upsets him. Apart from pain, illness or hunger, crying is either a reaction to fear, a signal to you to take action, or an explosion of frustration and rage. If you can work out which emotion is causing most of your baby's crying you may be able to offer what he needs most – whether it is extra security, a quicker response or greater freedom which will transform him into a happier baby.

# Using his body

Six-month-old babies usually give a distinct impression of being happy and at ease in their bodies. They use all four limbs smoothly and rhythmically. They enjoy physical movement for its own sake and they continually test the limits of their own strength as they struggle to roll right over or to lift their heads and shoulders even further from the floor. They have understood, now, that all the bits of their bodies form single, complete units. They have come to terms with them.

As we have seen, muscular control starts at the top and moves downward. So at this stage the baby's use of his upper half, his head, shoulders, arms and hands, is well ahead of his use of his lower half. He can use his arms and hands for accurate reaching out, and he can use his head to track moving objects with his eyes. He does not yet have similar control over his hips, knees and feet. It is the struggle for control over these muscle groups that the baby is now entering. The fight to stop lying around and become a sitter, a crawling quadruped and a walking biped is on.

*Sitting*  If you put your six-month-old baby squarely on his bottom on the floor, spread his legs apart, get him balanced and then slowly remove your hands, he will probably stay "sitting" for three or four seconds. His muscular control has already progressed downward to a point where he can hold himself straight from the top of his head to his bent hips. But it has not yet reached a point where he can balance himself in this position.

By seven to eight months, some babies will have solved this balance problem for themselves by leaning forward and supporting themselves with both hands flat on the floor in front of them. If your baby takes up this position he will be comparatively stable and he will certainly be sitting, but you cannot yet describe him as being "able to sit alone" because this form of sitting is not developmentally useful to him. Both his hands are occupied in providing balance, so he cannot play or even suck his thumb. And because he has to lean forward to get his hands securely on the floor, he cannot look around or see anything very interesting.

By eight to nine months, independent balance, without support from an adult or his own hands, is really coming. Now the baby can balance in a sitting position for as much as a minute at a time. But even now his sitting is more for practice than for use; he still topples over as soon as he turns his head or reaches out a hand. It will take him another month of constant practice before his sitting becomes a position in which he can carry on with his life.

*Helping your baby to sit alone*  The drive to sit is built in to your baby's development. You do not have to do anything to make him *want* to sit.

As we have seen, he will be ready to practice balancing in sitting position at six or seven months but he will not be able to *get himself* into sitting position without help until he is around nine months. Giving him the opportunity to practice, by getting him into position, is therefore up to you.

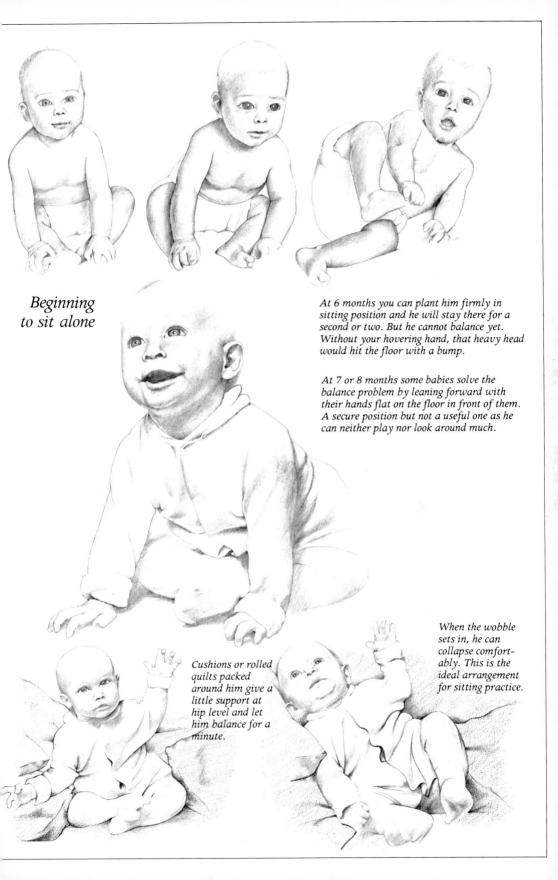

## Beginning to sit alone

At 6 months you can plant him firmly in sitting position and he will stay there for a second or two. But he cannot balance yet. Without your hovering hand, that heavy head would hit the floor with a bump.

At 7 or 8 months some babies solve the balance problem by leaning forward with their hands flat on the floor in front of them. A secure position but not a useful one as he can neither play nor look around much.

Cushions or rolled quilts packed around him give a little support at hip level and let him balance for a minute.

When the wobble sets in, he can collapse comfortably. This is the ideal arrangement for sitting practice.

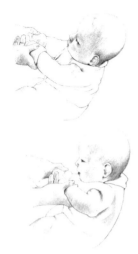

He will make it clear that he wants you to sit him up. While he lies on his back on the floor he will sometimes crane his head and shoulders up in a desperate but unavailing effort. If you kneel beside him, he will instantly grab for your hands and use them as levers to pull up by. Whenever you go to him as he lies in his crib or stroller, he will offer you his hands, hoping for another session of the pull-me-up-to-sitting game.

You cannot play the sitting game all the time, so you have to find ways to help him practice balancing alone, too. Where and how you do this is important. Sitting, as he is accustomed to do, propped in his stroller or strapped in a chair is no longer enough for the baby. It is still a good position for play but he cannot really practice balancing alone with that amount of back support available. On the other hand, sitting completely unsupported is not yet possible for him. He needs a compromise between the two.

The best compromise is to put your baby on the floor, surround him with cushions or with rolled blankets or quilts, and then sit him amongst them. When he is six or seven months you can wedge the supportive padding under his buttocks so that he has just enough support at the base of his spine to sit for a minute or two. When he goes over backward or tips himself forward into crawling position, the padding gives him a soft landing.

Experience of this sort of protection may mean that your baby never bothers to balance himself with his hands on the floor. Even if he does go through this stage it will be over quickly because he will be confident that he will not hurt himself. When he is around eight months, or when you can see that his balance is improving, you can arrange his padding so that it surrounds but does not actually support him. It will still make his fall comfortable when he waves both hands in triumph at finding himself sitting alone.

A month or so later the baby will be sitting steadily as long as he keeps perfectly still and concentrates on his balance. But sitting *still* is not his idea of fun. That padding will still be invaluable whenever he stretches forward just too far or falls over backward because he makes a wild gesture with his arms.

*Safety while your baby learns to sit steadily* Once your baby has really started to practice sitting alone he will try to get himself into sitting position by any "handle" he can get hold of, and he will try to balance himself wherever you put him to sit. This means that some of the equipment which was safe for him in the early months may now be dangerous.

**Beware of lightweight carriages.** If the baby wakes from a nap in a lightweight carriage, finds himself wedged against the side of it, gets hold of the edge and manages to get himself almost to sitting position, he may tip the whole thing over. If he is left propped sitting in such a carriage while you are busy, he may work his way forward and try to balance without support. When his balance fails and he flops forward with a thump, both the brakes and the chassis will be put under considerable strain.

Once he reaches this stage, a lightweight carriage is best used only for transport, or it can be replaced for this purpose by a stroller. If you want the baby to go on sleeping in a carriage, perhaps so that he can nap in the yard, you may be able to buy a second-hand, heavy carriage extremely cheaply. Few families want this type of carriage any more as it does not fit in a car or easily go up steps. Its cumbersome weight and solidity make it an ideal outdoor bed which the baby will safely be able to use all through his first and into his second year.

Another possible solution is a canvas camping crib for the yard. Although expensive, the purchase may well be sensible if you plan to camp or go away for weekends. It is easy to transport and it can be used, temporarily, instead of a dropside crib. On the other hand it will be less useful at home than a big carriage as the baby will not be able to sleep out in it in cold or wet weather.

**Beware of lightweight chairs.** A younger baby keeps up a steady pressure on the back of his chair (see p. 155). When he cranes forward he moves his head and shoulders but leaves his bottom and most of his weight squarely in the base of the seat. Now, he struggles to get right forward; he balances for a few seconds and then relaxes his muscles and hits the back of the chair with a thud that can make it tip. If the chair is on the floor, a fall will be frightening and painful. If the chair is on a table or worksurface, it may be a serious matter.

The infant seat should no longer be used for anything except perhaps picnic meals where you are constantly present. The baby must now have either a steady, safe high chair or a low chair-table combination.

**Use a safety-harness always.** The hazard of the baby falling right out of a carriage or chair is almost as great as that of his tipping it over. He should wear a safety-harness, as a matter of course, whenever you put him into anything that is meant to restrain him, such as a chair, carriage, stroller or car seat. The exceptions, of course, are his crib and playpen. It will be a long time before he can climb out of either of those and their design is in any case intended to provide safe freedom.

Using a safety-harness, always, is much less irksome if you have a separate one for each regularly used item of equipment. If you have to go into the yard and get the harness off the carriage in order to put it on the baby and his high chair, the day will almost certainly come when you will not bother. That will be the day your baby discovers how to tip himself out.

**Stop putting your baby to sit in armchairs or on beds.** Constant sitting practice means constant tumbles, but the best kind of tumble is from the floor to the floor. If your baby tumbles from a chair or sofa he is unlikely to do himself real physical damage, but damage to his nerves, morale and confidence can easily delay both his progress and his pleasure in sitting up.

**Don't leave your baby alone on the floor,** especially if he is surrounded by cushions while he practices sitting. If he fell face down into them, he would almost certainly lift his head and roll free, but he could fall with his arms awkwardly trapped; he could smother. Padded or not, your almost-sitting baby is also almost crawling. He should never be left free and alone in a room, not even for the few moments it takes you to answer the door.

*Crawling*  Many babies learn to crawl at the same time that they learn to sit alone. The two developments may parallel each other closely. At six months the baby can sit alone for a second but cannot balance, and can get into crawling position but cannot progress. At nine or ten months the baby can sit steadily and play at the same time, and can also crawl anywhere.

Babies who do not make these advances simultaneously will almost certainly learn to sit alone before they learn to crawl. Perfectly normal babies may still be immobile sitters on their first birthdays. Delayed crawling is nothing to worry about, especially if your sitting baby also shows signs of being interested in pulling up to standing position (see p. 237).

Although "crawling" is usually taken to mean progress across a room on hands and knees, quite a lot of babies adopt other maneuvers, either before, or instead of, a conventional crawl. Early mobility, for example, may come from skillful rolling over and over, with a slither to take the baby the last three feet to his objective. A slippery floor may help your baby learn to get about by pulling himself along on his elbows, with his legs straight out behind him. If he finds this satisfactory, he may be late in learning to pull his legs up and push with his knees.

Babies who learn to sit steadily comparatively early sometimes adopt a "bottom shuffle" instead of a crawl. The baby pushes himself around on his bottom using one hand to propel himself.

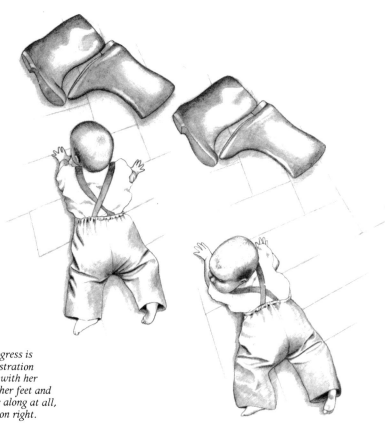

*A baby's first crawling progress is often backward. To her frustration she pushes more efficiently with her arms and hands than with her feet and legs. But once she can move along at all, she will soon get her direction right.*

From his point of view this method has a lot to recommend it. He saves himself the effort of going from sitting position to crawling position and back again, and he keeps one hand free even while he moves. He can see what is going on better than a conventionally crawling baby, too. Bottom shuffling babies often leave out conventional crawling altogether and go straight on to pulling themselves into standing position and cruising around furniture.

Some babies learn to crawl in the ordinary way but then discover that they can move faster on hands and feet than they can on hands and knees. A few leave hands and knees out altogether and "walk like bears" right away.

So while the following paragraphs describe average progress toward ordinary crawling, different rates of development or idiosyncratic methods of getting around do not suggest that there is anything amiss with your baby. He must learn to sit alone and he must eventually learn to stand and walk alone. How or whether he gets around the room in between is far less important.

If a desirable toy is put just out of the reach of a six-month-old baby who is lying on the floor on his tummy, he will pull his knees up under him, push up with his hands, and often manage to get his tummy right off the floor. For a moment he is in true crawling position but he will not get anywhere. Just as he still has a problem with balance when he is trying to sit, so he has a problem with actually moving *forward* when he is trying to crawl.

During the seventh and eighth month most babies clearly show their desire to crawl. If you watch carefully you can see the effort that is being made; see that the baby is "thinking forward." But very few will manage to cover any ground at this age.

Toward the end of the eighth month the baby will probably give up lying on his tummy altogether. As soon as he is placed face down, turns over or collapses from one of his sitting adventures, he gets himself on to hands and knees. He learns to do everything but move along. He rocks backward and forward and he swivels himself around and around, following your progress around the room or the cat's escape from his attentions. It is at this stage that he may be so desperate to get moving that he develops all kinds of peculiar ways of getting around, none of which is a true crawl. He may rock, swivel, roll over and squirm on his tummy, so that one way or another he does actually get from one side of the room to the other. But this is not useful progress any more than sitting by using his hands for balance is useful sitting. He still cannot choose to go in a particular direction, and if he sets off because he has caught sight of something he wants, he will have lost track of it by the time he has finished playing acrobat and come to rest again.

It is during the ninth month that most babies actually begin to make progress. To their fury it is often backward! The baby fixes his eyes on something he wants and makes a mighty effort. Because his control of his upper body is more developed than his control of his legs, he tends to push harder with his hands and arms than with his knees. Instead of finding himself closer to the thing he wants he finds himself moving backward away from it. Furious though the baby may be, this is a short lived phase. Once he can crawl backward he will soon get his direction and the power of his pushing right.

*Helping your baby to crawl*

A baby does not need help in getting into crawling position. He can get there himself either from lying on his tummy or by going forward from sitting. All he needs from you is opportunity. He will get plenty of that provided he spends a good part of his waking day on the floor. There are, however, a few things which you can do to encourage early crawling by making it enjoyable and safe for him:

**Protect your baby's knees.** Their skin is still soft and easily chafed. Even in summer he will be more comfortable if he wears cotton overalls or light trousers when he is trying to crawl on grass or rough textured carpet.

**Foresee possible dangers.** He will learn to crawl without learning any extra good sense to go with his mobility. Steps between rooms, staircases, splintery floors, and unsuitable objects left lying around can all cause accidents (Ref/ACCIDENTS AND SAFETY TIPS).

**Watch out for unexpected spurts in ability.** Even before he can actually crawl across a room the baby may roll and squirm himself out of the safe corner where you left him and into danger. Take action to child-proof the rooms he will use before he is fully mobile.

**Remember that part of the desire to crawl is a desire to get hold of things.** Something that looks really entrancing may give him just the extra surge of motivation he needs to get moving. Make very sure that when this happens it is not a pack of cigarettes or a pin cushion that has caught his eye.

**Don't leave your baby free, alone, in a room,** but don't keep him imprisoned in a playpen either. Being alone may mean that he gets into danger; being enclosed will frustrate him desperately because it will take away all the fun of crawling and much of the point of the tremendous efforts he is making. He needs a safe floor, safe interesting objects and constant supervision.

**Don't try to keep your baby clean.** Fussiness about hygiene is essential in the kitchen and the lavatory but out of place when your baby is playing on the floor (see p. 224). Ordinary household dust will not harm him and skin is the most washable of all materials. Don't dress him nicely if you are going to mind when his clothes get grubby. Treat him like a manual laborer; let him wear work-clothes and change him into party gear only on special occasions.

*Once she can crawl she needs space – as much as you can make safe for her – and the freedom to explore it.*

**Standing**　While learning to sit up and to crawl often go together, both being accomplished at around nine to ten months, standing and walking are definitely later accomplishments.

At six months most babies love to be held standing on a lap, and behave as if they were on a trampoline, "jumping" by bending and straightening both knees together.

During the seventh month they begin to use alternate feet instead of both together. They "dance" rather than "jump," and they often put one foot down on top of the other, pulling out the underneath one and then doing it all over again.

At this stage, the baby cannot bear anything like his full weight. Nor is he yet "thinking forward" as he does at this age when he tries to crawl. It is not usually until around nine months that he begins to get the idea of using his feet to go forwards. Now his dancing movements and the placing of one foot on top of the other give way to a definite placing of one foot in front of the other. The baby "walks" two steps to the end of your knee and then collapses, giggling. If he is held securely, with his feet on the floor and with you taking most of his weight, he may now enjoy making a few wobbling steps.

By ten months the baby's control of his muscles has usually moved downward to his knees and feet. At last he can take his whole weight, standing squarely on his flat feet, keeping his knees braced though still sagging forward a little at hip level. He has reached the same point in standing that he reached at six months in sitting. He can stand, but he cannot balance.

Once the baby can take his full weight and stand square on the floor provided somebody balances him, he will soon learn to pull himself up to a holding-on standing position. Most babies will do this before they are one year old, starting by pulling themselves, hand over hand, up the bars of a crib or playpen. If you give him the opportunity, your baby may use you in the same way, crawling up to you as you sit on the floor, and then hauling himself up by your clothes to stand triumphantly balancing by your hair.

Just as newly crawling babies are often flummoxed by their inability to crawl forward rather than backward, so newly standing ones often find it impossible to sit down again. For two or three weeks on end the baby may find something to pull himself up by as soon as he is set free on the floor, but shout piteously for help as soon as he reaches standing position because he cannot let go and sit down again. As soon as you come to the rescue and sit him down, he repeats the performance. It can be a tiresome phase because you have to go to his assistance every couple of minutes and both of you get tired and frustrated. Luckily it does not last for long. Don't just pluck him from his hold and dump him in sitting position. Lower him gradually to the floor. He will soon acquire the confidence either to let go with his hands and sit down with a plop or to lower himself by sliding his hands down his support, not releasing it until his bottom reaches the floor. In the meantime, if you are both getting fed up, extra rides to the stores or the park in his carriage or stroller may help. He has not yet got to the stage where he will even think about walking when he is out on an expedition. He will happily sit and watch the world going by, resting both his muscles and your nerves.

About a month after first pulling himself up to standing position the baby will learn the assisted walking we call "cruising." He pulls himself up as usual so that he is standing facing the back of the sofa or the bars of his crib. Gradually he inches both hands together along the support and then follows them by stepping sideways with one foot. Left straddle-legged, he will usually sit down, looking dumbfounded by his own achievement. It is a major one. That shuffle was his first step. Never again will he be a baby who cannot walk.

As long as the baby feels that he needs to take some of his weight on the hands that cling to his support, he will have to move those hands together. But practice brings confidence; within a few days or weeks of that first shuffling sideways movement he will have become convinced that his legs will bear his whole weight. He will then be able to stand further back from his support and pass himself hand over hand along it. Every time he moves a hand he moves his leading foot one step sideways and then brings the other foot up to join it. If you watch him carefully you can see that it is the moment when one foot is actually moving, leaving all his weight on the other one, which still worries him. Gradually his balance improves. By the end of the year you will probably see him standing right back, holding on to his support at arm's length, using it only for balance. Very soon now he will be ready to let go altogether and stand quite alone.

*Helping your baby to stand*

You cannot help your baby learn to stand by putting him in standing position as you sat him up to practice sitting. Given the opportunity and some careful attention to his safety, he will pull himself upright as soon as he feels ready to do so.

Giving him the opportunity is not difficult. If he is free in a room with furniture, he will hold on to that; if he is in his crib or playpen, he will pull himself up by the bars; if nothing better presents itself, he will grasp your hair or the family dog's neck. The problem is that many of these adventures will lead to falls and while some are inevitable at this stage of a baby's development, too many, especially when they take place from standing up, can hurt his confidence as well as his head. Later on, when he is walking freely, he will learn to put his hands out as soon as he feels himself falling. Toddler tumbles are usually no worse than grazed knees and palms. But at this early stage he is not good at protecting himself, because his hands are taken up with trying to hold on and his balance is so precarious that he is likely to fall awkwardly. It is worth planning protection for him.

**Consider the furnishings in the room.** Flimsy pieces are dangerous because they will support him as he first grasps them and begins the leverage part of his getting up, but they will topple over as his hands and his weight move upward and he pulls. He will then fall from his most unbalanced position – neither sitting down nor standing up, but halfway between the two.

Highly flimsy furniture – such as a small round end table or wicker plant stand – is the worst of all; it will not only topple over but, because of its height, will almost certainly fall on the baby. Even if it is light, it can hurt him.

Some obviously hazardous pieces can be wedged in place; others can be positioned in such a way that they are inaccessible to the baby. A few would be better removed to another room for a few months, until the baby can get to his feet unaided.

Watch out, too, for dangers above the baby as he pulls himself up. He will not be able to reach out for things while standing until he can spare a hand from holding on (probably at around a year), but he may try to pull himself up by a hanging tablecloth or dangling electric cord. Neither a coffee pot nor a table lamp will do his skull any good.

**Don't start using a sleeping bag at this stage** if your baby has not been accustomed to one. He will try to stand up while he is in it, will certainly fall and probably bang his head on the bars of his crib. But if he is accustomed to a sleeping bag, don't give it up now either. He will not attempt to stand in it if he has always worn one and this simple fact may keep him safely and happily in his crib later on when your friends' babies are driving them mad by trying to climb out! (See p. 313.)

**Don't put shoes on your newly standing baby.** He only needs shoes to protect his feet once he is really walking and doing so outdoors. Shoes at this stage will make it far more difficult for him to balance because they will cut down the sensations his feet receive from the floor and the sensitive adjustments of his toes. They can be slippery too and may cause an accident.

**Don't put socks on your baby without shoes unless your floors are carpeted.** Socks turn hard floors into skating rinks; your baby may fall and even if he does not, the difficulty of standing under these conditions will badly shake his confidence. He is safest in bare feet. If cold is a problem, use slipper socks which have a light non-slip sole on knitted socks.

**Don't try to make the baby walk holding your hands.** At this stage he will not like walking with all that empty space around him and only wobbly hands to hold on to. He feels safer doing his cruising around something solid. If you want to give him the chance to practice pulling himself up when you are out in the park where there is no furniture, kneel or sit on the ground and let him use your body as if it were inanimate.

**Don't try to hurry your baby on toward independent standing and/or walking.** Standing, cruising and eventually walking alone are all dependent on the baby's confidence and his motivation as well as on his muscles and coordination. If you try to hurry him you may slow up his development by causing falls that make him afraid. If he seems to have managed one stage, such as learning to pull himself upright, but does not seem to be moving on toward cruising or standing alone, it may be because he does not actually want to go further with the walking game at present. Pleasure in crawling all over the place at will may mean that he has no motive for learning to walk just yet.

Although most babies will pull themselves up and cruise before their first birthday, a large minority will not get on to two feet until their second year.

# Using his hands

Your baby spent much of his first six months in discovering that his hands were part of himself; that they were always there even when he could not see them and that by conscious effort he could make them reach out and get hold of things (see p. 157).

By around six months he has completed this stage of development. He has "found" his hands once and for all and he can wave them, reach out with them or grab with them as directly and immediately as you or I.

But the baby still has a great deal to learn about using his hands. Efficiency at reaching out and grabbing is not enough. He has to learn to make his hands perform complicated maneuvers and he has to learn to use different bits of them separately.

These developments are difficult to catalogue because the changes which take place in your baby's day-to-day use of his hands are minute, even though the overall change between six months and one year is enormous. Furthermore, the exact ways in which he learns his increasingly fine hand control will depend on the kinds of objects and opportunities he is given for practice.

*Touching as well as grabbing*

At six to seven months the baby begins to understand that he can use his hands to explore things by other means than grabbing hold of them and putting them in his mouth. While his most usual reaction to a toy will still be to reach out, grasp it, put it in his mouth and then look at it, he will sometimes simply use his hands to touch, stroke or pat. This small development is important because it enables the baby to find out something about things which are not graspable. As he lies on the carpet, for example, he will stroke it, exploring its texture. Even three or four weeks earlier he would have concentrated his energy on trying to pick up those bafflingly flat flowers in its pattern. The flowers would have defeated him by being ungraspable and the rest of the carpet would have gone unexplored.

Once your baby has discovered that simply feeling things with his hands can give him some information about them, you will probably notice him becoming increasingly interested in different textures and sensations through his fingers. He will stroke the tray of his high chair; feel the window pane and pat his blankets. You may even get your hair stroked rather than having it grabbed by the handful!

*Differentiating arms, hands and fingers*

At six months your baby still usually behaves as if he thinks his arms and hands are single units. If he wants to call your attention to something, for example, he gestures in its direction with a broad sweep from the shoulder.

Although expansive gestures will continue, because your baby characteristically reacts in a very physical way to things which interest him, he will gradually learn to use his lower arm, from the elbow, and his hand alone, from the wrist. By eight or nine months he will have a repertory of gestures and be able to wave goodbye royally from the wrist only.

*. . . a month or two later, the baby can
cope with two things at once, even if
they are a mouthful . . .*

*As manual skills develop, containers can be emptied and filled quite deliberately . . .*

*Hands are for touching and exploring,*
*but life can be baffling*
*– those flowers look pickable . . .*

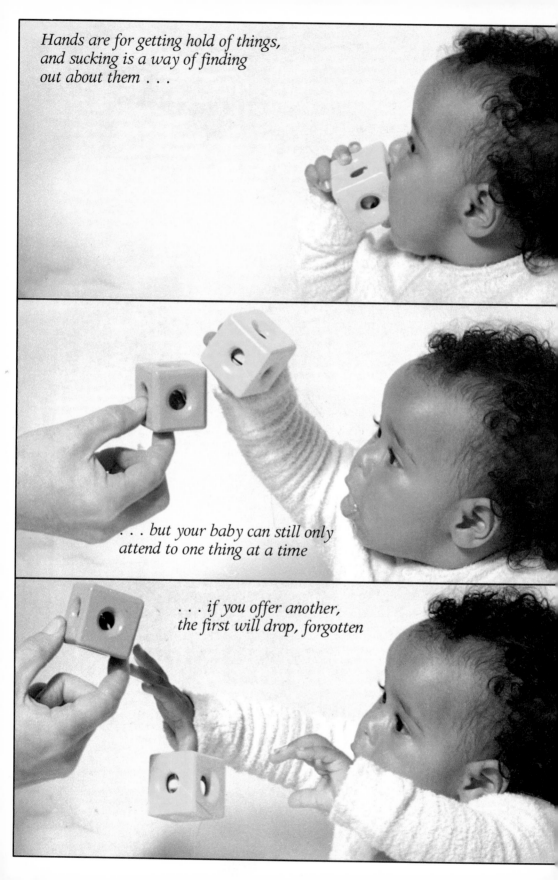

Hands are for getting hold of things,
and sucking is a way of finding
out about them . . .

. . . but your baby can still only
attend to one thing at a time

. . . if you offer another,
the first will drop, forgotten

*. . . though they may empty themselves
at quite unexpected moments.*

*As she gets control over her hands, she imitates what you do with yours. If you draw on the paper and give her a crayon, she will try too . . .*

*As she gets control over her separate fingers, she can use just one to point things out . . .*

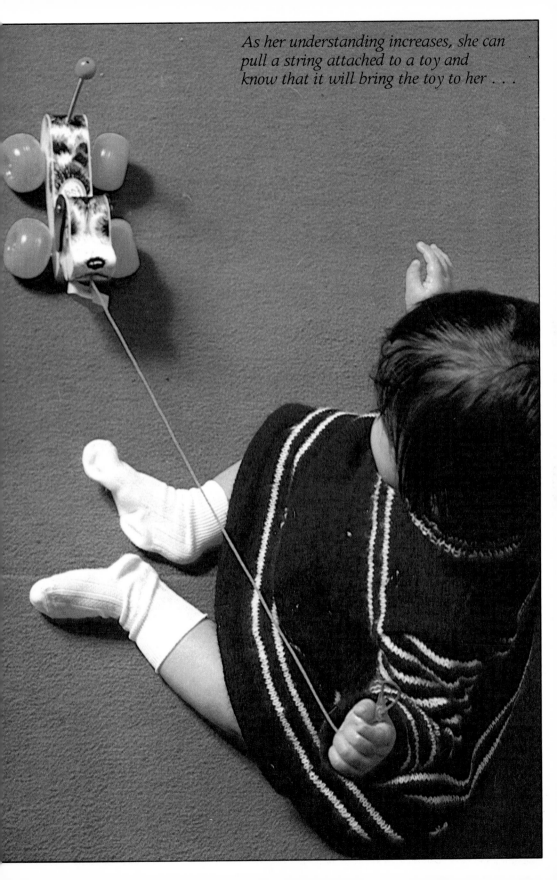

*As her understanding increases, she can pull a string attached to a toy and know that it will bring the toy to her . . .*

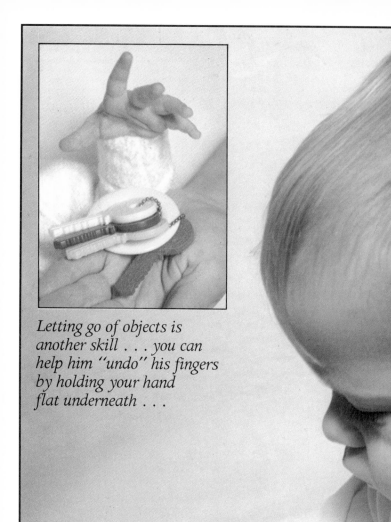

*Letting go of objects is another skill . . . you can help him "undo" his fingers by holding your hand flat underneath . . .*

*. . . eventually his control of his hands will be so fine that he can pick things up with his thumb and forefinger alone. By his first birthday he may well be able to retrieve the tiniest raisin or the smallest crumb . . .*

While your baby is learning to use different parts of his arms separately he is also learning to separate out the various sections of his hands. At six months he grasps objects with his whole hand and picks things up by using his cupped hand as a scoop. Large objects are tackled by using both hands together as if they were a pair of tongs. During the seventh and eighth months he begins to make use of his fingers and thumbs for grasping and for holding on to objects; by nine months he will probably have such fine control over his separate fingers that he can use an index finger to point or to poke.

*Opposing thumbs and learning to release objects*

During the last three months of the first year, the baby's new ability to use different parts of his hands separately from each other leads to the gradual development of a more mature grasp and grip. Instead of trying to pick up small objects by using his whole hand adjusted to a small cup or scoop, the baby learns to approach them with his forefinger and thumb using a pincer grip. This change may not seem to make much difference to his daily life and play, but it is interesting to realize that it is the ability of human beings to "oppose" their fingers and thumbs for pincer gripping which makes them so much more dexterous than other mammals. By the end of the year your baby will probably be capable of delicately retrieving the smallest crumb using this grip.

Simultaneously with acquiring these new and delicate finger abilities the baby also tackles the difficult problem of learning to let go of things he is grasping. At nine months most babies understand the idea of letting go. If you hold out your hand and say "give it to me," he will hold the toy out to you, clearly realizing that you want him to release it. But the actual process of uncurling his fingers in order to release what he is grasping is still very difficult for him. If he sits there holding out the toy but with his fingers still curled around it, don't assume he is teasing you. He probably does not yet know how to proceed. Releasing objects is no problem to the baby if he happens to be playing at a table. When he feels his hand and the object on a flat surface, he can relax his fingers easily.

Most babies will have discovered how to uncurl their fingers by the tenth or eleventh month. Once he has discovered how to let go of things the baby will practice at every opportunity. You may face weeks of toys being dropped from his crib; food being dropped from the high chair, washcloths and soap flopping over the edge of the bath and trails of shopping left behind his stroller.

*Helping your baby to use his hands*

Until he becomes mobile at around nine months, a baby has to rely on you to bring the world to him. He cannot go and get things for himself so he has to wait for you to bring things to him. Bring him plenty. Even while he is too young to *do* anything much with objects, he is ready to learn about them. If you provide him only with rattles, rings and woolly balls, while keeping all those interesting household objects out of range, you deprive him of endless fun and learning.

As he gets more competent with his hands, you can really help him by encouraging him to use his skills all the time. You can let him have a spoon at mealtimes and a washcloth at bathtime. You can show him how to pull off his socks and turn the pages of his board-books. He can put the potatoes in the vegetable rack as well as blocks in a box; bang the piano as well as his tambourine and throw a ball for the dog when you do. All these things, and thousands more, are new experiences for a baby. They are fun and learning and what is more they mean that he will feel properly involved with you and the things that you do. He does not really want to be kept separate from the rest of the household, with special toys and special games that are only for him. He wants to join in, and the more you can slow your pace down to his and put up with his messes, the faster and more happily he will learn.

**Give your baby plenty of objects to explore.** At six months your baby will not do more with a plaything than grasp, suck and inspect it. But he is learning about the objects you give him even though he is not using them. Let him handle as wide a range of objects as possible (see p. 183) but give them to him one at a time. A single toy takes up his whole attention. He literally cannot think about two things at the same time, even if they are two identical things like two little red blocks. If he is holding one of these in his left hand and you offer him another, he will not take it with his free right hand and hold them both. His attention will turn to the new block and the one he was holding will simply drop out of his hand and mind.

**Encourage interest in touching and stroking** as it develops in the seventh month. Let him play on grass, carpet, matting, wooden floors; let him discover with his hands the fascinating differences. Now that he need not grab and mouth everything he touches, you can bring him the pet rabbit to stroke and hold him up to pat the window, too.

**Give the baby more complicated objects** as he begins to use his fingers and thumbs separately. In the seventh and eighth month he will practice threading separate fingers through rings and handles; poking his index finger into indentations and using it to trace out the squiggly patterns of well-designed toys. Once he uses his hands in this way he will also be able to cope with two things at the same time. Now if you give him two rattles or two blocks, for example, he will probably hold one in each hand, which is good practice for him. He will still treat the two toys separately, though. It has not yet occurred to him that he could make each more interesting by combining the two. It will be a few weeks yet before he bangs those two rattles together to increase their noise.

**Give your baby lots of opportunities to watch adults using their hands.** The baby learns the properties of many different objects by handling them. He will learn how to use some of them by fortunate chance: his rattles sound when his arm waves so he learns to wave the arm deliberately to make the sound. But he also learns how to use objects by watching you. By late in the eighth month he may be ready to copy actual demonstrations. If you now give him a thick stumpy crayon and a piece of paper, for example, and then take a similar crayon yourself and scribble on the paper with it, he will try to do the same. He may not manage to make a mark, but his actions will imitate yours. Next time he gets a crayon he will try again, so beware of scribbles on walls.

Toys on strings also often produce a miracle of understanding for the baby. At seven months, if you give him the string attached to a toy car he will probably pull it more or less by mistake. Even when the car moves toward him he will show no understanding of what he has done. But only six weeks later his face will light up with amazement, and he will pull that car toward him as often as you are prepared to move it away from him again.

His willingness to copy what you do will increase steadily from now on. You can use it both for his benefit and for your own. If you will show him how to unscrew lids, thread rings on a rod, push toy cars and pour water, he will try to copy you. You will be giving him good ideas for things to try to do and he will be trying to do them. Because he is given the ideas and because he tries, his manual development will proceed as fast as it can.

As his manual skills increase, you can show him how to do things that will help you, like feeding himself, washing his own hands and pulling off his clothes. If you start him off on self-care at this early stage of learning-by-imitation, your baby will see no difference between these "tasks" and "play" with toys. You may avoid the usual battles that take place over teaching three-year-olds to wash their own faces when they would rather play.

**Help the baby to learn to release objects** by making sure that most of his play with small toys takes place at a table or other firm surface; by helping him to release things into your flat hand; and by providing toys he can practice on when he has finally got the idea at around ten months.

The phase when the baby throws everything out of his crib or stroller can be made educational for him as well as less tiresome for you if his small toys are fastened on with pieces of wool. He will throw them out and then discover, with joy, that he can fish them up again by pulling the wool. Don't use string or tape for this in case he gets himself entangled in it. Knitting wool is safe because it breaks well before strangling-point, but watch out for acrylics and other synthetics which might not. Just make sure that anything used will break under minimal pressure.

Toward the end of the year just dropping things will give way to a deliberate throwing and to an equally deliberate placing of objects. The baby needs a light ball to throw and he needs collections of blocks or other small toys which he can practice putting into a container and emptying out again.

# Listening and talking

This half year is crucial to babies' language development despite the fact that many will not produce a single recognizable word before their birthday. Babies learn language long before they can speak it. First they must listen to other people's words and learn to understand what they mean. Only then will they be able to produce meaningful words of their own.

The importance of a baby's listening and understanding is often underestimated because we tend to overestimate the importance of babies' own word production and try to force babies to produce word-sounds by imitation. But just saying a word or two is not useful language; we are trying to bring up a person, not a parrot. So try not to confine your interest to listening for sounds which sound like words, saying words for your baby to imitate, and identifying his or her first real words. Concentrate instead on giving him lots of talk to listen to; plenty of opportunities for grasping the meaning of the words he hears and an immediate and pleasant social response to the sounds he makes.

*Why babies learn to speak*

Most people assume that babies learn to speak because they must communicate in order to get what they want or need. The facts do not support this simple idea. Babies manage to communicate with their caretakers for the whole of their first year without using words. So why should they suddenly feel a need for them? When they do produce some words they are very seldom words which have anything to do with a baby's needs. He will not first learn to say "cookie" or "come" or "up," he will learn instead the name-labels of people or things which are emotionally important or pleasurably exciting to him.

Pleasant emotions may be the key to the development of speech. Babies are born with a built-in interest in listening to human voices and a built-in tendency to produce babbling sounds of their own (see p. 173). During the first six months, the baby comes to associate your gentle speech sounds with pleasure and with having his needs fulfilled. When he babbles, he hears his own noises as similar to your voice and so those sounds are associated with pleasure too. His own sounds make him feel pleased and happy because of their association with your sounds and you, so the baby is motivated to go on making more and more sounds, to elaborate his babbling into the more complicated form we call "jargon" (see p. 255) and eventually to develop actual speech (see p. 369).

This is only a theory, of course, but it is a theory which fits many observable facts. Deaf babies, for example, babble normally until around the middle of the first year (see p. 173) but instead of increasing in amount and elaboration, their sound making then dies away. It may well be that they stop making sounds because they are not receiving the affectionate feedback which motivates normal babies to go on. There are less extreme examples which support this theory too. One little girl who was born partially deaf also failed to develop sounds beyond the babbling stage. Examination later showed that her hearing loss was sufficient to cut her off from gentle speech sounds but was not great enough to cut out loud, angry talk or the sounds of her own crying. She could hear when her parents were cross with her or when she herself was miserable, but she could not hear when they were affectionate or she herself was happy. As soon as a hearing-aid restored the gentle sounds to her she developed normal speech.

If you listen to the development of your own baby you may well feel that his behavior also fits this theory. Throughout this half year he will do all his talking, whether it is to an adult or to himself, when he is pleased and excited or at least happy and content. When he is cross and unhappy he will not talk; he will cry. Whenever you hear him carrying on a "conversation" with himself, making a sound, pausing as if for an answer and then speaking again, you will find that his noises sound like pleasant, friendly or joyful speech, but never like cross or irritable speech. When the time finally comes for your baby to produce real words they too will be in a pleasant context. If "ball" is to be his first word it will not be spoken in angry demand but in pleased comment. If your name is his first word, he will not use it first as a reproving whine but as a delighted greeting.

*The development of speech sounds*

In the middle of this first year most babies will carry on long babble conversations with an adult, making a sound, pausing while the other person replies and then answering back again. The baby will continue for as long as you will go on looking and speaking directly to him. He cannot yet talk to you if he cannot see you or even respond vocally if you call across the room.

Most of the sounds are still single syllable cooing noises (see p. 173). He says 'Paaa" and "Maaaa" and 'Boooo." He intersperses them with laughter and gurgles and hiccups of delight. His conversations are all joy. If he is cross he will not talk; conversely, if he will talk to you he is not miserable.

During the seventh month the baby becomes increasingly on the alert for speech sounds. He begins to search the room with his eyes if you call him when you are out of sight. He will look for the source of the voice on the radio, too, ready to respond with conversation as soon as he can discover who is talking.

Toward the end of the seventh month you will hear elaborations of his own sounds. The first change is that he turns his cooing noises into two syllable "words" by repeating them. He says "Ala" and "Amam," "Mumum" and "Booboo." Gradually these "words" become more separate from each other, with less musical cooing between them. Once this happens, usually by the end of the seventh month, there are new sounds on the way. This batch is more exclamatory and less dove-like: he says "Imi!," "Aja!," "Ippi". . . . These new two syllable "words" seem to make the baby increasingly excited by his own sound making. Once they are in his repertoire, he will probably wake you each morning with a dawn chorus of delighted talk in which he behaves exactly as if you were in the room and talking to him. He will exclaim, pause, speak again, pause and then say some more, and he will go on for minutes at a time, entertaining himself until you choose to go and join in the conversation with him.

During the eighth month most babies begin to take an interest in adult conversation, even when it is not directly aimed at them. If your baby happens to be sitting between you as you talk over his head, that head will turn from one of you to the other as each speaks. He behaves as if your conversation were a tennis match he was closely following. But the talking game is too good for the baby to let himself be left out for long. Soon he learns to shout for attention. It is not a yell that he produces or a squeal or a cry: it is a definite and intentional shout. This is often the very first time that the baby uses a speech sound with a specific communicative purpose in mind.

*At 8 to 9 months the baby can take an active interest in conversation even when it is not addressed to her. But she will not let you leave her as passive audience for long: within the month she will learn to shout for your attention.*

Soon after the shout, many babies learn to sing. Of course the song is not elaborate: four notes up or down a scale is about average. But it is quite definitely musical and usually set off by your singing, by music on the radio or "theme songs" on television.

The ninth month usually produces exciting speech developments which all happen at once. The baby's forms of speech suddenly become much more elaborate, with long drawn out series of syllables being produced such as "Loo-loo-loo-loo." At the same time he begins to inflect and change the emphasis of his sounds, so that listening parents hear varied sounds suggesting questions, exclamations and even jokes among the babble. Then the forms of speech change yet again. This time the baby does not just add more and more of the same syllables to what he says; instead he combines all the syllables that he knows into long complicated "sentences" such as: "Ah-dee-dah-boo-maa." Once this kind of combination, which is technically called "jargoning," is heard, the baby is on the verge of producing real words.

For another month or so you may not be able to identify any words, but the baby's speech sounds become so clearly inflected, so varied and so expressive that he sounds exactly as if he were speaking, fluently but in a foreign language. The jargon sounds so realistic that sometimes, if your mind is on something else when he starts to talk, you may find yourself saying "What did you say, darling?," forgetting for the moment that he cannot really have "said" anything!

Most babies produce their first "real" word during the tenth or eleventh month. We cannot be exact, because first words are surprisingly difficult to identify. "Mommy" is a good example. When a seven-month-old baby says "Mom," few parents will be fooled into thinking it is a real word because they do not expect a seven-month-old baby to talk. But when that same baby makes the same sound at ten months, it is easy to be fooled. You are expecting words now so you tend to find them among all that babble, and to forget that the actual noises you are now considering for word-status are sounds he has been making for months.

*Identifying first words*

There is no particular point in trying hard to identify your baby's first words. It does not matter whether he uses any or not at this stage. His expressive, fluent, varied jargon is an absolute assurance that he is going to speak when he is ready.

But the stages the baby goes through in getting to words are interesting developments and if you find them so you will help the baby's language development along. Interest will make you listen carefully to what he says. Listening carefully will probably make you answer him with more adult talk. Being listened and replied to is what he most needs for his speech development.

In the tenth or eleventh month the baby is likely to get the idea of *using* a particular sound to refer to a particular object, but he may still take a while to "decide" *what* sound to use as a name for the object he has chosen. One child, for example, used the word "bon-bon" when asking for her ball. Later she used the word "dan" about the same ball. On each occasion it was clear that she meant that ball and did not mean anything else, but she behaved as if all that mattered was to use a word – any old word would do. After a week or two of this kind of confusion, the baby moves on a stage and starts to use one sound, and only one sound, to refer to one and only one object. But the sound he uses may still not be a "word" in the adult sense. It may be an "own-word," a sound that the baby has invented, and attached to a particular thing or a particular person. But even if the "own-word" has not the slightest similarity to the "proper" one, it should be counted as a word *if you know what he means by it.* After all, the whole point of speech is communication between people. If you know that your child means "bus" when he says "gig," then he is talking to you.

*How babies learn their early words*

Babies of eight to twelve months are highly imitative. As well as imitating actions they will often imitate word sounds. Because of this, many parents spend a great deal of time during these months holding objects up in front of their babies and saying "Say shoe; shoe; say shoe, darling," and so on. This kind of thing probably does not do babies any harm. They may enjoy the long "conversations" it gives them and they may enjoy the imitating game for its own sake. But they will not learn to talk that way. As we said at the beginning of the section (see p. 252), learning to talk is not a matter of learning to imitate sounds for their own sake.

A baby hears a word like "shoes" over and over again in daily life as the one constant sound in a large variety of statements. In one day you may say to him "Where are your shoes?"; "Oh, what dirty shoes!" "Let's take your shoes off"; "I'll put your shoes on"; "Look what nice shoes." That word "shoes" is the one sound which occurs in all those sentences and it is always associated with those things that go on his feet. Over days and weeks he will come to associate the sound with the shoes. When he has made the association "shoes" = what are put on his feet, he will know what the word means.

Your baby will probably learn the meanings of dozens of words before he actually says more than one or two. He will first use words which mean something joyful or exciting to him. Perhaps he has in fact understood that word "shoe" for several weeks but has never said it. When you take him to a shoe store and buy him a pair of bright red slippers, his pride in them as they glow on his feet may be what stimulates him at last to say "SHOES!" He may have known that the recurring word "Toby" referred to the family dog; a sudden rush of affection for him, as the dog plonks himself down beside him, may stimulate the first use of his name.

First words come slowly but understanding of words goes on apace. If your baby has only used a word or two by his first birthday, don't assume that he is not learning language. He is listening and learning to understand.

*Helping your baby to listen and to talk*

Lots of loving talk is the best overall help that you can give to your baby's language development, but there is talk which is positively useful and talk which is less useful:

**Talk directly to your baby.** A baby cannot pay attention and listen carefully to general conversation. If he is in a room with his whole family and everybody is talking, he will be lost in a sea of sound. You say something and he looks at you, only to find that your face is turned away to his brother. Brother replies, sister interrupts with a half-finished sentence that ends in an expressive shrug, and meanwhile somebody else has started a side conversation and the television has been switched on. Third or fourth children, especially in families where the children are born close together, are often actually delayed in their language development because they get so little opportunity for uninterrupted one-to-one conversation with adults. Even if you are coping with a baby, a toddler and a four-year-old who never stops asking "Why?" try to find at least some times when you can talk to the baby alone.

Don't expect him to learn as much language from strangers, or from a succession of caretakers, as he will from you and other people who are special to him. The baby learns the meanings of words by hearing them over and over again in different sentences and with varying tones of voice, facial expressions and body language from the speaker. The more familiar he is with the person who is talking, the more likely he is to understand. Even at the toddler stage (see p. 370) he may be quite unable to understand a stranger's *words* because the accompanying expressions and tones of voice are strange to him.

**Make sure that you use the key label-words when you talk.** The baby is going to single out label-words which continually recur in different sentences, like that label-word "shoes." So when the two of you are hunting under the bed, make sure that you say "Oh, where are your shoes?" rather than "Oh, where are they?" The child's own name is a vital label for him to learn. He will not think of himself as "me" or "I"; indeed as we shall see (see p. 434), English grammar makes this kind of word extremely difficult for a child to learn because the correct word depends on who is speaking. I am "me" to myself, but I am "you" to you. So at this stage, you use his name-label, too. Don't feel embarrassed because it is "baby talk." "Where's a cookie for John?" you can say as you rummage in the cookie jar. It will mean much more to him than "Where's one for you?"

**Talk to the baby about things which are physically present** so that he can *see* what you are talking about and make an immediate connection between the object and the recurring key word. "Wasn't it funny when that cat we saw ran up the tree?" will not mean nearly as much to him as "Look at that cat. Do you see her? The cat is going to run up that tree. There! A cat in a tree. . . ."

**Use picture books in the same way.** Big clear illustrations of babies and older people doing familiar things will entrance him: "look, the daddy's doing the washing up . . . can you see the mugs . . .?"

**Talk about things which interest your baby.** Not all your conversation can be about immediately visible things, but a long story about his sister's day at school will mean much less than the story of the squirrel he saw in the park that evening. Even if he does not understand everything you say, he will pick up the subject matter and, perhaps, the labels for the things he learned while they were visible, like "squirrel" or "nut."

**Overact. Use lots of gestures and expressions.** You can make your meaning much clearer to the baby if you point to the things you are talking about, indicate the thing you want him to crawl over and get, and generally "ham" your message a bit. Babies with vocal, outgoing parents often learn to understand and use exclamations first of all because they hear them used over and over again and with exaggerated inflections and infectious excitement: "Oh dear!" you may say when he falls down and "Up you come!" as you lift him from his crib.

**Try to understand your baby's words or invented words.** You will help to motivate him toward ever-increasing efforts at speech if you can make it clear to him, by your reaction to his sounds, that you care what he says; that it matters to your understanding whether he uses the right word or not; and that you will try to understand any attempt at communication that he does make. Of course this is a subtle message to try to convey to a ten- or eleven-month baby, but the general idea will get across to him if he sees you taking trouble. For example, if he makes a sound and gestures toward something when he is sitting in his high chair, you might look to where he is pointing, and list for him all the things that you can see which he might have meant. If you hit the right one his pleasure as he repeats his "own-word" will be immense.

If you see him crawling around looking for something, using a nonsense-word questioningly, join the hunt for the nameless object. Once again, when it is found, the baby's pleasure in your understanding will repay the trouble you have taken.

**Help your baby to use those few words in obviously useful situations.** If you are playing together and you can both see where the ball has rolled to, ask him to get it for you. When he crawls back with it you can confirm that he understood you correctly by thanking him, using the word again: "Good boy, you've brought your ball." If you then play ball with him the whole transaction of words and actions will have an obvious and pleasurable point for him, and the word will probably stay in his memory.

**Don't correct or pretend not to understand "own-words."** Correcting him, or trying to make him say the word again "properly," will only bore the baby. He does not want to say the same thing again better, he wants to say something else now. Your corrections will not have any effect anyway because, as we have seen, he is not imitating language but developing it. His "own-word" will evolve into something more correct in its own good time but not at your command. If you pretend not to understand the baby unless he says something "properly," you are cheating him. He has communicated with you, made you understand his meaning. He has therefore used a piece of language. If you refuse to acknowledge it, you spoil the flow of his language development. He cannot instantly produce the "correct" word, because that word has not evolved for him yet. His "own-word" is the best that he has to offer. Remember, too, that it is pleasure, affection and excitement that motivate early speech. Refusing to hand him his bottle until he says "milk" instead of "bah-boo" will make him frustrated and cross. You are more likely to get tears than words.

# Playing and learning

This is a very physical half-year. During it babies are learning to sit up alone, to get across the room on their own and to get up on their own two legs (see p. 230). Achieving these things takes enormous physical effort, and each has to be practiced endlessly before the baby is ready to pass on to the next. Luckily for children's continuing development, all babies have a tremendous innate drive to succeed. A baby who can crawl, will crawl. Nothing but actual confinement will prevent it. A baby who can pull up to standing position will do so and the persistence with which he will go on trying to stand alone, despite endless wobbling, falling and getting up again, is remarkable. We adults would send for a wheelchair after two days of it but the drive in your baby ensures that he will press on.

These new physical achievements earn babies a large new measure of independence. They no longer have to rely on adults to bring them bits of the world to handle and explore. They can go and find things for themselves. They need no longer accept passively whatever is offered to them but can begin to put their own ideas about what they want to do into action, and decide for themselves what they will play with.

Yet along with this new physical independence goes an increasing emotional dependence. Your baby wants and needs constant emotional support and encouragement as he learns the difficult lessons of growing up, through play.

*Safe physical freedom*

Sitting, crawling and standing are occupations in themselves for a baby. At this stage he is just as keen to practice crawling for its own sake as he is to crawl so as to get to somewhere else.

So the main thing he needs for his play is a floor and freedom to use it. If the household has not yet set up a playspace for him, it will need to now. He must have some area of floor which is suitable and acceptable for his constant use. The ideal floor is large, uncluttered (especially by any delicate, breakable or tippable furniture), reasonably soft and warm, easily cleaned and near to wherever you are likely to spend most of your time.

A few families will be lucky enough to have such a floor, perhaps in an already established playroom, perhaps in the family living room or even perhaps in a large open kitchen. Others will have to compromise and invent.

A hard, cold, stone or tiled floor can be partly covered with carpet tiles or even with cheap matting, which is hard on knees but not bad for heads.

A dining room opening out of the kitchen can often be made suitable for the baby, without losing its basic use, if the door between the two rooms is left open with a stair gate fixed across. This gives the baby a view of his mother without giving him access to a small and dangerous kitchen. With thought, a large kitchen can itself be made safe. Dangerous knives, cleaning fluids, etc., can live on wall racks or high shelves; electric appliances can be guarded and most cooking can be confined to the back burners.

If living space is very short, a corridor or hall is often usable by the baby if stairs are properly gated. And any kind of garden, porch or yard can be made safe for him with a little do-it-yourself work devoted to safety precautions.

If the baby has suitable floorspace close to you, he will occupy himself on it and around you for a great deal of his waking time. It is worth putting thought and effort into this space both because it will be basic to your lives together for many months and because some obvious-seeming solutions will not work well for any of you.

A special playroom in some out-of-the-way part of the house will not work, however beautiful it is. If you make him play there, he will be extremely lonely and bored, as well as at risk, without your constant presence. You will find that you either abandon it and let him play in the (unprepared) kitchen or that you take all your jobs from their natural places in order to do them companionably in the playroom. On the other hand he should not be expected to play in a crowded family living room unless it has been carefully adapted for him. He will inevitably damage and break things like books, records, ornaments and plants, and he will make life quite impossible for any older child who shares his space. A playpen in the living room is not the answer. Even a baby who willingly goes into it cannot learn all that he should if he is constantly confined. But imaginative use of everyday barriers may enable you to give the baby safe freedom without impinging on anybody else.

Of course the baby needs other kinds of play too, but these can be saved for times when you can pay him your full attention, protect him from dangers and keep other people's possessions from his clutches. Changes of scene and associated changes of activity are important. They broaden the play possibilities which are available to the baby, and stop him from getting bored. Changes can range from a simple move to another room, to an elaborate expedition. For example, a romp on a double bed is a marvelous game for a baby of this age. Play with toys on the carpeted floor of the living room makes a welcome change from the hard floor of the kitchen. Trips outdoors combining stroller riding with, perhaps, a crawl on the nearest available grass, are vital. The more you can take him out with you the better. A 20-minute trip which seems boring to you is full of new experiences for him.

*Playthings*     Actual toys are less important to babies during this age period than freedom to get moving and eventually to start exploring. Many of the playthings suggested for younger babies (see p. 183) will still please this age-group and they will seem different to them too, once they can sit up alone to manipulate them and crawl across the floor to find them. But a few new things will give your baby particular pleasure because they are especially appropriate to this particular stage of development.

Once he can crawl, he will much enjoy things that roll along, whether they are actual balls or wheeled toys. He will crawl after them, learn to push them and then give chase. Choose large objects and be sure that wooden toys have no sharp or protruding bits.

Once he learns voluntarily to let go of objects, two kinds of "game" become possible. He will enjoy actually throwing things.

*Company for both . . . space for each . . .*

*Let her join in your life . . .*
*Don't keep your cooking . . .*

*. . . your unwrapping*

*. . . your shopping*

*. . . and your sorting out*

*. . . all to yourself.*
*Your work can be*
*her play.*

He can have small cushions, beanbags, or balloons which are not blown hard enough to pop. He will also begin to enjoy putting things into containers and emptying them out again. Small blocks and a box or oranges and a paper bag are ideal.

As he learns about cause and effect and discovers his own power over objects, he will begin to enjoy simple musical instruments such as a drum, tambourine, maracas and xylophone. He will enjoy the noise itself (even if you do not) and he will revel in the realization that it was his own action that produced the sound and that he can produce it again whenever he pleases.

He will feel the same joyous sense of power if he is given toys which do something when a string is pulled or a lever is pushed, such as a jointed "dancing man" or a duck that quacks when he pushes it.

*Organizing toys*   The baby will not remember what toys he owns during these months except that he will notice if special things (like his "cuddly") are missing. If you keep toys put away out of sight, they will be out of mind too. You cannot leave it to him to go searching for what is not immediately available. On the other hand, if everything he owns is permanently strewn on "his" floor, he will get bored with all his toys just because he has seen them all so often. Some toys actually age without ever being used because the baby comes to regard them as totally familiar.

At this stage a very large shallow basket – such as the old-fashioned laundry basket – or a large smooth plastic tray, provides a good toy carry-all. If everything lives in there, and it is kept in a corner of "his" floor, the baby will quickly learn where to go when he wants something, and you will be able to do a quick clean up in between play sessions.

A baby who cannot yet crawl needs to be given a few toys at a time as he sits in his chair, his stroller or on the floor. Once he is mobile he can help himself from a small selection. When he is first put down on the floor, after breakfast or after a nap, get out a small number of toys for him, and just put them on the floor. Then, when he begins to get bored, pick those toys up and get him out a new batch, encouraging him to add to them from the carry-all.

Keep a few items on a high shelf or in a cupboard, to be produced occasionally. They might be toys that need close supervision, or toys that make so much noise you cannot stand them all the time. Either way they will keep their play value for longer by being produced only on special occasions.

Keep a box or basket into which you put things the baby might like as you come across them. Each shopping trip will produce some. Christmas will bring bright papers and labels and ribbons. Clearing out a kitchen cupboard might produce a plastic pot with a lid that can be filled with something rattly or a plastic scoop you don't want any more: you might save a cardboard box or plastic cup or an empty squeeze bottle he will enjoy in the bath. If you are clever about this, you will always have a "new toy" for the baby, ready to be produced on a grumbly day or when the weather keeps him in or a visitor comes and takes your attention from him. No "toy" will do *instead* of you, but a new one might allow you a few minutes' conversation!

## Including your baby in your "play"

Almost mobile, imitative and devoted, your eight- to nine-month baby will often prefer your "toys" and "games" to anything meant for him.

Watching and sharing adult activities help babies learn about the world, its objects and people. But unless you happen to farm, cook or breed dogs for a living, most of your important activities will probably be ones he cannot share. He cannot come with you to most office-based jobs and even if you do take him with you most office activities will be incomprehensible and therefore boring to him. Even your word processor will not interest him for long.

The activities which really will interest and involve him are domestic ones and it is because these are so peculiarly suited to entertaining and companioning babies and toddlers that people sometimes lump childcare and housekeeping together as if they were the same activity. They are not the same at all, of course. *Efficient* housekeeping means getting boring chores done as quickly as possible; companioning a child means slowing the pace of everything you do so that there is space and time for him.

Cooking will delight the baby, who will see it as "messy" or "water" play. It is easiest to work safely if he sits in his high chair and is handed odds and ends to mix, pummel and taste.

Housework can seem like a pleasant play all over the house if the baby is bounced on the bed that is being made, plays peek-a-boo around the furniture and has a duster to wave. Watch out for cleaning chemicals, though. Almost all will be dangerous if he tries to drink them, while sprays are dangerous to his eyes as well.

Gardening is also a good game, especially if there is earth he can scrabble in and grass to crawl on. Once again there may be danger from sharp implements or chemicals; an apron or coat with capacious pockets to secrete them in may be a good idea.

Laundry and ironing are neither much fun nor safe "games" for the baby. They are probably best saved for nap-time.

Shopping, whether it involves a saunter to a shop nearby for two items or a major supermarket expedition, can be a treat. He will enjoy riding in a cart, helping himself to things off the shelves, opening the packages and sampling the contents. . . . Accept the inevitable and let him help himself to something innocuous, like a small box of raisins, right at the beginning. Getting them open and eating a couple will distract him from destroying every shelf display and opening every purchase!

Unpacking shopping is almost the best game of all. If somebody deftly removes the eggs, tomatoes and any other squashy or dangerous purchases, he will unpack the cans and the oranges and roll them all over the floor. . . .

If you go out to work, leaving your baby at home with a caretaker, don't feel that it is wrong to expect her to replace you domestically because the baby ought to have her full-time attention. Some concentrated play with an adult *is* important, and you will want to be sure that your replacement would always give the baby priority if he especially needed a whole afternoon's cuddling or the two of them fancied the sunshine in the park. But babies find adults who do *nothing* but watch them play, and try to join in, both boring and intrusive. Your baby will enjoy his days more if he spends them in ordinarily busy company (see p. 274).

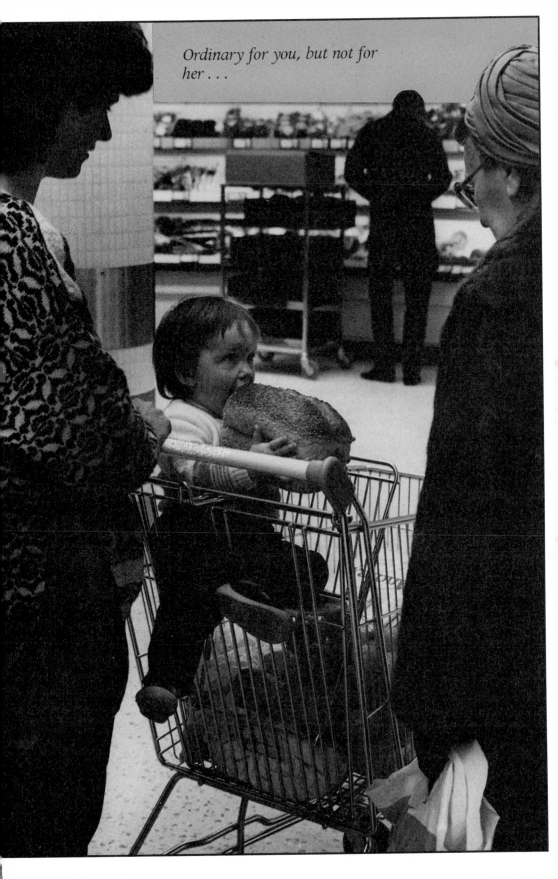

Ordinary for you, but not for her . . .

# *Enjoying your mobile baby*

Newly mobile babies are not always easy to live with. Being able to get around a room enormously increases their ability to get themselves into danger or to break and destroy things; yet the mobility does not bring even the smallest amount of extra commonsense with it. You have to watch your baby, every minute that he is awake. You have to prevent what you cannot allow as well as helping with the activities you approve of, and somehow you have to make space for the baby to do baby things while you preserve the space that rightly belongs to other members of the family. Many mothers find this the most difficult of all stages in child-rearing. Anything that you can do to make daily life easier for yourselves will be worthwhile. After all you are aiming to enjoy these months, not merely to survive them.

*Making life easier for all of you*
Try to arrange the easiest possible physical circumstances for yourselves and the baby. Even if it takes a whole weekend of hard work to reorganize the living room so that breakables and books are out of reach, it will be worth it. If you don't you will spend literally *hours* taking things away from the baby and the baby away from things, day after day.

Where one particular issue continually makes trouble between you, take action to make it totally impossible for the baby. If, for example, he is always escaping from you and trying to climb the stairs, put up a stair gate and leave it there permanently. The danger and the trouble are both removed together. If he insists on messing around with the magazine rack, remove it out of reach. Once it has gone it cannot cause trouble. Sometimes this kind of action takes a bit of thought. If trouble arises over something like opening the refrigerator door, you may have to buy and install a childproof catch. It is a bore for you but better than endless rows.

**Arrange basic safety precautions** (Ref/ACCIDENTS). Your nerves will stay in better shape if you know he cannot fall downstairs, electrocute or burn himself.

**Be positive with your baby.** Try to provide a permitted equivalent to every action you have to forbid. If he may not empty out that drawer, which may he empty? The answer "none" is bound to lead to trouble once he has got the drawer-emptying idea; the answer "this one" will satisfy you both.

**Use the distractibility of this age-group.** If he insists on playing with the wastepaper basket, remove it out of sight and give him something else. He will have forgotten in two minutes. If you can't move the object, move the baby. Five minutes in another room and he will have forgotten any but the most entrancing games.

**Put fun for everybody before pride in your home.** If you try to sweep every crumb and tidy each mess *as it occurs* you will go mad. Decide when you really want the place cleaned up (whether that is twice a day or once a week . . .); do it all in one almighty blitz and then don't worry until the next blitz is due.

However well you get yourself organized, life will not always run smoothly. You will have days when everything the baby does seems irritating. You will get angry. Don't be too upset if you find you have yelled at him. It is often easier for a baby or small child to cope with a parent who loses his or her temper from time to time than with one who bottles the irritation up and becomes silent and withdrawn. Your baby needs your cheerful companionship. If you withhold it from him he will be bewildered and lonely. He cannot flourish in an emotional vacuum. If you yell at him he will certainly be frightened but at least it will be quickly over. With your pent-up feelings relieved he will be able to see that you are ready to talk and to play again.

But try to remember that he will not have the least idea *why* you yelled and that your anger will therefore seem to strike out of the blue, like a thunderbolt. He has no way of knowing that just one more minor disaster was a "last straw" for you. He knows very little of your feelings which are not yet his concern. If you actually punish him physically, shaking him, smacking him or dumping him in his crib, he will be as amazed and horrified as you would be if the family dog suddenly turned on you and took a chunk out of your leg. Whatever you do to him in anger, he will not understand *why* and he therefore cannot learn anything from punishment.

Suppose he breaks an ashtray. You will probably justify your anger by saying that you have told him many times not to touch it and anyway he should have been more careful. But think a minute. He touched it because his vital curiosity told him to examine it and his memory and understanding are not yet good enough to tell him it was forbidden. He broke it because his manual dexterity is not yet adequate for handling delicate things gently. So was the accident really his *fault*? If the ashtray was really valuable, what was it doing left within his reach? He is being punished for being what he is. A baby.

Suppose he tips food out of his dish on to the freshly-washed floor. In fury you say that "he ought to know better." But ought he? A few minutes earlier you helped him to tip blocks out on the floor. Is he supposed to share your ideas about what is a "toy" and what is not? As to the clean floor, he probably watched you sloshing bubbly water over it. Is he supposed to understand that soapy water cleans things, but gravy dirties them? Once again you are being angry with him for being the age he is and for behaving as people in his age bracket are meant to behave.

Somehow, as parents, you have to find ways of staying on the same side as your baby, making the most of the good bits of each day and laughing at the misfortunes. An absolute determination to enjoy yourselves is what makes this possible. Find pleasure in being clever enough to guide him without his noticing, distract him before there is a clash and save him before there is an accident. Teach yourselves to look at life from his point of view as well as your own. Be intent, above all, on loving him and enjoying his passionate love for you. The last thing he wants is to displease you. You are his gods. But it will be a long time yet before he can understand what *does* please you. Your pleasures are not the same as his. You don't *like* gravy on the floor. . . .

# Thinking about the stressful times

Being a loving parent is tough emotional work as well as a hard practical job. The closer you have become to your baby during his first and most completely dependent year, the more you are going to mind when things don't go quite right for him. Of course you are upset whenever he is ill or unhappy, but there's more to it than that: you tend to feel guilty about anything you have done or have allowed to happen that makes him feel unhappy. Guilt is probably the least useful of the emotions commonly aroused by parenting. If you can keep it at bay, all of you will be happier.

Being parents does not make you all-powerful. Try as you may, sacrifice yourselves as you will, your power to force the outside world to give your child everything you want him to have is strictly limited. You long for the children next door to welcome him, for the scary thunder to hold off, for invading viruses to clear, for the bus to get you to his caregiver's house before he notices that you are late, but you cannot make those things happen. You can only trust in his ability to cope and find ways to help him do so.

## Going to the hospital

Coping with a young child who is badly hurt or seriously ill is definitely the down-side of parenting. If it is an accident that brings him to the hospital, you will probably feel desperately guilty, whether or not the incident was actually caused by anybody's negligence. If he is in the hospital because of illness, or even elective surgery, you are likely to feel frustrated and angry at your own inability to save him from discomfort, pain and fear. And if the matter is potentially critical, there will be your own unmentionable fear to deal with as well. The willingness of many parents to "leave him to the experts" or "keep out of everybody's way" probably springs from an entirely understandable desire to run away and hide until the whole thing is over and the child can be back home again.

But there are a few times when parents owe small children absolute priority and this is one of them. Your child may need hospital care for his scalded skin, his dehydration or his ear operation, but he also needs the personal kinds of care which nobody but you can give him (Ref/HOSPITAL). It is strange places and happenings combined with separation from you that will spell emotional disaster.

**If you wonder whether he can manage without you** ask yourself whether you would leave him in a camp while you went away overnight. If that idea strikes you as horrific or absurd, don't leave him in a hospital ward.

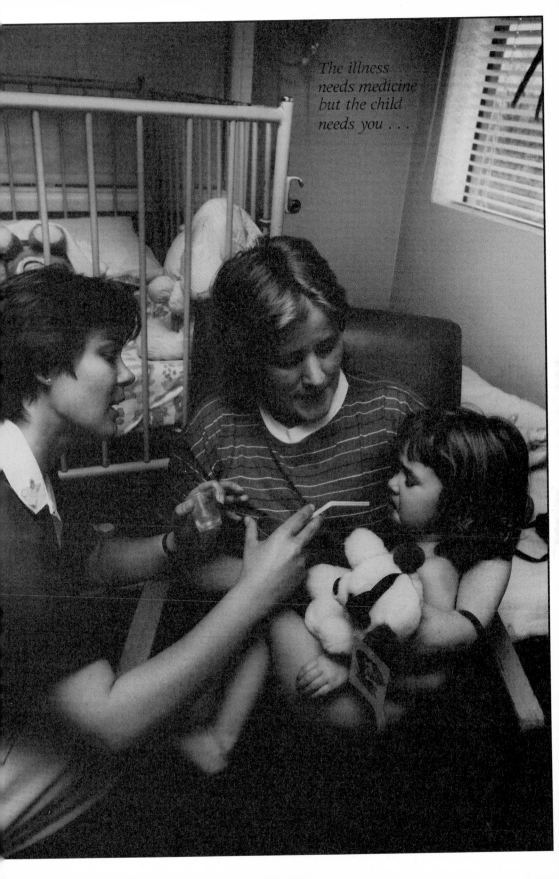

*The illness
needs medicine
but the child
needs you . . .*

**If you wonder whether other children can manage at home without you** remember that they are not ill and are not in a strange place. Of course someone must look after them while you are away, but if the choice is between leaving the well child with a less-than-favorite person and leaving an ill one with strangers, the decision should be obvious. If the child in the hospital is being given the real family priority he deserves, so that both parents are equally involved in coping with the crisis, that choice may not be necessary. Many hospitals are just as willing to allow fathers to stay as mothers, so that a two-parent family can cope with both ends for the necessary days with whatever swapping suits everyone best.

**If you wonder whether you can cope** tell yourself you've got to and then remind yourself that you are only there to keep your child as calm as he can be kept. You don't have to watch anything horrible the doctors or nurses do: give your attention to him rather than to needles or dressings.

Once the peak anxiety of the first 24 hours wears off, you will probably be desperately bored and claustrophobic, especially if your child sleeps a good deal or the two of you are alone in a room. As well as toys for him, take plenty to do for yourself – books, knitting, personal stereo or whatever. And try to arrange for people to visit both of you.

*Unexpected separation from you*

Young children feel secure when they have familiar people doing predictable things in the usual places. The people matter most, of course. But if you do have to go away without your toddler – to go into the hospital, perhaps, or to nurse your own mother – he will probably cope better with your absence if he can be in his own home, following his usual routine as much as possible. That is why the most helpful grandmothers are the ones prepared to move into your home rather than offering to have the deserted child to stay in theirs.

## Fragmenting the family

Nobody can be calm when real disaster – death, divorce – shatters life. Sometimes parents try too hard to batten down misery and rage for the children's sake. When you are under such extreme stress that you feel quite unlike yourself, quite "insane," you cannot be as your child expects you to be. If he is old enough to understand words at all, it will usually be less terrifying for him if you share at least the fact of your unhappiness. And if he must cope with you seeming strange and distant from him, he will do that better from home-base where everything else is familiar. If you cannot stand to be alone in the family home, it is better to have friends or relations move in with you than to flee to them with the children in tow.

After a death or divorce you may not want – and may not be able – to go on living where the child has always lived. But try to give him time to come to terms with the loss of a family member before you face him with the loss of his family base. If everything changes at once he will be totally bewildered.

At any one time about a quarter of all families have only one resident parent. Where children under five are concerned, many of the families will have been single-parent from the start, but some will be so because a parent has died and more because a marriage has ended, whether or not there is ever a formal divorce. Where one parent is absent it is almost always the father. There is no male equivalent to the single mother, after all: men are at greater risk than women of premature death and it is not only courts but couples who usually feel that young children will be better off with their mothers after a marriage breaks up.

Losing a father is a blow that can only be equalled or surpassed by losing a mother or both parents. For adults there is little parallel between the loss of bereavement and that of separation or divorce. But there *is* a parallel for a young child, who reacts to the parent's immediate absence and to the fragmentation of the family rather than to the loss of the parent's existence. There is much to be learned about helping very young children who are bereaved from research concerning marital breakdown.

Separation or divorce: becoming a one-parent family

Marriage-glue is not a good role for children, so staying together "for the children's sake" will not benefit them except possibly by buying time for a sick relationship to recover. On the other hand, once you decide to separate don't expect children – of any age – to approve your decision. All the available evidence suggests that divorce makes children extremely unhappy even where the father has been very distant, has sexually abused the children or has been violent to their mother. It appears that the only children ever to be relieved when a father leaves are those who have lived in constant fear of violent physical abuse.

**Don't expect a young child to believe in the separation.** Having steeled yourself to tell him, and perhaps having evoked tears in reaction to the extreme tension the child senses, it is easy to feel that you have "done it." By the next day he may appear so unmoved that you find him unfeeling. By the following week when he asks out of the blue "Where's Daddy?" you're liable to scream at him. He can't believe his father has really gone because he doesn't want it to be so; certainly at three and often at five he still half-believes in his own magical power to alter the world by wishing. You will have to keep on telling him.

**Allow for childish guilt.** Once a child does believe his father has gone he is likely to assume that he caused it. Young children are the center of their own lives and it takes years for them to realize that they are not the whole center of their parents'. Many three-year-olds do not even believe that mothers exist, eat supper, watch television and so forth, after they are asleep. So a child will instantly assume that any fragmentation of his family is the result of something concerning him which he has heard his parents arguing about: his noise, his tantrums, his impudence.

There are also subtler reasons for childish guilt. Small children are sexually aware creatures who, in the normal course of early development, dream of partnership with the opposite-sex parent and of replacing the parent of the same sex. The little boy who has wished his father out of the way believes, when his father leaves, that his wishes made it happen. The little girl clearly sees that her love-object has gone because he could not love a child so wicked as to want to supplant her mother. It is guilt of this kind that leads to the anxiety which bedevils children in newly fragmented families. If their wickedness has driven out one parent, can they count on the other to stay with them? Expect your child to be extra clingy and to keep the closest possible eye on you, and don't be surprised if his conviction that he is unlovable leads him to behave as if you and he do *not* love each other, inviting the abandonment he feels inevitable. It will be months before the child relaxes enough to stop watching you. Only then will he begin to believe that you will not desert him.

**Don't encourage your child to "forget all about it."** Fathers are psychologically essential even when they cannot be physically present. A separated child needs to talk of his father; try not to shy away from his pain as you may find that your less helpful friends do from yours.

More than half of the children of divorced parents lose touch with their fathers within a few months. In most families this is not because the fathers cannot be bothered to visit but because one or both parents decide that visits are too emotionally upsetting for the child. Don't let your child lose touch. However difficult it may be to make regular and frequent visits work – especially with a very young child – it is worth it for your child's happiness later on, in adolescence, even in adult life. Children need to find that the end of father-mother love is not the end of father-child love and that the fragmentation of the family does not break their relationships. This may require enormous efforts from the father and an almost unmanageable generosity from the mother, but for the child who is stressed by incomprehensible adult behavior it is a priority.

A child under five cannot maintain a relationship with someone based solely on a monthly trip to the zoo. He needs to see his father at least once a week and they need a base so that they can talk and play and cuddle, not just wander through the rain eating too many sweets. A two- or three-year-old may not even want to leave home with his father, especially while he does not feel safe with his mother out of sight. If visits in the home really cannot be tolerated, the home of one of the child's friends may offer a haven. As soon as the father has a "home" of his own – whether or not it has a lover in it – the child should become familiar with it, because until then he will worry about his father. Banishment from the family home seems to him a horrendous exile. You may find it difficult to respond sympathetically to questions like "But who will cook Daddy's supper?," but these are real concerns to the child. Only when he can see, and therefore believe, that both of you are "all right" as well as available, will he be able to be wholly happy again.

"Broken homes" are blamed for every kind of childhood problem from learning difficulties to delinquency. The link exists but it is not inevitable. Young children can survive even this extreme of pressure from the outside world if you can find the strength to help them cope. Nobody would bring a child into the world *intending* to face him with such disruption but, if you do not have the power to prevent it, you do have the power to see him through it, so don't waste unnecessary energy on feeling that you have failed him forever. You have not failed him by separating; you will only have done so if, between you, he loses out on love.

Being parents does not stop you being people, nor should it, because a person is what your baby is learning to be. As people you cannot always give your parenting absolute priority. However central to your life this baby has been so far, he is not your whole life for ever, and it is not necessary or desirable for his development and happiness to be so. Sometimes there will be things that you want to do in one of your many other roles: as worker, as wife, husband or lover, as daughter, son or friend or just as the individual on whom all these different roles depend.

As far as you can you will juggle the demands made upon you so that all get their share, but at times the share you offer your child will not please him at all. If he is to accept being put second to something else with reasonable calm, *you* have to be able to do it without guilt. Whatever the stresses in store as your child moves from the protection of babyhood into the realities of a bigger world, your loving best is all that he can have. Believe that it is good enough.

## Going out to work

Babies and toddlers only flourish when they are cared for by people they love. If you are the only people your baby loves you are probably right in thinking that it would break his heart to be left with anyone else, *tomorrow*. But that does not mean that you are committed to staying with him 24 hours a day indefinitely. It may just mean that it is time to help your baby attach himself to someone else so that he can comfortably accept her instead of you when you are not there. It does not matter whether the person who makes it possible for you to go to work knowing that you are not sacrificing your baby is called Granny, nanny, au pair, sitter or mother's helper. What matters is that your baby comes to love her and that you can accept their relationship with pleasure rather than uneasy envy. Your own acceptance is important whenever you want your child to accept arrangements he might prefer otherwise. If parents are relaxedly certain that they are doing the right thing, children can take almost any life pattern for granted, even a father who works away all week and comes home only on the weekend. So you can be sure that even the most clingy toddler will eventually take sympathetic daycare in his stride.

The kind of person and arrangement you need depends crucially on the kind of job you mean to take and especially on its hours. If you are only going to work for two or three half days a week, at least to begin with, your child's basic care and upbringing will remain squarely in your hands and all his caretaker needs to do is to ferry him across the chasm of your absence. Provided he is safe and contented with her it will not greatly matter if he is under-stretched or over-indulged during those periods. If you are going to take on a job that, even if it is officially part-time, keeps you out of the house from nine to five every weekday, though, you have to accept that you will be *sharing* your child's upbringing. His attitudes, discipline and education will be as much in his caretaker's hands as yours.

**Don't expect your baby to accept a new caretaker in a week.** He needs time to get to know her *with you* before he faces life without you and he needs brief times alone with her before he is committed to periods that seem to him endless.

**Do remember that once your baby has accepted an alternative caretaker he will have come to love her.** A change of caretaker does not just mean going through the getting-to-know-her process all over again, it also means losing somebody who has become important. Of course you cannot go on with someone who proves unsuitable, but do look for long-term arrangements and consider any change from the baby's point of view. It may be very irritating to come home from work to a messy house but, if it is occupied by a cheerfully chatting toddler, full of what he has been doing, you may need new plans for the housework rather than a new caretaker. There are very few paragons in the world. You *may* find someone who is perfect in all respects, but it's far more likely that you will have to settle for someone who is right for your child and tolerable for you.

*Caretakers who live in*

If you have enough space and money, somebody who lives in may seem to offer the ultimate freedom, not just to go out to work but to go out in the evening as well and maybe even away for the weekend. . . . Be careful. Your home will be her home. She will have every right to be there when you don't want her as well as when you do. By being there she may alter – even spoil – the relationship you have with your child, not to mention with each other.

**Nannies often undertake nothing but childcare** so that you end your working day cooking her supper and spend your weekends doing housework. All-day concentrated attention can be surprisingly boring for a toddler, too. He might be better occupied and happier playing alongside an adult who had other things to do (see p. 264).

**Mother's helpers** usually reckon to do anything you would do when you were at home, but may find the job just as lonely, boring and underpaid as you did (and after all it's *your* child!).

**Au pairs** *can* be marvelous but even the best of them seldom stay longer than about nine months, which means a succession of planned losses for your child. They can also be just as homesick, immature or downright lazy as you would have been at that age in a strange country. They seldom speak the fluent English you want your child to learn, and, if you expect more than the few hours of work they are meant to do, they haven't got time to learn it either.

*The right caretaker can mean happiness for everyone . . .*

| | |
|---|---|
| *Caretakers who come in* | Daily childcare arrangements often work better than residential ones. It's easier to maintain mutual respect and dignity when you neither have to share private lives nor draw awkward lines between time "on duty" and time "as family." But remember to allow for your caretaker experiencing some of your own difficulties in going out to work, especially if she also has children who will sometimes be unwell. . . . |

You may be able to share a daily nanny with another parent. Daily mother's helpers are sometimes happy with part-time work to match your hours away. If you only plan on being out of your home a couple of afternoons a week, a graduate student, desperate to pay her tuition, may be happy to play with your child and take him out.

| | |
|---|---|
| *Caretakers in their own homes* | Daycare mothers usually do the job because they want to be home-based for their own, probably older, children. Some are licensed and, if they are, the number and ages of the children |

they may take are strictly controlled and premises are inspected for basic safety and suitability. Although both your baby and you may find settling with a caregiver more difficult than settling with someone who comes in, there are major advantages.

**Your baby joins an ongoing household** where his new caretaker is in charge, has her own ways of doing things and a routine into which he is welcomed. That can be a lot less lonely and strange than his own home with no parents and somebody sitting watching him play.

**You cannot try to make her do things the way you do them** and although that will mean that they get done differently, it also means that you have to trust her, more fully, more quickly than someone in your house. She is not *your employee* but *your child's caretaker* and that may mean more equality and fewer pitfalls in the relationship. Certainly you will not be tempted into leaving her because she did not do your ironing while your baby slept!

*Caretakers in centers*  Daycare centers run by local authorities or by volunteer organizations are few and far between. They are usually over-subscribed by people in desperate need of daycare but if that might be you, ask advice from your doctor and from other parents and check at your Town Hall on what is locally available.

Some forward-looking employers provide work-place daycare centers at subsidized prices. These have the big advantage that you need only leave your child while you are actually *working*. You can visit during your breaks and be on the spot in case of illness or emergency. Rush-hour travel can be a snag, though, and remember that the daycare center and the job may go together so that if you want to change employment your child will lose his place.

Private daycare centers are also available in most communities though, once again, demand tends to outstrip supply, especially in cities. Centers range from informal community-based groups set up – and sometimes run – by parents themselves, to large-scale businesses with spreading networks of daycare centers. An informal group will usually cost much less but may demand more time and effort from you, in actual participation, fund raising and so forth. Full-time daycare in a center which is being run for profit will cost you a lot of money. It *should* be expensive because childcare is labor-intensive and the fees that parents pay should reflect adequate salaries to suitable – preferably trained – people. You do not always get what you pay for, though. Only personal visits and recommendations can ensure that you are spending your money on excellent daycare rather than on exorbitant costs for things that will not directly benefit your child, such as high rents or extensive glossy advertising.

By no means will all centers accept children under two. Those that do take younger children and babies do their best to provide consistent individual care but commonly find this extremely difficult. It is not enough to provide a good ratio of adults to children, such as 1:3; it is equally important that that one should be the *same* adult all day and every day because that is the caretaker your child knows and accepts. As soon as your child is being cared for by people with ordinary terms of employment, the *extra*ordinariness of what is required of mothers or their substitutes becomes glaringly obvious. An employee gets a vacation, time off for medical or dental appointments and perhaps for further training. She occasionally misses work because she is ill, too. Every time that happens in a daycare center, somebody else has to take care of ''her'' children. It doesn't happen in a home-setting because there isn't anybody else. If your caregiver or mother's helper *must* go to the dentist during working hours she will take your child with her, just as you would. If she is ill, you will probably have to stay at home.

*Relatives, friends and neighbors*   If a relative or friend will care for your child as an informal, unpaid sitter your plans for going back to work will be off to a flying start. But be a bit careful. Favors can be offered with more enthusiasm than forethought and then go sour. You told her it would be ''odd days,'' meaning two or three a week; she assumed you meant two or three a *month*. When the arrangement comes to grief, that means grief and a new start for your child. Ad hoc arrangements, using different helpful people at various times, can be invaluable with older children and emergencies like election days which close their school. But a baby or toddler is unlikely to cope well if he never knows who he is expected to rely on today. Try to set up a regular arrangement; make sure the ''terms'' are really understood and do everything possible to prevent your caretaker feeling put upon. Paying the going rate is good protection against this.

## Having a new baby

Having a new baby is the quintessential example of something that certainly *will* be stressful for your existing toddler or child but which you nevertheless have an absolute, human right to do if you want to. Don't spend any time wondering whether it would be fair to him. And don't waste much worry on the ideal age-gap from his point of view (Ref/FAMILY PLANNING). Whether he is one or four when the new baby is born (the problems are a bit different if he is eight or twelve) he *won't* like it but he *will* cope. And it's perfectly reasonable to expect that he will even be glad you did it – one day.

Parents who love their first child and look forward to the second often find the idea of the older child being resentful and jealous almost unbearable. They are pleased; they want their child to be pleased too. Natural though this is, pretending to yourselves that your present child looks forward to and will love the coming one will not make him more likely to do so. Things will go more smoothly if you can honestly accept the fact that you are asking your child to put up with feeling supplanted and that, however you dress the facts up, he is going to mind. Just for fun, imagine your husband coming home to tell you that he was proposing to take on a second wife as well as you and imagine him using the various phrases that are frequently used to break the news of a coming baby to a child:

| Parent to child | Husband to wife |
|---|---|
| *"We're going to have a new baby, darling, because we thought it would be so nice for you to have a little brother or sister to play with."* | *"I'm going to take a second wife, darling, because I thought it would be so nice for you to have some company and help with the work."* |
| *"We love you so much we just can't wait to have another gorgeous boy or girl."* | *"I love you so much I just can't wait to have another gorgeous wife."* |
| *"It'll be our baby; it'll belong to all three of us and we'll all look after it together."* | *"It'll be our wife. She'll belong to both of us and we'll both look after her together."* |
| *"I shall really need my big boy/girl now, to help me look after the tiny new baby."* | *"I shall really need my reliable old wife now to help me look after this young new one."* |
| *"Of course I shan't love you any less, we'll all love each other."* | *"Of course I shan't love you any less, we'll all love each other."* |

You wouldn't feel exactly mollified, would you? When we love people we want to be enough for them. The fact that they want another person makes us feel jealous and pushed out. So assume that your child is going to feel jealous and don't try to induce pleasurable anticipation of an event which he can barely understand and would not look forward to anyway. Concentrate instead on increasing the child's ability to cope with the stress of the new baby. That means making the relationship between all of you as secure and happy as possible; getting the child's own life running as smoothly and independently as possible and doing what you can to induce a general interest in babies.

*Preparing for the birth*

If your older child will still be under about 18 months, pre-verbal and really still a baby himself, there will not be a great deal you *can* do to prepare him. There isn't any doubt that he will be amazed, and probably furious, when you leave him and then come home with somebody else to whom you pay attention. On the other hand a child as young as this will forget very quickly that he ever was the only one. If he immediately turns into a truly terrible tantruming toddler you – and most psychologists – may wonder whether it was the new baby which transformed him. But you will never know. And if he isn't old enough for you to talk to him about the baby, at least he will not be able to suggest that she go home now!

**Foresee the things that will hurt him most.** If he often sleeps in your bed, for example, either resign yourselves to sleeping with both children or persuade the older child into his own crib well before the baby comes. If you are breast-feeding, tail off and stop several months before the birth, even if your milk supply would have continued throughout your pregnancy. If he still remembers, and half yearns for, the breast, he really *will* feel supplanted by the new baby.

**Make any lifestyle changes well in advance.** If having two children under two is going to mean that you have help in the house or that you give up your job and your sitter, do it well in advance. Getting used to having a stranger around will add to your child's stress and you certainly don't want him to feel that you stay at home *because of the baby* although you did not stay at home just for him.

If the child is talking *at all*, remember that he almost certainly understands far more than he says (see p. 256) and that his language will increase dramatically over the next few months. Talk to him about the baby even if he only understands half of what you say; that half is far better than nothing and *infinitely* better than not trying.

**Don't tell even a toddler or older child about the coming baby at once.** Use the early months of pregnancy for talking to him about families; point out his friends' brothers and sisters and find a very young one to talk about. The idea is to get him to accept that most families do have more than one child in them, so that when his does too he feels that it is a normal part of life, rather than a particular punishment for which he has been singled out.

**Tell the child yourself before someone else lets it out.** Wait until around six months if you can, but tell him sooner if you cannot trust friends not to drop hints or comment on your shape in front of him. He himself will notice nothing until you are too huge to play crawling games on the floor any more.

**Do everything you can to get the child's independent life going well.** If you plan pre-school for him and he will be three by the time the baby arrives, consider starting him a bit early (see p. 416). If he is not going to pre-school or is too young to start yet, work at establishing a network of friends he likes to play with and other houses he likes to go to. He is going to need things to think about other than you and that baby; places to escape to and ways of showing himself how different he is from the newcomer.

**Foresee the weeks around the birth.** He has time now to get used to whatever arrangements he will have to accept then, when he is under stress. If you are having the baby in the hospital and he will spend a night or two with Grandma, arrange a couple of preliminary visits and make them treats. If his father will care for him and does not usually take an equal part in his routine care, make sure he understands *exactly* how to get the bacon "just right." Tiny details will matter enormously when the child is missing you.

Wherever you deliver the new baby someone else will have to undertake a large part of the older child's care for a week or two. Two parents and two children can be an ideal solution but if full-time parenting will be new to your partner help him to integrate himself in advance. Nothing is more demoralizing than a pre-school child who wails "Mommy do it" whenever his father offers help.

**Tell the child where the baby is and let him feel her move.**
Once he has accepted the fact that there is going to be a new baby, physical evidence of her existence will help him to face the reality and to get interested in the whole affair.

Try to make the baby real for him by discussing names and speculating about sex, but don't describe it as "a brother or sister for you to play with." It will not be that for months. Instead, talk ruefully about how helpless it will be and how it will cry and wet its diapers. Tell him that he was just the same when he was tiny; show him some photographs of himself as a baby and think up some funny stories about his infant misdeeds like the time he peed on Grandma's dress, threw up in the bus or bit the doctor. Aim to inculcate an attitude of tolerant and amused superiority.

**Keep birth arrangements to yourself until you are sure of them** a couple of weeks before your due date. Even then, be careful not to make any promises you may not be able to keep. If you have promised to have the baby at home, your departure to the hospital will seem a betrayal. If you have guaranteed only to be gone for twenty-four hours, three or four days will seem a lifetime. Play safe, keep it vague.

**Think carefully about the child's involvement in a home birth.** Even if you want him to take part in this family occasion you will need to concentrate on your labor, undistracted by thinking about him: he will need a tactful companion and one who can take him away at the right moments.

**Say "goodbye" before you leave for the hospital** even if you have to wake the child to do so. It is better for him to face your departure than to wake one morning and find you gone.

**Don't promise that he can visit you in the hospital**, even if you know children are allowed. If you are away from him for more than twenty-four hours seeing you will certainly help, but only if you are able to seem like yourself. If you should have an intravenous set-up or so many stitches that you cannot move without wanting to screech, it may be better for him to wait.

*The early jealous days*

When you come home, remember that it is you the child wants, not the baby. He is going to have to accept that baby's presence and the care you give her, but there is no need to rub his nose in it. Come into the house without the baby and concentrate on the older child, leaving the new person to somebody else for a bit. During the first few days there are a few practical things you can do to ease him into the situation:

**Try not to breast-feed in front of the child** for the first day or so until he is used to having you safely home again. Whoever is helping you can be briefed to lure him away to some fascinating entertainment when the baby feeds. After a day or two, or when he refuses the lure, show him how a new baby feeds, reminding him that he fed like that too when he was tiny. He may ask to try some breast milk. You do not have to let him if you hate the idea, but try not to look shocked. You can always give him a taste on your finger so that he can see he is not missing nectar.

*Nobody likes being supplanted.*

**Do with the child as many as possible of the things you did before.** When you cannot, do not make the baby the reason too often. When the baby clearly is the reason, come right out into the open and say what you know the child is feeling: "I'm sorry but I've got to feed the baby first, I know that it must seem unfair, but little babies can't wait for their food as older people can, so I must do it now. She will go to sleep after she eats and then you and I will be able to play together."

**Accept any offers of help from the older child,** but don't make too much of the "you're my big boy" line. He may not be feeling at all big. Indeed he is probably feeling that his bigness is his whole trouble; if he were tiny he would be getting all the attention like that beastly baby. To have to help in order to get your approval may be the last straw.

**Offer the child chances to behave in a babyish way** for a bit, and make it clear that far from having to be "grown up" to keep your approval, you love him devotedly even if he decides to be more babyish than the newcomer. You could offer him a turn in the baby bath and a sprinkle of the baby powder. You can cuddle him, pat his back and sing to him. It may sound absurd but from the child's point of view it is not. You want him to feel that while the baby gets a lot of things he does not normally get, she is not getting anything he *cannot* have, but only things which he has *grown out of*. You want him to think "I can have a bottle too if I like, but I'm old enough to have orange juice and it tastes much nicer than that baby milk."

**Make sure that there are some practical advantages** to being "the oldest" to balance the inevitable disadvantages. This may be the moment for a few new privileges. Pocket money, perhaps, or a later bedtime or a regular Saturday expedition with Dad and without the baby.

Their father can make all the difference to the older child's reactions to the new baby if he is prepared to take a full part in the care and companioning of both of them. There are two children and two parents. He can make the pull between their differing needs much less obvious and painful by being prepared to cope with the baby while you do something with the older child and to do exciting things with the older one while you are busy with the baby. Some fathers find that they cement their whole relationship with the first child during this period; he is under stress and turns to his father because at this moment he feels let down by his mother's involvement with the newcomer.

**Don't make the older child feel guilty about jealous feelings.** Don't ask him to love the baby. He cannot. If you ask him to, he will feel guilty and think that you would hate him if you knew what he really felt. Accept, even suggest, that the baby is a considerable nuisance to him while assuring him that one day the two of them will be friends and companions.

**Don't let the child hurt the baby.** He will feel guilty however nice you are to him about it or however much you pretend to think it was an accident. So watch very carefully when he makes approaches to the baby and use a cat net, which he will think is against cats, to prevent those by-accident-on-purpose occasions when a ball gets thrown into the carriage.

**Work to make the child feel that the baby likes him.** We all find it easier to like people who seem to like us; your child will find it much more possible to love his new sister if the advances seem to come from her. Fortunately this is easy parent-upmanship. The baby will smile at the child if he puts his face close to hers and makes noises. Once she smiles you can play it up a little. "Mark is the one she *really* likes" you can say to admiring visitors. If the child says "I'll keep her quiet for you, Mommy, she'll stop crying for *me*," you are over the worst.

With any luck, two or three months of tactful handling and lots of affectionate attention from you both will carry the child through to a point where he can be amusedly patronizing about the baby. Try very hard to get him to this stage well before she gets mobile. While she lies in a crib she is only a nuisance to him in the emotional sense of taking up attention, but once she can crawl into games and snatch toys she will be a practical nuisance too. If your child can say "Oh isn't she silly!" or "She's trying to copy me!," their relationship will survive. If he simply dislikes her, you will be in for a difficult couple of years.

*Balancing both their needs*

Even when first jealousy has blown itself out and your older child has forgotten what life was like when he was the only one, balancing their needs goes on needing thought. If one starts school while the other starts playgroup, both will need all your emotional support and you will have to share it out or overdraw on your resources. There will be problems in suiting treats, expeditions and vacations to their differing age/stages; problems in nursing one without neglecting the other, and problems in coping fairly with one who gets her own way by charm while the other fails to get it by bullying. And as long as they both depend on you emotionally there will be jealousy *on both sides*. The younger one's can be just as painful, so don't go overboard in guarding the older child from the green-eyed monster.

Try not to assume, even as they grow older, that they love each other. Parents often take this love so much for granted that they insist that the children are "very close really" even when constant quarrelling and bitter complaints suggest otherwise. Both children have to tolerate each other and behave decently, but they do not have to love each other and, given the inevitable jealousies, they may not. Don't force them into each other's company. If you let them work it out, they may eventually surprise you with their mutual affection and loyalty.

Respect both children's dignity. If you can make it clear that you love them both as individuals and will never make them feel or look small to each other or to outsiders, you will not go far wrong. Do not compare them. There is no more point than there would be in comparing oranges and apples. They are simply nice-but-different. Never hold one up as an example to the other. The charming manners or neat habits that come easily to one may be almost impossibly difficult for the other to learn.

# THE TODDLER

## *From one year to two and a half*

Your toddler is no longer a baby feeling himself as part of you, using you as his controller, facilitator, his mirror for himself and the world. But he is not yet a child either, ready to see you as a person in your own right and to take responsibility for himself and his own actions in relation to you. He has begun to be aware that you and he are separate people. Some of the time he asserts this new-found individuality, crying "No!" and "Let me!", fighting your control and help each time an issue presents itself. But some of the time he clings to you, crying when you leave the room, holding up his arms to be carried, demanding with open mouth that you should feed him.

His in-between behavior is confusing for you but it is painful for him. He has to become a person in his own right but it feels safer to remain your possession. He has to begin to reject your total control over him yet it is easier to accept it. He has to develop likes and dislikes of his own and to pursue his own ends even when they conflict with yours, yet the conflict feels desperately dangerous to him. He still loves you with an unrivaled passion; depending on you totally for emotional support. The developmental imperative of independence conflicts with the emotional imperative of love.

If you expect your toddler to remain what he was – a comparatively compliant baby – you will be wrong; he will have to clash with you directly. He needs your love and approval but his drive to grow up will not allow him to accept them at the price of too much dependence. But if you expect him to change overnight into what he will be – a sensible child – he will feel himself inadequate. He needs your help and comfort and if they are withheld from him, he cannot manage. Babied, he is balky. Pushed on, he is whiny.

There is a middle road which allows him to adventure but insures him against disaster; helps him to try but cushions his failures; gives him a firm framework for acceptable behavior yet pads it so that it does not bruise his dawning sense of being his own boss. It depends on understanding and on a refusal to be fooled by appearances. In many ways he seems much more grown up than he feels. His walking, his talking and his play develop to a point where he seems little different from a three-year-old, but his understanding and his experience do not match up to them. If you treat him as a baby, you will hold him back. He must learn to understand. He must have experience. But if you treat him as you would treat a pre-school child, you put him under intolerable pressure. He has to be taught to understand. He must have experience made manageable.

The key to understanding him lies in understanding the development of his thought processes. It is only as these mature that those conflicting emotions and misleading abilities can come together to form the reasonable and manageable whole we call a child.

The toddler has a memory, but it is still very short. When he was a baby, doing baby things, this was neither very important nor very obvious. But now he is trying to do more grown up things it is both vital and conspicuous. Day after day he trips and tumbles over the step between kitchen and living room. Wild with irritation and plagued by worry over the bumps on his head, you wonder whether he will ever learn. He will, but it will take time. He cannot "bear that step in mind" until repeated experience has finally given it a permanent place in his memory. When he was a baby it would have been your job to prevent him tumbling. When he is a child it will be your job to point the step out to him. But right now your job is to modify the painful results of that series of experiences and to jog that memory. You may need to pad the step and issue endless reminders.

With little memory of events in the past the toddler is almost without forethought. If he can climb that step-ladder, he will do so. He cannot think ahead to the problem of how to get down again. Often lack of memory and of forethought combine to get him into trouble. He has been scolded again and again for twiddling the knobs of the television set, but as he approaches it again today he neither remembers past scoldings nor foresees the new one that is coming. Those knobs draw him like a magnet.

Because he cannot think ahead, he cannot wait a second for anything. If he wants it at all, he wants it *now* and the clamoring begins even as he watches you remove the wrapper from the longed-for lollipop. Unable to wait for things he likes, he cannot put up with even minor discomfort now, in order to be more comfortable later. Wailing with misery because the lollipop has made him so sticky, he will still fight off the washcloth that brings relief. He is a creature of this moment only.

Similar immaturities in his thinking get him into trouble in his relationships with people, too. He loves you. Everyone tells you that he loves you. He tells you that he loves you. Yet he cannot often behave in the ways we adults think of as "loving." He cannot put

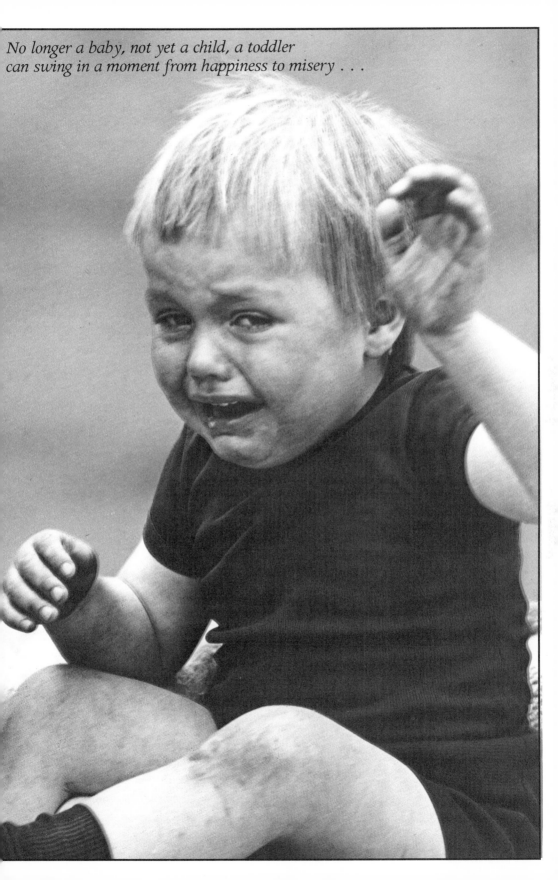

*No longer a baby, not yet a child, a toddler can swing in a moment from happiness to misery . . .*

himself in your place or see things through your eyes. He will hate it if you cry but it will be the feelings your tears arouse in *him* which he dislikes, not the feelings the tears represent in you. It is not his job yet to consider other people's feelings, he has to come to terms with his own first. If he hits you and you hit him back to "show him what it feels like," you will have given a lesson he is not ready to learn. He will wail as if hitting was a totally new idea to him. He makes no connection between what he did to you and what you then did to him, between your feelings and his own.

Even his own feelings are often still a mystery to him. He does not know what he feels now, and this, combined with being unable to remember what he felt last time or predict what he will feel later, makes decisions impossibly difficult for him. "Do you want to stay with me or go to the store with Daddy?" seems a simple and insignificant choice. But it is neither straightforward nor unimportant to the toddler. Which will he enjoy more? Which did he enjoy last time? Which does he feel like doing now? He does not and cannot know. He dithers and, whichever is finally chosen for him, he is miserable. He will have to learn to make his own decisions. Nobody can be mature who has everything decided for him. But practice-decisions should be ones where he has nothing to lose. If he has two jelly beans, "Which are you going to eat first?" is a question he can consider without stress. He has got them both. Nobody is going to take away the one he decides against. He can change his mind six sticky times if he pleases.

The child's language may get him into trouble by suggesting that his understanding is greater than it is. He learns new words and he uses them more and more freely, but many of them still lack the subtler meanings for him. He cannot possibly understand, much less keep, a promise. Yet he may well use the word. If you offer him five minutes more play if he will promise to come straight to bed afterwards, he will happily say "I promise." The word is an agreement label. But after that five minutes he wants a further five. He cannot understand the reproach in your voice as you say "but you *promised*. . . ."

Words make trouble over truth too. He may talk fluently enough to issue frequent accusations and denials while their accuracy still means nothing to him. He talks as he feels. It might have been the dog that made that puddle: he wishes it had been and says that it was. When in the course of a quarrel with his sister, he falls and hurts his knee, he says that she pushed him. She did not hurt his knee but she did hurt his feelings. He is telling a kind of feeling-truth which just happens to be different from adult truth.

Later on you will be able to demonstrate the value of promises thoughtfully made and reliably kept; of truth told and lies avoided. But it is too soon yet. Don't corner him with concepts he cannot understand. He is doing his best to please, but he is only just emerging from babyhood so, if nothing less than child-standards will please you, he will fail.

*. . . your role is to keep a balance*
*between her need for independence as she jumps in*
*and her need to be protected from going right under water*

Your child's developmental clock has told him that it is time to stop being a baby and move toward being a separate person. If you treat him as a baby, he will fight you every step of the way and, in the end, he will win his independence because he must. But he will win it at a terrible price paid in lost love.

That clock does not yet read "childhood," so attempts to discipline him as you discipline a child will not work either. You will be faced with a lack of comprehension that looks like defiance, and every battle you join will end with love lost. So don't try for absolute control and don't join moral battles. Your toddler will be "good" if he feels like doing what you happen to want him to do and does not happen to feel like doing anything you would dislike. With a little cleverness you can organize life as a whole, and issues in particular, so that you both want the same thing most of the time. Your toddler has his blocks all over the floor and you want the room tidy. If you tell him to pick them up, he will probably refuse. If you insist, a fight will be on and you cannot win it. You can scream at him, punish him, reduce him to a jelly of misery but none of that will get those blocks off the floor. But if you say, "I bet you can't put those blocks in their bag before I've peeled these potatoes," you turn the whole issue into a game. Now he wants to do what you want him to do, so he will. He did not do it "for Mommy"; he did not do it because he is a "good boy." He did it because you made him want to. And that is the trick. You conduct his life by foreseeing the rocks and steering around them, avoiding absolute orders that will be absolutely refused, leading and guiding the toddler into behaving as you want him to behave because nothing has made him want to behave otherwise.

The payoff now is fun instead of strife for you all. But the payoff later is even more important. This toddler, who does not know right from wrong and cannot choose to behave well or badly, is growing up. The time will come when he does understand your feelings and your rights; does remember your instructions and foresee the results of his actions. When that time comes he *will* be able to be "good" or "naughty" on purpose. Which he chooses will depend largely on how he feels about his "special" adults. If he reaches that next stage of growing up feeling that you are basically loving, approving and on his side, he will want (most of the time) to please you. So, with many lapses, he will behave as you wish. But if he reaches that stage feeling that you are overpowering, incomprehensible and against him, he may have decided that it is no use trying to please you because you are never pleased; no use minding when you are cross because you are cross so often, and too dangerous to let himself love you because you have so often seemed not to love him. If by the time he reaches pre-school age he is no longer seeking your approval, not feeling cooperative, not confident that he loves and is loved, you will have lost the whole basis for good and easy "discipline" right through childhood. At this stage, a happy child is an easy child and a child kept easy now will be easy to handle later.

# Eating and growing

Once past the first birthday your baby's weight gain will probably slow down to around 1–2oz (30–60g) a week. A faster or slower rate of gain may, of course, be perfectly right for your baby because, as we have said, there is a wide variation around the "average" at all ages.

Unless the baby has been ill or has had major feeding troubles during the first year, there is not much point in going on with regular weighing now. To weigh every week would be absurd as the scales may not be accurate enough to weigh to the nearest ounce and simple things like having a bowel movement before or after the weighing will be enough to produce a false gain or loss. It is probably best to weigh and measure every three months, so that you can see your baby getting heavier and taller both at the same time.

*Changing proportions*

The proportions of a newborn baby's body are quite different from those of an older baby. During this year they change even more. When a baby of around a year first gets up on his own two feet parents are often very worried by his appearance. His head is still large in relation to the rest of him and his neck seems non-existent. His shoulders and chest are thin, his belly sticks out, his legs seem bowed and his feet have no arches. But in the course of a year, all that will change. The year-old baby is still the right shape for life on all fours. By the time he is two his proportions will have changed so that he is much better suited for life on his hind legs. A year later still he will probably have slimmed down and elongated, so that he develops the lithe and leggy elegance typical of an active pre-school child.

*Suitable toddler foods*

By the beginning of the second year your baby will be ready to share most of the foods which you serve to the rest of the family and ready to have meals at the times which suit the rest of you.

If you are cooking fresh foods, you can make almost all of them suitable for a baby by a little last-minute adaptation. Any form of meat or fish, for example, can be cut into small pieces while you are serving. Vegetables can be puréed or cut into finger-sized cubes. Cooked fruits can be mashed, or strained if they are seedy. Fried foods which might be too fatty for him can be grilled or dry-fried in a non-stick pan, while rich sauces can be replaced at the last minute with plain stock.

If you are not doing much cooking for the rest of the family, you may find that some of the commercially prepared babyfoods are still useful. For example, if you do not provide a cooked breakfast for anyone else, a helping of baby cereal (see p. 202) will provide your baby with much more nourishment than a similar sized helping of adult breakfast cereal. If you do not usually provide dessert, "Toddler desserts" or "Fruit varieties" will save you stewing half an apple or cooking a minute rice pudding or custard just for the baby.

Adult convenience foods need to be used with some care. Although most frozen foods have the same nutritional quality as fresh food, canned and dehydrated foods are often nutritionally poor. A bowl of canned tomato soup, for example, may fill your baby's tummy but it will not provide many calories or many useful nutrients. Dehydrated meals, soups and sauces usually contain a great deal of salt. Although the baby's ability to cope with salt does improve with age, too much will still place a strain on the kidneys. Furthermore these foods usually contain a variety of preservatives, colorings and artificial flavoring agents such as the ubiquitous monosodium glutamate. Although most countries have stringent regulations to control the use of chemicals in food, many people believe that we should all be better off if we ate fewer of them. So while there is no need to go to extremes – the occasional gravy made with a bouillon cube will not hurt your baby now – it is not a good idea to feed him a steady diet of these manufactured foods.

The same caution applies to adult soft drinks. If you read the small print on a bottle of fruit drink, you will probably find that it contains a variety of sweeteners, flavorings and coloring agents and very little real fruit. An occasional drink of one of these products will not do your baby any harm but for regular consumption and plenty of vitamin C, stick to fresh orange juice or to one of the vitamin C enriched fruit juices. Of course if the toddler is simply thirsty, there is no drink to beat plain water.

## Worries about eating

After being bombarded with detailed advice about feeding a baby, parents who seek help at the toddler stage usually find themselves put off by the magical phrase "a good mixed diet." When they inquire what such a diet consists of they are told to "give plenty of meat and fish; eggs; cheese; milk and fresh green vegetables . . . ." Realizing that their toddler dislikes and refuses almost every one of those items, they wonder whether their child can be eating properly. The seeds of anxiety (and therefore of eating problems) are sown. So let us look a little more deeply into that good mixed diet.

## What is a "good mixed diet?"

A mixed diet is one which contains some of each of a wide variety of foods, eaten in different combinations, every day. Its virtue lies in the fact that a person who eats it will quite certainly get everything his body requires under all circumstances. If what you need is not in one food, it will be in another. If you do not eat enough of one nutrient at breakfast, the deficiency will be made good at lunchtime. So if your child *does* eat a good mixed diet, you do not have to worry about his meals at all. You need not even try to work out what your child needs or is getting because day by day and week by week the two are certain to match up.

This is a major advantage because working these things out is complicated. Total food needs and requirements for specific nutrients vary both from person to person and in the same person from one day to the next. Your own entirely adequate diet, for example, may suddenly fall short of the exceptional need for iron brought on by a series of heavy menstrual periods. Working out what you are getting from specific portions of food is even more complex. We know, for example, how much protein is in 6oz (170g) of lean beef. But how lean is lean? We know how much vitamin C is in 4oz (114g) of freshly picked raw spring cabbage.

But how much is absorbed by your body after the cabbage has been picked, transported, stored, cooked and kept warm? On a mixed diet these vexed questions need not concern you. If you have some meat or fish, some cheese, eggs and milk and/or some beans, nuts and lentils you will be getting adequate protein. And if that cabbage does not contain much vitamin C, it does not matter; there will be plenty in your potatoes and fruit.

So wide variety, that "good mixed diet," is the safe and easy way to feed any child well. Aim at it, by all means, as you gradually accustom yours to ordinary family meals, but don't feel that without it he must be poorly nourished.

Your child's diet can be both good and mixed enough without having to include normal quantities of all the foods that are conventionally considered "good for him." The value of any one food lies in the use which the body can make of its constituents. No food is magically good-in-itself; it is only as good as the sum total of what is in it. There is therefore no single food which is absolutely necessary, because anything which is in one food will also be in some others. Milk is an excellent example because it is often described as "necessary" for children. This is nonsense. Milk is an exceedingly valuable food and a very convenient package of the nutrients children need in an easy-to-take form. But even milk is not unique. The valuable proteins, minerals and vitamins it contains are in other foods too.

This argument carries over into the way in which you present foods to your child. Eggs (in moderation) are good for most children. But they do not have to be presented in the shell, or gazing one-eyed off a plate, in order to be nourishing. The egg in the pancake your child enjoys is just as nourishing as that breakfast egg would be if it was eaten!

So if your child does indeed eat a conventional good mixed diet, you are fortunate. He will certainly be getting everything he needs and you need not think any further about his food. Don't even bother with the rest of this chapter. But if he does not, don't worry. If you read on, you will almost certainly find that, whatever individual foods he rejects, he is getting enough of everything important from the combinations he likes.

## Calories

Whatever foods you offer your child will contain calories. He needs calories to keep his body's functions ticking, to fuel his activities and to provide a surplus for growth. However little he chooses to eat, it is enough if he is well, energetic and growing.

Foods vary in the concentration of calories which they contain. Those rich in fats contain most of all. One slice of bread thickly spread with butter gives the child more energy than two slices eaten plain; one french fried potato yields as much as three boiled ones. A child who seems to eat very little food may be eating it in a high-calorie form.

## Carbohydrates

Sugar is pure carbohydrate, but most of the carbohydrate foods are bulky ones like bread (and other flour products) and potatoes, pasta and rice. We get most of our energy from carbohydrate foods because we eat a lot of them.

If your child is eating at all, his appetite will see to it that he gets all the carbohydrate foods he needs for energy and bulk. Introducing him to wholegrain bread and other minimally processed carbohydrate foods will help to ensure a sensible diet later on, but he does not need a "high fiber" diet at this early age. Although too many *sweet* foods will be bad for his teeth and/or his figure, don't dismiss all these *starchy* foods as "just fattening." Potatoes and bread, for example, are excellent items of a diet.

*Fats* Many families now rightly try to keep down the consumption of animal or saturated fats. Provided your child has some milk, cheese or other dairy products, it does not matter if he eats no visible fats at all. He will get the minute traces of "fatty acids" his body requires from invisible fats in commercial foods. If he eats no dairy products, though, he could go short of the fat-soluble vitamins he needs. Make sure that he goes on having his daily dose of multi-vitamin drops.

*Protein* Protein is important in your child's diet as his body needs it to build new tissues. But the amount needed and the difficulty of providing it have both been overplayed by food manufacturers. "High protein" has become an advertising point. In fact a shortage of protein in a child who is offered as much of a variety of foods as he wants to eat is extremely rare.

The use of the terms "first class" and "second class" protein is partly responsible for this confusion. Protein is made up of a number of amino acids. Your child has to eat some of these in ready-made form because his body cannot manufacture them out of the others. These vital amino acids are present in the correct balance in animal foods like meat, fish, milk and other dairy products and these have therefore been termed "first class" proteins. But there are amino acids in other foods too. The vegetable proteins in bread, potatoes, beans, nuts and grains can complement each other so that a careful mixture results in a complete protein intake for an adult. Vegetarian diets are not inferior to diets which include meat and fish, but for growing children the imbalance in the amino acid composition of these "second class" proteins does need to be corrected by the addition of very small quantities of animal protein from dairy products. Bread (which contains vegetable protein) with cheese (which contains animal protein) would provide the child with a protein intake just as "first class" as that highly recommended, much-disliked slice of meat.

On this basis most toddlers get an ample supply of protein. They may refuse eggs, but they eat puddings and cakes with egg in them. They may refuse meat but they eat luncheon meat or ham, bacon or sausages, fishcakes or hamburgers. They may live in families where no meat products are served but they eat a range of bean, lentil and nut dishes and some cheese or yogurt. The protein they are getting is not as concentrated as it would be in butcher's meat, but balancing the sum total of other vegetable proteins it is ample.

If your child does not eat enough foods to make a good mixture of vegetable proteins or like any of the less concentrated forms of animal protein, don't forget milk. As long as he gets as much as one pint of milk per day, either as a drink or in cooking, he will not go short of protein whatever else he does or does not eat.

| | Calcium | Your child needs an adequate calcium intake both for the proper development of growing bones and teeth and for the correct functioning of muscles and blood clotting. There is a useful amount in bread, flour and other cereals, but a more concentrated source than this is needed. The obvious source is milk. A pint a day will ensure calcium intake. Even if your baby does not appear to *drink* that much milk, you can (and probably do) "lose" it in ordinary cooking, as shown in the following examples: |

| 1oz (30ml) milk per toddler serving | 2–3oz (60–75ml) milk per toddler serving | 4oz (115ml) milk per toddler serving |
| --- | --- | --- |
| Creamed/mashed potatoes | Baby cereal | Creamed soup |
| Scrambled egg | Breakfast cereal | Milkshake |
| Omelette | Cheese sauce | Cocoa/chocolate |
| Pancake | Custard | milk |
| White sauce for vegetables | Rice pudding | Yogurt |
| | Ice cream | |

Try cheese too, remembering that this is also a superb source of protein. Given the chance many small children develop a passion for cheese; in cubes to eat with their fingers, grated over vegetables, in sauces, or spread on bread. If your family is so strictly vegetarian that your child may have no milk, cheese or other dairy products, take advice from your doctor. Some mineral and vitamin supplement may be advisable while your child is still growing.

Other minerals
The other minerals your child needs are either so widely distributed (like phosphorus) that he is bound to get plenty, or, like iron, they are used and re-used by the body so that daily supplies are unnecessary, provided his stores are adequate.

Vitamins
Most vitamins are widely distributed so that your child automatically gets plenty. Giving the three vital ones as daily multivitamin drops or tablets ensures adequate intake, however peculiar the child's eating habits.

**Vitamin A.** The main sources in the diet are liver, then milk, butter or fortified margarine. Carrots yield "carotene" from which our bodies can make their own vitamin A. A child will probably get enough from these sources but a supplement is a safety measure.

**Vitamin D.** The only concentrated food sources are egg yolk and fatty fishes. Pale skins make their own in sunlight; but a supplement is essential, especially in winter and for black children.

**Vitamin C.** Widely available in fruits and green vegetables, this vital vitamin is nevertheless quite difficult to provide in adequate daily quantities because it is destroyed by both light and heat. Green vegetables displayed outside the greengrocer's in the sunlight, cut up ahead and then boiled in water will have lost most of their vitamin C by the time they are eaten. Quick cooking, instant serving and use of the cooking water, with its dissolved vitamin content, in soups or gravies, help, but it is still difficult to know how much has reached the child. Potatoes have plenty of vitamin C just under the skin. Served in their jackets some is lost because of heat; peeled and then boiled, even more vanishes.

Fruit is a better source because it is either eaten raw or with its cooking water served as juice. Citrus fruits, which are naturally packaged against light and always served raw, are an ideal source. One orange or its juice will give your child all the daily vitamin C that is needed. A daily serving of one of the commercially prepared vitamin C enriched fruit drinks serves the same purpose. There is no harm in giving this as well as the dosage of vitamin C that is in the multi-vitamins. Try not to let your toddler get into the habit of drinking "baby juices" ad lib, though. Even the brands labeled "no added sugar" contain enough fruit-sugar to put teeth and figures at risk.

*Mealtime behavior*

If you have done everything you can to set your minds at rest about your toddler's diet but you still find yourselves worrying, you may be worrying more about eating *behavior* than about actual food intake. Refusal of food, which has cost money and which has been prepared with care and love, is hurtful. The mess he makes as he plays with food he is not going to eat seems wasteful and goes against everything adults have been taught about "good manners." His anxiety to get down and get on with life after a few mouthfuls disrupts the family meal and prevents it from being a peaceful social occasion. But understandable though these feelings are, it is a mistake to get them mixed with worries about the child's actual *diet*. You are trying to feed him so that he can grow healthily. You are also trying to teach him to be socially acceptable. These are separate tasks: both important, but totally different.

When you insist that your child eat cabbage, is it for vitamin C or discipline? As we have seen there are many better sources of vitamin C. There are better issues for discipline too.

When you say that he "ought" to eat everything on his plate, are you thinking of him having enough to eat or of "not wasting good food?" As we have seen, he is the one who knows whether he has had enough or not. As to wasting food, isn't it just as much of a waste to force it down a reluctant child as to feed it to the cat?

When you say that he "ought" to eat his main course before he can have any dessert, is it because you really think the first course contains more important foods, or is it because you know he likes sweet things better and you think he ought to pay for them by ploughing through his meat and vegetables?

Of course it is up to parents to choose how and when to discipline their own children, but if you choose mealtimes you may pay a high price. I have talked to families who had got themselves into such a vicious circle over their toddlers' meals that the whole family's life was ruined by it, often for months at a time. Some families banned all mealtime conversation except stories and nursery rhymes designed to distract the toddler while mother ladled in some food. Others refused all invitations to visit friends for meals because the toddler would only eat at home. Some mothers regularly spent two hours over every meal and a great deal of time and money in between devising tempting little dishes for the next battle.

It is curious that we get ourselves into this situation, because toddlers get hungry just like everybody else. When they feel hungry their bodies are telling them to eat, and eat they do. Most toddlers with serious "eating problems" are actually rather fat. Very few are thin. But trouble begins because the child does not eat what you offer, when you say or in the way that you approve. The more you try to impose rules and regulations on eating and table manners, the clearer it becomes to the toddler that the mealtable is a marvelous place for a fight. Soon your child knows that it is one place where he can always get your attention and concern. That situation is irresistible to the child's growing sense of his own power and independence.

*Avoiding eating problems*

You are much cleverer than your toddler. If you foresee the possibility of mealtimes becoming a battleground, you can stay one jump ahead by resolutely refusing to become involved. It takes two to make a quarrel. The first steps are to do with your own feelings:

**Believe that your child will never starve,** if he is offered adequate food. This statement is not a careless generalization. It applies to all children and that includes yours. Somehow you have to persuade yourselves to believe it or you will not be able to follow the rest of the program for avoiding problems.

It might help to check your child's weight so that you can see that it is still following a steady upward curve. If that does not convince you, it might be wise to have the child checked over by your doctor so that you can be authoritatively assured that he is healthy and well-nourished. Go on seeking reassurance until you honestly believe that your job is only to offer good food, not to force it down your child. A long time ago a research study showed that year-old babies who were offered a wide range of foods three times each day selected for themselves, with no adult assistance, persuasion or instruction, diets which, while they were wildly unbalanced day by day, were perfectly balanced in the longer term. Like them, your child may have a bread jag and then a meat passion and then may eat almost nothing but fruit for a day or two without doing himself any harm at all. Trust him to know best. Once you have got yourself to this point the rest of the prevention program follows naturally:

**Encourage your toddler's independence in all areas,** especially at meals. Present his food in a form that is reasonably easy to manage, and don't help him unless he asks or gestures for help. If he does, don't scoop food straight from the plate into his mouth. Load the spoon for him and let him take it in his hand and put it in his mouth. Let him feel, always, that eating is something active which he does because he wants the food, not that being fed is something he accepts, passively, from you.

**Let the child eat by any method.** He needs to feel that getting the food he wants is the important thing, not getting it by tidy use of a spoon. If fingers are easiest for him, let him use them.

**Let the child eat in any order or combination.** If you will not give him dessert until he has eaten his first course, he will quickly realize that you care more about the main course than the dessert.

By the laws of toddler contra-suggestiveness, that will instantly make the dessert seem even more desirable. If you will not let him dip bacon in his cereal, he may well decide that he will not eat either of them. Just don't watch if you cannot stand the idea of the combination.

**Let the meal end when the child has had enough.** If you have accepted that what he eats and how he eats it is up to him, it follows that not eating any more or not eating anything at all is up to him too. You will ruin the effect of your whole campaign if you weaken at the last moment and try to feed him just a few mouthfuls to finish his meal.

**Try to keep mealtimes enjoyable.** Remember that sitting still is his least favorite occupation and that he still finds it difficult to join in a general family conversation which is not especially directed at him or his interests. Trying to make him sit up at the table for a whole family mealtime is bound to lead to trouble.

If you want him to feel part of a family group at the table, let him sit up with you, eat what he wants and then get down to play. For a while he may keep coming back for one more mouthful but he will soon learn that once he has got down his meal is over.

If you do not feel able to allow him to leave the family table before others have finished, feed him on his own. At three or thereabouts (see p. 390), he will be delighted to join you and will be able to "behave nicely" in order to earn the honor.

Many families will find that a compromise between these two positions works best. Perhaps you all have breakfast informally together before members of the family leave for work or school; lunch might be with mother and/or older brothers or sisters, while supper might be served separately to the toddler so that the older members of the family can enjoy a peaceful meal once he has been put to bed.

**Don't take an unreasonable amount of trouble over your child's food.** Of course it is vitally important that he should be offered a good diet (see p. 292) but the more money, time and trouble you take buying and preparing attractive and delicious food for the child, the more maddening you will find it when he is unappreciative. Keeping the child's meals simple often helps to keep the emotional temperature down. Why cook minced liver, three vegetables and a rice pudding when you know he will not eat them? Think what he is likely to eat. If the answer is "bread and butter and ham – again," give him that. It is perfectly adequate food; if he eats it, fine. If not, you will not have wasted much.

**Don't use food as reward, punishment, bribe or threat.** Remember that you are trying to keep the child's eating completely separate from his discipline. If he is hungry, he should eat as much as he wants of whatever is available. If he is not hungry, he should not eat. Food should be neither a treat nor a duty, and it should never be offered as a bribe or kept from him as a punishment. If he has ice cream, it should be because that is the dessert on today's menu, not because he has been a good boy. If he cannot have ice cream, it should be because it is not available today rather than because he has been naughty.

*Let him enjoy eating in his own way. Green beans dipped in ice cream may be unconventional, but if that is what he likes . . .*

*Candy* If you do not eat candy yourselves and your child has few older friends, you may be able to prevent him from even finding out what candy is until around the second birthday. It is probably worth trying. If the rest of the child's diet is sensible, even this period without candy will help those first teeth to get a good start.

But however careful you are, you are bound to meet the candy problem by the time of that second birthday. Children see the pretty packages in stores, see the advertisements so cleverly aimed at them on television, see other children munching and sharing. Your child will want to know what they have got. Once candy is known and recognized, he will demand to have some too.

There is no doubt that candy is bad for your child's teeth. But carefully selected, it does not have to be worse than many other foods; sensibly handled, candy does not have to become a major issue. Highly refined sugar makes enamel-attacking acid in the child's mouth. Every time sugar is eaten teeth are at risk; the more times per day they are put under attack and the longer the sugar remains in the mouth, the more holes there will eventually be for the dentist's attention. But this applies to *all* sources of refined sugar, not only to candy. A bottle filled with fruit drink and sucked over a long period will do just as much harm as the worst kind of candy while a slice of cake will produce as much acid as the least deplorable kind of candy. So to strike a moral pose and impose a ban on all candy while feeding the child the rest of a normal Western diet is foolish. It is much more sensible to take reasonable care over all sweet foods.

Sweet food which is eaten quickly will do little harm because the acid which is produced is gone from the mouth before it has time to eat into the tooth enamel. A slice of cake or a piece of chocolate are therefore much less harmful than a lollipop which the child sucks all afternoon. Chewy cakes and candy are usually worst of all since fragments tend to stick between the teeth and stay there until the next thorough brushing. This may also apply to many of the "healthy" foods which are often suggested as alternatives to candy; raisins, dates and other dried fruits – whether loose or in "health bars" – can cling tenaciously and although their sugar is not refined, it can do considerable harm. Some dentists even regret advocating finishing every meal with an apple as small pieces of sweet apple skin wedged between the teeth can do as much harm as the sugary film the apple was intended to remove.

So, when your child reaches the stage when he must have candy or feel conspicuously different from other children, select the particular candy carefully and control the manner in which he eats it. Choose types which dissolve quickly, such as chocolate or sugar wafers. Encourage him to eat all that you are going to give him in one short session, so that he eats a ration of six pieces of candy in a quarter of an hour rather than one every half hour throughout the afternoon. Try to arrange for him to have a drink of water as soon as possible after he has finished them, and make sure that his next tooth cleaning session is thorough.

Along with this kind of practical approach it is also important to monitor your emotional approach to candy because it is the emotional aspects of candy-eating which tend to make so many problems later on. Almost every human being likes sweet things.

Research has shown that even newborn babies can distinguish between plain and sweetened water and that most of them suck longer on the sugared bottles. But instead of calmly accepting that sweet foods are pleasant, we, with our copious supplies of cheap refined sugar, have made the buying and eating of actual candy part of our pleasure *rituals*. In many families boxes of chocolates are an accepted part of any outing and an expected purchase on any holiday. Candy is bought as a present, sent as a "thank you," hidden as a surprise, given to make banged knees better or disappointment bearable. It is used to convey or to stand in for love, and it is in this light that children yearn, whine and badger for it.

If you use candy as a reward and a treat during the toddler period, your pre-school child is bound to place an emotional value on it as well as liking the taste. If, when he grazes his knee, he gets a chocolate kiss along with your hug, that chocolate kiss will come to seem comforting to him. He will want candy whenever he is miserable or hurt and tired. If, when you are especially pleased with him, you buy him candy, he is bound to see the candy as being part of your loving feelings. He will want you to buy him candy to show that you love him. If, when he has to face something unpleasant like a shot, you pay him with a piece of candy, he is bound to see the candy as something he is owed whenever anything nasty happens. He will want payment in candy every time you make him do something he dislikes. If you can keep candy out of the emotional arena and treat it as coolly and calmly as you treat other particularly nice-tasting things such as strawberries or honey, none of this trouble will arise. Many children passionately enjoy strawberries and will eat as many as they can get during their short season. But how many of those children whine and cry and throw tantrums for strawberries?

*Snacks*  Many toddlers genuinely need to eat between the day's main meals. A mid-morning and/or a mid-afternoon snack may improve your child's temper as well as giving a welcome structure to the passing hours. And something to take the edge off hunger may prevent a late meal from becoming a major disaster. So try not to take a moralistic attitude to snacks. Food is food and there is no dietary law which says that it is better to eat three times a day than twice or six times. It is all a matter of commonsense and convenience mixed with social convention.

Part of the trouble over snacks arises from the vast market in fun-foods which has grown up during the last ten years. Like candy, fun-foods are heavily advertised and attractively packaged. Almost all children want them but many families react against them in ways which are really quite irrational.

Snack foods are said to be "junk food; no goodness in them." In fact these foods are neither more nor less likely to be nutritionally valueless than any of the manufactured foods you serve at the table. A pizza, for example, is a nicely balanced item of diet. Dairy ice cream from a reputable manufacturer is an excellent food, at least as good for your child as a home-made custard or pudding. Even the lowly potato chip (although too salty to be good for babies) is only potato, with the water removed, fried in vegetable oil. As such it is a surprisingly good source of vegetable protein and in no way worse for a child than a helping of french fries.

Snack foods are said to be "fattening." Of course all food is fattening if it is food in excess of the amount the child needs. A child who eats adequate meals *and* a lot of snacks will certainly get fat but a child who eats snacks *instead* of part of his meals will not. There is nothing devilish about snack foods which makes them more fattening, calorie for calorie, than the same kind of food which is served on a plate.

Snacks are said to fill children up so that they "cannot eat 'real' food." Again, this can happen, but it need not. If a child eats a non-nutritious snack when he was not really very hungry, he may well refuse that "good dinner" and indeed he ought to refuse it or he risks obesity. But the child who eats a nutritious snack and then refuses his meal may not be losing anything. It depends what the snack and the meal consisted of. So don't tar all snack foods with the same moralistic brush. As with candy, the real problem with snacks is an emotional one.

Snacks are almost always foods which, by definition, are bought because the child is hungry, are chosen by him, and are eaten because he wants to eat them rather than because anyone else cares one way or the other. They therefore escape the pressures to eat which, as we have seen (see p. 296), are so common with toddlers. This alone is enough to make them seem more desirable than "ordinary food." Snack foods are usually eaten under circumstances which are enjoyably different from sitting up at the table. Even the process of buying them is more fun for the toddler than the complex processes of supermarket shopping and kitchen food preparation. It is not surprising that many children would rather have that packet of "sesame crunchies" than their lunch, even if both are available simultaneously.

The answer is to treat snack foods as *food* (which is what they really are) rather than as *treats* (which is what will make trouble). A child should not get potato chips because he has been good any more than you would offer him cabbage for this reason. His ice cream should not be withheld because he has been tiresome any more than you would refuse to serve him meat. As with candy, if you keep the emotional temperature down in this way, remaining problems over snacks should be easy to handle.

The trick is to make sure that you offer the child the kinds of food he likes best as occasional parts of his regular meals, while keeping simpler foods freely available for eating between meals when he is genuinely hungry. Instead of waiting for him to nag you for chocolate while you are out shopping, serve him a couple of squares, with an apple, as a sweet course at lunch. Instead of taking a moralistic attitude to pleas for potato chips, serve them occasionally in place of that boring mashed potato.

Your child will still get hungry between meals from time to time. When he does, offer him something plain like bread and butter. If he is hungry enough to accept it, he is hungry enough for a snack to be sensible. He will not eat bread and butter from greed, and the cookies he might have eaten from gluttony are coming up on the supper table to be eaten or left as he thinks fit. The whole situation is emotionally defused.

*Fat toddlers*  A toddler can be plump without being fat. A lot of children are meant to be big; they are big babies, big toddlers, big children and eventually big adults. You cannot always judge whether your toddler is getting too fat just by looking. At this age faces are often very round and tummies almost always stick out.

If you think your child is getting too fat, look at the upper arms and at the thighs. If there are rolls of fat in those areas, so that the sleeves and the legs of the clothes strain tightly around them, then the child probably is too fat.

If you have been keeping up the weight and height chart, you can make a proper assessment by looking at that. Your child's ideal weight will go up in strict relation to height. If weight is being gained much faster than height, the child is bound to get fat.

*What to do*  Growing children should never be put on a diet which is designed to make them *lose* weight. You should aim to slow down your child's weight gain so that his height can catch up with his weight. If you try to diet a toddler more actively than this, you may actually distort his growth.

The fat toddler is almost certainly eating a diet which is high in carbohydrates. But that does not mean that the answer is to put him on the kind of low carbohydrate/high protein diet you might adopt if you were dieting. He needs his carbohydrate foods to satisfy his appetite and give him energy. He also needs the useful range of proteins, vitamins and minerals they contain.

**Look first at your child's consumption of fats.** You can cut a small child's calories very substantially without him noticing the difference at all or going without anything useful, if you just cut down his mealtime fats and fried foods. A 1oz (28g) slice of bread contains about 70 calories. If you add a normal spreading of butter you add another 70 calories with no extra value except some vitamin A which he is having in his multi-vitamins anyway. Roast potatoes have about twice and french fries about three times the calorie value of boiled ones.

**Look at your child's consumption of snacks.** You don't want to make him unhappy by suddenly forbidding all food between meals, but if he eats high calorie snacks all day he may actually be getting as many calories in the form of extras as he is getting from a complete diet of meals.

See whether you can substitute dried or fresh fruit for candy, Jell-O for ice cream, plain zwiebacks or water crackers for sweet ones, bread for cake or doughnuts.

**Look at your child's sugar consumption.** If he is a thirsty child who gets through a large bottle of concentrated vitamin C fruit drink in a week, he will be getting far more vitamin C than he needs and the sugar in those drinks alone will be giving him a lot of extra calories. Fresh orange juice will be better for him. Provided he gets enough vitamin C from multi-vitamin drops or tablets, an ordinary fruit juice, very well diluted, will be less fattening still, while water is the best of all drinks for fat children.

Does he have a lot of convenience baby fruits and desserts? Many of them are made extremely sweet; home-cooked or raw fresh fruit would be less fattening.

Does he eat a lot of candy? If so, try giving it to him as part of his meals (an apple with some chocolate or a few M & M's, as a sweet course for example) and then just not having any available between meals. If you want him to have some candy but he always insists on having a whole package rather than just a few at a time, you can fool him by taking the trouble to split a ¼lb (113g) package into eight tiny plastic bags. Once he has eaten the contents of one he will accept that they are "all gone."

**Look at your child's milk consumption.** If he is still drinking more than, say, 1½ pints (0.8l), it is worth trying to cut him gently back to somewhere nearer 1 pint (0.5l) – though not below this. If he is still having bottles, put 2oz (50ml) less in each. If he drinks milk from a cup just give him a bit less each time but remember to offer him plain water to make up the fluid.

Most of the calories in milk are in the fat of the cream while the valuable protein and calcium are in the milk. As we have seen (see p.194) skimmed or low-fat milk is not usually recommended for children under five, but if your toddler is really overweight and you cannot reduce his milk consumption without upsetting him, check with your doctor. Provided he has his multi-vitamins and the rest of his diet is good, she might think it sensible to change his milk for a few months.

**Look at your child's daily life.** Does he get the opportunity for all the exercise he wants? Is there somewhere for him to play actively? Do you let him push the stroller some of the way when you go shopping, or does he just sit in it? Is he free on the floor when he is at home and awake, or does he spend a lot of time in his stroller or playpen? Given the chance he will be constantly on the go, and the more exercise he takes the less chance food will have to settle down in his fat cells: it will be needed to give him energy.

# Sleeping

Now that your child is too big to sleep in a portacrib and too alert and mature to drop off to sleep while the outside world is offering entertainment, meeting sleep needs inevitably imposes some restrictions on your freedom. Keeping these restrictions to a minimum means making some decisions, now.

*The happy-go-lucky approach*

If you want to be able to take the baby with you wherever and whenever you go, you can. Your child will be happy to accompany you out to supper with friends, to be taken away for weekends or long day trips, even to sit on your lap at the movies. But you will have a price to pay. A baby who is kept up on occasion to suit your convenience is very unlikely to go happily to bed at a conventional hour just because that is what would suit you tonight. He or she will probably be the kind of toddler who is up until all hours most nights of the week, and whose daytime sleep pattern is also irregular because it depends on how tiring those nightly outings have been. None of that will hurt *him* (at least until he has to conform to the outside routines of school) but it is what *you* want?

*The regular routine approach*

If you want to be fairly sure of adult peace and privacy in the evenings and of a break from the baby's demanding company during the day, you can. A regular routine of naps and bedtimes will be accepted, but you, too, will have to pay a price. The routine approach only works if it is kept to almost all the time. That means arranging your evenings out so that you put the baby to bed before you go, and have a babysitter. It means keeping as close to the normal pattern as you can even when you are on vacation, and it means arranging most of your trips to fit in with that routine.

*Sleep needs*

As we saw earlier (see p. 207), babies vary widely in the number of hours they need to sleep in each twenty-four hour period. If your baby has always needed plenty of sleep, he will still need it. But if he has never slept for more than ten hours a day, he will not suddenly get sleepier.

Whatever his starting point, the overall number of hours slept will only drop very gradually during this age period. Between the first and second birthdays the baby will only reduce his total sleeping time by about one hour.

*Sleeping patterns*

Most toddlers sleep between ten and twelve hours at night (though seldom in an unbroken block, unfortunately)! The difference between those hours and the child's total sleep requirement is then made up in daytime naps of anything from twenty minutes to three or more hours.

At the beginning of this age period almost every baby will need two daytime naps arranged to break up his waking day fairly evenly. If he wakes at 5:30am he may droop by 9am and then need a second rest in the afternoon.

Around the middle of this year you may meet an awkward phase when two naps are too many and one is not enough. The baby makes it clear that he is not ready to be put to bed after the family breakfast. But if you let him stay up, he cannot last through the morning. By midday, just when his meal is cooking, he is exhausted, whiny and impossible.

If you realize that in this state he will not eat any lunch anyway and put him to bed at 11:30, he will go to sleep at once but exactly the same thing happens in the afternoon: he has his late lunch, does not want to go back to bed during the afternoon, but cannot stay comfortably awake until bedtime.

By the end of the second year this awkwardness usually resolves itself into a single nap taken either at the end of the morning before a late lunch, or at the very beginning of the afternoon after an early lunch. In the meantime you may find yourself serving your child lunch at 11:15 or putting him to bed for the night at 5:30!

There may be worse to come: some two-year-olds are so sensitive to daytime naps that even a brief afternoon sleep defers bed beyond a time you can tolerate. You may find yourself *refusing* him a nap, even avoiding a late afternoon car ride in case he drops off. . . .

*Waking from naps*  If you are to keep any kind of pattern to your own and your toddler's day, you will often have to wake him from his naps. A nap that begins at 11:30am might go on until 3:30pm if you left it to him. He has had no midday meal; you have not been able to go out shopping; and there may be an older child who needs meeting from school. Even if it suits you to let him sleep all afternoon, it probably would not be wise. After such a long daytime sleep he will not be ready for his ordinary bedtime.

Waking your toddler from a nap takes tact. He will probably bitterly resent being disturbed, and need at least half an hour of peaceful cuddling and conversation before he feels ready to face the world. If you try to wash or dress him, he will howl. If you hurry him to a meal, he will not eat it. If you rush him off to meet another child from school, he will whine and moan and make it impossible for you to pay proper attention to the schoolchild.

So, wake him gently while you still have plenty of time in hand and let him make a gradual transition from being asleep to being awake, from being cocooned in his crib to being loose on the floor.

*Getting overtired*  This is a very common toddler problem especially during the middle of the second year when the child really needs one and a half naps per day or at two and a bit when he needs half a nap!

Your toddler is working extremely hard. As he learns to walk and to climb he pushes himself to the limits of his physical strength. Because he is learning he falls down, bumps himself, surprises and hurts himself many times each day. His daily life at this stage must be something like an afternoon spent by an adult learning to water ski or to skate.

Like the rest of us, the toddler manages his body less and less well as he tires. Getting tired makes his physical coordination less efficient, so that he has to put more and more effort into everything he does. The more effort he has to make the more tired he becomes. If you watch a toddler in a public playground, you can see this happening before your eyes. When he arrives, keen and fresh from a rest, the child rushes around managing everything beautifully.

When you wake her from her naps,
be tactful; give her time to
re-adjust to the wakeful world.

The sand that he digs goes into his bucket and he can get three rungs up the climbing frame. An hour later it takes him ten minutes to fill that bucket; all his sandpies break and his hands slip every time he tries to climb.

Along with physical efforts the child is also making enormous efforts to understand and to manage the world. That playground is noisy; there are lots of other children; it may frighten him or it may excite him, but it certainly will not relax him.

Physical tiredness, excitement and tension can build up in a toddler to a point where he no longer knows that he is tired, does not see how to stop and rest, and cannot relax anyway. He needs rescuing before he reaches this point. Don't assume that a child who is still rushing around is not tired: look at what he is doing and see whether he is finding it more difficult than he was finding it half an hour ago. If he is, then he needs a rest. Don't assume that a child who has difficulty in getting to sleep at night (see opposite) is not getting tired during the day: he may be getting overtired, and it may be the resulting tension which is keeping him awake. The answer is not necessarily more sleep, but it is probably more rest.

*Resting without sleep*

Try to find some ways of giving your toddler both physical rest and relaxation from stress without actually putting him to bed. Quiet occupations that he enjoys now, between bouts of energetic and effortful play, will be useful for years to come. You will be able to build on them ways of keeping him occupied whenever circumstances make it desirable that he should keep still, whether it is because you are traveling, sitting in the dentist's waiting room or because the child himself is unwell.

Different families will select their own "quiet time occupations," but during this age period they will almost certainly depend on your doing something *with* the child. No self-respecting toddler will sit down alone to anything for more than five minutes.

*Draw a horse, read her a story,
play her a record or settle to a puzzle*

*. . . with your help, she can rest
even without sleeping.*

# Sleeping problems

*Trouble in going to sleep at night*

Many parents believe that every toddler except their own goes peacefully to bed at the right time every night. There is a general belief that if you are kind but firm no fuss should ever happen. It is a myth. When research workers give parents a chance to describe what actually happens in their homes, it becomes clear that at *least* 50% of all children between the ages of one and two make a major fuss about being put to bed. Night after night toddlers are rocked and sat with, cuddled, taken back downstairs, nursed to sleep on the parents' bed, fed, slapped, scolded and fed again.

So let us not pretend that it is easy. Let us think about the reality not the myth. The reality is that a fuss at bedtime wrecks the evening for the whole family. There is a meal to be prepared and eaten; there may be older children needing attention; there is news to exchange and everyone is tired. Most parents will do almost anything to get that toddler to settle down quietly. They know that bringing the child downstairs again is not really a solution but if it works for tonight, that is good enough – until tomorrow brings a new commotion.

*Putting your toddler to sleep*

If you have always nursed or rocked your baby to sleep, you may not be having nightly commotions but you are probably beginning to find that getting him to sleep takes longer and longer. He can keep himself awake in your arms for more and more songs and he can snap from apparent slumber into furious wakefulness the moment you try to put him into his crib. With the whole performance to be repeated every time he wakes in the night, you would probably be sensible to try to teach him to drop off by himself even if it seems to make your evenings worse for a while (see p. 141). The longer you go on nursing him to sleep, the more painful teaching him to do it for himself will become. In a few months' time he will not just cry if you try to leave him while he is still conscious: he'll beg for what he is used to with pathetic cries of "up-up mommy" and strict instructions to "walk about!"

Some parents find that the easiest way to teach a baby in this age group to go to sleep on his own is to give him his bottle in the crib and let him suck himself to sleep (see p. 327). You still need to think ahead, though. If he drops off with one bottle of milk he is almost bound to demand another to drop off with whenever he wakes in the night. Some babies get through three bottles a night in that way. That's at least two awakenings for parents, even leaving aside the effects on the toddlers' teeth and figures and the (faint) possibility of choking. If sucking seems to bridge the gap between you leaving and the baby sleeping, a pacifier might be a better solution.

*Leaving your toddler to cry*

If your baby is used to dropping off to sleep without you but won't, the most usual advice is to settle him down, leave and then refuse to go back into the room however much he cries. Parents are told that if they can only survive two hours of crying tonight it will be one hour tomorrow, half an hour the next day and peace after that.

Many families do not find that this works and indeed if you look at it from the toddler's point of view it is difficult to see why it should. What message does staying away convey to him? He is crying because he cannot bear you going away. So if you stay away you must seem to be saying "It's no good crying because I'm not going to come back no matter how sad you are." If that is the message the toddler receives, it is hardly likely to make him feel safer about bedtime tomorrow. It can only make him more sure that it is dangerous to let you go at all.

In fact very few families do pursue this policy. A determined toddler can keep himself awake and crying for much longer than his parents or the neighbors can stand. If you are going to have to go to him in two hours' time when he is convinced that you have abandoned him forever, you had much better go now.

*Staying with your toddler*  The opposite approach is to give the toddler what he wants, by staying with him or taking him back downstairs. Although it is kinder than leaving him to cry, it is not really any more sensible if you think again about the message your behavior will convey to him. "You're scared of being left and you're right, it is upsetting to be left all alone so I'll stay with you/take you with me. . . ." Once again this is not a message likely to make for easier bedtimes later on. How can the child come to believe that it is perfectly all right to be left to go to sleep if you suggest that he is right to mind? And how can he be expected to accept that bedtime is the end of his day if he has nightly proof that his day will go on if he cries?

*The middle path*  There is a compromise which neither leaves the child desperately alone nor gives him victory in getting some more day. The message it is supposed to convey is something like this:

"There is no need to cry. You aren't deserted. We will always come if you need us. But it is the end of today and time for you to go to sleep."

You settle the child down cheerfully, going through whatever rituals are usual and finishing up with your usual "goodnight" (see p. 210). If, when you leave, the child cries, wait to see whether it is just a "testing cry." The minute the crying starts to build up, you go back into the room and repeat just that last "goodnight." Then you leave again.

Between the two of you and the burning potatoes, you repeat this performance for as long as it takes the toddler to settle down. As long as the crying lasts you visit every few minutes, but on each visit you only stay for that 30 second "goodnight." "I am still here" you are saying, "but there's no more of today."

**Don't** get the toddler out of the crib, or stay in the room, or stay away for more than five minutes at a time.

**Do** try to get the toddler to see that you are there always, but that at this time of day you are completely boring.

I have known it take a week for this policy to work. I have never known it to take longer except when the parents weakened. If you get so fed up one night that you decide to leave your toddler crying alone after all, you will have the whole job to do again. Equally, if you cannot stand going up and down any longer and decide to take your child downstairs with you, the whole thing will start again.

| | |
|---|---|
| *Waking in the night* | Although the child is now old enough to keep himself awake on purpose he still cannot (and never will be able to) wake himself on purpose. Waking up in the night is not a "habit." You cannot teach your child not to do it, either by ignoring him when he wakes or by scolding him for it. In fact, night waking has nothing to do with discipline, and parents who tell you, smugly, that *their* children know better, are fooling themselves. Don't let them fool you. |
| *Waking without fear* | All children wake several times each night as they turn over. If nothing interests or disturbs them, they drop straight down into sleep again without anyone ever knowing that they have woken. If your child insists that you know about all his wakings, check some of the following: |

**Have you always put him to sleep?** If so, he will have to send for you until you can teach him to drop off himself.

**Do you go into the room whenever you hear a movement?** *You* may be disturbing *him*. If he wants you, he will let you know.

**Does your toddler go to sleep on top of the bedclothes** and then get cold in the small hours? If so, either put him in a sleeping bag or sleeper suit or keep a separate crib blanket to drape over him and his toys at your own bedtime.

**Is your toddler afraid of the dark?** If so, give him a 15-watt nightlight. It will not stop him waking, but it may stop him needing to call you when he does wake.

**Does the toddler use a pacifier?** If he does, put two or three pacifiers close beside him when you go to bed. With any luck he will be able to find *one* without crying for you/it.

**Is the toddler being disturbed by outside sounds?** As with a younger child (see p. 214) you may have to do something about traffic noise.

**Does your toddler get hungry in the night?** Some toddlers are so tired by bedtime that they cannot eat much supper. Breakfast then seems a long way off. An earlier supper with a drink of milk at bedtime may be a better pattern in these months.

**Does your toddler get thirsty?** A few parents, even at this early age, believe that restricting evening drinks will mean fewer wet beds. It will not. The child must drink as much as he wants right up until bedtime or thirst is very likely to wake him in the night.

| | |
|---|---|
| *Waking up afraid* | This is the more usual kind of night waking. Nearly half of every group of toddlers studied by research workers suffers from it. The waking is due to some form of nightmare, but of course we don't know what the child dreams, thinks of or sees while asleep. |

Some children wake up terrified several times each night for a while and then not at all for months. Others wake three or four times a week for months on end.

The waking may take the form of instant panic, so that you find the child sitting bolt upright in the crib, clearly terrified. On other occasions it takes the form of terrible grief, so that you find the child lying down, crying as if something dreadful had happened.

Either way, if you arrive quickly the drama is usually over in 30 seconds. One glimpse of your familiar figure, one soothing pat and the child is asleep again. He remembers nothing about it in the morning. But if you don't arrive quickly, things tend to be very different. The toddler becomes more and more afraid as he listens to his own frightened voice crying in the night-quiet. When you do come to him he is shaky, tense and sobbing. Instead of being reassured by a glimpse and a pat, he may need 15 or even 30 minutes' cuddling and talk before he can settle into sleep again.

*Dealing with nightmares*

Coping with the nightmares is simple: you just get to the child as fast as you can the moment you hear him crying. But preventing them is much more difficult; and it is prevention you will want when you have had to haul yourself out of bed in the small hours eight nights in a row.

Specific suggestions such as tiring the child out during the day or giving him more to eat at suppertime seldom work. An overtired child or one who has had an extra large meal forced upon him is likely to sleep less, rather than more, peacefully. But sometimes a more general approach to the child-as-a-whole does seem effective. We do not know exactly what causes nightmares either in toddlers or in older people. But we do know that they are associated with anxiety and stress. If your toddler is finding some aspect of his life a strain and you can relieve that strain a little, the nightmares may become less frequent.

Is there a new baby present or imminent? Have you recently taken a job so that the child is being cared for by someone else? Is his father away from home a great deal at present? Any radical change in his small world is liable to have made him anxious whether he shows it during the day or not. Even when you cannot remove the cause of his stress you may be able to help him, both by being extra-loving and tolerant and, perhaps, by talking to him about what is happening. Even a child who does not yet use many words can often be reassured by a simple acknowledgment from his parents that they know he is upset and understand why.

Are you in the thick of battles about eating, toilet training or his general desire for independence? However hard he fights you while he is awake, a baby-bit of him is liable to be worried about these battles. He is not sure that he can really afford to risk your displeasure. You may find it possible to relax the demands you are making on him for a while. This, together with lots of assurance that you love him, just as he is, may relieve the stress.

Have you just returned from a vacation? Has he been in the hospital or ill for a long time at home? Happenings which temporarily take him away from home or break up his accustomed routine can have a disturbing effect. Sticking carefully to a more than usually rigid nursery-type routine for a few weeks will give him back a feeling of structured security.

All these suggestions really add up to the same idea: that a toddler who is having a lot of nightmares may benefit from being treated, for a while, as if he were a little younger than he really is. Something is making him feel worried and unable to cope with the demands made by his life. Baby him a little so that he can meet all demands with ease, and the nightmares will probably ease off.

### Night wandering

Late in the second year a new reason for not leaving your toddler to cry alone at night often emerges: if you will not go to him, he will learn to come to you.

Climbing out of his crib at night is a development to be avoided at all costs. It is dangerous. Crib sides are high for a toddler who is only just learning to climb. If he gets out safely without you hearing, he is loose and unsupervised around the house. Even if no real disaster occurs, a child who discovers that he *can* get out of bed, and come to find you, will do so night after night. Thousands of families are driven mad by their toddlers appearing in the living room or, worse, in the bedroom, several times each night. If your toddler is going to share your bed it is probably both safer and less stressful for everyone if you *decide* that it is so and arrange things accordingly (see p. 84).

### Preventing night wandering

Prevention does not just mean physically preventing the child from getting out of bed, it means stopping him from ever thinking about getting out of bed alone. If it occurs to him to try to climb out of his crib, typical toddler persistence will probably keep him trying until he succeeds, so you have to make it seem completely impossible *and* make sure that he has no strong motive.

It is at this stage that a sleeping bag, started during the first year, proves itself valuable for more than keeping him warm. If he has worn such a bag, all night and every night for as long as he can remember, he will know that he cannot walk about until you have taken it off. A simple piece of parent-upmanship but a very effective one. But it only works if you start using a bag before he shows the least sign of trying to climb.

If he is always visited when he cries, whether it is before he has fallen asleep or during the night, he will not have an urgent and desperate reason for trying to get out. The times when he is most likely to try to come to you are the times when you have refused to come to him.

If he has never been taken downstairs again during the evening, or into your bed during the night, he will not have an alluring picture in his mind of the companionable pleasures he is missing by being in his crib. It is the toddlers who can envisage a cozy family group, or an even cozier sleeping couple, from which they are excluded, who try hardest to get out of bed.

### Dealing with night wandering

If the night wandering habit does start, it is extremely difficult to break. Nothing short of physical restraint will keep the toddler in. But physical restraints, such as locking the bedroom door, stretching netting over the top of the crib, or putting him to sleep in a safety-harness, are all potentially dangerous. Worse, keeping your toddler in by force makes it certain that he will regard going to bed as imprisonment. Once this happens there is little hope of contented bedtimes and peaceful nights.

Clever do-it-yourself parents may be able to solve the whole problem by taking the base of the crib out and putting it back several inches lower down the frame. The toddler will never notice the difference. He will just be surprised to find that he cannot reach to climb out of his crib tonight even though he managed to do so yesterday.

Failing that, the best way of teaching him not to get out is probably to make absolutely sure that he gains nothing by his exploits that he cannot get by calling. If you can get hold of a ''baby alarm'' so that you can hear over the loudspeaker when the child starts to climb, you can meet him before he so much as reaches his bedroom door. If he is always put instantly back to bed again, he will probably give up.

Even without quite such a quick response you can make sure that night wandering does not get him anywhere. If he appears in the living room, hustle him straight back to bed; do not give him even two seconds to be charming. If he appears in your bedroom, take him straight back to his own. Letting him cuddle in beside you is asking for nightly repeat performances.

A sleeping bag, a crib and parents who come when he calls are likely to keep a toddler in bed. It follows that this is not the time to promote him to a ''big bed.'' There is plenty of time for that later on (see p. 395). If there is a new baby on the way, plan to buy or to borrow a second crib.

*Early waking*  While early morning waking is even more common in toddlers than in younger babies, it is usually easier to live with. The toddler is at his best and most cheerful first thing in the morning. He may wake you up at 6am but it is more likely to be with loud singing than with crying or grumbling.

Some toddlers simply occupy themselves with talk and song and with bouncing their crib around and bossing their teddy bears. Others welcome older children, swapping charm for service until the grown-up world appears. If your toddler insists on you coming to him, try one of the following:

**Leave a small cardboard box of selected toys and books** beside his crib when you go to bed. Simply unpacking them will occupy him for a long time. And with any luck you will have chosen at least one object that he would actually like to play with.

**Leave a drink in a training cup and a zwieback or two.** Helping himself is half the fun and his crib will need changing anyway so the mess does not matter.

**Make sure there is enough light.** In summer thin curtains will let enough light through; in winter leave on a low-watt bulb.

**Teach the toddler how to know when it is really morning.** He will learn to recognize a signal which means it is time for you to get up and come to him. It might be your alarm clock going off or the radio being switched on.

# Toilet training

Learning acceptable toilet behavior is much more difficult for children than learning sensible eating or even sleeping habits, because the toilet behavior that is asked of them has no obvious reward. Children who are sat in high chairs get food for which they are hungry. Children who are put to bed get the rest that their bodies are demanding. But children who are put on potties just have bowel movements that they were going to have anyway. It is parents who care where the movements go. Eventually a toddler will get the reward of pleasing you and of feeling "grown up." But these are vague pleasures; behaving nicely on purpose is not your toddler's strong point.

Do not be in a hurry to start. If you begin before your child is physically ready you will be asking something of the toddler which he is simply not mature enough to give. There is bound to be stress. If you try to insist on cooperation before your child is emotionally ready, you will be trying to impose your will on the toddler's in an area where you cannot win. You cannot *make* him use that potty; attempts to force training invite the child to experience successful defiance and negate the whole purpose of the exercise. Toilet training is not a question of making the child do something *for you*. It is a matter of helping him do something *for himself*. You are not training him to use a potty or toilet but helping him to take independent charge of his own functions.

Remember that no matter when you start "training," your child is unlikely to be entirely reliable, even in the daytime, before the third year. An early start means that the learning process takes longer; if you start later he will learn faster and reach the same point at the same time. However late your child seems to be in acquiring control, he won't set off for big school in diapers.

*Judging the right moment to introduce a potty*

Until around fifteen months old your child still moves his bowels or passes water quite automatically. He neither knows when he is going to, nor does he realize when he has done so. Watch him if he happens to pee while he is naked: he does not even look at the puddle he produces because he does not realize that it is anything to do with him. He is not yet ready for a potty.

Somewhere around the middle of the year he makes that vital connection. Now he looks at the puddle and clutches himself. He has connected the feeling of urination or passing a movement with what is produced. He knows when he *has* performed but he still does not know when he is going to do so. At this stage the child is not ready to use a potty but he is ready to meet one.

*What kind of potty?*

The child's potty needs to be comfortable to sit down on and feel perfectly secure even if he wriggles while he is sitting. It must be virtually untippable and, of course, easy to clean. A boy needs a shape that shields the front.

A "potty-chair" is a good buy. Sitting down and getting up are easy for him and he has good back support. The actual potty lifts out for cleaning and taking on trips.

Gimmicky potties, such as those that play a tune, may amuse him or you. But the child will soon learn that a thrown toy produces the tune just as readily as a movement does.

## Introducing the potty

At this stage you only want to make sure that the child knows what the potty is for. Its use is obvious to you and, if he has older brothers or sisters, may be obvious to him too. But an only child may be totally mystified. After all he is accustomed to seeing you use a toilet, not a potty. The two items do not look at all alike.

Show him the potty, tell him that it is for putting urine and feces in when he is big enough to stop wearing diapers. Then put it in a corner of his usual playroom. Don't actually encourage him to use it as a hat, but let him make friends with it. If he is ready to be interested at all he may sit his teddy bear on it. Eventually he will want to sit on it himself. When he does, don't insist on taking his diapers off. He only wants to see what sitting on that potty feels like. He is not ready to use it yet.

## Judging when your child is ready to start using the potty

The right moment is the one at which your child becomes aware that he is *about* to produce urine or a movement rather than only being aware after the event. This awareness starts with advance warning of a coming bowel movement. The child may stand stock still, clutching himself and going red in the face. He may look at you and make sounds of anticipation. Now, if he chooses, he can put that movement in the potty instead of in his diapers. But remember that we are talking only about *bowel* training and that the choice is, and will remain, the child's.

## Bowel training

Becoming "clean" is far easier for a child than becoming "dry." Most children only move their bowels once or twice a day and many do not move them that often. Many children (especially if they have not been involved in too-early attempts at "training") are naturally regular in their timing. The signs of an imminent movement are quite clear to a watching adult, and the interval between the child first feeling the need and actually moving the bowels is quite long. If the toddler is emotionally ready to cooperate in using that potty, it is easy for you to help.

If you know that he is likely to move his bowels immediately after breakfast or on waking from a nap, delay putting on diapers, plastic pants, jeans or any other encumbrances, so that the whole matter is quick and easy. Make sure that the potty is in its usual place. Wait until the child tells or signals that a movement is on the way and then casually suggest that he might like to sit on the potty so that it goes in there.

If the child says "no" do not push it. If he does not seem to care either way or seems to like the idea, produce the potty, stay while he performs and be calmly congratulatory.

Many children who are introduced to the idea in this casual way and at just the right moment will bowel train themselves completely within a couple of weeks. But if your child does not take so readily to the idea, be cautious:

**Don't try to force the child to sit on the potty** even if you can see that he is about to have a bowel movement. Toddlers are extremely contra-suggestive. The clearer you make it that you really want him to sit there, the less likely he is to want to. Since toilet training can only succeed through his voluntary cooperation, battles will mean certain failure.

**Tone your reactions right down.** If you are thrilled when he "succeeds" and disappointed when he "fails," keep your feelings off your face and out of your voice. Above all don't make his use of the potty a moral issue by calling him "good" for using it or "naughty" for not doing so. Using a potty instead of diapers is just a new skill which he is learning. Feces in the potty deserve a quiet word about how grown up he is getting. Feces in his diaper or on the floor need an equally quiet word about the possibility that he might choose to put them in the potty tomorrow.

**Don't try to make the child share your adult disgust at feces.** He has just discovered that they come out of him. He sees them as an interesting product belonging to him. If you rush to empty the potty; change him with fastidious fingertips and wrinkled nose and are angry when he examines or smears the contents of his potty, you will hurt his feelings. You don't have to pretend to share his pleasurable interest – discovering that adults don't play with feces is part of growing up – but don't try to make him feel they are dirty and disgusting. If he knows his feces are disgusting to you, he will feel that you think he is disgusting too.

**Don't try to tamper with the natural bowel pattern.** Laxatives to make it "easier" or soap sticks to induce a movement at a convenient moment are totally wrong. It is his body. If you forcibly tamper with it, he really will feel that you are trying to overwhelm him.

**Help your toddler toward toilet independence.** If you have delayed introducing the potty until late in his second year, he will be able to go to it himself, manage his clothes with minimal help and get on and off the potty alone. The more he feels that the whole business is within his own control, the less likely he is to resent it.

*Bladder training* Although your child will learn to recognize the feelings which mean imminent urination at about the same age that he recognizes a coming bowel movement, doing something about those feelings comes considerably later.

Between noticing the sensations of a loaded rectum and actually passing the movement he has plenty of time to get to the potty and sit down. But there is no time at all between noticing a coming pee and producing a flood. The exclamation that means "I'm going to" is simultaneous with the puddle. It is too soon for training.

But your child will learn that urine can go in a potty as well as in a diaper because urine will often be passed while the potty is being used for a bowel movement. If bowel training is going smoothly, the toddler may be very ready to cooperate in urine training just as soon as he is physically capable of it.

*Judging when he is ready for bladder training* The first sign of readiness is your child's learning of the momentary control over coming urine which older children call "clenching your bottom." The child realizes, just in time, that urine is coming. He clenches the muscles around the urethra and the anus and stops it. But these muscles are too low down for efficient control; the pressure in the child's abdomen is already high; the urgency is extreme; the child can hold on only for a few seconds and only while standing stock still with legs crossed. While any control at all is a sign of progress this is not yet useful control because if the child moves toward the potty he will urinate.

Somewhere around the second birthday the child will learn to take charge of the coming urination at an earlier stage, by recognizing a full bladder and tightening the muscles of the abdomen. Now he can delay the flow for several minutes and can walk without losing control. The toddler is therefore ready to make for the potty – if he wants to.

*Helping your child to manage urination*

Even when your child can recognize a need to urinate while there is still time to get to the potty, becoming "dry" will probably be a long, slow process. Children urinate so many times in the day that many failures are inevitable, especially when they are absorbed in play and therefore do not notice their need in time. They still cannot wake themselves to pee so they go on being accustomed to wet night-time diapers and perhaps to nap-time ones as well. Unless you can be extremely tactful and gentle, your toddler may get very bored and discouraged about the whole matter.

Your first aim is to help him experience some "successes." Once you know that he can wait a few minutes after realizing that he needs to go, pick a day when he wakes up from a nap dry, and delay dressing him. Suggest that he sit on his potty but if he does not want to, or sits for a moment and gets up without doing anything, make no comment. Just leave him bare-bottomed, potty at hand, and encourage him to sit there when he feels the need. If he succeeds, be gently congratulatory and then put his diapers on as usual. If he gets absorbed in play and makes a puddle, mop it up without comment and dress him as usual. If the weather is warm and you can leave him naked in the yard, so much the better. Each experience of feeling and seeing himself urinate will help to clinch the connection between the feeling and what happens next.

After a few days or weeks of occasional casual successes, take the child out of diapers when he is *at home and awake*. Don't make a big thing of it or he may feel demeaned by having the diapers back on for outings, naps and the night. Just suggest casually that he would be more comfortable without them while he plays and that if he needs to pee, his potty is close by. Do realize that this is a puddly stage. Be actually sympathetic about his frequent accidents: "Bad luck, you left it a bit late, didn't you? Let's mop it up. . . ."

Once he manages to use his potty about half the time, buy him some terry-cloth lined plastic training pants. They will not absorb a whole urination but they will reduce flood-damage in the home; they are comfortable for the child and they are easy for him to take down and pull up. Go on using diapers for naps, nights and trips. You are still trying to prevent him from experiencing too many discouraging "failures."

During this stage it is a good idea to introduce the child to the toilet as well as the potty. If he will happily use that too, you will not have to spend the next six months carrying a potty with you whenever you go out! He will probably like the idea of peeing

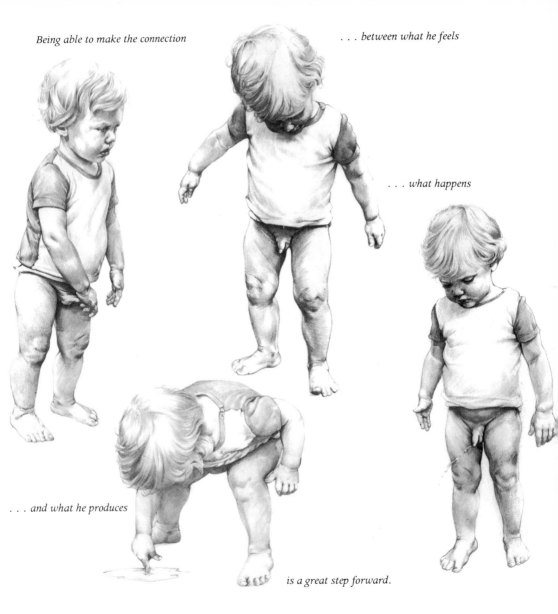

*Being able to make the connection* ... *between what he feels*

... *what happens*

... *and what he produces*

*is a great step forward.*

where you do, but he will need a firm stool or box to help him climb on and off, and a small seat clipped over the large one so that he does not feel that he is going to fall in. Be tactful about flushing the toilet. Many children hate the noise and are frightened of the idea of things being sucked away. They have so little idea of the relative sizes of things that they may actually think that they might be flushed away too. So let your child pull the handle himself if he enjoys doing so. If not, leave it until he is out of the bathroom.

Once he is more or less reliable at home in the daytime, abandon diapers as part of his regular clothes. He can have them on for naps if he prefers and he should still wear them at night, but that is all. Although you will still get a fair number of pools, giving up diapers is important. While he still wears them sometimes, the child cannot finally learn that *every* feeling of bladder fullness means a trip to his potty. You cannot expect him to think "I'm going to pee in a minute; am I wearing diapers or not?"

With many children, urine training will go smoothly from this point on. You will get fewer and fewer accidents until you suddenly realize that you have stopped taking mopping up for granted as one of your daily tasks. But there are some pitfalls:

**Don't continually nag and remind your child to sit on the potty.** You want him to feel that pants are more comfortable than diapers and that using a potty is quicker and easier than being changed. If you keep nagging, you will make him feel that life was easier when he had those safe old diapers on and that being put into pants has spoiled it all. Reminders ruin training anyway. You are trying to help him recognize his own need to go and do something about it for himself. If you keep reminding him, you are doing his thinking for him. You may actually delay the moment when he is fully and independently reliable.

**Don't expect a toddler to be able to urinate without feeling the need.** Until he is around three years old he will not discover how to urinate when his need is not urgent and therefore recognizable. So it is useless to send him to the bathroom before an outing "so that you won't need to go later," and it is bitterly unfair to be cross with him for an accident in the supermarket "because you ought to have gone before we came out. . . ."

**Cultivate your skill as a bathroom-finder.** Once your child wants to stay dry he must be able to rely on you to find him somewhere to pee, quickly, wherever you find yourselves when the need strikes. Get into the habit of carrying a potty when you go out for long periods and of noting the whereabouts of the facilities in stores and on the street. Be patient if you have to get off a bus, leave the highway, lose your place in the post office line or come home in a hurry. You are the one who wanted the child to stop wetting himself. Once he has stopped he will be really upset if too long a wait forces him to wet his pants after all.

*Bathroom talk*   Our language is full of euphemisms for bathrooms and the functions we perform in them. Adults find it easy to adapt their language to the company they are in, but children will accept whatever words you use when you first invite them to perform on a potty, and they will go on using the same words for years no matter where they are. So it is worth giving those words a bit of thought. An invented baby-name for a bowel movement may seem perfectly appropriate for a two-year-old but embarrass you when your child uses it at four and be incomprehensible to the school teacher a year later. Correct medical terminology from the beginning may seem the answer, but unfortunately both teachers and classmates will be amused and incredulous if he announces "I need to urinate."

There is no general answer to this minor problem because acceptable terminology will vary from place to place. Wherever you live there will be a fine line between the over-medical and the vernacular, the acceptable and the rude. It may help to listen in your local playground for the words somewhat older children are using among themselves.

# Everyday care

## Caring without bossing

Physical care involves looking after your child's body. Because toddlers are increasingly conscious of their own ownership of their bodies, it takes a lot of tact. They cannot do everything for themselves yet they bitterly resent being handled like objects or possessions. Take plenty of time and use lots of imagination. If you have time you will not be tempted to do things by force. If you use imagination, almost everything you have to do for your child can either be turned into a game or into something he can do with your help.

It is worth taking trouble. This is a very contra-suggestive and combative stage. If you let yourself get drawn into battles over face-washing or clothes, your child may use these issues as good excuses for thrice daily quarrels. The quarrels will cost you far more time and effort than the tact!

Toddlers get incredibly dirty and they should. Clean clothes, hands, face and knees at the end of the day either mean a swimming expedition or boredom. Of course a clean neat child with shining hair and pretty clothes is a pleasure to you, but save this as an occasional treat for yourself.

As long as your child is kept clean enough for health and comfort, it does not matter what he looks like between washes. The toddler is a laborer, working at the job of growing up. Like any other laborer he can start and end the day clean, but in between needs sensible clothes and freedom to get on with the job. If outsiders should look askance at your ragamuffin, don't make furtive attempts to clean that face wih spit and comb hair with your fingers: just tell yourself that they don't know how a toddler needs to live.

## Getting up in the morning

The toddler is a sopping wet bundle of energy. You cannot let her loose until you have changed that diaper but she is certainly not going to keep still while you "top and tail" her. Strip the wet things off as she stands in her crib: the bedding will need changing anyway. Then let her go naked to the bathroom and stand on a bathmat looking in the mirror while you wash her bottom, face and hands. If she prefers to do so, she can stand on a rubber mat in the empty tub while you help her to use a hand-shower.

## Dressing

Dressing her top half is easier than when she was younger because you can pull things over her head while she sits or stands, and if you get sleeves at the right angle she will push her own hands through. It may be a mobile business though. She will probably toddle off, laughing, leaving you to pursue her, tee-shirt ready, and pop it on when you catch up.

Getting diapers on is more of a problem as captured and laid on her back, she will probably roll away from you and suck her toes. . . .

## Diapers

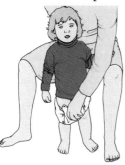

With washable diapers, distraction is the answer: lie her on the ready-folded diaper and then hand her a really interesting toy, kept especially for the occasion. She will become still at least for the few moments it takes her to examine it. Watch out for pins though when delight produces a sudden wriggle! Disposables are easier to manage on your lap or with the child standing down, momentarily captive and safe between your knees.

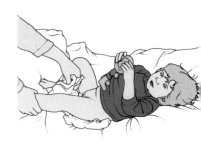

## Bathing

An evening bath is much the easiest way to remove the day's embedded grime. The toddler will probably object to being scrubbed with a washcloth, so try some children's bubble bath in the water. It will loosen the dirt and save you cleaning a grimy ring off the tub afterward. You need not hold the child in the water any longer; but don't move out of arm's reach or leave the room. A one-year-old may fall if he pulls up to stand holding the slippery tub edge. A two-year-old may turn on the hot water. Either could drown in 3in (8cm) of water because the reflex which makes us hold our breath when our faces submerge is not fully functional during this age period. If your child slips and gets that face in the water, he will take a big breath, ready to yell. But it will not be air that is drawn in, it will be water. If the tub bottom is very slippery, use a rubber mat. If the hot tap stays burning, wrap a washcloth around it.

With all safe, provide lots of floating toys and plastic cups and let your child have fun while getting clean.

*A double bath can be fun and save you time, but watch out for jealousy and those by-accident-on-purpose pushes. . . .*

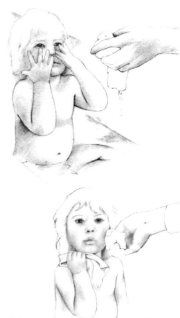

*It is your child's face, so don't wash it as if it belonged to you. Hand over a washcloth and let him have a go. You can touch up the edges with another one.*

## Frightened toddlers

Although most toddlers love baths, treating them as warm water play, a few are frightened. Don't try to force her. Use the methods suggested on p. 221 to re-introduce her to enjoyable bathing gradually. In the meantime you have to get the dirt off somehow and she certainly will not lie still for a blanket bath!

Try to work out what it is that frightens her. If it is the big tub itself, then water in any other container and room will do. If it is the amount of water, a smaller container or a hand-shower may put things right.

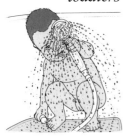

*If only water scares her, stand her in the tub, wash her and let her shower off the bubbles.*

*If the tub scares her, try sitting her on a towel on the drain board. She associates the sink with washing up, so she will probably enjoy dabbling her grubby feet.*

## Hairwashing

Many small children loathe having their hair washed. You may not find the answer here because there may not *be* a complete solution. Any of the tricks suggested for younger babies on page 222 may still work, but there are a few extra ones to consider now that your child is older. If hairwashing (and indeed brushing and combing too) makes real misery, are those budding braids or trendy curls really worth it? A short style can be *sponged* clean, is easily cared for and encourages thick, healthy hair growth too.

Taking your child swimming will get him used to water on the face and pay off at hairwashing time as well as being fun and good for the child too. If you go to a swimming pool, the hot showers provided for swimmers can make an ideal setting for a quick rub with non-sting shampoo. The child is wet already, wants to get warm and has you in there too.

If the child enjoys coming with you to the hairdresser, you can use the new passion for "let's pretend" games to set up a weekly hairdressers at home. With a little ingenuity, you can set up a "backwash." Provide "madam" or "sir" with a plastic bib, a choice of shampoos and much chat

about hair styles and water temperature and he will probably let you do the whole job with a hand-shower. If the game goes well, this is the moment to snip any straggly ends too.

If the child happens to have seen you having a manicure, coping with fingernails will follow naturally; the whole thing can turn into a pleasant weekly spring-cleaning. Don't push your luck by insisting on blow-drying the hair if, like many toddlers, yours is scared of the dryer. Once rubbed, the hair will dry quite fast enough if you just settle him in a warm corner for a story.

## Hands and nails

Short fingernails are important to hygiene, and hands really do need washing before meals and after the child has used the potty or "helped" you change diapers.

Try cutting nails with small, curved nail-scissors, keeping interest and cooperation by letting the child say which should be done next and how long each should be. Don't cut them uncomfortably short: you should leave just enough nail to clear the edge of the fingertip following its natural curve. If scissors are difficult, try nail clippers. Children who hate having their nails cut often prefer a nail file or an emery board and can soon learn to help.

A young toddler will like the feeling of handwashing if you get your own hands soapy first and then take the child's hands between them. Soon he will get the idea of making bubbles by soaping hands. You will have to give a bit of help and watch that soapy fingers don't go near eyes. But by the third year the child will make a good job of doing it alone. You can give extra confidence with a box or

stool like that used at the toilet, to stand on to reach the sink. Do guard that hot tap though. If the child can turn it on alone, you may need to reduce the temperature of the whole supply. 120–130°F (50–55°C) is safe, 150–160°F (65–70°C) is not.

## Clothes

Don't let clothes make trouble between you and your toddler. He will feel very strongly about them. The main concern will (and should) be comfort, but, boy or girl, the child may surprise you with strong feelings about what he or she looks like, too.

Clothes should protect the skin and keep the child warm and/or dry. They should never be stiff, heavy or physically restricting. They should not have to be "looked after" either; ban anything which is not easy-wash and permanent press.

Don't try to save money by buying clothes too big; they will not look or feel nice while new and by the time they fit they will be shabby. Buy cheap clothes; they will not last but the child will grow faster than they disintegrate.

## Top clothes

Don't spend money on a "good" winter coat. The child will grow out of it in one season; it will need dry cleaning; it will restrict movements and it will not do for all weathers.

Instead, buy a cheap, colorful waterproof parka with a hood. It is light, comfortable and warm, and extra layers underneath can make it warmer. You can wash it in a washing machine, dry it overnight and replace it when it gets shabby.

Mud-puddling demands special gear. Most children loathe stiff oilcloth. A waterproof suit or waterproof over-alls with the parka plus ankle-high rubber boots will ready your toddler for anything.

## Main clothes

Stretch materials – lightweight terry or synthetic mixtures – are ideal for you and your child. They are comfortable, they save you money (because stretch means a little more growth room) and they save time because they need no ironing. They are also available in a vast range of exciting colors. You'll probably want to stick to fairly dirt-concealing ones, though.

Both sexes will be least restricted and best protected in long pants while they spend their time crawling and falling. Overalls avoid tight waistbands and chilly gaps when tops separate from bottoms. You can buy these with snaps at the crotch for the younger end of this age-group. You will need elastic waisted pants once your child uses a potty independently; all-in-one garments or zip flies are too difficult. Sweatsuits are ideal. Avoid thick sweaters, especially scratchy turtle-necks. Add extra, light layers when it is cold.

Don't buy lots of different clothes for different occasions. Many will be outgrown after a couple of wearings.

Instead buy clothes which double up for many activities and can be gradually relegated down the grandeur-scale as they get shabby. A sweatsuit could start as a "best" outfit, give good service for everyday wear and finish life, too small and well-worn, as coveralls for painting. Consider before buying *anything* which needs separate treatment from the rest of your washing machine load. That hand-knit jersey may get handwashed the first few times, but you will then probably shove it in with the rest and ruin it.

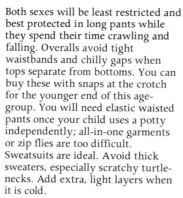

## Underclothes

Conventionally, children wear tee-shirts and, when they abandon diapers, underpants. Synthetic fibers prevent sweat evaporating from the skin; the child may well be less hot and clammy in cotton mixtures even though these are less easy to launder.

But you might like to abandon these items altogether and replace them with brightly colored stretch cotton tee-shirts and play-pants. Your child's innermost layer is then as pretty and serviceable as what goes on top and you can simply strip off or add layers as the weather dictates. On the beach, such an outfit is often better than swimming trunks, as the tee-shirt protects vulnerable shoulders, both in and out of the water (Ref/ACCIDENTS:SUNBURN).

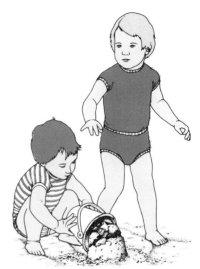

## Shoes and socks

Don't make your child wear shoes at all until he is walking out of doors. Bare feet are safer as the child uses the toes to help balance. They are more comfortable too unless floors are cold. If cold is a problem, find some playboots or "slipper socks," which are heavy woolen socks with a non-slip sole attached. Don't let the child wear ordinary socks without shoes: they are very slippery on a hard floor.

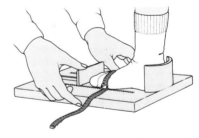

Once shoes are needed proper fitting and regular checking are vital. Your child cannot tell you if shoes are too short or narrow: the bones of the feet are still so pliable that they can be squashed up without causing pain even though damage is being done. Use a proper shoe store or specialist children's department and make sure the feet are measured for width as well as length. Have the size of those same shoes re-checked at least every 3 months; check wellington boots too. Provided shoes fit correctly they need not be grand leather ones with "good support." It is mucles that support feet. Sneakers are fine provided they neither squash nor chafe the feet.

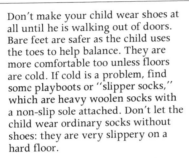

*Both length and width must be measured with the child's weight on the foot. If the shoe is not available in his size, don't buy it however pretty the color.*

Once hard shoes are worn your child will need socks to prevent rubbing and absorb sweat. The fit matters; socks which are too tight will soon distort toes. Watch out for shrinkage in cotton socks. When the child is standing, there should be at least $\frac{1}{8}$in (3.2mm) spare material over the longest toe. Buy socks according to your child's shoe size.

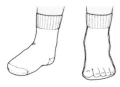

If it is a stretch sock designed to fit a range of three sizes, don't buy it if your child already needs the largest size: buy the next size-grouping up.

When you buy new socks which are bigger than the last ones, be sure to clear all the old ones out of drawers. It is no good having two pairs the right size and four more which are too small. . . .

# Teething

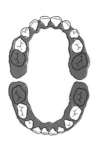

The toddler will be "teething" throughout almost the whole of the second year. The teeth which are most likely to cause discomfort are the first molars, cut between 12 and 15 months, and the second molars, cut between 20 and 24 months. The canines, cut in between, give no trouble.

While teething will not make a child ill, this second year teething will sometimes make him miserable and irritable. The cheek may be red and warm on the affected side, and the very things that give comfort (such as sucking or biting) may also cause pain. You may even find that the toddler's sleep is disturbed because sucking his thumb hurts. There is not a great deal you can do to help, and the trouble will only last a few days with any one tooth, but:

**Something cold to bite on may be comforting.** There is a type of teething ring available containing a special gel which can be cooled in the refrigerator. It can be very soothing, but watch out that the child (who is, after all, older than the age for which teething rings are designed) does not bite through the plastic.

**Rubbing the affected gum with your finger sometimes helps;** at least it makes the child feel that you are doing something.

**Sucking a bottle may make the gums hurt intolerably.** Give a bottle if that is what the child is used to, but offer drinks from a cup as well so that if sucking stops after a couple of painful minutes he will still get enough to drink.

**Cold wind often seems to make teething "toothache" worse.** If it is winter, keep the child in for a day or two or make sure that a hood or a scarf is worn.

If the child seems to be in real pain, teeth may not be the cause. At this age earache sometimes gets confused with teething pain. A child who keeps putting a hand to the side of the face and/or cannot eat or sleep should be checked by a doctor.

*Caring for teeth*    The formation of strong teeth which will resist decay depends on diet. The baby's first teeth formed during your pregnancy, so they depended on your diet then. But you can still do a great deal to ensure the strength of baby and later teeth.

**Make sure that your child gets plenty of calcium and of vitamin D** which enables the body to use it for laying down bones and teeth (see p. 295).

**Find out whether your local water supply contains adequate fluoride.** This trace mineral does more than anything else to strengthen tooth enamel and help it to resist decay. If there is an inadequate amount in the local water, ask your doctor or your dentist about giving extra fluoride.

**Brush the teeth regularly** especially once the molars, which have irregular surfaces to which food can easily stick, have been cut.

Your aim is to clear all food debris from on or between the teeth. You can do it with a small, soft toothbrush which should be used with an up and down motion rather than from side to side. Clean the teeth at least twice every day and make sure that the last time is after supper so that food debris does not stay in the mouth all night. Always use a fluoride toothpaste. The direct application helps the teeth and so do the traces of fluoride your child swallows!

Sticky sugary foods which stay on the teeth for a long time are the most likely to cause the acids which lead to decay. If you are not going to clean your toddler's teeth after a meal, try not to let it finish with this kind of food. Even an apple may not protect teeth (see p. 300). A rinsing drink of water is probably better.

**Don't give sweetened pacifiers or bottles of milk or sweet drinks to take to bed.** Pacifiers dipped in sugar are responsible for a horrifying number of decayed teeth in children under three. There is no need to start this pernicious habit; it is not one that will enter a child's head unless you offer it.

Giving a toddler a bottle to take to bed is a temptation if he or she is difficult about settling to sleep (see p. 309) but even plain milk contains enough sugar to cause dental trouble if it washes around the teeth over a long period, while sugary drinks from a bottle are just as bad as sweetened pacifiers. If you must give something to suck, make it a plain pacifier or a bottle of plain water.

**Take your child to the dentist some time before his second birthday.** Pediodontists or dentists who specialize in childhood dentistry are especially good with toddlers and will make familiarization visits fun so that any later treatment is more easily accepted. Don't decide that such visits are a waste of time because first teeth are going to fall out anyway. The health and spacing of the first set is vital to the second teeth and anyway these first ones have years of work ahead.

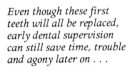

*Even though these first teeth will all be replaced, early dental supervision can still save time, trouble and agony later on . . .*

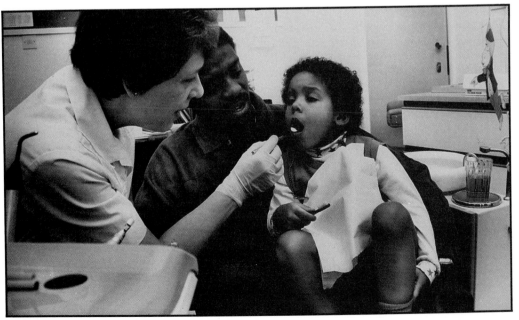

# Crying and comforting

Toddlers tend to live on an emotional see-saw with anxiety and tears on one end and frustration and tantrums on the other. Their feelings are as powerful at this age as they will ever be but they are very new. Children have not yet had time to grow a protective skin over them: they have not had enough experience to know how to cope with them; they cannot control themselves. It is the violent emotions of this age period which so often lead parents to talk despairingly of "the terrible twos."

Most of the toddler's troubles, tears and tantrums arise from a basic contradiction in what he wants from you, the parents. The desire to be independent, to shake off the absolute control adults have and to become a person in his own right, weighs down one end of the emotional see-saw. The contradictory desire to stay a baby, who can depend absolutely on continual protection from the adult world, weighs down the other end. Day by day, hour by hour, even minute by minute that see-saw tips. One moment the toddler demands that independence: "Let me" and "Go 'way!" the shouts resound. The next moment you do go away and the toddler turns back into a baby again, weeping bitterly because you have left the room.

That see-saw can only be kept in balance if you stand in the middle, adjusting to these rapidly changing emotional needs. If you surround your toddler with too much close care and protection, the need for independence will break out in anger and frustration. If you give too much personal autonomy, too much responsibility for self-care, the need to be close and protected will break out in separation anxiety. Keeping the balance between the two is the essence of your job as a parent.

*Anxiety and fears*

Anxiety and fear are normal human emotions but they are not comfortable ones. Most adults learn to cope with situations which make them anxious or to avoid things which make them afraid. But toddlers have neither the experience nor the power to do this for themselves or to force adults to do it for them.

If your toddler is anxious when you leave him at night, he will probably have developed some defenses against those uncomfortable feelings, like sucking his teddy bear's arm or wrapping his cuddly around his head (see p. 208). But even these simple defenses are not truly in his own power. If a jealous older sister hides that teddy bear or the cuddly gets lost at the supermarket, there is nothing he can do about it – except cry.

If he is anxious when you leave the room without him during the day, he can keep his anxiety down to a tolerable level by following you. But if you go into the bathroom and lock the door, he is powerless. He can never be quite sure of being allowed to feel safe.

Your toddler probably begins to feel anxious whenever his own feelings begin to get out of control. Anger, which he intended to frighten you, frightens him as it builds up. If you will change the mood, the anger and the anxiety will die down, but he cannot make you. There is nothing he can do to stop you answering his anger with your own until he is driven into a frenzy of furious fear. So the toddler is very much exposed to his own feelings and only you and the people who stand in for you can see to it that he gets help in managing them.

The very first step in giving a toddler this kind of emotional help is to watch and listen closely to him so that you pick up all the clues to his feelings that he can give out. It will be a long time yet before he can take you by the hand and say "Daddy, I'm scared of the thunder." In the meantime you have to notice without being told. Not all parents take notice of even the most obvious clues. I once spent an afternoon in a public playground, watching and listening. I saw 38 separate instances of children crying, screaming or shouting their fears of the various pieces of equipment, while adults blandly assured them that: "You aren't scared of that;" "This one isn't too high for you;" "You like it really, you know you do. . . ." Of course these phrases are only a "manner of speaking." Of course those adults did not really mean to suggest that they knew what their children felt better than the children knew themselves. But toddlers do not know about our strange "manners of speaking;" to them it must have seemed that the adult world refused to understand their feelings.

*Clues to general anxiety*

If your toddler is feeling rather anxious about life, a little pressured, perhaps, to grow up faster than he feels he easily can, you will be able to spot the signs:

**The toddler will probably be more clingy than usual**, choosing to go with you rather than to stay in the room alone; choosing to hold your hand rather than to run ahead; choosing to sit on your lap or your hip rather than on a chair or the floor.

**The toddler will probably seem less naughty than usual.** He is feeling extra-dependent on you so whenever he can remember what it is that you like him to do, he tries to do it. He does not feel very adventurous either so he does not get up to mischief as much as usual.

**The toddler will probably seem worried by strange places and people.** If you take him out visiting, he will turn shy and spend all afternoon with his head in your lap. If you take him to a new park he will be too busy keeping close to you to explore.

If you pick up this kind of cue from your toddler and offer a large extra ration of affection, attention and protection for a few days or weeks, the see-saw will swing back to the level again. If you miss the cues, it may tip further into anxiety:

**The toddler may have new or extra difficulty in going to sleep.** He may build up his bedtime rituals; add new members to the family of comfort creatures in his crib; cry piteously to have the light left on and call you, endlessly, after you have left him.

**The toddler may enter a phase of nightmares** (see p. 311).

**The toddler may seem to lose enthusiasm for food,** preferring the more "babyish" items in his diet and refusing to feed himself as independently as before.

Once a toddler's general anxiety is at a high enough level for it to affect sleeping and eating, he is very likely to produce sudden fears of specific things. It is as if all that general anxiety bottled up inside is looking for a means of expressing itself.

*Handling specific fears*

If a toddler is afraid of something which parents feel is "reasonable" he will usually be handled gently. Nightmares, for example, frighten us all, so the child who wakes screaming, sweating and shaky will usually receive instant sympathy and comfort. But many toddler fears do not seem "reasonable" to adults. Instead of sympathy and respect for genuine feelings, the toddler may get nothing but exhortations not to be "silly."

*. . . and does not want to stroke*

*To you it may be a dear, gentle, harmless tortoise. To him it is something strange and horrible that he has never seen before . . .*

*. . . or even look at.*

*And if you tell him that he is silly to be frightened, you are doing nothing to help him conquer his fear.*

**If your child shows fear, accept that fear.** It may not seem reasonable to you, but you are not the one who is feeling it. If you find yourself tempted to scoff, think over your own private fears and ask yourself whether they are all "reasonable" and how you would feel if you were not allowed to avoid them. Do you, for example, like large, harmless spiders?

**Tell your child when there is nothing to fear,** but don't tell him not to be afraid. If you say "It will not hurt you, but I can see it frightens you so we won't go any closer," your child will feel that you are on his side; but if you say "Don't be frightened, you silly boy," you offer neither reassurance nor support.

Most toddler fears are based on a natural and self-protective fear of things that are strange. Your child tends to be wary of new things until they have proved themselves harmless. Since most things in the environment either provide this proof or go away, the fears often pass as suddenly as they appeared. But some fears do not vanish so easily especially if they are not handled tactfully. Instead of coming to terms with the strange thing, making it part of the familiar world and accepting it, the toddler focuses more and more fear on it until it turns into the kind of fear which is technically called a phobia.

*Phobias*  Phobias in small children are very common and do not suggest that there is anything unusually amiss. The world *is* a frightening place to a toddler. There are a great many things which he cannot yet understand or cope with. It is not surprising that sometimes general fears should become focused in this way. More than half of all children develop at least one phobia during their second and third years. Research shows that a large number of them share fears of the same things. The most frequent objects of these phobias in Western countries are dogs. Darkness and the wide variety of monsters that flourish there come a close second. Insects and reptiles, especially snakes, come next, while loud noises like fire-alarm bells and ambulance sirens come last.

A phobia works differently on the child from an ordinary fear. Since dogs head the phobia list let us take them as an example: A child who is simply afraid of dogs will show his fear when, and only when, he meets one. The rest of the time his life is unaffected by his fear. Out of sight is out of mind. A fear like this will usually vanish when (and if) the child discovers that dogs are not hurtful. If he does not make this discovery spontaneously, you may be able to help by, for example, casually showing him the tiny puppies in the pet shop window or your neighbor's furry poodle safely on a leash.

A phobia of dogs works on the child through his new imagination. He is not only afraid when he meets a dog, he is afraid when he sees one in the distance, looks at a picture of a dog or even thinks about one. He not only tries to avoid going where he knows there are dogs, he tries to avoid going where dogs might be. If the phobia becomes very acute he may have to ride in his stroller in the street in case a dog should come by; keep out of the park because dogs play there; abandon a beloved picture book because there is a dog on page four and throw his toy monkey out of his crib because at night it reminds him of a dog.

*Handling phobias* Phobias are not open to rational explanations. You cannot help your child to get over this particular kind of fear by trying to show him that the thing he fears is harmless. If you try to do this, perhaps by taking him to visit that charming poodle, you provoke in him such horrible fear sensations that he is only confirmed in his phobia. It is not the actual dog-in-reality that is causing the trouble, it is the dog-in-his-mind.

Because it is his own sensations of fear which upset the child so much, you have to tackle phobias indirectly; by trying to lower his general level of anxiety to a point where he no longer has so much fear inside him that he needs to focus it on something:

**Help the toddler to avoid the fearful thing** but be careful not to let your behavior suggest to him that you are also frightened of it. If he wants to climb into his stroller in case there should be a dog in the street, let him do so, but make it clear that you are only giving him a ride because you understand that *he* is frightened, not because you feel there is any genuine danger. Fear is very infectious. If you yourself have an insect phobia, for example, do your very best to conceal it from the child. If the arrival of a spider leads you to snatch him up and rush from the room he will certainly feel that spiders are doubly alarming because they even frighten you, his calm protector.

**Look for specific causes of stress** in his life (see p. 312) and see what can be done to lessen the strain. You obviously cannot get rid of that new baby but you may be able to help the toddler with his feelings about her (see p. 280).

**If you can find no specific cause, baby the toddler for a while.** It may well be that he has forged ahead in growing up and becoming independent faster than is really comfortable for him. That emotional see-saw has hit the ground on the anxiety/fear side and you will have to work at making him feel safe again.

**If the phobia is taking over life,** limiting his play and making it impossible for him to go to places he used to like or to do things that he used to enjoy, seek help through your local clinic or through your doctor.

*Bravery and fearlessness* Sometimes parents find it difficult to handle anxiety, fears and phobias sensitively because they cannot accept that it is normal for a toddler to have any at all. They may even be ashamed of the child for being a "cry-baby" or a "coward." Little boys especially may suffer because their parents are afraid of them being "wimps."

It sometimes helps if you sort out in your mind the very real difference between being *brave* and being *fearless*. Being brave means doing or facing something frightening. You may ask your child to be brave about an injection or a thunderstorm. If you demand bravery, the least you can do is to acknowledge that he is afraid, show that you understand the feelings and make it clear that you recognize and appreciate the effort your toddler is making to control them. You will not help your child to behave bravely if you refuse to allow expressions of fear. You will not help your child to behave bravely next time if you deny that there was anything to be brave about in the first place.

Being fearless means being without fear. It follows that the less a child is frightened the more fearless he will be. To try to make a child adventurous and fearless by forcing him into the things that frighten him is a contradiction. When you carry your son, screaming, into the swimming pool because you want him to be fearless in water, you are really asking him to be brave. The more you demand the effort of brave behavior from your toddler, the more frightened he will become and the more effort it will cost him to behave as you wish. Continual fear and anxiety tip that emotional see-saw further and further toward the dependent end and away from the independence you are trying to encourage. Things can reach such a pitch that he cannot be the fearless, adventurous child you yearn for because your demands keep him too busy trying to get your protection and support.

*Independence and frustration*

Your toddler is rapidly developing a sense of being a separate independent person with personal rights, preferences and ploys. He no longer sees himself as part of you, so he no longer easily accepts your total control over his life. He wants to assert himself and it is right that he should do so. His "willfulness" is a sign that he is growing up and that he feels secure enough at present to try to manage things for himself.

But life is very difficult for a toddler to manage. He does not understand things very well yet; he often wants to do things which the adult world cannot allow and he is still very small and physically incompetent. His efforts at independence inevitably lead to frustration. While some frustration is inevitable, too much can damage the toddler's self-esteem and make him waste time and energy in fury which he could better spend in learning.

*Frustration by adults*

Adults can easily frustrate the toddler's new sense of independence, his feelings about himself as a separate person and his sense of dignity.

As soon as he feels himself harried, bullied, pressured, he digs his heels in. Any issue will do for a row. It can be his potty or his clothes, his food or his bed. If he feels you insisting, he will resent it. But if he feels he is being allowed to control his own life he will use that potty, eat the food, stay in bed, come when he is called, leave when he is told and love it.

Since there will be innumerable occasions when you must stop your child doing things for his own safety or the safety of other people's possessions, you will need all the obvious virtues of tact, humor and patience, but you will need talent as an actor too. Are you in a hurry to get home? If you swoop the toddler into his stroller when he wanted to walk all hell will be let loose. Act as if you had all the time in the world, offer to be a horse and pull him home and you will get there as fast as you can run.

*Frustration by objects*

The objects your toddler tries to use often refuse to behave as he wishes because he is not yet very strong and his muscular coordination is still not always accurate. Battles with objects or with frustrating toys are often educational. The toddler is finding out what things will and will not do and this is essential information for him (see p. 355). He may be frustrated, for example, because he cannot force his square blocks into the round holes of a hammer-peg toy. But the fact that they will not fit into the round holes is something he must learn; there is no point in concealing such facts from him.

A little frustration of this kind will keep your toddler trying and it will keep him learning. But too much works the opposite way. If he faces impossible tasks all alone and therefore faces continual failure, he will give up. Be ready to step in and help when you can see (and hear!) that your toddler is getting more and more frustrated and therefore less and less efficient. Try to see what his problem is and to offer the minimum help that will enable him to succeed; just doing it for him is not helpful.

*Frustration by his own body and size*

When a toddler understands what objects are supposed to do, understands how to make them do it, but cannot manage because he is too little or too weak, then he needs help. There is no pleasure or learning in such a situation, only grief and giving up. Children do not need rooms full of expensive toys, either for their pleasure or for their development. But any equipment they do have must be tailored to them physically. The toddler may long to push his sister's doll carriage but be too small to reach the handle. He may long to throw his brother's football but be too light to manage its weight. If he cannot have a push cart or a carriage of his own, and an inflatable beach ball or plastic "football," he is better off with none at all until he is bigger. We want him to feel as big and strong and competent to manage his world as possible. So we must keep at least his own possessions in scale with him.

*Tantrums*

You will not always manage to strike the right balance between the amount of frustration which is useful to your child's learning and the amount which is too much. When he is acutely frustrated the toddler is as liable to extremes of rage as to extremes of fear. Temper tantrums are the result of too much frustration just as phobias result from too much anxiety. More than half of all two-year-olds will have tantrums at least once a day while very few children will reach their third birthday without ever having experienced one. Toddlers who have a lot of tantrums are usually lively children who may be highly intelligent. They know what they want to do; they want to do a great many things and they mind a great deal when someone or something prevents them.

A tantrum is like an emotional blown fuse; it is not something which the toddler can prevent. The load of frustration builds up inside him until he is so full of tension that only an explosion can release it. While the tantrum lasts, the toddler is lost to the world, overwhelmed by his own internal rage and terrified by the violent feelings which he cannot control. However unpleasant your toddler's tantrums are for you, they are much worse for him.

Children's behavior during a tantrum varies, but your particular child will probably behave similarly each time: He may rush around the room, wild and screaming. Remember that he is out of control so anything movable that happens to be in his path will be knocked flying. If you do not protect him he may bang into solid walls and heavy furniture. He may fling himself on the floor, writhing, kicking and screaming as if he were fighting with demons. He may scream and scream until he makes himself sick. He may scream and turn blue in the face because he has breathed out so far that, for the moment, he cannot breathe in again. Breath-holding tantrums are the most alarming of all for parents to watch. The child may go without breathing for so long that his face looks greyish and he almost loses consciousness. It is quite impossible for him actually to damage himself in this way. His body's reflexes will reassert themselves and force air back into his lungs long before he is in any danger.

*If she will let you hold her through her tantrum, your arms will help her to be comforted when the monstrous rage within her drains away. . . .*

*Handling* You can prevent many tantrums by organizing your toddler's life
*tantrums* so that frustration stays within the limits of his tolerance most of the
time. Tantrums do no positive good to either of you: when you must
force your child to do something unpleasant or forbid something he
enjoys, do it as tactfully as you can. There is no virtue in facing
children with absolute "dos" and "don'ts" or in backing them into
corners from which they can only explode in rage. Leave an escape
route.

**Prevent the child from getting hurt or hurting anyone or
anything else.** His overwhelming rage already terrifies him. If he
comes out of a tantrum to discover that he has banged his head,
scratched your face or broken a vase, he will see the damage as
proof of his own horrible power, and evidence that when he cannot
control himself you do not have the power to control him and keep
him safe either.

It may be easiest to keep the toddler safe if you hold him, gently,
on the floor. As he calms down he finds himself close to you and he
finds, to his amazement, that everything is quite unchanged by the
storm. Slowly he relaxes and cuddles into your arms. His screams
subside into sobs; the furious monster becomes a pathetic baby
who has screamed himself sick and frightened himself silly. It is
comfort time.

A few toddlers cannot bear to be held while they are having
tantrums. The physical restriction drives them to fresh heights of
anger and makes the whole affair worse. If your child reacts like
this, don't insist on overpowering him. Remove anything he is
obviously going to break and try to fend him off from physically
hurting himself.

**Don't try to argue or remonstrate with the child.** While the
tantrum lasts, he is beyond reason.

**Don't scream back if you can possibly help it.** Anger is very
infectious and you may well find yourself becoming angrier with
every yell he utters, but try not to join in. If you do, you are likely
to prolong the outburst because just as the toddler was about to
calm down he will become aware of your angry voice and it will
start him off again.

**Don't ever let the child feel rewarded or punished for a
tantrum.** You want him to see that tantrums, which are horrible
for him, change nothing either for or against him. If he threw the
tantrum because you would not let him go out into the yard,
don't change your mind and let him out now. Equally, if you had
been going to take him for a walk before he had the tantrum, you
should take him all the same as soon as he is calm again.

**Don't let tantrums embarrass you into kid-glove handling in
public.** Many parents dread tantrums in public places but you
must not let your toddler sense your concern. If you are reluctant to
take him into the corner store in case he throws a tantrum for
candy, or if you treat him with saccharin sweetness whenever
visitors are present in case ordinary handling should provoke an
outburst, he will soon realize what is going on. Once he realizes that
his genuinely uncontrollable tantrums are having an effect on your

behavior toward him, he is bound to learn to use them and to work himself up into the semi-deliberate tantrums which are typical of badly handled four-year-olds (see p. 465).

Assume that your child will not have a tantrum; behave as if you had never heard of the things and then treat them, when they occur, as unpleasant but completely irrelevant interludes in the day's ordinary events. It sounds easy, but it is not. I once visited a friend whose 20-month-old boy asked her to take the cover off his sandbox. She said "Not now, nearly time for your bath," and returned to our conversation. The child tugged her arm to ask again but got no response. He then went to the sandbox and tried in vain to open it himself. He was tired and the frustration was too much for him. He exploded into a tantrum. When it was over and his mother had comforted him, she said to me "I do feel like a beast, I didn't know he wanted to play in the sand that badly." And she took the cover off for him after all.

That mother's behavior was easy to understand but also an excellent example of how not to handle tantrums! She said "no" to the child when he first asked for help without giving any real thought to his request. The child's own efforts to uncover the sand did not show her how passionately he wanted to play there because she was not paying attention to him. Only when he threw a tantrum did she realize that he really did want that sand and that there was no very good reason for forbidding it. She meant to make it up to him by giving in after all but she had her second thoughts too late. Hasty or not, she should have stuck to her original "no" because by changing it to "yes" after the tantrum she must have made her child feel that his explosion had had a most desirable effect. It would have been better for both of them if she had taken a moment to listen and think when he asked for help rather than giving in when he screamed.

It is not easy being a toddler rocking wildly between those anxious and angry feelings. It is not easy being a toddler's parent, either, striving to stay on the center of that emotional see-saw and to hold it in equilibrium. But time is on your side. The worst of the emotional turbulence will be over by the time you discover that you now have a pre-school child.

He will get bigger, stronger and more competent. As he does so he will learn to manage things better so that he meets less extreme frustration in his everyday life. He will get to know and understand things better, too, so that his life contains fewer frightening novelties. As he becomes more fearless he will stop needing quite so much reassurance from you. Gradually he will learn to talk freely not only about the things that he can see in front of him but about things he is thinking and imagining. Once he can talk in this way he will sometimes be able to accept reassuring words in place of your continual physical comfort. With the help of language (see p. 369) he will also learn to distinguish between fantasy and reality. Once he reaches this point he will at last be able to see both the unreality of most of his worst fears and the reasonableness of most of the demands and restrictions which you place on him. He will turn into a reasonable and communicative human being. Just give him time.

# Using his body

*Walking*  Learning to walk alone is a major landmark in human development. Those first staggery steps across open space mean that a new person has achieved one of the outstanding abilities of being human: walking on the back legs with the front "legs" free to do other things.

Babies go through several distinct phases between the day when they first haul themselves into standing position and the day when they first set off across open space. As we have seen (see p. 237) there is wide variation in the ages at which different children learn to stand and walk, so your baby may have reached any one of these phases on his or her first birthday. Whichever point has been reached, don't try to hurry your child into bypassing the next phase. Each one has to be gone through even though one child may spend only a few days, while another spends several months, on each one.

**Phase 1.** In the first phase the baby, who has already learned to pull himself up to standing position by crib bars or heavy furniture, learns to "cruise" along the support by sliding both hands to one side so that he is off-balance and then sliding his feet along one at a time until he is standing straight again. He does not trust all his weight to his feet or even to his feet supported by one hand.

**Phase 2.** The second phase ushers in a much more efficient and confident kind of "cruising." The baby stands back a little from his support so that all his weight is on his feet and he is using his hands only for balance. Instead of sliding both hands along together when he wants to move he moves hand-over-hand. By the end of this phase he is moving hands and feet in rhythm so that at critical moments he is relying only on one foot and one hand for support, the other member of each pair being in motion.

**Phase 3.** The third phase gives the baby an increased range of mobility because he learns to cross small gaps between one support and the next. If the furniture is conveniently arranged, he will now be able to get around the room, moving along the sofa back, crossing to the window sill and then to a chair. . . . He will cross any gap that can be spanned by his two arms, but he will still not release one hand until the other hand has first caught hold of something else.

**Phase 4.** The fourth phase brings the child's first unsupported step. Now he will face a gap between supports that is just too great for his arm span. He will hold on to the first support, move his feet out into the center of the gap, release his hand and then lurch a single step to grab his new support with the other hand. Once the child can cross a small gap in this way he will also be able to stand alone. Often he will discover this by mistake. Perhaps he is standing up holding on to the back of a chair when you cross the room toward him carrying his mug. Without thinking about gravity, he lets go of the chair to hold up his arms for the drink; he probably does not even notice that he has let go of his support.

5

6

*Helping your child toward those first steps*

**Phase 5.** Once your toddler can take a single step to get from one support to another he will soon be ready for the fifth stage. He will still do most of his walking with support, but he will toddle two or three steps to get where he is going if there is no convenient supporting furniture between him and his objective.

**Phase 6.** The sixth phase brings him to fully independent walking. He may not yet walk very far without a supported rest, but when he sets off to cross a room he moves in a straight line irrespective of whether or not there is anything to hold on to along his way.

Don't try to hurry him and don't get worried, however slowly he seems to progress. Once he has got on to his own two feet (Phase 1) you can be quite sure that he will eventually walk. If there were anything the matter with his legs, his muscular coordination, or his balance, he would have stayed at the sitting/crawling stage and never become a biped. Let him take his time.

**Offer opportunities to practice the phase already reached.** You can give him great pleasure in phase three, for example, by sometimes arranging the furniture so that he finds he can get himself all the way around the room or even from one room into an adjoining one. At phases four and five he will enjoy the "walk to mommy" game where you position yourself as a support and invite him to toddle two steps into your arms.

**Remember that the child is learning other things too.** Your baby is learning to walk during the same period that brings a spurt of learning about objects (see p. 354) and learning words (see p. 369). He has only a limited number of hours awake each day and he may have periods when he wants to use more of them on play than on trying to walk. If his walking does not seem to be progressing, ask yourself whether he is not making a spurt in some other aspect of his development.

**Protect your child from falls and the fear that they can bring.** Even though he is used to the kind of bump he gets when he topples over from sitting position, falling down from standing may frighten him, especially if he bangs his head. Several frights in a row may put him off the whole walking business for weeks, so protect him:

Slippery floors make independent walking seem as difficult to him as walking on ice seems to us. Never let him wear socks alone on a hard floor. Bare feet are safest because he can feel the floor and use his toes for balance. If it is too cold buy him playboots or slipper socks (see p. 325). He is not ready for real shoes yet.

Rowdy older children playing around him make the middle of the floor seem a very dangerous place. Make sure that he gets the chance to practice walking when there are no human trains around to knock him down.

**Don't worry about brief setbacks.** Once your child has got through phase one he will progress gradually toward independent walking. But as well as weeks or months when progress seems to halt while he concentrates on something else or gets over temporary nervousness, he may also have brief periods when his ability to walk seems to have gone backward.

A brief but acute illness, such as measles or a middle ear infection, can mean several days of high fever and little food or exercise. At this stage of his life the combination can reduce his muscle tone and his energy to such an extent that he reverts a phase or two for a few days. If he was cruising confidently before the illness, he may go back to crawling and pulling himself to standing. If he was walking two steps between supports, he may go back to cruising. There is no need to worry. He will repeat all the learning phases again but in a few days instead of months.

Even an emotional shock can cause your baby to abandon his newly acquired walking ability. If a separation from you or the arrival of a new baby causes him to go back to a bottle, it may also cause him to go back to crawling for a while. As soon as he feels safe again he will spurt ahead once more.

*Getting moving*  Most babies will reach phases five and six between 14 and 16 months. The child can now toddle at least a few steps and once he can do this his progress will almost invariably be very rapid. But he still cannot abandon crawling as his usual means of getting around because he still cannot get himself into standing position without first crawling to a support and pulling himself up. He will probably not be able to get from sitting to standing position without help until he is 16 to 18 months old.

He can be helped, at this stage, by a specially designed push-cart. The point of this "toy" is that it is balanced in such a way that the child can safely pull himself up by its handle without it tipping. Having got to standing with its help, he can then push it along without it running away from him. Obviously the design is vital. A pushcart or doll's carriage meant for older children will tip when he pulls up and rush away when he tries to walk. This kind of vehicle allows him to take his pull-up help and his walking support around with him. Used in the house or the yard or the park, it enormously increases the toddler's mobility. With years of use ahead as a block cart, first doll's carriage or wheelbarrow, it is a real best buy.

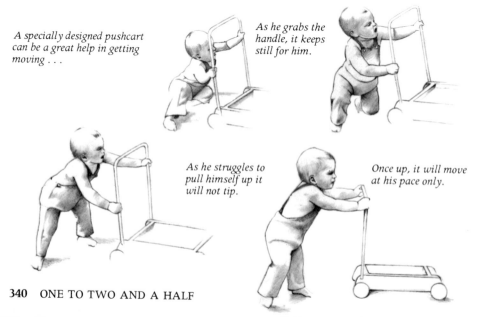

*A specially designed pushcart can be a great help in getting moving . . .*

*As he grabs the handle, it keeps still for him.*

*As he struggles to pull himself up it will not tip.*

*Once up, it will move at his pace only.*

Toddling is very uncontrolled at first. The child has no brakes and no steering. Once he has got up speed he cannot stop quickly enough to avoid falling down the steps or steer accurately enough to avoid the lamp-post. Indoors he may be reasonably safe because a restricted space does not allow him much acceleration. Out of doors, a big open space, such as a park, will delight him, but practicing his walking in busy streets or crowded stores is liable to be dangerous. If he sits in his stroller while you shop and saves his walking practice for a visit to the park on the way home, that is fine. But if most of his outdoor life has to be passed in streets, he will have to be held. Holding hands will be extremely uncomfortable for both of you. Your arm is not long enough to allow you to hold his hand at a comfortable angle so his shoulder will be continually wrenched upward and he will not be able to follow his natural inclination to stop and look at things and then to dash ahead. You will both be far more comfortable if you use a harness. This useful invention has been unfairly maligned on the grounds that it restricts the child's freedom and keeps him a prisoner. In fact it gives freedom to children in this age group.

By his second birthday the child's brakes, steering and general control over his legs will have improved a great deal. He will be able to walk steadily over quite long distances (although children vary, at all ages, in the distances they are *willing* to walk!) and he will be able to start and stop without needing support.

*Doing other things while walking*

When a child first learns to walk a few steps alone, the business of moving along on his own two feet takes up all his energy and concentration so that he cannot do anything else at the same time. If he wants a toy he will have to stop, sit down, get the toy and then find something by which he can pull himself up again. If he wants to listen to something you are saying, he will stop, and probably sit down, to do so.

But once walking has really begun, constant practice soon makes it easier for the baby. By 17 months or thereabouts he will have learned to get up without pulling himself to his feet and he will have become so steady that he can pay attention to other things at the same time as walking. He will learn to stoop down, pick up a toy and walk along while he carries it. He will learn to turn his head so that he can look at things while he walks and listen to you when you talk to him. He will learn to glance back over his shoulder, too, and once he can do that, a pull-toy to take along with him will be very popular.

A few months later the toddler will have discovered that he can walk backward as well as forward and that he can actually run rather than simply toddling fast. Once he can run, he will soon be able to jump so that both his feet leave the ground at the same time.

By the time he is two years old, your child will probably be so dexterous and sure on his feet that you will almost have forgotten those staggery steps he took only six months or so earlier. He will like to play running-away games, dashing off, glancing back at his pursuer, dodging to avoid your catching hand. He will be able to play games that mean sudden starting and stopping, like "Simon says" and "statues." He will be so pleased with his new agility at getting up and down off the floor that "musical chairs"

*At first she must hold on to reach down, but soon she can stoop, carry things and even kick a ball. . . .*

and "ring-around-the-rosie" will be among his favorite games. He will even be able to kick a ball after a fashion but because he cannot yet balance on one leg for more than an instant, it will be a shuffling kind of kick.

*Using mobility*

Adults think of walking as a means of getting from one place to another. Toddlers do not. It is no use expecting your child to use walking in the same way as an older child. He will not because he cannot. Understanding the limitations and the peculiarities of his walking can save you a lot of irritation and friction.

*Adult caretakers as home-base*

For a toddler, walking is not a going-along activity but a coming-and-going around a central adult. The toddler will do most walking when you are still and least if you are moving around. Mothers often say "he makes me wild; this morning I was busy doing the chores and he kept whining and clinging around me until I thought I'd go mad. Now I've sat down all ready to play with him and he's rushing around all over the place as busy as a bee." That is being a toddler. In the morning the child had to keep a close eye on you because he never quite knew where you were going to be next. Now you have fixed yourself and he can go adventuring, come back and go again safely. He knows you are there. He knows he can get back to you in a hurry if he should need to.

*Distance limits*

If you do fix yourself, perhaps on a park bench, the toddler will at once go away from you. He will toddle off in a straight line in any direction. He will not go further away than about 200 feet. There is no need for you to get up and follow him. He knows exactly where you are. When his outward journey reaches his own personal distance limit, he will start back again, often making several stops along the way but always getting closer. The homeward journey may end before the child actually comes into contact with you. He may stop several feet away, closely examine a twig or a leaf and then set off again without ever looking at you. He will go on like that all afternoon.

## The "come to mother" problem

The toddler's coming-and-going pattern is built in to him. It has a logic of its own which is very different from your logic. If you move to a different bench or a new patch of sun, you disrupt the toddler's pattern. Although he can see where you have moved to and although there is no logical reason why he cannot use this new base as easily as the old one, he will not. His built-in rails lead back to where you *were* not to where you *are*. So he freezes where he finds himself; he may even cry. You can call, you can wave, but whatever you do the toddler will not come. You will have to go and get him, bring him to your new base and let him start out all over again on a new set of rails.

## The "walk nicely" problem

A toddler does not learn to follow or to stay with a moving adult until he is around three years old. Until that time he will ask for transport as soon as you signal your intention of moving off. Unfortunately very few people understand that the toddler, who plants himself squarely in mother's path and holds up his arms to be carried, is not being lazy or tiresome but is simply following his natural instinct. He knows that once you walk off he will be unable to stay close to you. If you watch the apes at the zoo, you will see that the moment an ape-mother moves purposefully away, her baby will become motionless and cry. Sometimes the mother will call angrily to the baby. But it will not move until she fetches it and it will not accompany her without riding on her back.

Many a pleasant afternoon in the park has its ending ruined by a toddler's apparently willful refusal to walk home. You know that he is not too tired to walk; he has been rushing to and fro for the past hour and could clearly go on rushing toward home. But attempts to make him do so will cause sad trouble.

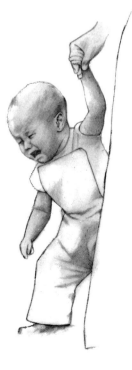

If you have no stroller with you and you do not want to carry the toddler, you will probably take his hand. Being physically joined on to you helps him to stay close, so for a few yards he will manage. But holding hands is not enough. Progress will be slow and jerky. The child will keep stopping, be yanked on again, will steer off in the wrong direction and be pulled back. A few minutes of this will probably be enough for both of you. The toddler will keep getting in front of you, holding up his arms, begging for a lift. You may lose patience and drag him along by the hand or you may decide to let go and leave him to follow at his own pace. He will not, because he cannot.

Left to his own devices while you move slowly on, the toddler will lag, stop, go off on side tracks and probably sit down. His behavior looks like teasing and most people would describe it that way and tell you to keep moving because "he'll follow soon enough when he sees that you mean it." But although he will try, he does not know how to follow you. If you really move off purposefully, you will lose him. If you go slowly, you will have to keep going back, retrieving him and setting him on the right course again. It would save time if you carried him from the beginning. It would save time, effort and irritation if you took the stroller with you on these expeditions and let him ride whenever you wanted to move on. He does not want to get separated from you; to lose you is his dread. He is only asking you to help him stay where you both want him to be: close.

# Playing and thinking

For a small child there is no division between playing and learning, between the things that he or she does "just for fun" and things that are "educational." The child learns while living and any part of living that is enjoyable is also play.

Toys and other playthings are fun – if they were not, children would not use them and so they would learn nothing from them – but they are also tools for finding out about the world and for gradually acquiring the hundreds of skills which will be expected from the child when he becomes an adult member of society. While all children enjoy and learn from toys, they have a particular importance for children who live in highly mechanized, urban societies. Selected playthings can reveal to such children many aspects of their world and the way it works which life in a city environment conceals from them.

Even a century ago a country child was part of a family who worked and played around him at activities whose point he could clearly see. Cows were milked so that everyone (including the toddler) could have milk to drink; musical instruments were played so that everyone (including him) could dance. He could see, and soon understand, adult concerns – the corn flattened by unseasonal weather, or water coming through the roof – and he could "use" most of the adults' tools, from spades to washtubs. But, in contrast, a modern urban toddler is cut off from most of the meaningful basics of life. Productive work goes on away from home in a mysterious place called "the office," or even more mysteriously "downtown." Instead of producing obviously useful stuff like milk, it produces incomprehensible stuff called money. Adult play is usually equally mysterious – evening classes, or meetings or the drinking of special drinks – while adult worries are inexplicable, concerned perhaps with layoff, promotion or the landlord. Activities which do go on at home mostly involve gadgets which are too complex for him to understand or too delicate or dangerous for him to handle. He can neither comprehend nor may he touch the VCR or the washing machine.

While nothing you can do will make an urban apartment the ideal environment for a new human being, a wide range of playthings can do a great deal to ensure that your toddler understands the natural world which is concealed under concrete, and the principles of how things work which are hidden in all those gadgets. By giving your child things to play with you can give him the opportunity to practice the many skills which are not made familiar by being used at home. By providing the child with his own possessions you can make sure that his development does not suffer because your possessions are forbidden.

There are thousands of toys on the market and there are many playthings available at the cost of only a little imagination. Making good choices depends on taking a thoughtful look at what the child already has, but it also depends on an understanding of how your child's thinking is developing and the stage he is reaching, as well as on the observation of what is already being enjoyed.

*Your toddler will turn from explorer to scientist,*
*finding out for himself what happens . . .*

*. . . the way natural materials behave — like clay, which squishes*

*. . . and water, which can be seen and felt but not held*

. . . and the various weights and textures of things, and how they change shape as they move.

*She becomes an engineer too . . .*

*. . . discovering how to build at the top*

*. . . and what happens if you take from the bottom.*

**The world of the one-year-old**

At one year most of your child's play will probably be home based but once he is fairly steady on his feet and has grown through any acute anxiety about strangers (see p. 192) you can probably enrich his playing and your own social contacts by finding a "mother and toddler group" to take him to (see p. 377). There may be a group connected with a local playgroup, church or health center; if you don't know of one, ask at your local library.

Mother and toddler groups are not only for *mothers* and toddlers of course; this usual name only reflects the fact that they are for toddlers *with an accompanying adult* who stays all the time and takes full responsibility for the child. Any regular caretaker can take your child and will probably enjoy it. Fathers still often feel conspicuous in this female world, but should, of course, be especially welcomed, as most toddlers suffer from the imbalance between male and female adults in their daily lives.

The one-year-old's world is a world of reality taking place in the here-and-now. He is not yet interested in the worlds of imagination; he is too busy making sense of what *is*, to be ready for what *might be*. He cannot cope with the past or future. He cannot yet remember yesterday or plan for tomorrow; his job is to come to terms with real people and real things as they come before his eyes.

He has already learned an enormous amount about the real world as it is revealed to him by his five senses. He can recognize familiar objects even when he sees them at peculiar angles, like his bottle, presented end-first so that all he sees is a white disc. He can recognize familiar sounds so that he knows his father's voice even while he is still out of sight. His sense of touch is well-developed: if his hand touches his cuddly, he knows it by feel alone and gathers it to him without bothering to open his eyes. The good smell of baking is enough to tell him that something nice to eat is coming up and his sense of taste will differentiate the chocolate cookies from the plain ones.

But his interpretations of the world are by no means always accurate. The world is an unpredictable place and he can still be fooled by people and things which do not appear as he has learned to expect. He has clear expectations of your appearance, for example. If you come home from the hairdresser with a new style, or emerge from the swimming pool dressing room in a bathing cap, you will contradict those expectations. He may not know you. He may even be alarmed by your combination of strangeness and familiarity. He may expect his father's homecoming around that corner and on foot. If his father emerges from a friend's car, the child may go on gazing up the road for him. Even as his father greets him, the child may glance puzzledly from his face to the point where he expected him to appear. But he is ready now to learn to cope with these inconstants in his world.

**One year to eighteen months – being an explorer**

Sometime during the first half of his second year all the child's new abilities come together to make it easy for him to learn. He is mobile. He can go and find things and angles on things which you could not bring to him as he sat. He has seen that table many times but now he can view it from underneath.

His reaching out, grasping and letting go are competent. He can get hold of the things he wants to find out about. His "jargoning" is highly expressive. He can question and exclaim, even without words, and you will answer him; tell him things, show and help him. Soon he will use real words himself and they will both help him to understand and help him to remember what he finds out.

His need for sleep is diminishing a little and, when something really interests him, he can keep himself awake. So he has more hours for finding out, for learning. He learns by exploring. When you set him free in an interesting room he moves around from object to object, looking, touching, tasting, smelling and listening. He has no particular purpose in view. He examines an object as a mountaineer climbs a mountain: because it is there. But he may examine a hundred things in an hour.

Because almost everything is new to him, he does not easily get bored. Tiny changes in that interesting room start him exploring it all over again. The dining table was bare this morning; now it is laid for a meal. The ashtray was full but it has been emptied and moved; the wastepaper basket he emptied has been (wisely) hidden; his spread-out blocks have been piled up and it takes him quite a while to recognize his truck because it is upside down.

He cannot have too much exploring time or too much variety to explore. As he picks things up for the sake of picking them up, drops them because dropping things is fun, puts them in his mouth to understand them better, he is playing and learning.

*The explorer turns research scientist*

After months of pure exploring, the toddler begins to experiment too. He still picks things up and puts things in his mouth, but now he is trying to find out what he can do with them, what they taste like. He fingers, drops and squeezes things *to see what will happen*. He is carrying out an endless series of basic experiments.

His experiments gradually teach him the rules which govern the behavior of objects in our world. It is not fanciful to call him a "scientist" because most of these rules are ones which real scientists examined and explained generations ago. The toddler does not understand them but he discovers them for himself.

When he drops something, it falls down. Always down, never up. He does not understand the idea of gravity, but he discovers its effects. When he pushes a ball or an apple, it rolls – always; but when he pushes a block it does not roll – ever. The ideas of solid geometry mean nothing to him either but once again he is discovering its rules.

When he tips a cup of water, he gets wet; when he tips a cup of sand, he does not. The water soaks into his clothes but the sand cascades off when he stands up. He could not describe to you the different properties of liquids and solids but he is finding them out all the same.

*Discovering group identities*

As he discovers how different objects behave, the toddler also begins to realize similarities and differences in what he can do with them as well as in how they look. He may have blocks in several different colors and shapes, but he comes to realize that all those various blocks are more like each other than any of them is like any other object. Foods look very different from each other, yet that slice of bread has a greater similarity to a strip of bacon than to a sponge or a sheet of paper. Gradually he will learn to make more and more differentiations and if you watch carefully you can see him doing so. When he was newly crawling, he tried to treat the family dog and cat as if they were toys. He rushed at them and tried to grab as he grabbed a ball or a toy car. You could see his surprise when the animals failed to behave like toys but instead did a bit of rushing themselves and escaped him. Now he knows those pets are not toys. He treats them differently.

*Forming mental "concepts" at around two years old*

Once your toddler is able to recognize similarities and differences in things and to make them into groups in his mind, he is on the way to making a vital intellectual stride. Adult human beings organize their perceptions of an extremely complex world by using a more sophisticated version of the same sorting technique.

Each one of us sorts, compares, contrasts and groups innumerable objects, facts, people, feelings and ideas. Having "sorted through" what we know of the world, we form complex "concepts" in our minds which allow us to join new information up with what we already know and allow us to communicate freely with each other on the basis of shared knowledge. If I speak to you about an "insect," for example, you will know at once what class of creature I am talking about. I shall not have to spend the first minutes of the conversation explaining to you that an insect is a living creature rather than a man-made one or that it is smaller than an elephant. We share a concept of insects and we can start talking from that basis. In the same way if you want to talk to me of "jealousy" I shall know that our discussion is in the area of uncomfortable feelings of envy and loss. You need not explain the concept of jealousy to me because we already share it.

Because we label our concepts with words, it is difficult to see how your toddler's concept-formation is progressing until or unless he uses at least some language. If you watch and listen carefully, you will see that while he is learning to differentiate "dogs" from all other objects he is also learning name-labels (see p. 370). Eventually he may learn the name-label "dog" and attach it to the family pet. Has he therefore acquired a "concept" of dogs? Not necessarily. His use of the word starts as a simple label for one particular thing – that individual dog. To make a concept of dogs he has to put *all* dogs, your own, the ones he sees in the park, picture book dogs and toy dogs, into one single category in his mind and

*Early concepts can thrill; these are quite different yet they are both "DOG!"*

use that label "dog" for the whole group. He has to recognize that although each member of that mental group is different, they are all more like each other than they are like anything else. You may suspect that he has reached this stage when he turns from the family dog to his picture book and points out all the dogs on a page of mixed animals. Later, you can be sure he has got there if he says something like: "Dog, Bow-wow! Horse go Neieieigh!" He will have picked out one of the characteristics that differentiate dogs and horses (the sounds that they make), generalized them to all members of each group (all dogs bark, all horses neigh), and contrasted the two groups (dogs don't neigh, horses don't bark).

Once his thinking has reached this stage the toddler will spend a great deal of time sorting and classifying in play. But his concepts are still firmly attached to the visible world. If you show him a page of mixed pictures or a box of mixed toys, he will find you all the dogs or all the cars, but not all the "nice" or "heavy" or "round" things. These are *abstract* ideas and they come slowly.

## *The beginning of abstract ideas in the third year*

Abstract concepts, which describe things that are not real or visible, are still impossible for the two-year-old. He may, for example, have a vague understanding of the meaning of "more" and "less," but actual numbers defeat him. Any number of objects which is more than one is likely to be "lots!" He may vaguely understand "soon," but any more distant time concept like "next week" is impossible for him. Even ideas like "food" are beyond him, although he will know what you mean if you re-phrase the idea in terms of known reality: "things you like to eat."

But as he feels his way toward abstract concepts he begins to be able to think and play in a way which is further removed from real objects in his hand or in front of his eyes. He begins to be able to think about familiar objects when they are not there; to remember them and to make future plans for them. Out of sight is no longer always out of mind. Called in for lunch from a game in the yard, he can leave the game, eat the meal, and return to the game afterward. It may not sound very clever but it demonstrates remarkable advances in his thinking. He had a picture of that game in his mind. He remembered it through the meal; he planned to go on with it in the future and he was able to do so without prompting.

## *Being an inventor in the third year*

Once your child can think like this, he will begin to imagine and invent; you will see the beginnings of imaginative play. Don't belittle the original ideas that he now produces. A saucepan used for a hat does not look brilliantly original to you because you have often seen children wearing saucepans on their heads. But your child has not. He invented that hat out of and for his own head.

Early imaginative play sometimes looks like the kind of imitative play which has been going on for months, but if you watch carefully you will see the difference. At 18 months a little boy loved to be given a cloth so that he could help his father clean the family car. A year later he took a pair of underpants off the clothes-rack, dipped it in the dog's water bowl and cleaned his pedal-car with it. He was not imitating a present father; he was being the absent one. He was *inventing* his cloth and bucket, *pretending* the toy car was real and *imagining* he was his father.

*New imagination
enriches her
imitative play. . . .*

# Learning about his world

Children will play with whatever is available to them. They need raw material to explore and experiment with but they do not care whether it comes from a toystore, is passed on by a friend or is assembled from junk materials.

It is impossible to generalize about which of the thousands of available toys a child should have. It depends what yours already has, and chooses to spend time on. This list will show you the types of plaything every child will enjoy and learn from during this age period.

A real understanding of the world and how it works must be founded on a knowledge of natural materials. Country life or a yard and a tolerance for mud mean that a child acquires this automatically. But if you live in a city apartment, it could take your child years to discover that concrete is man-made and that not all water comes out of taps. . . .

| The materials a toddler needs | The discoveries they lead to | Ways of providing them |
|---|---|---|
| **Water:** Plain, bubbly, colored, warm, ice.  | *It pours, splashes, runs, soaks; it feels warm, cold or icy. If you blow, it bubbles. Some things float, some sink, some dissolve in it. It can be carried in things with no holes but it leaks through a sieve or cupped hands. . . .* | *The child will play in scale with the quantity you provide, so while a paddling pool is glorious and a bath is obvious, a washing-up bowl on lots of newspaper, with small containers to fill and empty, provides a lot of fun. Emphasize the changes with ice cubes, food coloring, a whisk. . . .* |
| **Earth:** Mud, clay or a practical dough.  | *It squishes gloriously in the hands; it can be rolled and pounded, shaped and molded. More water makes it sticky; less makes it powdery. When it dries it changes; it sticks to hands and hair; water removes it. . . .* | *Clay is hard to handle and almost as messy as real mud. Commercial doughs and plasticines are expensive and the colors soon get reduced to overall brown. Make your own dough (see p. 544); provide an apron, protect the table and let your child explore.* |
| **Sand:** "Washed" or "silver sand." Avoid cement or chemicals. | *Wet sand behaves rather like dough but with interesting differences; dry sand behaves like water but is different again. A solid that is not solid and a liquid-like substance that is not liquid.* | *While a beach is heaven and a sandbox is an excellent buy for the yard, a child can have a couple of pounds of sand on a tray in the kitchen even in mid-winter. Failing sand, a couple of pounds of cornmeal is a worthwhile extravagance. Don't use salt; it will get in the eyes.* |
| **Stones, shells, leaves, twigs.** . . .  | *The toddler is not ready for formal botany, but shiny stones dull as they dry; green twigs bend but later snap, and the world is full of fascinating shapes and textures. . . .* | *Let toddlers find things for themselves and bring them home to be kept while interest lasts, not thrown out as "rubbish."*  |

## Basic engineering

The child has to learn both *how* things work and how to *make* them work. He or she must discover the principles and perfect the fine manipulations. The toddler needs some bought toys here because materials must be light, smooth and unbreakable, even when they are subjected to the forces of many mistakes. Make sure that everything is well-designed so that once he discovers how two objects fit together, they do actually fit.

| The materials a toddler needs | The kind of thing learned from them | Ways of providing them |
| --- | --- | --- |
| **Blocks** 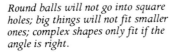 | *Tip them and they are higgledy-piggledy; put them end to end and make a line; pile them with the smallest underneath and they fall, build on the largest and they stand. . . .* | *Blocks make one of the most valuable and longest-lasting "toys" and the child needs at least 60. Different colors are fun but different shapes are more important. They must all be in scale so that tiny ones are quarters and small ones are halves. If you make your own, sandpaper them very carefully. If you paint them, use safe, lead-free paint.* |
| **Fitting toys of every kind**  | *Round balls will not go into square holes; big things will not fit smaller ones; complex shapes only fit if the angle is right.* | *There is scope for making and for buying here. Make a first "posting box" by cutting block-and-ball-sized holes in a cardboard carton; follow up with a more complicated bought one. Find some plastic cups that will build up as well as being used in the bath, or buy a "nesting doll." "Play people" that fit into holes on a range of vehicles, etc., have a long and varied play life. Simple "formboards" are the first step to jigsaw puzzles. Make your own by cutting squares, triangles and so on out of cardboard and helping to put them back in the holes. Later the child will like the kind of jigsaw where whole figures lift out by a knob, perhaps revealing a picture and leaving their self-shaped holes for re-fitting. Putting a key in the lock is fun, too.* |
| **Hook-together toys**  | *Any hook and ring will join together; two hooks will too but two rings will not. Why?* | *The toddler will hook a ring with your umbrella or experiment with a train with simple couplings. There are plastic chains whose links join and come apart and one of your doors may fasten with a "hook and eye." Stick to a large scale for those small hands. . . .* |
| **Threading toys**  | *Closed circles have all kinds of interesting properties, such as the way they can be threaded on to anything longer and thinner than the hole.* | *Start with rigid rings to thread on a rod. The child can have a cucumber and the rings from your preserving jars, or a toy which builds up into a pyramid when (at last) the right threading order is learned. He will learn to put the dog's leash over the fence and the toothbrush into its holder. Eventually he will enjoy threading curtain rings or big beads on to a piece of string or a shoelace. Both sexes will enjoy wearing the results, too.* |

## Beginning to classify

One of the toddler's most important thinking-tasks is noticing the similarities and the differences between things and gradually learning to group them mentally. Doing it with hands as well as brain will help, as well as being fun. If you watch carefully you will see your child beginning to classify things in obvious ways like "my cars" versus "everything else." Later you will see oranges separated from potatoes. Later still you may watch the child consider universal dilemmas such as whether the apple goes with the ball, because they are both round, or with the biscuit, because they are both edible.

## Things to sort and group

All your child needs for sorting and grouping play are collections of objects which are safe and of a manageable size. These can be colored blocks, big counters, little cars, miniature farm animals. But the child will be just as happy and absorbed with more mundane objects like cotton spools or big buttons. Natural objects with less definite differences, such as stones or shells, make a change. A grocery bag (with the eggs removed!) is best of all.

## Things to fill and empty

Apart from the skill involved, there are all kinds of lessons to be learned about how much water will fill that mug; how many blocks will fit into that box and what happens to them all when the containers are overturned. The child will discover interesting things about weight and about what can be carried, too. You will see it happen: see the toddler set off with half a pail of sand, having found a full one too heavy. . . .

*At the beginning containers that are full just have fascinating ways of getting themselves emptied . . .*

*Later on she will find out how to fill and empty deliberately; as one cup gets fuller the other gets emptier. . .*

*She can then discover sophisticated methods of getting things out of one container and into another.*

## Miniature worlds

At the same time that the toddler is learning to sort and group objects, to understand their behavior and to manipulate them by hand, he is also becoming able to *imagine* the objects and to *pretend* their behavior. Although much of this kind of play will take place with the child as the main actor, a miniature world in which to play God is also valuable. If you give little cars, farm animals, etc., your toddler will start by sorting them, but eventually will move through that to creating situations and disasters. Lambs will frisk in fields in his head and cars will crash on the roads of his mind.

## Domestic play

Domestic chores may bore you, but they are among the few adult activities whose point the toddler can easily understand and in which both sexes can join. At first your child will simply want to be given a duster like yours so as to dust too. Later the child will want to pretend that he or she *is* you, and will need a "house" in which to do his own "cleaning up. . . ." If you buy domestic toys rather than sharing your tools with your child, don't go for the gaudiest versions. Choose toys that most resemble the real tools you use yourself.

## Dressing up

Around the second birthday, your child will increasingly experiment with "being other people." The roles of bus driver or construction worker will be tried out just as the child tries out your domestic roles.

At this stage elaborate clothes are seldom the point. The toddler neither wants nor needs an accurate cowboy outfit. Needed instead are the "props" which, for the child, identify the character. Hats are often the key item. A good buy is a collection of plastic helmets, hats, caps and headdresses, as supplied to nursery schools. Otherwise the toddler needs the use of your handbag or shopping basket, your tie or your running shoes, together with a collection of adaptable cast-offs. An old nightgown makes a bride or a queen. A jacket that is no longer even good for gardening automatically makes its wearer into a grown-up man.

## Dolls and soft toys

Don't reject soft toys as too babyish or dolls as too girlish for either sex. Apart from the familiars who guard the crib at night a large family will be well-used for a long time. The toys will people imaginary games from tea-parties to rides on chair-trains. They will receive and relieve a lot of uncomfortable feelings as your child inflicts on them some of the bites and pinches he is learning not to give to real people. Don't be surprised if your child subjects them to harsh discipline, shouting and smacking them; children try out the exasperated as well as the loving aspects of parenthood as they think about themselves in relation to you.

If there is a new baby on the way, a realistic baby doll can be useful to bathe or drown, love or hate.

# Physical play

Your toddler must run, climb, jump, swing, push, pull, roll and generally leap about. It is only by using their whole bodies to their physical limits that children can learn to control and manage them. The more practice your child gets at this stage the more agile, well-coordinated and safe he or she will be as a pre-school child. And using up energy in physical play is relaxation from the stress of new thinking and the efforts at control which must be made when play uses hands without the rest of the body. Your child will find plenty of opportunities for physical play in ordinary daily life, but furniture is not really made for daily gymnastics. The child and your possessions will be damaged less if there are some special facilities and equipment. While no one family could buy or house all the suggestions listed below, you can select what is possible and desirable for your child. A friendly apple tree is the best thing for climbing, but it is easier to build a frame in your yard than to produce a tree where there is not one already.

**Climbing frames**

*These give most children a great deal of pleasure and valuable varied play over many years. A fold-away version making a 4ft (1.2m) cube can be used indoors and out. Larger models need permanent installation in the yard. Chrome has a long life but tends to get rusty when the paint chips and to feel unfriendly on wet cold days. Wooden frames need occasional weather-proofing. Both need an annual safety inspection.*

*Once you decide to invest this much money it is sensible to think ahead to your child as an 11-year-old. Buy the biggest frame possible. You will be able to add all kinds of swinging gear, slides and scrambling nets when he is older. You can transform it into a tent or a house now by throwing an old sheet over it. Unless teased or pushed, your toddler will be safe on a climbing frame. Let the child do whatever he feels able to do, but pander to your own nerves by siting it on grass or earth, not concrete.*

**Stairs**

*Stair climbing "lessons" are important to your child's safety. They are fun, too. Teach your toddler to turn around at the top and come down backward on his or her stomach. When that becomes too easy, teach him to come down on his bottom. Adult stairs will be far too high for a toddler to walk down during this age period.*

*If there are no stairs in your child's life, make a point of going to find some occasionally. If you don't, the toddler may fall head first when you visit two-story friends.*

*A bought or home-made set of double-sided steps, three to four high and with a small platform at the top, makes a surprisingly adaptable plaything if you have the space. You can use it to support a slide, a see-saw plank or a balance beam and it serves well as a ship's bridge, too.*

**Balancing**

*Putting one foot directly in front of the other instead of in front-but-to-the-side is difficult for a toddler. He or she can have fun practicing trying to walk along the lines of your floor tiles or the sidewalk.*

*A board about 8in (20cm) wide and 6ft (2m) long, put flat on the floor, is fun to walk along and can be made more exciting later if it is put across two piles of magazines. It is worth getting hold of such a board as it will stay in use for years. By the time your child is two he or she will walk up it with one end planted on a chair, and across it with both ends on chairs and your hand to hold. Children can learn to jump off it, too.*

*A see-saw gives a different kind of balancing play. That same board placed across a sturdy box will do to begin with, but supervise it closely or it will work its way off.*

*Once children have got the idea of balancing along things they sometimes want to walk every wall they meet. For safety's sake don't help much. Staggering along, clutching your hand, the child uses your balance instead of finding his own. Walking it with only your fingertip to lend confidence, the child finds personal balance and will probably be safe.*

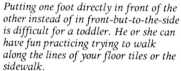

### Swinging

Swinging gives children a glorious sense of power and freedom as well as appealing to their innate desire for rhythm. While loving it, they learn a lot about weight, balance and gravity.

An ordinary yard swing is a passive toy which children can only use when you will push. Later on it is hazardous when more than one child is in the yard: flying feet are the cause of many bashed-in baby teeth. Outdoors, a convenient tree branch or the central rung of a climbing frame will take much easily-available swinging equipment. An old car tire on a rope is among the most popular. Indoors, a couple of sturdy hooks in the ceiling above the usual play-space give a vast potential for physical play which can grow up with the child. Such hooks can take a baby bouncer to start with. Later there can be a thick, soft rope with a big knot on the end to hold on to and try to straddle. Later still there are rope ladders, a monkey swing, a climbing rope. . . .

### Push/pull toys

Large-scale toys to push or pull are a "must." That pushcart (see p. 340) is still a good buy – usable indoors or out, for dolls, sand or a friend.

The toddler will enjoy pulling something while walking. You can choose from a vast range of toys including a realistic dog on a leash!

Don't buy doll carriages or other free-wheeling and lightweight toys until your child walks absolutely steadily. Tipping and running away are both vices in toddler equipment.

### Ride-on toys

In the second year the best buy is a low stable toy on swivel castors which he can sit on and push along with the feet. This is preparation for the tricycle for which many children are ready by the time they are $2\frac{1}{2}$. Do watch out, though, if he rides on a toy with ordinary wheels. The toddler can easily tip these horses, etc., over as he pushes sideways on corners.

### Throwing and catching

Few toddlers can manage a game of ball, but all enjoy and need big, light, inflatable balls to toss around, capture and practice catching. Balloons, kept fairly soft, are fun too. Bean bags, easily made at home and filled with rice or lentils, make an interesting change because they neither roll nor float.

### Acrobatics

Toddlers fall down all the time and it usually hurts. A situation where falls are fun instead of being painful is bliss.

A double mattress is a fabulous playground. Toddlers learn to turn head-over-heels, to look between their legs, to roll over and over and to bite their toes. . . . It may not sound grand and educational but it all helps to give knowledge of and confidence in his body as well as to relax and get rid of tensions. If you are one of the fathers who has the knack of throwing your child around without anyone getting hurt, this kind of roughhousing will probably become one of your child's very favorite games.

If you cannot stand the idea of the child on your bed, even without shoes and its cover, a couple of bean bags or giant floor cushions are almost as good. When opportunity offers, don't forget the bliss of throwing oneself into a giant pile of leaves or even a haystack. . . .

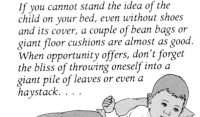

# Watching and listening

Although your toddler will seem to be on the go all day and every day, quiet play is important, too. This is the time to introduce the peaceful joys of books and music. They are things that will be more obviously important later, but the child can get great pleasure and benefit from them now if you will help. Watching and listening activities need your participation to help understanding and concentration.

## Books

Books are going to be vital to your child's education. Help him make friends with them and learn to value them. Picture books with big, detailed illustrations of familiar scenes will hold the attention even if a toddler is alone if you give them when circumstances (such as being in a crib!) mean that he is forced to keep relatively still.

Being read to is a lasting pleasure for every child. Take it slowly; teach yourself to adapt difficult words or put in explanations as you go. Show the pictures and encourage talk about what is happening.

If your child does not already have a library card, do get one now. He needs fresh books week by week, as well as old favorites. The children's librarian can help you choose and going to the library is a popular expedition.

## Drawing

Drawing is the first step to writing. Let your child watch you sketch a cat on paper or a blackboard, or with felt-tip pens on a piece of plastic laminate. Toddlers will want to try scribbling for themselves, but most of all they will probably enjoy finger painting, with no instrument to form a barrier between themselves and those glorious colors and textures.

## Music

A sense of rhythm seems inborn in every child but musical sense can also be taught. Listen with your toddler to whatever music you prefer as well as to children's songs and nursery rhymes. Encourage dancing or marching or clapping. Help the child to hear how the melody rises and falls and to feel its meaning through the body. Help him to make music too.

Percussion instruments range from saucepan lids to tambourines, but the child will need something accurately tuneful, too. A good xylophone (from a music store) will be used spasmodically for years. You will hear the difference between "just banging" and "making a tune" during this age period.

## Professional entertainment

Toddlers are barely ready to enjoy television, cinema or live entertainment because instead of moving at their pace, waiting while they take it in, it moves on without them and they get lost. But there are a few special TV programs directed at the end of this age-group which your child will enjoy and get new ideas and words from, especially if you will watch too.

If your local park or playground offers summer children's shows, with puppets or the simplest comic magic, a toddler will probably enjoy them, especially if they involve shouted participation: they are the first experience of the magic of being part of an audience. . . .

*Helping your child to play and think*

If you provide the space, equipment and time for your child's play, he will see to the development of his thinking for himself. He is the scientist and inventor; your job is merely to provide the laboratories, the facilities and a research assistant – you – when he needs one. What he actually does with the play materials you provide or allow is his business. He needs the true scientist's independence to work as he pleases, involving you or showing you results only as and when he thinks fit.

**Make sure the toddler has basic play-space which is close to you.** He is still better off with a suitable corner in the living room than with a special room that is tucked away (see p. 260).

If you, or other children, share that space, you must make sure that he can play freely without driving you mad. His relationship with a four-year-old sister will be loudly ruined if the toddler snatches her pencils whenever she tries to draw. If you have space, a playpen can protect her (inside) from the roving toddler (outside). You and your typewriter or sewing machine would be sociably safe in there too. If space is short or you have no playpen, a clothes-rack opened out can be used to toddler-proof a corner.

He will need changes of scene, especially if he does not go out often. Make use of the kitchen or bathroom for messy play and break the day up with sessions in a different room, perhaps listening to music in the living room or romping on your big bed.

**Outdoors is important.** Make use of any outside space you have. Making a balcony safe is a problem, but it can usually be done by stretching strong nylon mesh from the railing to hooks set into the masonry, thus encaging the balcony completely. If the resulting cage will take your weight, you can be certain it will take his, even if he tries to monkey-climb it. Backyards and gardens can usually be made safe with a little thought, but they will not be much use if your home is several floors up so that he can only go out if you go too. If you live on the ground floor, you may be able to make it possible for him to move freely in and out through a window. A stool on the inside and a slide down the outside give him a route that is also a plaything. Parks and countryside give him a wholly different range of experiences from those he can get indoors or in the streets. He needs to know about wind and rain and sunshine, about grass and mud and twigs, about puddles to splash in, banks he can climb and the half-frightening freedom of wide open spaces.

A toddlers' group or playground set aside for children under five will probably be a favorite place for your toddler, but think carefully before you take him to ordinary playgrounds intended for older children. The crowds and the noise may be too much for him, the equipment will be too big and fierce and he will find no peace for his small experiments. He is only just discovering how to make a sandpie; he will learn nothing useful from having his early efforts trampled on.

**Even routine outings can be fun.** He is at the age and stage where the combination of familiar routes with the novelty of the small changes that take place day-by-day is ideal. He will not get bored with local shopping expeditions even if you do. Yesterday he saw a bus, a dog, Mrs. Jones and triplets. Today he sees a motorcycle,

two cats, Mr. Smith and a mailman. Let him join in with this ever-changing world: let him greet Mr. Smith, load the clothes at the laundromat and feed the end of his roll to a pigeon. If you do, he will enjoy and learn from that ordinary little walk as much as from an elaborately arranged trip to the zoo.

**Use local facilities and your imagination to prevent winter boredom.** Unless you live in a very fierce climate, wintry weather is an ordinary part of his world and he needs to discover it. A waterproof suit and boots for him and enough clothes and good cheer and courage for you can make howling winds, rain and puddles into adventures.

When you want to stay dry there are all kinds of improbable public places which will give your toddler new and exciting experiences. Riding on buses and trains is always popular and so is watching them at their terminals. Stations have escalators too. . . . Large department stores can seem like fairyland to a child, especially when you are not actually trying to accomplish useful shopping but are only there to have fun. They are warm, bright, full of people and fascinating objects and the expedition can finish with a ride in the elevator. Museums and art galleries are usually empty on weekdays and a lot have not yet followed the mean trend toward charging entrance fees for children. They can give your child a quarter of a mile of warm carpeted running space and you a chance to look at the exhibits.

But if winter palls, what about sharing the load by starting an informal house-swap system with one or two neighbors? If they and their children come to your home one afternoon, you will have fun and a mess to clean up. If you then go to each of their houses that is two more afternoons of fun and *no* cleaning up. . . .

**Organize play materials.** He cannot play well if he has to hunt for what he wants and when he finds it half is missing. His things need organizing just as efficiently as a kitchen or a real laboratory.

Toy cupboards hide a mess from your visitors, but they also hide his possessions from the child and encourage you to let them get in a mess. Many parents grumble that their children have hundreds of toys that they never play with. Usually it is because the toys are incomplete, broken or simply forgotten. Try to arrange to have toy shelves in his main play-space and take pride in their organization. Big toys stand at the bottom so that he can get them without breaking his toes; other toys can stand directly on the shelves where they will look very attractive; vital collections of small objects – cars, stones, chips, Legos – can be kept sorted into cardboard boxes, plastic cartons or plant trays. If you stick one of each item on the outside of the box, the toddler will be able to see for himself what lives where.

The child's toys stay interesting to him for longer if he cannot see all of them all the time. He will feel that he has more variety if some of his things are kept in the particular places where they are used. A special drawer in the kitchen for his "cooking" things will keep him from turning yours out. A basket of bath-toys could live by the tub, while outdoor toys could have their own place on the balcony or in the shed. Especially nice books, difficult puzzles and records will probably be better appreciated if they are kept in the living room, to be used when he has an adult's attention, while things he likes to use in bed can live in his room. The toddler is only just old enough to have his own new ideas about what to do with playthings or how to combine them to make them more interesting. An "odds and ends" box in which you squirrel away packaging materials, scraps of cloth, ribbon and string, cardboard tubes, plastic jars, etc., will ensure that you can produce a new cereal-box garage for cars that have become boring or a new costume for a doll who has lost her novelty-value.

*Joining in with your child's play*
Your toddler wants to be near you as he plays and often he will welcome your help and participation in what he does, but he does not need or want to be told what to do. His play is exploration, discovery and experiment. If you insist on showing him what particular toys are "for," demonstrating the "right" way to do things and telling him the answers to questions he has barely formulated, you will spoil the whole process. The art of joining in a toddler's play is to let him be play-leader.

Provided your dignity will allow you to take this subordinate role you can enrich his play enormously:

**Give physical help.** He is very small and physically incompetent. Often he has a plan in his mind but is frustrated by his physical inability to carry it out. Lend him your coordinated muscles, your height and your weight, but make sure that you stop when his immediate problem is solved. He wanted you to carry the watering can to the sandbox, but did he ask you to wet the sand?

**Offer partnership.** Some games require a partner – and you are elected. He cannot play "chase" if nobody will run (slowly) after him. He cannot practice rolling and receiving a ball if nobody else will play.

Try, sometimes, to offer unlimited time for these games. Many toddlers have to nag ceaselessly in order to get a grudging game from an adult. Then they spend most of the ten minutes allotted to them waiting for the dread words "That's enough." You cannot play with him all day but try sometimes to seem willing, or even eager, to play, and let him have the luxury of going on until *he* is ready to stop. He learns by continuous repetition. If ball-rolling is on today's play–work agenda, he may need to roll a ball for half an hour at a time.

**Offer casual demonstrations and suggestions.** He can use any number of these provided they are not made bossily or at tactless moments. If he is playing with ping-pong balls and you happen to have the cardboard tube from a toilet paper roll at hand, pick up a ball and show him the interesting thing that happens if you roll it through the tube. He is free to take up the suggestion or not, just as he pleases.

If he is playing with some paper, show him what happens if you scribble on it with a chalk. He may or may not want to have a try himself. But don't bustle up with the ping-pong ball or the chalks when he is busily engaged with his blocks. If you do, you are rudely implying that what he is doing has no importance. You are interrupting him.

**Help the toddler to concentrate.** He will find it difficult to work for more than a few minutes at a time on anything that he finds at all difficult – especially if it means sitting still. That means that he will not be able to get very much satisfaction out of his most advanced new activities like puzzles or fitting toys. If you will sit with him, talk, support and encourage him, he will be able to go on for longer, perhaps for long enough to get the tremendous satisfaction of completing his self-imposed task.

**Help your child to manage with other children.** He is not ready to play *with* other toddlers but he will get great pleasure (and many new ideas) out of playing alongside them. Be prepared to conduct the party for them both. They are not old enough to be left to "fight their own battles" or to "play fair," "take turns" or "be nice to guests." They need protecting from each other so that neither has to watch a "friend" destroy a mysterious arrangement of counters or break down a careful sand castle. Give them similar materials and let each do what he wishes, guarded from interference. Both will play, pausing now and then to watch the other; enjoying each other's presence and making the interesting discovery that there are other children in the world who do the same kinds of things but do them just a bit differently. . . .

Older children can be wonderful company for a toddler but playing at the younger level comes very hard on the older ones. They have their own play, different from, although just as important as, the toddler's. An eight-year-old may let the toddler "catch" her three times in a game of tag but the fourth time her natural desire to win will overcome her. The game will end in tears. Older children should not be expected to entertain toddlers except for short periods as a spontaneous gesture of affection.

Where circumstances demand that a mixed age group play together, you can help them to find a game which has a natural role for the toddler. He can play at his level, the older children can play at theirs, and everyone will be satisfied. On the beach, wave-jumping suits everyone from the ripple-splashing baby to the breaker-jumper. At home, any variety of playing "house" or "doctor" gives the toddler a natural position as baby or patient.

*Playing alongside another child is the first step toward making friends. But each child will need his own materials and you must be ready to act as peace-keeper.*

*Outdoors brings freedom to her play . . .*

*. . . freedom from restrictions about making a mess*

*. . . freedom to create miniature worlds of her own*

. . . freedom to play alongside others, and make a noise,
— and maybe find it's tuneful.

# Learning language

Toddlers cannot really join the human race until they can understand and use language. Until that time they are part of a babyrace, needing to be "talked to" with special gestures, little words, lots of physical contact. And until that time their needs and wants have to be guessed at too. He is whining. What does he want? Is he tired? Hungry? Bored?

Once a child can really understand and use speech, you can discuss things with him. Things that are there to be seen like that naughty dog stealing the chicken off the table; things that are not there but will be, like Jane who will soon be home from school; things that will never be "there" in the sense of being visible, like thunder or electricity or joy.

*Understanding language*

Language is for communication; for people to talk with each other. It is not just one person saying words. A few separate words on their own are not even very useful, as you will know if you have ever faced a foreign country armed with a phrasebook. The book will tell you how to say "where is a hotel?" but it cannot tell you how to understand the answer.

Understanding language is far more important to your toddler than actually speaking it. Once he really understands, he will communicate with you. If you try to teach him to imitate word-sounds before he understands their meaning, you are treating him like a parrot, not a person.

*Helping your child's understanding*

As we have seen, a baby has an inbuilt interest in human voices with a natural tendency to listen and to concentrate when someone is talking. You can build on this as you did earlier.

**Talk as much and as often as you can directly to the child.** Look at him while you talk. Let him see your face and your gestures.

**Let the toddler see what you mean,** by matching what you do to what you say. "Off with your shirt" you say, taking it off over his head; "Now your shoes" – removing them.

**Let the toddler see what you feel** by matching what you say with your facial expressions. This is no age for teasing. If you give him a big hug while saying "Who's mommy's great horrible grubby monster then?" you will confuse him. Your face is saying "Who's mommy's gorgeous boy?"

**Help your child to realize that all talk is communication.** If you chat away to yourself without waiting for a response or looking as if you want one, or if you don't bother to answer when he or another member of the family speaks to you, he is bound to feel that words are just meaningless sounds.

**Don't have talk as background noise.** If you like to have the radio on all day, try to keep it to music unless you are actually listening. If you are listening, let him see that you are receiving meaningful communication from the voice he cannot see.

**Act as your toddler's interpreter.** You will find it much easier to understand his language than strangers do and he will find it much easier to understand you and other "special" people than to understand strangers.

**Help the child to understand your overall communication.** It does not matter whether he understands your exact words or not. If you do some cooking, set the table, take off your apron and then hold out your hand to him saying "It's lunch time now," he will understand that his lunch is ready and will come to his high chair. He probably would not have understood the words "lunch time now" if he had not had all those other cues to go with them. He will learn the meanings of the words themselves through understanding them, again and again, in helpful contexts.

*Using words*  As we have seen (see p. 255), babies' first words are almost always labels; they are names for people, animals or other things that are important to them. Once babies have attached name-labels to a person or an animal or two they are likely to add a label for a favorite food. It will not be a word like "supper," produced out of hunger. Hunger will lead to whining, not talk. It will be a name for some treat food or for something giving special emotional pleasure. "Bopple" and "gooky" are very usual ones.

Toddlers' attention often turns next to their own clothes. Shoes are a firm favorite for early naming. They have novelty value because the first pair has only just been introduced and they stay in sight much more than do sweaters or pants!

Many children do not get further than this before the middle of their second year. New words come very slowly at first, being added, perhaps, at a rate of only one or two each month. But the child is storing up understanding of language and eventually, often at around 20 months, will burst out with a positive spate of new words. It is not unusual for a child who says only ten words at 18 months to be using 200 by the second birthday.

The new spate of words will almost all be centered on the child himself. He is most interested in the things which are part of, or concern him, and these are the things he chooses to talk about. He will learn the names for parts of his own body. He will find his hairbrush and name it, avoid his face cloth while naming it and escape from his crib, by name. When he begins to extend his words to things that belong outside his own home they will still be things that are important to *him*. He may learn to name the birds he enjoys feeding with crumbs but he will not bother to speak of the school that is important to his sister!

Although these single words are all simple name-labels for familiar objects that the child can see, he uses them in an increasingly varied way as he readies himself for the next stage of speech. You can help him along by paying attention not only to the word he says but to the way he says it. He may label the family pet "dog" and you acknowledge that he is indeed a dog. But next time he uses the word he puts a question mark after it. "Dog?" he says, watching him trot across the yard. Answer the question mark: tell him where the dog is going. He may even make moral judgments with his single words. Watching the dog scratching in your flower bed he may say "Dog!" in tones of deep disapproval. Make it clear that you have understood him by agreeing that the dog is doing wrong.

*Using more than one word at a time*

Once he has acquired a good collection of single words and has learned to use them with varying intonations and meanings, your toddler will move on to the two-word stage without any prompting. But do not expect his first phrases to be grammatically correct. He adds a second word in order to communicate a fuller or more exact meaning, not in order to speak more "properly." He will not go from "ball" to "*the* ball" because "the" adds nothing to what he wants to say about the ball. Instead he will say "John ball" or "more ball." Don't try to correct him. If you do, you will limit his pleasure in communicating with you. It's important to help him feel that each new effort he makes in this difficult business of talking is worthwhile. When he says "ball" he may mean one of a number of things, but when he says "John ball" it is much easier to guess that he means "Is this John's ball?" or perhaps "Will John play ball?"

Two-word phrases make it much easier to understand the toddler's thought processes. You will be able to see, for example, that he is beginning to be able to think about things which are not actually visible (see p. 352). If he wanders around the room saying "Ted? Ted?" you may guess that he is thinking about his teddy bear, but once he wanders around saying "Where Ted?" you will know that he is searching for it. You will be able to hear his early concepts forming too (see p. 351). He has been at the stage where all animals were called "Pussy;" he may now meet an Alsatian dog and say, in tones of doubtful amazement, "*BIG* pussy?" You will know that while he still does not have a separate word for dogs or for any animals-that-are-not-cats, he does have a sufficiently clear concept of cats themselves to be quite aware that this large dog does not in any way fit into it!

*Sentences and grammar*

Once he has begun to make and use two-word phrases your toddler will soon add another word or two so as to make sentences. But he will not do this by copying the things he hears you say, so some of what he says may surprise you. His sentences will follow strictly communicative and *logical* rules of grammar which will usually be quite different from the "correct" grammar of whatever language you happen to speak.

Don't try to correct your child's grammar. He will not alter what he says to suit your instructions, but your disapproval will put him off. He needs to feel that any message he communicates is welcomed for itself, so just listen to him instead.

**Listen to the order of the child's words.** He rarely gets this wrong. If he wants to tell his sister she is naughty he will say "naughty Jane." But if he wants to tell you that his sister is naughty, he will say "Jane naughty." If he wants to tell you that he has seen a bus he will say "see bus," but if he wants you to come quickly to the window and see the bus for yourself, he will say "bus, see."

**Listen to the way your child makes past tenses.** Most English verbs are made into the past tense by adding a "d" sound. The toddler extends the rule and says "he goed" and "I comed."

Sometimes for good measure he adds the "d" sound to a verb that is already in the past tense so that he says that he "wented" or that she "beened."

**Listen to the way plurals are made.** Most English words are made plural by adding an "s" or a "z" sound. The toddler extends this logically to all words and says "sheeps," "mans" and "mouses."

**Listen to your toddler using phrases as if they were all one word.** Phrases which the toddler has understood for many months often seem like single words to him. When he comes to use them with another word, he cannot separate the first two to get the grammar right. He has heard "pick up," "put on" and "give me" over and over again. Now he says "pick up it," "put on them" and "give me it."

*Learning to get grammar right*

A toddler's early sentences are his very own original telegraphese, developed out of his desire to communicate interesting and exciting things rather than imitated from teaching adults. Convincing evidence of this came from a small boy who was taken to see a football game. Thrilled by the scene he said "See lots mans!" It was the first time he had ever said anything of that kind and he could not possibly have copied the sentence from adult speech. An adult would have communicated the same message with the sentence: "See what a lot of men." If you compare the sounds of the two sentences you will find that they have almost nothing in common. In his excitement the little boy had thought up his sentence all for himself.

Your child will speak his language and he will listen to you speaking yours. Your quick and understanding response to the things he says will keep him interested in communicating with you, while your correct speech keeps a model in front of him to which he will gradually adapt his own. When he rushes into the kitchen saying "Baba cry, quick!" you know that he means his baby sister is crying and you should go to her at once. You show that you understand his language but you answer in your own: "Is Jane crying? I'd better come and see what's the matter."

If you insist on correcting your toddler's telegraphese and making him say things "properly," you will bore him and hold up his language development. He is not interested in saying that same thing more correctly; he wants to say something new. Let him speak in his own way and don't pretend that you do not understand him when you do.

If you reply to your toddler only in his own "baby talk," you will also hold up his language development because you will not be providing him with new things to say. So along with letting him speak his way, make sure that you speak your way, too. Let him ask you for a "gooky" if that is his word for it; let him tell you that he has "eated it." But you offer him a "cookie" and ask him whether he has "eaten it" yet. As long as you both understand what each other means and say plenty to each other, all will be well.

*In the toddler years . . .*

*She looks to you to interpret talk, just as she looks to you to interpret the world.*

*the language of strangers is always hard to understand.*

*Only when you have translated for her can she respond for herself. In this way she will learn in time to meet the outside world without your mediation. . . .*

# Thinking about early learning

Your child has been learning with and from you since the moment he was born and he will go on doing that, whether or not you are conscious of teaching him. But as he emerges from the personality crises of toddlerhood, and as his language burgeons, giving you a window into his increasingly sophisticated mind, you will probably find yourself thinking about his education in a more formal sense. A "good education" is certainly important to later happiness in any Western society, but try not to let yourself equate that education with school, or its value with examination success.

Once school becomes an educational goal – instead of an eventual educational tool – it is easy to put too much emphasis on the formal aspects of the learning that will go on there – on reading, writing and numbers, for example – and to feel that you can and should give your child a head start: "When my child starts school she will learn to read and write. If she learns to read and write at nursery school she will be a school success from the beginning. But if she's going to learn to read and write at nursery school she'd better go to a playgroup first so that she gets a flying start at nursery. Maybe I can persuade the playgroup to take her quite soon, when she's two and a half, but they'll have to be able to see that she's ready so we'd better go to the toddler group and practice playgroup skills. . . ." There's much more to education than literacy, numeracy and the skills that follow them. You and your child will both have a more relaxed time and he will become more mature and confident if you let each stage in his education do its own job. Toddler groups are not meant to prepare children for playgroup or to teach them anything specific. They are intended for parents' benefit and children's fun; the social learning is just a useful extra. Playgroups are not meant to prepare children for nursery schools. They are an alternative approach to a stage in children's lives when they learn most through self-motivated play. And the legal starting age for full-time school is set where it is because educationalists believe that *that* is the most generally appropriate time for the very beginning of formal academic learning.

At this age-stage there isn't a distinction between playing and learning. Play is any activity which a child engages in for himself because he enjoys the *activity* (rather than the gold star kudos which a teacher might graft on to it). If he goes on with the activity – for two minutes or two hours – it is because he enjoys it. If he is enjoying himself he will certainly be learning whether or not you can see any "educational value" in his game.

There often is a distinction between playing and *lessons* but it is not a distinction from which pre-school children can benefit. Later on in your child's life there will be lessons which he has to do and the best teachers in the world will not be able to help him enjoy them all. Part of the point of formal education is that its knowledge and skills require practice; part of the point of schools is that they make it easier for children to give effortful work today to something such as legible handwriting which will not be of pleasurable use for months or years. But it is far too early in your child's life for that. If your three-year-old enjoys banging the piano she may be thrilled if you show her how to pick out a tune she can already sing. But make her practice and you will almost certainly bring her interest in that piano to a brisk halt.

Pre-school children want to know, so they ask. They want to see – what and how – so they watch and listen. They want to do it too so they copy. But most of all they want to find out, for themselves, what things will do and what happens if they. . . .

*What about teaching at home?* If you let your child lead, you cannot teach him too much, too young. But if you go ahead, dragging him along behind, you risk putting him off the whole business of being taught. The simple answer to "how much should I teach my child at home?" is "as much as the child himself invites."

Your two-year-old is not likely to invite you to sit down with flash cards and teach him to read, but he may well become fascinated by what the postman brings, irritated by everybody vanishing behind the Sunday papers and amazed by your desire to sit and gaze at a book with no pictures in it. Let him into the secret of reading and let him decide whether to accept it as information about adult behavior or to experiment with the idea for himself. If the reading-game takes off with advertising billboards, television slogans and road signs, by all means play it with him. Many pre-school children can recognize "exit," "stop" and "walk" long before it occurs to anyone to *teach* them to read. Once your child understands that those squiggles mean something, that they constitute a useful and enjoyable code-system in older people's lives, he may try to follow with his finger the words you read aloud to him and want his name written on everything from his door to his tee-shirt. He may, but he may not. It doesn't matter either way. It is his interest in, and understanding of, the point and process of reading which will give him a head start, not the level of his skill.

If yours is a child who *does* lead you into teaching him academic skills, do try to do it by putting him in the way of discovering interesting things for himself rather than exercising his slowly improving memory in rote-learning. Saying, "One, two, three, four, five . . ." isn't *counting*; it's a useless, boring chant until he knows that those words are the names for *numbers of things*. Let him start with the things themselves, like a spoon for you, a spoon for him and a spoon for Daddy. One day he'll find the word "three" useful and discover that four comes after three because it is one more spoon, needed just today because Grandma is coming. . . . Once your child is interested in numbers at all he will not just be *counting* but adding, taking away and dividing (or splitting up). Every time you divide an apple or a chocolate bar between him and his sister he will be "doing fractions" as well because he will see one whole being turned into two halves. . . .

*Offer the materials and trust her to use them. . . .*

Children cannot get interested in things they have never seen, or lead the way toward activities they have never thought of. Introducing your child to what is available in his world, offering him opportunities, is probably your most important and enjoyable educational job during these pre-school years.

You do that every time you buy your child a toy he had not asked for because he did not know of its existence. You may have to help him unwrap it; you may have to translate instructions or give a demonstration so that he can see its potential, but you don't then insist that he use it as the manufacturer intended or that he play with it for a given period each day "because it's educational." In the same way, you introduce your child to the library and to the idea that he can have any number of new books to look at and to listen to. You hope that he will enjoy books. You probably try to build them in to pleasant routines like bedtime, but you don't try to *make* him listen to stories when he would rather be doing something else. You introduce him to many different skills as well. He could not *invent* the idea of a huge pool of cold water to immerse himself in, but if you take him and show him, swimming may become his favorite game and an early skill. The more ideas, activities and skills you can offer your child the richer will be his choices, as long as you keep those choices genuinely open. The apocryphal story of the father yelling at his toddler on the beach "I've brought you here to paddle now damn well *paddle*" vividly illustrates the risk of pressurizing your child because you have spent so much (money or effort or time) that he must repay you with his pleasure. Your practical circumstances, personality and mood will dictate what you can offer your child. Beware of sacrificing so much that you obligate him. If an afternoon at the zoo will so strain your resources that you will be really upset if he only looks at the pigeons and the people, stick to your local park.

Your child cannot discover the vast potential of group play for himself unless there are other children in his age-group at home and in neighboring homes. Small families, working parents with a range of childcare arrangements, and the danger of city streets often mean that today's small children have to have their social lives organized to an extent that more home-and-community-based generations find extraordinary.

*Parent and toddler groups*

Parent and toddler (or mother and baby) groups are not primarily designed for children's benefit but for the adults. Their intention is to provide mothers, fathers and other caretakers with a pleasant place to meet and talk with others and with the companionship and play for the children which, hopefully, will make some adult relaxation possible. In some towns and most cities there are also at least a few other meeting places, such as playgrounds, drop-in centers, and children's rooms at the local library or Y. Describing the variety makes the provision sound far better than it is. One small area may have a choice of such groups while another may have only one, and vast areas have nothing at all.

If you can find an informal group which meets even once or twice a week, it will certainly reduce your own or your home-care person's isolation while introducing the child to social life. If there is no such local group, you could even consider starting one, perhaps with like-minded parents you met in child-birth preparation classes. But however good the play-arrangements (and some parent and toddler groups, especially those run in pre-school playgroups' premises, have excellent facilities), such a group will not serve similar educational purposes to a pre-school group and is not meant to do so.

In a parent and toddler group your child remains entirely in your charge or in the care of whoever takes him there. However friendly the other adults, or however skilled the "hostess" that a well-established group may employ, your child does not *have* to have anything to do with any adult but you. He will go on depending on you for emotional matters like sorting out fights or kissing banged knees and for personal service in the bathroom or at juice time. The group compels no expansion of his input from the adult world or of his communication with it.

Although such groups usually refer to themselves *as* groups they seldom function that way. There is no membership or subscription payment so parents tend to bring children when it suits them to do so and not otherwise. If a group is the one-and-only in the district and open only once a week, its membership may in fact be fairly consistent, but a drop-in group that is available all week may contain different combinations of children at each session. Your child will probably always find playmates for the afternoon but he gets no chance to find out about real, individual friendships; about being part of a little gang within a bigger group or about ways of coping with children whom he finds difficult.

But the most important difference between parent and toddler groups and pre-school groups is the basic difference between the kinds of play-learning experience they can offer. The toddler group may have many of the same toys and activities as a pre-school group and your child may much enjoy the chance to use equipment he does not have at home, but the toddler group does not have the trained play-leader or teacher who makes the pre-school group into something much more than "just play."

| *Pre-schools and nursery schools* | If your child attends a day-care center, whether full- or part-time, pre-school *education* should be built in to its program so that by the time he is approaching three, your child will be spending part of his time there in nursery school activities. Do remember to check on the center's educational provision when you first enroll him though. When a child is three-months- or fifteen-months-old and you are desperate for day care so that you can work, it can be hard to imagine his future educational needs. But if the center takes many infants, its resources may be biased toward their care and its pride may be in its hygienic milk-preparation and toileting areas rather than in its entrancing play-learning facilities. If you have to move your child in his fourth year because he is bored and obviously needs a more grown-up program, you will have to reorganize his daily care and help him live through the upset of losing the second home to which he has become accustomed. |

*A parent and toddler group makes
a break for both of you . . .*

*. . . but at playgroup he joins a world beyond the family. . . .*

If your child is at home with you, with a relative or with a caretaker, or if he is in family day care, you will probably want him to attend a pre-school or nursery school from about the time of his third birthday. Most nursery schools put a lower age limit of two years nine months but it may be more appropriate for your particular child to start later, especially if he is getting plenty of companionship already (see p. 417). Most nursery schools are privately owned and run by large-scale businesses or by individuals. The range of quality and cost is enormous and you would be ill-advised to assume that there is a positive correlation between the two. Nursery schools also vary widely in their philosophy and practice. Some are like "mini" schools, with considerable formal teaching, internal promotion by age and performance, and a deliberate separation between the worlds of home and school. Others aim to make the group an extension of home-experience for the child *and* for his parents so that everybody involved learns with and from everybody else. They stress social skills and learning through self-discovery under a *play leader* rather than a *teacher*. Parental involvement should not only mean a rotation of volunteer mothers to serve drinks and clean up. Volunteers should be genuinely involved in the work of the group so that their own experiences of children's play, and their opportunities to see their own children interacting with others, are expanded and fed back into the family. Parents who cannot serve on a rotation should still participate in their child's playgroup via fund-raising or serving on its committee.

You may find pre-schools within private day-care centers, within community centers run by local authorities, or in your nearest church hall. If you cannot identify available local groups via your own network of friends and acquaintances, perhaps because you are new to the district, your town hall or library might know of most of them. Also check your local newspaper.

Pre-school groups are intended for children's benefit. They are not primarily a source of part-time daycare for parents' benefit. Of course the time that your pre-school child spends at a group may be invaluable to you, but don't build too much on the freedom it will give. Most sessions will, and should, be short. Two and a half hours is about average and since your child will need taking and picking up your period of liberty will be brief. Children who are newly entered into groups tend to pick up innumerable colds and other minor illnesses so there will probably be a lot of days when your child cannot go. And some groups offer children only two or three sessions per week. If you want to do a part-time job or fulfill other regular commitments you would probably be sensible to look into, or continue with, *day-care arrangements* to combine with your child's pre-school group attendance. It will certainly be better for him to go to his group from his usual day-care worker, and go on spending the other days with her as he did before, than to be sent, as some children are, to two or three pre-school groups each week. Starting at a group is stressful enough for many children (see p. 417) without the additional stresses of thinking "is this the one where the toilet's down there or around there and is it Jane or Sue who helps me with my pants?"

*Dovetailing pre-school with big school*

Unless you plan to educate your child outside the school system, making your own arrangements to satisfy the education laws once he reaches six-years-old, your child's pre-school experience will end when he starts at "big school." You will want to make arrangements that leave him neither bored and under-stretched nor pushed and over-stressed. Every child in the United States must start all-day school (or suitable alternative education) by the term after his sixth birthday. But many children will be offered places long before that simply because a falling birthrate has left many schools with empty classrooms. In some districts your child may be able to start kindergarten in the term after his *fourth* birthday: a quarter of his life earlier than you began.

You do not *have* to accept early kindergarten for your child if you do not think he is ready for it. But the decision to defer his entry may be a difficult one. If he is then at a nursery school or playgroup, being kept back and separated from his friends may upset him badly. On the other hand it could give him an invaluable period as "top dog" and he might then move on to school with a new batch of friends with whom he is actually happier and more confident. If he is not at a pre-school group when early kindergarten is a possibility, you may feel that you must defer it and quickly arrange at least a few months of group experience for him first. But if he is not already at a group, simply because there isn't one within reach, you may feel that he will benefit from the earliest possible placement at school.

Decisions like these depend on your child and your circumstances but they will also critically depend on what the

*. . . a world which, one day, will lead him into school.*

school(s) will offer him when he does start. Very few just-turned-fours are ready to cope with a full school day designed for six-year-olds, but happily, fewer and fewer schools expect them to do so. As you explore the local pre-school group possibilities, try to identify the local primary schools as well so that you have the best possible chance of meshing the end of one and the beginning of the other without grating the gears of your child's confidence.

**Does the school have a pre-kindergarten class?** If it does, four is certainly not too early for most children to join it. Pre-kindergarten classes – sadly rare – are not organized and staffed as part of the rest of the school, but like nursery schools which happen to share school premises, equipment and support. Such a class is often the ideal setting for a four-year-old who can get used to going every day to "his" school while still enjoying the short sessions and routine appropriate for a pre-school child.

A child with a place waiting for him in a pre-kindergarten class may enjoy a nursery school between three and four but if you are doubtful about his readiness, or if there is no group available, it does not matter. The pre-kindergarten class is meant to be *pre*-school experience even though it is on *school* premises.

**What are the school's kindergarten arrangements?** Although there is no legal obligation to send a child to school before he enters first grade at six, most elementary schools accept children into kindergarten at five and some will accept them sooner. If your child is to be ready to make this vital move as soon as it is offered, you need to know what the offer will entail: What is the class size? How much extra adult help is available to the teacher? Are play, lunch and toilet facilities separate from those of the rest of the school so that the very youngest pupils do not have to cope with the whole age range?

**What concessions can be made if very young children need them?** Some schools believe that once a child starts it is important that he accept the routine of a full-school day, every day, unless he is sick. Others recognize that some children become overtired and are willing to be more flexible about half-day attendance or the occasional day off. You also need to know what help the school can offer to children with medical or learning difficulties.

Questions like these need authoritative answers. However much information about a school you amass from the local parents' grapevine, don't hesitate also to make an appointment with the head teacher, through the school secretary. You need not feel diffident about taking up her time, or about letting it be apparent that you are trying to exercise a positive choice among any schools available to your child. Head teachers *want* parents to be involved in vital decisions about their children's education and what could be more vital than that very first school? Some schools print information leaflets for prospective parents; some hold "open houses." The secretary may first offer you such information but she will easily accept that you need to meet with the person who will be in charge of him there.

# THE PRE-SCHOOL CHILD

## *From two and a half to five*

A pre-school child does not emerge from your toddler on a given date or birthday. He becomes a child when he ceases to be a wayward, confusing, unpredictable and often balky person-in-the-making, and becomes a comparatively cooperative, eager-and-easy-to-please real human being – at least 60 per cent of the time.

Children change and grow up gradually. They do not transform themselves overnight, turning from caterpillars to butterflies under our eyes, but this particular change from toddler to pre-school child does have a sudden and magical quality about it. The pre-school child has, in some almost mystical way, "got there." He has made it safely through infancy and toddlerhood into the beginning of real childhood. The changes that take place within him between, say, two and a half and three and a half, are not actually as great as the changes of the second year, but they seem tremendous because he is suddenly so much easier to live with and to love.

A lot of the magic lies in his language. Grown-up people do very little and say a great deal. We use words instead of actions, berating ourselves and others with conscience-searching and with scolding rather than with hair-tearing and blows. We tell our troubles rather than howl. We make lists rather than buy ten items one at a time. Everything we feel and do is mediated through words. Toddlers say very little and do a great deal. They express themselves in action and demand action from us. With a toddler you cannot explain, you have to show. You cannot send, you have to take. You cannot control with words, you have to use your body.

Although pre-school children are still very physical in their reactions to their feelings and to the world, still readily capable of tears and tantrums, they have learned enough language and enough of the thinking that goes with it to be able to join us in using words as well.

At last you can talk to your child, have what you say listened to, understood and accepted, get reasonable answers back. The great block in communication between you has finally come down, and this, more than anything else, makes the child seem like a "real person."

Compared with the toddler, your pre-school child has built up a lot of experience and a lot of accomplishment. He can wash his face (if you tell him); put on his boots (if you leave them in the right position); get his own drinks (if he can reach the tap) and climb in and out of chairs, cars and trouble. As his abilities increase, your routine work diminishes. As he feels more able to manage his world and himself in it, so you can devote increasing time and energy to the exciting business of introducing him to a wider world and its ideas.

As he uses the kaleidoscopic pieces of what he has learned, shaking them together in his mind to form and re-form different patterns of thought, he begins to remember from day to day. He applies what he learned yesterday to what he does today and he looks forward to tomorrow. Because he can look forward he can wait a bit, too. The offer of a game when you have finished what you are doing does not always drive him into a frenzy because he wants to play *now*. He can enjoy simple choices, asking himself what he enjoyed last time, wondering what he feels like now. He can begin to understand (though not necessarily to keep) promises, to recognize (though not reliably to tell) the truth, and to acknowledge (though not always to respect) the rights of other people.

He can begin to acknowledge your rights because his feelings of individuality have extended from himself to you. He not only sees himself as a separate person from you, he also sees you as a separate person in yourself. You are no longer simply an appendage or slave whose desire to do other things than look after him is at best incomprehensible, at worst bitterly hurtful. He may not understand *why* you should want to talk to adult friends, but he sees that you do; sees that your wish is similar to his own desire to play with his friends; sees the reasonableness of your case. So this is the age of bargaining, of practical and emotional trade. "If I do this, will you do that?" appeals directly to his finely balanced sense of justice and makes it easy to find ways around almost every potential clash.

Seeing you as a real whole person gives his love for you a new quality and one which brings it much closer to adult ideas about love. He becomes capable of genuinely unselfish sympathy and concern; capable of offering something because he thinks you might want it rather than because he feels like giving it. If he should see you crying, he will not simply be frightened and angry at the feelings your tears call up in *him*, he will be sorry for you because of the feelings the tears suggest you are experiencing. He would like to help you, like to have some part in making you feel better. If he comes and hugs you, it will not always be an attempt to reclaim your attention from whatever is

*She is able now to recognize how you feel*
*— and she can offer you sympathy too . . .*

bothering you back to himself, but an attempt to soothe you with his own attention. He gives as well as takes.

As he watches you and the other adults who are close to him or who catch his imagination, the pre-school child strives to understand your roles and your behavior toward each other. This is the age of identification. Your child will "be" all kinds of people from his own baby sister to the elevator operator, but above all he will try to "be" you. However hard you try to keep activities and play bi-sexual (see p. 454), the child may insist, during this period, in adopting the most sexist aspects of family life, seeming always to be involved in domestic play when he is 'Mommy" or with mechanical matters when he is "Daddy." The accuracy of his observations may be uncomfortable. As he looks at you, you will sometimes see his father's, supposedly private, coaxing expression on his face. As he cares for his doll-family you will hear your own turns of phrase and the expressions you are least proud to recognize as your own!

It is through identification with adults in general and with you, his special people, in particular, that the pre-school child takes in and makes part of himself the instructions and demands which have previously come from you, outside him. Now he begins to scold himself (and anyone else below him in status) for carelessness you had not even noticed. He warns himself against actions you had not known he was contemplating and he tries to run everything just the way he thinks you want it. Because he is very young and inexperienced, he will sometimes go too far so that he sounds bossy and smug. Sometimes you will find yourself positively looking forward to his more babyish and less virtuous moods, or even being tempted to squash him when he asks yet again: "That's right isn't it, Daddy?" or "Aren't I good?"

But this new behavior, even if it is sometimes irritating, is a triumph for his development and a gold star for the relationship between you. It means that he at last consciously wants your approval, wants you to be pleased with him and is actually prepared to put some effort into seeing that you are. You knew that your toddler *needed* love and approval but he often seemed not to care whether he got it or not and never seemed to know how to earn it. Your pre-school child is positively asking you to tell him what does and does not earn approval, so he is ready to learn any social refinement of being human which you will teach him. Since that was what you were aiming at all along, his obvious desire to please should make it easy to be patient and gentle with him. He knows now that he wants your love and he has learned how to ask for it. Give it to him in full measure.

# Eating and growing

The pre-school period sees a further slowing in growth rate. Your child will probably gain around 5lbs (2.3kg) and 3½in (9cm) in the third year, dropping to 4½lbs (2kg) and 2½in (6.5cm) during the fifth. Don't worry if the gradual change from being a stocky, curvy two-year-old to a slimmer, straighter five-year-old makes the child look comparatively thin for a while. The toddler plumpness will eventually be replaced by muscle but this takes time. In the meanwhile legs and arms may look positively fragile.

*Weighing and measuring*
There is no point in frequent weight and height checks now. But twice yearly weighing and measuring is sensible. If both rise together (Ref/GROWTH), you will know that growth is proceeding normally. If weight rises much faster than height, you will know that the child is getting fatter. If the height does not rise perceptibly during six months, you should measure your child again three months later. If there is still no increase, take chart and child to the doctor. A very few children do lack a particular hormone which is vital for growth. It can be given to them at a "growth clinic" and will re-start normal growth, but it may not be able to make up for the height the child has already failed to gain. So get advice before much growing time has been lost.

**How to measure.** Measuring a child's height accurately is difficult. Don't try to use a tape measure directly. Instead, stand the child up against a wall or door, heels flat on the floor and touching the wall, head straight so that he or she is looking directly in front. Now put something flat and rigid (such as a book) on the top of the head so that it flattens any sticking-up hair. Make a mark on the wall, and then use a tape to measure from the floor to your mark. If you always use the same wall or door for measuring your children, you can name and date your marks so that over the years you accumulate a permanent record of who measured what at which age.

*Lithe and leggy, the pre-school child's proportions are quite different from the dumpy toddler or large-headed baby. . . .*

# Food and eating

Pre-school children who have not got food and eating mixed up in their minds with love and discipline (see p. 296) are often very big eaters. They use up an enormous amount of energy in their daily lives and they eat to match it. Provided there is enough food available, a child like this will certainly take in enough calories. Hunger will see to that. If the offered food is adequate in proteins, vitamins and minerals, the child will also select a diet that is well-balanced for his needs. As we have seen, refusal of particular, valuable foods like meat, eggs or green vegetables will not matter provided that the child can get their value from other sources such as cheese and fruit. As a useful "rule-of-thumb," a child who is eating as much as he wants of an ordinary family diet and is having a pint of milk and a correct dose of multi-vitamins every day will be getting everything needed.

So you need not push particular foods, but neither need you hold back. There is no food which is ordinarily served to your family which your child should not have. If he likes curry and you like serving it, let the child have it too. A few foods may still disagree with him, but unless your doctor confirms an allergy to one of them (Ref/ALLERGIC CHILDREN) you need not worry unduly even about these. The child will not "eat himself sick" either. A child who always eats enthusiastically will stop where greed ends and gluttony begins.

*Helping your child to eat sociably*
Your child is enthusiastic about food because you have not spoiled the natural relationship between feeling hungry and enjoying food. He is ready, now, to start to fit in with the social aspects of mealtimes. But go easy. If you suddenly change your attitudes, refusing to cook alternative dishes, or insisting on a vast improvement in table manners overnight, you could still spoil eating for the child and make problems for yourself.

**Teach table manners by example rather than by exhortation.** On the whole he will come to behave as the rest of the family does, so if you are suddenly irritated by his eating with his fingers and leaning his elbows on the table, make sure he is not watching the rest of you doing the same thing!

**Promote the child to eating arrangements like your own.** He will imitate adults more readily if he sits on an ordinary chair (or a small but extra-tall version specially made for young children) rather than in a high chair, and if he has a place setting like everybody else. He cannot learn to take care of china and glass and to manage a fork, spoon and eventually a table-knife if he is only given plastic.

**Help your child to acquire a sense of occasion.** Few families can have every meal together, elegantly served at a perfectly set table. Life is not long enough. But if every meal is a kitchen-scramble, with mashed potatoes dolloped from saucepan to plate and people coming and going at different times, your pre-school child will get no chance to see how people behave on more formal occasions. He is bound to "let you down" when you most want him to behave nicely. In a busy household it may be a good idea to make one weekend meal deliberately more formal. The child could be involved in making the table look pretty – perhaps picking flowers for a centerpiece or folding paper napkins – and he could change into clean, tidy clothes for the meal. If the grown-ups have a drink beforehand, a special drink for him adds to the fun. During the meal food is served on dishes and everyone, including the child, helps themselves and each other. It is obviously an occasion for something especially nice to eat and for at least some conversation which will particularly interest him.

In this kind of atmosphere the child will not feel nagged at if you show him a more conventional way to manage a fork or get peas to his mouth. He will feel honored that you are letting him in on the grown-up world. It is realistic too. Why shouldn't he eat french fries with his fingers when he is having supper alone in front of the television? What matters is that he should be able to behave inoffensively at table when the occasion demands it.

**Help the child to acquire new tastes.** If your pre-school child knows, from bitter experience, that he will be made to eat anything that is put on his plate, he will probably refuse even to try new foods, in case he does not like them. He will feel much more adventurous if you allow him to taste before the meal or to have a tiny bit of the new food on a teaspoon and decide whether he wants to be served with it or not.

**Get the child used to foods which will make life easier for you.** A child who is generally enthusiastic about food will accept new foods if you start off by introducing them as part of ordinary family meals. Accustom him to whatever will be available on camping trips, picnics or in restaurants. Above all, try to get him used to eating cheese. Bread or crackers with cheese and an apple is a perfectly balanced meal which takes 30 seconds to prepare and another 30 seconds to clean up. It is easily portable and available in any convenience store in any Western country. If he will happily eat that combination you need never interrupt a day's activities in order to think of something for his meal.

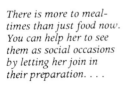

*There is more to meal-times than just food now. You can help her to see them as social occasions by letting her join in their preparation. . . .*

*"Fussy" eaters*  Real eating problems now are almost certainly a hangover from the toddler period and need handling similarly (see p. 297). But a lot of pre-school children get labeled "fussy" or "difficult eaters" when they are only trying to exercise the same rights to personal taste and appetite which adults take for granted. In our well-fed society most of us would rather stay hungry than eat what we dislike. Yet because we are adult we seldom face the choice. We buy and/or prepare what we do like. Only young children are faced with food chosen and prepared by someone else and are then expected to "eat what is put in front of them."

So allow for the child's dawning tastes in food. Where those tastes are similar to yours they will be accepted without question; it is when a child's tastes differ from everyone else's that he tends to be called "fussy." If no member of the family eats bacon fat, the child's rasher will be trimmed without question; but if other people eat the whole rasher, the child may well be labeled "fussy" when he leaves the fat.

While every family will work out its own attitudes to individual food tastes, there is a reasonable middle-road which will go a long way to avoiding mealtime trouble for all concerned:

| From the child's point of view | From your point of view |
|---|---|
| *It is unreasonable to serve a meal or dish you know the child dislikes and then be irritated when she leaves it. Make sure you serve something she normally eats, even if it means substituting an egg or some cheese for the family main dish.* | *It is not reasonable to pander to momentary whims. The child must make her meal out of whichever items she normally eats that are available today. If the menu is liver and bacon which she normally enjoys, she does not have the right to demand egg and bacon instead. If she does not want liver today she must make do with the bacon.* |
| *Remember that you will never help her to like a particular food by forcing her to eat it. Many adults still cannot face foods which were forced on them because of war-time or other restrictions.* | *It is not reasonable to allow the child all of the best part of a family dish. If she only wants the crisp brown top of her helping, fine. Don't give her any underneath. But don't feel that you have to give her the crisp brown top of everyone else's helping too.* |
| *It is unreasonable to insist that the child eat all the food on her plate if you put it there. Let her say how much she wants or help herself. She may then come back for more.* | *It is not reasonable to let the child spoil food. If there are iced cupcakes and she does not want any cake but only icing, she has the right to the icing off one cupcake – she has simply eaten what she wanted of it – but this does not give her the right to nibble the icing off a plateful.* |
| *It is unreasonable to insist that the child eat at all if she says she is not hungry. She may be coming down with something or having an unhungry day. She has the right not to eat, just as you have.* | |

*Eating between meals*  Most pre-school children genuinely need to eat more often than the adults in the family. If you are using up that much energy, it is a long time from breakfast to lunch and from lunch to supper.

Children who are hungry at other times need food-fuel. A formal mid-morning and mid-afternoon snack will almost certainly be routine, but problems arise because hunger gets confused with greed. Usually it is our fault. The child says he is hungry and we give him a chocolate cookie. Next time, he does not say he is

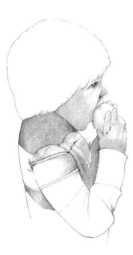

hungry, he says he wants a chocolate cookie. Hunger or greed?

The easiest way to keep out of this kind of dilemma, once your child is old enough to understand, is to have certain foods which the whole family knows are available at any time they want them. There might, for example, be a cookie jar which is kept filled with plain crackers, and a fruit bowl with apples and bananas. Equally there might always be bread and butter for the asking or a piece of cheese or a handful of raisins. Different families with different tastes and budgets will find their own basics, but for all families the point is the same. These are "I'm hungry" foods. Anyone who cannot wait for the next meal can have some.

If you do follow this idea, other foods which the child asks for between meals can be seen as being asked for from greed rather than need and you can decide for yourself whether you feel indulgent or not. If you have just baked a batch of cookies and the smell is driving the child mad with greed, you may decide to give him one at its warm best or to make him wait until supper. Either way you are not depriving him of food when he is hungry.

*Candy*  If you have managed the kind of approach to candy which was outlined in the previous section (see p. 300), it will probably never be a major issue in your household. But sometimes, as children get older, spend more time with other children and are able to compare what they get with what others get, candy-trouble does begin. If you have to formulate a candy "policy," remember that it is usually the parents who try for the strongest and most righteous line who have the most trouble. Strict rationing, for example, tends to focus attention on what is *not* allowed. Those who can stay coolest about the matter suffer least.

The policy which most often seems helpful is the simple one of never keeping candy in the house. If you do not have any candy you can say so, calmly and honestly, when the child asks. Willingly buying the child a small package of the least damaging type of candy (see p. 300) at some regular times (such as on the way home from shopping) also gets you out of a lot of difficulties. The child knows there will be some candy then, so your refusal to buy any right now will probably be accepted quite calmly. You can also make candy seem nice-but-ordinary by occasionally using it as part of meals — serving chocolate with dessert or using jelly beans to decorate a cake. When your child does have some candy, you can reduce the damage it does both by banning the most damaging types (such as toffees and lollipops) and by encouraging him to finish what he wants of it all in one go just as he would finish with a slice of cake.

Your whole attitude to especially-nice-things-to-eat will have an effect on the ease or difficulty with which you handle the candy problem. If you want him to regard candy as just one more nice thing in a life full of nice things, some of which are foods, encourage him, sometimes, to buy himself a different kind of food-treat. The actual shopping is half the point. Many small children only get the chance to shop for themselves from the candy store, but being allowed to choose to buy a beautiful red apple from the greengrocer or a fresh roll from the baker can be just as much fun.

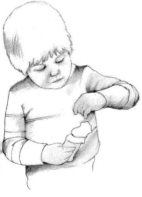

The natural growth pattern tends to slim children down now, so obesity becomes less usual and fat children all the more conspicuous. Really fat children are often teased by others, so try to produce a slimmer contour before it is time for your child to start kindergarten.

The aim of slimming fat children should be to slow their weight gain down so that as they grow upward, less and less of them bulges out. Over the next 18 months or so your child will get about 5in (15cm) taller. If you can hold the weight gain over that period down to only 2–3lbs (1–1.5kg), you will end up with a much thinner-looking child.

It may be a good idea to start your "slimming campaign" by taking your child to the doctor. Take the growth chart with you so that he can see whether the obesity is new or part of a long-term pattern, and so that he can help you to work out by how much the weight gain is outstripping the gains in height.

*Slimming* The principal ways in which you can help a pre-school child slim down are similar to those suggested for toddlers (see p. 303). But the child's greater age makes some differences:

Fat consumption has probably gone up because the child now shares family meals which may mean more fried foods and more bread and toast. Remember that almost all foods you normally fry in butter or oil can be dry-fried with no extra fat at all if you use a non-stick pan. Frying by this method is better for everybody. Remember, too, that many foods which your child likes crisp can be made that way by being dry-baked in an oven. Crisp bacon cooked by this method actually *loses* most of its fat.

Not everything that is spread on bread need be fatty and fattening. The child is old enough to experiment with spreads that need no extra butter such as peanut butter or cottage cheese.

Although the child may drink less milk than before it might be sensible to give him low-fat now (see p. 304). He may be drinking a great many carbonated drinks, too. Serve plain water at meals. If fizz is the point of treat drinks, mix juice with plain soda water. Ice cubes often make simple drinks seem fun.

Obviously you will try not to let a child who is already fat eat a great many candies and fattening snack foods which are extra to meals. But cutting down on these sweet and enjoyable foods takes tact if the child is not to be made miserable. A very useful trick is to buy, make or serve miniatures. Ten tiny pieces of candy seem more to a child then three big ones. Three finger cookies seem plenty yet will not contain the calories of one full-sized one. You can even make home-made cupcakes in paper candy-cases. . . .

By the time fat children are three or four years old, they may have fallen into a vicious circle over exercise. They do not run about much and this is partly because they are fat, but they are fat partly because they do not run about much. Where a *toddler* will normally be very active provided he is allowed physical freedom, a *pre-school child* may have grown out of running for its own sake – and have become addicted to television. Your child needs people to run with, after and away from. When he must play alone, encourage kicking a ball, rolling a hoop or skipping rope. Even indoors he can dance to music and learn to turn somersaults.

# Sleeping

Problems over going to bed are almost universal among toddlers, but pre-school children tend to divide neatly into those who make no fuss about it at all and those who make a very great deal. If your child is in the first group, you are lucky. Go on doing whatever it is that you have been doing up to now and hope that it lasts! If your child is in the trouble-group, it may help if you take an honest look at the whole business of bedtime.

A lot of children spend a great deal more time in bed than they spend asleep. They are put to bed because their parents want peace in the evening. If you can admit that it is you who wants the child in bed rather than the child who needs to be there, you will see that it is worth it to you to make bed, and going there, as pleasant as possible for the child.

*Making bedtime pleasant*

Pre-school children are rapidly developing a sense of ownership and the beginnings of feelings of privacy. They really need a place they can call their own. Whether you decide to do up a room specially or merely to spend a weekend reorganizing to create a sleeping corner, consult with the child about the grand new arrangements, and make it clear to the rest of the family that this place now belongs to him. Older brothers and sisters should not be allowed to barge in without permission and it should be left to the child to show it to any visitors if, and only if, he wishes.

Remember that the child will spend at least half his time in this special place. It should therefore be kept just as bright and clean and pretty as the more public parts of the house. However much children like their rooms they will not, at this age, keep them tidy themselves. If you do not do so, the room will soon become so littered that it is totally unappealing.

The child's bed should be the centerpiece. This is probably the sensible moment to promote him from a crib to a "big bed." Avoid bunk beds if you can. One or other child will always feel that the other one has the best layer and it is difficult to feel private when two of you sleep one on top of the other. Another disadvantage is that caring for a sick child in a top bunk is impossible so every time your child is ill he will have to be moved. Bunks can cause accidents too. Two separate beds are infinitely better, even if they make the room crowded. Don't buy a "junior" bed. Your child will grow out of it long before its useful life is over. Buy a full-sized single bed and if the absence of the accustomed crib sides worries him, use a removable safety rail for a while.

Make the bed itself as attractive as you can. Don't decide that it is not worth buying pretty bedding and smart pajamas while the child still wets the bed: the pretty ones wash just as well as shabby old ones. If you are buying new bedding, consider a washable Continental quilt. It suits a small child's instinct to snuggle, and makes bed making easy too. Make the bed properly whenever the child gets up, whether in the morning or after a nap. A child will not want to return to a mixed-up mess of bedding any more than you would. A careful arrangement of possessions around the bed will complete a sort of "mini-home" to which – you hope – your child will look forward to returning each night and in which he will be happy to spend time awake each morning. Tastes vary, but these are some of the things which make their sleeping quarters attractive to many children:

A light, safely screwed to the wall and within the child's reach. It can have a 15-watt bulb for leaving on all night or a dimmer switch he can work for himself.

Pictures on the wall or on a bulletin board, and mobiles over the bed and hung in the airflow from the window.

A bedside table or shelf stocked with his own books. Picture books meant for pre-school children are fine; comic books meant for older children are also excellent because a non-reader can follow the picture-stories.

Special bed-toys which usually fall into two groups: soft toys for friendship and comfort, and puzzles and fitting toys which he may attend to better in bed than he does during the day.

A musical box or children's cassette player. The source of friendly noise will probably be switched on the moment the child is left for the night and the moment he wakes in the morning.

A means of communicating with you. This may just mean an open door or it may, in a large house, mean a baby alarm or intercom.

*Using this special place*

The point of all this trouble is to make your child a place which feels pleasant for relaxing, playing and going to sleep. You will ruin it all if you *ever* use it as any kind of punishment. Don't send your child to the bedroom or to bed because of naughtiness. Don't even suggest such a thing indirectly by saying "you must be overtired or you wouldn't be so silly. I think you'd better go to bed early."

Try instead to make nice things happen in his room. If a letter or postcard should come for him, put it on his bed for him to find. If you have bought him a new sweater, spread it there ready for him to try on. Keep magazine pictures for him to put on his wall or draw him a message sometimes and put it there for him to see at bedtime. If he asks to play with something of yours which he is not normally allowed – like your costume jewelry or a pack of cards – tell him he can borrow it to play with in bed.

If you are going to put all this thought into making bed a nice place to be, you obviously want to make the business of getting there enjoyable too. Make sure that the child has plenty of notice when bedtime is coming up. As with younger children (see p. 208) a definite evening routine usually works best, but, whatever your family pattern, don't expect the child to break off in the middle of a game or television program and come instantly to bed.

Tell or read a bedtime story with the child actually in his bed. If you tell or read it downstairs, the story is just one more nice thing which has to be left at bedtime. Read upstairs it is something nice to look forward to in bed.

When you leave the child in bed give (and keep) a definite promise of your return. You might say something like "I'm going down to have my supper now. I'll pop up and see if you're asleep when I've finished." The child knows that if he does not go quickly to sleep you will be back before long. As a result he is likely to be fast asleep before the allotted time is over.

Once the child is in bed, getting out again should be banned or, better still, never considered. But if you want him to take it for granted that once he is in bed he stays there, you will have to be prepared to wait on him a bit. If you expect him to get out of bed to fetch his own drink of water you cannot be surprised if he also gets out to tell you something interesting. He must know that if he wants something and calls, one of you will always come. At around three and four, urination may cause difficulty. The child may worry in case he wets himself or he may use needing to go to the toilet as an excuse for getting up. A potty beside the bed with permission to call for company if he needs to use it, together with a plastic sheet on the bed and a relaxed attitude to "accidents" will usually avert problems.

## Sleeping problems

However attractive you can make going to bed, there are some night-time problems which are very common during this age period. You will all be exceptionally fortunate if your child never experiences any of them.

*"Nasty thoughts"* These are a kind of half-asleep nightmare which many children experience when they are drowsing off. The child himself will not be sure whether he was awake or asleep. After quite a long period of silence from his room (so that you probably thought he was fast asleep) the child either starts to cry or calls you and says that he cannot go to sleep.

It sometimes helps to ask the child what is bothering him. He may be able to tell you what monster is besetting him and make himself feel better by talking about it. But your reassurances need to be very simple and definite. If the trouble is "nasty men getting in . . ." remind him that nobody who does not belong in his family could possibly get in; the doors are locked and need a key to open them, the windows are too high even for a ladder to reach. . . .

*Preventing "nasty thoughts"* Unlike nightmares (see p. 398), nasty thoughts often arise directly out of stories the child has heard, or seen on television. It is as if his mind replays the story to him and then, as his controls relax toward sleep, his powerful imagination takes over and embroiders it. Censoring his viewing and his bedtime stories, so that he goes to bed with his head full of pleasant everyday matters rather than mysteries and miseries, may help.

Overheard snippets of real life can cause "nasty thoughts" too. A half-understood telephone conversation about Aunt May's operation, a half-heard quarrel between you two or the sound of his mother in tears can all impinge on the child so that as sleep approaches he is flooded with anxiety. Once again it may help to talk and explain but it will not help to lie. If he did overhear a quarrel or tears, it is much better to admit it and tell him a suitable version of what it was about. He will accept that quarrels and upsets need not be frightening and do not mean that you don't love each other any more, if you remind him that he too sometimes has quarrels with his friends, or his brothers and sisters, and that grown-ups, too, can cry.

*Nightmares*  Sleep alternates between cycles of lighter "paradoxical" sleep and deeper "orthodox" sleep. Dreams go on all through the "paradoxical" phases even though it is only the frightening or disturbing dreams – the ones we call nightmares – that are usually noted. Dreams are part of the child's inner life. If they seem to relate to external events, stories and so forth, it is only because real happenings are serving as a language for fantasy. You will not prevent nightmares by banning a scary television program; their material comes from the child and can only be affected by general measures which reduce his overall level of anxiety.

Almost every child sometimes has nightmares; from time to time your child may have a patch during which he has them almost every night. Unless he shows signs of stress when he is awake as well, don't worry about them. Just get to him quickly when he starts to cry. The sight, sound or touch of you will soothe him instantly back to peaceful sleep. It is only if he has time to be terrified by the sound of his own fear, or if the babysitter who comes to comfort him is a stranger, that the nightmare is likely to become a memorable event, which may make him afraid of going to sleep.

*Night terrors*  Night terrors are quite different from nightmares and, fortunately, much rarer. They arise during a phase of "orthodox" sleep and not from fantasy but from a breakthrough of emotion – fear or panic. Most children never have them; very few have them more than once in a while. They are sometimes precipitated by traumatic events such as operations.

When you answer the scream that heralds a night terror you will usually find the child sitting up, eyes open, "looking" at some non-existent "thing" in the room. He seems terrified. Any anger mixed in with the fear will be hating anger. Any grief will be desolation.

Although he looks awake, the child is not really conscious and he is difficult to "bring to himself." Instead of being instantly comforted by your arrival he will either ignore your attempts at comfort or actually involve you in his terrified fantasy. He may make you into one of the enemy with horrified screams of "go 'way, go 'way," or make you into a companion victim, crying "look, oh look. . . ." Sometimes he will actually scream piteously for you: "Mommy, Mommy, I want my Mommy" even as you hug and pat him and try to make him conscious of your presence.

*Handling a night terror*  Such extreme fear is infectious and there is something eerie, too, about a child who seems awake but is not in touch with reality. You will probably feel uneasy and have to fight a tendency to gaze with the child into the corner he has peopled with horrors.

**Put all the lights on.** This will steady your nerves and may alter the room enough to begin to dispel whatever images the child is seeing. Even if the light has no effect on him now, it will reassure him if he comes to full wakefulness before the incident is over.

**Don't argue with the child.** He is not awake so he is not open to reasonable statements about monsters being made-up or there being no huge wolves in the room. Just burble soothingly along "it's all right darling" lines. If he is conscious of your voice at all, it will only be the tone he hears.

**Don't take any notice if the child says hurtful things.** He is not conscious, so he is not responsible for anything he says. If he shouts about hating and killing you, ignore it. He doesn't mean *you*, he means whatever you stand for in his night terror.

**Don't do anything in particular to awaken a child who stays in bed.** The terror will probably recede, letting him drift straight back into normal sleep without ever knowing what has happened. You are the one who will probably take time to calm down, but he will be quite unharmed.

If he gets physically involved in the terror so that he gets out of bed, runs away or begins to throw himself about or knock things over, see whether he will let you pick him up without increased panic. If he will, carry and rock him so that he wakes to warmth and comfort rather than to the shock of pain when he runs into a door. If he fights you, don't capture him by force, but follow him, putting on lights as you go, and pick him up as soon as he will permit it. If all else fails, a warm wet washcloth wiped over his face will probably wake him by its cooling evaporation.

If you do have to wake the child from a night terror, especially if he has ended up in a different room, he will probably be very surprised. Don't let relief at having him "normal" again make you at all dramatic. Just tell him he had a bad dream and ask if he would like a drink or to go to the bathroom. He may now be so wide awake that you have to put him to bed all over again as if it were the beginning of his night. If he remembers his strange awakening the next day, dismiss it matter-of-factly: "You had a nasty dream. . . ."

Nobody knows exactly why some children have night terrors and others do not, or even exactly where a nightmare ends and a night terror begins. Children who do have them seem to be most susceptible when a high fever is already making them a bit "wandery" (Ref/FEVER); when they are given a sedative medicine for any reason, or when they have had a severe physical and emotional shock such as being involved in a car smash. Night terrors need to be handled by calm and experienced adults. Don't leave your child with a teenage babysitter, let alone a stranger, if previous experience or present circumstances give you any reason to suppose that he might have one tonight.

*Sleep talking*   A great many children mutter in their sleep. Some speak clearly enough for you to hear words. The child may even laugh, or talk in a tone of voice that suggests teasing. It all sounds a bit eerie, but it does not matter unless the child is obviously having a nightmare or starting a night terror.

Night-talking children who are calm don't need waking and they don't need listening to either. It is better not to tell them funny stories next day of the peculiar things they said, as most children find the idea of talking when they were not conscious rather scary. A talking child may wake a brother or sister who shares the room. A very young one may be frightened. If so, you may have to find other sleeping arrangements because once children start to talk in their sleep, they usually go on doing it from time to time right through childhood.

*Waking in the night for no obvious reason* Occasionally a child will wake, after several hours of sleep, for no reason that either you or he can see. He has not dreamed – as far as he knows – he is not afraid and does not need anything. He is simply wide awake and so amazed at finding himself the only conscious being in a silent house that he has to call you to make sure that the world has not emptied around him.

A reassuring visit and permission to look at a book until he is sleepy again will be all he needs, but if it happens often you may be able to explain to him that most people like to stay asleep all night and that it is a pity to wake them unless he really needs something. His room can be arranged like the early waker's room (see below) and he can be encouraged to look after himself.

But he may not be able to bear the solitude. He may have to see that there are other people left in his world. If so, being put to sleep with a brother or sister (even a tiny baby one) may work wonders. He is asked not to wake the brother or sister so he stays very quiet, but he can see his or her sleeping, breathing form and he knows he is not alone.

If you have no brother or sister available, there are other forms of "company" that may work. I have known various families successfully use each of the following:

A bowl of goldfish; a hibernating tortoise; a "noddy clock" with a friendly face that moves with each tick; a special lampshade (designed for a low-watt nightlight) with stars or pictures which flick on and off, and a photograph of the whole family.

If all this fails and the wakeful child simply has to announce that he is conscious, you may not have to get out of bed if his room is nearby and doors are open. Just calling to him may be enough.

*Early waking* If your child is fond of his special place and his bed with all its things around it, early waking need not be a problem now. He cannot stay asleep just to please you – so it is no good being irritated with him for waking up – but he can play quietly without disturbing you. Soon after his third birthday he will probably be able to understand that he must not wake you, except for a special reason, until he hears your alarm clock or the radio or hears you moving about.

Of course he may wake you by mistake because you hear him talking to brothers or sisters, dolls or teddy bears. That is different. He cannot be expected to stay totally silent. You will just have to put your heads under the pillows and revel in your last half hour. If he insists on calling for you, it may be because he wakes wet, urgently needing the bathroom, hungry or thirsty.

If he calls because he is wet, it is not fair either to ignore or to scold him. It is a good sign that he is aware of being wet (see p. 404), and once he begins to move around in play he will get very cold in wet pajamas and sheets. You will have to go to him but you need not go through the trouble of changing his bed until later. Hand him dry pajamas to struggle into while you put an old sheet or towel over the wet patch on the sheets.

If hunger and/or thirst is the problem, try leaving a drink in his old training cup and a couple of crackers or cookies by his bed. Helping himself to this morning mini-picnic is good entertainment as well as meeting the need.

# Toilet training and after

Many children will be completely reliable about using the toilet or a potty, both for urinating and for bowel movements, before they reach their third birthday, but some will not be. When and only when your child has reached this point, you can help him to *generalize* his accomplishment so that he can manage the whole business of excretion under almost any circumstances.

*Getting used to toilets*

Your child may have been using the toilet for months, but many children infinitely prefer their potties. Now it is time your child got used to toilets so that he will be able to manage anywhere, without your having to carry a potty with you.

The first step in the switch-over is to give that familiar potty a permanent home right next to the toilet so that the child gets used to going there. When the child is calm about this change in routine, buy a child-size toilet seat that clips over the big one and find a box that is the right height for climbing on and off the toilet alone and for planting the feet on while sitting there. If you buy a stepstool, he will be able to move it himself to reach the washbasin. Encourage your child to use this new set-up, but don't remove the potty until it is voluntarily abandoned.

Once he is happy to use the toilet at home, you can cultivate interest in toilets all over the place. Show the bathrooms at friends' houses; take the child to the restrooms in stores or at the swimming pool. He should even make the acquaintance of less elegant toilet facilities in public places, so that he is not surprised and distressed when faced with a dirty, smelly bathroom on a train or in a gas station. Eventually the bathrooms at school may upset him unless he has met a lack of privacy and hygiene before.

Most three- and four-year-olds will prefer a parent to go with them to a strange bathroom and should always have an adult caretaker with them in a public toilet. No one will object to a very little boy accompanying his mother to the "Ladies" room but fathers and little girls are in a more difficult situation as rows of strange men using urinals can be a bit put-off and off-putting. Most of Europe already has unisex public facilities. Let us hope it spreads to become the norm here too.

*Managing out of doors*

However reliable the child is, his waiting time will still not be very long. Every child needs to learn how to urinate outdoors if family picnics or long drives are not to be ruined for everybody.

Boys don't usually find this difficult. They can copy Daddy and urinate against a tree or even next to the car on the side of a road if necessary. Girls are at an unfair disadvantage. One who went on an outing with a boy cousin expressed it neatly: "Why won't Mommy get *me* one of those useful things to take on picnics?"

Very small girls may find it easier if they are "held out" with a parent supporting them in a squatting position. Four- and five-year-olds may prefer to remove their pants altogether as they find it difficult to hold pulled-down pants out of the way. All ages will be thoroughly put off if they find themselves amid thorns!

*Urinating positions*

Most little boys urinate sitting down during the toddler years but begin to copy fathers, older brothers and friends during these pre-school years. It is a good idea to help him to pee standing up before he starts at a pre-school group. If you point out that urinating standing up means that he need not take down his pants, the ease and speed will probably appeal to him. Do keep him in elastic waisted trousers or shorts until peer-group fashion makes him yearn for zipper flies. Elastic is both easier and safer for him. Once he stands to urinate, start teaching him to lift the toilet seat beforehand. Make sure the surrounding floor is easy to clean; his aim will often be inaccurate.

If a little girl sees a boy standing to urinate, she will probably try too. When that experiment proves messy and frustrating she may urinate sitting backward astride the toilet. Don't fuss. She will soon realize that her body works best if she sits normally. Accepting this is part of accepting that she is female and that female bodies are not the same as male ones.

*The child's bowel rhythm*

Remember that many children do not need to move their bowels every day but will do so quite naturally every two or three days. Equally naturally, some will regularly go twice or three times a day. The child's pattern is individual and, ideally, it should be none of your business.

If the child seems to like to go after breakfast, this makes good physiological sense, as eating after the long fast of the night often sets up a reflex need to move the bowels. Later on it may make social sense, too. Many children do not like using school bathrooms for anything but a quick pee so are better off if they move their bowels at home. But if this is not your child's natural pattern, do not try to impose it. Children should go when they feel the need, just as they urinate when they need to.

*Managing alone*

At home, the child will feel more secure and independent when he can manage completely alone in the bathroom. Most will still prefer a parent to wipe their bottoms after a bowel movement. They should gradually learn to manage even this alone so that they are not caught out later on, at school, but don't try to hurry it. Most three-year-olds *cannot* wipe themselves, simply because their arms are not long enough relative to their bodies.

Little girls must be taught to wipe from the front backward, never the other way round. Wiping forward brings traces of the feces into contact with the vaginal area and the urethra and can lead to the urinary infections which are so much more common in girls.

*Problems with staying dry*

Children vary widely in the age at which they can manage to stay dry all day. If your child still shows no signs of being "trained," he may simply be a late developer in this respect. Look back to the toddler section (see p. 317) and see whether he is following the ordinary *sequence* for learning control, even if he is doing so later, or more slowly, than most. If he is, you have nothing at all to worry about. All children, except the severely mentally or physically handicapped, learn to stay dry in the end. So will yours. If despair makes you doubt this, ask yourself whether you have ever seen a child start big school in diapers. . . .

There is some evidence that being late in acquiring bladder control runs in families. If you can check up on your own achievements, by asking your respective mothers to search their memories, the answers may comfort you. There is also evidence that boys tend to be later than girls in perfecting control – so if your worry is partly due to comparing a girl who was dry early with this sopping wet boy, stop. They are not comparable.

If your child constantly dribbles urine so that he is always damp rather than occasionally soaking, it is just possible that there is a physical reason why he is not yet "trained." His sphincter should function in such a way that it is either firmly closed or entirely open. If it is permanently in-between, he cannot learn to control it. Brief your doctor privately so that the child need not suffer the embarrassment of listening to you describe his damp pants, and then take the child to see him.

If the child seems totally oblivious to potties, toilets or indeed to urine, make sure that he does in fact understand what you want:

**Take the child out of diapers altogether in the daytime.** Those accustomed wads of padding may be concealing the whole business from his attention.

**Make it clear that you want the child to use the potty or toilet.** You may have been so anxious to avoid toilet training pressure that you have quite neglected to convey this message!

**Make sure that the child sees family and friends using the bathroom.** You do not want to rub his nose in the fact that everybody else stays dry, but imitation can be a great help.

Otherwise there is nothing you can do to hurry the process. Relax and help your child as if he were a two-year-old (see p. 318).

*"Accidents"*  Many three- and four-year-olds have frequent accidents. Even five- and six-year-olds have enough to make a supply of spare pants standard equipment in kindergarten.

Once a child is basically "trained," wet pants are much more embarrassing for him than they are for you. They are uncomfortable too. So be sorry for the child.

Some children, especially boys, have a small bladder capacity. They need to urinate very frequently until their bladders mature both in their capacity and in their ability to concentrate the urine. Some authorities believe that you can speed up this development by getting the child to tell you every time he needs to urinate and then to wait a few more minutes by the clock. Although this seems to work for some children it inevitably focuses a great deal of attention and anxiety on what should be an entirely natural and matter-of-fact part of life. It is probably better to let his bladder mature in its own time.

Like most adults, children urinate most frequently when they are nervous or excited so don't be surprised if your child chooses all the worst times for accidents, such as birthday parties or weekends away. Many also ignore full-bladder signals if they are deeply involved in play. A tactful reminder may save a flood.

Very occasionally a child under emotional stress will hold urine for so long that the bladder becomes overfull and he is unable to empty it. This sometimes happens, for example, if an unready child is left with strangers and is determined not to use the bathroom without mother. The answer is water. The sound of a fast-running tap may release the flow. If it does not, put the child into a warm bath. It is easy to urinate there.

*Urinating at night*

Many children need diapers at night well past their third birthdays. If your child still urinates every couple of hours during the day and always wakes with a wet diaper in the morning, you can be quite sure he is not ready to stay dry. After all, the urination that takes place while he is asleep is not within his control. You cannot *teach* him either to hold all the urine until morning or to wake up to the signals from his full bladder. Only greater maturity will enable him to do either or both. Wet beds seem more of a "problem" than wet diapers, so don't hurry.

*Timing the giving up of night diapers*

Wait until he sometimes wakes up dry after a whole night's sleep, sometimes goes for three or four hours without urinating in the daytime, and occasionally wakes in the early morning because he needs to urinate. Even when you see some or all of these signs of growing up, don't insist on leaving diapers off if he prefers to wear them. If you make him anxious about night-time urination, you will make wet beds and eventual problems more likely.

When you and he together do decide to abandon diapers, do encase the mattress in a proper plastic protective cover. Small plastic sheets get horribly wrinkled and uncomfortable and they usually manage not to cover part of the flood area. Show the child the covered mattress and explain that because it is there it does not matter at all if he should wet in his sleep.

If you have just bought new pajamas and/or bedding, casually emphasize their washability, and *don't* describe them as making a "lovely bed for a grown-up, dry boy." If he gets the idea that wetting his bed will spoil these nice new things, he will be anxious before the event and heartbroken after it.

*Helping your child to stay dry*

Distinguish between trying to keep the child's *bed* dry and helping him to keep *himself* dry. "Lifting" a child to urinate late at night and early in the morning may help avoid wet sheets, but it does nothing for the child's control. If he wakes when you lift him, he will be aware that you, not he, are responsible for his night-time urination. If he does not wake, but urinates, almost asleep, while you hold him out, you are actually encouraging the very thing you are trying to avoid: peeing in his sleep. It is probably best to avoid lifting, at least until a five- or six-year-old becomes worried about wet beds and asks for your help. At that point you can agree, but make sure you wake the child enough to register full bladder signals for himself.

Never restrict evening drinks. A child who goes to sleep thinking thirstily of water is far more likely to wet the bed.

If a child wakes because he needs to pee, this is an excellent sign that control is coming. Make sure he has a potty in his room and enough light to keep the monsters that live under the bed in their places. He may need company, though. Getting out of bed alone frightens many small children. If he is not allowed to call, he may not get out until too late. He is bound to have some wet and some dry beds. Don't comment on either. Congratulation for dry beds and silence on wet ones is almost as bad as scolding him for wetting. If you tell him he is "good" when he is dry, he himself will feel that he is "naughty" – or at least "not good" – when he is wet. You can avoid praise and blame altogether by explaining honestly that people's bladders grow up along with the rest of them and that eventually his will be able to hold all the urine all night.

*Coping with wet beds*

Night-time accidents are very common until around five and not unusual at seven – especially in boys. Don't be in a hurry to decide that your child has a problem.

If you find that you worry about wet beds when your child is four or five, you have to decide whether you can afford to keep calm and keep the child calm, while he matures, or whether you ought to seek help from your doctor.

If the child is wet because of a continuous dribble of urine, there might be a physical problem. A medical check would be worthwhile.

Sometimes children will themselves become worried about bedwetting – usually following tactless comments by overnight guests or hostesses. They may find it difficult to accept your assurances about soon growing out of it, and put more faith in the identical message given with more authority by a doctor. If you brief your doctor privately, explaining that it is your child who is concerned, not you, he can concentrate on reassurance, and the promise of further help being available if it is needed later.

If your bedwetting child can be kept unconcerned – which means you being able to control your natural irritation *and* protect him from being shamed by visitors – he will probably become dry spontaneously by the time he is seven. If he does not, that is quite early enough to seek help from an enuresis clinic.

If bedwetting suddenly starts again when your child has been dry for months, it may be a reaction to stress in daily life. A new baby in the family may give the child an unconscious wish to be a baby again even though his conscious wish is to be grown up enough to stay dry. A separation from you, a stay in the hospital, the loss of a beloved grandparent or any other major upheaval can shake a child's confidence and make him temporarily less able to cope. If there is any obvious stress, you may be able to relieve it by talking about it and babying the child a little. If you can see that the child is tense and anxious but you cannot quite see why, your doctor may be able to help you work out the cause.

*Soiling*

Bowel control usually comes earlier and more easily than bladder control so frequent "accidents" in a child who has been clean, or perpetually soiled pants in a child who seems to be fighting against using the bathroom, need to be taken a bit more seriously than wet beds. Feces smell. A child who soils his pants at school will probably be shunned or labeled "smelly" and it will not be long before the situation affects his self-image, making him *feel* disgusting and unlovable. Soiling is often said to be a sign of emotional disturbance but in many children it is the soiling which *causes* the disturbance (Ref/SOILING).

# Everyday care

During the pre-school years, children will and should become increasingly aware of their own individuality: it shows clearly in their sense of physical dignity. They resent it if you treat their bodies like poodles to be brushed and be-ribboned.

Of course you still have overall responsibility for your child's general cleanliness, health and well-being. But the more you can help him to manage the details of daily routines alone, the less you will offend that sense of autonomy. Practically this will be good for both

of you. Every task the child performs is one less for you. Every piece of self-care is preparation for school when you will not be there to do it. And habits set up now may last a lifetime.

Don't expect fast learning; the chores are boring and repetitive. But there will be gradual progress. Children who will wash their faces, with a parent standing over them, at three, will wash, if they are told to, at four, and may go and wash just because they are dirty by the time they are five. . . .

## Making things easy at home

If your child is to try to do things independently, you need to make it physically possible. In a dark house most children will refuse to run their own errands; lit corridors make it possible. If a child is to cope in the bathroom the door handle must be in reach and the lock manageable or out of reach. Walk around considering your child's size and safety. Is the water hot enough to scald? Are the drawers too heavy to open? Can the child reach that toothbrush without touching razors or pills, reach a cup without breaking your best glasses? Children cannot do the impossible and will not do anything that is accompanied by frantic exhortations to "be careful" so arranging their independence is up to you. If there are no coat hooks they can reach, how can you expect them to hang their coats up?

## Giving choices

Making decisions is part of growing up. Your child must learn to think, rather than simply doing (or not doing!) what you say. But in these early days you cannot leave choices entirely to the child, because he will often make decisions that are bad for health (like "deciding" only to clean teeth weekly) or intolerable to you (like "deciding" to play in the mud in "best clothes").

The trick is to organize life so that your child has complete freedom of decision between a carefully limited set of choices. He can clean teeth now or after a story; go to the bathroom now or later; wear any of the clothes you have left in the drawer or choose between the two dishes you are offering for supper.

## Making clothes easy to manage

Your child is developing a taste in clothes and he or she will loathe garments which are heavy or "smothery." Stretchy materials will still be most comfortable while adding extra light layers will avoid the heavy sweaters most children hate. Avoid heavy overcoats in favor of quilted parkas which allow freedom of movement and freedom to get dirty. Buy in the color the child prefers and always with comfort and independence in mind.

Go for buttons or toggles the child can manage alone or coats with giant zippers rather than tiny ones which are difficult. Until he or she pleads for zipper flies, try for elastic waisted jeans, shorts and skirts. Keep tiresome extras like gloves and hats to a minimum and sew on essentials so they do not get lost. Buy Velcro or buckle shoes and slip-on boots so that the child need neither face those knotted laces nor come for help.

## Coping with the boring chores

Most pre-school children still hate having their hair washed or even thoroughly combed through, while fingernail and toenail cutting is boring and teeth are often brushed in a hurry. A weekly "spring cleaning," undertaken on a regular, agreed evening, chosen *not* to clash with a favorite TV program, and conducted with pleasant ceremony, is often the easiest way for both of you. Set aside plenty of time; rushing will make the child balky. You must have time to let him try everything and the child must feel that there is lots of relaxed attention in return for cooperation.

**Nailcare:** At this stage children cannot cut their own nails; but you can give them some control over the process. Let your child use an emery board to smooth the results of your cutting. The child can clean them himself with an orange stick. Toenails should be cut straight across, not in a curve.

**Teeth:** To finish off, make a game of "how well have you cleaned your teeth this week?" Your child will enjoy using a disclosing agent which stains areas of remaining plaque bright pink. Getting that pink off is a real challenge and when it is done you will know that the teeth really are clean, for now.

**Hairwashing:** Hair has got to be washed but if washing it causes problems let the child decide the easiest way. He may choose any of the tricks suggested for toddlers (see p. 323) but just being allowed to choose is what matters. Offering a choice of shampoos or the use of your personal comb may help too. At the foamy stage, let the child do the rubbing, design soap "hairstyles" and have a mirror to look in. Teach him to check adequate rinsing by "squeaking" hair between the fingers. A cream rinse afterward will help with tangles, but if knots are a problem a short style might be better both for the hair and your tempers.

Clean all over and taught some useful things, let the spring cleaning end in little luxuries: a sprinkle of your talc; clean pajamas; a story while the hair dries . . . not spoiling but a way of ensuring cooperation next week.

# Teething

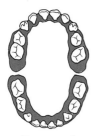

At around two and a half years old your child will have a complete set of first (milk) teeth consisting of ten teeth in each jaw: two molars (double teeth) on each side, one canine (eye tooth) each side and four incisors across the front.

The second molars, the double teeth right at the back, are the last to be cut. Like the first molars cut at around a year (see p. 326) they can make a child's jaw ache while they are coming through.

*Preventing cavities*

The completion of the set of teeth makes tooth cleaning even more important than before. Each tooth now has another one butting up to it and food debris can easily become trapped in between. A small toothbrush, used with an up and down motion, will clear it. Even better is a battery-operated toothbrush which makes tooth cleaning more enjoyable and does a more thorough job. Make sure the back teeth are cleaned as well as the front ones! Make sure that his teeth are thoroughly cleaned after his last food in the evening so that he does not spend all night with food debris between his teeth. Make cleaning them after breakfast a regular habit too, and then try to see that he has a drink of water, which will at least rinse his mouth, after meals.

Remember that sweet foods which stay in his mouth for a long time are the worst for his teeth, so try to keep sticky candy like toffee and long-lasting ones like lollipops away from him and, when he does have candy, encourage him to eat what he wants and get the whole thing over with rather than nibbling off and on over a long period.

Fluoride has a strengthening effect on tooth enamel, making it far more resistant to the acids that otherwise eat into it and let in bacteria. Levels of naturally occurring fluoride in drinking water vary widely from area to area, and the routine fluoridization of supplies is not generally approved because of the faint possibility of overdosage. Some health authorities will be happy to advise you on local levels so that you can, if you wish, fluoridate your child's drinking water, using tablets available from pharmacies. But experience is beginning to suggest that routine use of a fluoride-containing toothpaste is enough – and that these pastes have already reduced the decay rate among children, who inevitably swallow some as they brush. Your dentist is also likely to apply "topical" fluoride to your child's teeth if the enamel seems especially vulnerable.

*Going to the dentist*

Having made a familiarization visit to the dentist during his second year (see p. 327) your child should start regular check-ups at least every six months by the time he is two and a half.

First teeth are vitally important. The second set does not even start to come through until he is around six, so these first ones have to last for years. Furthermore they keep the proper spaces open for the later teeth, and help his jaws to grow to their intended shape. So don't take a happy-go-lucky approach to early dentistry. Above all, don't wait to make an appointment until the child has toothache. Pain means that you have missed the stage where only superficial enamel was affected and a repair would have been easy and painless. The pulp is damaged and the cavity is much larger than it need have been. Try to find a dentist who enjoys working with very young children (Ref/DENTIST). If your pre-school child can build a relationship with his dentist before he first needs treatment, he is likely to accept later fillings trustingly.

*First fillings*  However much your child likes his dentist he is not going to enjoy his first filling. Don't make a drama out of it but don't pretend that it is nothing either. A superficial cavity in the enamel probably will not hurt even when it is drilled, but a cavity as deep as the pulp may. Even if there is no pain, the piercing whine and water pressure are hard for a child to bear, especially if a top tooth is affected.

Explain what the drill is for and, with your dentist's cooperation, show the child his cavity in the mirror. It feels like an enormous hole while it is being drilled; seeing how tiny it really is can be comforting to the child.

Help him to feel that he has some control over the situation by arranging with the dentist to stop drilling at once if the child signals (perhaps by raising his hand) that he needs a rest. This is really important. If he feels helpless and tortured he may panic, now, or the next time he sits in that chair.

With tactful handling most pre-school children will tolerate any dental treatment that is needed, but a few will find it impossible to cooperate. Discuss any problems privately with the dentist. He cannot work on your child by force so the two of you have to decide whether to leave the cavity for a few months, hoping that the child's nerve will improve, or whether the treatment is urgent and should therefore be carried out with the help of a mild sedative or even a very light general anesthetic.

*Accidents and teeth*  Teeth are not rooted directly into the child's jawbone but into a strong pad of highly elastic tissue which acts as a shock absorber. It takes quite a hard bang to knock a tooth out.

Occasionally a direct blow will drive a milk tooth back into the gum from which it emerged. You will probably be able to see or feel its top, just as you could when he was first cutting it. In most cases the tooth will emerge again of its own accord. If the nerve has been damaged, the tooth may "die" and this will mean that it turns a dull yellowish color. Show it to your dentist, but don't be too worried about it. Even a "dead" tooth can usually safely be left to do its job until the second teeth begin to come through.

A tooth which gets broken or chipped is more serious. The sharp edge may cut the child's tongue as he eats or even cut through his lip next time he falls. Take him to the dentist. He will file the sharp edge down or he may decide to "cap" it.

If a tooth is knocked out, or if it is left still attached but out of place, take child and tooth and go straight to your dentist or to the nearest emergency room. Baby teeth can sometimes be put back into position, so that they re-attach themselves, if you get dental help quickly enough. If the tooth cannot be replaced, your dentist must decide whether to leave your child with a gap until his second teeth arrive to fill it, or whether to make a single false tooth for him.

# Coping with stress

Becoming a pre-school child implies that some of the acute emotional stresses which are typical of toddlers have been left behind. But the child has not changed his personality. If he was tense before, he will probably still be tense. If he was irritable before, he will not have become entirely sweet and compliant. But whatever he is like, his ability to cope with the stresses of everyday life and with the feelings they call up in him will have improved.

You will probably see the improvement most clearly in his reactions to separation from you. A few months ago he was bedeviled by separation anxiety. Now, although his passionate dependence on you is as strong as ever, he is able to hold himself calm through minor separations.

Words help him to cope. When you leave the room saying "I'm just going down to the clothes line" he can understand you and see the clothes line and you going to it in his mind.

The beginnings of a sense of time help too. If you say you will be home by lunch time, he cannot count the hours that must pass but he knows that they will.

Experience of other adults makes the world seem more secure. He has discovered by now that there are other nice people in his life. A grandmother can mend a hurt knee or a broken toy, a babysitter can bring a drink of water, and an older child can hold hands on the way to the swings.

His own growing competence is reassuring too. He knows that he can manage a good many things for himself. He is no longer dependent on you for anything he might need at any moment of the day. He is beginning to value playmates of his own age, too, and when he is involved in play with them he accepts that you are only a background figure.

But perhaps it is time and experience which give him most help in coping. He has lived as your child for long enough now to begin to trust you. Over and over again you have left him (for a minute, an hour or a day); over and over again you have come safely back to him. As long as he feels absolute security in your dependable presence and can take your affection for granted, he can afford to take some of his concentrated attention off you and focus it instead on the outside world.

If you can make your child feel that it is safe to venture a little away from you now, to make tiny flights out from under your protection, you will be laying the best possible foundations for the time when he has to venture out into school. But take care. His ability to cope without you is only in the bud and it is rooted in security. If you make him feel that you expect more independence than he can comfortably manage, or if something happens to make him feel less secure, such as a change of caretaker, the coping will shrivel and he will revert to anxious clinging. You have to allow him all the independence he wants without forcing too much on him, and foresee the things which are likely to worry him without being so over-protective that you deprive him of the opportunity to try to manage them.

# Getting on with other children

Although a two-year-old is usually interested in watching, and then in playing alongside, other children (see p. 364), he will not be ready for the beginnings of cooperative play until well into the third year. If he has always played where there are other children, he may slip into an active participation without you even noticing, but if he is not used to others there may be problems. He has to learn the vital lessons of taking turns, of sharing, of giving way. He has to discover that it is all worthwhile; that many games are more fun with a group and two can often succeed at a self-imposed task where one fails.

Gentle, cooperative, social behavior is a tremendous effort for most small children and those who are making the effort successfully tend to be hard on a child who cannot yet manage. If a group has just discovered how to make a sand village without trampling each other's contributions, it will be quick to turn on the big-footed newcomer who does not know the rules. So don't expect other small children to "be nice" to yours. If there is trouble, don't waste energy on being hurt and angry with them for "picking on him." Look at his behavior; see what it is that he does or does not do which makes him unacceptable to the group, and teach him how to manage better. He can learn acceptable group behavior just as easily as he can learn table manners or new words.

*Behaviors that make for trouble*

Some pre-school children take out on other children all the stresses they are feeling at home.

If your three- or four-year-old bites, hits, kicks, attacks younger children, pockets other people's toys and generally makes it impossible for anyone to like him for a playmate, look to his life at home. Is he hitting other children because he longs to hit the new baby and dare not? Does he steal their toys because he feels he has unfairly few of his own or because he feels that their toys mean they are loved, while he is not sure that he is? Does he disrupt their games and bully them because he wants to get back at you for being too bossy over him?

Some children have been over-carefully handled at home so that they find the rough-and-tumble of group life amazing. If you have always arranged for your three-year-old to win at "Go Fish," have the biggest strawberries and think himself stronger than you, he is not going to take kindly to playing with other children who expect justice and reality. "But I *want* to go first" he will say, stunned that anyone else should claim the privilege. "Fall *down*" he will command, pushing at a stalwart opponent.

*Helping your child to learn to get on with others*

As he comes out of toddlerhood, it is important to teach the child the basic principles of "do as you would be done by," especially if he is not attending any kind of pre-school group. If you can help him to understand that every child wants to win and only one can; that each would like to lead and only one can; that all would like the biggest piece of cake and only one can have it; he will at least see *how* to play nicely, even if he cannot manage to play that way all the time. It may seem obvious to you that it is wrong to kick other people. It is not obvious to your child at this age.

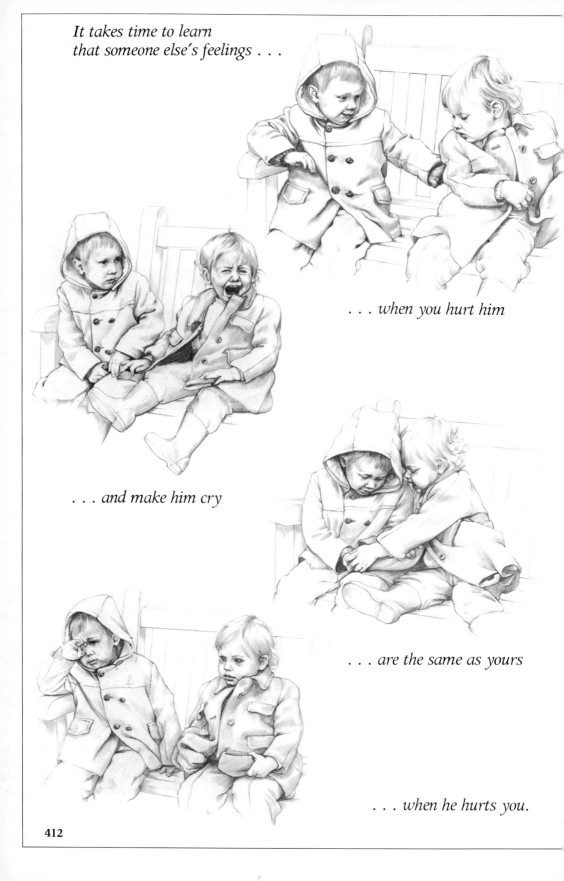

*It takes time to learn*
*that someone else's feelings . . .*

*. . . when you hurt him*

*. . . and make him cry*

*. . . are the same as yours*

*. . . when he hurts you.*

412

He will learn it best if you take every opportunity to show him that other people's feelings are generally the same as his. For example, if he complains that a particular little boy is a sissy and a tattletale, always running to Mommy, suggest that the child may be a bit shy and not very used to other children yet. Remind him of a time when he felt a bit like that. If he pops someone's balloon and gets clobbered for it, kiss the bump but then point out that everyone likes to keep or pop their own balloons.

Don't expect pre-school children to play in company without supervision. Their social controls are not strong enough. Tempers are still precarious and new forethought can be lost in the heat of the moment. If one child hits another's head with a tennis racket, both will suffer. It is your absolute duty to keep everyone reasonably safe from their own and other children's aggression.

But supervision needs to be subtle. Do not sit and watch them like a policeman watching a demonstration. Find something to do within their vicinity; busy yourself but be prepared to step in before things get out of hand. If everyone is armed with a plastic sword and battle is heating up, it is no use exhorting them to "be careful." Take the swords away and suggest something else.

If a group is playing on something – such as a climbing frame – which could be dangerous, you cannot rely on their good sense to take turns and not push. Go and supervise directly, saying "you can only use this if you do it properly; it's one at a time up the ladder, and one at a time down the slide, now, who's first?"

When things go wrong, concentrate on getting them going right again, rather than on finding out the rights and wrongs of the situation. It does not matter who began the fight. It matters only that the fight has spoiled play for everyone, so it must stop.

*"One at a time" is a valuable lesson in taking turns as well as a safety precaution when groups are using large equipment.*

## Helping your child to find friends

An easy relationship with the children who live nearby is beginning to be important to your child now and will be increasingly important all through childhood. So think carefully before deciding that the local children are not suitable friends. If you really cannot accept your local community on your child's behalf, you may have to more rather than commit him or her to a lonely and isolated childhood.

But the children you see around and with whom your three-year-old tries to play may be too old for him. He cannot mix well with a group of schoolchildren, for example. They may tolerate him from time to time as slave labor – fielder of the ball but never pitcher – but they will hurtfully reject him most of the time. He needs younger friends. There may be other pre-school children living close by whom he does not know because they seldom appear except in a family group. If so, a well-timed birthday party or a few invitations to coffee issued to child *and* mother when you meet at the store or chat over the back fence, may help him.

If there really are no young children available, you may have to make the effort to take him where there are some. Absence of playmates is a good reason for seeking out some form of playgroup for him.

Once he is old enough to spend much of his time playing with other children, make it clear to him that he is welcome to bring them in. If he seems to prefer visiting their houses to using his own with them, ask yourself why. He may feel that you do not really like having lots of children in and out, that you resent the noise or the mess. He may be afraid that you will embarrass him in front of them or that the customs and discipline he is accustomed to will seem strange or severe to them.

If he is to have a comfortable, secure feeling about his own community and his own street, all the way through his childhood, it is important to get these things right, now, while he is feeling his way into the outside world. Pride in you both and in his own home is going to be important to him. You do not have to be grand; it does not have to be luxurious. But he does have to feel that it is truly friendly and welcoming.

*You cannot make friends for her but you can help her to make her own. . . .*

# Typical fears and worries

Although every individual child has special fears and worries of his own, there are some anxieties which are very general among children of both sexes at this particular age and stage.

*Worry about disasters* — The child is riding on a crest of imagination in everything he does. This makes him liable to all kinds of "supposing . . ." fears. Where a toddler does not worry about getting lost until he sees a likelihood of being so, the pre-school child looks at his small self in the big park and wonders *what it would be like* to be lost. He may worry about all kinds of improbable possibilities like the house catching fire, both his parents dying or the dog going berserk.

*Worry about injury* — Awareness of self, as a whole separate person inside a body which belongs to him, tends to make the child temporarily very anxious about getting hurt. Sex comes into this exaggerated fear of even minor injury. The child is aware now of which sex he or she belongs to. A little boy usually feels that his penis is both a precious and a vulnerable part of him; despite explanations, he finds it hard to believe that girls are meant to be without these organs, so the removal of his own seems to him to be a real possibility. A little girl is usually also puzzled by her own lack of a penis for which an invisible "special hole" seems poor compensation; despite explanations she may believe that her body has already been damaged by having its penis removed. So for both sexes, injury seems to start up terrible images of being broken, damaged for ever or having lost a part of their precious selves.

The focus of terror is often blood. Pre-school children get through more boxes of bandaids than any other age-group because they cannot get on with their lives until that dreaded blood is safely hidden. But pain is a focus too. A routine injection, which would have evoked nothing but a brief cry a year ago, may be dreaded, hated and remembered with horror. It may take all your tactful skill to get a splinter out of that finger.

*Worry about breakages* — This fear of injury to themselves spreads, in many children, to a shivery horror of injury to anything else. Your child may be disproportionately upset if he breaks anything. If he comes across a headless doll, he may react as you would react to a dead rat. A few children cannot even enjoy jigsaw puzzles because they so dislike the incomplete and "broken" pictures.

*Worry about adult words* — Although the child's language helps him to tell of his fears, his understanding of language also causes some. He overhears fragments of adult conversation and understands the words without their context and without allowing for the dramatizations and shorthand which adults allow themselves when they are gossiping. If he hears you reply to a conventional "How are you?" with "Not long for this world I'm afraid . . .," he may not take it as the wry joke which you intended. He may panic. The same applies to half-heard and partially understood fragments of radio or television programs. Pathetic child-victims of war or famine confirm his anxious feelings that the world is a dangerous place.

| *Worry about you seeming strange* | The security your child gets from being with you comes partly from communication: from his comfortable feeling that you are there for him in spirit as well as available to him in the flesh. A child can *feel* separated if his mother is sunk in depression when a new baby arrives (see p. 36), or even when she is temporarily distracted by other people. Your child may be at his most clingy and demanding whenever there are guests in the house. He is more likely to relax and give you space if he feels he can have you if he needs you. The more he senses a barrier between you, the more he will keep pushing at it. |
|---|---|
| *Worry about strange places and routines* | Relationships have contexts. You feel most readily available to your child when you are in familiar places doing familiar things, and even being both emotionally and physically with him may not protect him from anxiety when everything else is strange. Don't be surprised if he weeps and whines to go home from an eagerly anticipated vacation. The beach-bronzed four-year-old who announced "I don't like it here cause Mommy don't do cooking" spoke for many! Don't be upset if a house-move is even worse than you had expected. The intended improvement in family life may well make it worthwhile in the end, but that will not prevent the beginning from being horrible. |

You can keep your child's personal disorientation to a minimum if you keep his most treasured objects with him. Don't pack his toys and clothes and books in advance and don't let a moving firm do it. Let him "help" you pack the day before (so he knows where everything is and can keep an eye on it) and transport that lot, with him, in your car or in your hand-luggage. When you get to the strange new place concentrate on building a replica-nest – including a corner that feels like a place to play – and try to save enough time and energy to put yourself into the context he expects by cooking an ordinary supper and making him brush his teeth.

In a hotel, keep up as much of his home routine as will allow you to feel you are having a break. In a new house remember that you have to rebuild your context for him and that you will probably do it fastest if you actually encourage him to follow you about while you find your own way. Don't expect him to assume that you will come if he calls in the night, just as you have always done. He hasn't got your bedroom and likely whereabouts mapped in his mind; if he cannot see you, he does not know where you are. Don't try to make him sleep alone if he is homesick that first night. You don't want his new room marked with misery. If he ever sleeps with you, this is a good time to let him. Even if he has not slept with you since he was a baby it may lower the stress for both of you to invite him, "just this once, while we all get used to it. . . ."

| *Dealing with your child's fears* | You can best help your child with his fears by letting him lead the way toward independence whenever you can. You can help him too by keeping a firm and even control over him and his life, making it clear that you do not expect him to take the responsibility for his own safety; that is still your job. If he asks permission to do something – such as go to the playground alone with a friend – and you can see that he is not happy about it, say "no" quite firmly. He will be enormously relieved to find that you don't feel he *ought* to be ready for the new experience. |
|---|---|

When he is afraid, give him reassurance in full measure. Do not ever tease him or let anyone else mock his fears. If you do, he may learn to hide them, or to mask them under a layer of cockiness, but they will still bother him inside.

Your pre-school child's fearfulness will cure itself when he has had enough experience of being able to cope with whatever happens to him. Gradually he will discover that grazed skin always heals, that falling off a tricycle does not break him into pieces, that mother never loses him, forgets him or goes off without telling him, that bad guys do not break into the house at night and that he stays quite safe and in control of whatever is asked of him. But the less he is frightened in the meanwhile, the faster he will reach that happy state of confidence in himself.

Pre-school children face many new experiences that are an integral and proper part of growing up and into the world outside their families. You know your child best so you are best placed to guess what will provide exciting stretch without despairing stress, as well as being best able to provide the kind of support which keeps things manageable. Don't put your child in for a race toward independence. There is no particular virtue (and there may be some risk) in having a two-year-old who will go anywhere and do anything with anyone. And there is no shame in having a shy clingy three- or four-year-old, or the kind of five-year-old who adapts slowly to new situations and people.

## Starting at a group

With your child's third birthday in sight you will probably be thinking about pre-school education (see p. 374). Are you going to look for a regular pre-school group for him? Is there a group available and will it suit your child and your way of life?

Starting at a pre-school group does not have to be an acutely stressful experience. For some children it is a welcome widening of horizons in the shape of a twice-weekly treat. It *is* stressful for a lot of children, though, especially if going to the group presents them with several important new experiences all at the same time. If you work out which aspects of starting at a group might bother your child, you may be able to do some useful familiarization in advance. And if your advance thinking makes you quite sure that there is going to be major trouble, you can arrange to have the time available for a lengthy settling-in period. Having arranged to be available, you may get a nice surprise when your child sails happily in without you from day two. . . .

Going to a pre-school group means separating from you or from the other caretakers to whom your child is accustomed. However gently your chosen group takes this separation – encouraging you to stay with the child and so forth – he will be fully aware that the eventual plan is to leave him there. After all he can see that the established group members do not have a special adult each.

Separating from you means accepting help and care from adults who are not (yet) "special." A shy child may be agonized by having to answer when they speak to him. A newly dry child may wet himself and then be appalled that a comparative stranger should change his pants.

Whatever a child feels about the adults in a pre-school group, its basic point, the other children, may present him with major stresses. He may still be so focused on his relationships with adults that he is scarcely ready to see the benefits of friendship with children. And until he can see the point of cooperative play, the necessary social skills, turn-taking and speaking-before-you-hit, will probably escape him.

Some two-year-olds are already accustomed to all that from regular time spent in a day nursery or center. Others are used to aspects of it. Regular time with a sitter, for example, may have helped your child to accept care from several different adults and to accept being out of his own home, but it may not have prepared him for the shock of a room with 15 or more children in it. Lots of social life with other families or regular attendance at a toddler group may have accustomed your child to lots of caring adults and to lots of other children, but it may have done nothing to prepare him for the idea of managing all that without you. . . .

If you decide that going to a pre-school group is likely to be very stressful for your particular child, think carefully about the timing and your own circumstances. Does he have to start at the first moment that the group will accept him? If freedom from a part of his daily care is important to you the answer may be "yes" and you may have to help him put up with a difficult start. But if you are considering a group only from *his* point of view, because from yours his daily care is already satisfactorily catered for, things may be far easier if you wait a while. Quite a lot of children who start at a playgroup as soon as they are three are bored with it before they can move on to school. And quite a lot of children, who are sent to playgroups at three to prepare them for the nursery school which will accept them at four, would do better if that nursery were their first experience of pre-school (see p. 374).

*Judging your child's readiness for pre-school*

One of the most important signs of readiness is your child's willingness to be away from you and/or from his home for short periods. If he still clearly prefers to spend every waking moment within your sight, managing without you will be a strain for him.

Being willing to be away from you will probably mean that he is able to talk easily with other familiar adults, no longer needing you as constant interpreter (see p. 370). A child who has reached this point will obviously find it easier to make friends with a teacher than a child who is still desperately shy.

Interest in other children whom he sees playing in the park or playground is also a sign of readiness for group life. Even if he has not yet had much opportunity to join in their play, his interest means that he is ready to try out relationships with people his own age rather than devoting his whole attention to adults.

Apart from these psychological points, you also need to consider more practical aspects of his readiness. He needs to be more or less clean and dry, for example. Although a few puddles will be calmly accepted in any good pre-school group, the child will feel uncomfortable if he cannot use the potties or toilets provided just as the other children do.

If you decide that your child is not ready for any kind of group (or if there is none available) don't let the whole matter slip from your mind so that his life goes on indefinitely in its present mold. One day it will be time for him to go to school. When that day comes he will *have* to go, however much he dislikes it and, unless you are particularly fortunate in your individual school, he will have to go all day, every day and manage without you almost from the beginning. It's fine to delay any kind of pre-school education, but as a three-plus he will need alternative ways of getting to know other children and of getting used to managing without a "special" adult for short periods. And as a four-plus he really will benefit from some more formal group experience if you can possibly arrange it for him (see p. 378). You would be wise to look for a group and get his name down a year before you plan to send him.

*Assessing a group*

However popular and over-subscribed a group may be, you do not have to accept it at face value. Make an appointment to visit the group, without your child but during its open hours. Meet the person in charge, by all means, but if the group is split into various sub-groups or "classes" make sure you also meet the person who will be directly responsible for talking to, comforting and disciplining your child. Do you like her? Does she seem really to like small children, speaking sympathetically of them and not being too ready to joke with you at their expense or to dismiss them as "all the same at that age?"

Ask to be allowed to watch the group in action. Do the children seem happy and busy? Do they talk freely to each other, to themselves and to the adults? Does there seem to be some choice of activities so that a child who does not want to join in a song can play, rather than sit in a corner as if in disgrace? Is there adequate tactful supervision during "free play," or are these periods a chaos of fights, tumbles and tears?

Consider the accommodations. A dreary building is not a sensible reason to turn down a group that is otherwise good: it is people who make or mar a pre-school group, not buildings. But if you have any choice, you will obviously prefer a group whose facilities offer things which you feel your child particularly needs. Outdoor play-space may not matter to a child with a yard at home but it can be a big plus to a child from a high-rise apartment. A large multi-group school might overawe a shy child but be an advantage to a confident one who needs a wide range of children to make friends with and the possibility of "promotion" with age.

*Getting ready to start pre-school*

Rising threes who have never been cared for in a group before cannot usually be directly prepared for this big experience. It is totally new so there is nothing similar in their previous lives with which you can compare it in talk or with which the child can compare it in his mind. Unless he is unusually advanced in both speaking and understanding you may even put him off the whole idea if you make too much of it. Take him to visit the group; make sure he registers "his" teacher or helper by some permanent (you hope) feature, like her long dark hair, and then be content with occasional references to the group: "Look at that rocking horse. It's just like the one they have at playgroup. . . ."

But if his first days are going to go smoothly, you may need to think ahead about how *you* are going to manage:

**If you are pregnant, arrange for him to start well before the birth,** or resign yourself to keeping him at home until several months after it. If you launch him into group life just when the new baby comes into his life, he is bound to feel banished and rejected. If you try and launch him immediately afterward, you will not have the time or energy to support him properly through his first weeks. If you confide your pregnancy to the group leader, she may even agree to take a child who seems ready before his third birthday so that he can settle before the baby arrives.

**Get the taking and picking up organized.** If the group is only a short walk away and only meets weekly, you may be able to manage alone, but if it is far, a double daily journey at 9:30 and again at midday will drive you mad. If you do it by car, there will be days when it is being serviced. . . . You need a carpool, a friend who will share, or at least somebody who will take and pick up for you in emergencies. Making this kind of arrangement may be an excellent excuse to strike up acquaintance with other parents whose children are starting at the group. They will all benefit by getting to know each other on their home ground.

*First days at a pre-school group*

Most three-year-olds reckon to be able to cope with almost anything as long as Mom or her accepted substitute is there, so if your child is starting in a group that encourages you or his regular sitter to stay with him until he is ready to be left, you should not have much difficulty.

Mention casually, about a week ahead, that his first day is coming up. Remind him the day before, and answer any questions. Make it clear that you will be with him. If, for example, he asks what the other children will be like, you can say something like "I'm sure they will be very nice, but anyway we shall see tomorrow shan't we?"

Be honest with the child about your movements. If you mean to stay all morning, every morning, until he is happy to be left, tell him so and mean it. Don't suddenly decide to slip away after all in the middle of the session because he seems so happy. Later on, if you mean to stay for half an hour, tell him that too and say "goodbye" when you are leaving. He cannot concentrate on group activities if he is continually looking over his shoulder to see if you have vanished.

Try, over the first few sessions, to become more and more invisible. If you play with the child, get things out for him and take him to the bathroom, you make yourself into a barrier between him and the other adults as well as between him and the other children. He may need you to stand between him and them on the very first day, but after that you have to help him behave as if you were not there, ready for the day when you will not be. If he keeps coming to you to show you things, try saying "It's lovely, why don't you show it to Miss Jones?" If he tells you he needs to go to the bathroom, say "I'm sure Mary will take you, just as she does the others." Above all, don't interfere between your child and the other children. The teachers will protect him if he needs protecting, or control him if they think that he is being too rough or aggressive.

When you and the teacher or group leader decide that the time has come for you to leave him for the first time, do tell him. Remind him, by name, of all the people he knows there now and of all the things he likes doing. Point out that only new children have their mothers with them and that he is not new any more.

Give him something from home to take with him. If the group prefers children not to bring toys from home in case they get lost or appropriated, he can have the handkerchief out of your handbag to keep in his pocket, or even just an apple out of the home fruit bowl to eat at snack time.

Take the child to the group yourself, leave him with the adult he knows best and say that you will be there, on that same spot, to take him back again at going home time. The idea is to make him feel quite sure that there will be no gap at all between his being in your care and in the teacher's:

**Go back early on the first two or three days.** He does not, of course, know the actual time, but you should aim to arrive there before the last activity of the session ends and therefore before he even has time to start looking for you.

**Do not be late in collecting him, at least during his first few weeks.** Children left waiting after every other child has gone feel abandoned. The adult's justified irritation (which the child will sense, however kindly she conceals it) will not help. Your child may then decide that it is not safe to let you leave him at group in the first place.

**Don't tell him about interesting things that happened while he was away.** If you tell him about beloved visitors who came and have now left or fascinating dramas involving plumbers or stray dogs, you may make him feel that he is missing too much by going to his group. Make your routine sound as ordinary as possible. You can even be clever and mention casually that you have finished up all your most boring jobs or your work so that you now have time to bake a cake or play a game.

**Once he is settled, don't take parting tears too seriously.** Many children who are genuinely enjoying and benefiting from group life find the parting moment hard. A good teacher will tell you honestly whether your child cheers up and joins in as soon as you have left. If you are not sure you believe her, arrange a bit of spying over the playground fence or through the door crack. If he is drearily watching the door and sucking his thumb, spy again the next day in case you picked a bad moment. If it is the same sad sight, talk to the teacher again, making it clear that you do not want the child to come to group unless he enjoys it. If worst comes to worst, you may have to take him away altogether for a time and see whether, after a few weeks of finding home rather boring, he asks to go back to group again.

But probably, if you spy, you will see your child happily doing whatever the others are doing. If it is only "goodbye" which is causing trouble, don't let the child think you take his tears too seriously or he may deduce that letting you go really is dangerous. Instead, try to find another mother and child to travel with so that the two children can rush in together. If that is impossible, experiment to see whether he finds it easier to part from his father, having left you where (in his view!) you belong: at home. Either way, confide in the teacher. She may find a regular job – like paint-mixing – for your child to do the moment he arrives. His busy importance will probably solve the whole problem.

## Getting ready to start school

Starting school is the beginning of a new life for your child, whether he does it at four or at five. School will dominate his life for the next twelve or more years and the imperatives of its hours, mid-term breaks and vacations will probably dominate yours, too. A good start may affect his attitude to school and your Monday mornings for years to come and there is quite a lot you can do to ensure it provided you start early enough. You can equip him with school clothes and a school bag in the week before he starts but confidence and competence take longer.

Very few children in the U.S. now start school without *any* preliminary experience in some kind of pre-school group. If yours will be one of these you will need to find ways of letting him practice managing without you *or* his usual sitter for a few hours at a time, of managing himself with only a small fraction of an adult's attention and of managing a group of other children. Make sure that he understands the basic social rules like taking turns (see p. 411). And even if he has never been a group-member before, do try to make sure that he has been a playmate and friend (see p. 414). If he actually resents being with a lot of other children, because he knows nothing of what they can offer him, he will have little motivation for settling in.

**Teach him to manage on his own until it is second nature to him.** A sense of being able to cope with whatever will be expected is a vital part of self-confidence for all of us at any time. Your small child cannot know *what* will be expected of him at school so it is up to you to know for him. You know, for example, that he will be expected to manage his own pants and underwear in the bathroom. Of course there will be an adult who can be *asked* for help but, unlike playgroup, there will not be an adult automatically *offering* it. Having to ask for help will make your child feel very helpless. And it's worth making it easy for him with elastic waisted pants rather than zippers, suspenders and overalls. The same argument applies to all kinds of practical aids from slip-on shoes to easily opened lunch boxes and school bags and to practicing techniques which are peculiar to school such as drinking from a drinking fountain or finding the coat-hook with the right name on it. A child who copes confidently with these everyday matters saves the teacher time and trouble but he saves himself something even more important: the anxiety of needing help and the asking for it which many shy children find so painfully difficult.

**Help him to practice talking to adults outside the family.** In the months before he will go to school, teach your child to greet visitors to the house and perhaps show them his room or his guinea pig. Shopping is good practice too, whether it is for his own candy or your bread, and he can have a go at speaking for himself to the doctor, the bus driver or the librarian. The practice is not just in making the effort to face strangers but in finding out how loudly he needs to speak in order to be understood; in learning to repeat himself (rather than burying his head in the nearest skirt) if he is not understood the first time and in remembering to listen to the answer and "de-code" it even when the voice or the accent is unfamiliar.

**Try to build some crowded *fun* occasions into his pre-school life.** A lot of small children dislike crowds, especially noisy ones. Even twenty small children in a classroom can seem like a noisy crowd when they are all strangers, and when a new schoolchild is fighting for self-control it is often the larger and noisier groups at Assembly, at lunch or in the playground which finally defeat him. If he can cope with the swimming pool and its café on a Saturday morning and join in the noise at a puppet show, a circus or a pantomime, he'll be less inclined to panic the first time he sits down to lunch in the big school cafeteria.

Whenever your child first leaves you to enter group life, you want him to move happily into a larger world than he has known before and to expand the range of his friendships with children and adults. None of that should involve abandoning him to total strangers in a strange place. Some parents have such an exaggerated respect for professional institutions like schools and hospitals that they will hand over to perfectly strange teachers and nurses children whom they would not dream of leaving with unknown people anywhere else.

Pre-school playgroups usually pride themselves on serving as extensions of children's homes. Most will encourage – even insist upon – a parent or sitter staying with a child through as many sessions as it takes him to feel "at home" in the group. Beware of the occasional nursery school which actually forbids parents to stay with their children, even on the first day. And as you investigate your local schools, ask what arrangements they make for all of you to get to know each other before you pass your child into their care. Although it is important for your child to identify his teacher, his room and the bathroom on a preliminary visit, that is not enough. He needs to feel that you, his most basic and trustworthy person, know the school, know the teacher and *approve of them*.

Once your child makes the school world into his world, you may feel that you have lost him to it because you will never again know and control every detail of his days. But making his own a world that does not contain you is a triumphant piece of growing up and on the way to it your child needs to feel that you go with him into school and that you confidently swap yourself for his teacher. At first you may do this literally: taking him all the way into the classroom and swapping his hand from yours to hers. Then you may do it symbolically: taking him as far as the cloakroom where he sheds the coat that brought him from home, and then waving him down the corridor that separates you from his teacher. And even after that you will need to do it in spirit and in talk, so that home and school still make a whole for your child and so that he can always leave you without losing you.

# Using his body

Pre-school children have won the battle to get on to their feet and to get their bodies under reasonable control. Now they are ready to use those bodies. They *are* their bodies; that arm does not only belong to the child, it is the child.

Because pre-school children feel at one with their bodies they do not separate physical activities, thinking activities and feeling activities as adults tend to do. Doing helps them think; thinking makes them do. Doing helps them to understand what they feel and to stand the strength of their feelings; so feeling also makes them do. This is why attempts to modify a child's physical behavior – to make him use his right hand for activities in which his left naturally dominates, for example (Ref/HANDEDNESS) – often lead to considerable confusion and emotional upset.

Children are always on the go. But as they rush around they are learning. Physical activities are just as important to a child's development and intelligence as other kinds of play (see p. 448).

*Testing self-limits*

Since children feel that their bodies are "themselves," bodily strength and efficiency are very important to both sexes. A child whose body fails at a task feels that he personally has failed.

So he sets himself challenges, testing his own limits. He knows he can walk, but needs to see how far; he knows he can run, but needs to find out whether he can run faster than his friends. He knows he can climb, but he has to find out whether that particular tree will defeat him. While he measures himself against these continual challenges, he learns vital lessons about managing his physical self. He learns where the main strength of his body lies. He finds, for example, that a bed which he cannot move when he pushes from the wrist, shifts a little when he pushes from the shoulder. If he lies on the floor and pushes with his feet, his straight legs, powered by his hips, can move it freely.

He learns how to nurse his body along so as to get the most out of it. If he carries something heavy in one hand, the muscles tire; when he changes hands, the fresh muscles work better. When he changes back again, the first set of muscles are rested and ready for more. He discovers his most vulnerable spots too. He learns to guard his head with his arms when he falls and to let his knees take the brunt of life rather than falling flat on his belly. Painfully he discovers that his private parts need respectful clearance when he climbs over sharp chair arms or climbing frame bars.

Gradually he discovers more about what he can and cannot do with this body. It is solid enough to stop a rolling ball if his feet are together but if they are apart the ball will roll through. His hands can make a cup efficient enough to carry wet sand but inefficient when the sand is dry and hopeless for water. Gravity affects his body: he can run downhill and jump down steps but he learns that he cannot get far upward. He experiments continually with balance or, as he probably sees it, "how not to fall down!" He can walk along a bench with both arms outstretched but if one hand comes inward to put a lollipop in his mouth he will wobble. He can lean just so far over a fence to reach something but when he leans farther he is off-balance and cannot get back. By the time he is three he can stand on one foot but only while he concentrates; doing anything else at the same time is impossible.

## The child's body and feelings

Pre-school children have to involve their bodies as well as their minds in order to understand the world and its experiences. Watching television, the four-year-old shoots the bad guys, cheers the hero and gallops around the room with the horses. He neither can nor should sit quietly. If he may not engage his body as well as his mind, he will switch off his brain, if not the TV set.

His own emotions affect him in the same way. He must vent his anger in shouts and stamps, howl out his misery as he throws himself dramatically on the floor, or hop and squeak to let out just enough joy to stop himself exploding.

Unfortunately for small children, this kind of emotional display shocks and embarrasses many adults. We tend to take pride in controlling ourselves, in using words instead of actions and in concealing our feelings from others. So many parents try to impose a separation between body and feeling on children who are at the stage where the two are totally intermixed. Imposing physical restraint of this kind can totally spoil things for him. If he may not roar with laughter and drum his heels when the clown enters the circus ring, he will stop finding him funny. It can make feelings harder to bear, too. If a sudden disappointment leaves him crying bitterly and you say "Oh don't cry," he may feel that it is his actual tears that distress you rather than his disappointed feelings.

If, instead of trying to squash his physical displays of feeling, you can accept and even encourage them, you will help him to recognize what it is that he feels and to learn to cope with it. Instead of telling that disappointed child not to cry, you could say, "It has made you sad, hasn't it? Come and sit with me for a bit until you don't feel cryey any more. Then when you feel better we'll do something else. . . ." You show the child that you accept his disappointed feelings; that tears are a perfectly acceptable response to them; that you will support him through the feelings/tears; and that when the tears end, the feelings will have become manageable. On happier occasions you can even play pretend-feelings with him. He is a natural actor and will throw himself eagerly into a game of "Be a very tired old woman; be a very angry man; be a child who's lost his puppy. . . ." He will deliberately tense and distort his face and body, striving for the feeling-image your words have conjured up. As he does so he is learning to understand the feelings through his body; making them familiar; making them safe.

This total intermingling of body and emotion makes small children especially vulnerable to adult abuse of either. Almost every parent recoils from the idea of sexual abuse – whether incestuous or otherwise – but there are less horrendous and less obvious kinds of abuse which may nevertheless be damaging. Being physically punished or forced, for example, cuts into the core of the child's new sense of self. He cannot yet say (as some prisoners of conscience have said) "Do what you like with my body; you cannot touch my mind." Whatever is done to the body is done to the mind as well. Of course any child will sometimes have to be restrained or forced, fleetingly, to prevent him from harming himself or others. And of course even the least violent parent can be reduced to delivering a smack. It will do no good (see p. 463) but it will do no permanent harm provided you make it clear to the child that you lost your temper and did something you regret: "I'm sorry. I lost my temper. I shouldn't have hit you but . . . ."

Being forced to make gestures of physical affection can be almost as bad as being physically punished. The child who is made to kiss Aunt Mary whom he dislikes is being asked to betray himself through his body; to use it to express an emotion he does not truly feel. Even a parent whom the child does love can demand too many kisses and hugs. The little girl who loves to sit on Daddy's knee wants to (and should) do so when she feels like it. If he grabs her and snatches kisses as she passes on other business she feels that he is using her body for his own pleasure rather than responding to love when it is offered to him. Don't demand or force physical affection. If you truly yearn for a cuddle, ask.

Your child's body and the feelings it evokes are his very own and what is done to them should be up to him. A child has a right to masturbate and almost certainly will, whether you are aware of it or not (see p. 212). You may gently persuade him to keep this pleasure to private times, as a matter of good manners, but if you scold or shame him for the activity itself you are interfering between body and child. But if children have a right to masturbate because their bodies and their feelings are their own, the same reasoning gives them the right *not* to be sexually stimulated by adults or asked to stimulate them. A child who is brought up, from the very beginning, to have this dual sense of his body's worth and its privacy will have a basic protection within himself against uncomfortable approaches in the years to come.

*Your body and your feelings*

Pre-school children are so tuned in to bodies and to physical behaviors that they read the "body language" of adults with uncanny skill. Where a toddler needs to see your face to know whether you are happy or sad, a pre-school child will often read your headache in your drooping back.

He will hardly ever be wrong about *what* you are feeling but he will often be wrong about what you *want him to know* you are feeling. If you are trying to conceal a serious quarrel, an illness or work problem from him, he will know that you are miserable. Your bright, forced smile will not fool him but it will confuse him. He knows you are sad, yet you pretend to be happy. You make him doubt the evidence of his own senses. He will be better reassured by a simplified version of the truth than by attempts at total concealment of it. "Mommy is sad because her Daddy is ill" is a far less worrying thought for a small child than: "There's something odd about Mommy and I don't understand her today. . . ."

The child who detects sadness in your body will use his own to try to comfort you. The best comfort he knows is the comfort he himself wants when he is miserable: a big hug. Tied up in your own problems you may feel quite unable to use a hug just now. If you reject his efforts too often, he may stop trying. Try to accept what he offers with a good grace. Giving your stubbed toe over to be "kissed better" is part of parenthood!

When you begin to think about how you can teach your child to keep safe from strangers, don't exclusively dwell on the ultimate horrors of abduction, rape and murder. These disasters do happen but they are much rarer than other kinds of sexual abuse and there is much less that you can do to protect your child against them. Think about daily safety not headline tragedy.

The conventional teaching is "Never talk to strangers" but when you think about it from a child's point of view that is neither an easy nor a useful message. Which strangers? You *want* the child to speak politely to the nurse or the storekeeper he has never met before and you want him to be able to ask what is his fare from a bus driver or for help from a policeman. Just *talking* will not put a child at risk, anyway. It is what may follow the talking that matters. And when a child is at risk, it is rather unlikely to be from a total stranger. More sexual abuse takes place within children's homes – whether from parents, relations or "friends" – than outside them; and when there is abuse outside the home it is far more often at the hands of family acquaintances or neighbors than the hands of complete strangers.

A more useful kind of teaching avoids the whole concept of "strangers" and who they are, avoids the idea that talking is risky and makes it unnecessary to induce fear and suspicion in a trusting and sociable small mind. All you have to teach your three-year-old is that he must never *go anywhere with anybody* without coming to tell you, or whoever is looking after him, first.

The message is particularly easy for this age-group to understand because it fits with the development phase. Small children always want to know where *you* are – even if you have only gone to the bathroom – so it seems entirely reasonable to them that you should feel the same way. The lesson is easy to remember because the child practices it every day rather than only in unusual and dramatic circumstances. If you are sitting on a bench while he plays on the swings, he is to come and tell you before he moves into the sandbox. If you know he is next door, he must come and tell you before the next-door parent takes his little gang for ice cream.

If your child will never deviate from his stated activities or planned path without checking in with somebody, nobody will ever be able to lure him into a car, take him to see a puppy or bribe him away with the promise of candy. He does not have to judge whether he should go or not; the judgment is up to you when he comes to tell you what he proposes. And he will never have the confusion of "I thought it was all right 'cause it was Daddy's friend . . ." because he has to come and tell *whoever* it is. Later on you will probably want to teach him about the real risks; introduce him to the idea that not all adults are trustworthy. But for the next few years it will be enough for him to know that the "rule" established between you is absolute and anyone who tries to persuade him *not* to come and tell you must be disregarded.

Physical adventures mean a chance of physical accidents, but while it is your job to keep your child safe, it is also your job to keep your caretaking to a minimum. If you continually fuss at the child to "get down from there" or "hold my hand or you'll fall," you get between him and his body. You prevent him from finding out what he can and cannot do: by preventing him from learning, you may even provoke exactly the kind of accident you are working so hard to avoid.

It is often helpful to remember that you could only certainly prevent all possibility of accidents by literally imprisoning your child – following him around and holding on to him all day. So try to accept the fact that a few bumps and grazes are all in the day's work for a pre-school child. Concern yourself with preventing *serious probabilities* but don't drive yourself mad thinking about the thousand and one *trivial possibilities.*

**Trust a child who is playing alone.** He will almost certainly stay within his own limits. He will not climb four rungs of the climbing frame until he can manage three. Let him set his own pace. Remember that muscles improve with use; balance improves with practice; and nerves steady with experience of success.

**Watch out when other children tease.** The taunt of ''baby'' will drive the most sensible child to heights of idiotic daring. He needs you to remind him – and the children with whom he plays – of the line between bravery and folly.

**Be wary of leaving your child in the charge of older children.** He will long to emulate their exploits and they will find it easier to take him with them to the lake than to find him a safe occupation nearer home and keep coming back to check on him.

**Be careful of machines.** At a stage when he is discovering the workings of his own body you cannot expect him to have much idea of the workings of machines. They have quite different properties. Pedal cars will amaze him by being more difficult to stop from high than from low speed. He will not remember to keep his fingers out of tricycle spokes or his toes away from wheelbarrow wheels. Objects like lawnmowers and hedge clippers will be highly dangerous because he will not easily understand the relationship between switching a switch and distant blades whirling around.

**Above all, watch out for traffic.** However sensible he seems about ''road drill,'' he is totally incapable of assessing the speed or intentions of a moving vehicle. However obedient he seems to your instructions to stay on the sidewalk, he will forget when anything distracts him.

*Vacations and trips away from home*

A lot of small children who can keep themselves reasonably safe at home come to grief when they are away. A new environment offers new hazards. The child has never met them before and therefore can neither anticipate nor even recognize them. You have to do both for him. At the shore, for example, local children will have learned about tides and collapsing sand tunnels. Your child has not learned. He will see no significance in a dwindling beach, the increasing pull of a current around his legs or the tell-tale trickles of sand from a tunnel that is about to cave in.

When you take your child on vacation you will probably long to let him run free, but if his freedom is to be unsupervised you need to choose your place very carefully indeed. Even that innocent country cottage may have a bull in the next field, poison ivy in the hedge, a well in the garden or a delightful haystack with a pitchfork for him to jump on.

**Put yourself in your child's shoes.** Think of this new environment and all the things in it he has never met before. Try to foresee how they will strike him.

**Make a tour of inspection when you arrive.** Visualize your child running around and try to spot the traps lying in wait for him.

**Be an undemanding but willing escort,** ready to go with him over the rocks or down to the pool, into the ocean or over to the farm. With you as his watchdog he can have freedom.

*Fatigue and illness*

Your pre-school child, whose whole life involves maximum effort, is more liable to accidents when he is below par. The more tired or unwell he becomes, the more liable to frustration. If he has been trying to ride a two-wheeler all afternoon and his performance gets worse as suppertime approaches, he will be furious. "I can, I can do it" he roars, setting off yet again. Left to fail and try again, he will get bolder as he gets crosser. If you mind him coming to grief, you have to find a tactful way to make him stop until he is rested.

*"Accident prone" children*

Some children seem unusually accident prone all the time. The local emergency room may even come to know them by name, so often do they appear for a couple of stitches, a cast or a night's observation.

A few of these children may be being distracted by worries or anxieties or made careless of their own safety and bad at managing their bodies by long-term unhappiness. If you suspect that your child's liability to accidents is due to unhappiness and tension, you may need to offer extra protection while you try to discover and sort out the trouble.

Some children are just less well-coordinated than many others, so that they come to grief during ordinary play. You can offer practical help. Show him safe ways to climb a ladder; teach him to wait until he has got his balance before trying to walk along a wall and to sit down when he feels himself wobbling; set him little obstacle courses on his bike to improve his steering.

If he seems really clumsy, he may benefit from actual lessons in bodily control. You may be able to enroll him in "music and movement," dancing, gymnastic or even judo classes.

A few children seem neither unhappy nor clumsy but unreasonably fearless. They do not only climb too high into trees, they also jump out again and break their legs. Speed does not frighten them so they win all the bike races at the expense of bits of skin.

A child like this will learn his own lesson in time, but you want him to do it as cheaply as possible. Never congratulate him on his outrageous performances even when relief that he has come through safely makes you want to cheer. Instead of applauding his Tarzan leap, point out that his success was pure luck and that trying was stupid. If you can make him feel that you really care about his safety, he may be able to care about it too and see his rashness as babyish and silly.

## Physical anger and aggression

Even the most tolerant parents rightly draw the line at being hit [or] kicked because the child is angry. He has the right to use his bod[y] to act out his feelings, but he does not have the right to use it to hu[rt] anyone.

A lot of parents believe that a child who deliberately hur[ts] should be hurt back. The idea is that if he is shown what a goo[d] smack feels like he will not do it any more. If he does still do it the[n] he deserves painful punishment.

This is a completely illogical argument from the child's point [of] view. If he smacks you and you smack him back, he sees that yo[u] have done exactly the same thing as him. He cannot possibly tak[e] you seriously when you punctuate your slaps with "I will *not* hav[e] you *hitting* people!"

The force of your argument is much stronger if nobody in you[r] house ever hits anyone. When he hits you, you take his hands an[d] say "No, I know you're angry but we don't hit people. Hittin[g] hurts and that's horrid. . . ."

You are bigger and stronger than the child. That means that yo[u] never have to hurt him to stop him attacking you because, [if] necessary, you can simply hold him until he calms down. If you the[n] suggest some other way that he can vent his pent-up fury, he wi[ll] probably accept that instead. Some families have a special pillow [or] cushion for angry pummelling. Some actually encourage othe[r,] harmless, signs of anger, saying "go on, shout, see how loud you ca[n] shout. . . ." The vital thing is to make it clear to the aggressive chil[d] that it is not the *anger* you disapprove of but only his particularl[y] painful way of showing it.

## Aggression against other children

The child who is accustomed to using physical violence to get hi[s] own way, or to having it used against him when other people wan[t] their way, is the one who is most likely to hurt other children o[n] purpose. He may accompany cries of "that's mine" with a goo[d] wallop to reinforce the point, or he may gratuitously attack smalle[r] children just because he feels angry inside. Although problems [of] this kind can arise however carefully you teach your child non[-]violence, they are much less likely if you teach him that there ar[e] no circumstances under which it is right to hurt anyone de[-]liberately, and that accidents which hurt merit apologies al[l] around. It goes without saying that this philosophy will only b[e] effective if he sees it continually applied by and to all members o[f] his family.

Once he starts at playgroup or mixes freely with other childre[n] you will meet the "hitting back" dilemma. Morally, it is obviousl[y] less reprehensible to hit *back* than to hit *first*. But even hitting bac[k] is not useful. A hits B so B hits A. Inevitably A will hit B again an[d] the fight could go on forever because neither child can bear t[o] accept the last blow and retire. I actually overheard one pantin[g] four-year-old plead "Just let me hit you one more time so that I ca[n] stop . . .!"

You need to give your child a basic framework now that he ca[n] build on as he grows up. You might want to suggest, for example, tha[t] straight revenge is never a good reason for violence, but hitting [a] bully in order to escape or pushing a child so as to get out of hi[s] clutches is acceptable.

*Physical sex differences*

An only child takes the shape of his or her own body for granted. He tends to assume that all other children are made in the same way. Mommy and Daddy are usually also taken for granted; they are just themselves and the child sees no similarity between their big hairy bodies and his own smooth little one.

First questions usually come up when the child notices a child of the opposite sex naked. "What's that?" All he wants is its name – vagina – and perhaps the matching name for what he has – penis.

There is no reason why the subject should get loaded with embarrassment if you take it calmly and concentrate on giving accurate information that exactly answers the specific question you have been asked. You do not have to "get the whole business over" by telling all. It is much better to let the child realize which parts he does not understand and ask, in his own time, for the missing links. He may be six or seven before he asks that crunch question: "How does the Daddy put the seed in the Mommy's va-what do you call it?" After years of brief specific answers you will find it perfectly easy to reply "By putting his penis into it."

If you do let a deadly serious "special" atmosphere build up every time your child asks a question that touches on sex, you may land yourself with pure farce. One child rushed into the kitchen saying "Quick, Mommy, tell me where I came from. Sarah's waiting to know." Taking a deep breath, her mother launched into her long-prepared lecture, watched with amazement by her daughter who at last interrupted: "Mommy, I only said where did I come from? Was it Chicago like Sarah?"

Some families make a point of letting their young children see them naked so that they get the chance to see the difference between the sexes when they are adult. Other families make an equal point of not displaying themselves. Where sex and young children are concerned it is probably best not to make a point of anything. It does not matter whether or not your child sees you naked as long as the atmosphere is relaxed and casual. So behave as you always have behaved and don't be deliberately "old-fashioned" or self-consciously modern.

Deliberate displays which are intended to show children that they are made just like their parents of the same sex can misfire badly. To a child's eye there is no similarity between a small, smooth hairless girl and a fully developed woman or between a little boy with a tiny penis and almost invisible scrotum and a fully mature man. Looking at a same-sex parent, the child may actually worry about his or her own inadequacy. Looking at an opposite-sex parent, he may actually worry at the thought of making a baby with someone like that. If your child says anything which suggests that he is bothered in this way, it is comforting to say that all the parts of people's bodies grow at just the right rate to keep up with the rest. The child is just the size and shape he is meant to be now and as he grows his body will change so that it is still just the right size and shape when he is grown up.

But at this stage it is better if children are not especially encouraged to think about *themselves* and the sex act. Intercourse is just one more peculiar thing people get up to when they are adult. That is why sexy teasing and jokes about "boy friends" and "girl friends" are much better avoided.

# Language

Most parents are as thrilled with their children's first words as with their first steps. But just as it is wrong to assume that a newly walking child will now use walking just as adults do, so it is wrong to assume that once the first words come, the rest of language will follow automatically.

Using language becomes more, rather than less, difficult once children have passed the toddler stage. They learned their early words as labels for, and comments on, interesting things that they could actually see. But now they begin to use language for its uniquely human purpose: for talking about things that are not in the room but in their heads, and for expressing things that come *into* their heads: ideas that are theirs alone.

Pre-school children are tremendously busy finding out how things work, finding out what they themselves can do, and putting themselves, imaginatively, into other people's places. The more language they have, the faster thinking will progress. But the more thinking they are doing, the more language they will use. So language and thought, even language and "intelligence," are intimately entangled. A very bright child will be, or at least will become, advanced in talking: he will need language for his thoughts. A child who is helped to use language well will use all the brightness he has to good effect. His talking feeds his intelligence.

*How you can help*   The more conversation you have with the child the better. But to be really useful, it must be genuine, two-way conversation, not just talk. If you let him babble at you while you keep the flow going with "uh-huh" and "really?" the talk is not true communication. He will realize that you are not really listening to him. Monologues from you are not very useful either. If you do not leave pauses for his contributions, and listen and react to them, your talk is no more than pleasant background noise like a radio left on when nobody is listening. He will soon realize that you are not really talking to *him*; that you do not care whether he listens or understands you or not; he will stop bothering.

Provided you are having plenty of attentive two-way talk, you can help your child enormously by providing him with labels for things or ideas at the moments when he needs them. Whether he already has a large vocabulary or still uses only a few words, he needs more and more.

Suppose that he is struggling to move a fresh bag of sand toward his sandbox. He obviously needs physical help, but you can give him language-learning help at the same time by labeling his problem for him. If you just say "Let me help you," he learns nothing new. If you say "Let me help you carry that bag of sand, it is too heavy for you," he is offered several new language ideas. It may not previously have occurred to him that sand in a bag is called a "bag of sand." Above all, he will probably not have realized that he was unable to move it himself because it was "too heavy." You have just taught him the label for an idea (weight) which he could sense but could not express.

You can do the same with all kinds of other ideas. You reach something for him because you are "taller;" you take some ketchup off his plate because he has taken "too much;" you dropped a dish because it was "very hot" and you rejected one of his sweaters because it had got "too small."

You can help him with words about color, shape and number in the same way. If you offer him a bag of candy and he selects a pink one, you *could* say "You're going to have that one?" – friendly chat, but not actually helpful. If instead you say "You're going to have the pink one?" you supply him with the word for a color he obviously likes the look of but probably did not know was called "pink." Two candies give you the chance to elaborate with "Two candies! One candy for this hand and one candy for that hand. Two candies for two hands. . . ." If both are pink but one is oblong and the other round, you can add the colors and shapes into your comments as well.

His imaginary games give you scope for providing words, too. Equipped with a tiny pair of gloves and a huge umbrella, he announces "I'm Daddy." He knows that his father often goes out and he is obviously playing a Daddy-going-out-game in his head. "Is Daddy going to the office or is he going for a walk?" you ask. You have supplied him with name-labels for two of the places Daddy might go; you have helped him to elaborate his thinking within his own game.

You can carry on with this kind of elaboration almost whenever your child speaks to you. There is nothing difficult or phoney about it. Indeed if you are *really* listening to what the child is saying, what he is trying to communicate, you may find yourself doing it automatically. It is the opposite of the "uh-huh" approach to children's talk. He says "Look! Big dog!" It is clearly an exclamation; he has obviously seen something notable about the dog. You try to see what it is and to offer him an elaboration both of the thoughts and of the words that will express them: "Yes, it is a big dog isn't it? And just look how fast he is running. . . ."

He runs to you, showing his grazed knee, crying "Bad bang, bad bang." Embroidery and comfort can go together with "Poor love, you have banged your knee haven't you? But it isn't really very bad; it's only a little bit bad. See, there isn't any blood, just a bump. . . ."

Although your child probably does not need you now as constant interpreter when he speaks to other people (see p. 370), you can still help him to get the most out of conversation with them. If his father comes home and asks "What have you been doing today?" he probably means the question to be rhetorical. Without your help the child will not answer because the question was incomprehensibly general. But you can help him. "Are you going to tell Daddy about the squirrel we saw in the park?" Launched into telling, the child's account will be jerky and incomplete, but you can smooth it out and keep it unrolling for him with the same elaborating technique:

"Squirrel comed . . . frightened . . . I say 'OOOH'. . . ."

"Yes, you did say 'Ooh' didn't you? And then what happened? The squirrel ran back into the . . .?"

"TREE!" supplies the child delightedly.

*Learning to use pronouns*

With this kind of conversation going on, the child adds the nouns which label things, the adjectives which describe those things and the verbs which tell what they do, at a rapid rate. But he finds words like "me," "you," and "him" extremely confusing because their meaning depends on who is talking and your ordinary elaborations therefore get in a mess. *I* am writing this book for *you* to read. But if you tell someone else about it, you will say "I am reading this book that she wrote." I am still me and you are still you. But I have become "she" and you have become "I!"

Because this is so confusing, children usually go on using proper names (their own and other things), thus avoiding pronouns altogether: "Johnny will get Teddy" rather than "I will get him." Trying to correct this will get you both into a monstrous mess. You say: "Say, 'I'll get Teddy', darling." The child will look at you in amazement and reiterate his first statement: "Johnny will get Teddy." What he means is that it isn't *you* who will get him, but he. Yet you said "I." Oh dear.

Don't try to make him use pronouns but take trouble, now, to use them correctly yourself, saying "Shall I help?" rather than "Shall Mommy help?" He will gradually sort it out for himself.

*Asking "What's that" and "Why?"*

By the time he is three the child knows that he needs more words and he asks you for them by continually demanding "What's that?" He is asking you to tell him or remind him of the *name*, so don't confuse the issue by launching into elaborate answers to the different question, "What's that for?" If it is the washing machine he is pointing to, say "That's the washing machine." Don't embark on "That's my special machine for washing clothes. . . ."

Soon you will be into "why?"

Several hundred "why?" questions per day of the "why can't I?", "why is it hot?", "why has Daddy gone out?" type can be very wearing. But remember that the child is asking because he *needs to know*. He is adding to his store of knowledge and understanding and he is doing it in the most efficient possible way – by using words. "Why's" are a clear sign of growing up. As a toddler he would either have tried to find out by doing or he would not have thought of the question in the first place.

Some "why's" are unanswerable either because the child, without realizing it of course, is tapping the edges of human knowledge, or because he is tapping the edges of yours!

"Why does it thunder/rain/blow?"
"Why is Daddy a man/big/brown?"
"Why is that lady on my TV?"
"Why do lights switch on?"
"Why won't the sun switch on?"

Try not to fall back on "because that's the way it is." If the question is answerable, answer it briefly. But don't muster everything you know about the workings of television and launch into a lecture. His question is casual; the phenomenon of the TV showing that particular picture has just caught his attention. "Because she is the lady this program is about" is probably all he needs. If the question is answerable, but not by you, don't be afraid to say so.

There is nothing but good in telling the child: "That's an interesting question but I don't know myself; let's ask Mommy/let's look in a book. . . ."

Some "why's" end up landing you in a sort of "Alice in Wonderland" world.

"Why am I Rick?"
"Because when you were a new baby we decided we liked that name, so that's what we called you."
"Why?"
"Because it seemed like a nice name for a super boy."
"Why?"

The "why's" may simply be a device to keep your attention and keep the conversation going, or the child may have long ago stopped meaning literally "Why?" and be meaning "Tell me more." You can break it up by saying "Shall I tell you more about when you were a new baby?"

Often, he asks "Why?" but is unanswerable because "Why?" is not the right question. He is using the word wrongly so it is meaningless: "Why are bulls?" Try not to say "I don't know what you mean." Try instead to think what he is likely to mean. Is it *what* are bulls? What are bulls for? Are bulls dangerous? Are you frightened of bulls and should I be? . . . A general "I'm not quite certain what you want to know, but let's talk about bulls and see. Do you know what a bull is? It's a man cow . . ." will start him off on the conversation he is really seeking.

*Using words to control his own behavior*

After years of having their behavior controled and managed by you, pre-school children begin to take over for themselves (see p. 456). You will probably notice this new self-discipline first in what he says to himself as he plays. He uses the same kinds of controlling phrase he hears from you to his toys or imaginary companions: "Careful now!", "Up you come," "Don't touch. . . ." He is a hard taskmaster. You will overhear much fiercer tones than you are conscious of using.

Later on he begins to talk to himself in the same way, but his warnings come after the event. He kicks his ball into the flower bed and scolds himself: "Not in the *flowers*, Harry." A little while later he warns himself in advance. Poised to kick that ball, he says "No Harry, not in the flowers" and just as if someone else had spoken, he turns and kicks it the other way.

This is an excellent sign that he really is taking your instructions and rules into himself and applying them alone. But if you often hear him fiercely instructing himself but *disobeying his own instructions*, saying "Mustn't hurt the dog, John" as he yanks its tail, try to listen to yourself for a few days. You may be issuing streams of nagging instructions without making the reasons clear or making sure one is obeyed before the next is given.

*Using words to control the behavior of others*

Being on the receiving end of controling talk, the child is bound to try out this use of language for himself. Four-year-olds, in particular, tend to sound very bossy. "Stop it at once," he yells at the surprised baby; "Come here immejitly" he commands the unheeding dog. He is trying to find someone below him in the status hierarchy so that he can be boss as well as being bossed. He is also trying to see whether his words have as much power over other people's behavior as yours have over him. So be tolerant of this tiresome phase. He does not mean to be unpleasant. If his bossiness really upsets you, teach him to soften his commands and exhortations with "please" and "thank you" and look to the way you both speak to him. . . .

*Using words to boost self-esteem*
Boasting is another typical four-year-old trait and not to be taken too seriously. Two children together will often have a boasting session that is almost a verbal tennis match – and recognized by both to be a game:

> "My house is bigger than yours."
> "My house is bigger."
> "My house is as big as a palace."
> "My house is as big as a park."
> "My house is as big as, as, as *everything*!"

Although listening adults often sadly recognize that one or the other child does, in reality, have a smaller house, father or income than the other, you need not worry about hurt feelings. This kind of thing is recognized by both children as verbal play.

If your child boasts continually, you may wonder whether he needs to make himself sound very grand and big and rich because he really feels rather humble and small and poor. Lots of love, and more congratulation and praise than criticism and reproof may be the right prescription.

*Using words to ask for approval*
Four-year-olds often sound goody-goody as well as bossy. "John's a *good* boy" he says, smugly. Try not to be sharp with him for being so. It is a good sign for his future behavior that he wants you to think him "good." And it is also a good sign of language development that he wants to use words to talk about the idea. Don't sit on him, saying "Well, I don't know about that. . . ." You will hurt his feelings and confuse him.

Sometimes this talk means that the child wants assurance that you love *him* even when you do not love what he *does*. He is still very literal about language, so these distinctions are important to him. If he and his sister have been racketing around until you feel that the noise will drive you crazy, try to avoid saying "Go out into the yard, you two, you're driving me crazy." Separate *them* (whom you love) from their noise (which you do not) and say "Go out into the yard, you two, if you are going on with that game. The noise is driving me crazy."

*Talking about abstract ideas*
Once a child is confident that words will work for him, that he can express anything he thinks and understand the expressed thoughts of others, he will begin to use them for their uniquely human purpose: the exchange of ideas. Not every child asks about God at four or five or tries to tell you how a piece of music makes him feel at five or six. It certainly doesn't matter if you don't share this kind of conversation with him for a long time yet, but it does matter if he tries it and finds himself laughed at, quoted around the family – "the things they come out with . . ." – or blocked by your obvious

embarrassment. It matters because any of those reactions is likely to shut him up. And however much you may sometimes wish that he *would* shut up for a minute, talking and listening and thinking and talking some more are essential parts of his education in its widest sense.

It's easy to squash small children without meaning to as this mother almost did:

"It was the winter she was four. I found her gazing out of the window, tears pouring down her face. I asked her what on earth was the matter, thinking she didn't want to go to bed. But what she said was 'Oh Mommy, I don't know how to think about the moon.'

It was so unexpected that I nearly laughed and said 'Don't be silly' or something. I'm glad I didn't though. We talked about things being too big or too far and why moonlight was the kind of beautiful that was sad . . . *I* don't know how to think about the moon either. But the point was that she wanted to share."

Sharing thoughts and feelings with someone of such limited experience and understanding isn't always easy, especially if you are not a person who often has in-depth conversations even with adults. But if you make the effort, you may be surprised by how much you both get out of it. Potentially difficult conversations usually come into one of the three following groups, each of which has its own useful techniques.

**Talking about facts.** When your child asks you about complicated questions of fact, you don't have to pretend to know everything. Part of your tremendous grown-up skill is that you know how to find out things you don't already know. And part of your unique value to your child is that you're interested enough to try. So if he notices flocks of birds in early winter and, not satisfied with being told that they are going to fly to a warmer climate, asks where they are going, find out together from a book or from a friend who knows more about birds than you do. Often your child will ask about things you do understand but cannot think how to explain to him (nursery school teachers are taught how to teach, after all).

"Why don't airplanes fall out of the sky?", "Why do plants go yellow when we keep them on the table instead of the window-sill?" and "Why is this tooth wobbly?" are the kinds of question that may leave you groping. You need reference books which are written for young children. Finding them in the library, and perhaps enlisting the help of the children's librarian, can be fun and good practice for later on when your child will be doing projects for school.

**Talking about beliefs.** Questions about beliefs can be even more difficult. You are being asked to explain your attitudes and you cannot look those up in a book. On the other hand you are being given the chance to pass on to your child some of what makes you the person you are and that's a precious part of being his parent. These questions come up in many different ways. Whether or not your household practices any kind of religious observance, your child will eventually notice that other families behave similarly or differently. Friends may go to different kinds of "church" on different days of the week. His best friend may never be able to sleep over with him on Fridays. An older friend may even tell him "We don't have God, silly, we have Allah. . . ."

If you have a clear belief, share it, but try to make clear to your child that it is a belief rather than a set of facts. That will allow you to acknowledge respectfully the different beliefs held by different people and it may protect the two of you from the kind of religious discussion which is most difficult with small children. At this stage children's thinking is still too concrete, too based in what can be observed, experienced and proved, for easy understanding of faith. They are therefore very liable to over-literal ideas about heaven and hell and to picture-postcard images of grandfatherly gentlemen in blue robes sitting on clouds.

If you have no religious belief yourself, by all means share that fact with your child, but try to help him avoid offending his grandmother with Sunday lunch stoppers like "God's just silly, my Daddy said."

**Talking about death.** Questions about taboo subjects are usually the most difficult of all. A couple of generations ago the most general taboo was the "facts of life" (see p. 431); now, it's the facts of death. Our culture is peculiarly bad at accepting the simple fact that death is the inevitable and universal end of life. Many people live all their lives in an unacknowledged, semi-conscious terror of events they know must take place: their own deaths and the deaths of people they love. Terror makes us bad at talking, so terror and taboo can pass from generation to generation unless parents begin to break that cycle.

You cannot alter the facts of death for your child. And you cannot protect him from thinking about death because he will notice it – in plants, insects, fledglings and squashed animals on our roads, if nowhere else – and he will wonder. You may be able to protect yourself from his questions, by letting him sense, the first time he asks, that death is the unmentionable. But wondering, alone, will make him more liable to anxiety and deprive him of any intellectual context within which to face the first death – whether of a pet or a person – which matters directly to him.

The starting point is the most difficult. Once you have acknowledged that all living things die, your child will certainly ask – if he feels he can – "Will I die?" or "Will you die?" If you can cope with this you will be able to let him go on asking, at his own pace, so that he gets more information as and when he has a use for it. Remember, when you face these first questions, that a small child cannot anticipate or empathize with grief (see p. 426). He does not really know what "die" means – that is the question he is trying to explore – so although the word vibrates with pain for you it does not do so for him. You have to give him the factual answer but you can offer other facts to help guard his emotional distance. He will be fascinated to know about the different time-scales on which creatures live – from the lifespan of hours of that butterfly through the brief gestation and life of tiny mammals (like his pet mice) to the longevity of people or elephants. In that factual context you can honestly tell him that parents usually live not just through all the eons of childhood lying ahead of him, but on into the time when children are parents themselves.

Natural death is linked with aging. Even a small child observes objects, animals and people wearing out and hears adults using phrases like "past her prime" of everything from cars to dogs to neighbors. If you are therefore asked "Will Grandma die soon?" try to avoid a shock-horror reaction which will make nonsense of everything you have said so far. You can be both reassuring and truthful if you say something like "Most people live to be 70 and some live to be 100 so we don't have to worry about that. . . ."

Childish (and not so childish) anxieties about death usually focus around the manner of dying and on what happens afterward. Insofar as a young child has any concept of death at all it is usually violent death off the TV screens. He needs to know that natural death is usually a peaceful drifting into oblivion, a giving up of life rather than a killing. He may see a butterfly come to a permanent stop on a flower. He may find one of the goldfish just floating on the water, or go to feed his guinea pig and find it, still apparently asleep, in its nest. That may be dreadfully sad for *him* but he can be helped to realize that it was in no way dreadful for the guinea pig. Whatever you wish to teach him about a possible afterlife, it is vitally important that he understand that *physical death*, of insects, animals or people, is always final; that the dead never come alive again or have any awareness or feeling. Ghost stories are *stories* and funeral trappings are for the living not for the dead.

If it is important that children be helped to accept the inevitability of natural death as an end to life, it is even more important that they do not take for granted the casual slaughter of TV drama and the reported carnage on our roads and in battle-zones. If your child can ask you about death, you can talk to him, in ways he will understand, about reverence for life and the importance of people looking after themselves, other people and creatures. And if this kind of talk lands you with questions you find awkward, like "Why is it all right to squash wasps?", maybe finding answers will clarify your own thinking!

Learning about dangers and safety measures is part of your child's learning to keep himself safe (see p. 427). Learning about the people we pay to help us keep safe, like doctors, nurses, police and ambulance staff, is basic to his learning about his community and how it works. But help him also to accept human fallibility. He will sense it anyway as soon as he begins to bring you baby birds that have fallen from their nests or fieldmice that the cats have mauled. You and he together can try to save them and you are right to try. But you will not always succeed. As Jessica, then six, put it "I tell you the trouble Daddy. Birds don't know about seat belts and parachuting thingies. . . ."

# Problems with language – large and small

As we saw in an earlier chapter (see p. 370), there is an enormous variation in the age at which individual children learn each stage of speech. One child may stay wordless until he is two and a half and then produce three-word sentences; another will have several words at ten months and add very few more during his second year. Yet another will start talking at around a year and progress fairly steadily.

The most common reason for delayed speech development is some degree of deafness (see p. 173). Babies' hearing should be regularly checked (Ref/EARS) but any child who is not talking *at all* by the age of two should have it checked again, by the doctor, as part of a developmental assessment. You may be referred to a special speech clinic. If nobody finds anything amiss (and they probably will not) they will suggest that you give him time and bring him back in six months if he is still not talking.

*Slower than average speech development*

If your child has a few words, you almost certainly have nothing to worry about. Take him for a check-up by all means if it will prevent you from worrying, but the child is probably acquiring speech more slowly than average for one of the following reasons:

| | |
|---|---|
| He is giving his concentration and energy to acquiring some other skill. | *He cannot do everything at once. He may talk more when walking is perfected.* |
| He is a twin or has a brother or sister very close to him in age. | *The problem is not "private language" but too little individual attention from adults.* |
| He is a boy and not a girl. | *Boys' developmental programming is slightly different, so don't compare across the sexes.* |
| He has several older brothers and sisters. | *Older children may interpret too skillfully, so that he has little need or time to speak for himself. Their talk may be so continuous that he has little chance for face-to-face talk with you.* |
| He is in group care with too low a ratio of adults to children. | *He may lack face-to-face talk with a familiar caretaker and/or be unhappy.* |
| He may be cared for by a foreign helper or "au pair." | *Both may find gestures easier than words. He needs a fluent adult model.* |
| His family may be bi-lingual. | *Learning two languages at once will take him longer than learning one.* |

*Stuttering and stammering*

The pre-school child's ideas are bigger than his vocabulary. He finds it difficult to express his thoughts smoothly, especially when having to search for the right word holds up the flow of what he wants to say. When he is excited or upset, he wants to pour something out but the words keep hiccuping.

Jerky uneven speech happens to almost every pre-school child sometimes but only rarely does it turn into a real stutter or stammer which lasts. The important thing is to stay calm yourselves (even if one of you stuttered as a child so that you are sensitized to the possibility) and remain completely accepting of the way the child talks. If you can avoid making him nervous or self-conscious about speaking, he will almost certainly talk his way out of this phase.

**Listen to what the child is saying not to how it is said.** Don't hurry him; don't finish sentences for him and don't tell him to speak more slowly. Speech is conscious but the processes which produce speech sounds are not. If you make him think about how he produces a word you will cause him to stumble just as you become breathless the moment you try to count or control the rise and fall of your chest.

**Make it clear that you enjoy his talking.** If he feels it is not good enough for you he will become self-conscious.

**Make verbal communication easy for him.** If he always has to shout down his sister and repeat everything six times to make you listen, repetition and a word-jam become more likely.

If you are trying to decide whether a pre-school stutter *is* turning into a real problem, consider the following points before you seek the speech therapy that will certainly make him aware of it:

**Does he deliberately try to control the muscles** of his face, lips and tongue so that he grimaces whenever he stumbles? If so he is already conscious of some difficulty with speaking.

**Does he speak fluently to himself when he is alone?** If so his stuttering when he speaks to other people is almost certainly due to anxiety caused by too much pressure.

Reducing stress in every area of his life and providing extra, warm, fun companionship for a while may produce an easy flow of talk again. If not, ask your doctor to refer the child to a speech therapist so that he gets help before lack of confidence in this new skill of communication saps his confidence in all his other skills as well.

*Baby talk*    Some children go on with baby talk for a very long time. It is as if they refuse to accept adults' words and expressions in certain areas and insist on going on using the "words" they started out with a year or more ago. "Gooky-a-baby" demands the four-year-old who is perfectly capable of saying "I want a cookie."

Usually such a child has discovered that grown-ups think his baby talk is "sweet." Maybe when he uses it, your face softens. Perhaps you use it back to him. Perhaps he has overheard conversations in which you have proudly maintained to uncomprehending visitors that you "understand every word he says."

Suddenly you realize that most people *cannot* understand him and that that will make trouble when he goes to pre-school or to big school. Or you look at him one day in his new jeans and sweatshirt and realize (rather late) that his talk is not appropriate to his age.

Obviously it is very hurtful to the child if you suddenly take against talk which up to then you have seemed to encourage. So don't do anything dramatic. Vow never to imitate or melt to baby talk any more, and translate everything he says in it into proper English, so that you put his version alongside yours. Over a few months he will drop it.

Some other kinds of baby talk are positively useful though. When the child does not know the word for something he wants to mention, he will often coin a highly descriptive word. That cereal which is advertised as going "Snap, crackle, pop" was christened "snapples" by my own children long before advertisers had the same idea. A small girl who was anxiously excited by the sound of an ambulance asked if it was the "bellvan." Words of this kind show that the child is actually *thinking* about words and making them *work for him*. They often get adopted into family speech, and why not? They make a bridge between the child's language and the language of adults, and their use by other people shows him that he can produce good, meaningful words of his own. It is easy to tell him the "proper" name for it while letting everyone have some pleasure out of his.

*The chatterbox*    Most three- and four-year-olds talk all the time. With perhaps 500 words in his vocabulary, the child may utter 20,000 words in a single day. That is an awful lot of repetitions. Some parents get extremely bored with it.

But he *must* talk, because he has to practice *making* the actual sounds. He has to try out different inflections for his words and he has to try them in different combinations.

The child will practice using every word he can think of that will go with one particular one. He may say "Daddy gone" as father leaves for work. Then, he starts casting around the room for other words he can use with "gone." "Breakfast gone," "water gone," "dog gone." When he has run out of things he can see that have gone he produces more "gone" things out of his mind: "tree gone, Jack gone, bed gone, house gone, me gone. . . ." It is nonsense, of course, in that what he says is not *true*, but it is sense all the same because he is making sense of the use of the word.

Join in and make a game of it. He does not *really* think the tree has gone; after all, he is looking at it while he says it. He is playing with words, so you play with them too. Look straight at him and say "pants gone?" or put yourself half behind the curtain and say "Mommy gone?" He will probably roar with laughter and embroider the game even further.

*He talks to communicate . . . he needs you to join in*

**Nonsense and naughty-nonsense**

Words are powerful things. Being able to use them makes the pre-school child feel much more able to control the world.

If he can find some words which have a particularly powerful effect on other people, he is liable to use them over and over again. "Pee-pee" he shouts. If he gets a nice strong reaction, he will add in "Wee-wee" and "Piss, piss, piss" for good measure.

If you ignore him, it will probably not get out of hand. If you scold, you will get into very deep water. What are you scolding for? A word? *Can* a word be naughty? No, obviously not. If you start trying to explain that this particular word is naughty except when used in its "proper" context, you will really confuse him.

If this kind of thing bothers you, the best way to cope is to substitute your own equally absurd but less "naughty" nonsense for the child's. "Squashed tomatoes to you" is the kind of response that never fails!

All pre-school children love nonsense rhymes and nonsense words. "Niddle, naddle, noddle nee" they chant, enjoying the rhythm and the sounds and practicing both difficult consonants and new emphases. If this chant drives you crazy, suggest a new one: "double, double, toil and trouble," for example.

A child who enjoys nonsense rhymes is ready to be introduced to the sounds and rhythms of poetry too, even if he cannot understand all the words. You could read him some of "Hiawatha" with its regular beat and lovely sounds. It will all help him to listen and think and enjoy words. He will be off to a flying start when he meets "creative writing" at school.

**Insults and angry talk**

We try to teach pre-school children to use words instead of blows. The trouble is that having taught these lessons parents often don't much like the angry *words* either. The child gets into trouble for going for you as if he would like to kill you, but he also gets into trouble for standing stock still shouting "I'll kill you. . . ."

A child who says this kind of thing is usually frightened. His own powerful fury frightens him and he is still very unsure just how great his power is. He does not know that it would be virtually impossible for him really to damage you. He longs for you to prevent him, to keep control of him while he is out of control of himself. If you let yourself get angry because of his words and shout back at him, you add to his alarm. You have no real reason for anger. He is using great self control in using words instead of physical attack. Try calmly to assure him that he will not kill you, could not kill you, but that you realize he feels very angry just at the moment and you are sorry for him.

Lesser insults can usually be turned into a joke if you can remember that it is a little *child* who is calling you a "silly old cow." You really don't need to react as you would if an adult insulted you! "If I'm a silly old cow, you're a cross little calf" will often bring the whole episode to a giggly close.

It is important to avoid giving the child the idea that words are ever bad in themselves. You want him to use words, to like words, to enjoy his own and other people's words. So try to apply – even teach – that old adage "sticks and stones may break your bones but words will never hurt you." It is not entirely true, of course, but it is useful with this age-group.

# Playing and thinking

The stages through which your child's playing and thinking will pass during the pre-school years are neither so clear-cut nor so easy to see as those that passed during the toddler period. As an explorer discovering his small world and then as a scientist experimenting with its properties and behavior (see p. 349), he learned an enormous number of separate facts and facets. At the same time he began to develop the ability to think about the things he was finding out. Now, in the pre-school years, it is this ability to think, to imagine, to create and to "play in his head" which dominates his play-learning. It is rather as if his toddler years had been spent gathering together the separate tiny pieces which go into a kaleidoscope, and his pre-school years see him able, at last, to put all the pieces into his kaleidoscopic mind and shake them around to form new and different patterns at will.

It is not only his ability to think which is maturing. His body, and especially his manual dexterity, is growing up too. Increasingly he will be able to do the things he can now think of. He can think about how something works and make it work; he can think about color and apply it to paper; he can imagine himself as Mommy or the mailman, the doctor or Mr. Jones, and manage the "props" which help the game along.

*Expanding your child's world*

The play-conditions which were suggested for your toddler in the previous section will still be entirely appropriate for him. He still needs that suitable play-space, the undemanding company, willing partnership and varied equipment which he needed then. But it will not be enough for him. His immediate world has become familiar, he needs more scope. With home and all its familiar things as a solid background, he needs new experiences, new people, new objects, to feed that imagination.

*Organizing an expanded world*

Your family circumstances will dictate how much you need to do deliberately to broaden his daily life. If you live in the country, with adult activities like farming or gardening going on around him and the seasons bringing their own change and drama to life, he will promote himself at his own pace. He will move gradually from the shelter of the house toward the barns and fields, joining in with adult activities, making relationships with whoever is around working the land. You do not have to plan special trips for a child who has haymaking or root clamping, sheep shearing or the apple crop coming up.

If you live in a close community with many other children around, the same sort of automatic expansion of his life may take place. He will join the other children more and more, gradually being included in their group movement from house to house, yard to yard. Sometimes you will find yourself setting up an impromptu tea party for seven; at other times you will have no child at all because he will be "camping" in the Jones' yard or setting up a lemonade stand or made-up fairground with the Robinson children. . . .

Sadly, most children live in cities, and few of them experience a close community. You are likely to have to choose between expanding your child's life through some form of pre-school group or working at it yourself. What is needed from home if home is the whole world will be totally different from what is needed from home if it is the backdrop to a new group experience.

| What your child needs from home when home is all of every day | What your child needs from home when a group is added to it |
|---|---|
| The whole of her enjoyment, occupation and learning is in your hands. She will experience nothing new unless you arrange it; she will go almost nowhere unless you take her; she will have no fresh play materials unless you provide them or friends of her own age unless you find them for her. Each day you have to ask yourself what new material for thought and action you have fed her. | Much of his interest and his energy is being mopped up at the group. His teachers present him with new experiences, take him on expeditions, provide fresh play materials and help him to work with a group of children his own age. He is probably stretched to his limits. Your job is to keep home and its familiar objects and people just as they were before. |
| Her day is no longer broken up by naps so it needs breaking up and structuring by complete changes of activity and place. Solitary play indoors while you are busy in the morning needs a recognizable end with a morning snack and then something different – a walk or active play in the yard. She needs a routine both predictable and varied. | His day is totally broken up by group attendance. Time before group in the morning is just waiting time. After group, at lunch time, he may need an actual nap or at least a rest. For the remainder of the day he needs time just to be himself; to contemplate, to mess around. |
| Although you are the most important people in her life you are not enough. She needs to meet every sort and kind of person. She needs individual adults to make friends with; she needs individual children to be a pair with; she needs groups of children to see what group life is like and how it works. | He did not have you at group. He will need a chunk of your time and attention now. He may have had enough of all other people and need peace and solitude rather than tea parties. |
| Without your direct and concentrated help she probably will not muster the effort and persistence needed to conquer tasks she finds really difficult or frustrating. She needs time with you to master that puzzle, cut out a crown neat enough to satisfy her or to finish her clay model with paint. | Group activities will usually include all the concentrated careful work of which he is capable. Spurred on by the other children and by skilled teachers he will be stretching himself on "educational" play. Home play will need to be easy, as well as fun. |
| Without ideas and information from you whole worlds of play-learning will stay closed to her. She cannot conjure the idea of a book, a record or a radio program out of her head. She needs you to introduce her. | Different groups will emphasize different types of activity. He will need from you what the group does not provide. He may have had enough of stories and music and may need yard-romps instead or he may have climbed and swung and pedaled all morning and need stories from you. |
| Every human being needs high-spots and holidays in life. Break up her week, her winter and her year as well as her days. Saturdays or Sabbaths may be special; people's birthdays are important. Even the official first day of spring can make a marker. | Group life may be full of special days; there may be Mother's Day celebrations, little concerts, end of term shows, exhibitions of children's work . . . let the home-weeks roll calmly on. |

*When it is all up*
*to you*

Gradually broadening your child's horizons without much help from outside demands a new level of communication between you. By listening to him and thinking about his questions (see p. 434), you can keep abreast of his thought processes. By talking to him you can both feed in information and ideas and you can involve him directly in the things you do and see together. If you can stay alert to the way he is likely to be thinking, and awake to his comments, you can make even the most casual encounters fascinating. An ambulance, for example, is likely to cause comment. "Why" he asks you "does it make that noise?" You can use his question to bring alive the whole drama of hurrying sick people to the hospital. You could talk to him about the fact that ambulances take priority over other traffic. If he goes on asking questions you could take him, then or another day, to see your nearest hospital with its uniformed nurses.

You can involve him in routine things too. The supermarket has long been a favorite place but now he can look for specific items for you, get things which are within reach, push the cart instead of riding in it, and even choose which particular kind of fruit juice you should buy.

With words you can help him to think about people. The mailman, to a toddler, is a man with an interesting cart and a uniform. To your pre-school child he can also be somebody who has to get up very early in the morning, carry bundles of letters and magazines, and cope with people's barking dogs. You, too, can become "real" to him. Let him think about you as a person. Which of the things that he sees you doing every day do you enjoy? What are you looking forward to? How do you spend your time at that mysterious place called "work"?

With his interest and his imagination well fed by new things to see and feel and understand, you will notice his play change. If you watch and listen, unobtrusively, you will be able to find areas in which he is ready to use help and ideas from you.

*Dramatic play*

The pre-school child is usually being somebody else. He tries out every activity he notices among adults, not simply copying what they do (as a toddler might) but trying to put himself into their place and be them. When he is a builder, it is not just sand and blocks he is thinking about but sweat and language too.

Although he may love dressing up, he does not need elaborate costumes. He changes character in his head. More useful than clothes are "props." A detective needs a magnifying glass, a storekeeper a cash register and a knight a sword.

Sometimes he will use dramatic play to re-live incidents which were emotionally important to him. With practice you can see these coming. A night in the hospital, for example, is bound to mean a spate of hospital games, and merits a doctor set or nurse's outfit. You will hear him assuring his Teddy that "this is only my listening thing; keep still, it won't hurt – much."

Don't insist on listening to, much less taking part in, dramatic play. There is only room for one author and that is the child. If he plays hospitals, he does not want you to be nurse while he plays patient. This is his script and he is the doctor. His patient will be a junior and shadowy figure, a doll or soft toy or even an imaginary someone from out of his head. If you have a role at all, it is entirely subordinate. You may be required as dresser, or as provider of "pink medicine." Otherwise keep discreetly away. This is his private world which he is making for himself out of the raw material of the real world you show him.

*Arts and crafts*

Making and creating things with his hands is vitally important to the pre-school child. As a toddler he wanted to discover how things like scissors and felt-tipped pens worked. Now he gradually discovers how to make them work for him. The child deliberately snips a piece of paper. Don't ask him what he has made. The obvious answer is a piece of paper with snips in it. But by asking for an identification you suggest to him that it "ought" to be something else. After some practice, he may look at his most recent piece of snipped paper and decide that it is "lace." He will have reached yet a further stage in creation when he decides *in advance* that he is going to snip the paper into lace. The same applies to drawing and painting. He begins by exploring the materials. He wants to paint in order to make a painting, not in order to make a painting of a house. For a long time the medium is the message.

Colors are important. As he learns their names and relationships, finding that pink is somehow linked with red, he will explore them deliberately. He may paint 57 rainbows in a week. Give him the materials and stand back. If he asks for comments, stick to what you can see on the paper. "I like those colors" is safe. "Is that Daddy?" is a question which will either make him think you ineffably stupid (since representational painting has not entered his mind) or make him feel inadequate: "Ought it to be Daddy?"

His drawing goes through definite learning stages without anyone teaching him. At three, he finds vertical lines and circles much easier than horizontal lines. His drawings are therefore either up and down scribble or round and round scribble.

Soon the day comes when he sees something in the scribble that reminds him of a person. If he has made a circular drawing, he will add some lines for limbs and perhaps some dots for eyes. Then he will announce his first representational drawing: "A man."

By the time he is four, he will actually set out to draw a person, rather than scribbling first and labeling afterward. His man will have a big roundish head, with eyes and perhaps a nose and mouth too. Straight out of the head will poke legs. The man has no separate body yet and probably no arms either. During his fifth year, his man gets more and more lifelike. By the time he is five it may have a separate head and body; legs with feet, arms with hands, and even some clothes indicated by buttons or a waistband.

*"Messy" play*

Play with water, clay, mud, dough or sand often spans dramatic and creative play. It can be either one or both together. To some extent your child can expand these activities for himself using only his own imagination. He may spend all afternoon in the sandbox but now he is not just experimenting with the sand, he is mixing "cement" and using it to fill every crack in the sidewalk.

But he needs help in expanding and applying the lessons he has learned about natural materials. His knowledge of volume is growing, but he need not think about it much when he is pouring water as part of water play: an overflow is just part of the game. He needs to discover that his mug will overflow in just the same way if he does not stop pouring milk in time.

He needs to use all these skills in ways which are obviously useful as well as "just" fun. He has messed around with dough. Now it is time for real scraps of pastry. He has mixed sand and water, now it can be cupcakes and endless questions about why they "blow up" in the oven.

*Building, fitting and counting play*

This is the most obviously "educational" play and, perhaps as a result, it is the kind for which most toys are bought. But it is also a kind of play which many pre-school children find pointless. Where there is a cupboard full of barely-used toys most of them will be construction sets, jigsaw puzzles and fitting toys. Think carefully before allocating money to more of these.

Your child need not use "educational" toys to educate himself. He will carry out all the intellectual activities which these toys are supposed to encourage if he is given materials which lend themselves also to more imaginative and multiple uses. He probably already owns a good many, such as blocks and Lego.

Expanding this kind of play means helping him to use his knowledge and skills in contexts where he can see that they are useful. Counting on an abacus is a game. But counting out spoons for supper or cans of cat food at the supermarket has obvious point.

He need not use a construction set to construct. He can build with his blocks; make your clean sheets into a neat stack in the linen closet or put together a castle out of cardboard boxes.

Careful, exact fitting is part of managing life. If he can fit the cutlery into its compartmented drawer and learn how to open the front door with your key, he may scorn a "mere toy."

Gradually he can be helped to use an increasing number of adult tools. Your sharing will give him pleasure; the lessons will teach him manual dexterity, and learning how to use these things will mean fewer careless accidents later on. He can use a whisk to beat eggs for his omelette; learn to handle a table knife and make a start with lightweight gardening and carpentry tools.

*Physical play*

As we have seen, the child continually tries out his physical limits as well as having to involve his body in all his activities. But even here you can help him to expand his play so that some of it overlaps the real and serious adult world. If he can climb a ladder, he can go up the step-ladder to fetch what you need from that high shelf. If he can run fast, he can be the one to get to the telephone before it stops ringing. If he can jump, he can ford the stream by those stepping stones and he can add his small proud strength to yours in mastery of that shopping bag.

Physical skills acquired in the pre-school years are seldom completely lost. Look ahead: think what he will need to be able to do later, that you could teach him now. He can certainly learn to swim – the earlier the better. He can master a two-wheeler with patient help. He can enjoy the basic playground games like hop-scotch or skipping which will make him feel at home when he goes to "big school," and given the chance he can learn to ski or skate.

*Play belongs to the child.*
*It is not for us to know who*
*he is being when he dresses up . . .*

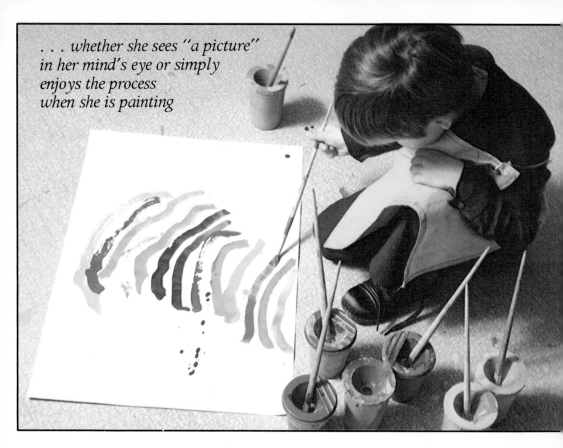

. . . whether she sees "a picture"
in her mind's eye or simply
enjoys the process
when she is painting

. . . who inhabits this, her own small
world, as she plays "house"

*. . . how she feels as she hands on to others the care she herself receives*

*. . . and what she is thinking as she builds.*

*Music* Every human being has a sense of rhythm; all life, after all, is based on it, from the seasons to our heartbeats. But while every child with normal hearing can also perceive the different sounds that make up music, it has only recently been discovered that teaching can help him learn to interpret them; to hear them as music and reproduce them as such with his voice. The music of completely foreign cultures tends not to sing to us because we have not learned to hear it. The more music your child hears the more it will mean to him.

The older child who cannot carry a tune or sing on key is not a child with an inbuilt defect, but a child who was not taught. You can teach your child to be musical even though you cannot teach him that still-mysterious thing called "musical talent." Listening with you and singing simple melodies is part of it. But your child needs more structured teaching too. A tuneful xylophone, bought from a music store rather than from a toy store, is probably his best tool. With and without your help, he will make and listen to pure sounds which get higher and lower, louder and softer, are the same as or different from each other. He will discover for himself that two notes an octave apart are the same-only-different, while two notes seven tones apart are simply different. Two- and three-year-olds learn to play violins in Japan; British primary schools teach the recorder as a matter of course. If your three- or four-year-old gets as interested in those sounds as in colors or somersaults he could soon learn to play the piano. . . .

*Books* Where books are concerned the child really does need your direct help. He does not know what books there are or what they say. He cannot imagine what pleasure they can give him. He cannot "invent" them out of his own head.

Almost every toddler enjoys looking at picture books as well as hearing stories read aloud. But the pre-school years are the ideal time to expand your child's acquaintance with and affection for every kind of book and all that they contain. They are going to be vital to his later education.

He needs at least three kinds of book. Picture books are important. By "reading" pictures he prepares himself for reading words later on. Both are symbols after all, the words are just a further abstraction from the pictures. Look at them with him. Help him to milk each illustration of its last detail. How many birds are in that tree? What is the little boy in the background doing? Try to find him books with big, colorful, detailed illustrations rather than the sterile conventional A is for Antelope type.

Highly illustrated story books are important too. If you choose good ones, he will be able to follow the story you are reading him on the picture pages, or at least stop you in mid-sentence to study the highlights of the plot. You have read about the children getting ready for the party. Now on this page he can study the party itself, discover what the children wore and had to eat. . . .

Your books are important too. He needs to get the idea that books are important to you – to the adult world – as well as to children. If you read for pleasure anyway, this will happen automatically. If not, try sometimes to look up the answer to one of his questions in a book, or to find him a picture of something that interests him. Help him to see books as useful as well as fun.

# Problems with play

A child's play-world is his very own. Ideally what your child does within it should be nobody else's business provided the child does not hurt anybody or anything. But there are some troublesome issues which do arise.

**Guns, war and violence**

Pretend-war and blood-curdling deeds are part of the universal currency for play for both sexes in all cultures. If it makes you uncomfortable to have replica guns and nuclear video-games in your home you certainly don't have to buy them. But don't be disappointed when your child uses a stick for a gun or turns a harmless game of "tag" into World War III. Our history, and therefore our culture, with all its fairy tales and folk-heroes is full of blood and battle. Even if your child only heard stories from the Bible, he would find plenty of war games to play from it.

At this stage it is usually best to accept games as games, realizing that your child has no concept of the realities of slaughter. "Zap-Bang your dead" means no more and no less than "I'm it." The behavior of the people in and around home *is* real to your child and it is from them that he will form attitudes to violence and non-violence. Eventually you can help him to differentiate between fantasy and reality; between TV-news policemen and TV super-heroes; between behaviors you consider right and wrong. But you will do that through your own behavior and talk, not by arbitrary-seeming bans on particular toys and games.

**Sex differences**

The fact that children are either boys or girls should clearly not deprive them of the opportunity to explore every aspect of being human. Try not to differentiate between "boys' toys" and "girls' toys" but to offer whatever playthings or play ideas you think your child will enjoy at a particular moment. It is not as easy as it sounds. Plenty of families who are happy to take a daughter out to the stores dressed up as a King, quail at the thought of taking a son out dressed as a Queen. . . . Some fathers who will push babies in strollers will still not be seen with a little boy pushing a doll's carriage. Your child's eventual sexual orientation will not be skewed by role-play in childhood. If you try to make a boy stick to the "right" sex, you deprive him of half the world and if you are happy to let a girl swap over but not a boy, you inevitably contribute to the basic sexual inequalities that still bedevil us all.

Deliberate anti-sexism in playthings does not work any better than deliberate pacifism, though. You cannot force a little girl to abandon dolls and model ponies for trains and model cars by banning one and buying the other. If you want your children to grow up believing that the only areas of human experience closed to them by their sex relate to particular reproductive functions, look to the sex role-models they see all around them!

**Television**

It is easy to moralize against television in children's lives. Its combination of sight and sound, movement and color makes it an easy medium, requiring less concentration than reading or listening to the radio. Unlike a game with real people or even objects, it demands no active physical participation or manipulation. A lot of parents and educators therefore see TV as a seductive time-waster; a medium which deprives children of time that would be better spent with books or music or in active play.

Of course television *can* take an overwhelming and therefore negative part in young children's lives. But it can also play a positive part. The very qualities which make it seductive also make it a superb medium for education in its very widest sense. Because television itself is appealing, the child who will not yet sit still for an excellent book on natural history will watch a wildlife program and emerge with mental pictures of otherwise inconceivable wonders. The child who loves to be read to can hear good children's fiction read by the best narrators of the day. The city child can find out where those cartons of milk come from and the country child can see bustling cities or the President. And every child can discover that there are other people and lifestyles in a world far bigger and more complex than he could otherwise know.

What matters, of course, is *what* your child watches and the balance between viewing and other activities. And this depends on parents. *If* you offer only the few short programs you truly approve of and resist the temptation to let him go on watching for an extra fifteen minutes while you get some vital job done, your child will accept limited, highly selective viewing. If it has never occurred to him that the television set is a source of constantly dripping, easy entertainment, he will not bully you for more and more at least until he is old enough to read the program guides and play out soap operas with other children in the school playground. And by then, with any luck, his life will be too full of people and activity for television to take a disproportionate part. But, if you switch on the set for him to get yourselves half an hour's peace from his conversation, let other caretakers use it to "entertain" him while they save their energies, or let the set babble half-watched nonsense as a background to life and a mechanical alternative to company, he will turn to it more and more whenever he finishes with one activity and has not yet thought of another. Trapped by those half-understood images and attractive jingles, sucking his thumb and drifting, the child finds it more and more difficult to break away and get on with life.

Selective and companionable viewing *ought* to be made far easier by a VCR, which allows you to shift your child's special programs to times that fit with your family routine. But don't start doing that unless you are sure you can use the medium and not be used by it. Once your child realizes that his favorite episode of a series is available at *any* time at the touch of a button he will ask for it again and again. And if you find yourself thinking "well why not?" when he asks at 10am, you may find yourself reacting in the same way at 3pm and so allowing his viewing to build up.

If *you* only watch programs you truly want to see – and you take the trouble to identify those in advance – you will find it easy to teach your child to do likewise. And if you use a VCR to time-shift everybody's programs to suit the whole family's activities, there is no reason why the weekend's sports should deprive a child of his father's company or the after-school children's programs prevent him from playing with his friends.

# Learning how to behave

As children move out of toddlerhood and into childhood, they have to begin to learn behavior which will enable them to be accepted by a wider world than the family. Society has countless expectations for people's behavior and while nobody will expect a three-year-old to meet all of these all the time, the pre-school years are the ideal period for coming to terms with them.

Small children will learn almost anything adults try to teach. They like to learn because they want to know and they particularly want to know how to behave because they very much want to please you. But a process which ought to be agreeable and interesting both for you and the child is often bedeviled by the heavy word "discipline" with all its related specters such as "disobedience" and "dishonesty."

If you like your child, if you are proud of him and pleased with yourselves for having done a good job as parents so far, you may be able to get right through his childhood without ever thinking about "discipline," as a topic, at all. The child has moods and so do you. He makes mistakes just as you do and he sometimes does what he wants instead of what he ought, just as everybody does. If you are just moving along happily together treating each other as human beings, that may be all there is to it. If so, do not bother with this chapter. It is meant for the millions of parents who do not feel able to take this casual approach because they feel that they have problems with discipline.

*What is discipline?* Dictionaries define the word as "teaching rules and forms of behavior by continual repetition and drill. . . ." A disciplined person is defined as "one whose obedience is unquestioning. . . ." The word itself, with all those grim, punitive connotations, has bedeviled our attempts to show children how to behave. You can make sure that your child obeys you, tells you the truth, behaves as you say and fears your displeasure. But none of that will help to keep him safe, honest and good when you are not there to tell him what to do. And you are not going to be with him forever.

True discipline is aimed at building up within the child what we call a conscience. This is the *self-discipline* which will one day keep him doing what he should and behaving as he ought, even when there is nobody to tell him what to do or to notice if he does wrong. Telling a child what he must and must not do is only a means to that end. The things that you teach him are only of value once he takes them inside himself and makes your instructions to him his own instructions to himself.

Learning self-discipline takes time. When he was a baby you had to *be* him. You acted for him in all the ways he could not act for himself and thought for him when he could not think for himself. When he became a toddler you had to combine letting him begin to be himself with keeping a total control over his safety, his security and his social acceptability. Now that he is a pre-school child he is ready to begin to learn how to keep *himself* safe, secure and socially acceptable. You will show him how to behave in countless different situations and circumstances. You will teach him that all those different items of behavior add up to a few basic and vitally important principles. Then, bit by bit, you will withdraw your control, leaving him to apply the principles for himself because he has taken them in and made them his own.

*Showing your child how to behave*

The very first rule for trouble-free and effective discipline is "do as you would be done by." The child will not give you more politeness, consideration and cooperation than you give him. There can be few double standards here. If he asks for help with his puzzle and is told you are too busy; trips over your feet and gets screamed at, he will not readily help you to lay the supper table or quickly forgive you when the comb pulls his hair.

**Make sure that good behavior gets rewarded and that bad behavior does not.** It sounds obvious, but it is not. If you take your child shopping and he whines for candy, you may well buy him some for the sake of peace. If you take him shopping and he does *not* whine for candy, does he get any pleasurable reward – whether candy or an especially companionable outing?

**Be positive: "do" works better than "don't."** Small children like action and hate inactivity. They respond much better to being told something positive that they should do than to being told *not* to do things. "You can't leave your tricycle there" is a challenge. It makes him think "I can, too. Just watch me." But "Put your tricycle over by the wall so that nobody trips over it" tells the child something positive that he ought to do.

**Be clear.** Even positive instructions don't work very well if they are vague. "Behave yourself" sounds like a positive instruction, but it is meaningless to a child of this age. What you really mean is "don't do anything I don't like" which is an impossible command because he does not know what you don't like!

**Always tell your child why.** Apart from emergencies, when reasons must wait until later, it is an insult to the child's intelligence to tell him to do something without telling him why. "Because I say so" is the kind of answer that makes sure that the child will not learn anything useful from what you say. Without a reason, he cannot fit this particular instruction into the general pattern of "how to behave" that he is building up in his mind.

"Put that shovel back" you say crossly.

Why? Because it is dangerous? Dirty? Breakable? Because you want to be sure of being able to find it next time? If you tell him that it belongs to the builders who have a right to find it where they left it, he can apply that thought to other occasions. But if you just say "Because I say so," you teach him nothing.

**Keep "don't" for actual rules.** Telling the child not to do things really only works when you want to forbid a specific action once and for all. If you only want to forbid a piece of behavior now, under these particular circumstances, you will do better to turn it around and phrase it positively. For example: "Don't interrupt while I'm talking" is useless. There are lots of times when you actually want him to interrupt – to tell you the potatoes are boiling

over, his sister is crying or that he needs to go to the bathroom. Better to say "Wait a minute until we have finished talking."

Specific "don'ts" become rules. As long as you keep them to a minimum the child will probably accept them easily, especially if you explain your reasons.

"Don't ever climb in that tree, it's not safe." If you stick to it and don't let him risk it "just for once," that particular tree will be recognized as forbidden.

"You mustn't cross any roads without a grown up." Once again this is an acceptable rule just as long as you don't send him to the corner store for a newspaper because the road concerned is only a small one and anyway you want the paper!

Rules are very useful in keeping a small child safe. But they don't really play much part in teaching him how to behave. They are too rigid and inflexible to be very useful in ordinary life. So try to keep rules to definite, here-and-now issues and try not to make them about issues of principle that will matter all his life.

**Trust your child to mean well.** If your child feels that you are always standing over him, ready to correct or instruct him, he probably will not bother to think very much about what he ought or ought not to do. So within the limits of his age and stage try to pass as much responsibility for his own behavior as you can over to him, and make him feel that you know you can trust him to handle it.

If he is to go to a friend's house, for example, don't smother him with anxious instructions such as "Remember to say thank you for having me" and "Don't forget to wipe your feet." If you are willing to let him go at all, you must be willing to let him take charge of himself. Your exhortations will not help him to behave nicely, they will merely make him feel uneasy about going.

**Be consistent in your principles.** You obviously cannot show your child how to behave if you are not yourselves sure how people *should* behave. But this is the only kind of consistency that really matters. Your child is not a circus animal, being taught always to respond to a specific signal with a particular trick. He is a human being, taught to respond as best he can to a vast range of signals. He will accept that circumstances alter cases. Candy ad lib at Christmas will not make him expect it when the holiday is over, nor will permission to jump on Grandma's bed make him demand to jump on your forbidden one. Even disagreement between parents need not matter if it is honestly discussed in his presence so that he cannot play you off against each other.

**When you are wrong, admit it.** Since small children are watching how you behave, and modelling themselves to some extent on you, it is important to be willing to admit and apologize when you make a mistake.

A useful family phrase, used in excuse, apology or forgiveness, is "Everybody's silly sometimes." If your child is brought up to accept the truth of this statement, he will not set unreasonably high standards for you, for himself or for his friends, and he will not be shocked and disillusioned the first time he catches you in a real mistake, an injustice or a "white" lie.

Suppose you accuse him of breaking a glass and refuse to believe his denial. You later discover that you were wrong. By all the standards you are trying to teach your child, you owe him a sincere apology. There is no escaping it. No way to save your face. You were wrong; you were unfair and you refused to believe him when he was speaking the truth. If you ask him to forgive you, he will respect you more, not less.

## Problems of behavior

The overwhelming problem of small children's behavior is that it is so difficult for adults to live with. Children are noisy, messy, untidy, forgetful, careless, time-consuming, demanding and ever-present. Unlike even the longest-staying visitor they don't go away. They can't be put away for a few weeks when you are extra-busy, like a demanding hobby. They can't even be ignored when sleeping in on a Sunday, like a pet, because they have an unfailing ability to make you feel guilty. Loving magnifies the pain of them as well as the pleasure. Loving may even make it difficult for you to admit that they *are* a pain.

It is important to be able to admit that, at least to yourself, because a lot of parents' worries about children's behavior are not really about specific crimes but about general irritation. We all have days when we can hear our own nagging voices going on and *on* saying "Don't *do* that . . ." and "*Stop* it" and when we can hear the glum silences buzzing between outbursts. We all have times when children are removed from objects, or objects from children, with more than necessary force, and when we hate those children for making us be so hateful. But if you let yourself decide that your children are disobedient, ill-disciplined and spoiled, you risk blaming yourself for being a bad parent – which really *will* make you feel guilty – and you risk giving your children the kind of problem-labels which can easily become self-fulfilling prophecies. Give a child the impression that you think he is naughty and nasty and he will confirm your view and probably come to share it. But hang on to the truth, which is that he is very young and that family life is difficult, and he will change, because the one thing you and he can both be quite sure about is that he is going to grow older.

*Disobedience*    If you are truly thinking about "discipline" as a matter of showing your child how to behave, you will find that most of the problem issues of discipline cease to look like problems at all. Disobedience becomes an irrelevance, because you will not be issuing un-explained orders nor will you resent questions of the "why should I?" kind.

Instant and unquestioning obedience probably kept life peaceful for Victorian parents, but it cannot produce children who think for themselves and can therefore be trusted to look after themselves from an early age. The difference was sharply illustrated when three small girls were abducted in a car from outside their nursery school. A fourth child ran home, and raised the alarm. They were home again four hours later and one distraught father asked:

"Darling, why did you go with the man in the car? We've *always* told you not to go with strangers. . . ."

"But the man said 'Your father says you're to come with me at once. He sent me to get you.' So I did. You always say 'You must do what I tell you.' You always say it."

The child who raised the alarm was questioned by police:

"What made you run home instead of going too?"

"I don't know, but Daddy and Mommy are always saying 'think!' They say 'You've got a mind of your own, use it.' So I thinked. I thinked that if Daddy really wanted us he'd have come and I thinked that the man only said one Daddy and we've got three Daddies, all of us have I mean. So I ran."

Getting rid of "obedience" and "disobedience" and thinking instead of the child cooperating, defuses the whole issue.

Sometimes he will not do what you want because he wants to do something different. He will not go to bed because he wants to finish his game. It is not his disobedience that is causing trouble, it is a simple conflict of interests. Instead of yelling "Do as I say this moment," find a compromise like "five more minutes."

Sometimes he will not do what you want because he has not understood what you do want. Told to stay at the table until lunch is finished he may get down when his plate is empty. He did not realize you meant that he was to stay put until everyone had finished. He has not failed to obey, he has failed to understand.

Occasionally he will not do what you want because he is out to annoy you. He feels like showing his independence. He feels balky. You tell him not to touch your new book and he goes straight to it. This, and out of all these examples *only* this, is true disobedience. It is a deliberate attempt to provoke you and how well the attempt succeeds probably depends on what damage has been done. If the shiny dustjacket is torn, you will be furious with him. That's reality. He would be cross if you had spoiled something of his; he has provoked a universal human reaction. But it is the sad damage that merits wrath, not the "disobedience." If no real harm has been done you can defuse the whole situation by refusing to rise to his bait: "Imagine going off and doing the one thing I asked you not to. You must be in a silly mood." Where is the argument he was looking forward to?

*Lying* Denying wrongdoing is the kind of lie that usually gets children into trouble. Your child breaks his sister's doll by mistake. Faced with it he denies the whole incident. You are probably angrier with him for the lie than you are about the breakage.

But what matters is that he should recognize the mistake he has made. Confessing is not nearly as important.

If you do feel strongly that your child should confess when he has done something wrong, do make it easy. "This doll is broken, I wonder what happened?" is much more likely to enable him to say "I broke it, I'm sorry" than "You've broken this doll, haven't you, you naughty, careless boy."

If your child does admit to something, either because you force it out of him or of his own accord, do make sure that you don't overwhelm him with anger and punishments. You cannot have it both ways. If you want him to tell you when he has done something "wrong," you cannot also be furious with him. If you are furious, he would be a fool to tell you next time, wouldn't he?

Tall stories get some children into trouble too. Pre-school children are not often very good at telling reality from fantasy or what they wish had happened from what really did. They can happily accept stories about the Easter Bunny while keeping a quite unmagic rabbit of their own; they see no conflict between the two.

If you are going to read your child fairy stories and help him to enjoy Santa Claus, it is unreasonable to jump on him for lying when he comes in from a walk with an elaborate story of his own about meeting a lion and taking a thorn out of its paw. Enjoy the story. Such fantasies are not *lies* in the moral sense.

Parents sometimes complain that their children simply seem to have no regard for the truth at all. They may overhear them mentioning Mommy's new dress when she hasn't got one, or announcing that they were sick last night when they weren't, or just telling a friend that they are going out for lunch when they aren't.

There are lots of reasons for this kind of casual inaccurate talk. But an important one is that the child hears his parents doing it. Adults lie out of tact, kindness, a desire to avoid hurting other people's feelings. The child hears them. He hears you agreeing with Mrs. Smith that the weather is much too hot when you have just told the child how much you like the heat. Unless the reasons for these "white" lies are explained to him, he cannot be expected to see why he must never exaggerate or falsify when you can.

If your child tells so many stories and adds so much embroidery to his accounts of daily life that you really cannot be sure what is true and what is not, then it is time to make it clear to him *why truth matters*. Don't fall back on it being "naughty" to tell lies. Instead try him with the story of "The boy who cried wolf." It is a good story. He will enjoy it. Having told it you can discuss it with him. Point out that if you cannot distinguish between what is true and what is untrue, you might not know when something really important had happened to him or when he was really feeling ill. Phrase the whole conversation so that he feels you only care about him telling the truth because you care about *him* and want to be sure that you look after him properly.

*Stealing*  Pre-school children are as vague about property rights as they are about truth. Within the family there will be lots of things that belong to everybody; some that belong to particular people but can be borrowed and a few that are "private possessions" for the owner only. Outside the family there are complications too.

It is all right to keep the little ball you found in the bushes in the park but it is not all right to keep money. It is all right to bring your painting home from nursery school but not a piece of plasticine. One can take leaflets from stores but not packets of soup.

Obviously you want to be careful that your child does not appear to steal, because other people are liable to make such a song and dance about it. But don't make it a moral issue at this age. Probably it is a good case for rules:

Don't bring anything away from somebody else's house without asking. Always ask a grown up if you can keep anything you find.

Try not to be especially moralistic about *money*. If he takes some from your handbag, stop and ask yourself what you would have said if it had been a lipstick that he took and then say the same

about the money. To him it is the same. It is treasure. He knows money is precious because he hears you talking about it and sees you exchange it for nice things. But to him it is like one of those tokens you put in slot machines. He has no concept of *real* money.

The child who is forever swiping things, behaving like a magpie, collecting other people's possessions in a bottom drawer, may be in emotional trouble. In a symbolic way he may be trying to *take* something that he does not feel he is being *given* – it is probably love or approval that he feels short of. Instead of being furious and upset and making him feel disgraced, could you try to *offer* what he needs? If you cannot, and if his stealing goes on, you would probably be sensible to ask for help from your local child guidance clinic. They will help you to see the problem calmly and to sort it out.

*Arguing and bargaining*  Some children, especially rather intelligent ones, catch on to the idea that if you want them to do something they don't want to do, they have bargaining power. Rather than go silently upstairs to change into a clean shirt, your son may say "If I get clean cos you want me to will you get out my paints cos I want you to?" Unfortunately, parents often feel that this is in some way impudent. They have the right to tell him what to do and they don't want to concede him the right to do the same. "Do as your mother tells you and don't argue!" roars father. We are really back with instant obedience.

Bargaining can be a very useful form of human exchange – as every adult society throughout history has discovered. But you will obviously get bored with it if the child tries to exact a return for every single thing you remind him to do. Keep bargains for *exceptional* requests or ones that are unusually tiresome for the child, and then use them yourself, sometimes, rather than always waiting for him to propose them. "I know you're comfy in those jeans but they're dirtier than I can stand. Will you go and put on some clean ones if I get your bike out for you to save time?"

## Problems of handling

*Punishment*  The idea of formal punishment sits better with "discipline" than with "learning how to behave." Older people, who know how they should behave but do not always want to do so, may be persuaded by the cost of transgression – detention for talking in class or a fine for parking by a fire hydrant – but young children cannot weigh future penalties against present impulses. They are learning how to live with real people in real situations and the only sanction that works for them is other people's disapproval. Whatever "punishment" you choose to declare when you get cross, it is your crossness that punishes. If that statement makes you laugh because your child is currently testing the limits in an especially defiant phase, think how he would react to a formal punishment announced in two different ways. The punishment is that he should have no ice cream for lunch today. Tell him so in cheerful, matter-of-fact tones and he is unlikely to turn a hair. (Does he *usually* have ice cream for lunch? Does he especially *want* ice cream for lunch? What *is* he going to get for lunch?) But tell him angrily

"That's it. Just for that you'll get no ice cream for lunch . . ." and he will probably cry or rage. Whether or not he expected or even wanted ice cream, he does *not* want you to be cross with him.

You made the angry statement about the ice cream in the (righteous) heat of the moment and it had the desired effect of making your feelings clear. But so would any other statement of those feelings, like "I'm simply not enjoying this walk because you're being so stupid, so we might as well go home." The trouble with the "no ice cream" version is that by the time lunchtime comes the whole row will probably be long over and forgotten. In order to stick to your formal guns you have to drag the whole episode up again and, in effect, punish him a second time. How awkward if he has been especially charming and helpful ever since. . . .

Your disapproval, or anger, is your most effective sanction. If it leads you to immediate and spontaneous "punishment" so that the child can clearly see that his behavior has directly caused it, the punishment may strengthen your point. You will not go on standing in the line for ice cream while he behaves so badly, so he doesn't get the ice cream right now. He has done himself out of it rather than being "punished" for his behavior. You cannot let him go on pulling boxes out of the supermarket stacks so you pick him up and put him in the cart seat. He has abused his liberty and thus sacrificed it. You will not have your make-up emptied out so, since he cannot stop himself doing it, you stop him by putting him out of the room. All those actions would count as "punishments" if they were cold and calculated. As genuine reactions to an immediate situation they are the logical results of the child's own ill-advised actions.

A lot of small children get smacked as the direct result of driving their parents beyond endurance. If you are ever going to smack him that is certainly the best way to do it, especially if the smack pulls you *both* up short and leads to apologies and a fresh start. Be very wary of smacking as a way of teaching your child how to behave, though. If you look around, you will see that most smacks are administered to under-fives who are either whining or screaming. It really is *not* very logical to expect a stinging bottom or leg to make a child cheerful or stop him being angry. Small children learn their behavior partly from parents so you have to ask yourself whether you actually want your child to learn that violence is a legitimate way to make a point. And smacks and other physical punishments can be unexpectedly dangerous, too. A light smack can catch a child off balance and knock him down; a boxed ear can mean a burst eardrum; while shaking a child while his head is still relatively heavy compared with his body can lead to whiplash injury to his spine or even to concussion.

But the real danger in physical punishments is that, because they are ineffective in teaching children how they *should* behave, they tend to escalate. Most of your child's wrongdoing is caused by impulse and forgetfulness. Today you spend all afternoon yelling at him not to run over the flower bed. Finally you smack him. Tomorrow he does the same thing again. Logically you have to smack him again – harder. If you let yourself get into the beginning of that particular vicious circle, this year's smack or half-hour in his room can easily become next year's real spanking or hour locked in the closet. Research shows that children who are smacked or confined can never remember what they were punished *for*. Physical punishments make them so angry and helpless that they go away seething rather than full of repentance. One of the most telling reasons for banning corporal punishment in schools is that the punishment books show the same handful of children being beaten over and over again and therefore clearly *not* "learning their lesson." So whether or not you ever take a swipe at your child's backside because you have lost your temper, don't try to use physical punishments as a way of teaching him. You cannot get the cooperation you need merely through using your superior physical strength.

Be wary of your superior emotional strength, too. Punishments which are designed to make children feel silly or undignified are just as ineffective and emotionally dangerous as the physical kind. If you take away a child's shoes because he ran away, or force him to wear a baby's bib because he spills food down his clothes, you make him feel helpless, worthless and quite incapable of learning the growing-up lessons you are trying to teach. If untidy eating is making a real laundry problem he needs showing how to manage better and perhaps an apron or overall of his own to wear "because that gravy is so drippy. . . ."

If you are genuinely trying to show your child how to behave, you will not need to hurt or shame him. He will learn most of all through praise and congratulation on the things he gets right (and you will usually be able to find *something*!), a great deal from your displeasure when he gets things wrong and something from the explosions that occur when you all get cumulatively across each other. Formal punishment for a child in this age group smacks of revenge and power-mongering and will make him less, rather than more, inclined to listen to what you say and try to please you. You are trying to teach him to control *himself* and to take responsibility for his own behavior. Later on, when he faces problems without you, there will be nobody to jog his memory with a sharp slap so try to manage without that now and keep him on your side and learning willingly.

*Bribes and prizes*  People who are shocked at the idea of bargaining with a small child will probably find the idea of bribing one even more horrifying. After all, a child *ought* to do anything you say without question. . . .

But bribery or, if you think it sounds less immoral, prizes, can be very useful. Small children have a clear sense of justice and are clear-sighted about other people's goodwill. If you have to make the child do something he very much dislikes, offering a prize will both make it seem worth his while to cooperate and make him realize that you are trying to soften the blow.

Suppose, for example, that it is a hot afternoon and he is enjoying himself in his paddling pool. You have run out of potatoes and must go to the store. You cannot leave him behind because there is nobody in the house. What is wrong with a simple bribe honestly proposed? "I know you'd rather we stayed at home but we can't because I've got to get some potatoes so we'll have to go to the store. What about coming home by the bakery and choosing a cookie for supper? Would that help?'' It is a bribe but it is also a perfectly reasonable bargain provided he wants a cookie.

An actual prize sometimes makes all the difference to a child who has to put up with something genuinely unpleasant. A child who has to face an anesthetic or stitches in his head may be carried through the experience by thoughts of the prize to come. It is not the *object* that matters, it is having something nice dangling just the other side of the nasty few minutes. Don't make this kind of prize conditional on good behavior though. If you offer a prize ''if you don't make any fuss,'' you put him under terrible strain. He may *need* to make a fuss. And he certainly needs to feel that you will support him however he behaves.

*Spoiling* Everybody knows that spoiled children are a misery to themselves and to everyone else, and most people assume that they reflect badly on their parents' good sense. But few people stop to consider what it is that makes them consider a child ''spoiled'' or what it is that the parents have done to him. As a result, ''spoiled'' is a sort of specter haunting parents who live in dread of hearing the word used either of their child or of their child-handling. Some even deliberately withhold treats and presents from their children because ''we don't want him getting spoiled. . . .''

This is sad because true spoiling is nothing to do with what a child owns or with the amount of attention he gets. He can have the major part of your income, living space and attention and not be spoiled, or he can have very little and be spoiled. It is not what he gets that is at issue. It is how and why he gets it. Spoiling is to do with the family balance of power.

The pre-school child sees himself as an individual among other individuals and he is deeply concerned about the extent to which he can manage them as well as himself. So this is the age when power-games begin. He tests the limits of his influence just as he tests the limits of his muscles.

It is right that he should discover that he has some influence over people; he cannot grow up if you keep him totally subservient. But it is not right that he should discover that he can override your power by bullying. There is a balance to strike.

The secret lies in deciding what *you* consider reasonable or sensible for him to have or do, and then in being honest. If he manages genuinely to change your mind by reasoned argument or charming persuasion, that is fine. He is using real influence to good effect. But if, despite tears and tantrums, he does not alter your real opinion, don't give in. Think of yourself as a judge. You are always prepared to listen patiently to your child-witness, but you insist, as a judge does, on reasonable behavior in court, and your final verdict depends only on the evidence. Has he convinced you that he needs another popsicle because he is so hot and thirsty, or do you secretly still believe that he is just being greedy? Another popsicle will not spoil him, but winning things he wants against your better judgment may.

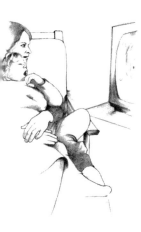

**React more favorably to reason and charm than to tears and tantrums.** Although self-control is still very difficult for him, you want the child to realize that while you are never prepared to be frightened into saying "yes" to a request, you are often prepared to be charmed into it. "Getting around people" is a very valuable skill to teach him. Encouraging him to use reason is important, too. If he can think and say why he so badly wants something, he not only gives you a chance to weigh his wanting against your policy, he also makes it possible for you to soften an eventual "no" by thinking of some other way of meeting his clearly expressed need. If he simply whines "play with me" over and over again, he is likely to get anger as well as no game. If he says "I'm bored of being by myself, will you play with me?" you can say "I can't come and play just now because I'm ironing, but if it's company you want why not bring your teddy over here and iron his clothes too?"

**Let your child join in decision-making processes.** As he gets older there will be an increasing number of policy-decisions to make. He will discover what is permitted to other children of his age, hear about television programs he has never seen and generally seek new privileges. Because these are new issues you will not have ready-made answers. Don't pretend that you have by giving quick answers off the top of your head. Discuss them with your partner *and* your child. Whether the matter goes for or against him, he will know that the two of you are agreed and he has had his chance to speak too. He will not feel that a spontaneous "no" can probably be altered by an equally spontaneous yell!

**Balance the child's rights against yours** just as you balance the rights of one child against the rights of another, or your partner's against your own. You all live together and the downside of loving companionship is that you all have to leave each other space, and sometimes shift over a bit to give somebody a temporary extra share. Your child will not always do as you wish. You do not always have to do as he wishes. The clashes have to be sorted out between you. If you want to read and he wants a walk, there's a problem. Discuss it honestly. If you simply can't stand the idea of a walk, say so. It's better to refuse him than to go every inch with dragging footsteps, feeling a martyr and ensuring that he does not enjoy it. But if you feel he's entitled to his walk, as you are to your reading, compromise on a half hour each and feel entitled to insist that he, too, fulfils his half of what amounts to a bargain.

**Help your child to understand other people's feelings.** The more interested you can make him in how you and other people feel and in how similar others' feelings are to his own, the more sensitive to them he will be able to be. Understanding the feelings of others is the root of unselfishness and therefore the opposite of being spoiled. When an opportunity comes up, grab it. Talk to him about what the little girl next door felt when the big ones stole her bike. If he says, calmly, that she can buy another, point out that parents often want to buy things for their children but cannot always afford to. When you are making family plans, let him in on the difficulties of arranging outings and vacations so that all the different people involved get what they enjoy. You can even help him see that while it would be unfair to *him* if you served the cabbage he hates every night of the week, it is unfair to his *father* if you never serve what happens to be his favorite vegetable. . . .

Your pre-school child longs for conversation with adults and for information of all kinds. As long as you don't do this kind of teaching as a set of lectures, each cued off by some misdemeanor of his own, he will enjoy it enormously. You are doing him the honor of discussing feelings with him as well as things. You are helping him in the age-appropriate task of putting himself into other people's shoes. And you are calling his attention to a whole area of experience he might not yet have noticed for himself. The more you can do this, the sooner and the more clearly will he come to understand that he is one very important and much-loved person in a world of equally important other people.

*Your child is not spoiled if . . .*

Whatever you may overhear people saying when your child throws a tantrum in the supermarket and however guilty you may feel about that pile of birthday presents, your child is not spoiled if you enjoy him and he enjoys life.

If you enjoy spending time with him, arranging treats and buying him things he wants, he must be a nice person. If he were spoiled you might still do these things, but they would be duties and trouble averters, not pleasures.

If he enjoys everything extra-nice, nice and just ordinary that you offer, he cannot be spoiled. If he were, his mind would be on how to get the next thing rather than on enjoying this one.

If he accepts a "no" with reasonable grace – usually – he cannot be spoiled. However many things he asks you for, he clearly understands that you have the right of decision.

If he changes your mind – however frequently – by reasoned or passionate argument but never – or *almost* never – by obnoxious scenes, you are not spoiling him. And if you aren't sure where to draw the line between "passionate" and "obnoxious," consult your own feelings. He has persuaded you to read yet one more chapter. Do you now read it willingly and enjoy it with him or do you still privately feel it is ten minutes more than he ought to expect of you? If you can enjoy it with him, all is well.

If you can face a scene when you must, even in public, you are not spoiling your child by distorting the balance of power between you and leaving him without the security of limits. Giving way, with a bad grace, to avoid living through a semi-deliberate tantrum, is something every parent does sometimes but no parent should do too often. After all, you do not want to teach your child that *that* is the way to behave. . . .

# Launching into life

Your child's world with you, with his family, his home and his immediate community, is now secure. His foundations are laid in his relationship with you and all that you have taught him. They are steady, solid, confident. Ready to bear the weight and balance of whatever superstructure of life and personality is to be built upon them.

The wider world is waiting for him, waiting to add its part to what you have already made. With it wait some of the greatest pleasures you will ever know. The pleasure of watching him become a child among children; leader, follower, one of the gang. The pleasure of watching him try out on teachers and other adult friends the techniques he has perfected on you; the charm, the wheedlings, the arguments and explanations. The pleasure of watching that lithe, coordinated body that you have cherished and nourished, cleaned and patched, arching through the air in its first dive; gliding, giggling across the asphalt on its first roller skates or parading proudly in its first real play. The pleasure of watching him through the eyes of other people; seeing him regarded as "my friend;" as "always sensible;" as "such a sweet child" or, quite simply, as "the nice-looking one over there." The pleasure, above all, of his pleasures; so intimately entangled with your own that you no longer know whether you enjoyed that circus, because he enjoyed it with a joy that was more than enough for you all.

His sadness will be yours too and there will be some. But even here there is gladness. Because he has you; because you care and he knows that you care, his sadness need never be solitary; his despair need never be desolation. Whatever the world must do to him, he has a safe haven in you.

You have made the most important thing there is: a new person. New though he still is, he is ready to start being a person among other people just so long as you are always there for him to come back to. When he was a crawler he left your feet to journey to the sofa and bring you a ball. When he was a toddler he left your side to journey across the grass and bring you a leaf. When he was a preschool child he left your yard to journey next door and bring you back his neighbor's doll. Now he will journey into school and bring you back pieces of his new world.

He will bring you his teachers, holding them up to you for comment with cries of "my teacher says. . . ."

He will bring you his friends and his enemies, recounting their games, boasts and exploits, waiting for you to help him fit them into the jigsaw puzzle of people.

He will bring you proud and disunited facts to be admired and put into context. Above all, he will bring you himself, to prepare for his next launching.

His journeys are all outward now, into that waiting world. But he feels the invisible and infinitely elastic threads that still guide him back to you. He returns to the base that is you, seeking rest and recharging for each new leap into life.

*With you they have built security.*
*Now they will go out into a wider world . . .*

*. . . and from that world they will bring you
their bangs and bumps and scratches*

*. . . their triumphs and their new-found strengths*

*. . . returning to recharge the bond for each new leap into life.*

# Reference

This section is designed as a quick guide to those medical matters which are most likely to concern you in everyday life with a basically healthy baby or child.

It is intended to be useful in emergencies and in preventing them; to help you recognize and cope with common illnesses and to contribute to your understanding of health and safety issues.

It is not intended so serve instead of advice from your doctor, to give you all the information you will need in a serious ongoing illness or to serve you as a glossary for rare conditions or medical terminology.

# Emergency

If your child's life was in danger, would you calmly do everything that could be done or would you be frozen to the spot? None of us can know the answer to that question in advance. Luckily most of us will never discover the answer because there will never be such an emergency, but this is not an excuse for remaining unprepared.

Emergency first aid procedures are on the pages listed below. Read about them now, while you are feeling calm and strong – there will be no time to turn to a book for help during a crisis. . . .

> For **Bleeding, see p. 478**
> **Burns and scalds, p. 480**
> **Choking, p. 481**
> **Drowning, p. 482**
> **Electric shock, p. 483**
> **Head injuries, p. 486**
> **Poisoning, p. 487**
> **Shock, p. 490**

*If a child is unconscious but breathing*
If a child is unconscious, whatever the reason, you have to do what you can to keep his circulation and his breathing going. Provided that he has no injuries which would be made worse by being moved, he will be safest in the "recovery position." It will ease the job of his heart and ensure that his tongue cannot fall back to block his air passage and that he does not choke on any blood or vomit.
☐ Very gently turn the child onto his stomach.
☐ Turn his head to one side so that his ear and cheek touch the ground.
☐ Bend his upper arm at the elbow, so that the hand is at about face-level.
☐ Bend the upper leg at the knee, so that the foot is level with the other thigh.

Moving a child who has damaged his spine – including his neck – is dangerous. Such injuries are likely if he has fallen from a height or been injured in a car crash or road accident. As long as his breathing remains easy, leave him as he fell. If his breathing begins to falter or if he vomits so that there is a risk of him inhaling it and choking, try to move him into the recovery position *without twisting* his neck or his spine.

*If a child has stopped breathing*
The life of a child who has stopped breathing may be saved by mouth-to-mouth resuscitation if this is started soon enough and continued without a break until help comes.

The technique is easy once you know how but it is impossible to learn effectively from the pages of any book.

☐ *Please* have yourself shown how to carry out CPR. Organizations such as the Red Cross and local hospitals run courses designed to teach this and other emergency first-aid procedures. Your doctor can advise you where to find a local course. Do it now, because if the unthinkable ever happens to, or near, you, it will be the most worthwhile thing you ever learned.

*Calling an ambulance*
If you are on your own with a child, emergency first aid must be your priority. Make sure he is stable and safe before you leave his side even to dial 911.

The first person who answers will be the dispatcher for *all* emergency services and will ask "what service do you require?" Don't waste time at this stage in telling your story; just say in reply "ambulance please."

The next voice you hear will be the ambulance dispatcher. Stay calm and take your time answering her questions. As soon as she knows yours is a real emergency she will be dispatching an ambulance even while she talks with you. Tell her your address and add any tips for finding your home, especially if it is part of a big complex. She will also want your name and some details of the emergency.

Make sure you know the whereabouts of nearby public phones. This is important not only if you have no phone of your own; it is a safeguard against the day when yours is out of order. Also make sure that you know the location of your local hospitals. It is sometimes quicker to take a child to the emergency room yourself than to wait for an ambulance to arrive.

# First aid supplies

If you are going to follow the kind of advice given in this book you will not need elaborate supplies because you will leave all complicated dressings, bandages and slings to your doctor, nurses or your local emergency room.

It is sensible, though, to keep the few things you might need gathered together, so that you don't have to leave a crying child while you search the house for scissors or bandaids and so that anyone left temporarily in charge knows where to find them.

A lockable medicine cabinet is the obvious place. Make sure that the locked section is large enough to take everything that is potentially dangerous as well as all other medicines, contraceptive pills and so forth used in the family.

You might like to include:

☐ A large box of assorted sizes of adhesive bandages – the kind that has each one sealed into a sterile packet is best. These should be used for covering small wounds while scabs form and for concealing blood from a scared child until he has forgotten his fright.

☐ A 1″ and a 2″ bandage. These can occasionally be useful to hold a cold compress in place over a bruised area or to wrap around an injury, such as a head wound, while you are on the way to the doctor or hospital.

☐ A package of sterile gauze – useful for cleansing dirty grazes; for helping grit out of eyes.

☐ A package of sterile non-stick bandages, useful for wounds, especially grazes, too large to be covered by bandaids.

☐ A roll of adhesive tape – use in strips to hold non-stick bandages in place, or to make a neat finish for a bandage.
NB Never put tape all the way around an arm, leg or finger. It could hinder the circulation.

☐ Special "finger" splints with their own applicator. Once you've worked out how to put them on they make the neatest possible covering for all finger and toe injuries, including those otherwise impossible-to-dress cuts on the tips of fingers and thumbs.

☐ A large, freshly laundered, ironed (and therefore sterile) handkerchief, in a sealed plastic bag – this is for emergency use to cover a serious wound, such as a burn or a compound fracture, during transport to the hospital.

☐ A pair of scissors – for cutting gauze, etc.

☐ An insect sting reliever spray.

☐ A soothing lotion such as calamine, for cooling sunburn, heat rash, poison ivy rash.

☐ A clinical thermometer.

☐ A pair of square-ended tweezers and a package of needles (and the matches for sterilizing them) – for getting thorns and splinters out.

☐ A pain-and-fever reducer. Aspirin and compounds containing aspirin should not be given to children. A liquid acetaminophen is easy for babies and toddlers to take. Bigger children who would need several teaspoons may prefer chewable tablets. Tablets are safest when each is separately wrapped in foil.
NB Stick faithfully to the recommended size *and frequency* of doses.

☐ A travel-sickness remedy if this is one of your child's problems. Ask your doctor's advice; buy the type he prescribes or advises and use strictly according to instructions.

☐ An antiseptic liquid – for your own hands.
NB Don't stock laxatives unless you use them yourself. Your child should never need them.

Don't keep things like eye ointment or nose drops in stock. Buy and use them when they are prescribed but throw away what is left.

Don't bother with cough medicines. Cough syrups are ineffective (although soothing): expectorant or codeine-containing cough medicines should only be given on your doctor's advice.

Don't keep antibiotic medicines prescribed for one child or illness for use in another. Leftover antibiotics are a reproach to you since a course is only effective if completed. Furthermore most lose their efficacy with storage and none should be given without a doctor's instructions.

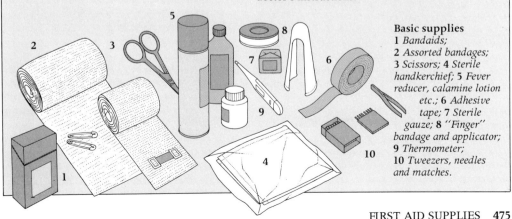

**Basic supplies**
1 *Bandaids;*
2 *Assorted bandages;*
3 *Scissors;* 4 *Sterile handkerchief;* 5 *Fever reducer, calamine lotion etc.;* 6 *Adhesive tape;* 7 *Sterile gauze;* 8 "Finger" bandage and applicator;
9 *Thermometer;*
10 *Tweezers, needles and matches.*

# Accidents A–Z: first aid and safety tips

Minor bangs, bruises and grazes are a normal part of a child's life. If yours never had *any* kind of accident you would probably be over-protecting him and depriving him of his rightful share of exploration and adventure. Of course it is your job to protect your child from serious hazards, but don't let yourself be overwhelmed with guilt every time he is even slightly hurt or you will not be in a fit state to do what you need to do: assess the situation, give sensible first aid and comfort your injured child.

Do remember that while a baby or small child reacts to any pain he feels, he does not have the experience to assess the seriousness of that pain for himself so he will take his cue from you. If you are frightened for him, he will be terrified. But if your sympathy is tempered by quiet assurance that the whole matter is trivial and will soon be better, he will calm down more quickly this time and will gradually learn that the pain of a banged knee can be shrugged off.

*Coping with minor accidents and wounds*
Most everyday mishaps require no medical treatment at all. Bodies are good at healing themselves and over-enthusiastic first aid often hampers the process. Antiseptic creams, for example, often delay wound-healing while doing little to prevent unlikely infection. Bandaids can keep a cut unnecessarily soggy when exposure to the air would have helped it to heal up far more quickly.

Your child will probably like you to do *something*. Cold water is your ally. Use it from a running tap to wash the visible dirt out of a graze or cut, or to cool the area of a coming bruise *while you inspect it carefully to make sure that the matter is not more serious than you thought*. If it obviously *is* trivial, confine any interference to making the child more comfortable. Bandaids may be needed to protect a graze from rubbing clothes. Sitting down with a book may be right for a child who has had a nasty fright. Even kisses and hugs can help to make things better.

If you cannot decide whether the injury needs medical attention or not, does your doctor's practice have a nursing station? If so, you can probably take the child there without an appointment. If the nurse thinks a doctor should see the child, she will arrange a consultation for you or send you to the nearest hospital emergency room; if not, she will do whatever is necessary herself.

*Coping with more serious accidents*
Remember that first aid should be exactly what the name suggests: the *first* help that you give your child before getting professional attention for him. First aid can save lives; more often it can ensure that an accident victim reaches the hospital in better shape than he would have done without it. But outside these rare dramas first-aiders often do too much rather than not enough. Once you have decided to take your child to the emergency room, don't waste time and misery on trying to establish whether his arm is fractured or dislocated, or on cleaning and bandaging a deep and dirty wound – whatever you do to him will be redone by the hospital staff.

☐ The following articles are intended to help you decide when you *should* seek medical help and to suggest things that you can do to help your child in the meantime.

---

## SAFETY TIPS: Bites and stings

*Animals*
● A few dogs (usually long-established pets) are bitterly jealous of a baby, occasionally even to the point of attacking it. Watch out for warning signs like the dog always jumping up and demanding attention when you are holding the baby.
● Dogs vary in how much mauling they will take from a small child. Some will put up with anything, others treat the crawling child like a puppy (and that means a few reproving nips), a few get cross and snap. To play safe, don't leave dog and child alone together.
● Various skin and parasitic complaints can be caught from dogs and cats. Keep yours in tip-top health; clean, regularly "wormed" and free from fleas. Mention your pet's existence to your doctor if your child comes down with any puzzling illness.
● Cats are not usually emotionally concerned about a baby, but use a cat-net over the carriage to make sure the cat cannot curl up on top of him,
and watch out for scratches if an older child manages to capture the cat and upset it by teasing and tail-pulling.
● Small mammals like hamsters and guinea pigs should not be given to a tiny child to hold – for both their sakes. Let the child watch them, and stroke them by all means, as long as someone else does the holding.
● Fish tanks are unhygienic: fish are prone to various fungus diseases. A child should not be allowed to dabble in the water.

*Insects*
Bites from mosquitoes, gnats and so forth are easier to prevent than to treat. In places or seasons where biting insects are prevalent:
● Dress the child in light-colored long-sleeved and long-legged clothes and *socks*.
● Use screens or nets when available.
● Apply insect repellent cream to all exposed skin.
This includes the face, although you should take care to avoid the area around the eyes.

# Bites and stings

Families which travel outside their own area, and especially those which head off into the wilderness, should always get advance information about specific hazards in particular places and seasons. Even those vacationing in well-populated areas should pay attention to local media and any warnings or advice they may be carrying.

If you are going to an area infested with venomous snakes, scorpions or spiders, you need local advice on avoidance, recognition, first aid and sources of local emergency aid. If rabies is endemic in the area, children must not be allowed to attempt to touch wild creatures such as raccoons or oppossum (especially as a wild animal which permits such contact is rather likely to be sick), and even the most trivial bite or scratch from a dog or cat must be treated as an emergency, taking you straight to the nearest emergency room. And if this is a place and a time when ticks are active, you may need to restrict children's freedom to explore freely in the countryside because while ticks themselves are not dangerous some carry diseases which are.

## Animal bites
*Cats and dogs* Barring any risk of rabies, a bite or scratch which has only just broken the skin can be treated at home.
☐ Wash the wound under cold running water, dry it and cover with a dry bandaid.
☐ Inspect it next day to make sure there is no redness around it which might suggest infection.
☐ A deep bite, a single tooth puncture whose bottom you cannot see, or a severe scratch should be treated as above, but also shown immediately to a doctor or the hospital emergency room. Treatment may be needed to prevent infection and the child may have to have an anti-tetanus booster injection, especially if the injury was caused by a dog.

*Guinea pigs, hamsters* These small pets often bite but very seldom do more than make a tiny graze in the skin or a pin prick puncture.
☐ Wash the wound under cold running water. Dry and cover with a bandaid.

*Horses* Many ponies and horses "nip." Such a bite may bruise but seldom breaks the skin.

*Snakes* General treatment is as follows:
☐ Reassure and comfort the child. Fear may induce shock even if there is little poison in the system. The bite will hurt.
☐ Lie him down. If he keeps still the spread of poison will be delayed.
☐ Wash the wound to get rid of any venom which may still be on the skin around the puncture. If you have no water gently wipe it, using saliva.
☐ Get the child to the hospital, keeping the bitten limb as still as possible. An injection of anti-venin or anti-tetanus may be given and a small child may be kept in the hospital overnight.
NB Avoid heroic measures such as cutting open the wound. You are more liable to do harm than good.

## Insect bites
Bites cause most swelling where skin is loose – around the eyes, for example. Otherwise the main problem is usually itching – and associated broken nights. Cold water or calamine lotion will reduce itching for long enough for the child to get back to sleep.

## Stings
Fear and panic are usually the worst aspect of insect stings.

### What to do
☐ Calm the child. Tell him that the pain he feels now, this minute, is the worst he is going to feel.
☐ Remove the stinger if you can see it.
☐ Spray the area with one of the special products available, if you can reach it quickly. Otherwise cool the area as best you can.

A little swelling is to be expected, but if there is a great deal take the child to the doctor.
*Stings in the mouth* These may lead to swelling which can obstruct the child's breathing. Give him a piece of ice to suck and take him straight to the doctor or hospital.

Very occasionally a child reacts to a sting with general collapse, becoming pale, sweaty and faint. This is called "anaphylactic shock" and is a full-scale emergency requiring a rush to the hospital. A child who reacts in this way once may need further treatment, once the emergency is over, to "desensitize" him so that later stings do not have the same effect.
*Multiple stings* These may lead to so much poison being injected into the child that his body cannot cope. He will be in severe pain. Remove clothes from the affected area and wrap him in a cold wet sheet to relieve the pain. Rush him to the hospital.
*See also* ALLERGIC CHILDREN/Allergic reaction to wasp or bee stings.

*Ticks* Ticks live by attaching themselves to a victim and sucking his blood. Although the very idea is unpleasant, a tick-bite is not dangerous or painful *in itself* but can pass infection directly from the bloodstream of one victim to the bloodstream of the next. Tick-borne diseases, such as Rocky Mountain Spotted Fever and Lyme Disease, used to be confined to particular parts of the United States but are now spreading widely. The following precautions should be taken in all areas where ticks are active.
☐ Make sure that everybody is clothed from head to foot, including socks. Sleeves with close-fitting cuffs and pants tucked into socks are helpful. Light-colored clothing will make it easier to see the *tiny* deer ticks which carry Lyme Disease.
☐ Inspect each other for ticks at intervals through the day and brush them off. At the end of the day inspect children carefully – in the tub, maybe. If you find a tick, the risk of infection will be negligible if you can persuade it to release its hold. But if you remove its body, leaving the head embedded in the skin, the risk will be high.
☐ To remove a tick, try gently grasping the body

and rotating it *counter-clockwise*. It may let go. If it does not, try touching a very hot match-head to its body. If it does not let go, or if the head is left in the skin, take the child to the nearest emergency room.
*Lyme Disease* Although light-colored all-over clothing may keep the tiny ticks off your child's skin, an inspection of her naked body may not reveal one which penetrated that defense, as the ticks are no larger than black dots. Make sure you look her all over each day for a week after possible exposure so that you will spot any sign that she *has* been bitten:

☐ The tick-bite will produce a small red patch on the skin which rapidly spreads to produce a distinct red circle with normal-looking skin in the center. If you see such a circle, or any rash which seems composed of circles, take her immediately to the doctor or emergency room.

☐ Treatment with antibiotics can halt Lyme Disease in its early stages. Untreated, it can produce a generalized rash with fever, malaise, chills, headache and signs of central nervous system irritation. Left to progress it can affect the joints, tendons and bones.

# Bleeding

Although your child may hate the sight of it, blood which oozes or drips is never dangerous and usually carries dirt, germs and so on out of the wound.

*Heavy bleeding* Blood pouring steadily from a cut or running down an injured limb will take a very long time to reach critical levels. You can easily control it with pressure which will seal the cut edges of the blood vessels while the escaped blood clots to form a self-seal.
*What to do*
☐ Quickly inspect the wound to make sure there is no glass or other foreign body sticking out of it. If there is, *do not press on it* and *do not remove it*. Seek professional help.

☐ Press firmly on the wound through a gauze pad, the inner folds of a clean handkerchief or, in emergency, with your bare hand. If the site of the wound allows, raise it above the level of the child's heart. If the wound-edges gape open, try to hold them closed as you press. Maintain the pressure for at least three minutes.

☐ Release the pressure gently but do not remove the pad or you will disturb any clotting which has started. If blood still runs steadily, try two more minutes' pressure. If bleeding is still not controlled, follow the next instructions but take the child to your nearest emergency room. The bleeding itself is still not dangerous but the wound may be deep enough to require stitches to help it close.

☐ Dress the wound, even if blood still oozes, *over the existing pad*. If this dressing becomes soaked, add another layer over the top. Do not remove the layer nearest to the wound until all bleeding has finally ceased.

*Dangerous bleeding* If blood spurts from a wound, it suggests a cut artery. Each heartbeat is sending blood through the cut as it pushes it around the body. Because of the blood pressure, such bleeding cannot clot to seal the wound.
*What to do*
This is an emergency; a time to forget hygiene and even to ignore the child's pain.
☐ Press directly on the spurting wound – hard. Use a handkerchief if you have one, your fingers if not. Raise the injured part above heart level to reduce the flow of blood.

☐ If blood spurts around your pressure, you must find an underlying bone to compress the cut vessel against. Try just above the wound. If the spurting slows, you have found the right "pressure point." Don't move your fingers or relax the pressure.

☐ If the wound is in a place you cannot span with pressing fingers, such as the groin or armpit, lie the child down and use your closed fist or a balled handkerchief to press the wound up against the bone.

☐ If you can carry the child without releasing your pressure, take him to the telephone with you or to a place from which you can shout to someone else for help.

☐ If you must leave him to get help, replace your pressure with pressure from a firm pad and bandage improvised out of whatever you can reach. Check that your "pressure bandage" has stopped the spurting as your hand did, then go for help – fast. NB Don't drive the child to the hospital yourself if there is any other hope of help. If the pressure should fail and spurting start again, you would have to stop.

---

## SAFETY TIPS: Bleeding

When your child is very small, everything sharp enough to do damage, especially if he puts it into his mouth and falls down, has to be kept completely out of reach.

● Knives, scissors, screwdrivers and all sharp or pointed tools are best kept along a magnetic rack which can be screwed to the wall out of the reach of the child.

● Cutlery, especially forks, need to be kept safe too. If he plays in the kitchen, keep them in the dining room – or vice versa.

● Sewing materials, especially needles, should be kept in a high or locked drawer or cupboard. A Victorian writing box makes an excellent workbox and has a lock.

● Be especially wary of electrically powered appliances such as grass cutters, hedge trimmers, or saws that have been known to cause serious injury to children who suddenly ran into them.

● Plate glass windows and French doors can lead to horrible injuries. Glass with panes is safer, but expanses of glass reaching within two feet of the floor should be replaced with safety glass or plexiglass.

Don't try to use a tourniquet to control arterial bleeding. It is far more difficult than old-fashioned first aid manuals imply and it is also very dangerous, as a successful tourniquet cuts off blood from all the vessels to the damaged area, not just from the cut one.

## Blisters

Apart from burns, friction is the most usual cause of blistering. The outer layer of the skin separates from the inner layer. Fluid from the inner layer seeps out to make the typical blister. Eventually the fluid inside the blister is reabsorbed, and the dead outer skin peels away leaving a new layer of healed skin underneath.

*What to do*
☐ Don't remove or prick the blister. The skin underneath it will be raw and extremely sore. The intact blister protects it from infection.
☐ Protect it from further friction by covering it with a "doughnut" shape of dry gauze with a bandaid over it, or with a ring-shaped corn pad.
☐ Check the shoes that caused the blistering. If the fit is wrong, discard them. If the child simply wore them without socks, try them with socks, but not before the foot is completely healed. Meanwhile, let the child go barefoot as much as possible because he is likely to find any further rubbing very painful.

## Bruises

A bruise appears when blood vessels under the skin are crushed or broken and blood escapes into the tissue. The area looks red at first then bluish-black. As the escaped blood is broken down and reabsorbed the area looks greenish-yellow. It may take as much as two weeks for a bruise to disappear.
*Trivial bruises* These are a normal part of childhood needing no treatment, except perhaps a kiss and a cuddle. A very cold wet cotton ball or gauze swab held over the place for half an hour may make the bruising less dramatic, but few children would think the effort of keeping still worthwhile.
*Extensive bruising* If a child has a fall so bad that he bruises himself over a large area, you will probably have to treat him for minor shock, and it would also be sensible to have him checked by a doctor.

Remember that the bruising still means that the child is bleeding even though he is doing it under his skin so that you cannot actually see the evidence of damaged blood vessels.
*Excessive or unexplained bruising* Parents sometimes worry because a child seems to bruise very easily, with blue marks following even minor knocks. If you are worried about this, by all means check with your doctor, but unless the child also bleeds excessively or for a long time from every minor scratch, it is most unlikely that the bruising is due to any blood disorder. Some people simply do bruise more easily than others. And small children's skin is soft compared with older people's. The child will show fewer bruises as the skin toughens up.

Be wary of bruises for which you cannot account, though. Everyday life can damage knees, shins and elbows but bruises on backs and buttocks or around upper arms *can* suggest that somebody is being rough with the child. And a black eye or a bruised face demands explanation.
*Black eye* A blow around the eyebrow, nose or cheekbone may lead to rapid swelling and a black eye. The eye itself is seldom damaged: eyes are set in bony sockets to prevent just this. But if eye-damage seems possible, take the child to a doctor or emergency room quickly. The swelling may close the eyelids and make effective examination impossible.

None of the traditional treatment for black eyes (such as the application of raw steak) has any merit, but a cloth wrung out in very cold water (or a pack of frozen peas wrapped in a cloth) and held against the place for ten minutes may minimize swelling.

Because of gravity, the swelling around an eye often travels downward during healing. Don't be surprised if, by the time the bruising is greenish, it is the nose which has come to look misshapen.
*See also* FINGER AND TOE INJURIES; HEAD INJURIES, SHOCK.

# Burns and scalds

These affect more than the skin you can see. Heat penetrates to blood vessels below the skin, dilates them and lets the colorless part of the blood (the plasma) escape. In a minor burn this escaped plasma becomes trapped in a blister. In a burn that removes the skin altogether plasma weeps from the raw area. Although only the clear part of the blood is lost, its loss reduces the total volume of fluid available to the circulation. This is why large burns and scalds so often lead to shock and why fluid-replacement by transfusion is such an essential part of hospital treatment. Judge the seriousness of a burn or scald by its area, not its depth.

☐ If a burn covers more than half a square inch of skin, show it to a doctor.

☐ If a burn covers an area more than the size of your hand, it is potentially serious. Rush the child to the hospital.

*What to do*

☐ Stop heat from burned skin penetrating deeper tissues by instantly cooling the whole area. Put a finger under the cold tap or a seriously burned child into a cold bath. Continue cooling for ten minutes. This will help blood vessels which have been damaged already to close up again and prevent further loss of plasma. Cooling will also stop the pain – temporarily.

☐ If clothes are soaked in boiling water, oil, acids, or alkalis, the heat or chemicals will be trapped by them. Tear the clothes off as you run the cold tap.

☐ If the burn or scald merits medical treatment, wrap the cooled area in a freshly laundered smooth fabric (a handkerchief, pillowcase or sheet) to keep airborne bacteria from the raw skin. Get the child to the hospital immediately.

For burns small enough to treat at home: don't interfere with a blister. It protects raw skin from infection and prevents further plasma-leakage. Don't use any ointment or grease. Apply nothing but a sterile adhesive bandage to protect the burn from rubbing.

*Scalds can mislead you* If a large area of skin is reddened but no blisters form, you may be tempted to assume no damage has been done. Don't. Fluid leakage is taking place slowly under the skin. Cool the skin and rush the child to hospital. Scalds in the mouth are best cooled by sucking ice. If none is available or if the child is too young, get him to sip icy cold water through a straw (so it emerges near the burned area) or from a bottle.

*Electrical burns look trivial* You can usually only see a blackened pin-point because the electrical contact has closed up the skin's blood vessels so there can be no superficial blister. But underneath the current will have fanned out. There may be a big wedge of burned tissue under that normal-looking skin. All electrical burns should be seen by a doctor at once.

---

## SAFETY TIPS: Burns and scalds

● All fireplaces must have fixed safety approved guards. If you must use a portable heater, use a warm air convector or fan-heater rather than a bar electric one.

● Even guarded fireplaces need caution. Don't put anything on or above the mantelpiece that might make the child want to climb up there. Don't let the child see you poke things into a fire, use a spill of paper to get a light for your cigarette from it, use a newspaper to make it draw or do anything to the fire that he might imitate. Gas fireplaces should be self igniting in case the child turns on the gas tap.

● Watch out for children around wood stoves. A stove's closed-in fire *looks* safer than a fireplace but the child who touches or falls against the hot metal may in fact be badly burned. Stoves must be screened.

● Take extra care around barbecues. Your child will enjoy watching his hamburger cook but his face may be just at the level of the hot spitting fat.

● Watch your stove: there are "pan guards" on the market which are safety rings that drop over the burners, and then hold saucepans safely so they cannot be tipped over. Failing that, always turn the handles of pans inward, and use the back burners if possible. Remember that some ovens are so badly insulated that a child can burn himself just by leaning on the door. Never leave a child in the kitchen with anything frying on the stove.

Hot fat can spit, hot oil can catch fire and an oil burn is even worse than a boiling water scald.

● Watch out for anything which dangles within the toddler's reach or which he can pull down on himself – an iron for example.

● Remember that things like irons and heaters hold their heat for some time after you have turned them off. They are not safe until cool.

● Never fill a hot-water bottle with water hot enough to scald the child if it should leak or burst. Better still, only use it to warm the bed – take it out when the child gets in.

● Check your hot water temperature. If your domestic hot water or central heating runs at too high a setting, radiators and hot taps can lead to burns and scalds.

● Discipline yourself if you are a smoker. A lit cigarette can inflict a painful (if minor) burn; your lighter or your matches must not be left lying around. A lighter on a chain around your neck is safest if you have no pockets.

● Tea or coffee can scald a child even if not actually boiling. Teapots and coffee pots should never be put on low tables where a child could reach or knock them, or on a high table with a cloth. Pulling off the cloth and the pot has scarred many a little chest and tummy for life.

● Remember that oven-to-table dishes stay hot for a long time, hot enough to cause damage. Keep high chairs well back from the family table; don't use table clothes that could be pulled off. Serving from a side table may be safer.

*Pain may surprise you* Burns and scalds hurt more than any other kind of wound. Even tiny ones upset children badly. Muster all the calm comfort you possibly can.

# Choking

Choking occurs when food, drink or a foreign body goes into the passage to the lungs instead of the passage to the stomach. Coughing and spluttering is the body's very efficient method of getting it back up into the throat.

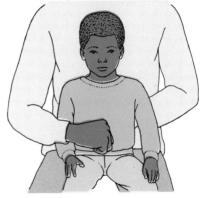

*What to do*

☐ As long as the child keeps coughing and is not turning blue or grey in the face, there is nothing to worry about. He is getting plenty of air and he will almost certainly "cough it up" for himself. A series of sharp pats on his back, between his shoulder blades, may speed things up. Coughed back food or drink may be expelled so violently that it actually goes up into his nose. It is painful (especially if the substance is acidic) but not dangerous.

Choking on objects can be much more serious as something round, such as a button or marble, can become wedged at the back of the throat blocking the air passage.

☐ If the child is coughing, don't worry too much: he must be getting some air past it or he could not cough. Put him across your forearm or knee so that his head and chest are lower than his legs and hips, and pat him smartly between the shoulder blades until the object is coughed out. It is a good idea to give this help quickly because if the child goes on choking *without* clearing the blockage, the muscles of his larynx *might* go into spasm – even clenching around the obstruction – making it far more difficult for him to breathe.

☐ If the child is not coughing but is gasping, turning scarlet and then greyish, with an expression of panic, he cannot breathe so you must act fast. Open his mouth and put your finger boldly into the back of his throat in case you can hook out the object. If you make him retch so much the better; this may dislodge it.

☐ If this doesn't work, your best hope of enabling him to breathe in time is the "Heimlich maneuver." It *is* risky. You might possibly cause damage. But you might save his life. Get your doctor to show you the technique. If you are ever faced with an adult in the same situation the procedure is exactly the same except you use both *fists* instead of your fingers.

The moment the obstruction shoots out the child should take a huge breath and at once start to recover his color. However well he seems, phone an ambulance, tell the dispatcher what happened and take him to the hospital to be checked over. And be proud of yourself.

---

---

# Cuts and grazes

*What to do*

Minor cuts need little treatment. Bleeding carries germs out of the wound and seals it as it clots.

☐ If you want to do something, put the injured part under a gently running cold tap. Don't use antiseptic. If it is strong enough to kill germs it will damage cut tissue too. Don't use ointment. It will delay formation of a protective scab.

☐ If a bandaid is needed to conceal the wound

from the child, remove it as soon as he will let you, so that the wound can harden in the air.

*Cuts on the face* These should be seen by a doctor if they penetrate more than the top layer of skin. Even if the wound is trivial, stitches may be advisable to minimize scarring.

*Gaping or jagged cuts elsewhere* While serious ones should be seen by a doctor, even trivial ones will leave scars unless stitched. With these you can balance beauty against the trauma of stitching. A scarred knee may not matter. You can help such a cut to heal neatly by cleaning it under running water, laying gauze over it and then using strips of adhesive tape to hold its edges together.

*Puncture cuts* The kind of wound made when a child steps on a nail is very liable to infection because it is deep for its size. Any germs have been carried well into the tissue; there is little bleeding to carry them out again and you cannot reach the bottom of the "hole" with running water. A deep wound, especially made by something dirty, should be seen by a doctor. He may decide to give the child an anti-tetanus injection.

☐ A smaller, cleaner wound, made perhaps by a glass splinter, should be considered carefully. If it is deep, play safe. Take him to the doctor. Thorn or needle punctures do not need medical aid.

*Grazes* While trivial, these are usually painful because a large area of raw tissue is exposed to the air. If the child does not show you a graze at once leave it alone. Bleeding and oozing will have carried out most of the dirt. Any that remains will be incorporated and lost in the scab.

*Grazes with embedded grit* These usually come from falls on gravel, some of which penetrates deeper than the superficial skin. If the surface is open and the grit visible, remove what you can with moistened gauze under a running tap. It will be painful. An older child may prefer to do it himself.

☐ The graze needs protection from friction but the more air it gets the faster it will heal. Cover it with non-stick gauze taped to the skin.

☐ The scab may be yellowish, showing local infection and dirt, but this will clear by itself.

☐ If the surface has pockets of skin with grit beneath them, cleaning and dressing is a professional job, as the pockets must not be allowed to heal with dirt trapped inside. Take the child to your doctor or emergency room.

☐ Any graze on the face which has visible dirt or grit in it should be professionally cleaned. Dirt can stain the tissues leaving an unsightly scar.

# Dislocations

In theory any movable skeletal joint can become dislocated. The hip joint, for example, is formed with a "ball" at the top of the thigh bone which fits into and rotates within a "socket" of bone at the base of the pelvis. If the "ball" is wrenched out from its socket, the joint is dislocated.

In practice dislocations are rare without fractures because the muscles and ligaments which hold them together are stronger and more resilient than the bones themselves. There are two exceptions to this. First, the shoulder joint is extremely mobile. The "ball" at the top of the upper arm bone can be twisted out of its socket in the shoulder, especially if the arm receives a sudden jolt when fully stretched above the head. A child who falls from a height and, on landing, instinctively throws up his arms to protect his head may dislocate his shoulder. Second, the lower jaw can sometimes be dislocated by an extremely deep yawn (although an injury to the jaw is more likely to fracture the bone).

*Recognizing a dislocation.* Only a skilled doctor and an X-ray can differentiate a dislocation from a fracture or see whether the child has suffered both together. Re-aligning the joint is a comparatively simple job provided it is done within two or three hours of the injury. If more time passes, the surrounding tissues tend to swell.

*What to do*

☐ The child needs comfort and urgent medical attention because he will be in great pain. The displaced parts of the joint press on nerves and over-stretch ligaments and muscles at the slightest movement. The pain of a "simple" dislocation may in fact be greater than the pain of a simple fracture of one of the long bones. If his jaw is dislocated it is just possible that it will click back into place of its own accord as he cries. If so, and if the child can then open and close his mouth freely without any pain, assume that all is well.

☐ If the shoulder is dislocated, secure the child's arm across his chest with a sling made out of a big scarf folded into a triangle and tied around his neck. Take him to the nearest hospital emergency room as soon as possible.

☐ Don't give the child anything to eat or drink – he will almost certainly need an anesthetic. Don't let him use the dislocated part; any attempt at movement may lead to further damage.

Although fractures are commonly considered more serious than dislocations, the opposite is often true. Even after a joint has been slipped back into place there will be torn ligaments and bruised tissues to heal. The joint may have to be immobilized for several weeks, and be more painful meanwhile than a fracture.

Occasionally a bad dislocation leaves a joint weakened and more liable to further dislocations, because the holding ligaments and muscles fail to heal to quite their original strength and elasticity. In such cases, the child may need treatment by a physiotherapist to strengthen the joint.

# Drowning

A baby or toddler can drown in the smallest quantity of water it takes to cover his mouth and nostrils when he falls face down in it – a couple of inches. He drowns because he does not put his arms out as he falls and does not hold his breath when he feels his face covered. Instead he opens his mouth to yell and fills his lungs with water instead of air.

☐ Snatch the child out of the water.

☐ Hold him head downward to drain any water out of his lungs and/or stomach. If he vomits water, the vomiting will press on the lungs and may help to get more water out.

If the child is coughing and spluttering he is getting some air into his lungs and some of it is getting into his bloodstream. Therefore, he will probably be all right.

☐ If there is someone else to telephone for an ambulance, put the child either head down across your lap or lying face down on the ground with his head well turned to one side.

☐ Cover him with any warm clothing that you have to hand.

☐ Watch him carefully to make sure that if any water or vomit comes up he does not breathe it back in and choke.

☐ Take him to the hospital even if by the time the ambulance arrives he seems perfectly all right. If the water he breathed or swallowed was dirty and polluted, he will need watching in case of pneumonia. If it was fresh water or swimming-pool water (rather than seawater), enough may have got from his lungs into his bloodstream to upset the biochemical balance of his body and he should be examined thoroughly.

If you snatch your child out of water so fast that you think the two of you may have got away with a nasty fright, ask yourself "did *any* water come out of him during those first desperate seconds?" If the answer is "yes," play it safe and have him checked at the hospital. If the answer is "no" and he *seems* perfectly all right, he is . . . this time.

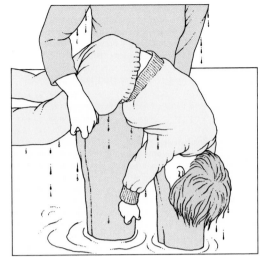

# Electric shock

The severity of an electric shock depends on a large number of factors, such as whether the victim touched the power source with wet or dry hands or was wearing rubber-soled shoes at the time.

If a child simply *touches* a live appliance, there is a good chance that the jolt he receives will be over before you even realize what happened. He may be shaky and a poor color, and will need treating for shock with warmth, comfort and perhaps a nap, but if he is all right enough to yell his outrage, it is certain that he is all right.

Very occasionally an electric wire is acting as a short-circuit. If a child touches this it will burn his fingers. You may only be able to see a tiny bluish mark. The action of the electric current closes up the superficial blood vessels. Don't be deceived. Underneath that mark there may be a wide area of damaged tissue. *All electric burns should be treated by a doctor.*

☐ AC current tends to clench muscles. If your child's hand should clench itself around the source of an electric shock (or if he should become entangled in live wires, even of DC current) so that he is receiving continuous current, *don't* follow your instinct to snatch him away. His body will be "live" and if you expose yourself to the current as well you will not be able to help him. If there is a switch, throw it. If not, don't waste time looking for the main switch. Push him clear using the nearest object which will not conduct electricity – such as a wooden chair – or protect yourself with something rubber, such as rubber boots or shoes or even a rubber doormat.

☐ If the child is unconscious he must be rushed to the hospital. If he seems to be dead, start mouth-to-mouth resuscitation and heart massage if you know how. If you do not, don't waste a second: get him to the hospital.

---

## SAFETY TIPS: Electric shock

● Make not touching plugs or switching on appliances one of your few definite rules.
● Don't buy toys that are powered from an outlet even via a transformer, at least until he is old enough to appreciate how the power source works. Transformers can go wrong.
● Don't let a child use an electric blanket – a wet bed or a spilt drink can make it dangerous.
● Have all appliances grounded: this means three-core cable and three-pin plugs.

● Keep switched sockets in the "off" position – then even if the child turns the mixer on, it will not mangle his fingers.
● Buy dummy plugs and keep one in every unused socket so the child cannot poke things into the holes.
● Use correct ampage fuses as indicated on electrical appliances.
● Have fraying cords of appliances repaired.
● Use "cord holders" to keep trailing wires completely out of the way of tripping feet or clutching hands.

---

## Finger and toe injuries

Fingers and toes are richly supplied with nerves so injuries to them are especially painful. Apart from tiny burns and cuts on fingers, the most usual injury involves bruising under the nail. Fingers get trapped in hinges, car doors and folding chairs; toes get heavy objects dropped on them.
*First aid for damaged nails* If there is bruising underneath the nail, so that blood is seeping from the nailbed, the child is in for a painful time because the bruised area will swell against the unyielding nail. You may be able to minimize the bruising if you quickly put the finger or toe under a cold water tap, or hold a well-wrapped package of frozen peas against it. Ten minutes' cooling will do all that can be done to keep the small blood vessels closed up so that as little blood as possible seeps out to blacken the nail.

When you have finished cooling, consider the nail. If there obviously *is* blood under it, and the child is still in a lot of pain, take him immediately to the nearest emergency room. A doctor can make a tiny hole in the nail and release the free blood. With the pressure will go most of the pain.
NB The nail-drilling procedure only works if it is done while the escaped blood is still liquid – within about an hour of the injury. Try to explain your need for immediate treatment (even though the child is obviously not seriously hurt). If the emergency room is so busy that you are kept waiting for a couple of hours there is little point in staying any longer.

*First aid for other injuries* The tiny bones in fingers and toes are quite easily damaged. It is very important that fingers are carefully treated to make sure they do not heal out of shape or alignment. The slightest suspicion should mean a visit to the emergency room. Toes are rather different. Even if a bone is fractured it probably will not be set with plaster of Paris but will be left to heal itself. Nevertheless it is worth getting professional help, because the pain of a damaged toe can be much reduced by taping it to the natural "splint" of the toes next door.
*Dressing fingers and toes* Finger and toe injuries almost always need protecting, from life or from socks and shoes. If you make a dressing with strips of adhesive tape you will probably make it impossible for the child to use the finger or wear his shoes. The "finger and toe bandages" suggested for the first aid box on page 475 make a neat and comfortable protective covering.

---

## SAFETY TIPS: Finger injuries

● Things that pinch fingers: deck chairs, ironing boards, clothes horses, etc., can all blacken nails or break fingers if the child tries to set them up or play with them.
● Door hinges pinch worse than the closing side and it is much easier to miss the fact that the child's hand is at risk. "Hinge protectors" are worth considering.

---

## Foreign bodies in ears, eyes, nose, vagina

*Ears*
☐ A round object, such as a bead, which fills the ear canal should not be touched. Attempts to remove it could push it further in and damage the ear drum. Take the child to your doctor for its removal.
☐ A soft, irregularly shaped object may be removable with tweezers. Have one gentle try at getting a grip on it. If you fail, take the child to your doctor.
NB Thick discharge from an ear that is not wax

should always be shown to a doctor.

### Eyes

☐ Copious watering of the eye (and/or crying) will float most foreign bodies out. Don't let the child rub it. Encouraging rubbing of the other eye often helps him leave the injured one alone.

☐ If the child neither forgets about it nor can be distracted, take him into a good light and try gently pulling down the lower lid and pulling up the upper lid. If you can see the foreign body, try gently to remove it with *damp* tissue. Even if you see nothing, lifting the lids may free it to float out by itself.

☐ If you can see something but it does not move, *leave it* and take the child to the doctor or emergency room. If it is embedded it must be removed professionally.

☐ If you can see a scratch or mark on the white of the eye (an "abrasion") take the child to the doctor or emergency room. Eyes heal very well but antibiotic drops to protect against infection might be indicated.

NB If a child squirts any stinging or abrasive fluid into the eye, washing it out with masses of gently running water is the immediate treatment. Hold the child under the tap with the damaged eye lower than the other so that the substance is not washed into the unaffected eye. Use force to keep him under the tap for several minutes, if you must. Gently open the lids so that every fold is rinsed repeatedly.

☐ When you have thoroughly irrigated the eye, pause to consider. If it was "only" detergent, all will now be well. If it was toilet bowl cleaner, bleach, battery acid . . . rush to the hospital emergency room, taking the container with you.

### Nose
Proceed as for ears.

### Vagina
If a little girl "loses" something in her front passage you will probably only know about it when a foul-smelling discharge appears on her diaper or underpants. Take her to the doctor.

☐ If you can see an object in the vagina you can probably gently remove it.

## Fractures

*Greenstick fracture* A greenstick fracture is not usually as serious as a fracture in an older person. Because the affected bone only bends and cracks like a green twig rather than snapping like a dry one, there are no sharp ends of bone inside the limb to damage blood vessels and muscles. The bone cannot get out of alignment so it does not need complicated "setting." Nor will movement make it much worse.

*Symptoms* Your child will complain of pain in the limb and probably refuse to use it. The limb may look swollen or bruised. But many of these signs may be present in a severe sprain too. For definite confirmation that there is a fracture an X-ray is usually needed.

*What to do*
If you want to avoid taking the child to the hospital unless it is absolutely necessary, you can afford to wait for half an hour or so to see whether he starts to use the injured limb.

☐ Comfort the child and lie him down if he seems at all shocked.

☐ Put the affected limb in whatever position seems most comfortable. Don't encourage him to use it, but don't stop him either.

NB Don't give him anything to eat or drink because if the limb is fractured he may need to have an anesthetic.

☐ If after an hour he can use the limb and does not complain any longer of acute pain it is safe to assume that all is well.

☐ If he cannot use it, or if it hurts very much when he tries to do so, take him to a hospital emergency room. Even if it is only a sprain it is obviously bad enough to merit some prompt medical attention.

*Serious fractures* The fractures will be more serious if the break is complete. There may be a real risk of damage to the blood vessels, muscles, etc., as the broken ends of bone move around. If the fracture is "compound" with a wound exposing the broken bone to the outside world there is a major risk of infection.

*Symptoms* The child will clearly be badly hurt, scared and unable to use the affected part: you will need to get him to a hospital emergency room right away.

*What to do*
☐ Don't move him unless he himself gets up and you are therefore quite sure he has not damaged his spine or his pelvis or a bone in his thigh. Make him as comfortable as you can where he is and try to keep him calm and still until an ambulance arrives.

☐ If the child can walk, but has obviously damaged an arm, collar bone or ribs, get him as comfortable as his injuries allow and then keep him still. The more he is allowed to move about the more those ends of broken bone will damage him, and the more difficult the fracture will be to set.

☐ If you have to take him yourself to the hospital (perhaps because the accident happened miles from anywhere) try to keep the injured part from moving by fastening it to the child himself. If he has broken his collar bone he will instinctively hold the arm bent at the elbow across his chest. Tie it in that position with a scarf or large handkerchief. An injured leg can be tied to the sound leg in several places well away from the apparent break, so that the sound leg splints the broken one.

☐ If he must be carried, carry him flat as if he were on a proper stretcher. If there is no convenient board to use as a stretcher, an adult's coat will do provided you and your helper keep it stretched tight so that the child is lying completely flat.

A bone which has broken through the skin, or a wound which goes right through to the broken bone, does carry a very real risk of the bone itself getting infected.

☐ If you are at home, cover the whole area with a big sterile dressing. Don't attempt to wash or interfere with such a wound; whatever you do will be redone at the hospital.

☐ If you are out, try to think of something which is sterile or at least clean. The inner folds of a newly laundered handkerchief will do fine.

☐ Your child will almost certainly be shocked. Keep him calm, quiet, lying down and covered up until help arrives.

NB Don't give him anything at all to eat or drink. He is bound to need an anesthetic.

*Plaster casts* A child with his limb in a cast can believe that the limb has actually been removed or at least that it will be permanently stiff and heavy. Try to prepare for this common emergency by talk and play at home in advance. If it happens, warn the child, before he has the anesthetic for setting the limb, that it will be in a cast when he wakes up. Point out, when he comes around, that his thigh is still visible at one end of the cast and his toes at the other; the rest of his leg is still there. It is just safely covered up to keep it from moving while it heals.

*Traction* Sometimes, after a bad fracture, your child's arm or leg has to be stretched for a while so that the bones are held end-to-end, rather than overlapping, while they re-fuse.

Lying on his back with his leg raised on a pulley and weights suspended from it, the child is trapped. He cannot sit up, turn over or do anything for himself. He may have pain in the limb during the first days, and muscle discomfort later. He needs constant reassurance that his leg is still whole under the cast and that when he next sees it, it will be perfectly normal. He also needs careful explanations as to what is happening to him and why, and is likely to demand continual company and entertainment. Do room-in with him if you possibly can, even though traction usually means a long stay. *See also* HOSPITAL ADMISSION.

# Head injuries

Falls or bumps on the head cause more worry to parents than almost any other common type of accident because they often *look* serious and parents know how they *can* be serious. Most of them are not serious, however, and if you understand something about them, you can be certain that you would know if a particular bang *was* serious.

Head injuries often look horrible because the skin of the scalp and face is well supplied with blood vessels and tightly stretched across the rigid skull so that a graze bleeds a lot and even a tiny cut gapes wide open.

☐ Bleeding from a graze on the forehead is no more serious than from a graze on the knee. Wash it, then press on it gently with a clean swab to stop the bleeding.

☐ You can stop cuts on the scalp bleeding by pressure, even through the hair, but because such cuts gape open they may need a stitch where a comparable cut elsewhere would not. If blood does not clot within ten minutes, seek advice.

☐ Cuts on the face should be shown to a doctor. Stitching may be advisable to minimize scarring.

☐ Bruises on the forehead (the usual result of babies rolling off beds or toddlers standing up under tables!) often come up in enormous "goose eggs." Once again bruises on the head are no more dangerous than bruises elsewhere. All that matters is what, if anything, has happened to the brain under that skull.

*Concussion*
Such an injury to the brain is called "concussion." Only if the skull is actually smashed in is concussion caused by a direct blow. Much more usually it is caused by the fall or blow jolting the brain so that it is banged against the inside of the skull. The seriousness of concussion depends on the severity of the bang and on the exact area of the brain which is affected. But *any* child who is, or may have, a concussion should be seen by a doctor, so all you need to be aware of are the signs that there may be concussion of any degree:

☐ Unconsciousness or being "knocked out," for a moment or more, always means concussion. Send for an ambulance. Keep the child lying down, warm, quiet and comfortable until it arrives. Make sure he cannot inhale any blood or vomit. Move him into the "recovery position" on page 474 unless you think he may have damaged his spine.

☐ Shock and confusion after the accident are probably the result of fear and pain. Try comfort and quiet distraction. A baby may cry furiously for as much as ten minutes; a toddler may want to lie on the sofa and be told a story. If he is conscious and coherent, you can afford twenty minutes to wait and see.

---

## SAFETY TIPS: Head injuries

● Falls from windows still happen. If you don't want bars, fit "acorn fasteners" which allow the window to open only a few inches.

● Watch out for balconies. Safety fences should be high and strong, with *no* cross-pieces between verticals. Children climb.

● Beware of rugs on polished floors, especially near stairs.

● Until your child can go safely up and down stairs, you need safety gates at the top and bottom. If you only gate the top he may climb all the way up and tumble all the way down.

● Steps outside are a particular hazard for a child on a tricycle or other ride-on toy. You may need a safety fence across the top until he learns to use his brakes and can always judge a halt completely accurately.

● Ban socks without shoes; they make an ordinary plastic floor into a skating rink.

● Watch out for banisters: older children will slide down them if they are slideable. If there is a real drop you need a safety net or uprights at frequent intervals ruining the run.

---

Seek medical advice, at least by telephoning your doctor, if:
- [ ] He is still (or becomes) very pale or grey.
- [ ] His breathing is noisy and like snoring, even when he has stopped crying.
- [ ] He seems "odd" – does not recognize you; seems not to see properly; talks nonsense if old enough to talk or makes odd noises if not.
- [ ] He vomits (though this may just be shock).
- [ ] He complains of headache (although he may be confusing it with the pain of the bruise).

If none of these symptoms appears and the child wants to get up and get going, let him. If he seems all right he *is* all right.
NB Babies and small children often drop off to sleep after a shock, an efficient way of relaxing and recovering. Let him nap but just check, over the first hour, that his color and breathing are normal, that he *is* asleep, not unconscious. If you're not sure, wake him. If in doubt, seek help.


## Poisoning

If a child eats or drinks something poisonous he must be treated quickly. The longer the poison stays in his stomach, the more of it will be absorbed into his bloodstream and the more seriously ill he will be. Call your Poison Control Center for advice.

But treatment will be frightening and unpleasant for the child. It will involve making him vomit and/or passing a tube into his stomach and siphoning out the contents. He will probably be kept in the hospital overnight to be watched for effects of poison already absorbed. So while you must play safe, do be sure that he really has taken something dangerous before you rush him to a hospital. It would be a great shame to put him through all that, if the pills you thought he had eaten were on the floor all the time.
*Pills and medicines* Assume that anything your child takes from the medicine cabinet may poison him: e.g., very few sleeping pills/tranquilizers/anti-depressants are needed to kill a child. Painkillers, such as aspirin, kill many children every year. Antihistamines and travel sickness tablets contain powerful and dangerous drugs. Even medicines (like vitamins or iron tablets) which may be good for a child in controlled doses can harm or even kill him if he takes much more.
*Household cleaning products* Assume that all are potentially dangerous. They may be alkalis such as bleach, ammonia or caustic soda, acids such as carbolic soap, or disinfectants, or petroleum products such as dry cleaning fluid. The first two groups burn the throat and stomach. The third group releases poisonous gas which can be fatal.
*Lawn products* Any insecticide, weedkiller or fungicide is dangerous. Some can be fatal if even a tiny quantity is tasted.
*Garage and workshop* Oil-based paints, paint removers such as turpentine, car polishes, metal polishes and gasoline are only a few of the serious poisons he might find and take.
*Garden* Yew berries, laburnum seeds, deadly nightshade (and the more common woody

## SAFETY TIPS: Poisoning

*Medicines*
Children between about one and five years old will eat any pills that they "discover," however difficult they are about taking medicines they have actually been prescribed.
- Buy a medicine cabinet with a safety lock made to "safety approved" standards. Nowhere else is really safe. A high cupboard can be a challenge to a climber, an ordinary lock and key can be an entrancing game to a fiddler, while a hiding place will be discovered in the end by your favorite explorer. Keep all medicines, even "harmless" ones like the children's own vitamins in the cabinet, and put them back after use.
- Don't keep medicines (even oral contraceptives) in the room just to remind you of a regular dosage; write yourself a conspicuous message instead.
- Don't carry medicines in your handbag unless they are essential. Always use a childproof container.
- Don't let the child play with empty medicine containers. It only increases the chances of a mistake occurring and of him learning how to open those "safe" lids.
- Don't get caught out in other people's houses. Grandparents' houses can be especially dangerous: all too often there are sleeping pills by the bed, "heart pills" in the pocket and laxatives beside the washbasin.
- Be extra careful when traveling. A vanity case or briefcase which locks is safest.
- Guard against your own mistakes as well as the child's: don't give medicine in the dark, check the label. Don't give medicines from one illness or one child to the next. Don't rely on breaking adult tablets to arrive at a child's dose. Rewrite any label which gets smudged so that you know, for sure, what is in the bottle.

*Poisons*
Cleaning, gardening and beauty products are so many and various that you cannot hope to know exactly what is in everything. Play safe. Assume that all these things could harm a child who swallowed them.
- Keep all cleaning materials in a cupboard too high for the child to climb up to. Remember that even if he did not actually drink the bleach or the oven cleaner, he could spray it in his eyes and blind himself.
- Garden sheds, garages or workshops must be kept locked. Even so the really dangerous things like insect and weedkillers, paint-strippers and cleaners, etc. should be kept in locked cupboards in case you leave the door open "just for a minute."
- Keep potentially dangerous beauty products in the medicine cabinet. A good go at your surplus hair remover will do the child no good.

nightshade and enchanter's nightshade) are all extremely poisonous. Privet and laurel berries are less dangerous but they still constitute a serious matter.

*Adult pleasures*  Tobacco is a lethal poison if swallowed. A single cigarette could kill a one-year-old. Alcohol is also surprisingly poisonous to children. As little as a good swig of straight liquor can kill a toddler.

### What to do

If your child has swallowed any pills, medicine, tobacco, alcohol or berries, clear his mouth of any bits he has not yet swallowed and give him syrup of ipecac. Put him face down across your knee with his head lower than his hips, then put two fingers right to the back of his throat and wiggle them until he vomits. If he retches but nothing comes up, make him drink a big glass of water and then try again. Be bold.

☐ Whether you have managed to make him vomit or not, give up your first aid after three minutes and get him to the hospital. Take the poison with you. NB Don't give him an old-fashioned emetic like salt or mustard and water. Syrup of ipecac is a safe and effective emetic. Don't make him vomit lying down on his back, or if he seems drowsy. He might breathe his vomit and choke.

If the poison is any form of household cleaner, garden spray, paint solvent or gasoline, vomiting it up will burn his throat more and he might breathe it in, so don't make him vomit.

☐ Try to dilute the poison so that it does not damage his stomach so badly. Give him as big a drink of milk as you can persuade him to sip quickly. Don't force him to drink it, though, or he may vomit.

☐ Swill his mouth out and sponge his face to get rid of any chemicals still damaging his skin. Rush him to the hospital. Don't forget to take the poison with you.

## Road safety

A toddler can begin to learn that the curb is a safety line between him and traffic. But don't trust him there any more than you would trust him on the edge of a deep lake. Hold on to his hand or reins, he can dart out in a second.

Until you can absolutely trust your child to stay on the sidewalk, don't let him on the streets alone at all. Children under five should never be allowed to cross any road alone. Even when concentrating they cannot usually distinguish right from left, judge how far away approaching traffic is, how fast it is moving or whether it is parked. They cannot anticipate unexpected driving maneuvers such as U-turns or right-turns across the traffic.

Older children who are ready for school still only learn these things gradually, and through example and experience. They may be fully able to learn and apply safety rules yet still be caught off guard by unexpected failure of traffic lights or the non-appearance of a crossing guard. They are subject to distractions and fatigue, especially if the school day

has gone wrong. Don't regard them as road-proof until you have collected months of evidence.

*Safety Rules*  If you live in a quiet area, you may be able to teach your child to use this code as a set of absolute rules. If so you must obey them too – always. In a city it may be difficult for the child ever to follow it: you will have to adapt it.

● First find a safe place to cross such as a cross walk, patrolled crossing, underpass or at a traffic light. (There may be none.)
● Stand on the pavement near the curb. Look all around for traffic and listen. (There may be traffic everywhere.)
● If traffic is coming, let it pass. Look all around again.
● When there is no traffic near, cross. (There may always be traffic in daytime.)
● Keep looking and listening for traffic all the time you cross.

*Adapting the rules for your child*  Decide what regular journeys you want the child to make alone on foot and work out yourself:
● Where he should cross.
● When he should cross: find markers that the child can use as his signal that approaching traffic is too close, like "don't cross if there is anything closer than the big red house" or "don't cross if there is anything your side of the bridge."
● How he should cross: if there are likely to be parked cars, you may have to teach him to stand between them holding the outside edge of one bumper while he peers both ways.
● What he is to do if he cannot cross because of road work, etc.: is he to walk on to an alternative crossing place or wait until an adult comes and then ask for help? (What about your "don't go with strangers" rule?)

Walk each route several times with the child. Make a game out of testing him – when he thinks he knows one you should make him take you. Next, you could let him walk it alone within sight and calling distance of you. Then you could let him do the easiest half of the walk and meet you half-way. Continue until you are sure he is no more likely to get run over than you are yourself.

Gradually, generalize this very special teaching which has kept him safe on particular roads, to other roads. Don't worry if it is two years from the time he first goes to school alone before you give him the freedom of local roads.

*Tricycles*  Tricycles and other self-propelled vehicles are toys. They are not meant for riding on roads, even quiet ones.
☐ On the sidewalk, watch out. He is bad at steering, bad at using brakes (even if he has them) and slow to spot or react to emergencies. He may go off the curb.
☐ In the park, watch out for hills. Putting his feet down to stop can pitch him over the handlebars on to his head.
☐ In the yard, guard steps if you have them. A temporary safety fence or set of bricks 4in (10cm) high and set at least 2ft (60cm) back from the top step of the flight may be needed.

that the play in your own seat belt will not prevent him from being crushed.

☐ From birth to about nine months, babies are safest in a backward-facing car-seat. These seats, with a five-point harness and restrained by the

adult safety belt, can safely be carried on the front seat of the car so that you and the baby can see each other and you can concentrate on your driving. The seats are easy to carry and to put in and out of the car, complete with baby, and they are useful indoors as well.

☐ Once a baby outgrows his backward-facing seat and can sit steadily by himself he needs a car safety seat in the back of the car. There are many types available, requiring different kinds of fitting. Whichever you buy, make sure that it is properly fitted to your own particular make and that it is government approved.

*Bicycles for fun* Your child may manage to balance a two-wheeler by the time he is five: it may be a status-symbol and heart's desire.

☐ If there is safe fun-riding space in parks, etc., teach him to push the bike along the sidewalk to it. Make it clear that if he rides it on the road it will be confiscated.

*Bicycles for use* Big cities are just not safe for cycling any more except where special "bike lanes" have been made. Whatever your child's road sense on foot, he will be in danger on a bike with traffic. It is easier to teach a young child safe use of public transport for necessary journeys to school, etc. If you live in the country and he really needs a bike:

☐ Buy one that fits him, not one he will "grow into" unless it is the kind that can be made larger.

☐ Have it safety-checked even if it is new; many come from factories with faulty brakes and other such defects.

☐ Have him properly taught to ride it; most schools have courses.

☐ Take or have him taken on several trial rides before you let him go alone.

☐ Don't allow him to ride after dusk. Teach him to telephone if something keeps him late at school during the winter.

☐ In case of unforeseen circumstances keep his lights in top condition (don't make him buy batteries out of pocket money) and sew reflective strips on his clothing.

☐ Have your child wear a helmet.

*In the car* No baby or child should ever ride in a car without a properly fitting and fitted safety restraint.

☐ Never hold a child on your lap in the front seat. This practice is almost universally illegal because the position is the most dangerous in the whole car. In a crash, the child's body protects the adult's.

☐ Never drive while carrying a baby in a sling or front-carrier. He is so close to the steering wheel

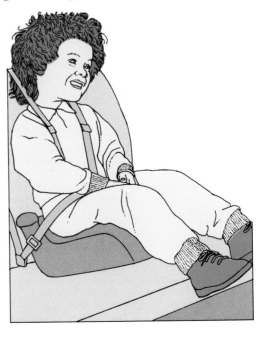

☐ Don't go on using a car safety seat once your toddler reaches its maximum safe weight. Between about 36lbs (16kg) and 75lbs (34kg) (when he can use an adult seat belt) he will need either a "junior safety harness" or an adjustable "generation" belt with a booster cushion.

☐ Booster seats are also available for use with adult back seat belts. These seats are inexpensive and a good buy for the use of extra children whom you might otherwise be tempted to carry unrestrained, but for regular use by children of the family, junior or "generation" harnesses are safer and more comfortable.

☐ When your child graduates to an adult seat belt, insist that he travel in the back of the car and check that the belt fits him safely and comfortably. Kits are available to adjust the relative length of the shoulder strap.

☐ Think carefully before you carry in your car a child for whom you have no restraint. And think equally carefully about letting your child ride unrestrained in someone else's car. If you and other parents are going to share a nursery or school run, *all* the cars should be equipped for *all* the children. There should be no exceptions.

☐ Have childproof locks fitted to your car.

☐ Remember it can be dangerous to let a child lean out of the window, or put out an arm.

# Shock

The brain has overall control of all bodily functions, including the heart and lungs. The brain's own functioning is dependent upon an adequate supply of sufficiently oxygenated blood. If the brain is deprived of blood, various physiological reactions follow. If the deprivation is temporary, as in a faint or in minor shock, the situation can be easily reversed. But if the brain is being deprived of blood by circulation failure, with heavy bleeding or burns causing medical shock, treatment of the condition is a matter of urgency.

*Minor shock*
Hearing bad news, seeing a bloody accident or getting slightly hurt in especially frightening circumstances can reduce the blood supply to the brain. The child's body reacts by closing up the blood vessels near the skin's surface to conserve the blood supply to the internal organs so he becomes very pale and his skin feels cold and clammy. His nervous system is affected so he is shaky and feels "odd." He cries and may vomit.

Minor shock reactions are much increased by fear and pain. A child may have a shock-reaction to a frightening car crash which left him uninjured and he may react with greater shock to a small but painful burn than to a more serious but in fact less painful injury.

Multiple minor injuries can cause this kind of shock even when each on its own would be trivial. A child who has had the fright of falling off his bike and then finds himself with a bleeding hand, a very sore grazed knee and a bump on the head can definitely be shocked.

*What to do*
☐ Lie him down with his head lower than his feet to help adequate blood return to the brain.

☐ Keep his head turned to one side so that if he should vomit he will not choke.

☐ Loosen any tight clothing so that his breathing is not restricted.

☐ Cover with a blanket or coat to preserve his body warmth.

☐ Comfort and make much of him so that he stops being frightened.

NB Do not give hot, sweet drinks or indeed anything to drink at all until he is completely back to normal. He cannot digest anything while his body is fighting shock. Do not warm with hot-water bottles. Artificial warming will force the blood vessels in the skin to re-open. His color will improve, but at the expense of his vital organs which for the moment need extra blood.

☐ Even five minutes lying quietly should reverse minor shock. The child's color will improve and he will either drop off to sleep (in which case you have to watch that he does not vomit and/or choke) or sit up and get on with life.

If he does not seem normal within half an hour, call your doctor. The incident which led to the shock may have been more serious than you had thought.

*Medical shock following serious accident or acute illness* The child's brain is being starved of blood as in minor shock, but simply lying down cannot give it adequate help because some physical cause such as very heavy bleeding (external or internal), extreme dehydration, a severe scald or burn, uncontrolable sickness or diarrhea, has reduced the amount of blood or body fluid in circulation. Damage to the brain or nervous system may also disrupt the brain's control of the heart and circulation, producing a state of medical shock.

Because the circulation is short of blood, the heart automatically pumps harder but because it has less than the optimum amount to pump, it gets less efficient so that decreasing amounts of blood reach the brain whose control circuits therefore get even more inefficient. Without treatment, acute medical shock leads eventually to failure of the circulation and of breathing.

The signs of serious medical shock are similar to those of minor shock but more pronounced. The child looks and acts "collapsed." Dizziness and faintness may be so pronounced that the child is barely conscious. He may behave as if delirious, rambling and not recognizing you. He may be very restless and anxious, behaving like a child with a night terror.

NB Lying down does not produce any noticeable immediate improvement: the child is getting worse.

*What to do*
☐ Recognize the likelihood of shock developing.
☐ Send urgently for medical help.
☐ Treat the cause if this is obvious (by stopping heavy bleeding for example) and minimize the effects while waiting for help by treating the child as for minor shock.

# Smothering

It is impossible for a baby to smother himself just by lying face down in a bed that has no pillow, or by going under the bedclothes. He will turn his head clear when he needs air, and sufficient air will come through blankets and sheets even should he get tangled up.

*Plastic*
Plastic may cause smothering because it is both airtight and clingy. If a child puts a plastic bag or thin plastic sheeting over his face, the first breath he takes in causes the plastic to cling and mold itself closely over his mouth and nose so that he cannot rip it off.

*What to do*
☐ Speed is what matters. Rip off the material. He may take a great gasping breath at once and all will be well.
☐ If he does not breathe, don't waste a second. If you know how to do mouth-to-mouth resuscitation, start instantly, and give him six full breaths. Phone for an ambulance, dialing 911 in between breaths.
   Continue until help arrives. If you don't know how to give mouth-to-mouth resuscitation don't waste time trying. Rush him to the hospital or phone for an ambulance, whichever will be quicker.

*Earth, sand or cement*  Fine grainy material can collapse on the child, covering his chest and head and filling his mouth and nostrils. Efforts to breathe only pull the material into his air passages.

*What to do*
☐ Speed is essential. Dig him out, clearing his complete chest as well as his face. He cannot breathe with weight on his rib cage.
☐ Rapidly clear all the sand you can out of his mouth, throat and nose. He may start to choke and splutter in which case all will probably be well, though he should be rushed to the hospital as he may have sand in his lungs.
☐ If he shows no sign of breathing but is still a normal color, rush him to the hospital.
☐ If he shows no sign of breathing and is already greyish blue, start mouth-to-mouth resuscitation if you know how to do it. The risk of blowing more sand into his lungs is worth taking if his color tells you that immediate oxygen is the only chance. Otherwise don't waste time. Rush for the hospital.

---

## SAFETY TIPS: Smothering

Even a new baby will turn his head if he cannot breathe, but this will not remove all obstructions. Avoid plastic – especially the thin filmy kind that clings. Take it off crib mattresses, etc., before you ever use them. Tear up and throw away plastic bags – or if you want to re-use them, lock them away like poisons. Use stiff plastic bibs and take them off as soon as a meal is over. Keep plastic pants well out of the way of his face and hands.
● Never let a child tunnel in sand or piles of earth. Don't even encourage games of burying each other in the sand at the beach. Sand dunes make heavenly playgrounds but sand falls are always possible; he should be watched every single moment.
● Be careful of anything he can get into but not out of. Ice chests make a deadly hiding place. You will not even hear him call because of the insulation. Keep them locked. Be sure that if he can get into cupboards he can also get out of them.

● Don't give him a pillow when he is sleeping. If you want to prop him when he is awake use a pillow under the mattress.

---

# Splinters

*What to do*
☐ If the end of a splinter or thorn stands out from your child's skin it can be removed using square-ended tweezers.
☐ If there is no end to get hold of, but the splinter is clearly visible lying under the skin, look carefully to see the direction in which it entered. Wash the area and numb with an ice cube. Squeezing gently from the other end may persuade it to come back through its own hole. If not, you may be able to tease it out, using a fine needle, sterilized in a match flame. If your efforts fail, wait a day or so; if the child is still complaining of discomfort from the splinter, take him to the doctor.
☐ If the splinter has penetrated below the skin into the tissues, or if it has entered directly downward so that only the pin-point head is visible, the needle-technique will hurt. It may be best left alone. It will work its own way out.
☐ Splinters of glass or metal should always be removed by a doctor. All sides will be sharp. Attempts to remove it may cause damage.

# Sprains and strains

These are rare in babies and small children. Their own weight and activity are seldom enough to cause this sort of damage, while damaging force exerted by somebody else will usually cause a dislocation or a fracture.

In practice you do not need to differentiate between injury to joints, bones and the ligaments and muscles associated with them. All you need to be able to do is to recognize an injury that requires professional help and get your child to the doctor or hospital which can provide it the most speedily.
*A sprain* means that some of the ligaments that support a joint have been torn. The ankle, knee, wrist and shoulder joints are the ones most commonly affected. The signs are:
- [ ] Pain.
- [ ] Swelling.

*A strain* means that some muscle-fibers have been over-stretched or torn. Strains are usually less serious than sprains but unless the pain is trivial and the child uses the affected limb freely after a few minutes, don't try home diagnosis.

*What to do*
- [ ] Comfort the child – the accident will have frightened him and until you have calmed him down you cannot differentiate between his fear and possible damage.
- [ ] Let him put the limb in whatever position seems most comfortable. Don't try to make him use it. If it is not damaged he will start to do so spontaneously after a few minutes. Otherwise it should not be used.
- [ ] If he still does not use it or forget the pain once he is calm, call your doctor.
NB Don't bother with cold compresses and bandages. If the limb turns out to be fractured, you may make matters worse. If it is sprained or strained your treatment will do no good and the hospital staff will have to undo it all when you get there anyway.

- [ ] In a more serious case blisters may form. The child will be in real pain. He will need a doctor's attention unless the area is small and he seems perfectly well. Get a doctor at once if he is feverish and/or seems ill. An appropriate dose of children's acetaminophen will help the pain. At night stretch his under-sheet very tightly to help prevent friction, and use a silky covering if you can, rather than ordinary bedclothes.

# Sunburn

Sunburn needs to be taken very seriously.
*What to do*
- [ ] In a mild case, the child's skin will be red and hot to the touch. Apply calamine lotion liberally, and cover him with something really soft – such as his softest tee-shirt or a cloth diaper.
NB Keep the burned area out of the sun. The merest touch of the sun's heat will be painful.

---

## SAFETY TIPS: Sunburn

Sunburn does not show or hurt until after the damage is done, so don't rely for prevention either on looking at your child's skin or on what he says.

*Babies*
- Babies burn extremely easily as their skins have not been toughened by long exposure to air and friction. Don't deliberately expose a baby to full sun. If you keep him in the shade and use a carriage canopy when he naps outside, he will get enough sun as you carry him around to build a little protection. By the end of his first summer you will probably be able to expose his legs under a coating of high-factor sunscreen cream.
*Toddlers and older children*
- Remember that fair-skinned children burn more easily, and take longer to build up a protective tan, than those who are naturally darker.
- Sun is reflected off water as well as beating down onto it so take particular care when you are beside or on the ocean or a lake.
- Air temperatures need not be high for sunburn to occur. A cool breeze can keep a child feeling chilly while bright sun is burning him. Lightweight clothes will deal with both.

- Skin that is least often exposed to air and sun is most liable to sunburn. Watch out especially for your toddler's bottom as he digs, naked, on the beach. If you plan a beach vacation with a child under five, try to accustom him to playing naked in the garden during previous warm days.
- Protective sunscreen, lotions or oils do help. More sophisticated and selective lotions are being produced all the time, especially in the ranges designed for children. Factor numbers represent the extra time for which "normal" skin can be exposed without burning. So Factor 2 is meant to double safe exposure-time and Factor 15 to multiply it accordingly. But fierce midday sun could redden your child's bare shoulders in two minutes, so that even that high protection factor will not protect him for long. Start him off with the less direct sun of early morning and late afternoon. Reapply a protective sunscreen every time he goes into the water. Make him wear a light cotton shirt or tee-shirt and make sure there is shade available whenever he wants to sit still.
- A wide-brimmed hat will shade the back of his neck and shoulders. If you cannot persuade him to stay covered up enough, cut down your time on the beach.
- Keep gradually-tanning skin well-moisturised. After sun products are a worthwhile investment.

# Allergic children

If your child is allergic (or "atopic"), his body over-reacts to something (or to many things) that he eats, breathes or touches. The cause of the reaction is called an "allergen." Allergens are usually proteins although this does not mean that they are always – or even most usually – foodstuffs. The trillions of micro-organisms that share the world with us, the skin cells in shed animal fur and the plant spores that blow around in autumn are all partly proteins.

Allergic people react to their allergens rather as the rest of us react to the bacteria and viruses that cause illness: they manufacture antibodies against them *as if they were dangerous*. The allergic reaction therefore creates a physical problem where in a non-allergic person there is none: it *makes* otherwise harmless substances dangerous – or at least unpleasant for the sufferer.

Nobody knows exactly why some children are born with, or develop, allergic sensitivities, although much research is being conducted and progress is being made. It is known, though, that allergic tendencies run in families and that the child of two parents with allergic problems is very likely to have at least some allergies of his own.

Allergy can be a confusing topic because the single tendency to develop allergic reactions can manifest itself in a wide range of apparently different conditions. The main allergic conditions are dealt with alphabetically below but some general points apply to them all:

☐ The nature and severity of allergic symptoms tend to change with age so that, for example, a baby who suffers from infantile eczema may "grow out of it" to develop allergic rhinitis ("hay fever") and then asthma, which becomes milder in adolescence. Whatever your child's symptoms *now* you can expect them to change with time.

☐ Although a substance that is an allergen for a particular person will always provoke a reaction, the degree of that reaction will often depend on the degree of his exposure to the allergen. The obvious example is that of the hay-fever sufferer whose symptoms may increase in direct relation to the pollen-count. Less obvious is the example of the baby who proves allergic to cow's milk protein when weaned from the breast to a formula. Although he will continue to be sensitive to cow's milk protein (until or unless he "grows out of it"), replacing his bottles of cow's milk formula with a soy-based milk may enable his body to tolerate small quantities of cow's milk in the rest of his diet without obvious symptoms.

☐ Infections play an established (though ill-understood) part in most allergic disorders. The asthmatic child is more likely to have an attack, and the attack is more likely to be a bad one, if he already has a cold or other illness.

☐ Stress and excitement often exacerbate allergic complaints, but zealous attempts to *avoid* stress sometimes rebound. If an allergic child is over-protected and made to feel different from his peers, this may in itself cause stress and an increase in the symptoms.

*The handling of allergic complaints*

Allergy cannot be *cured*: the bodies of susceptible individuals cannot be persuaded to make antibodies only against dangerous substances.

☐ Since no *cure* is possible, attempts at exact diagnosis and identification of the particular allergens which cause symptoms are not always worthwhile. If a child suffers from asthma, for example, a large number of allergens may cause symptoms. Endless testing to identify them would be expensive, time-consuming and stressful. At the end of such a program it would not be possible to de-sensitize him against all of them or for him to avoid them all. The sensible course of action may therefore be to avoid the most likely allergens (cutting down the dust and therefore the house mites in his bedroom, for example) while treating his asthma symptomatically.

☐ Some allergic complaints are so transient that no diagnosis is possible. Urticaria, for example, can seldom be accurately diagnosed (unless it chances *only* to occur after eating strawberries) because the itching weals go down of their own accord before a doctor can investigate them.

☐ In a few conditions – such as allergy to penicillin – the allergic reaction is potentially life-threatening and avoidance is essential "treatment." Such a child must never again be given penicillin. The fact will be recorded on his medical and school records and a medic-alert bracelet may be given to him so that penicillin is not administered during emergency treatment by doctors without access to those records.

☐ In rare conditions – such as allergy to wasp stings (anaphylactic shock) – the allergic reaction is potentially life-threatening, but the allergen cannot certainly be avoided. De-sensitization is then vital. A series of tests with much-diluted allergen will be used to find the minimum dose to which the child reacts. A series of injections containing the allergen in much-diluted form will then be given, increasing in strength but always staying within the child's rising tolerance. By this means his body can be persuaded gradually to produce special extra antibodies which will bind to the injected allergen and thus prevent a violent reaction to any further wasp sting.

The doctor who looks after the allergic child will often use combinations of these main treatment approaches: some symptom control; some attempts at identifying allergens; some avoidance and some de-sensitization. It is important for parents to understand that over-enthusiastic attempts to hunt down allergens are not always in the child's best interests and that inability to diagnose the exact cause of an allergic rash does not suggest medical ineptitude. It is also important to understand that the stress components in allergic illnesses often make it necessary for doctors to inquire into aspects of family life which are not obviously relevant. If your doctor is to do his best for your allergic child he needs to know him and all his circumstances well. You need to trust that doctor with the family skeletons as well as the family flu for him to do his job most effectively.

## Allergic reaction to wasp or bee sting (anaphylactic shock)

*Very* occasionally the chemicals in these stings cause an allergic reaction. The stung child develops widespread inflammation and acute pain at the site of the sting and collapses, feeling faint with a poor color and perhaps with breathing difficulties.

Any child who reacts badly to a sting should be rushed to the hospital. A telephone warning that a child with "anaphylactic shock" is on the way will help the staff to be ready to cope quickly with the affected child.

Once the emergency is over, "de-sensitization" treatment (see above) is essential as a further sting is likely to provoke an even more serious reaction.
*See also* ACCIDENTS/Bites and stings.

## Allergic rhinitis (hay fever)

The child is allergic to something he breathes. The mucous membranes in the nose swell and discharge clear fluid. The eyes may also be red and watery. He may sneeze frequently and will certainly keep rubbing his eyes and nose because they itch.
*Hay fever* This is the most common type, the allergens being some of the many pollens released during spring and early summer.
*Seasonal allergic rhinitis* This occurs in the autumn. The allergen is one of the molds which form on plants as they die down and on root crops brought in for winter storage.
*Perennial allergic rhinitis* This can be due to many allergens. The house mite is especially suspect if the condition worsens in winter. Attempts to reduce the population of house mites in the child's bedroom may well be worth the considerable trouble (see below: Asthma).

You will not confuse allergic rhinitis with a head cold or with "catarrh" if you remember that rhinitis is itchy, which a cold is not and that in a cold the nose is obstructed by a thick discharge. In rhinitis it is obstructed by internal swelling and the discharge is thin and watery.

Although seldom more than tiresome in itself allergic rhinitis can presage asthma in a child generally prone to allergy. So consult your doctor during his first attack.

Avoidance of the allergen if it is known is the best "treatment," otherwise medically supervised use of nasal decongestants and/or antihistamine medicines may give some relief.

## Asthma

The allergen is in the air the child breathes and the reaction with his antibodies takes place in the bronchi (breathing tubes), leading to an outpouring of mucus, which gives his breathing the characteristic "wheeze," and to muscle spasm, which makes the process of breathing (especially breathing out) difficult. A severely asthmatic child may always be wheezy and breathless on exertion, but an asthma attack is a different and unpleasantly dramatic event.

*Attacks* These usually take place at night. The child wakes, unable to release his breath in order to take in the next. Panic tenses muscles and tears take breath he cannot spare.

*What to do*
☐ On the first occasion ring the doctor urgently. There are other causes for frightening breathlessness. He must make sure that it is asthma and decide, with you, if the child needs immediate medication to stop the attack.
☐ While you wait, sit the child up and calm him as much as you can. If he is old enough to understand, assure him that whatever it feels like enough air will get through. Explain that the more he can relax the easier it will be. Reading aloud may provide some helpful distraction.

*After the first attack* With your doctor's help, identify at least the principal allergens so as to avoid heavy concentrations. Feathers, down, animal hair and natural wool are all common ones, but most common of all is the "house mite," a microscopic creature which lives off shed dead scales of human skin in house dust.

You cannot clear any house of mites but you can reduce the population, especially in the child's bedroom. Plastic foam mattresses and upholstery, hard floors with washable rugs laundered weekly, unlined cotton curtains and synthetic quilts instead of conventional bedding will all prove inhospitable to the mites. Damp dusting will prevent their precipitation into the air, while frequent washing of clothing, etc. will prevent a build-up. In a serious case the child may have to keep toys, books, etc., elsewhere so that he does not spend all night breathing the dust that they inevitably accumulate so quickly.

Work is being carried out on de-sensitizing children to the house mite.
*Treatment of subsequent attacks* It may not be necessary to call the doctor for each attack once the diagnosis is established. He will instruct you on the administration of drugs to relax the muscle spasms, liquify the mucus and/or relieve anxiety. They can be administered by mouth or from special inhalers. During a severe attack administration by a doctor via injection or suppository works faster; the child may even need to be admitted to the hospital for some treatment.
*Overall treatment of the child* Repeated severe attacks of asthma can eventually damage a child's lungs and produce a "pigeon chest." Physiotherapy to clear mucus from the bronchi and to teach the child correct breathing techniques is vital in such a severe case.

If the asthma is often precipitated by infections your doctor may ask to be called at each sign of illness so that he can give antibiotics early if they are appropriate. Long-term antibiotic treatment is sometimes given to protect a child during the winter months.

The doctor will also want to discuss emotional and environmental precipitating factors. Don't be offended when the consultation turns to your discipline and your dust.

# Eczema

Infantile eczema tends to run in families. There will probably be a close relation susceptible either to eczema or to some other allergic complaint such as hay fever or asthma. Like all allergic conditions it will be made temporarily worse by anything which upsets the child: a separation from home, for example. The vast majority of children outgrow the eczema (although not necessarily the tendency to allergic complaints) by the age of three.

The disorder usually begins with bright red scaly and wildly itching patches on the cheeks. There may well be scurf on the scalp and this may lead to bad patches of itchy rash behind the ears. Occasionally the rash spreads to cover large areas of the body, but it is usually concentrated in the moist creases: in the groin, behind the knees, etc. When the eczema is very active, acute inflammation makes the scaly red patches moist. Eczema itches continually and scratching will make the patches sore and may infect them. The baby is likely to be desperately miserable.

*What to do*
There is no cure, but you can do a great deal to keep infantile eczema manageable.
☐ With your doctor's help, look for a cause. Extensive testing for allergens is not helpful, but occasionally the child is allergic to cow's milk protein. Suspect this particularly if the eczema began when he was weaned from breast milk. Your doctor may recommend you to try feeding him on soy bean "milk" instead of cow's milk.
☐ Soap and water often make the skin worse. Use mineral oil or baby lotion on cotton balls instead.
☐ Avoid rough or scratchy clothes: several layers of thin silky materials will be better than a big woolly sweater.
☐ Keep fingernails very short and clean, so that scratching rubs the skin rather than cutting it. NB Don't put him into mittens or splints however bad his skin becomes. It will be torture for him if he cannot even rub the place.
☐ Provide masses of entertainment and occupation to distract him from the itching. He must have special attention for the moment; when you cannot give it to him yourselves try to find someone else who will share the burden. If you don't expect him to play peacefully by himself or to drop calmly off to sleep every night you will not be quite so maddened by his continual frenzies of itching-scratching-crying.
☐ Stay in touch with your doctor. If you get desperate or the eczema suddenly gets very bad there are extreme measures he can take to help you all over the bad patch. He may, for example, prescribe a cortisone preparation for the skin or give the child a sedative for a few days to help the itching and get him (and you) some rest. For an older child he may be able to arrange a priority place in a playgroup if you and he both feel this would help. Severe infantile eczema can be an overwhelming burden for all of you, so don't suffer alone and in silence.

# Food allergies, intolerances and reactions to additives

Sometimes a child who is allergic to a certain protein in his food or drink may produce symptoms which seem entirely unrelated to his digestive tract; eczema, for example, or asthma or urticaria.

Where food or drink leads to symptoms which are clearly digestive, it is often difficult to tell whether the problem is a true allergy or whether it is one of many kinds of intolerance. If cow's milk gives your baby acute diarrhea you may feel that it does not matter whether his body has actually made antibodies to cow's milk protein or whether he is simply unable to digest the stuff. But it may matter very much. If his symptoms are caused by allergy to the protein, his diet will need to be altered accordingly. But if he is not allergic to the protein but just intolerant of the lactose in the milk because his body lacks the enzyme, lactase, which normally breaks it down, he will need different handling. Food allergies and intolerances are complex and often interrelated. It is important not to leap to conclusions but to seek medical advice with an open mind, prepared to accept that there may not always be a simple solution to a problem and that it may take a long time to solve.

An open mind is also necessary when a child seems to react badly to colorings, flavorings or other additives. The range of ill-effects which may be expected from these substances has been so widely broadcast that many parents are ready to ascribe almost any behavior problem, from sleeplessness to "hyperactivity," to these chemicals. Some children certainly are hypersensitive to some of them, and a smaller overall load of added chemicals would certainly improve most people's diet. But it is often a mistake to attribute particular kinds of problem-behavior to specific chemicals without good evidence. There are many small children who are not allowed to have any orange drinks because tartrazine is thought to keep them from settling in the evening and sleeping through the night. Few of their parents realize that there is also tartrazine in many other completely ordinary foods that the children are eating regularly, such as custard or canned peas.

If banning certain foods makes those families feel they have banished a problem, perhaps it does not matter if the cause and effect relationship does not really hold. But banning particular foods, or categories of food, is not something to be undertaken lightly, because not only does it deprive the children of those items, it also makes them feel "different" and anxious about their own bodies. If a child really is allergic to strawberries, intolerant of milk or hypersensitive to tartrazine, then clearly he will have to accept appropriate dietary limitations. But aim, with a doctor's help, to make the limitation temporary and incomplete. There are very *very* few children who need to be embarrassed by detailed inquiries into the contents of a birthday cake or to feel anxious about what will happen to them after they have munched a furtive, much longed-for chocolate.

## Urticaria (hives; nettle rash)

This is a general term for an allergic skin reaction. White weals surrounded by reddened areas appear. The skin itches furiously. If the reaction is intense, the weals may become large swollen white patches which have the effect of making the child's face or body look quite misshapen.

The weals and the itching usually vanish within a few hours but new ones can appear as the old ones wane so that the child has urticaria for several days at a time.

Many children have a single attack of urticaria and nobody ever knows the cause. If it recurs frequently, however, the misery of the itching and the damage done to the skin by scratching may make it necessary to search for the allergen. This is frequently a food (such as shellfish or strawberries), a drug (such as penicillin) or an insect bite. In a few allergic children emotional tension clearly predisposes the skin to react in this way. Your doctor will help you discover the cause of your child's urticaria, if this is not at once obvious.

*What to do*
☐ Relieve the itching with calamine lotion or a bath containing two tablespoons of sodium bicarbonate. If the urticaria goes on for several days your doctor might prescribe antihistamine medicines like Benadryl Hydrochloride. These medicines directly help a few sufferers and their sedative side-effects can help others to sleep right through the irritation.
*Angio-neurotic edema* An uncommon but dramatic form of urticaria. A single large area of the skin, commonly around the eye, lip or penis, suddenly puffs up into a large white weal. The swelling usually goes down in a few hours and the allergen is seldom discovered.

Occasionally angio-neurotic edema affects the soft tissues of the throat and causes difficulty in breathing. Any sign of obstructed breathing should, of course, lead you to take the child without delay straight to the nearest source of emergency help.
*Papular urticaria* An allergic reaction of the child's skin to the protein in animal fleas. The white weals on reddened skin look a little like normal urticaria except that each weal is topped by a round spot with a little blister of clear fluid on it. The weals will disappear in a few hours, but the spots may stay longer and, since they itch, it is likely that the child may scratch the blisters off the top and infect the spots.

Calamine lotion will help the itching, but the trouble will recur if the child has any contact at all with animal fleas. Touch is enough.
☐ Dust all pets against fleas.
☐ Keep the child out of places like hay barns, desirable play areas though they are, because they are likely to have a flea population.

If you have real trouble with this minor but tiresome complaint take your child to the doctor. He may think it worth giving antihistamine drugs such as Benadryl Hydrochloride, which is sold over the counter, a trial.

# Appendicitis

The appendix is a small blind tube leading off the lower part of the intestine. It seems to serve no purpose and, being a "dead end" with no through drainage, is liable to infection. Infection leads to inflammation, with pain, often vomiting, sometimes fever. The child has appendicitis.

When a doctor sees a child with acute abdominal pain but few other symptoms, it is usually because parents know that, if he has appendicitis, it is essential to remove the appendix before it becomes so inflamed and infected that it bursts, spreading infection throughout the abdomen. In fact, appendicitis is unusual in children under five (it is much more common in later childhood and adolescence). In very young children the symptoms that suggest appendicitis are quite often caused by tonsilitis, which causes inflammation and swelling of glands in the abdomen as well as in the throat. But since any child who is ill and in pain should be seen by a doctor, don't let the likelihood that it is *not* appendicitis delay your call. Even doctors and surgeons find diagnosing appendicitis difficult and, knowing how serious a "missed" diagnosis can be, they often play safe by acting on suspicion. So don't feel that your doctor "made a mistake" in arranging to have your child admitted to the hospital if he turns out not to need an appendectomy. And don't be angry if a surgeon does operate and removes a normal appendix. Even an unnecessary operation is infinitely better than the life-threatening peritonitis, which results when an inflamed appendix is allowed to burst.
*See also* STOMACH ACHE.

*Appendectomy*
Provided the appendix has not burst, the operation is simple and the child recovers quickly. Although he will have considerable pain for two or three days after surgery, it is important that he should breathe deeply and cough freely to prevent pneumonia. Constipation can be a problem, too, as the child is terrified to strain. If you are rooming-in at the hospital or at least spending all day with him, you can help with these vital matters under direction from the nurses. They know what should be done, but you know the child.
*See also* HOSPITAL: TONSILS & ADENOIDS.

# Athlete's foot

This is a form of "ringworm," a fungus infection which can also affect the scalp and the body. Athlete's foot affects the skin between a child's toes, making it wildly itchy. When his scratching draws your attention to his feet and your examine them, you will find that the affected skin looks white and sodden and that scratching or rubbing removes it to reveal raw, sore areas underneath.

Athlete's foot is usually spread from victim to victim, one depositing fungus on the floor, the next picking it up. School locker rooms are obvious sources of infection and so are swimming areas if children are allowed to walk around the footbaths designed to prevent such infections! Nobody with athlete's foot should go barefoot, but sweaty shoes and socks will provide a hospitable environment for the fungus, so open sandals are the best indoor wear while the infection is active. If wearing socks, use cotton and not synthetics.

*What to do*
Various special creams are available over the counter. Applied regularly according to the instructions, they usually clear active infection within a couple of days, also reducing the itching so that the child is less likely to spread infection from one foot to the other.

Powders are also available but seem less effective. Powdering the inside of all the child's shoes may, however, be a useful adjunct to treatment with one of the creams.

NB Very occasionally athlete's foot can be spread to another part of the body as ringworm. If a child has been scratching his infected toes, make sure that his hands are washed thoroughly and immediately – before he scratches elsewhere!

*See also* RINGWORM.

# Boils and pimples

Every hair grows from its root to the surface of the skin along a channel called a "hair follicle."
*Pimples* If an infection starts where the hair emerges from the skin a white pimple forms containing a tiny amount of pus which will discharge itself in a day or so. Let it alone.
*Boils* Infection occurs lower down near the root of the hair. The boil starts as a hard red tender lump that gets bigger and more painful until it makes a "head" and the pus escapes. This usually takes two or three days. Since infection spreads very easily from one hair follicle to another, boils often appear in crops. They are especially likely if a child has been ill or is below par for some reason.

*What to do*
Take the child to the doctor if:
□ A boil does not come to a head in five days.
□ It is in an awkward place such as the ear, the armpit or on the bottom of a child in diapers.
□ You can see red streaks under the skin running away from it.
□ The child has swollen tender glands in the area.
For home treatment:
□ Clean the skin around the boil with alcohol: this may help to prevent one boil turning into a whole crop of boils.
□ Dress the boil by stretching an adhesive bandage across it: this will lessen the pain by preventing too much movement and pulling.
NB Don't squeeze a boil until it has made a yellow head on its own. You may force the pus downward. Don't use hot compresses. They hurt a great deal and may also spread the infection. Don't use antiseptic or ointments unless prescribed by a doctor. They do no good, and they too may spread the infection.

# Circumcision

There is no rationale for "routine" removal of the foreskin from the tip ("glans") of the penis in newborn boys. We know, now, that the foreskin and glans are *meant* to be fused at birth and that the foreskin only gradually becomes separated. It may not be possible (or necessary or desirable) to wash the smegma from under a little boy's foreskin until he is four or five years old.

Circumcision is still carried out as part of religious ritual and observance, however. If your son is circumcised in his first couple of weeks, the tip of the penis will be dressed with gauze. Urine will sting so expect some distress. You can lessen it by changing his diaper *very* frequently so that the sore place is not left in contact with the urine. Ask your doctor or pharmacist whether he or she can recommend a cream which will act as a barrier between raw skin and urine.

Very occasionally circumcision is *needed* later in a boy's life. Sadly, this is usually because of unwise attempts to pull back the foreskin before it has loosened, leading to bleeding and scar tissue which may permanently *fix* the foreskin to the glans. Sometimes, though, circumcision is recommended because the boy has had repeated episodes of infection under the foreskin which are both painful and difficult to clear.
□ Once circumcision is recommended, think carefully about its timing. Little boys feel possessive and proud of their penises – and so they should. The younger they are, the more difficult it is for them to understand that removing the foreskin will not damage the organ, and that the painful and humiliating procedure is not carried out as a punishment for masturbation or general wickedness. Circumcision is rarely urgent. Wait, if possible, until the boy is over six.
□ Circumcision is upsetting even though it is a minor operation. Try to arrange for your son to be admitted to the hospital only as a day-patient. In this way he can usually be spared the additional trauma of a hospital stay with lots of strange nurses looking at his private parts.
□ Older boys often find the few days after circumcision extremely painful. There are many ways in which you can help to keep pressure off his sore penis. If sitting in a chair is agony, for example, a bean-bag chair may be the answer. An athletic supporter may enable him to tolerate underpants and pants which are unbearable without.
*See also* HOSPITAL.

# Colds

These are caused by virus infection. Sitting in a draft, having wet feet, or going out without a coat cannot cause a cold, although severe chilling might possibly lower a child's resistance to an infection that his body was already fighting.
*Babies* Young babies have little resistance to common colds: they catch them easily and may be quite ill. For a few months, at least, it is worth

doing what you can to protect them from outsiders' colds although there is no point at all in trying to protect them from family ones.

☐ Take the baby to a doctor if he seems ill, whether or not he has fever. Babies *can* have extra-*low* temperatures when they are ill.

☐ Remember that he will find mouth-breathing difficult and that he will *have* to breathe through his nose to suck from breast or bottle. Ask your doctor if he recommends decongestant nose drops before feedings (*never* use them if he does not) and/or clearing the nose with a nasal syringe.

☐ Keep an eye on the quantity of milk/water the baby manages to take while a cold is bothering him in this way. If sucking is really difficult and his appetite is also reduced, he just might become dehydrated (short of fluid). Don't hesitate to take him back to the doctor if he should seem floppy, lethargic, dry-skinned, or if his diaper should still be dry after two or three hours, or be wet only four or five times in 24 hours.

*Toddlers and children* Children often run a fever, or even vomit, at the beginning of a cold. But once it is established they are seldom ill – only uncomfortable. It helps if the child is shown how to blow his nose effectively, by closing one nostril with a finger while he blows down the other. If he relies on sucking a pacifier or his fingers or thumb for getting to sleep, there may be a case for using nose drops at bedtime too. But don't use them more often than your doctor recommends.

*Complications* Colds often get worse before they get better, because once the viruses have a foothold, they lower the child's resistance and can therefore multiply. Complications occasionally set in if, because of this lowered resistance, harmful bacteria enter, leading to "secondary infections," like bronchitis, pneumonia or a middle ear infection. Suspect secondary infection if the child runs a fever after the first day, has a thick greenish-yellow nasal discharge; a thick or wheezy cough, sore throat, earache or deafness, or seems ill, lethargic, lacking in appetite.

While a doctor cannot prescribe medicines which are against cold viruses, he can prescribe antibiotics against bacteria. Call him as soon as a common cold begins to look unusual.

# Cold sores (herpes simplex)

Some people, children and adults, are carriers of a virus called herpes simplex. Most of the time the virus remains dormant, although the child can pass it on and nothing can be done to stop this.

When he is run down, usually when he has a cold (which is where this infection gets it popular, but inaccurate, name) the virus attacks. The first attack usually takes the form of a crop of extremely painful ulcers in the mouth. Later attacks take the form of unpleasant sores round the mouth or nostrils, starting as red patches, becoming open and weepy and then forming scabs which tend to crack.

*What to do*
Cold sores are very liable to become infected. Your doctor may prescribe special ointment with a greasy base which will protect against infection and cracking. The cold sore will probably vanish in about a week.

If your child, or you, suffer from recurrent cold sores, ask if your doctor will prescribe a specific ointment which, applied as soon as the first signs (redness, itching) appear, may abort the attack. NB The same virus which is responsible for cold sores can also be responsible for a form of genital herpes. If you or your partner have active cold sores avoid having oral sex.
*See also* MOUTH ULCERS.

# Color blindness

This affects about eight in 100 boys and one in 200 girls. The usual confusion is between red and green with both appearing as a similar brownish hue. Confusions between other colors are possible but rare. Diagnosing color blindness early is difficult as children often confuse the *names* given to colors and may seem color-blind when they are not. The problem should be obvious by the time the child is four years old.

☐ Warn all teachers. Color coding is extensively used in teaching – especially math. Help will be needed.

☐ Remember that traffic lights are red/green and that "red for danger" is a common signal on machinery, etc. Protect him.

# Constipation

Left to themselves the bowels open, by reflex, when the rectum is full. The reflex can be inhibited by the voluntary control of a toilet-trained child but will recur, from time to time, until he accepts that it is a convenient time to pass a motion.

Children's bowels have their own particular rhythm and only in a minority does this involve daily opening. Two motions a day or one every four days are perfectly normal *provided that when the motion is passed it is soft enough for ease and comfort, yet formed.*

☐ Don't decide that your child is constipated because he hasn't "gone" for several days.

☐ Only a motion which is so hard that it is difficult and painful to pass suggests constipation.

If your child does become constipated *don't* resort to laxatives. Whatever your own adult habits, you can save your child a lot of grief in later life by steadfastly refusing to expose his bowels to insult. If you are a laxative-user yourself – or somebody whose idea of good health has to include daily bowel movements – pretend to yourself that laxatives for children are available only on prescription and consult your doctor before giving them to your child. Treat painful hard motions by:

☐ Increasing the amount of fiber ("roughage") in a child's diet, offering additional raw fruit, vegetables, salads, wholegrain bread and so forth.

☐ Increasing the fluid intake of a baby or child.
☐ Making sure that he has plenty of opportunity for exercise.

If these measures do not work and the next motion is also painfully hard, consult your doctor. He may suggest a "stool softener" which will make the process of defecation comfortable for the child without ruining his natural bowel rhythm.
*See also* LAXATIVES.

# Convulsions or seizures

Convulsions or "fits" in young children are usually caused by a sudden rise in body temperature at the beginning of an illness. The sudden fever irritates the brain, which is less stable in young children than in older people. The irritated brain gives abnormal "messages" to the nerves which, in their turn, "instruct" the muscles to clench and contract in quick succession.

The tendency to feverish convulsions usually runs in families. The first episode generally occurs between the ages of two and three, and once the child has one, he may be liable to have another any time he runs a high temperature. He will outgrow the tendency completely by the time he reaches school age.

*Recognizing a convulsion*
Since it is *sudden* fever that most often provokes a convulsion you will not always know in advance that your toddler or child is unwell. He may suddenly "have a fit" while playing. Often, though, you will have been aware that he was unwell and he may be in bed, or resting on the sofa, when he begins to convulse. If his fever rises while he is asleep, the disturbance of you waking him or lifting him may start the convulsion off.

In a "typical" febrile convulsion the child's body suddenly stiffens and then the muscles of his body, arms and legs clench, relax and clench again so that he jerks and shudders. His whole body may be involved or only his limbs. His face may be involved so that he grimaces and his teeth clench. The whole convulsion may only last for a few seconds or may last for a minute or two but however long or short it may be it will seem like a lifetime to you. Convulsions are not dangerous. Your child will not die during this one however terrible it looks. But "fits" *do* look horrible and you may find yourself seized with a passionate desire to get away, with a superstitious terror of the whole episode.

*What to do*
☐ Don't leave a child who is convulsing: he might fall or roll off the bed; he might vomit and choke on the vomit; he could be terrified when he comes around after the "fit."
☐ If he isn't on the floor already, put him there, preferably on his side so that any vomit runs harmlessly out of his mouth. If he is on a bed or sofa, protect him from rolling off but don't try to restrain his limbs; you might wrench a muscle or even cause a fracture.

☐ Don't try to force open his mouth to protect him from biting his tongue; you are much more likely to break his teeth or injure his jaw.
☐ Remember (because it may comfort you) that while the convulsion lasts he is unconscious. When it is over he will probably drop straight into deep sleep but if he rouses first he will need reassurance. He will not remember the "fit" but may feel extraordinary and be amazed to find himself on the floor.
☐ As soon as he is peaceful and safe again, call your doctor.
☐ While you are waiting for the doctor to return your call, start cooling the child. Don't bother to take his temperature because the convulsion will have raised it. Just assume that it was too high and start reducing it. Take off warm clothing or bedding; cool the room if necessary; fan the child. Don't try to give him fever-reducing medicine or to reduce the fever by sponging him. Disturbance just might start the convulsion off again and you should therefore wait until you are in contact with the doctor.

While one convulsion does the child no harm, a big one every couple of months is not good for him. The doctor may advise you to try to keep the child's temperature down whenever he is unwell and to give him a prescribed sedative medicine at the first signs of illness. During a period when the child is completely well the doctor may suggest that he should be tested to make quite sure that the convulsions are only fever convulsions, with no epileptic illness behind them.
*See also* FEVER.

# Coughs

A child coughs because there is extra mucus somewhere in his upper respiratory system. The cough is designed to rid his body of the mucus and is therefore valuable in itself.

The most usual reason for couging is a simple cold. Mucus which does not appear as nasal discharge trickles down his throat, tickles and makes him cough. But the mucus may not be in his nose, it could be anywhere from deep in his lungs upward. And it may not be caused by a cold. It could be caused by asthma, croup, bronchitis, whooping cough, pneumonia . . . so don't try to diagnose a cough yourself. Let the doctor do it after an examination.
*Coughs with vomiting* Usually mean only that the child has swallowed enough coughed-up mucus to make him sick. As he vomits, his stomach muscles will press on his lungs and air passages, pressing out more of the mucus that is bothering him. So although unpleasant for the child, the vomiting is not a bad thing.
*Coughs with difficult breathing* If the coughing child's breathing is noisy, difficult or painful, sucks in his lower ribs and/or distends his nostrils, he may have serious respiratory trouble. Call the doctor immediately.

# Crib deaths (SIDS)

After the first month of life, more babies under six months old die from Sudden Infant Death Syndrome (SIDS) than from illnesses and accidents put together. Despite much research these deaths are still not understood. Until they are, little can be done to prevent them. But accurate information can do a little to help anxious parents or even those who must suddenly come to terms with inexplicable bereavement.

All crib deaths are unexpected deaths but not all unexpected deaths are crib deaths. This point, often missed by media reporting, is essential for any understanding of SIDS.

When a baby is put to bed healthy, or with a mild "cold" which has just been pronounced unimportant by a doctor, and is subsequently found dead, investigations sometimes reveal a previously unsuspected condition – such as congenital heart or kidney disorder or a fulminating infection – which has proved fatal. Such an unexpected death is tragic and shocking but it is not a crib death. It is unfortunate that it may be counted into the statistics for SIDS. It is even more unfortunate that the media sometimes apply the cause of one such death to all unexpected infant deaths, so that headlines appear in the newspapers saying "Crib death caused by heart disorders." If the cause of a death can be ascertained, then it cannot be said to be a crib death.

If all unexpected infant deaths are lumped together, statistical "risk factors" appear and lead to media statements about crib deaths which are as misleading as they are terrifying. It has been stated, for instance, that crib deaths "are more common amongst deprived families." Unexpected infant deaths *are* more common where medical, social and educational standards are lower, but the incidence of true crib death is the same for all social classes. It has similarly been stated that SIDS is more common among bottle-fed than breast-fed babies. Breast-feeding offers protection against many potential infant ills; breast-fed babies are likely to be "healthier" and therefore the incidence of unexpected death is slightly lower. But surveys have shown that there is no relationship between true crib death and breast- or bottle-feeding. So do not be alarmed by scare headlines, such as "Mothers who smoke risk crib death." Above all do not decide that your smoking caused your recent bereavement.

Anything you can do to promote your good health in pregnancy (including giving up smoking!) will be good for your unborn child, and everything you can do to ensure that he is well-cared for will be good for him after birth. But nothing you do, have done in the past or can do in the future will specifically cause or prevent a true crib death as far as we yet know.

Any unexpected death must legally be investigated by the police and made the subject of a coroner's inquest. After an infant death such inquiries sometimes add to parents' agony because they, or their neighbors, feel that they are under suspicion of child abuse or neglect. But it is only through such investigations that parents can hope to find an explanation for the death of their baby. Together with careful assignment of the cause of death on death certificates, posthumous inquiries are the best way of supplying accurate information about true crib deaths and therefore of helping to prevent them one day.

In the meantime, parents whose previous baby died from genuine SIDS, and who cannot face the months of worry that their new baby might also simply stop breathing, may be offered a more or less sophisticated home version of the "respiratory monitors" used in hospital intensive care units. These "crib death alarms" sound if the baby's breathing is interrupted. There are reported instances of babies being stimulated to start breathing again when, left unattended, they would have died. But there are also families who found life with the crib death alarm intolerable and who feel that the need to use it and monitor it constantly distorted the early life of a baby who, with hindsight, was not at risk.

# Croup

A form of laryngitis which has dramatic effects in babies or small children simply because their breathing tubes are so small. Infection from a virus cold moves downward to the voice box (larynx) and the windpipe (trachea). In an older person this would lead to hoarseness, a tickly throat and a cough. In babies and small children, the inflammation of the larynx can cause enough swelling to obstruct the passage of air through it. Instead of ordinary laryngitis the child has croup. If a baby or small child sounds hoarse, and his breathing makes a rasping noise, you would be wise to take him to the doctor even if he does not seem particularly ill. You may be able to save yourself and him from the nasty experience of acute croup in the middle of the night, which is an emergency. *Symptoms* The child wakes in the night with a hard, painful hacking cough, usually followed by crying. As he draws his breath to cry he makes the extraordinary barking noise which is diagnostic of croup. In severe croup the child's breathing will be extremely labored and his lower chest will suck in with every breath. He will be able to speak only in a hoarse whisper, if at all.

*What to do*
Call your doctor urgently. Follow the emergency steps below to relieve the child's breathing while you wait for him to get back to you.
☐ Try to calm the child. He is short of oxygen and the feeling makes him panic, but the more he struggles and cries the more oxygen he will need. If you can get him to keep still and quiet (and even better to relax), he will discover that the reduced amount of oxygen he is getting is enough.
☐ Take him to a window and let him take six breaths of night air. Cold or moist air will reduce the swellings of the larynx enough to get a little more air past.
☐ Then carry him to the bathroom (or into the

shower stall), close the window, and turn on every hot tap so that the room fills with steam. Stay in the steam-filled room for ten minutes. If you have no hot water supply an electric kettle will steam up a small room quite quickly.

The cold air and the wet air will usually relieve the child's breathing within ten minutes, so that you can talk to the doctor. Your doctor will help you to decide whether the emergency is now over or whether the child's breathing is sufficiently obstructed that the child should be brought to his office or taken to the hospital.

If the cold air and steam treatment relieved his breathing but the croupy distress starts again, a cold air vaporizer, which blows a stream of cool moist air, may keep him comfortable. Used routinely, whenever your child has upper respiratory symptoms and fever, it will often abort attacks of croup.

# Dehydration

It is far more important for people to have enough to drink than to have enough to eat because human bodies have better reserves of energy than of fluid. Babies need to drink more than older people, per pound of their bodyweight, and they need to drink more frequently. Their turnover of fluid is more rapid and they have a smaller safety margin protecting them from serious ill-effects if water is scarce. The very few newborn babies who do not demand feeding during the night need to be woken to suck for just this reason: even if they are not hungry, managing for a whole night without fluid is far too long.

Dehydration is not the simple "drying out" which the name suggests. A body that is seriously short of water cannot maintain the complex and delicate balance of chemicals on which its functioning depends. This is why a baby or very young child who has become dehydrated will not instantly be restored by a drink of water. He will need a careful mixture of chemicals and fluid dripped directly into his bloodstream.

*Ensuring an adequate fluid intake*
You cannot rely on a baby to recognize and communicate his own need for extra fluid, especially while milk constitutes both food and drink in one:
☐ Never add extra milk powder or concentrate or any cereal to a baby's bottle. Always offer extra water to a baby who refuses a milk feeding.
☐ Remember to offer your baby extra fluid when he begins to reduce his milk intake in favor of "solid" foods.
☐ Offer extra fluids to babies and toddlers whenever they are feverish or the weather is hot.

*Preventing dehydration*
Diarrhea and/or vomiting, *especially* if accompanied by fever, make a baby very liable to dehydration because each episode may deprive his body of more fluid than his last drink put in.

The younger the child, the greater this risk. Babies under six months should be seen by a doctor as a matter of urgency. Babies under a year should be seen on the day the illness begins. You should consult your doctor, at least by telephone, about any child under three who has had diarrhea, with or without vomiting, for more than the duration of twenty-four hours.

Doctors often recommend "rehydratant fluids" rather than ordinary drinks. They provide a drink which the child's body can easily retain and absorb and which will help to maintain its biochemical balance. They are widely available over the counter. Don't use rehydratant fluids *instead* of seeking medical advice, though.

*Emergency treatment of possible dehydration*
If a baby or child should become ill with diarrhea and/or vomiting or an older child or adult feels giddy and unwell after violent exertion in hot conditions, when you are far from medical help and have no rehydratant fluid, the following mixture will be better retained and used by the body than plain water:

Take 1 pint drinking water.
Add $\frac{1}{4}$ level *teaspoon* of salt.
Add 1 level *tablespoon* of sugar. Stir well and give small drinks ad lib.

# Dentistry

Not every dentist works happily with children under five or feels able to give the time a toddler needs for familiarization visits at which the teeth may not even be fully inspected, let alone treated! If the dentist who treats you does not specialize in work with small children, look for one who does. Dentists who specialize in children's care are called pedodontists.

Many parents defer children's first visits to the dentist because they remember their own with horror. Things have changed. A child who is given the chance to get used to visiting a dentist in his second year and is then taken regularly, every six months or so whether he is likely to need any treatment or not, can take the whole matter in his stride. Even when he does, one day, need a filling, new techniques mean that it should bother him no more than his immunization injections from the doctor. He may not like it but he does not have to be terrified.

Some parents neglect early dental appointments because they do not think it is worthwhile to keep checking on first teeth which are going to fall out and be replaced. But healthy first teeth are important. They keep open the proper spaces for later teeth and, by allowing a proper "bite" and facilitating the development of the jaw, they make later orthodontic problems much less likely.

A dentist is also the best person to advise you about fluoride. Fluoride certainly strengthens tooth enamel whether it is given orally or applied topically to the teeth themselves. If the drinking water in your area is low in fluoride, you may be advised to give your baby and child a supplement. If your dentist considers this unnecessary but recommends a fluoride toothpaste, he or she may be one of many who believe that the paste children swallow while cleaning their teeth is as valuable as the paste that goes on them. Treatment with fluoride gels is also sometimes used to help weakened tooth enamel to repair itself, thus preventing the otherwise inevitable development of a cavity.

A good relationship with a friendly dentist can be an important educational influence on your child, giving authoritative reinforcement to everything you are trying to teach about good diet, especially the importance of limiting the intake of sweets and sugary drinks.

# Diarrhea

In diarrhea the contents of the intestine are hurried through so less water is absorbed through the intestinal walls and the bowel movement remains "loose" or liquid.

☐ Diarrhea can be caused by a variety of infections, by different forms of food poisoning, by dietary indiscretion or even by an emotional upset. A baby or toddler with diarrhea should be checked by a doctor, and any child who has diarrhea *associated with vomiting* requires medical advice because the two together can mean that the body loses more fluid than it can afford (see DEHYDRATION). Otherwise you need only consider diarrhea as a symptom of illness if the child does not seem entirely well in every other way.

*Giardiasis*
The parasite "Giardia Lambia" lives and feeds in the human bowel and can be passed from one "host" to another via contaminated food and drink. Victims excrete the parasite in the form of cysts which can contaminate fresh water and remain infective to the next human host for months on end.

Many lakes and rivers in remote areas of the United States are known to be contaminated with Giardia Lambia and it is thought that the increasing popularity of back-packing and wilderness trips was originally responsible for the increased prevalence of Giardiasis, which is now an extremely common cause of diarrhea among children in day-care centers and kindergartens. Once the parasites are introduced into groups living closely together, the disease is hard to control, as symptoms may be minimal, the diagnosis unsuspected and the patient infective for as long as cysts remain in her feces which may be for many months.

Giardiasis produces persistent diarrhea in which the stools smell particularly unpleasant. It often (but not invariably) produces a falling off of the appetite. There are sometimes colicky pains.

If there has been an outbreak, or even a single case, of Giardiasis in your child's group, take her to the doctor promptly at the first sign of diarrhea even without other symptoms. Treatment will render her non-infective and help control the spread of the parasite.

☐ It is safer not to drink water from lakes or streams, however pure they appear, without using chemical sterilizing tablets or boiling it thoroughly before using it.

# Diet

Babies and young children who are basically healthy do not starve themselves in the midst of plenty. However limited your child's diet or however eccentric his food fads, his natural appetite will ensure that he selects from what you offer a diet that is adequate for him, just as long as you can avoid turning the meal-table into a battleground.

It's hard to seem relaxed when you are worried, though, and hard *not* to worry if you think your child is going short of vital necessities. The following reminders of the basic nutrients children do need, and of the comparatively tiny quantities of various foods which will provide them, may help.

## What nutrients your child needs

|  | For babies of 14 lb (6.4 kg), i.e., large baby at 3 months; average at 4½ months; small at 6 months | For babies of 19 lbs (8.6 kg), i.e., large baby at 6 months; average at 9 months; small at 12 months | For toddlers weighing about 25–30 lbs (11.4 kg), i.e., aged about 1–3 years | For pre-school children weighing around 35 lbs (15.9 kg), i.e., aged about 3–5 years | Notes |
|---|---|---|---|---|---|
| Energy | 760 kcal | 950 kcal | 1,200 kcal | 1,600 kcal | ☐ Minimum protein levels, i.e. those below which there is a possibility of protein deficiency, are approximately two thirds of these figures. |
| Protein | 20 g | 20 g | 30 g | 40 g | ☐ kcal = kilocalories (often incorrectly abbreviated to "calorie" in nutrition). This is the amount of energy required to heat 1 liter of water 1°C (1 pint of water 3°F) |
| Minerals Calcium | 600 mg | 600 mg | 500 mg | 500 mg | |
| Iron | 6 mg | 6 mg | 7 mg | 8 mg | g = gram = 1/28 oz |

| Vitamins | | | | |
|---|---|---|---|---|
| A (Retinol) | 450 µg | 450 µg | 300 µg | 300 µg |
| D | 10 µg | 10 µg | 10 µg | 10 µg |
| Thiamine (B1) | 0.3 mg | 0.3 mg | 0.5 mg | 0.6 mg |
| Riboflavin (B2) | 0.4 mg | 0.4 mg | 0.6 mg | 0.8 mg |
| Niacin (Nicotinic acid) | 5 mg | 5 mg | 7 mg | 9 mg |
| C (Ascorbic acid) | 15 mg | 15 mg | 20 mg | 20 mg |

mg = milligram = 1/1000 g
µg = microgram = 1/1000 mg
□ **Vitamin A** in a diet consists roughly of 2/3 retinol and 1/3 carotene, a related chemical. The measure is therefore in "retinol equivalents."

| Need | Source | Examples |
|---|---|---|
| **CALORIES (energy)** | | |

**CALORIES (energy)**

Calories are a measure of the amount of energy our bodies take in. We need energy to keep our bodies ticking over and warm, to keep our hearts, lungs and digestions working. We need more when we are awake and moving around. We need most when we do heavy physical work. Children need more calories than adults, weight for weight, both because they use a lot of physical energy and because they need a surplus for growing. If your baby gains no weight at *all* week by week or if your child gains no weight for three months, or actually loses weight, you should check with your doctor.

*All* foods contain calories. Whatever your child eats will provide him with calories. His appetite will accurately control his intake, so if he eats as much as he is hungry for he will be taking enough, while if he eats from greed not hunger he will get fat. Some foods contain more *concentrated* calories than others. Fats are the most concentrated, then sugar, and other processed carbohydrates like white flour and cereals; least concentrated are leafy vegetables.

1 oz **butter** = 211 calories; 1 oz **sugar** = 112; 1 oz **beef** = 89; 1 oz **bread** = 72; 1 oz **boiled potatoes** = 23; 1 oz **boiled cabbage** = 2.

But looking at calories per ounce of food is not very useful, because you would probably not eat a whole ounce of butter or sugar at once, whereas you would eat much more than an ounce of potato or beef.
So the calorie content of a meal made from the above might be:

3 oz **beef** = 270 calories; 6 oz **potatoes** = 138; 4 oz **cabbage** = 8; 1 oz **bread (1 slice)** = 72; $\frac{1}{4}$ oz **butter spread on bread** = 53; 2 **teaspoons sugar in tea** = 50.

**CARBOHYDRATES**

Carbohydrates provide energy for maintaining body functions and for powering activity. If not enough carbohydrates are eaten, the body will burn proteins instead. In a growing child especially, this can mean that protein needed for body growth is used for energy. Carbohydrate foods also provide the bulk of our diet, and this bulk is important in proper digestion/excretion. Sugar is, of course, pure carbohydrate and offers the body nothing except calories. But most carbohydrate foods contain other nutrients as well. Although the nutrient concentrations may be low, large quantities are consumed, so they are useful sources.

Apart from sugar and products sweetened with it, potatoes, other root vegetables, bread, all flour and flour products, all cereals and cereal products are high in carbohydrates.
There are lower proportions of carbohydrate in milk and in other vegetables and fruits.

2 oz **orange juice** = 69 g; 10 oz **milk** = 14 g; 1 oz **bread** = 15.5 g; 2 oz **boiled potato** = 11 g; 3 oz **French fried potatoes** = 32 g; $\frac{1}{2}$ oz **dry spaghetti** = 12 g; $\frac{1}{2}$ oz **flour** = 11.5 g; $\frac{1}{2}$ oz **dry rice** = 12 g; 1 oz **cereal** = 25 g; 1 oz **bar of chocolate** = 15.5 g; $\frac{1}{2}$ oz **sugar** = 15 g.
The "protein sparing" function of carbohydrates will best be fulfilled when he eats traditional combinations of foods, such as a hamburger in a bun, a hot dog in a roll, or milk and cookies.

| Need | Source | Examples |
| --- | --- | --- |

**PROTEINS**

Our tissue and muscle are made of protein. We therefore need it so that our bodies can heal and repair themselves. Children especially need protein because they are making new tissue. Proteins are made up of various combinations of chemical substances called "amino acids." There are 9 particular amino acids which a child must eat complete, and all at the same time, because his body cannot construct these out of others.

We call certain high-protein foods "first-class" because they contain these essential substances in the correct balance. Proteins in other foods are called "second-class," because, while the amino acids they contain are just as useful in themselves, the balance between them is not exactly right or else one or more of the vital 9 is missing.

"First class" protein is animal protein. Most concentrated in meat, fish, eggs, milk, cheese and other dairy produce, it is available also in any food manufactured from animal foods, such as fish sticks, sausages, or luncheon meats. Many foods which are not commonly thought of as high in protein contain egg, milk, etc., with the other ingredients. "Second class" protein is from vegetable sources. Both the concentration and the balance of the various amino acids vary so that, for example, soy bean protein is an almost-perfect substitute for animal protein; nuts are excellent sources and the amino acid balance of both potatoes and wheat (from which pasta as well as bread is made) has been shown to sustain growth well over long periods. Vegetables such as beans and peas contain high concentrations of some amino acids, although some of the vital ones are lacking. Combinations of vegetables eaten together can give the child protein which is just as good for his growth as the protein in animal foods. This is the basis of a good vegetarian diet. Since many sources of vegetable protein only just fall short of the body's requirements, a very small quantity of animal protein can balance the mixture. The addition of milk to potato, for example, produces an amino acid combination which is just as good for the child as butcher's meat.

A toddler is adequately served by 25 grams of protein (first class or completed second class) each day. Ordinary cow's **milk** yields almost 1 gram per fluid ounce so if he takes 1 pint of milk (in drinks and/or cooking) he will get 16 grams of protein. At this level he could not go short of protein whatever else he did or did not eat. If he hates milk, or is allergic to it, and takes none at all, each of the following food portions will give him one-third of his day's requirement:

1 tablespoon **minced beef**; 1 tablespoon **minced liver**; 1 tablespoon **white fish**; 1 standard 2 oz **egg**; 1 tablespoon **grated cheese**/1 slice from vacuum pack; 1½ large **sausages**; 2½ slices **luncheon meat**; 2–3 **bacon slices**; 2 slices **ham** from vacuum pack; 8 oz (2 containers) natural **yogurt**; 7 oz (3 small brickettes) **ice cream**; 3 oz **milk chocolate** (medium bar).

The following food portions will each yield one-third of his day's requirements, either in the form of a mixture amounting to first class protein, or by containing vegetable proteins known to be adequate in the presence of minute quantities of animal foods: 3 slices from cut **white or brown bread**; 4 medium size **potatoes**; 6 level tablespoons **baked beans**; 1 heaped tablespoon **roasted peanuts**; 8 average sweet or **chocolate cookies**; 4 small slices **madeira cake**; 4 individual (1 oz) bags **potato chips**.

**FATS**

The only *need* human beings have for fats is for tiny traces of three "fatty acids," which occur in all animal or vegetable fats and oils. It would be impossible to go short of these as long as you were eating anything at all. There is therefore no need for table fats and frying oils. Because they have so many calories concentrated in them, fats can be useful in feeding a child who cannot eat much bulk. They also contain the "fat soluble" vitamins A and D.

Most of our fat intake comes from butter and margarine, cooking fats and oils, lard, dripping and meat fat. There is also a considerable amount of fat in cream, milk and egg yolk. Vegetable sources include most nuts and seeds.

Fats are the most concentrated of all sources of calories.

1 slice of **bread** = 72 calories, but, with ¼ oz of **butter** added to it, equals 125.

A serving of two **boiled potatoes** = 80 calories, but with ½ oz butter added this becomes 185, while turning the same potatoes into **French fries** makes them yield 240 calories.

An 8 oz glass of full cream **milk** = 144 calories. A ½ oz serving of **heavy cream** = 64 calories.

| eed | Source | Examples |
|---|---|---|
| **TAMINS**<br>**Group**<br>ıe process by which our bodies<br>t a smooth and continuous<br>pply of energy from our<br>rbohydrates is controlled by<br>ese vitamins. We need a daily<br>take as the body cannot store<br>em. | These vitamins are distributed in such a wide variety of foods that a shortage would be most unlikely in anyone except an adult on a crash diet. Most of our intake comes from milk and milk products, flour and flour products, other cereals and cereal products. | Almost everything he eats will contribute to his daily intake of these vitamins. |
| **tamin A**<br>tamin A is important to the<br>ocesses of vision and in the<br>otection of mucous membranes.<br>ıildren need it especially as it<br>ɩo contributes to the processes<br>growth. It is stored in the liver.<br>your child drinks milk, likes<br>ɪtter, margarine or cheese, eats<br>rtified baby cereal or liver<br>casionally, he will not go short.<br>he rejects all these things *and*<br>ɪslikes carrots, he could go short.<br>ɪat is why vitamin A is included<br>ɩth the recommended<br>ultivitamin supplement. | Liver and fish liver oils are a rich source of this vitamin. Milk and milk products are a good source too. Carrots contain a substance called "carotene" which can be converted by the body to vitamin A. | A pre-school child needs about 450 micrograms daily.<br>1 pint of **milk** = 220 $\mu$g<br>2 oz **butter** = 564 $\mu$g<br>1 **egg** = 170 $\mu$g<br>1 oz **cheddar cheese** = 119 $\mu$g<br>1 small **carrot** = 500 $\mu$g |
| **tamin C**<br>ɪis vitamin is important in<br>ɑintaining the structure of the<br>ɪdy's connective tissue; it aids<br>ɔund healing and possibly helps<br>developing resistance to<br>ʃection. The body cannot store<br>tamin C so daily supplies are<br>ɪportant. | This vitamin is present in most fresh fruits and vegetables, but unfortunately it is soluble in water, destroyed by heat and destroyed by sunlight. This means that cooked vegetables and fruits are not a reliable source because they lose much of their vitamin C in the cooking water and have much of what is left destroyed by heat. Salad greens displayed outside the greengrocer may have lost most of their vitamin C through being exposed to sunlight. Citrus fruits are probably the best source. | Your child needs about 20 mg per day. The juice of one orange (2 oz of orange juice) will meet this need.<br>If fruit juices or fortified fruit syrups do not agree with your child, you will have to rely on vitamin drops or tablets. |
| **tamin D**<br>ɪis vitamin enables the child's<br>ɪdy to absorb and use the<br>lcium and phosphorus it needs<br>ɛe below) to build bones and<br>ɛth. The body can store this<br>tamin. | The body can manufacture vitamin D for itself through the action of sunlight on bare skin, so a deficiency is unlikely in a white child who spends a good deal of time outdoors during the summer months; the pigment which protects a dark child from sunburn also prevents efficient manufacture of this vitamin, so even in summer such a child risks deficiency. It is present mostly in fatty fish – like herrings and sardines – and in eggs. Supplements are added to fortified baby cereals, margarines and to milk. | Your child will get enough from these sources but milk-hating children who have abandoned baby cereals will need a supplement.<br><br>He needs about 10 micrograms each day.<br>1 egg = 1 $\mu$g<br>1 oz **herring** = 6 $\mu$g<br>1 oz **sardines** = 2 $\mu$g<br>1 oz fortified **margarine** = 2.5 $\mu$g<br>1 quart of **milk** = 10 $\mu$g |

| Need | Source | Examples |
|---|---|---|
| **MINERALS**<br>**Calcium**<br>Calcium is vital to the proper clotting of blood and to muscle function. It plays a vital part in building healthy bones and teeth. A baby's need for calcium starts in the womb, so pregnant women must eat enough. | Milk is by far the most useful and adequate source. There are useful amounts in bread, flour and other cereals too, but not enough taken on their own. If he rejects milk other milk products such as yogurt are good too, but cheese is the best and most concentrated. | He needs about 500 mg per day<br><br>1 pint of **milk** = 540 mg (more than the requirement)<br>1 oz **cheese** = 230 mg<br>1 oz **white bread** = 28 mg<br>1 oz **white flour** = 41 mg |
| **Phosphorus**<br>Phosphorus is also important to growing bones and teeth. | This is found in the same foods as calcium. | A child who is getting enough calcium will be getting enough phosphorus too. |
| **Iron**<br>Babies accumulate stores of iron in their livers while they are still in the womb, enough to last three or four months, which is lucky, as milk contains almost none. So you will only need to provide an "iron rich" diet during weaning. Iron is a vital part of the hemoglobin, the constituent of red blood cells which carries oxygen around the body. People who are anemic as a result of iron deficiency feel exhausted and weak because their muscles are not receiving enough oxygen. | Fortified cereals and flours, eggs, meat, some fruits and vegetables, all contain small quantities of iron. Chocolate and cocoa powder are rich sources, and drinking water contains variable amounts. | The average recommended daily intake is about 8 mg, but this is only approximate, as various types of dietary iron are variously absorbed.<br>1 portion of fortified **cereal** = 3 mg<br>1 small slice of **liver** = 6 mg<br>1 tablespoon of **minced beef** = 1 mg<br>1 **egg yolk** = 1.5 mg<br>1 small bar of **chocolate** = 1 mg<br>1 slice of **white bread** = 0.5 mg<br>1 slice of **wholewheat bread** = 1 mg |

**Problems of weaning**

Weaning usually means a drop in the baby's milk intake and hence his nutrient intake. Switching from breast/formula milk to cow's milk will add to this problem, since ordinary (cow's) milk is less nutritious than either breast milk or formula. If you look at the table below you will see that even if your baby drinks 32 oz (910 ml) of cow's milk (his maximum capacity) he will be short of calories, iron and vitamins A and C. If his milk intake goes down to 1 pint (16 oz/455 ml) he will not be getting enough protein or calcium or thiamine either. If his milk intake goes down to ½ pint (8 oz 227.5 ml), he lacks some of every single vital nutrient. He will need a complete solid diet.

| | Energy (kcal) | Protein (g) | Calcium (mg) | Iron (mg) | Vitamin A (µg) | Vitamin D (µg) | Thiamine (mg) | Riboflavin (mg) | Niacin (mg) | Vitamin C (mg) |
|---|---|---|---|---|---|---|---|---|---|---|
| What the 6-month baby needs | 800 | 20 | 600 | 6 | 450 | 10 | 0.3 | 0.4 | 5 | 15 |
| What the baby gets: From 32 oz (910 ml) of a formula milk | 640 | 14 | 522 | 11 | 747 | 9 | 0.6 | 0.9 | 6.3 | 49 |
| From 32 oz (910 ml) of cow's milk | 576 | 29 | 1,000 | 0 | 350 | 10 | 0.3 | 1.2 | 9.6 | 13 |
| From 16 oz (455 ml) of cow's milk | 288 | 15 | 500 | 0 | 175 | 5 | 0.15 | 0.6 | 4.8 | 6.5 |
| From 8 oz (227.5 ml) of cow's milk | 144 | 7.5 | 250 | 0 | 88 | 2.5 | 0.075 | 0.3 | 2.4 | 3.25 |

# Ears

The opening of each ear leads, by a short passage, to the ear drum. On the other side of this membrane is a small "compartment" known as the middle ear. It is connected by a long passage, the eustachian tube, to the back of the throat.

Beyond the middle ear lies the inner ear, which contains structures that are concerned with both hearing and balance.

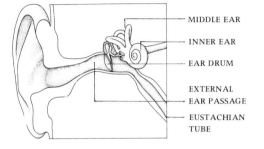

MIDDLE EAR

INNER EAR

EAR DRUM

EXTERNAL
EAR PASSAGE

EUSTACHIAN
TUBE

## Hearing disorders

*Deafness* New babies can be born completely deaf or with any degree of "hearing loss." Deafness is difficult to detect because until at least six months a baby will make a normal number and range of sounds himself even though he is not hearing them. It is only later that a deaf baby's sound making will begin to seem different from others of the same age. The earlier you can detect problems the more the baby can be helped and the less hearing time he will miss out on at a crucial stage of his development, so it is worth making a definite effort to be sure that he can hear totally normally from the earliest weeks of his life.

At around five to six weeks a baby should react to a sound by turning his eyes or even his head toward it. Try speaking to the baby or shaking a rattle when he is unaware that you are beside him. Don't use very loud and sudden sounds; not only will the baby be startled but he may be able to hear loud noises while still being deaf to all the normal speech tones.

By around three months most babies will be able to smile back when you smile at them and "talk" back when you talk to them. Of course these reactions depend on the baby's mood and state at the time, but if you are in the slightest doubt about the results of your "tests" mention them to a doctor straight away.

Older children can become temporarily partly deaf after a middle ear infection or even after a heavy cold which blocks the eustachian tubes. If the child seems deaf after, say, a week, take him to see a doctor.

The residue of repeated middle ear infections (see below) can sometimes cause permanent damage to the hearing. This is why any acute pain in a child's ears should always be reported immediately to a doctor.

# Infections

*The middle ear* In a small child the eustachian tubes are relatively wide. Since a baby spends much of his time lying down, it is easy for germs, or even part of a vomited milk feed, to find their way from the throat up the eustachian tube into the middle ear. This often leads to middle ear infection (otitis media). This can make a baby or child extremely ill very quickly, with high fever and great pain. A doctor should be called immediately if an ear infection is suspected. Treatment, usually with antibiotics, will prevent a burst ear drum and possible damage to hearing. The child may be ill without making it obvious that his ear is the cause: this is why a doctor will always examine an ill child's ears even if they do not appear to hurt.

NB Don't try home first-aid for earache even while you are waiting to see the doctor.
☐ Painkillers may confuse the picture and make diagnosis more difficult.
☐ "Folk-remedies" such as warmed oil dropped into the ear are useless if the source of the pain is the middle ear and dangerous if the source of the pain is the outer ear.
☐ External heat, such as a warm hot water bottle to hold against his ear, may make your child feel comforted and cared for but may also speed an abscess toward bursting. . . .

*The outer ear (otitis externa)* Inflammation can be due to infection, perhaps after swimming or because the child has poked something into the ear, or even scratched the ear passage with a dirty fingernail. It is extremely painful; moving the ear or even lying on it will hurt; you may also be able to see inflammation or discharge. The child should see a doctor immediately.

NB Babies can have severe ear infections without being able to localize the pain to the ear. To complicate matters further, a baby who happens to be teething may be thought incorrectly to put his hand to his face because of teething discomfort.

If he keeps pawing at his face, grizzles and seems off-color, take him to the doctor.

If he also has fever and/or loss of appetite, contact the doctor urgently.

*"Glue ear" (serous otitis media)* This is becoming increasingly common as a result, it is thought, of frequent (and not always completed) courses of antibiotics for middle-ear infections. Where previously such acute infections would have led to a burst ear drum and a runny ear, they now leave an accumulation of sterile gluey stuff in the middle ear. It is not infected but it is trapped and, by preventing the ear drum from vibrating as it should, it makes the child partially deaf.

The gluey stuff is too thick and sticky to be let out through an incision in the ear drum or to drain through the tiny plastic tube which is usually inserted in a minor operation. What the tube does is to equalize the pressure on either side of the ear drum. The improvement in the child's hearing is often so marked that parents find it difficult to believe that the tube is only an air tube and that no "glue" has been physically removed.

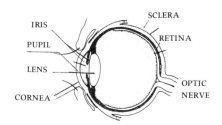

Many children these days have tubes in one or both ears. Some are forbidden to swim or go under water in the bath. Others are allowed to swim with ear plugs and caution. The tubes usually fall out of their own accord after a few months. A tube which does not fall out spontaneously will usually be removed by the surgeon after a maximum of eighteen months. The tiny hole in the ear drum will then heal itself.

## Other ear problems

*Wax in ears* Sometimes it is difficult to distinguish between wax and pus. Wax coming from the ear is perfectly normal – the body's way of clearing dust from the passage – but if you are uncertain whether it is wax, take the child to a doctor.

*Water in ears* This may feel uncomfortable or even make a child temporarily deaf, but it will do no harm unless he has an infection of the outer ear. If it worries the child get him to lie with the affected ear downward, so water can drain.

*"Blocked" ears* Changes in air pressure, which occur for example when traveling in an airplane or when driving in high mountains, can make the ears feel blocked and deaf. Swallowing will equalize the pressure and cure the problem. A candy to suck will force a child to keep swallowing. A baby can most easily be kept comfortable under these circumstances by being given the breast or a bottle to suck on.

*See also* ACCIDENTS/Foreign bodies.

# Eyes

The eyeball is covered with a thin, transparent membrane called the "conjunctiva" which extends to form the inner lining of the eyelids. Beneath this is the opaque white of the eye known as the "sclera." Its center is transparent and forms the disc-shaped "cornea." The cornea helps to bend rays of light as they enter the eye and also serves to protect the parts of the eye which lie directly beneath it. It is highly sensitive, its reactions ensuring that any foreign bodies are removed before they can do damage.

Beneath the cornea lies the circular colored portion of the eye – the "iris." (At birth the iris is usually blue-grey. Permanent eye color is not established until six months of age.) The iris contains many tiny muscles which control the opening and closing of the "pupil," the little dark hole in the center of the iris. It is through this opening that light rays enter the eye. If light is bright the pupil closes up; if dim it opens fully.

Directly behind the pupil lies the "lens" whose muscles adjust shape so as to focus light rays from objects at varying distances to the light-sensitive "retina." Layers of sensory nerve cells within the retina respond to impinging light rays by building up images of the thing being looked at. These are transmitted along the optic nerve from the back of the eye to the brain. Here they are interpreted and converted into a "picture."

## Problems with vision

Most vision problems, especially in babies and small children, are caused by faults or peculiarities in the shape of some of the eyes' working parts and merit examination by your doctor.

*Astigmatism* A child may be born with a cornea which does not refract (bend) light rays uniformly as they pass through to the pupil and lens. If the cornea is not perfectly curved, for example, light rays will not reach the retina in a point, as they should. If this is the case the shapes of objects may be distorted so that, for example, round objects look oval.

*Focusing problems* Occasionally the lens of the eye does not become adequately adjusted to focus on objects, whatever their distance from the eye. If the lens allows an image to fall in front of the retina, the child will only clearly see objects close at hand. He will be "near-sighted" or "myopic." If an image falls behind the retina the child will only see clearly objects at some distance from him. He will therefore be "far-sighted."

*Treatment* Problems of this kind can all be corrected with glasses. Small children adapt surprisingly well to wearing glasses, but many will also accept contact lenses, whose design is being rapidly improved. If you prefer the idea of these lenses for your child, ask your ophthalmologist to consider their suitability.

*Squinting* Although a baby should focus briefly on objects brought within eight inches of his eyes, from birth, one eye may "wander" from the focus of the other. The muscles are not strong enough to hold them in alignment. By three months the eyes should be permanently aligned. A "fixed" squint or "wandering" eye merits a visit to the doctor for examination.

*Fixed squints need urgent treatment* The retinas of normal eyes receive images from slightly different angles. The two fuse to give the brain a single composite picture to interpret. If the eyes squint, these images cannot fuse. The baby's brain receives two images but because it cannot interpret both at once it rejects one, interpreting, for example, only the "messages" from the left optic nerve. If this continues unchecked over time the right eye will go blind from lack of use.

Don't let the phrase "lazy eye" make you feel it is not serious. It is. The baby may have to wear a pad over the good eye to force his brain to accept images from the other. When old enough he will be given exercises to strengthen the eye muscles. Later he may, in fact, need surgery to adjust the lengths of the eye muscles.

# Eye infections

*Conjunctivitis ("Pink eye")* The conjunctiva which lines the outside of the eyeball and inside of the eyelids is inflamed. The eye may be weepy and reddened. After sleep, the discharge forms dry yellowish crusts in the eyelashes. There may be pain and/or gritty discomfort.

Irritation from dust, etc. can cause conjunctivitis, but so can a variety of infections including the "pink eye" which rages through schools. Take your child to the doctor; drops or ointment will quickly clear up the infection. Make sure the infected child uses only his own washcloth and towel – the infectious varieties can easily spread.

*How to give eye drops/ointment*
These may be prescribed for minor eye irritations or infections. If giving eye drops, do not expect much cooperation from the child because however much he means to keep still and hold the eye open, reflex action will make him blink and turn his head when he sees the dropper coming. The doctor may prescribe an ointment instead. This is usually sold in tiny tubes with a very fine nozzle on the end. You should have a tube for each eye and keep them distinguished; otherwise nozzles can transfer infection from one eye to the other.

*Eye drops*
☐ Lie the child across your lap, or, if he is old enough to be cooperative, lie him down flat on a bed instead.
☐ Draw up the right amount of the solution into the dropper.
☐ Put your left arm around the back of the child's head so your hand reaches around his face.
☐ Gently use your finger and thumb to hold the eyelids apart.
☐ Poise the dropper about two inches above the eye, and then wait until he blinks. As he does so, drop the solution into the inner corner of his eye.
☐ Keep him lying still for a few seconds to allow the solution to spread over the whole eyeball. Repeat for the other eye.

*Eye ointment*
☐ Lie the child down, bring the nozzle to the inner corner of his eye, and squeeze out the correct amount. Don't worry about the child blinking; the ointment can even be applied when his eye is completely closed.
☐ Keep the child still for a few minutes: the feeling of the ointment in his eye will be uncomfortable; if you let him free he will probably wipe it away. As he blinks you should see a fine film of the ointment spreading around the inside of the lids over the surface of the eyeball.
☐ If the ointment does not go inside the corner of his eye, but simply stays on the outside, repeat the application. Treat the other eye similarly.

Eye drops and ointments have a fairly short shelf life: they should never be kept and used again. Furthermore eye infections are highly contagious. Never use the same dropper or ointment tube for anyone else.

*Sties* A sty is a tiny boil developing from infection at the base of an eyelash. The infection often passes from one lash or eye to another, producing a succession of sties. Your doctor can prescribe an ointment to prevent this.

*What to do*
You can relieve the pain of a single sty if the child is old enough to cooperate and keep still.
☐ Look at the sty carefully in a good light until you see precisely which specific eyelash is growing through it.
☐ Remove the lash with tweezers – it will come out easily as the root is infected; a tiny drop of pus and complete relief of pain follow.
☐ Wash away the pus with a cotton ball, avoiding the other eye.
☐ Sterilize the tweezers before using for anything else. Any child with a sty must keep to his own washcloth and face-towel to avoid infecting anyone else.

# Eye injuries

Any injury to the eyeball itself should be seen at once by your doctor or local emergency room. A tiny scratch on the white of the eye may not be serious but may need treatment to prevent infection. Even the tiniest scratch on the pupil is very serious indeed; treatment is urgent.

Cover the affected eye if that makes the child more comfortable. Do nothing else. Don't even bathe it; hurt eyes are for experts.
*See also* ACCIDENTS/Foreign bodies.

# Family planning

Whatever the size, shape and structure of your family, the happiness and security of each of its members depends largely on yours. If you enjoy each child, each will enjoy being himself. If you truly love (and like) each child, each will grow up feeling both lovable and able to love. So if you plan your family to be right for *you* there is an excellent chance that it will work out well for the children. If you want one child, have one child. Arranging for him *not* to be lonely, spoiled or "precocious" is far, *far* easier than having a second child "to keep him company!" There cannot ever be valid reasons to have a child you do not want for his own sake, or to risk finding yourself with a child you do not want because it is another son when you were taking an emotional gamble on having a daughter.

If you should lose a baby, through miscarriage, stillbirth, newborn or crib death, don't let anyone persuade you and your bereft body to "replace" him by getting pregnant again as quickly as possible. The bulge in your belly or the bundle in your arms was a real person – even if he did not seem so to anyone but you. Real people have to be mourned and they are irreplaceable. You may want another baby one day. You may want another baby quite soon. If so, be sure that you know with your whole self that it will not be that same baby or none of you will even stand a chance of happiness.

Should people criticize your family planning, worrying you with the horrors of being the only child, the one squeezed in the middle or the baby of the family, remember that we do not know nearly enough about the characteristics of children born in different family positions to be able to make confident predictions about this complex subject. *Every* first baby is an "only" after all (*and* the baby of his family)! How quickly must another baby follow if he is to take on the characteristics of an eldest child? And once you have that second child, is he supposed to be "squeezed" by a third, irrespective not only of the age-gap but also of the sexes of the children either side of him?

Planning for children's companionship is equally complicated. A close relationship with a brother or sister can illuminate childhood and enrich the whole of adult life. But not all brothers and sisters even *like* each other and it is often the apparently ill-assorted pairs who get on best. If you want two or more children there is far more you can do to help them like each other than merely arranging to have them a specific number of years apart.

You could start by being hard-headed and practical. If you plan two or more children, do you want to pack them into the minimum number of years so as to get the having-babies stage of life over, or will you all need time to regroup in between? Do you plan to go on with a part-time job? That is probably easier with one baby at a time than with two under three. Do you mean to stay at home until your children are ready for school or employ full-time help for that period? If so, it may be more economical of effort and money to fit two children into five or six years rather than the same number into seven or eight.

Don't forget to allow for physical factors though. If you have two babies eighteen months apart you will be pregnant again when the first is only nine months old. You may ask your body to go straight from breast-feeding to intra-uterine feeding. You may be overwhelmed with nausea and/or sleepiness when your first child is at his most clingy and crawly, and when you are at your heaviest he will still be young enough to need a lot of carrying. After the birth you will have two babies. Two in diapers, a double stroller, two cribs and high chairs, two small people for whom you are the universe. Yet two babies at quite different stages and with different needs. . . . The advantages of a small age-gap tend to come much later. When the older child forgets that he was ever your only baby and when the younger one becomes mobile and vocal, you can *hope* that they will begin to companion each other and to share.

A longer gap – perhaps two and a half to three and a half years – is usually much easier, physically and emotionally. Your body belongs to you for a while between the two children. The first baby can have all of you until you have steered him through toddlerhood and he can be launched into at least the beginnings of pre-school friendships and adventures before the new baby is born. But although the two children may become, and remain, devoted friends, the age-gap between them will never close. You will have a baby and a child and one day they will be child and teenager, and then adolescent and adult.

*Contraceptives*
Whatever interval you plan between your children, plans can go awry. A three-year gap can turn into four for no obvious reason or into two against the statistical probabilities. Just don't let a planned two-year interval turn into a ten-*month* gap, by relying on breast-feeding to prevent you from getting pregnant again or by assuming that you will not ovulate until after menstruation has re-started following the birth. Breast-feeding does reduce the likelihood of ovulation and pregnancy by raising the levels of the hormone prolactin in the bloodstream. But who wants to base important plans on a likelihood? If you are going to ovulate while you are breast-feeding it is possible that you will do so for the first time before you have menstruated. So don't assume that you are infertile until your periods have begun again.

Most forms of birth control pill reduce the supply of breast milk. Some women breast-feed successfully while taking the mini-pill but others prefer to avoid hormonal contraceptives altogether until the babies are weaned.

If you plan to use an intra-uterine device this can often be rather easily fitted at your post-natal check-up six weeks after the birth. If you have not used an IUD before, though, this may not be a good time to start. Some women have heavy bleeding and other uncomfortable side-effects.

A diaphragm will need careful fitting – don't even try to use one which fitted before you became pregnant – but carefully used is a highly reliable and fairly unobtrusive form of birth control.

If you resume sexual intercourse before you have your post-natal check-up or can get to a family planning clinic, use a condom.

# Fever

A rise in temperature is part of the body's reaction to most infections. Almost every parent uses the presence or absence of fever, and its height, to judge whether a child is ill and whether to call the doctor. But don't overplay it.

☐ *Small* rises in temperature – 99°F (37.2°C) or even 99.4°F (37.4°C), say – are often not caused by illness at all but by the child's activity, the warmth of the room and so forth.

☐ Babies can have very high temperatures with insignificant illnesses or no fever at all (even a subnormal temperature) with serious illnesses.

☐ Any child who *feels* ill deserves attention, even if the feelings turn out to have more to do with school than with germs. Using the fact that he has no fever as a way of dismissing his complaints will not help.

Taking a child's temperature is usually more

important in an established and ongoing illness, where you and the doctor can use its rise or fall as a part-index of his progress or lack of it, than it is in home diagnosis.

*Taking temperatures*
For an accurate reading babies' temperature are often taken "rectally" – that is by inserting a

clinical thermometer about one inch into the rectum and holding it there for a minute. But although doctors and hospitals use this method, you need not unless your doctor asks you to. A reading from a fever-tester or from a mercury or digital thermometer used under the arm will be accurate enough for babies and toddlers. As soon as your child is old enough to cooperate by keeping still and keeping his mouth closed you can take his temperature in his mouth. This is not the dangerous business it once was, for you can now buy a non-glass, non-mercury thermometer. The child will not harm himself even if he bites it and the digital read-out is easy to understand too.

*Coping with high fever*
Most children can have a high temperature without seeming especially odd or ill, but have a sort of "critical level" above which the fever seems to overwhelm them, affecting their level of consciousness and their nervous systems. For many children past babyhood the level seems to be somewhere around 103°F (40°C).
☐ Once your child's fever has gone too high for him he may, if he is inclined that way and the rise has been sudden, have a febrile convulsion.
☐ Even if he is not liable to convulsions he may be trembly; his limbs may judder; he may overreact to everything you do, jumping when you touch him, crying as though in pain when you sponge his mouth.
☐ Without becoming completely unconscious, he may "wander" so that in the middle of a normal conversation he says something quite irrational.
☐ He may talk in his sleep and then, when you try gently to waken him, be completely delirious.
☐ He may vomit back any pills, medicine or even drinks which you try to give him.
☐ He may vomit anyway, sometimes quite suddenly without apparent nausea.
☐ Unless his control has been established for a long time, he may wet himself.

*What to do*
☐ If your child suddenly shoots a high temperature you cannot foresee it. But once you know he is ill you have to try to keep the fever down below his critical level. Keep his room fairly cool – 67°F (19°C) is enough for a very feverish child. Dress and cover him lightly.
☐ Try to stay calm because if he is very jumpy

obvious anxiety from you will make him much worse. Nursing a delirious child is alarming, but fever alone is not dangerous; it will drop eventually and he will then either suddenly wake and seem normal again or go off into natural sleep.
☐ If he has ever had a convulsion you will naturally be terrified that it is going to happen again. It is only likely to do so at the very beginning of the fever. However, once your child has had a febrile convulsion you have every right to call your doctor any time he has a high fever. Even if he does not see the child he will stay in touch with you and tell you where he can be reached.
☐ Stay with the child in case he gets up and wanders about in a delirious state or is sick, but let him sleep or doze as much as he can. You will get more rest at night if you either sleep in his room or bring him into yours, so that you are right there if he needs you. If you are alone in the house with him and really worried, consider calling a friend or relative. Someone to share the watches of the night with you can make all the difference. Choose the child's least feverish moments to give him the water he must have and any medicine that has been prescribed for him.

*Reducing fever*
☐ Make sure that the room is cool. Open all windows and turn down heating.
☐ Take all coverings off the child's bed or "nest" and replace them just with a sheet.
☐ Take off the child's clothes, down to the minimum in which he feels comfortable. In the hospital he might be stripped naked, but most children find this very distressing because they feel so exposed. A diaper or underpants and short sleeved tee-shirt will do.
☐ Get a bowl of warm water and a face-cloth; sponge the skin where you can see blood vessels close to the surface: his face, neck, the inside of his arms and legs. Leave the skin wet. The warm water helps those blood vessels to open up (cold water would make them contract) then cools the blood in them as it evaporates.
☐ If the sponging makes him cry, shiver and generally seem very distressed (which it may do as the skin can be hypersensitive to touch in high fever), try using a fan to cool him instead. Most hot air blower heaters have a cold setting and this is very satisfactory; alternatively a small electric fan can be used, or even hand fanning.
☐ Acetaminophen will reduce fever but don't give it: to a baby without orders to do so from your doctor; within four hours of giving a previous dose; if he is vomiting; or if he has any stomach symptoms at the time.
   Any fever over 102°F (38.5°C) should drop a little with these measures. Take his temperature again half an hour after you have finished ministering to him. If it has risen further, call your doctor. If it has stayed the same, do everything all over again except the acetaminophen.
☐ If this second bout of nursing still does not reduce the fever, call your doctor and report.
*See also* CONVULSIONS.

# Growth

A growth plan and goal are laid down in the genes of every individual – and closely related to parental size – but reaching it depends on how the child thrives: on the use he makes of the food and care he is offered and on his ability to withstand the illnesses and traumas that may come his way.

Growth involves the whole body. Monitoring the growth of bones, brains and internal organs is not practically possible, but monitoring height as well as weight is essential. Weight gain alone cannot provide an index of growth, since large weight gains without height increase suggest that the child is becoming fatter rather than larger.

But even weight and height together can only give useful information about growth when they are considered over time. A child's total growing period is finite. He will reach his adult height through a growth spurt that relates to puberty, but the inches gained during that spurt are added to the inches accumulated through childhood. Whenever a child is weighed and measured the results tell you how big he is *now* but you also need to know how big he was on the last occasion – what his growth *rate* has been – and how fast and how much he should be expected to grow in the future – his expected growth rate.

*Percentile growth charts (pp. 510–13)*
The old charts gave a series of static "averages" for children of different ages and led to statements with little relevance to growth, such as "this child is very small/big for his age."

Percentile charts build in growth rates so that individual measurements show whether a child is the expected size for *him*, and what can be expected of his growth in the future.

Percentile charts are produced by weighing and measuring thousands of children at many different age points and then dividing the resulting measurements so that a stated proportion of the sample children fall above and below particular measurements at particular ages. Five "bands" will serve to illustrate the following distinctions.

*The 50th percentile is placed so that 50% of children are above it and 50% below it at any given age.*
*The 75th percentile will always have a quarter of all children above it and three-quarters below.*
*The 97th percentile has 3% above it and 97% below.*
*The 25th percentile has three-quarters above it and a quarter below.*
*The 3rd percentile has 3% below it and 97% above.*

*At any age, then, and for any measurement, the 97th percentile will represent large children: only 3 in a 100 will be larger and the remaining 97 will be smaller. At the other extreme, the 3rd percentile will represent small children. Only 3 in 100 will be smaller and the remaining 97 will all be larger.*

Percentile points are still static: they cannot show how growth proceeded on the way from one measurement point to another. Percentile graphs or curves are made up with further research, which follows the week by week growth of thousands more children to see at exactly what rate they gained either the pounds or inches separating the measurement points.

The final result is a percentile chart whose printed curves give a background picture of normal growth over time, from the starting point of the lowest birthweight baby to the final size of the largest adult. Boys and girls need to be charted separately because boys tend to be slightly heavier at birth and the timing of their final growth spurt is different from girls, but a percentile chart for the appropriate sex enables any child's personal growth to be monitored in perspective.

*Percentile charts for babies*
Modern doctors record babies' weight and length, and some other aspects of growth such as head circumference, on percentile charts like those on the following pages, but a lot more detailed.

At this age weight gain, week by week, gives an indication of the adequacy of diet. A baby who is not gaining at all is not getting – or at least absorbing – enough milk. A baby who is gaining at, or above, the expected rate *and* is being offered as much milk as he willingly takes, can be reasonably assumed to be having plenty. Length changes slowly and is difficult to measure accurately but its rate, in relation to weight gain, is an important check on obesity.

*"Catch up growth"*
Underfeeding, illness or emotional trauma or neglect can push a baby off his expected growth curve. He will not entirely stop growing – you will still see gains over time – but because he gains slowly, his upward curve will be flatter than the percentile curves and, if growth continues slowly the percentile curve below may cross over his.

As soon as conditions improve the baby will enter a phase of accelerated "catch up growth." After a brief set-back the extra growth will quickly put him back onto his old curve and all you will see on his chart will be a dip and then a rise. When his growth is back to the old pattern its rate will drop back to the norm.

Long-term deprivation can be different, though. After months or years better circumstances will indeed produce "catch up growth" but it may be too late for the baby to catch right up to his intended size: the field has left him behind. This is why a baby or child who grows much more slowly than you expect, so that his personal curve flattens over a long period, dropping him through the percentile lines, should be medically checked. There are a few (rare) conditions which can reduce the growth rate for a long period before producing other symptoms. There are malabsorption syndromes which make it difficult for a child to thrive on a normal diet and there are a few children who lack naturally produced growth hormone. If a child is to be treated for a condition that is slowing his growth, the sooner he begins the better. Treatment can help him build the expected number of inches in the future, but it cannot necessarily give him back the inches that he has already failed to grow.

# Growth charts

The printed curves charted on these and the next two pages map the expected gains in weight and height, over time, for both boys and girls from the time of birth to the age of five. You can see that they all tend to grow at the same rate, gaining similar amounts over similar periods of time. And you can therefore see the crucial significance of a baby's starting point: his birthweight and length.

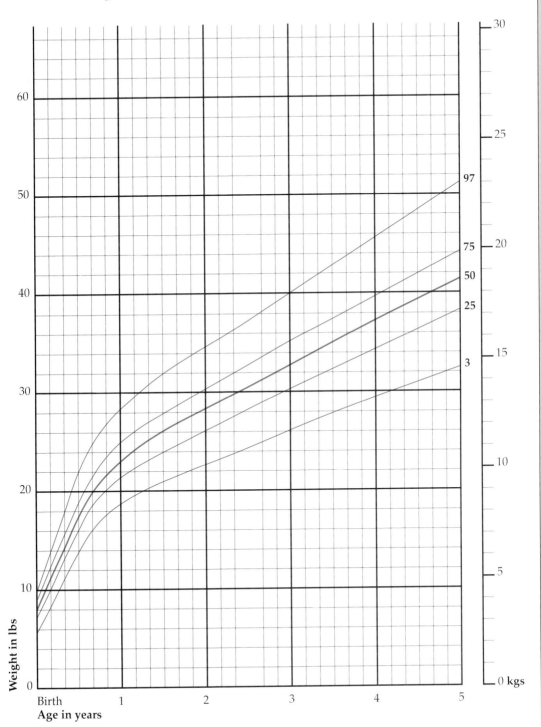

Weight in lbs

Birth
Age in years

## Growth patterns

An individual child's week-by-week measurements would not form smooth curves, of course. There would be jiggles when he gained slowly and then caught himself up. But smoothed out on to a bi-monthly graph like this, the shape of the curve would be similar for every child, whether it began at the very bottom because he weighed less than 6lbs at birth, or at the very top because he measured 22in in length.

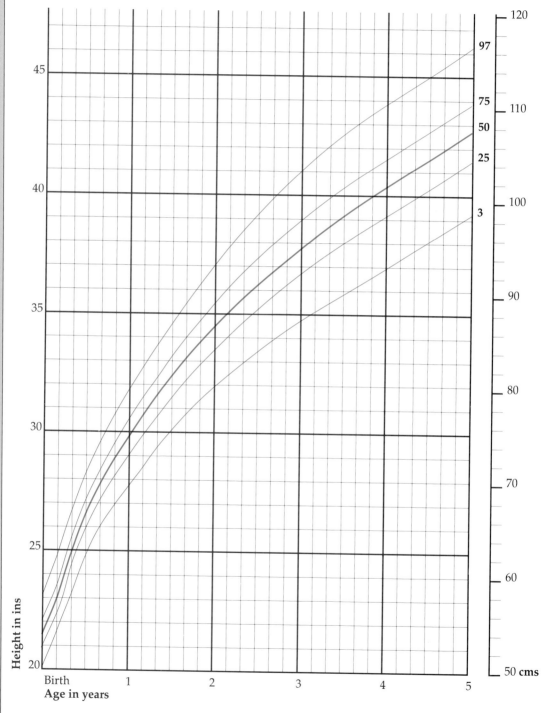

## Using the charts

If you would like to see your own child's route through this growth map, get her birth weight and length from her birth records and enter them as accurately as you can on the appropriate chart.

Then every few months, get her current weight and length from the doctor, find her age across the bottom of each of the charts and the height or weight up the side of each chart and mark where the two meet on the grid.

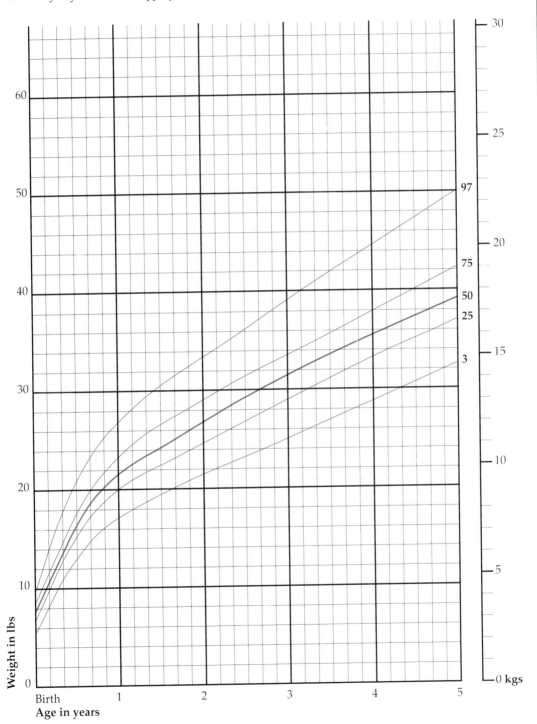

Weight in lbs

Birth
Age in years

## Growth curves

A premature baby or one who was sick may start well beneath the 25th precentile line but settle above the 50th. Any baby may drift from just above one percentile line to just below it. But on the whole you will find that your child's curve is neither steeper nor flatter than the printed ones over *time*. And if it should become a different shape, your chart will be useful to whomever you choose to consult about possible obesity or very slow gains in height.

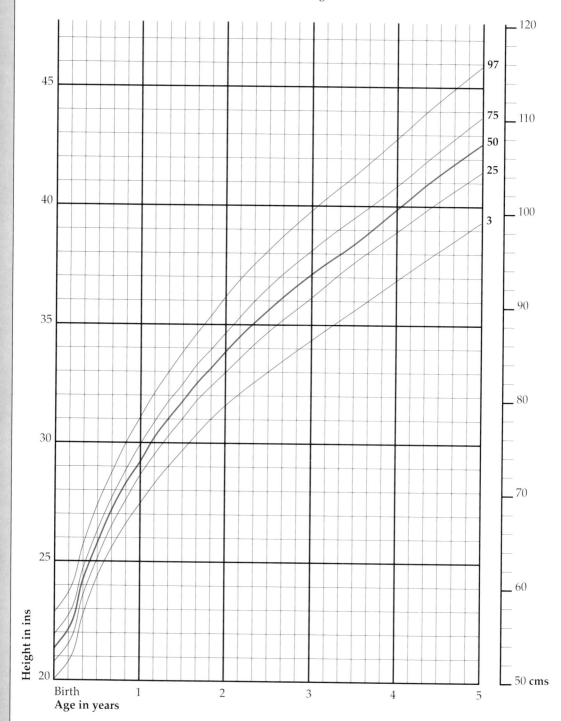

# Gum boils

These are hard, painful red swellings at the margin of the gum, where a tooth sticks up. They are not really boils at all, but abscesses under the tooth which are trying to make a "head" right through the baby's gum.

Make an emergency appointment with the dentist that same day. If you delay, your child may lose the affected tooth as well as having an extremely painful night.

# Handedness

Babies start out ambidextrous and toddlers go through phases of using a particular hand for particular activities. Your child's handedness will not be decided until the third year so conduct life right-handedly unless he begins to swap spoons and crayons from his right to his left.

Left-handed children form about 10% of the population. Although they are at a slight disadvantage in a right-handed world, don't try to interfere. Handedness is controlled by the part of the brain dealing with language: spoken as well as read and written. Trying to reverse left-handedness can cause major problems.

Help instead: lay his place-setting the right way around for *him*; get him left-handed scissors; show him the easiest way to manage pencils and paper and make sure other adults and teachers take the same approach.

# Headaches

A baby or toddler whose head appears to hurt him may have a headache but equally he may have earache, toothache or swollen sore neck glands. Neither of you will know which so you need a doctor to look at him.

An older child may tell you that his "hair hurts," or he may now copy your term.

Headaches can mean nothing or almost anything. If the child seems well in every other way and the pain is transient, you need offer nothing but sympathy. If the pain persists, keep an eye on him: the headache may herald a fever. Don't give him pain-relievers at this stage; they may mask symptoms of illness. If the headache is so bad that you cannot bear to withhold relief, take him to the doctor for an examination.

If he does become ill and headache remains a tiresome symptom, a pain-reliever such as liquid acetaminophen will ease it.

Headache severe enough to make the child want to lie still, especially if it is associated with high fever, unusual sleepiness, dislike of light or a stiff neck should always be reported to your doctor straight away. The whole group of symptoms is often associated with nothing worse than tonsillitis, but he should see the child now, rather than tomorrow morning, as it is possible that the symptoms could be due to one of the illnesses that affect the central nervous system and are serious enough to require immediate treatment.

Headaches are never due to "eye-strain." A child who frequently announces that his head aches, especially in association with going to playgroup, is more likely to be in need of help in coping without you than of spectacles. Have his eyes tested if it will relieve you, but look for the solution to the headaches in some aspect of his life which is causing him tension.

*See also* MENINGITIS/ENCEPHALITIS.

# Homeopathic medicines

Homeopathy is still regarded as a poor (though well-behaved) relation by most orthodox medical practitioners, although it is increasingly popular with people who feel that too many powerful drugs are responsible for some of the ills for which further drugs are then prescribed. Homeopathic medicines are prescribed on quite different principles from orthodox medicines. Their major attraction is that they are given in "micro-doses" so that there is no possibility of overdose or of unwanted side-effects.

Whether these micro-doses have the wanted effects is the crucial question. Homeopaths maintain that their medicines' effectiveness cannot be assessed by the only means orthodox medicine accepts – the "double-blind" trial – because such trials ask inappropriate questions such as "does substance A have more effect on the symptoms/disorders of a large group of patients than substance B?" That question will differentiate between aspirin and pretend-aspirin when given to patients with arthritis without either the patients or their doctors knowing which tablets they are taking. But it will not "prove" the efficacy of a homeopathic remedy because such remedies are not *intended* to affect all similar patients similarly; indeed they are not intended directly to affect *symptoms* so much as the patient's bodily balance including his symptoms.

Homeopathic practitioners say that the efficacy of their remedies must be judged by their beneficial effects on individual patients and many patients are happy to accept this. If you are considering a homeopathic approach for your child for the first time, don't buy remedies over the counter. They will certainly not do him any harm, but since homeopathy is an individualized, whole-patient approach, you cannot give it a fair chance unless you first take the child to a reputable practitioner. If homeopathy does your child good, somebody will doubtless tell you that it was just the "placebo effect" of the doctor's attention. But if you are trying to clear up your child's chronic catarrh, rather than prove a professional point, you may not care *why* the medicine works as long as it does work. . . .

# Hospital admission

Being admitted to the hospital is no longer the dreadful trauma for babies and small children that it was once. Most children are cared for on special children's floors where a relaxed atmosphere and regime try to cater to their needs. (Indeed the nursing staff may be so tolerant of toddlers with trikes and bigger children with personal stereos that you feel the whole place is chaos!) Children's floors (and children's hospitals) have at least some nurses who are specially trained in the care of babies and children and many of them are remarkably good at getting medicine down or giving injections with a minimum of fuss. Above all, most children's wings will arrange for parents to stay with babies or small children, sometimes in special units, sometimes on cots (or even armchairs) beside the cribs.

If your baby or child faces a planned hospital admission (perhaps for an operation such as tonsillectomy) do talk to your doctor about your staying with the child. If the admission is not planned, but an emergency, discuss with the admitting doctor or the social worker the possibility of your staying. Hospitals usually are – and should be – sympathetic to your request.

*Why being with your child in the hospital is so important*
Hospitals are big, frightening places full of strangers who *do things* to children, even hurt them sometimes. A baby or child who is left alone in a hospital is absolutely certain to feel scared, lonely and, above all, abandoned. At one, two or three, he has no idea when (or whether) you will reappear. His understanding just isn't good enough to allow him to hang on to the *idea* of you when you have vanished or to go on believing in "two o'clock tomorrow" when it is 10 pm today. Furthermore if he is without you, he must submit to intimate care from people he does not know and this doubles his trouble. He wanted his ordinary breakfast in his own familiar kitchen from you. Now he has got to have (or refuse) an unfamiliar breakfast in a strange room from a nurse. . . . Even if nobody does anything *medical* to him, he will despair. If the terror of injections is added to that despair it is certain to redouble.

Your presence cannot protect your child from every aspect of being in the hospital which may be frightening or unpleasant. If he must have tests, dressings or surgery, he must live through them. But by being there you can protect him, explain to him, help him with every other aspect of his life so that the strange bathrooms become an adventure, the nurses' caps an observation game and the hospital food – well, interesting perhaps. With you there, he may not *like* it but he will tolerate it and your reward for what may be a very stressful few days will be that when he is better and comes home he will be himself rather than the angry, babyish, clinging small person he will be if he has felt deserted in hospital.

Rooming-in is ideal for your child but it may be difficult for you to arrange and hard to bear. Sharing with your partner may make it possible and the hospital should certainly be equally accepting of fathers and mothers. If you are torn in two between the hospitalized child and others, or between the child and your work, don't hesitate to call on the help and goodwill of other family members, friends and colleagues. This is a time of genuine family

crisis and you deserve all the help you can get.

If rooming-in is completely impossible, try at least to organize things so that you can be with your child in the hospital all day, only leaving him to put up with "babysitting" from the nurses at night. Some hospitals will allow you to bring a healthy brother or sister to play in the playroom. All should accept complicated turn-taking between yourself and other relations and friends. It will doubtless be hell to organize and live through, but it will be worth it.

Don't, *please* don't, decide that your child is so upset each time you leave him that it would be better to visit less often or for shorter periods. If he is calm in your absence, it is probably the calmness of despair and he has the right to protest when you leave because he needs you to stay.

*Preparing your child for the hospital*
If you are going to stay with your child you need not try to prepare him for every detail of hospital life because you will be there to share, explain and cushion him. If you are *not* going to stay but are only going to visit for a couple of hours in the afternoon, preparation will not be very much use if your child is under three. He will not understand much of what you tell him and anyway you cannot prepare him for the most important part of the experience: his own feelings of loss when you leave him and of anger when you visit and leave again.

Some kinds of preparation are still worthwhile:
☐ Make sure your child knows what a hospital is and what doctors and nurses do (make people better. . .). If he is over 18 months, get some of the excellent picture books about hospitals which are designed for just this purpose. The children's librarian will pick some out for you.
☐ Prepare toddlers and pre-school children for hospital routines, like having their chests listened to with a stethoscope or having their temperatures taken, through play. A "doctor set" is a good buy in preparation for hospital and will probably be played with for days while the child is coming to terms with the experience afterwards.
☐ If you are preparing for a planned admission (rather than "just in case") and you *know* some of the things that are going to happen to your child, do talk to him about them as honestly as you can. If he is going to have his tonsils out, for example, you *know* that he will have a pre-med and a general anesthetic and that when he comes around he will see blood from his mouth and have a desperately sore throat. Don't keep quiet *or* tell him it won't hurt. Tell him that his throat will be sore but that it won't last very long and that the nurses will give him medicine to make it better.
☐ Do everything you can to ensure that the child *knows the hospital stay is temporary*. He may assume he has been taken away from home forever. Just before the day of admission, buy a nearly flowering plant for his room and tell him "that will be right out when you come home . . ." or take his coat to the cleaners "to be all nice for when you come home" or let him hear you making plans for parties "afterward."

# Immunization

When a child "catches" an infectious disease his body fights the invading "germs" by producing antibodies. When a child is immunized, he is given the "germs" in a very much weakened (or a killed) form. His body produces antibodies just as it would do if he had been infected with fully active "germs," but because they were so weakened he is not ill. If he later comes into contact with the infection he will have the weapons to fight it already formed and will either not get the disease or will get it in a very much reduced form.

If whole populations of children are immunized, that particular infection becomes rare but the "germs" still exist. If parents then decide not to bother with immunization because "children don't get that any more . . .," they risk being partly responsible for starting it up again.

Immunizations are carried out either by pediatricians or by the community doctors who work in clinics. Your doctor will remind you when the immunizations are due but deciding whether or not to accept them for your baby or child is up to you. Do decide carefully. A few families refuse immunization on principle – and that is their right. But many more don't exactly refuse them but don't have them done, either.

☐ Don't let your very natural (and widely shared!) distress at the idea of your beloved baby being injected put you off. The injections are so quick that many babies don't even have time to cry before they have forgotten that anything happened. It is *far* worse for you than it is for your baby.

☐ Don't let worry over reactions to the injections put you off. Most babies have none. Some do have a slight fever, a sore arm and perhaps a cranky day after the injections, but these are *nothing* compared to the illnesses that they prevent.

☐ Don't let publicity about whooping cough immunization and possibly disastrous after-effects put you off. Go and talk to your doctor about them instead. While nobody will try to pretend that no babies have ever been damaged by this vaccine, you will come away very clear that the chances of *whooping cough* killing or permanently damaging a baby or toddler, are far higher than the risks of the vaccine to him.

*Your baby's immunization schedule*
Suggested programs vary a little from pediatrician to pediatrician and many vary from state to state, especially when particular epidemics are expected during a given season. The approximate schedule will be close to the following:
☐ Triple vaccine (DPT) against diptheria, pertussis (whooping cough) and tetanus. Three injections at roughly six-week intervals starting at the age of around two months.
☐ Polio vaccine (in the form of drops) on the same schedule as DPT.
NB If you are late with the second or third injection, the course does *not* have to be started again. These are minimum effective intervals. Longer intervals do not reduce protection, they simply delay the time when it is completed.

NB Premature babies, even those who have not yet reached 10 lbs, should be immunized on schedule unless your doctor recommends otherwise.
☐ A single injection, the MMR, against measles, mumps and rubella (German measles) given at about fifteen months old.
☐ A single booster injection of DPT given at about eighteen months old.
☐ A single injection of HIB vaccine, against "Haemophilus Influenza Type B" (Not flu at all but a serious bacterial infection often causing meningitis) usually given at the age of two years.
☐ Pre-school boosters against diptheria and tetanus, and against polio, given between the ages of four and six years.
The only contra-indications to immunization are:
☐ Acute illness.
☐ An acute reaction needing medical attention to an earlier injection in the series (in which case the baby should just have the diptheria and tetanus parts of the triple vaccine).
☐ Brain damage at birth or convulsions or fits.
☐ Some neurological problems.
☐ A family history of certain kinds of epilepsy.
These should be discussed with your doctor.

*Immunizations against other diseases if you mean to take your child abroad*
Your travel agent will tell you the recommended immunizations against such diseases as typhoid, cholera and yellow fever for any particular country, but only your doctor can help you decide about your baby or child.

If your work takes you to a tropical country and you want to take the child with you then the reactions which can follow full immunization have to be weighed against the alternative of the family being divided. If you are only considering a brief vacation in such a country, your doctor may advise you to wait until the baby or child is older. A full course of these primary immunizations may make him quite ill over a longer period than you are planning to be on vacation.
*See also* INFECTIOUS DISEASES OF CHILDHOOD.

# Impetigo

The first signs of this disorder are little red spots usually on exposed parts of the skin such as the hands, legs or face. They quickly develop little watery heads, then large brown crusts.

Impetigo can be cleared up by antibiotics (ointment, medicine or both) so take your child to the doctor the moment you suspect it. Left untreated it will spread rapidly, to other children in the family as well. So act promptly. Keep the infected child's face-cloth, towel, etc., separate from everyone else's.

# Infection in wounds

You cannot keep wounds bacteria-free (sterile) because there are bacteria everywhere including on the broken skin and on whatever injured it.

Washing and covering with a sterile dressing will prevent more bacteria getting in, but minor infection in small wounds and grazes is common. The wound may look wet and weepy. The scab that forms may be yellowish. But the body's defenses are coping. Only the superficial skin layers are affected and when the scab falls off healing will be complete.
*Warnings* If a wound is infected and the body is not coping well, the wound will become more painful and the edges will be red and inflamed. There may be some oozing of yellow or white pus. If the wound is small, keep a check on it. If it is large or does not start to heal cleanly in a further 24 hours, show it to your doctor.
*Danger signs* Occasionally, instead of infected material being carried up out of a wound to harden into a scab, it is carried into the bloodstream. This can be extremely serious. Take the child immediately to the doctor if:
☐ Reddish streaks run away under the skin from the edges of the wound.
☐ The skin around the wound is hot and shiny.
☐ There is continuous, throbbing pain.
☐ There is swelling around the wound.
☐ Pus is oozing from beneath a hardened scab.

# Infectious diseases of childhood

These are thought of as "childish complaints" because they are highly infectious and the immunity your baby gets from your body wears off during the first year so that he is likely to "catch" each of them the first time he comes into contact with it. Although some of these diseases are extremely unpleasant in childhood – and dangerous in babyhood – they tend to be even worse in adult life. This is why it is often thought a good idea for schoolchildren to "go ahead and get it over with" while a local epidemic is raging.

*Preventing the spread of these infections*
Most of these infections can now be prevented by immunization. It is tragic that two serious ones – measles and whooping cough – remain common because not much more than half the baby-population receives all the protective injections.
Immunization against mumps and rubella ("German measles") in the second year, along with vaccine against measles (MMR), is comparatively recent. If your child missed it in infancy, do ask if it can be given now. One way or another it is vital that all girls are immune to rubella before they reach an age where pregnancy is remotely possible because the effects of the disease on a young fetus are often disastrous. If your daughter has neither received immunization nor suffered an attack of German measles by the time she leaves school, she should be given the injection at that point.
NB Rubella seldom makes the victim ill but if one of your children gets it do make strenuous efforts to keep him or her away from any woman who *might be* pregnant. Avoiding visibly pregnant women is useless because any damage done to a fetus will take place in its earliest weeks, possibly before pregnancy has been recognized. So keep rubella-ridden children out of public places and warn adult female visitors to your home.
A couple of generations ago the families and contacts of children with infectious diseases were stringently quarantined. Nowadays only the ill child himself is kept out of circulation because contact quarantine is not effective in controling these diseases. The reason is simple: a child who is going to have (say) measles is at his most infectious *before* he shows any symptoms. By the time measles is diagnosed he will probably have passed it to other children.
For this same reason, infectious diseases cannot be effectively controled by quarantine within a family. If one of your children gets chickenpox the others will almost certainly be incubating it.
A child who has an infectious fever should be kept at home and his playgroup, sitter or school should be told the diagnosis so that other parents can be informed and susceptible children can be watched for early symptoms.
Other children in the family can pursue their ordinary lives, but you should not take them to *new* places where there are other babies or children who may not have been exposed to their pool of infection. Don't, on any account, take them to visit hospitals, for example.
Let other parents judge whether they want their children to exchange visits with yours. A family with a young baby, an older child with asthma or a teenager facing exams, may prefer not to add contact with your infected child to the chance that their own are already brewing the illness.
When a child first develops an infectious fever, do tell the parents of children with whom he has recently had contact but who do not go to the same group. They can then work out, from the incubation period, *when* their children are likely to develop the disease if they are going to.

## Chickenpox

Incubation period 10–21 days.

*First signs*
☐ Possibly slightly off color for one to two days, but often no warning at all.

*Definite signs*
☐ Small dark red pimples appear and within hours turn into blisters that look like drops of water on the skin. The fragile blisters rub off, leaving raw places which then scab. While the first batch are changing, a new batch of pimples is appearing. This goes on over three to four days so that the child has spots in every stage of development and healing.

*Degree of illness*
☐ Usually very minor; child may not feel ill at all. Older children *can* be very ill with high fever.

*Possible complications*
☐ A really copious rash may cover the child including the scalp, inside the mouth, ears, penis or

vagina and anus. The tremendous itching/scratching can mean very disturbed nights and infected blisters which will leave scars.

*What the doctor may do*
☐ Prescribe an ointment to help prevent infection of scratched spots in diaper areas.
☐ Possibly consider a sedative for extreme itching at night.

*What you can do*
☐ Help the itching by giving frequent lukewarm baths with a cupful of bicarbonate of soda dissolved in each. In between dab spots with calamine lotion – a pre-school child may like to have his own lotion and cotton balls; being allowed to do it for himself may prevent him from scratching. It's also available as a cream in a tube, which is easier for the child to apply himself.
☐ Leave a baby without diapers as much as practically possible.
☐ Keep the fingernails short and clean.
☐ Give antihistamine after seeing the doctor.

## German measles (Rubella)

Incubation period 14–21 days.

*First signs*
Usually none.

*Definite signs*
☐ Flat pink spots start behind the ears and spread to the forehead and then over the body, merging, often in a few hours, so that the skin merely looks flushed. The whole rash may pass so rapidly that you never notice it and/or have no time to show it to a doctor.
☐ Swollen glands high up on the back of the neck, just below the skull, may be sore to touch. They often stay swollen for weeks.

*Degree of illness*
☐ Usually nil. This "illness" often passes completely unnoticed.

*Possible complications*
☐ None for the patient, but infection of a mother in the early weeks of pregnancy can be disastrous to her baby. This is why this mildest of all infectious diseases is the subject of a campaign for the immunization of all girls before or at puberty.

*What the doctor may do*
☐ Nothing for the child but he may encourage you to warn any possibly pregnant women who have had contact with the child.

*What you can do*
☐ Nothing for the patient. Keep him away from places where young women congregate; warn anyone you know to be in early pregnancy or who later tells you that she is pregnant, having had contact with your child. The worst fetal effects happen if infection takes place in the first weeks.

## Hand, foot and mouth disease

Incubation period 3–5 days.

*First signs*
Usually none.

*Definite signs*
☐ Sores in the mouth: tongue, throat, lips, cheeks.
☐ Small clear blisters on fingers, hands, toes and feet. Sometimes a more widespread rash.

*Degree of illness*
☐ Usually minor; some children have mild to moderate fever.
☐ Young babies may be badly affected; sore mouth makes sucking difficult and can lead to dehydration.

*What the doctor may do*
☐ Nothing unless patient is a baby.

*What you can do*
☐ Provide bland food and drink while the mouth is sore.
*See also* DEHYDRATION.

## Measles

Incubation period 8–14 days.

*First signs*
☐ A "bad cold" with runny nose, reddened, watery eyes and a cough.
☐ Fever which gradually rises rather than dropping as you would expect in a genuine cold.
☐ Child complains of feeling ill.

*Definite signs*
☐ "Koplik's spots," which look like grains of salt, appear inside the cheeks about day three or four.
☐ Rash proper appears on day four or five, as small dark red spots, starting behind the ears and becoming blotchy all over the face and body.

*Degree of illness*
☐ He may be exceedingly ill from about day three until day five or six when the rash is fully out.
☐ Very high fever with delirium is quite usual.
☐ Dry irritating cough disturbs him.
☐ Sore eyes are distressing.

*Possible complications*
☐ Acute conjunctivitis with intolerance of light. (Light will not damage his eyes but may make them feel worse.)
☐ Sore throat spreading to middle ear.
☐ Secondary infection leading to bronchitis or pneumonia.
☐ Inflammation of the brain, encephalitis.

*What the doctor may do*
☐ Confirm the diagnosis.
☐ Prescribe lotion for eyes.
☐ Prescribe antibiotics to protect against/treat secondary infections.

*What you can do*
- ☐ Free yourself from other commitments for intensive and continuous nursing for at least a week; much longer if there are complications.
- ☐ Bathe eyes often, using prescribed lotion or boiled water on cotton balls.
- ☐ Keep fever to reasonable level.
- ☐ Keep fluid intake up with frequent drinks.
- ☐ Report immediately to the doctor if: he has earache; breathing becomes labored; cough becomes thick, with sputum; fever rises sharply once it has begun to drop; he seems suddenly sicker after seeming a little better; he becomes semi-conscious or difficult to rouse.

## Mumps

Incubation period 14–28 days.

*First signs*
- ☐ May seem off color for one to two days.

*Definite signs*
- ☐ Swollen, painful gland running from behind the ear to beneath the jaw bone.
- ☐ Dry mouth (the affected glands normally make the saliva and now do not).
- ☐ Acute stinging pain on swallowing anything acid such as fruit juice.
- ☐ Increasing swelling, changing shape of his face.

*Degree of illness*
- ☐ Minor, unless there are complications, but pain on swallowing will be troublesome and he may be self-conscious.

*Possible complications*
- ☐ The illness may affect each side of his face in turn so that the other side swells just as you thought he was recovering.
- ☐ Deafness; often overlooked, so check.
- ☐ Very rarely inflammation of the spinal cord "mumps meningitis" about 10 days afterward with high fever, delirium and stiff neck.

*What the doctor may do*
- ☐ Diagnose; check hearing.

*What you can do*
- ☐ Be tactful; don't let other children laugh unless he himself thinks his face looks funny.
- ☐ Remember that opening his mouth/swallowing are really painful. Give bland nourishing drinks (ice cream milkshakes, chocolate milk, etc.) through a straw. Help him rinse his dry mouth.
- ☐ Give pain relievers if pain keeps him awake.
- ☐ Keep an eye on him during the week after recovery so that you recognize the rare complication of meningitis quickly.

## Roseola infantum

Incubation period 7–14 days.

*First signs*
- ☐ Inexplicable high fever for about three days.

*Definite signs*
- ☐ Small, separate pink spots appear all over the body but vanish so quickly that they may be missed altogether.

*Degree of illness*
- ☐ Depends on the height of the fever and his reactions to it. In a susceptible child, it may cause febrile convulsions. Once the rash appears there is no further illness.

*Possible complications*
- ☐ None.

*What the doctor may do*
- ☐ Nothing, unless you need his help early on because of convulsions.

*What you can do*
- ☐ Nothing is needed except nursing of the fever.

## Scarlet fever

Incubation period 1–5 days.

*First signs*
- ☐ Scarlet fever is a strep (streptococcal) throat infection which happens to produce a rash. First signs are similar to an attack of tonsilitis. There may be fever, loss of appetite and vomiting.
- ☐ Complaints of stomach-ache may be due to swollen glands in the abdomen.

*Definite signs*
- ☐ On day two or three, tiny red dots appear on skin which has an overall red flush. The rash starts on the chest and neck, then spreads to the whole body. There are no spots or flushing around the mouth so, in contrast with the rest of the face, this area always looks strikingly pale. When the rash fades after about one week, the skin flakes.

*Degree of illness*
- ☐ He will be about as ill as with tonsilitis.

*Possible complications*
- ☐ Middle ear infection.
- ☐ Without treatment, there is a chance of the bacteria spreading to infect the kidneys or cause rheumatic fever.

*What the doctor may do*
- ☐ Give antibiotics or sulphonamides to control the bacteria and prevent complications. Although the illness is not severe the complications can be.

*What you can do*
- ☐ Nurse him as you would for any tonsilitis. Watch for earache or for signs of acute illness.

## Whooping cough

Incubation period 8–14 days.

*First signs*
- ☐ An ordinary-sounding cough which may, or

may not, be accompanied by a runny nose. The child may seem slightly off color and the whole phase may drag on for several days.

*Definite signs*
(In an immunized child diagnosis may be very difficult as the typical features are lacking.)
☐ The cough worsens and becomes paroxysmal so that the child coughs several times on one breath.
☐ Typically, the cough takes him unaware, with no time to breathe in before coughing out. As a result he becomes distressed for air. The diagnostic "whoop" is a trick he learns to cope with the situation. He forces air in while the larynx is still in spasm. Because the larynx is partly closed the inrushing breath makes the whooping sound.
☐ Very young babies may never learn to whoop. As a result they do become very short of oxygen with each coughing fit. They may turn bluey-grey in the face during the attack and vomit after it.

*Degree of illness*
☐ Very ill indeed and for a long time, especially if he is under one year old and/or is not immunized.

*Possible complications*
☐ The frequency of coughing bouts and the vomiting after them may make it extremely difficult to get and keep enough liquid and food down the child. Exhaustion, dehydration and prostration are real risks.
☐ Middle ear infections and broncho-pneumonia are common.

*What the doctor may do*
☐ Confirm the diagnosis with throat swab and/or blood test, especially in a child who has been immunized or is too young to whoop.
☐ Give antibiotics which are effective in modifying the disease if they are given early.
☐ Show you how to tap the child's chest while he lies head down, so as to move the phlegm to a position from which he can more easily cough some of it up.
☐ Recommend hospital admission if the child (especially a baby) is getting dehydrated or exhausted, or if you have nobody with whom to share continuous, demanding nursing.

*What you can do*
☐ Nurse him continuously, making sure he is never left alone even at night. Panic makes breathlessness worse so your reassurance during coughing fits is vital. Inhaled vomit is dangerous so you must be there to hold his head.
☐ Keep him quiet, especially during the acute phase. Active play will make him cough.
☐ Give tiny drinks and things to eat immediately after a coughing/vomiting fit. This gives the best chance of at least some nourishment being absorbed before the next attack bring it up again. Keep accurate notes of the quantities of liquid the child has had. Even though you do not know how much he has vomited, these will help your doctor decide if his fluid intake is likely to be adequate.

☐ Be prepared for a long bout of intensive care and, even after that, for what may be weeks of convalescence.
☐ Protect unimmunized or very young babies from contact with the patient.

# Jaundice

In someone with jaundice, the skin and – most obviously – the whites of the eyes take on a yellowish tinge. This yellowness is always caused by a build-up in the blood of breakdown products from red blood cells which have reached the end of their lifespan. Red blood cells last for about three months. After that the cells are broken down, their hemoglobin is released, processed in the liver into bile and then passed into the intestine for excretion. If the liver is not working to full capacity it may not be able to clear red cells as fast as they are broken down; jaundice results.

Jaundice, then, is a symptom relating to liver function. It is not, in itself, a disease. The seriousness of jaundice can only be assessed when the condition of the liver – the reason for its failure to perform efficiently – is known.

*Newborn ("physiological") jaundice*
A newborn baby's liver is often rather inefficient. Mild jaundice is common and especially so in premature babies.

As the baby's liver becomes more efficient, the jaundice clears, often without any treatment. Hospital staff do not rely on measuring the yellowness of the skin by eye: they will test the baby's blood for a substance called "bilirubin." Repeated tests will show whether the bilirubin level is falling and the jaundice therefore resolving.

A baby with mild physiological jaundice that is clearing on its own may be a little sleepy and slow to feed. Since plenty of fluid is an essential aid to the liver, he may be given extra water as well as whatever he will take from the breast.

If the jaundice deepens – or is slow to clear – it can be lessened by exposing the baby to cool, blue, fluorescent light ("phototherapy" or "light treatment"). He is undressed, so that the light can act on his whole skin surface. His eyes are bandaged to protect them from the bright light and a special box, containing the light-tubes, is placed over his crib. He will probably only need to stay under the light for two or three days but although this is not distressing for him, it may distress you.
☐ The baby and his treatment box may be kept in the nursery instead of by your bed. It is worth *asking* whether he can be treated beside you.
☐ The bandaged eyes mean that you cannot see his face properly and cannot interact with him. You will be allowed to take him out of the crib and remove the bandages for feedings, but it is still very distressing not to be able to pick him up whenever you wish.
☐ The combination of his sleepiness and the extra water he has to be given can make for difficulties in getting breast-feeding started.

☐ His father may scarcely be able to make contact with him since his periods without bandages and out of the crib are so brief.

☐ The jaundice may foil all your plans for an early discharge.

☐ Don't be surprised or angry with yourself if you find these days depressing; just hang on to the fact that once the bilirubin level in the baby's blood begins to drop it will soon be over and the baby will be none the worse.

*Jaundice caused by infections*
Babies *can* get various forms of "hepatitis" (infection of the liver) but these are rare. Formerly, when a mother had one of these virus infections of the liver she used to be isolated from her baby, adding the agony of separation to the misery of the infectious hepatitis. The incubation period for hepatitis is so variable and often so long that if a baby is going to catch it from his mother he will probably have done so long before the mother shows signs of illness, so separation of mother and baby is no longer routine.

Infectious hepatitis in an older baby or a child is always cause for concern, but the course of the illness may be mild or very serious. The yellow jaundice will not appear until the illness has been present for some time.

In a young baby, infection of *any* organ can cause jaundice because the efficiency of the liver is impaired by the general infection in the body. Yellow jaundice, appearing after a period of illness, does not therefore necessarily indicate liver infection but may be because of the effects of infection elsewhere.

*Breast milk jaundice*
This rare type of jaundice in the newborn period deserves a special entry because it can cause misunderstanding and misery to mothers.

The presence of an unusual chemical in the breast milk (which does the mother no harm at all) impairs the efficiency of the baby's liver in dealing with finished red blood cells.

The doctor makes the diagnosis of "breast milk jaundice" by *excluding* every other possible cause for the baby's yellowness. Once she or he is certain that this chemical is the only possible cause, there is no further reason for concern because *breast milk jaundice is never dangerous*. The baby can go home, yellow though he may be, and, within a few weeks of full breast-feeding, his body will adapt, his liver will build up its full efficiency and the jaundice will clear. *Breast milk jaundice is not a contra-indication for breast-feeding*. It does not mean that you, after all that you have heard about breast milk being the perfect food, are poisoning your baby.

*Congenital defects causing jaundice*
In very rare cases malformation of the liver or bile duct may cause jaundice. The yellowness will usually not appear before the baby is ten days old.

If it is only the channel (bile duct) outside the liver which is missing or deformed, surgery may put matters right. If the trouble is within the liver itself there may be nothing that can be done.

# Laxatives

No baby or child should ever be given a laxative (or a suppository) without specific instructions from the doctor. His intestine will empty itself when it needs to do so. That may be twice every day or once every four days. There is no relationship between daily bowel movements and good health.

Trying to force a daily pattern with laxatives may upset the whole system, and laxatives tend to be habit forming too. You dose your child on Tuesday because he has not passed a motion since Sunday. He will pass a large motion on Wednesday and his bowels will then be abnormally empty. It may be Saturday before they are ready to empty again, but you have dosed him again on Friday. . . .

If a child is genuinely constipated, so that his motions are not only infrequent but also hard and painful to pass, then the doctor may prescribe stool softener to make things more comfortable for him.

# Lice

## Head lice

Given the chance, head lice live on the scalp and stick their eggs (called "nits") to the bases of individual hairs. These lice do not need much of a chance. Infestation with head lice is now extremely common among children in playgroups, nurseries and schools. It is just as common in "nice" neighborhoods as in less privileged ones, and keeping your child's hair extra-clean with frequent shampooing will not help unless you use the shampoo as a time for *inspecting* his scalp: lice don't mind clean hair and their nits are not killed by ordinary toiletries. Lice itch *frantically*. If your child is scratching his head, take a look. . . .

*What to do*
☐ Check your child's head by parting the hair again and again across different parts of the scalp. If there are living lice you will see them as tiny brownish-black *things* moving against the paler scalp. You will probably be horrified but try not to shriek, for the child's sake.

☐ If your child's hair *is* washed frequently, most of the living lice may have been washed out but you must look carefully for minute white dots sticking to the base or on the shaft of individual hairs. These are the nits and shampooing will neither kill nor remove them. Left there they will hatch.

☐ Ask your doctor for the chemical lotion or special "shampoo" that is currently being recommended in your area. Lice have become resistant to some. From time to time schools send out warning notices about lice with recommendations for treatment. If in doubt about what to use (especially if this is your child's third infestation in as many months) call the school for current advice.

☐ Most of the chemicals have to be left on the hair and scalp for at least two hours and then shampooed out. It is sensible to treat yourself and other family members at the same time, especially other children.

☐ All sheets and pillowcases, as well as hats, should be thoroughly washed.

☐ After treatment the nits will be dead, but still there. Your pharmacy can sell you an especially fine-toothed comb to get them out. Most small children object violently to this procedure.

## Body lice

Body lice are a different species from head lice. They live and lay their eggs in clothing and only go on to the body to feed. They make minute red puncture marks, which itch so frantically that the child scratches ceaselessly and therefore may infect the bites.

*What to do*
☐ Chemicals similar to those used for head lice are available as creams and dusting powders for body lice but, since these lice live in clothing and bedding, you will need advice on getting rid of them permanently. Ask your doctor.

# Medicines

Your doctor prescribes a course of medicine because your child needs it. If he needs it at all he needs every dose. Don't stop giving it because he seems better or because he dislikes it. If you really cannot get it down him or he vomits it, tell the doctor immediately. Most medicines (such as antibiotics) are supposed to be given at regular intervals so that the level of the drug in the child's bloodstream stays constant. Ask the doctor whether the child must be woken at night to take medicine, or whether the stated number of doses can be fitted in while he is awake. Write down the times you give it. It is easy to forget a dose or to get muddled, especially if you are giving two drugs on different dose schedules.

If your child always finishes the prescribed course of a medicine, you should not have any left. If you have, say, some cough syrup prescribed for use "as needed" left, *throw it away*. Many medicines have a short shelf-life. Anyway you should never use the same medicine for another child or illness without consulting your doctor.

*Medicines for babies*
Exact doses are critical and tiny quantities may be difficult to measure. Medicine for a baby may be prescribed as drops: easy to measure and to give.
*Liquid medicines* These are usually prescribed for small children in preference to pills but often taste nasty with synthetic fruit "concealing" a bitter drug. Sit him up on a chair or on your lap (never give medicine with the child lying down; he might choke) and put a glass of his favorite drink beside him ready to wash the taste away. Measure the proper dose using the pharmacist's 5ml spoon, but put it into a big spoon or "medicine tube" so that it does not easily spill. Get the child to open his mouth and pour it in gently.

If he simply hates it, try concealing the taste by mixing the proper dose into a spoonful of something soft but strong tasting like apple sauce or chocolate mousse. Tell him it is medicine but that it does not taste nasty this way and then proceed on the assumption that he will take it. Don't pretend it is just apple sauce or the funny taste may put the child off apple sauce as well as medicine. Don't try to hide the medicine in a drink. It will only sink to the bottom and stick to the sides of the glass or bottle. Even if he empties it he will not have had the full dose. If he still will not take the medicine you can try the following:
☐ *Force* Wrap the child in a blanket so that he cannot bat the spoon out of your hand and then calmly wait him out. Pop it in the minute he opens his mouth either to cooperate or protest.
☐ *Bribery* With an older child you can often strike a bribe/bargain, perhaps a candy immediately afterward, a comic book he badly wants or the promise of a game.
*Changing the medicine* Your doctor may sound a bit scornful if you admit that you cannot get the medicine down the child. But it can be extremely difficult: maybe he has not had to try recently. He can prescribe the same drug in a different form.
*Pills and capsules* If the child wants to cooperate, but simply loathes the taste of the liquid, try capsules or pills (sugar-coated if possible). Some children manage to swallow these at a surprisingly early age. Wetting the capsules to make the gelatine coating slippery makes them easier to swallow. Explain that the bit of his tongue which tastes things is at the front and that if the pill or capsule goes at the back of his tongue he will not taste it. Give him a drink to hold, get him to open wide, pop it right back on his tongue and encourage him to empty that glass.

If he cannot or will not cooperate, capsules are useless as they must never be opened or crushed. Tablets can be crushed to a really fine powder. Put a layer of anything slippery and strong tasting that your child really likes – jam, honey, peanut butter – in a small spoon. Dump the powder on top, all in one place, and cover it with another delicious layer. The spoonful should simply slide down the child's throat and he will never taste the powder at all. If you cannot think of anything the child will want to eat a whole spoonful of, try *mixing* the powder with a very small amount of yeast extract or something with an equally strong or salty cover-up taste to make a sort of pellet no bigger than a salt spoon. If you are still stuck, there is one more trick to try with a whole pill. Push it into the tiniest piece of banana which will hold it. Pop it in and encourage him to swallow this "banana pill" straight down. Don't use this technique with a grape or cherry, because it could lead to choking.

*Over-the-counter medicines*
☐ Babies should not be given *any* medicines without the advice of a doctor.
☐ If you want to be able to give a baby or small child pain relievers, teething medicines and so forth, ask your doctor which of these he recommends and check the dose and its frequency with him.

☐ Remember that vitamins, minerals and other "health supplements" *are* medicines. Ask advice about those, too.

☐ Skin applications (such as cream prescribed for a rash) are medicines too: the active ingredients may be absorbed through the skin into the bloodstream. The size and frequency of the dose are just as important as they are in medicines given by mouth.

☐ *Never* rely on breaking an adult pill to arrive at a children's dose. You cannot be sure of the accuracy of the dose.

# Meningitis/Encephalitis

Meningitis means inflammation of the "meninges," which is the lining surrounding the spinal cord and the brain. Encephalitis means inflammation of the brain itself. Neither is really a disease in its own right, with its own causative organism. A variety of viruses and bacteria can cause this kind of inflammation.

Diagnosis (and planned treatment) depends on examination of a sample of the cerebro-spinal fluid which bathes the brain and spinal cord. Doctors obtain these samples by carrying out a lumbar puncture, in which the patient is curled up so as to widen the spaces between the vertebrae and a hollow needle is then inserted into the fluid-filled space below the bottom of the spinal cord itself. A local anesthetic is injected before the hollow needle is introduced. Although the doctor who carries out a lumbar puncture may get some information from the pressure of the fluid and from its appearance, anxious parents may have to wait some time for a diagnosis as the fluid has to be examined in the laboratory and any organisms found in it have to be cultured.

*Meningitis in babies*
A baby with meningitis will be obviously ill but it may not be at all obvious what kind of illness he has. He is likely to be off his feedings; he may vomit; he may have convulsions; he may be miserable and irritable or detached and withdrawn; in short, he will seem very much like a baby with an acute infection.

None of the "classical" signs of meningitis – such as headache, stiffness of the neck or dislike of bright light – are customarily seen in babies with meningitis. Occasionally the fontanelle (the soft spot on the top of the head) becomes tense or even bulges and you may see the doctor looking for this. Otherwise he must diagnose meningitis by excluding other likely sources of acute illness (ears and urinary tract especially) and then by admitting the baby to the hospital where a lumbar puncture can be carried out and the cerebro-spinal fluid examined for raised pressure and for infective organisms.

*Meningitis in toddlers and older children*
The "classical" signs – headache, stiff neck and dislike of light – are unlikely to feature in meningitis in a child under three, so if a toddler *has*
one of these signs, don't jump to the conclusion that meningitis is likely. In an older child the trio together are suggestive (though by no means absolutely conclusive).

Toddlers with meningitis are obviously *ill* and may well have fever, vomiting and perhaps convulsions. Meningitis becomes a likely explanation for all this if a child also displays a sudden and conspicuous change of mood, almost a change of personality. He may be uncharacteristically cross, clingy, frightened, aggressive . . . whatever he is, if he is "quite unlike himself" a visit to the doctor is urgent.

Whatever the age of the child, a presumptive diagnosis of meningitis will always be confirmed by lumbar puncture but, while lumbar punctures are quite often carried out on babies who turn out *not* to have meningitis/encephalitis, the clearer symptoms in older children mean that negative lumbar punctures are less frequent.

☐ Don't allow yourself to be haunted by the possibility of meningitis/encephalitis to the extent that every headache or stiff neck frightens you. *Any baby or child with meningitis will be obviously ill*. If the child is ill you will be seeing a doctor. These are not illnesses that you are likely to miss by failing to take a symptom seriously enough.

☐ If one of the virulent forms of meningitis is affecting children in your area and you are anxious neither to risk reacting too slowly to symptoms *nor* to be over-fussy, go and discuss the dilemma with your doctor in detail and ask him for guidelines.

☐ Meningitis/encephalitis can sometimes be caused by viruses that have already made the child ill with one of the infectious diseases of childhood, such as mumps. If a baby or child with one of these complaints suddenly seems more ill, when you have expected him to be better, and especially if a mood change or uncharacteristic behavior is part of the picture, call the doctor even if he only saw the child the day before.

☐ Remember that although these illnesses are serious and can leave after-effects such as partial deafness, *the majority of babies and children recover absolutely unscathed*.

# Mouth ulcers

Single mouth ulcers may appear as a sore red area with a yellowish-white center on the inside of the child's cheek, on the gum or beneath the tongue. They are very painful indeed. They take about ten days to clear up. The most useful treatment is usually a cortisone ointment which your doctor may prescribe for your child.

Several shallow white ulcers appearing together on the roof of the child's mouth, inside the cheeks, or on the gums, may be a first attack of the herpes simplex virus; later attacks will take the form of cold sores. This first attack is extremely painful. The child will probably refuse all solid food: he may even find it difficult to drink. A straw will help. Vaseline applied gently to each ulcer may help a little by preventing friction against the teeth.

# Nosebleeds

Nosebleeds caused by a blow on the head or nose should be seen by a doctor. Spontaneous nosebleeds can be caused by the child picking his nose, or by the spontaneous rupture of a tiny blood vessel inside it.

*What to do*
☐ Reassure the child. Most hate the sight of their own blood so sit him up leaning forward over a washbasin with the tap running fast so that it is continually washed away. Don't let him swallow the blood: it will make him feel sick.

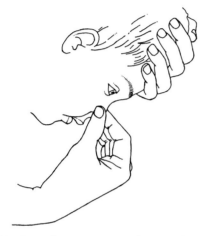

☐ If bleeding is heavy or goes on for more than two minutes, pinch the nostrils firmly together for about two minutes during which time the blood should clot.
☐ Don't let the child blow or fiddle with his nose for at least an hour even though the clotted blood will feel uncomfortable.
☐ If the child has repeated nosebleeds for no apparent reason he may have a fragile blood vessel in his nose. It may eventually have to be cauterized by a doctor.

# Nursing or caring for sick children at home

Nursing a baby with a heavy feverish cold, a toddler with chickenpox or a four-year-old with the flu can often be an unpleasant combination of worry and boredom. Nursing a baby with measles or a toddler with whooping cough can be a nightmare. The following tips are intended to make these inevitable parts of family life just that bit easier for *you*.
*The sick child's basic needs* Babies and pre-school children who are ill need masses of company. If you are the nursing-person that means *you*; your presence, your company and entertainment and your arms. The more relaxed you can be about being so absolutely necessary, the less irksome it will probably seem:

☐ Be realistic (with your doctor's help) about the probable length of the illness. A child with a bad cold may be back at nursery school in two days but one with measles is likely to be quite ill enough to matter for at least a week.
☐ Re-arrange any commitments within that period so that you aren't constantly worrying about whether or not you will be able to leave him tomorrow.
☐ Call on any other available help, from your partner, relations and friends, not only so that you can keep engagements that are important to you and have a break yourself but also so that you have support and company during worrying times like the small hours' watch beside a child who is delirious. If your partner's firm is amazed when he says he needs time off because his child is ill – well, maybe it will teach them something. Why should children's illnesses only interrupt the *mothers'* work-lives?
☐ If you are the kind of person who can't bear to spend whole days just chatting, making drinks, telling stories and cutting out paper dolls, think of a project you've been waiting to have time for and which you can carry out *while* doing some of those things. Guitar practice can be child-entertainment. Cleaning out closets may be boring for you but entertaining for a child. If you're going to be bored anyway you might prefer to end up with clean closets.
*Food and drink* Unless your doctor tells you otherwise, the sick child can have anything he wants of what is available and need have nothing except *drink*.
☐ Remember that drink is especially important if there is vomiting and/or diarrhea, especially if the child is also feverish. If you are not sure the child is taking in enough liquid, ask the doctor for a target quantity for the 24 hours.
☐ Most small children drink more if they are given tiny glassfuls of varied fluids.
☐ An almost-weaned baby will probably drink more if he is allowed to use his bottle – or, alternatively, have your milk.
☐ Older children may drink more through a straw – they may suck ice with pleasure too.
*Warmth* An ill child needs his energy for getting better. You don't want him to have to use it on getting warm *or* getting cool. Your aim is not *extra warmth* but a steady temperature.
☐ Try not to let him go from a warm room to an icy bathroom. If it is icy he could wash in the kitchen. . . .
☐ Don't overdress him. If he is in bed the pajamas that keep him comfortable every night will be right now; why add a sweater? If he is up, ordinary indoor clothes are fine.
☐ Don't snuggle feverish children up. Their overheated skins cannot shed heat if they are insulated by layers of clothes and bedding.
*Bed or not* Children are seldom *kept* in bed nowadays because doctors know that they can use more energy on bored bed-gymnastics than they use playing in the living room. But that doesn't mean that a sick child with a headache and a temperature might not be happier in some kind of "bed." Unless

you are happy to sit in his room with him or to run up and downstairs every five minutes all day, try to think of a "bed" he can have in the room that *you* want to use.

☐ Babies will want cuddling. When they can't use your arms and lap as a "bed" they will want to be near you. Bring the carriage into the kitchen or the carrier into the living room.

☐ Toddlers and small children need "nests." The sofa may be ideal but if it is in the wrong room, a bean-bag chair or nest of cushions may be better.

☐ Older children who really feel better lying down may be happiest on a cot or air mattress. You can easily move it for a change of scene – perhaps to the television or even into the yard in summer. . . .
*Handling the child* Feeling unwell will make him irritable and easily frustrated. While you do not want him to feel that persuading you that he is ill means total license and your undivided attention, it is no good expecting his most reasonable and grown up behavior. A happy medium means treating him as if he were one stage younger than his actual age, dropping the top demands of the moment. Treat a crawler like a baby, a toddler like a crawler, a pre-school child like a toddler. . . . But within those concessions, ask for, or rather just behave as if you take for granted, ordinarily civil behavior.
*Routines* The child will feel more ordinary and behave more normally if you keep some pattern to his day. Don't let the hours drift past unmarked.

☐ Get him up in the morning even if it is only into clean pajamas and his nest instead of bed.

☐ Make small ceremonies of meals even if he is only having a drink.

☐ Put him to bed for his usual naps and keep bedtime just as usual even if you know that you will be up and down to him all night.
*Play* While your company and attention will be what he really craves, the following ideas may help to relieve his boredom and give you at least a little time to get on with other things.

☐ A "being ill box" is a good idea, especially during the pre-school years when many children seem to get one cold or throat infection after another. Save all the surplus things your child is given, like his second painting book or those felt-tip pens. Assemble odds and ends that he has had and

lost interest in, like trinkets won at a fair; things you might have put in the "odds and ends box" but did not because they were too good – like pretty boxes or tinsel ribbon from Christmas – plus a few small items you buy from time to time, like a new drawing block, some plasticine, colored sticky labels and transfers.

☐ If you want to be more elaborate than this, order a parcel of "tiny toys" from a wholesaler; they are mostly junk (and unsafe for children under about three), but just right for novelty for a bored, miserable child. Add one or two toys that your child is not usually allowed to have. They might be things that you find too expensive to keep replacing, like a battery-operated flashlight, or something too noisy, like a harmonica. A "comforting person" will probably be popular. It can be any soft toy that you have prevented from becoming part of your child's regular "family" but which appears each time he is ill. You may also like to lend anything entrancing of your own that the child would not normally be allowed to play with like costume jewelry or discarded make-up.

Put the whole lot into a box and hide it. The whole point is lost if the child knows what is in it. Dip in, or let the child dip in, either at regular intervals through the day, or just whenever you think he really needs a new distraction.

☐ A small child who feels too ill to *do* much needs interesting things to look at and to fiddle with. Try a mobile; the family goldfish bowl to keep him company, and something "fiddly" like a small abacus, a string of beads or a squeaky toy.

☐ When you cannot be with him he may enjoy the radio, preferably tuned to something like a "call-in" rather than just music which will soon become a background blur. If he is in the same room with the television, this is one exceptional time when slightly-less-than-selective watching might possibly be allowed!

☐ When he is a bit better but does not want to be up he must have a proper play surface. A large tray on his knee will do but a swing-across bed-table is better because he does not have to keep still. A good compromise between these two is a large cardboard box with two-semi-circles cut out of its long sides. Placed across the child's knees it makes a satisfactory and comfortable temporary play table.

☐ If you put a large plastic tablecloth right over the bed, he can do almost anything in bed that he likes doing out. Try a bowl of sugar or rice for "sand play," a mixing bowl and marbles to whiz around and around it, pastry to make into "men," your old make-up and a mirror to watch his own transformation in, and a propped up tray to whiz his cars down.

☐ When you cannot play with him, try starting him off on activities and then setting him tasks to complete while you are busy. Show him old photo albums and ask him to find all the pictures of himself; make a string of paper dolls and then ask him to color them; set all his toy animals out and then ask him to put them in their proper families; help him find some pictures of cars in a magazine and then ask him to find as many more as he can; start a bead necklace and leave him to finish it or bring him the shells you collected on vacation and ask him to sort them out.

☐ A child who is confined and inactive often learns a lot because he does not get distracted by his desire to rush off and be physically active. Read to him; show him how to cut out neatly or to trace accurately; talk to him and use books to look things up in; introduce him to a new puzzle or bring out a construction set that he has never taken much interest in and see if now is the time for him to find he can do it.

☐ Choose some playthings that do not slide about and get lost in the bedclothes all the time. He may enjoy those cut-out shapes that miraculously stick, all by themselves, on to sheets of special felt. He may enjoy a magnet and things to "catch" with it.

☐ Glove puppets are excellent company in bed. You may find that the child will use a glove puppet to tell you what he is feeling: some children find it much easier to express misery, headache, dread of medicines, etc., through "someone" else. You can make glove puppets very simply (start with a sock!) or, if bought puppets are too expensive, you can gradually accumulate a collection of "finger puppets" which most small children find much easier to use.

See also FEVER.

# Pediatrician

Choosing a pediatrician for your first baby is not easy because you do not yet know the baby (who is only a bulge inside you) or know yourselves as parents.

If you like and trust your obstetrician, he is a good person to ask for a recommendation; so is your own doctor. If either or both of them work in a group, with a pediatrician as a colleague, that pediatrician may be the obvious choice for your child. Teachers giving childbirth classes can also sometimes give you useful information about children's doctors in your area, and so can other parents who are your neighbors and friends.

Do go and talk to any pediatrician you are considering. It's important to make sure that you are comfortable with her, adult to adult, and that her location and back-up services are likely to suit you. If she does work in a group practice or health center, for example, there are advantages and disadvantages to weigh. You may welcome the idea of constant night, weekend and vacation cover by the group, or you may feel that you would only want to speak to her, personally. Some pediatricians work closely with nurse practitioners who screen calls and can give reassurance and explanation. You may find that idea very comforting or you may feel that having a third party stand between you and contact with the doctor would be frustrating.

Many new parents make a good choice first time around and stay with the same pediatrician as long as they remain in the area. That's ideal because the better that doctor knows you and your family, the better the job she will be able to do by your growing child. But if you find – after a few months, or as your infant turns into a toddler, or even later when he needs to make his own relationship with the doctor as a schoolchild – that you are not comfortable and satisfied, don't despair. There need be no embarrassment about leaving one pediatrician and consulting another provided you are not casting aspersions on the first doctor's professional competence. She knows, even better than you do, that where your child's health care is concerned you must have a doctor with whom you feel personally at ease. Do be honest, though. If you go from one pediatrician to another *without formalizing the changeover*, you will be asking the new doctor to work without your child's full history and medical records. If the child is to change doctors that information must go, too.

*Using your pediatrician*
You need a real relationship of mutual communication and trust so do try to get to know the doctor, during your early visits, and give her the chance to get to know you. You can set the whole relationship off to a good start if you ask directly about some of the issues that often cause misunderstandings. Ask how (and under what circumstances) you should contact her outside office hours. Ask what you should do if you are ever unable to reach her in an emergency. Are there circumstances in which she would expect you to take the child directly to the emergency room or would she always prefer you to reach her, or a colleague first? And do ask what she feels about being consulted over the telephone. You may find that she will call back for emergencies all through the day but has special "telephone hours" when she is willing to deal with non-urgent matters. Once you know how she prefers to conduct her practice you can tell her what you feel and reach an agreed compromise.

Your doctor has an absolute duty to explain things to you so that you understand, but you have an absolute duty to listen and then tell her if you *don't* understand. If you say, meekly "I see, doctor" when you don't see at all, subsequent misunderstandings are as much your fault as the doctor's. If she makes you feel stupid, or doesn't seem to have time to explain, you need to change your doctor.

### Contacting your doctor
Many parents go through unnecessary agonies of indecision about whether to contact their doctor. Your child's health and wellbeing are your responsibility. Society recognizes that and provides pediatricians to help you fulfill it. If you are concerned about your child you have not only the right but the duty to seek medical advice. If your concern turns out to have been ill-founded (this time) it does not mean that you have "wasted the doctor's time" because checking that all *is* well is just as important a part of her work as coping when all is *not* well. So try to trust your own judgment and feelings. If your child "doesn't seem right" to you, contact your doctor even if you cannot pinpoint any particular symptom or assess its seriousness.

### New babies
Until babies' bodies have settled into life outside the womb and their physiological functions have settled into rhythms, their wellbeing is often hard to assess and some parental anxiety is almost inevitable. Doctors all know this and all also know that worrying will do nothing for your recovery from the birth or for your breast milk. Ask for help whenever you feel anxious and let your medical advisers act as educators. If today's consultation was not necessary from the baby's point of view, it was from yours, and may have taught you something which will help you to stay calmer tomorrow.

If you need a lot of support during your baby's first weeks, your doctor might suggest that you join a post-natal support group. Don't feel that you are being "passed off." She is recognizing your need and trying to meet it.

### All babies
The younger a child is the more vigilance his health requires because:
☐ He cannot talk, and may give conflicting signals so that you confuse acute earache with teething or abdominal pain with temperament.
☐ His immune system is comparatively inefficient so that he is both more liable to pick up infections and to suffer severely from them.
☐ His small size and infant characteristics make him extra-vulnerable in many respects. He is more liable than an older child to dehydration in gastro-intestinal illnesses; to convulsions in high fever; to respiratory difficulties with colds. . . .

Play safe. If he *seems* unwell, assume that he is unwell and don't wait to "see how he is tomorrow" as you might sensibly do with a school child. And if he *doesn't* seem unwell but doesn't seem "like himself," watch him carefully. A baby who usually

sucks well and won't suck at all today is probably brewing something. A baby who is usually active and demanding and seems quiet and withdrawn may be in trouble. And a baby who is normally happy and sociable must have some reason for two hours' screaming. Major changes in established behavior patterns are an important cue to baby illnesses and you are the only people who can spot them before major symptoms develop.

### All children
A list of symptoms for which a doctor should be consulted tends to imply that a doctor should *not* be consulted ("bothered") in their absence. You will not miss obviously worrying signs; don't ignore others if they worry you or the child.

As your child gets older, though, you will find that you often "wait and see" because you will learn that there is little point in taking a six-year-old to the doctor with generalized malaise associated only with a raised temperature. The time to seek advice is next day when symptoms have developed or the fever has stayed obstinately high with nothing to explain it.

Within the limits of proper vigilance, do try to give your growing child a sense of confidence in his own body's ability to throw off minor ailments. If you are calm and sensible about illness and can avoid implying that every pain needs a pill and every sniffle a prescription, you will be teaching him to keep himself well in the future even while you keep him well in the present.

### Night, weekend and vacation calls
Anxieties tend to be most acute in the small hours but obviously no doctor would choose 3 am or Sunday lunchtime to give you reassurance! If your child is sick, try to anticipate *during* office hours what you may be going to feel when they are over.

If you are trying to decide whether to call right now or wait until the next morning, ask yourself the following questions:
☐ If you were unable to contact the doctor, would you feel that you had to call an ambulance or drive the child to the nearest emergency room?
☐ If you reached the doctor and she agreed to meet you at her office immediately, would you be eager to dress yourself and the child and go there?
☐ If your doctor listened to your story, either over the telephone or in person, and recommended admitting the child to the hospital, would you accept that advice without hesitation?
☐ If two out of three answers are "yes" your emergency call to the doctor is legitimate. If you do not feel your child is as ill as that, your call can probably wait until the next morning.
*Telephone advice* Once you and your doctor know and trust each other, time may be saved by telephone contact, especially in continuing illnesses where it is a question of "is he progressing as well as can be expected?" Ask your doctor what she feels about being consulted by phone and ask what time of day she prefers. Do remember, though, that if you report new illness by telephone, you put her

under heavy pressure to see the child even if you do not ask her to. If she does not, and the child later turns out to be seriously ill, she will feel very responsible. If you are concerned enough to want to speak to her it is better to take the child to see her.

# Rashes

Babies and young children quite often produce dramatic skin rashes without accompanying symptoms. A lot of them go away as suddenly as they arrive and nobody ever knows what caused them. Some are probably allergic reactions to something the child touched or ate; others may be caused by viruses.

You may want to show such rashes to your doctor so that he can exclude the possibility of one of the childish infections. It is certainly worth knowing whether or not your child has German measles, even if he is not ill.

A doctor will usually be able to tell you if a mysterious rash is *not* caused by a recognized infection but do not be surprised if he cannot then tell you what it *is* caused by. Transient skin conditions are extremely difficult to diagnose and extensive investigations of a first episode in a well child are scarcely ever worthwhile. If such investigations were undertaken the rash would probably have vanished long before there were any results available.

*See also* ALLERGIC CHILDREN/Urticaria; INFECTIOUS DISEASES OF CHILDHOOD.

# Rhesus disease

About 15% of women have blood which is Rhesus negative. If such a woman has a baby by a man who is Rhesus positive their baby's blood group may not match her own. While the placenta is under pressure during labor some of the baby's red blood cells can be squeezed through into the mother's circulation. If this happens and if the baby's red cells are Rhesus positive, the mother's blood will form antibodies to deal with these "invading" cells.

Although this does no harm to the mother or to that first baby who is born before he can be affected, a second or later child who is Rhesus positive may not be so lucky. As the mother's blood crosses the placenta to nourish the new fetus, the antibodies in it will attack his red blood cells. In the past, when Rhesus disease could not be prevented, many such babies died in the womb and those born alive were often so anemic that their brains were damaged by lack of oxygen. Since the killed red blood cells have to be disposed of by the liver, such a baby was also deeply jaundiced.

*Preventing Rhesus disease* Most problems of Rhesus incompatibility can be prevented by good prenatal care, and it is essential that the baby be delivered in a modern maternity unit.

Rhesus negative women who deliver Rhesus positive babies are immediately given an injection of Rhesus positive antibodies prepared from the blood of another person. These antibodies neutralize any "foreign" blood cells from the baby's circulation and thus prevent the mother's body from reacting to them by making antibodies of her own. She will need an injection after the delivery of each Rhesus positive child so as to protect the next.

While first babies are not usually at risk from Rhesus incompatibility, excellent antenatal care is important for Rhesus negative women in the first pregnancy as well as in later ones. There is a chance that an earlier miscarriage or termination might have been of a Rhesus positive fetus and that blood cells from it got into the maternal circulation. In such a case a first live baby could suffer from Rhesus incompatibility.

Every girl with Rhesus negative blood should be brought up to be aware of her particular need for sophisticated obstetric care.

*Treating Rhesus disease* A Rhesus negative woman will be carefully watched during pregnancy and her blood tested to see if she has any Rhesus positive antibodies. Her baby must be delivered in the hospital. A baby born with Rhesus disease may receive an "exchange transfusion," his own blood being gradually taken out while fresh Rhesus negative blood is put in. The transfusion washes out most of the antibodies that have reached him in the womb, while giving him Rhesus negative blood ensures that if any antibodies are left they will not attack the new red blood cells which will also deal with his anemia. This will be repeated until the level of jaundice drops.

# Ringworm

This is a fungus infection which has many forms affecting different parts of the body. Infection can occasionally come from animals, so if you have a case in the family get your vet to check any pets. Usually it is passed on from another child.

*Tinea capitis* (ringworm of the scalp) The child has one or more small bald areas usually round or oval in shape. They are covered with dry greyish scales and you can see the stumps of broken off hair among the scales. The doctor will confirm the diagnosis by shining a special light on the scalp and/or looking at a scraping of the flaky scales under a microscope.

Treatment with a recently developed antibiotic prevents further growth of the infecting fungus. The hair will recover completely in about three weeks. During this time the child will have to be kept away from nursery, playgroup or school. Other children in the family are likely to catch it, but the risk can be minimized by strictly separating his hairbrushes, towels, etc. If the bald patches embarrass the child, he can wear a cap or scarf.

*Ringworm of the body* This produces circular or oval areas with tiny bumps around the edges. Your doctor will probably prescribe a special ointment or paint. Treatment is easier and quicker than for the scalp, but you must check for hidden sites of the infection such as between the toes.

*See also* ATHLETE'S FOOT.

# Soiling

Bowel training is always assumed to be easier and quicker than bladder training and so it is – for the child who is eager to cooperate in becoming independently clean and dry. Quite a lot of toddlers do not feel cooperative at exactly the moment their parents choose to introduce potties instead of diapers. Problems with bowel training, including various forms of soiling, are far more common than most involved families realize. A conspiracy of silence helps nobody and helps least of all a child who is sent into nursery school to be labelled straight away "stinky."

Few children seem to feel possessive about their urine but many feel extremely possessive about their stools. The stools, after all, are part of the child's body. When they emerge he may still feel that they belong to him and he may well feel that he would like to handle, explore and smear them. Adult reactions – including disgust at their smell, speed of "cleaning up" and instant disposal down the lavatory – may not only surprise the toddler but hurt his feelings.

If he is not feeling cooperative with adult demands – and especially if he is looking for an arena in which to fight the power adults have over him – he may easily discover that in bowel training he can both fight and win. However great the pressure, nobody can *make* a child pass his movements in a potty or on the lavatory. He can pass them in his pants or on the floor in unconscious but active resistance, or he can withhold them altogether for long periods in equally unconscious passive resistance.

*Active resistance and soiling*
The child passes his movements almost anywhere except in the potty or lavatory and at almost any time except when you are trying to persuade him!
☐ He is not resisting you on purpose. Being angry – even though you will probably *feel* angry – will make matters much worse.
☐ Instead of increasing the pressure on him to open his bowels when and where you say, re-read the first paragraph of this entry and *take the pressure off*. It may help if you make your new position clear to him in words: "You obviously don't feel ready . . . so OK, it's up to you. . . . Remember that toilet training is supposed to hand responsibility for his toilet functions over to the child, not force him to follow a set of adult commandments.
☐ Help yourself to tolerate the situation by making some compromise solutions, like putting him in plastic-backed trainer pants (*without* shaming comment) or asking him to tell you when he has soiled himself so that he can be changed and "made comfy."
☐ Don't put him back into diapers unless you are at the very beginning of the whole toilet training process and he is still wearing them anyway a lot of the time. You cannot possibly encourage a child to feel more grown up by treating him like a baby if he isn't one.

*Passive resistance and soiling*
In order to avoid passing his movements in the potty or lavatory, the child has to withhold them until he gets up again. If that phase of active resistance is not defused, he may become more and more efficient at withholding and discover that he can avoid being scolded for putting his feces in the wrong place by keeping them inside his body. Remember that there are pleasant sensations involved, too.

If a child withholds his bowel movements for a period of days after he first feels the need to go, feces collect in his lower bowel and rectum, more and more fluid is taken from the waste-matter by his body so that the feces become harder and harder, and the rectum expands to a point where he actually stops receiving "need to open" signals.

In this situation a child's bowel is effectively blocked. He could not pass a normal movement even if he wanted to but, because he is still digesting food and producing more waste matter, he will begin to get leakage of semi-liquid feces from higher up above the log-jam. This is often the physiological mechanism behind the soiling of the child whose pants are always a little bit dirty but who never seems to pass a complete bowel motion in them.
☐ He is not resisting you on purpose. He probably is not conscious of withholding his stools and certainly makes no connection between doing so and defying your wishes. Anger is completely inappropriate.
☐ Ignoring the situation is not appropriate for long, either. Even slightly soiled pants smell and his friends will not be slow to point this out.
☐ You would probably be wise to seek advice from your doctor because if there *is* a blockage of hard feces, she or he is the one to advise on handling the matter. The days of repeated enemas are (almost) over but the child may need help with stool softeners. He will certainly need explanation of what has happened and why and this is often more convincing when given by an outside authority-figure. When the doctor explains that it is not the child's fault, he may be able to believe him although he cannot believe you.
☐ *Occasionally* the withholding begins because a child has a minute "anal fissure" or tear in the skin around the edge of his back passage. Passing a movement hurts acutely and this is what first makes him avoid doing so. Such a split is easily cured but, once again, you need a doctor's diagnosis, prescription and thoroughly sympathetic explanation to the child.
NB If you are consulting a child's doctor about a soiling problem, try to speak to him or her privately, on the telephone or in person, before you take the child to the office. A long description of his soiled pants and smell, given to a comparative stranger in front of him, will do nothing for his dignity and nothing to assure him that you are on his side.
NB Although soiling is often described as being deeply rooted in serious emotional disturbance – and although it certainly *can* be a serious symptom

of this kind — remember that soiling can also be the *cause* of emotional disturbance. However oblivious a school-aged child may appear, he is all too well aware of his own odor, his "difference" from other children and their reactions. Often his "don't care" attitude is because he *feels* that he is dirty, smelly and different and therefore is not particularly angry when others share his poor opinion of himself.

## Stomach-ache

Stomach-ache is a difficult symptom to cope with because it can herald an acute abdominal emergency (such as appendicitis); an illness in some quite different part of the body (such as tonsilitis); or nothing at all. Don't try home-diagnosis. Decide whether or not to call the doctor on the basis of:

☐ How severe the pain is.
☐ How long it lasts.
☐ How ill the child seems.
☐ Any other symptoms.

*Babies* Stomach-ache makes a baby scream and draw his legs and thighs up to his tummy. But so does anger. If cuddling comforts him and he seems otherwise well, you can afford to wait for other symptoms to appear.

If cuddling does not comfort him although he seems otherwise well, he may have colic. Talk to your doctor but not as an emergency.

If he has fever, diarrhea, vomiting, loss of appetite, and/or seems ill, call the doctor.

*Young children* They often cannot locate pain accurately or differentiate pain from nausea. If the child seems very ill, has other symptoms as well or has such severe pain that he cries, lies curled up and walks bent double, call the doctor at once.

If the pain is milder and there are no other symptoms, you can afford to wait and see. Call for advice if the pain is still bothering him after two or three hours.

*Acute intussusception* This is a very rare but acute abdominal emergency in babies between three months and two years. A small portion of the intestine telescopes into the portion in front causing total blockage. When natural intestinal movements press on the blockage the pain is so intense that the baby goes grey/white and seems beside himself. It goes off after two or three minutes, but happens again about 20 minutes later. He may vomit between attacks. Rush him to the hospital.

*Emotional causes* Some children get periodic bouts of stomach-ache and/or vomiting as a reaction to stress. Have him checked by the doctor the first time, to make sure there really is no physical cause. Then treat him with sympathy (the pain hurts just as much as if it was caused by a germ) and try to relieve the stress-cause. If the idea of a party gives him stomach-ache he probably should not go. If pain recurs each Monday talk to his teacher.

Although you need not bother your doctor for every one of your child's periodic stomach-aches, be careful. Proneness to stress pains does not protect him from all other possible causes. You will have to consider each one on its merit or you may miss the one that is appendicitis.

## Thrush

The fungus candida albicans is a normal inhabitant of the mouth, intestines and vagina. Usually harmless, it can set up the infection called thrush.

If you have a candida infection of the vagina, the fungus can reach your baby's mouth during birth or later on via ill-washed hands or inadequately sterilized bottles and nipples. It produces white patches on the inside of a baby's cheeks and sometimes on his tongue and the roof of his mouth. The patches look like milk but if you try to wipe them off they either stick or come away leaving raw patches underneath. The mouth is usually extremely sore so that the baby cannot suck comfortably.

Treatment consists of dropping a special antibiotic solution on to the patches.

A baby with thrush should have his diapers changed very frequently, as his stools will contain the fungus, and if they are left in contact with his warm wet bottom for long he may develop thrush around the anus. Treatment is by painting with a special cream that contains the specific anti-fungal agent.

## Tonsils and adenoids

Tonsils and adenoids are two pairs of bodies of "lymphoid" tissue, which act as filters to trap potentially harmful organisms. They are carefully sited in the path of bacteria and viruses that are breathed in through the nose and mouth: the tonsils can be seen on either side of the back of the throat while the adenoids are just out of sight at the base of the nose.

Until quite recently the tonsils and adenoids were regarded as *sites of infection* that were likely to cause ill health. As soon as they became enlarged, they were surgically removed in an operation which, for middle-class children at least, was almost "routine." In fact the tonsils and adenoids *always* enlarge after the first year — as do other bodies of "lymphoid" tissue, such as the neck glands. It is during early childhood that strong defenses against upper respiratory infections are needed and the tonsils and adenoids enlarge to meet the challenge: they enlarge to *help keep the child well*. Tonsils and adenoids enlarge even further when actively engaged in trapping organisms. If your child's tonsils are much enlarged during a bad cold, they are doing their job by preventing viruses penetrating further down the throat to the bronchi or even the lungs.

*Trouble with tonsils*
Acute tonsilitis can be caused by various viruses and bacteria. Although the tonsils are inflamed and the throat is red, small children seldom complain of sore throat as older children do. Very often you will consult the doctor because the child is obviously unwell, with flu-like aches and pains, fever, perhaps vomiting. Only when the doctor checks his throat — as he does whenever a child is unwell — will the source of the trouble be discovered.

Tonsilitis is infectious, often highly infectious since the victim is breathing out "germs" with every breath. It may be worthwhile to try to keep other children away for the couple of days of acute illness and it will certainly be worthwhile to try to keep a small baby protected from infection. A baby will not catch *tonsilitis* but the germs which have inflamed her brother's tonsils may easily set up another form of upper respiratory infection in her.

Acute tonsilitis can lead to infection of the middle ear. If it is caused by the organism called "streptococcus" (as in "strep throat") it can lead to later complications involving the kidneys or the heart. This is why your doctor will quite often prescribe antibiotics for tonsilitis even before the results of throat swabs sent to the laboratory are available to tell him whether the tonsilitis is in fact caused by this organism.

Expect the child with diagnosed tonsilitis to be quite ill for a couple of days and at home recovering for about a week.

*Trouble with adenoids* Although infection of the adenoids does not produce a specific illness comparable with tonsilitis, chronic or recurrent infection and resulting enlargement can cause problems. Swollen adenoids partially block the drainage from the back of a child's nose into his throat. Poor drainage can be associated with recurrent infection in the middle ear. Less seriously it can contribute to "catarrhal problems" sometimes including habitual mouth-breathing and, some people believe, indistinct speech.

If an ear, nose and throat surgeon decides that your child's adenoids should be surgically removed ("Adenoidectomy") before he is four years old, he will probably not remove the tonsils which should still have useful work ahead of them. If an older child has a tonsilectomy, however, his adenoids will often be removed at the same time.

*Tonsilectomy*
The decision to remove a child's tonsils must be taken by an ear, nose and throat surgeon to whom your doctor will refer him.

The surgeon has to decide whether the recurrent bouts of tonsilitis which have led to the consultation, and the state of the tonsils when he examines them, suggest that they are doing the child more harm than good. The tonsilitis makes him ill. If it recurs several times a year it may lead to him missing a lot of school and becoming generally "run down." But if the action of the tonsils is preventing each episode from being a bronchitis, the tonsilitis may in fact be the lesser of two evils.

Nowadays tonsilectomy before the age of five is very unusual. Often the surgeon will suggest a "wait and see" policy, making preliminary plans to remove the tonsils when the child is seven or eight and their most active life is over. Sometimes attacks of tonsilitis cease spontaneously around that age so that the deferred operation never becomes necessary, in fact.

A few children who have been occasionally subject to tonsilitis suffer a new series of severe attacks when they are in their teens. Tonsilectomy at 16 or 17 can be an extremely worthwhile procedure.

Tonsilectomy (or T & A as it will be called if the adenoids are also to be removed) is not a pleasant procedure because there is almost always some visible bleeding from the raw places in the throat, as well as considerable soreness for three or four days. Plan the operation so that you can be with your child and so that you can keep him at home, away from sources of infection, for at least a week after he is discharged from the hospital.

# Travel sickness

Almost everybody can get sick on a rough sea voyage, but travel sickness can afflict young children to such an extent that it makes buses or trains impossible forms of transportation and use of the family car a misery for everybody.

Travel sickness (or, more accurately, motion sickness) is thought to be associated with upset to the delicate balance mechanism of the inner ear. Perhaps this mechanism is more sensitive in children than in older people. Certainly travel sickness, however occasional or extreme, tends to improve with age.

If your child is going to be liable to car sickness you may know by the time he is six months old or not until he is nearer two years. Once he starts feeling, or being, sick on most car trips, the sickness is likely to go on until puberty. After that it will probably decrease.

*Preventing motion sickness*
There are many folk-preventatives such as hanging a chain from the back of the car or sitting the child on layers of brown paper. If one of these works for your child, fine. It probably will not!

☐ The exact form of the motion may be important. A rough choppy motion is often tolerable when a smoother, rolling motion makes the child sick. This is probably why ships affect most of us and why trains make few people sick. If you are desperate enough to consider changing your car, try the child in a model which is harder-sprung than yours. A car with soft suspension is usually a mistake.

☐ Heavy traffic and therefore stop-start driving is usually the most nausea-provoking. Your family may do better if most of its driving is undertaken at night, when traffic is lighter, and on highways where you can (usually) keep going.

☐ The child's own motion, added to the car's, may make matters worse. Once he graduates from a car-seat, fasten his seat belt firmly so that he does not roll on corners and encourage him to fix his head against a cushion. Active play (and back-seat scuffles) will usually make him more liable to be sick.

NB A lot of people – children *and* adults – feel sick always (and only) when they try to read in a car. Listening to a personal stereo or to tapes on the car's system may be a better choice of quiet in-car entertainment.

☐ Large greasy meals before traveling increase the tendency to sickness but so does hunger. Most families find that a light, non-greasy meal beforehand and a ready supply of sugary candy, plain crackers and iced water for consumption in the car work best.

☐ There are effective drugs against travel sickness but some of them have unpleasant side-effects like a very dry mouth or overwhelming sleepiness. Consult your doctor (rather than buying over the counter) and consider trying out his prescription in advance of an important trip or treat. Giving the medicine the recommended time in advance of the journey is important.

NB Side-effects will probably not matter if you can arrange to make longer trips while the child sleeps.

NB If you have a car-sick child who is of an age to unfasten his own seat belt, *have childproof locks fitted in the back of the car*. Children have been killed because they have leapt out of cars that were still moving, or into following traffic, in order not to vomit in the car.

# Verrucas and warts

Warts are growths on the skin caused by viruses. They are harmless. Most types eventually vanish by themselves and this probably accounts for the many "miracle cures" in folk medicine: the "cures" happen to coincide with the spontaneous disappearance of the warts.

Warts on the soles of the feet (plantar warts or verrucas) used to be considered highly infectious.

A child with a verruca was not allowed to go barefoot and was often banned from swimming, school PE and so forth. Nowadays plantar warts are regarded as trivial and self-limiting. Treatment is only needed if they cause pain by being pressed up into the foot as the child walks.

Verrucas can be treated by daily application of a special antiwart solution or application of liquid nitrogen. Consult your doctor.

# Vomiting

The forcible expulsion of the contents of the stomach always means something, but what it means or whether it means anything important, is often hard to tell. In any particular episode of vomiting you will need to consider the context, the child's general wellbeing and the presence or absence of any other symptoms.

*Vomiting in small babies*
Some babies are much "sickier" than others. There are babies who bring back a portion of almost every feeding. They may drive their parents mad with worry and leave the smell of partly curdled milk on every sweater in the house but they very seldom do themselves any harm at all. This is not true vomiting but regurgitation or "spitting up." Although you will certainly consult your doctor about it, your real evidence that the baby is doing himself no harm is on his weight chart.

However much milk he seems to you to lose, he is not losing more than his body can afford if he is gaining steadily.

A quicker additional check is the number of times he wets his diaper. If he were really bringing back more milk than his body could spare he would be short of liquid as well as short of food. If his diaper is soaking almost every time you pick him up he is certainly not going short of essential fluid.

Like older babies and children (see below) small babies can vomit at the beginning of an infection. *If your baby seems ill before or after he vomits, consult your doctor.*

*Projectile vomiting (pyloric stenosis)*
Some babies – more boys than girls – are born with a tendency to pyloric stenosis. During the first couple of weeks after birth (whether he was born premature or at full term) the muscles around the "pylorus," which is the channel at the bottom of the stomach, begin to thicken. This narrows the passage from the stomach into the gut, slowing up the milk's escape route. As he fills his stomach he vomits. After a few days, the entire feed is forcibly ejected. If you ever see this kind of vomiting you will recognize it. It is so forcible that far from just ruining your clothes, it may even hit the wall behind you.

Pyloric stenosis must be dealt with urgently because the baby really does lose almost all the food and water he takes in and would therefore become dehydrated and lose weight if left untreated. Luckily, though, a doctor can easily diagnose the condition by feeling the thickened pylorus while the baby is feeding. Once diagnosed it is dealt with, once and for all, in a short and simple operation.

NB If a baby is going to develop pyloric stenosis he will do so during his first two months and probably much earlier than that. Vomiting after two months of age must therefore be caused by something else and, if it is forcible enough to make you wonder if it is "projectile," it should certainly be reported at once to a doctor.

*Vomiting in older babies and children*
Some possible causes of vomiting are listed below: only you can put the whole picture together and decide whether or not this vomiting is part of a picture of illness and therefore requires you to call medical help.

☐ The vomiting may be a reaction to infection. If it is, the child will probably seem unwell. He may have nausea before the vomiting which is only partly relieved by it. He may have fever.

☐ Some children vomit easily in reaction to "digestive difficulties" – often simply eating when excitement makes digestion difficult. Such a child may vomit quite unexpectedly and without suffering from nausea beforehand. If he has been on an outing or to a birthday party, he may vomit in the middle of the night. You may clearly be able to see undigested food. If he feels perfectly all right afterward and the vomiting does not recur, you can forget it.

NB Despite appearances, this kind of vomiting is not due to *overeating* and it is very unfair to label the child "greedy" and unnecessary to warn him off treat foods on other occasions. Normal digestion cannot take place when the body is in a high state of excitement, anxiety or stress (think of yourself in early labor); in childhood, excitement and party food often go together. As he gets older he will both get used to social occasions so that they are less stressful and learn to recognize a stomach that is saying "no."

☐ Some children react to emotional stress by vomiting, whether or not there has been any insult to their digestions. Monday morning vomiting, for example, may be associated with going to playgroup or school, or a child may always vomit just before he was meant to go to a party or out with a parent who is separated from the family. It is the stress that needs dealing with rather than the vomiting.

☐ Travel sickness may cause vomiting as early as six months.

*Seeking medical help because of vomiting*
Your child needs a doctor if he is *ill*. Vomiting alone cannot tell you that he is ill but vomiting in association with other signs and symptoms can be part of a picture of illness. Seek medical help if:

☐ The child is sick and the vomiting does not make him feel better shortly afterwards.

☐ He is sick several times in succession – three or more times in half a day, for example, certainly merits a phone call.

☐ He is sick and also has other symptoms such as fever or diarrhea. If sickness is the first sign of an infection, other symptoms will certainly follow within a couple of hours.

☐ He seems generally "laid out" by the vomiting, exhausted, a poor color, un-hungry and unenthusiastic about anything.

NB The younger the child the more important it is to seek advice quickly for that combination of vomiting, diarrhea and perhaps fever. Taken together they will almost certainly take more fluid from the baby's body than he will put back by drinking. The result is dehydration – or "drying out" and this is a serious matter often requiring the replacement of fluid intravenously in the hospital. In a baby, the first sign of incipient dehydration is often a dry diaper.
*See also* DEHYDRATION; DIARRHEA; TRAVEL SICKNESS.

# Worms

Anyone, child or adult, can become infested with worms. There is nothing shameful about them and they are not associated either with squalor or "dirty habits."

*Pinworm (Threadworm)*
This is the only worm infestation which is at all likely outside the tropics. Pinworms look like tiny white threads and can be seem moving in the stools of an infested child or sometimes moving around the anus.

Although we pass millions of "living" organisms in our stools, including bacteria, funguses and so forth, we cannot see them. Seeing these obviously living, moving things coming out of our bodies gives most of us the horrors. If you are the first to see that your child has pinworms, try to control your revulsion so that the child does not pick it up from you. It may not even be necessary for him to *see* the pinworms he has produced. This is quite important because the various physical symptoms (such as stomach-ache) which are often said to be due to worms are not in fact caused by the worms themselves but by the disgust they arouse.

*Treatment*
A single dose of a medicine prescribed by your doctor will kill all the living worms and all the eggs. She or he may recommend a second dose two weeks later just in *case* any fertilized eggs managed to escape the first time.

☐ Treat the whole family at the same time. If you do not, infestation could be passed around and around the family for months.

☐ The medicine has to be taken in a dose matched to body weight and that can mean a large number of pills or a large dose of liquid for the larger members of the family. Some of them cause nausea in some people. Once you have all taken a worm-medicine which you found tolerable, keep a note of its name so that you can ask the doctor for it next time. (Yes, more than one infestation is extremely common while children are at school.)

☐ Some worm-medicines cause slight diarrhea in some children. Ask your doctor about the drug he is prescribing. If one of your family is recently toilet trained and would be horrified by an "accident," it might be kind to warn him of the slight possibility.

*Prevention*
You cannot prevent a child from picking up the infestation because he may do so whenever he holds hands with a child who has pinworm eggs under his nails, and then sucks his own fingers. But you can prevent the infestation from going around and around the family.

Pinworms live and fertilize their eggs in the bowel but the female prefers to lay the eggs in the slightly cooler environment of the skin around the anus. This is why you may see worms there as well as in the stools.

The worms tickle. If the child scratches his bottom and then puts his hands to his mouth he will take in some eggs and re-infect himself. If he scratches and then feeds you part of his banana, he may infect you.

☐ Keep children's nails short and take particular care with cutting the nails of a child who is being treated for pinworms.

☐ Persuade the infested child to wear close-fitting underpants or swimming trunks for a few nights until the medicine is certain to have worked and any eggs laid around the anus are certain to have been washed away. You want to be sure that however much he scratches, he cannot actually get eggs from the skin around his anus on to his fingers or under those nails.

☐ Be extra careful about washing hands after using the lavatory.

*Other worm infestations*
Infestation by tapeworm is a theoretical possibility. It usually results from eating undercooked pork. Don't.

*Toxocara* is the roundworm which infests cats and dogs so that they pass eggs in their stools. A child can be infected by a family pet so make sure that it is regularly wormed from the moment it comes into the household.

More often (though very rarely) a child is infected with toxocara when he plays on grass where untreated animals have been.

Because toxocara is only rarely a human problem, many people do not realize how serious this infestation is. Eggs transferred from the animal's excrement into a child's digestive system hatch into larvae which penetrate the intestinal wall and can migrate to any organ of the body. Wherever they end up, they cause acute local irritation and they can therefore cause a wide range of serious conditions, extending from liver problems to blindness.

The larvae can be killed by a single dose of medicine, as in pinworms. But killing the larvae does not undo any local damage already done.

Greater public awareness of toxocara is needed so as to encourage regular de-worming of animals and to raise people's perception of children having to play on animal-fouled ground from merely "disgusting" to "intolerable."

# Playthings

The following pages will help you to provide the playthings that will keep your child interested, happy and learning fast at each stage of his development.

| | What he needs | Why he needs it | Suitable "toys" |
|---|---|---|---|
| **First weeks** | *He needs as much contact with people as possible. Objects mean nothing to him at this stage. Physical and visual contact are what matter.* | *His survival depends on human care. He is programmed to attend to people's voices and faces.* | *He does not need objects. His "entertainment," apart from sucking etc., is in listening to your voice and in studying your face. His best focusing distance is only 8–10in (20–25cm) from the bridge of his nose.* |
| **From about five weeks . . .** | *Contact with you and the chance to study faces are still his prime needs. Hold him close, put his carriage or chair near you so he can watch your activities.* | *He has seen nothing, so variety and change are what matter. He will practice focusing his eyes on things at different distances, and begin to learn the appearances of things.* | *Mobiles, washing, or moving leaves, seen from his carriage; things strung across his crib. His own hands, left free to suck when he can "find" them.* |
| **From about three months . . .** | *He needs things to hold as well as to look at, and things which sound as he waves them about. Go for variety of shape and color.* | *When his random waving makes a rattle sound, the sound makes him look and see the clever thing he is making happen. He is learning to find his hands by touch and by eye; they are his best toy, don't conceal them in mittens or wrappings.* | *Small plastic or metal pots filled with dried peas, sugar or paper clips all sound different and give variety. Make sure the lids are securely on. Fill a transparent plastic bottle with colored water and detergent. It looks pretty and makes an interesting swooshy sound as well.* |
| | *He needs things to reach out for and things to swipe. His best reaching out will take place when he is supported sitting on your lap or in his chair.* | *Batting at hanging objects gives him practice in getting his hand to something he can see and the lovely power of making it move.* | *Woolly balls, partially blown-up balloons; a shiny plastic ball, tiny soft animal toys, paper streamers, a chiming ball.* |
| | *He needs things to get hold of. They will go into his mouth, so watch out for toxic paints, etc. as well as for sharp edges.* | *Once he can get hold of things, mouth and handle them, he can explore his world, object by object.* | *Seal a marble in a plastic bottle (such as a washed out detergent bottle). It thuds and alters its balance as the marble moves. Make bean bags with crunchy cornflake or dried pea filling. Make chewable books by putting magazine pictures into clear plastic wallets. Provide some big objects to get hold of; soft toys or cushions or loaves of bread.* |
| | *He needs physical play – give him games like "this little piggy" counting his toes, or "this is the way the farmer rides," bouncing his whole body.* | *He is learning about his whole body, where it ends and the "outside me" world begins, how it feels, what he can make it do.* | *Your lap is his best gym, his own body the perfect floor toy, with rolling over to practice. Bounce or roll him on your bed: it is as exciting as a trampoline. Buy or borrow a baby bouncer, it will stay in use through toddlerhood.* |

|  | **What he needs** | **Why he needs it** | **Suitable "toys"** |
|---|---|---|---|

**From about six months . . .**
Many of the playthings he already has will still be popular, but he will increasingly *use*, as well as merely examine, them. So provide at least some toys with which he can actually do something and from which he can learn something specific.

*Everyday household objects especially those used in his care.*

*He is deeply attached to you and will soon be highly imitative. If he is encouraged, through play, to take part in his own care he will feel less overwhelmed and bullied later.*

Bath equipment: washcloth, toothbrush. Feeding equipment: own spoon, cup, etc. "Helping Mom:" dusters, brushes, etc. Clothes: a try at getting his own socks on, etc.

*Toys with a definite cause and effect.*

*He needs to feel that he has power to affect his world. He needs to feel "because I do this, that happens. I do it; I make it happen."*

Toys that squeak when squeezed, pots and pans or drums and tambourines to bang. Miniature cars to pull, paper to tear.

*Objects that behave in different ways when they are treated in the same way.*

*Once he has grasped his own power to make things happen he can learn a lot about his world by discovering that objects have basic characteristics which differentiate them from each other whatever he does.*

Things that roll when they are pushed and things that don't: a ball and a block. Things that crumble when banged and things that don't: a cracker and a piece of bread.

*Toys which are fun at the baby level of looking, sucking, banging, but have built-in potential for more advanced play.*

*He will often acquire new skills by first making something happen by accident and then, because it was fun, teaching himself to do it again on purpose.*

A pull-string musical box, nesting toys, containers and things to put in and out of them. Boxes, jars and bottles with lids to remove; "pop-up" toys.

*Games you can play with him.*

*He learns by watching and by imitating what you do. The ability to watch and copy will be important to all his later education. You can foster it now.*

Build block towers for him to knock down; soon he will build too. Post ping-pong balls down a cardboard tube. Eventually he will learn to angle the tube so they roll in particular directions. Roll a ball for him to retrieve; soon he will roll it back to you. Play the piano and let him bang the keys, and make loud or soft, high or low discords.

*Once the baby can crawl, much of his play will be crawling for its own sake, but some kinds of playthings are ideal at this stage. He needs toys big enough to see across the room and crawl to, and toys he can have fun with when he reaches them.*

*Being a crawler can be frustrating. He needs to work off on suitable objects the inevitable frustrations of having unsuitable ones removed from his explorations.*

Big wheeled toys, wooden trucks, etc. Really big soft toys and cushions that will stay still while he pummels them. Beach balls or balloons which may escape when he pushes them. Rings which he will eventually learn to pick up and throw.

*He needs his own special possessions, like, but distinct from, everyone else's.*

*As he nears his first birthday he begins to feel himself to be a separate and unique individual. Possessions can help to encourage this vital sense of self.*

A safety mirror set in a molded frame with finger holes. He can see something he is realizing is "me." Eventually he will make faces at himself. Photographs of himself with and without you. His own special plate, mug, books, pictures, etc.

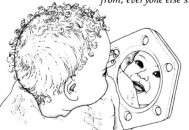
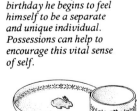

## Playthings from about one year . . .

Your child is ready for more elaborate toys, but safety is a very real factor, for he is pulling himself to standing and about to become a biped. Almost every child will enjoy the following types of toy; they are safe and he will use them long enough to make the investment worthwhile.

*Toddle truck* This small push-cart is designed so that it neither tips when the child pulls himself up by the handle nor runs away when he toddles with it. It gives him mobility indoors and out during the cruising stage and has years of life ahead as first doll's carriage or wheelbarrow. The design is crucial – don't try to make your own.

*Pull-toys* Once he walks steadily he can pull a wheeled toy along at the same time. Would-be pet owners will enjoy a realistic dog with wagging tail and wobbling tongue.

*Ride-on toys* Any toy for him to sit on, and push himself along by his feet, should have castors, which will safely take pressure in any direction, not wheels, which will tip when he pushes randomly.

*Push-toys* These are unsafe until he can get to his feet without using anything to pull up by, and understands that when riding, he must push straight with his feet. Then a wheeled animal with a handle will be very popular.

*Romping toys* Soft toys nearly as big as himself are fun to romp with and a safety valve for feelings too, as they get punched and strangled. Save money by using a ready-to-sew "novelty cushion kit." There are huge snakes, teddy bears and even a snail big enough to ride on.

*Fitting toys* Although he is concentrating largely on getting mobile, hand control is developing too. He needs a few toys which hold his attention while he sits still for a change. Follow the rule: the smaller the hands the bigger the pieces should be. Of the many available the following best combine fun and lasting play value.

☐ Rods-on-a-stand, with big colored balls that slide on to them. The rods take different numbers of colored balls – a first counting and color learning toy.

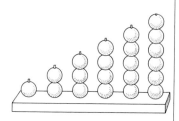

☐ Very simple nesting toys, such as a set of graduated cups.

☐ A version of the traditional hammer peg toy – wooden frame with holes through which pegs are banged with a mallet. Then the frame is turned over and they are banged back again.

☐ Simple take-apart toys, such as wooden vehicles with interchangeable top parts which can be lifted off a hole and peg attachment, or with interchangeable peg "men" fitting into holes in the body. Molded plastic "people" sold with a variety of vehicles and equipment, into which they fit, are even more versatile, and the "people" can populate later games.

## Playthings suitable for toddlers and pre-school children . . .

The bewildering variety of toys on the market together with claims to special educational advantages makes choosing good toys hard.

The more a toy is played with the better its value. As a fun-guide, you can work out play value, by dividing purchase price by minutes of play. You may find that expensive equipment such as a climbing frame, that is played with over years, and small cheap toys, that are played with intensively over the first days of their novelty, both work out better than the medium priced toys – such as construction sets. One such "educational" set only received two hours' play in total over a year. Those two hours cost over $7 per hour. . . .

*Choosing toys* While every child should sometimes have a particular toy just because it fulfils a heart's desire, many such yearnings will be inspired by misleading advertising. If possible, have the package opened before you buy. Does the toy work? Does it do what the child expects? Will he be able to use it or does it need more space than you have available, more help from you than you are prepared to give, or weather you cannot expect at this season? Consider whether the toys will stand up to your particular child's play-of-the-moment. A plastic plane used as a missile can turn into a lethal weapon when it breaks. A "talking" doll will not "talk" for long if all dolls in your house have frequent baths!

Don't refuse to buy "more of the same." If a child likes dolls his or her idea of enough will not be the same as yours.

If you want to buy something he has never had before, choose something that particularly suits a time in his daily life when he is often bored, such as a sitting-down toy for the early morning if he is bored in his crib.

Try not to buy toys that are too delicate/expensive/noisy for him to use as he pleases. If you are going to say "shh" or "careful" every time he uses that drum or doll's house, don't buy them. If you buy a toy with many pieces which are easily mislaid, check the availability of spares and if possible buy some extras; a marble run that will only take its own marbles can be useless in a week if they all get lost.

Provided they look nice, children don't care if toys are second-hand or home-made. Buying from garage sales or ads in your local paper may mean you can afford more and better toys for him. Many toys are ludicrously over-priced. Lift ideas ruthlessly from toyshops and catalogues and provide the same play value for much less money by making things yourself (see Presents).

## Playthings to save up for, or make

These comparatively large and expensive items are not, of course, *necessary* to your child. But each will give him hours of fun over many years. In terms of value for money they will be worth every penny....

*A wading pool* Buy the biggest you can afford. The inflatable type is safest as there are no sharp sides to fall against.

*SAFETY NOTE* – stay close by. Empty between sessions.

*Splasher pool* You might save money in the end by buying a "splasher pool" (10ft/3m in diameter, 2ft 6in/75cm deep) instead of a wading pool. It will last for years, your children can learn to swim in it and because it is above ground you can safely leave it full all summer without fear of them falling in.

*SAFETY NOTE* Go in with toddlers, provide water wings for older non-swimmers and stay close.

*A home-made "wallow"* Take the biggest plastic sheet you have got, spread it on the lawn and roll the edges up around garden stakes or whatever you have. Fill from the hose and you have a large expanse of water only about 1in (2.5cm) deep. It will leak away but not before the child has had a lot of fun. Provide ping-pong balls and paper boats to float on it.

*SAFETY NOTE* It will be slippery, so make sure there is nothing he can bang his head on when he falls.

*Climbing frame* A climbing frame will cost a lot of money but will repay it over and over again. Don't try to make one yourself unless you are an experienced carpenter. The child's safety for years to come depends on its stability. A freelance carpenter might make you one to fit your particular yard (perhaps even incorporating a well placed tree) for less than a shop will charge you. Choose between tubular metal and wood. Metal lasts longer but is cold, slippery when wet, and does not easily allow you to make your own accessories.

Wood will outlast your family if you periodically check that all joints are still tight and perhaps add a coat of wood-preservative every couple of years. Buy the biggest frame you can get. Choose a position that gets all the sun there is and is in full view of the house: you may want to keep an eye on it.

*SAFETY NOTE* Put your frame on grass if you can. Falls are rare, but more likely to be serious on concrete or paving.

*Extras* Your small child will be safer just climbing at first. Later you can buy a slide to fit.

*Platforms* You can make your own: measure across one of the bays of the frame; buy a rectangle of wood one inch bigger than the space. Sandpaper and paint it with wood-preservative. Mark on its underside exactly where it crosses the bars, and screw on stout clips that will fit the bars tightly. It can now be clipped securely in place, and is easily removed when the frame is wanted for climbing.

*Swing* A rope about 1½in (3.5cm) in diameter can be tied to the top of the frame for climbing. A big knot at the bottom makes a simple swing. Turn it into a monkey swing by cutting, or getting cut, a circle of timber about 1in (2.5cm) thick and 15in (40cm) across. Drill a hole in the center, thread the rope through and knot the end. You can suspend a small car tire for standing or swinging on, but if you leave it out it will fill with water which is surprisingly difficult to get out.

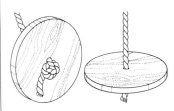

*Cover* A cover (an old double sheet will do) right over the frame makes a fantastic house or tent.

*Gym set* A rope ladder, trapeze bar and swinging rings can be bought as a set, complete with ropes fitted with clips at either end, so they are interchangeable and easy to hang, indoors or out.

*Balancing planks* Make these exciting extensions to the frame. Buy 8in × 1in (20cm × 2.5cm) planks 6 to 8ft (2 to 2.5m) long. Sandpaper them and paint with wood-preservative, and screw a pair of clips to the underside of one end to clip safely to the climbing frame bars.

On a low bar a small child can balance up the gentle slopes. On a higher bar you can make an exciting angle for older children.

### Playhouses

A proper playhouse made of wood and designed to live permanently in the yard will cost as much as a garden shed. A plastic or cotton "playhouse" cover that slips over a collapsible metal frame is a better and cheaper buy, but check that the material is fire resistant.

A small tent makes a good house out of doors. A wigwam is more adaptable, since it is self-supporting and can be put up anywhere, including the living room! If space and money are no problem, wooden fold-away houses designed to serve as houses, shops and puppet theaters, suit a wide age range. A competent handy-person could copy one of these designs easily. The structure is no more than a a series of hard-board panels hinged together, with refinements like doors, windows and counters added. You could make a simpler version by cutting windows, etc. in an old-fashioned screen. Even easier is a "clothes horse" house, made from the kind of clothes horse that opens into three wings. Cover each wing by stapling material around the top and bottom bars, and across the top if wanted.

If you buy a new stove, refrigerator or freezer, make a house from the box it comes in. It will not last forever but will give enormous pleasure until it collapses. If you like handiwork you could transform one of these boxes into something a bit more permanent. Seal the whole thing with sizing and then with paint, and strengthen all edges and folds with insulating tape. Use simulated brick wallpaper, stick-on flowers, etc. to decorate it. Treated like this your house should stand up to months of use.

### Making blocks

Blocks are irreplaceable. He must have them, and he must have plenty. Choose a big plain set sold by a good toy suppliers in their own kit bag rather than a cheap small colored set. Try to buy enough all at once. If you add more later their measurements may have been changed so the child cannot learn, for example, that one big one takes up the same space as two medium or four small.

To make your own: Decide on your basic "module." A 2in (5cm) cube is about right. Buy 2in × 2in (5cm × 5cm) wood – each block will need only one saw cut. Cut a few "doubles" of 4in × 2in × 2in (10cm × 5cm × 5cm) and a few "halves" 1in × 2in × 2in (2.5cm × 5cm × 5cm). You may like to add some flat pieces too, cut from ½in (1.3cm) thick wood and measuring 4in × 2in (10cm × 5cm) or 2in × 2in (5cm × 5cm). Sandpaper each block so that it is safe for sucking, and paint or varnish (with non-toxic material) so they can be washed. It is easiest to spread them all on newspaper and spray the lot with aerosol varnish. Don't do the underside until the tops are dry. Provide a container which comfortably holds the whole lot – a drawstring bag or a plastic laundry basket will do.

### Making a sandbox

If you have a yard, a sandbox is a worthwhile investment. It should be at least 4ft × 4ft (1.2m × 1.2m) with seats in the corners. It can be wood or molded plastic.

You can save money by making a wooden one. Buy four lengths of wood each measuring 4ft × 9in × 1in (1.2m × 23cm × 2.5cm). Screw them together at each corner. Screw a further piece of wood across the two front corners to give added rigidity and make "seats."

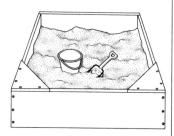

Use washed or silver sand, not ordinary builder's sand which stains everything orange. Provide a cover to keep out animals, leaves and so on. A sheet of hardboard

will do, or a sheet of heavy plastic folded over the corners of the sandbox as if wrapping a package, and stapled so that it can be slipped on and off. Use something (perhaps a bucket) in the center to act as a "pie funnel" so that water runs off the cover.

If you install your sandbox on concrete or pavement it will drain adequately. On dirt, you will need to put a plastic sheet down first, studded with little drainage holes. Choose a sunny place close to your own yard activities.

Provide buckets and spades, a rake, a sieve, a big plastic spoon or flour shovel, and a variety of plastic containers. Provide somewhere to store the toys so the child can get a clear start at the sand.

*SAFETY NOTE:* Teach the child never to throw sand and don't let two or more toddlers play in the sandbox on their own. Sand in the eyes can be dangerously scratchy.

### Playing and long distance travel

Every form of transportation has its problems with young children, but cars are the worst as well as the most usual. Adapt these ideas if you are going by train or plane.

*Safety comes first* Babies should have their own car-safety seats. *Comfort is vital* Define shares of the back seat with rolled blankets or pillows between children; these double as head rests for sleeping and prevent physical fights, if not quarrels. Keep clothes comfortable. Tee-shirts and stretch trousers are better than fiddly belts and tight sweaters. Give each child a large plant tray as a play-table and don't forget his "cuddly."

*A surprise bag* Although it may seem extravagant, a "surprise bag" full of small cheap treasures collected over previous weeks makes all the difference. The collection can be used in various ways to suit different ages. You might collect:
- ☐ A balloon to blow up and let down with a squeal.

- ☐ A tiny notebook and crayon.
- ☐ A small car, doll or animal.
- ☐ Plasticine or playdough.
- ☐ A bubble blowing kit – bubbles stream beautifully from a partly opened car window.
- ☐ A new book or comic book.
- ☐ A puzzle or coloring book.
- ☐ A kaleidoscope to hold to the window or a telescope for looking out of it.
- ☐ Carefully chosen snacks – not chocolate!

*Using the bag* Give a very small child a package whenever his boredom drives you to screaming point. Build older children's packages into a game to last the whole journey. Tell him he can have one at each of the following place names, write out the names for him and make him compare the letters on town signs and say when a package is due. Or set a number of miles apart for each package and make him consult the odometer or milestone. Say he can have a package each time he sees a school bus full of boys or a car with out of state license plates or six horses in a field. . . .

*More toys specially for cars* The side windows are an excellent surface for drawing on with felt-tip pens. A new set and a damp sponge will pass minutes. Stick-on peel-off plastic shapes sold to make "scenes" on a background will stick on the window too. Pocket puzzles of the kind that let the child compete against his own record are a good idea: "pin ball" lets you set challenges like "try and score 500 with three balls." Many children (of both sexes) travel happily if allowed to "shoot" passing motorists out of the window. Perhaps this sure-fire game shocks you, but if not, include a toy gun in the surprise bag.

*Games* Car games depend on family tradition and your patience. Try the "silence" game. Hand a watch with a second-hand to an older child, a kitchen timer to a younger one. Challenge him to keep silent for a whole minute. He enjoys watching time pass, you get at least 20 seconds peace and it sometimes ends in sleep. Elaborations include timing breath holding or nursery rhyme-chanting.

*Using a tape recorder* If you have a portable cassette recorder or car tape-deck, record a tape specially for the child in advance. You could include stories read by each or both of you, favorite songs off a record, idiotic jokes and riddles. . . . You may find that a tape like this stays in demand long after the journey is over.

*Even if you have no yard, you can teach your child about the living world,*
*by bringing outdoors indoors and displaying it for her benefit . . .*

**Plants** You can buy many kinds of children's "propagator," ready supplied with suitable seeds.
*Mustard and cress* will grow on any piece of absorbent paper or material, if it is kept damp. The child could sow someone's name for a birthday. Or eat his own harvest.

*Mung beans* are quick and easy to grow. After the first two days the child can see daily progress, and eat the shoots a week later . . . .
*A bean or pea,* put between the sides of a jam jar and a lining of damp blotting paper, grows fast too. No crop, but fun to watch the roots going down, the shoots up.

**Creatures** Leaving "real pets" aside, the child can get a lot of interest without giving you much work through:
*A snailery* Collect snails off the plant they are eating and make a note of it; they may eat nothing else around. Keep in a shallow plastic tray with food-leaves, stones, other greenery.

*A wormery* You can buy these, but a small aquarium or large pyrex dish filled with earth will do. Use fine wire mesh for a lid. If the worms stay invisible water the soil lightly and they will surface.

**Ant farm** It is best to buy special containers (from school equipment suppliers or pet shops) as it is difficult to make an ant-proof one yourself. If you manage to get a colony established it is fascinating to watch and the child will enjoy feeding them.
*Tadpoles* Collect frog spawn and water. Put into a large container and add rocks, gravel and pond weeds. Top up with pond water if possible, rain water if not.

Once they are swimming free feed them tiny quantities of fish food meant for baby fish. Raw meat leads to stinking water and dead tadpoles. When they have become frogs, return them to their pond.

*Whether you have a yard or not, your child will benefit, especially during*
*the winter months, from having somewhere to climb and swing indoors . . .*

*Climbing set* Failing a climbing frame you can make your own climbing set. You need at least two (more if you have space) sturdy wooden boxes big enough for the child to get right inside. Orange crates are the easiest to find. Be careful to remove all nails, and to flatten down any sharp pieces of metal binding before using.

Now buy a board, about 6ft (2m) long by 8in (20cm) wide and at least 1in (2.5cm) thick. Sandpaper it carefully, and paint it and your boxes with long-lasting, non-toxic paint in a bright color.

The child will use this collection separately and together, for years. The boxes will be hidden in, climbed on, jumped off, put together for a train and on top of each other for a ship's bridge. The board will be walked along on the floor, put across the boxes for a bridge, jumped off and balanced along. With one end on a box it is a slide; with the middle over a box it is a see-saw.

If you cannot store such a set, it is still worth making just the board. A pile of magazines at each end makes it a bridge and balancing bar, one end propped on a chair makes a slide. When the child is not using it himself he will run cars down it or sit dolls on it.
*Hooks in the ceiling* You may already have one of these from his baby bouncer. If so, add another about 15in (38cm) away and you have tremendous potential for years to come. A gymnastic set consisting of rope ladder, trapeze bar and swinging rings is the best bet to use with them. The quick-change clip-ropes make the various items quick and easy to hang. An ordinary rope about 1½in (4cm) in diameter can have a permanent loop made to slip over the hook at the top, and a big knot for sitting on at the bottom. It can even have a monkey-swing seat (see p.541) for a change. Elastic cord left over from his baby bouncer or bought (for luggage racks) from a car-accessory shop will give him

quite a new experience. Holding on to this he can jump, and seem to defy gravity.

If the floor beneath your hooks is stone or tile, you may be happier if you provide the child with a soft landing. A sheet of 1in (2.5cm) thick foam rubber will do a great deal to protect him and can be neatly rolled away in an elastic band for storage. Such a gym mat will also encourage lots of physical adventures on its own, like learning to turn head over heels and to stand on his head.

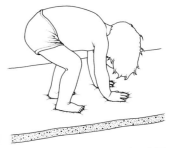

# Pre-school Presents

*Collections of things can make presents which are cheap, original, geared to your child's particular tastes and infinitely more fun than most "bought" toys. Even if your child already owns some of the separate items, she will enjoy using them together with others as part of the collection. Make the objects in the collection as elaborate or as simple as you please.*

## Play cooking

A sophisticated version of mud pies helps the child to find out what happens when she mixes this and that, and is good practice in measuring and using utensils.

Collect many small plastic containers – and lids. Scrub off labels (scouring pads remove print from the plastic).

Fill pots with flour, sugar, cereal, chocolate vermicelli, with as much variety of texture and color as you can manage.

Collect small plastic spoons, measuring scoops, miniatures of salt, jam and so on.

Provide a plastic mixing bowl. Add extras like pie tins, a toy food mixer, or egg whisk.

Buy a plastic tray about 18in × 12in × 3in (45cm × 30cm × 7.5cm). Assemble and present everything in it. Washing up is part of the game!

## Store

The stock for a shop will delight any child of this age. It can be simple, or as ingenious as you like.

Refill the jars of a toy "candy shop" with real sweets, such as chocolate drops or jelly beans.

To make a general store fill containers as for play cooking. Stick-on labels make it seem more real.

Dolls' house cakes make a baker's shop. Or bake tiny loaves from flour and water dough.

Make fruits for a greengrocer's department with marzipan and food coloring.

For a grander present, buy scales, a cash register and play money. A box covered with sticky-backed plastic holds everything and becomes the counter when emptied and turned upside down.

## Post office

Your own set, using real stationery, can be cheaper as well as better than a ready-made one.

Collect trading stamps, play money, paper clips, sticky labels. Use bank slips for official looking forms.

A date stamp, or inkpad and stamp set add a final touch of grandeur.

## Play dough

Make dough from equal parts plain flour and salt, enough water for pastry.

Color, using food coloring in the water or powder paint with the flour. Pack in matching lidded pots – ½ pint (285ml) ice cream pots are perfect. Stick on colored labels to match the contents.

Add pastry-making "extras." Pack in a box, with a plastic tablecloth. Keep in the refrigerator.

## Montage

Give a special collection for cutting, sticking and making pictures and patterns. The basics: different colored drawing paper, a glue pen, round-ended real scissors. The extras: colored tissue and foil, lacy doilies, stiff card, sticky papers, shiny and matt. The trimmings: pipe cleaners, sticky stars or labels, paper streamers, small balls of wool, scrapbook pictures.

## Finger-paints

Mix small quantities of non-toxic wallpaper paste, made up to cheese-sauce consistency, with dry powder paint.

Choose bright and subtle shades, black and white too. Put in plastic jars with close-fitting lids or in screw-top jars covered with sticky-backed plastic (so the glass will not splinter free if it breaks).

Leave a strip clear to see the color. Keep in the refrigerator.

Add a square of white formica covered board, plastic mirror or glossy linoleum to paint on, a comb, plastic fork or cookie cutters to vary the patterns she makes.

Painting sets can give your child new ideas. Even if used with ordinary poster paints and brushes, he will enjoy some of these.

**Folded paintings**
Buy big sheets of drawing paper. Crease each one down the middle.

Provide an eye dropper, plastic spoon, drinking straw. Help him to drop paint on one half,

then fold for a mirror-image "print."

**Drippy paintings**
With same tools as for folded paintings, the child drops paint on thin paper and tips it to make patterns.

**Air paintings**
The child drops paint on shiny card and disperses it by blowing through a wide plastic tube

or uses a "squeeze bottle" to apply it. Or (more exciting) he can apply thin paint from a plant sprayer.

**Print painting**
Letter printing sets are too awkward at this age. Buy ink pad sets with animal stamps, or make your own set. Saw $\frac{1}{2}$in (1.3cm) softwood cubes. Chip away all of the surface except the shape to be printed, which stands proud of surface.

Or glue shapes to the block: curtain rings, matchsticks, string squiggles or balsa wood chips. For the pads, line pots or cans (such as bandaid boxes) with $\frac{1}{4}$in (0.6cm) sorbo rubber. Soak each in a different brilliant color of washable ink. These pads can also be used with potato cuts.

Other prints can be taken from any textured object:
□ A sponge, dipped in paint and pressed on the paper.

□ A paint roller, tied to make stripes or with chunks cut out to make a line with holes in it.

**Negative paintings**
The child puts an interesting shape on his paper, paints over paper and shape and then removes the shape which appears as white amid the color.

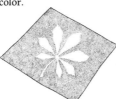

Lacy doilies, paper dolls or leaves (stuck with a dab of glue to remain steady for painting) all make lovely patterns.

**Making things**
Pre-school children long to make things, but are not ready for most commercial "kits." You can prepare one to fit his interest and abilities along the lines of the ideas given here.

**Woodwork**

If you cut out the basic shapes of boats, doll's house furniture, etc. from softwood (balsa is easiest) and present them with dowelling strips, sandpaper, glue, scraps of material for cushions, etc. the child can finish and decorate them himself.

**Dressing up**
Cut masks, crowns etc. out of stiff cardboard.

Make holes for eyes and give with paint or sticky paper, and elastic for the child to complete. He can even adapt the shapes with scissors.

**Sewing doll's clothes**
Make basic dresses with elasticized necks so that they fit a wide variety of dolls.

Present with a collection of pretty buttons, fringe, lace, ribbons. The child can then make them as elaborate as he likes with little sewing.

**Soft toys**
The boring part for the child is making the basic shape. Sew this for him and give with a bag of foam crumbs for stuffing, buttons for eyes, bits of fur fabric, etc. for him to finish.

Felt needs no hemming and can be glued. You can even cut felt shapes ready to stick on.

**Styrafoam**
Buy styrafoam balls and blocks and present them with orange sticks, dowelling, glue, paint, wool and material scraps.

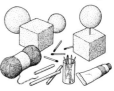

He can assemble "people" by pushing the sticks into the styrafoam, and then give them hair and clothes. The balls can also be painted gold or silver for Christmas decorations.

**Box modeling**
For extra glamorous junk modeling, collect sturdy, pretty boxes (chocolate and shoe boxes are best), matchboxes, cardboard tubes.

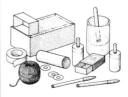

Add a good paper glue, felt-tip pens, paints, stickers and stamp hinges, paper fasteners and ring reinforcements. Colored string, sticky tape and a small stapler are useful too. Give him a good start by presenting a model with the kit.

# Index

joints, dislocation 482
jumpy babies 96–7

# L

labor 20–33
language
  newborn 106–7; settled
    172–5; older 252–8;
    toddlers 288, 369–73; pre-
    school 295–6, 432–43
  babbling 173–4, 253
  baby talk 441–2
  and behavior 388, 435–6,
    443, 454, 460–1
  cooing 108, 173, 253
  first words 255–6, 370
  and ideas 351–2, 436–9, 446
  jargoning 255
  late talkers 439–40
  questions 434–5
  sentences and grammar
    371–2
  stuttering and stammering
    440–1
  talking to babies 107,
    172–5, 252–8
  words for bodily functions
    320, 431
  worries about adult 415
laryngitis 500
laxatives 524
  and bowel training 317
  and constipation 218, 498
lazy eye see EYES
learning see EARLY LEARNING;
  PLAYING AND
  UNDERSTANDING
''let down'' reflex see BREAST-
  FEEDING
lice 524
light babies see BIRTH -
  WEIGHT
listening see HEARING AND
  LISTENING
looking see SEEING AND
  LOOKING
love see ATTACHMENT
lumbar puncture 526
lying 460–1
Lyme disease 478

# M

masturbation 212, 426
measles 521
  immunization against 519
meconium see STOOLS
medicines 475, 525
  homeopathic 517
meningitis 526
milk see BOTTLE-FEEDING;
  BREAST-FEEDING; DIET
minerals see VITAMINS AND
  MINERALS
miserable babies 95–6
mixed feeding see
  FEEDING/EATING
molars see TEETH AND
  TEETHING
Montgomery's tubercles see
  BREAST-FEEDING
Moro response 101, 105
mosquito bites see BITES AND
  STINGS
motion sickness 534
mouth
  exploring with 158–9
  in newborn 41
mouth-to-mouth
  resuscitation 474
mouth ulcers 526
moving (relocating) 412
multi-vitamins see VITAMINS
  AND MINERALS
mumps 522
  immunization against 519
music 360, 453
myopia see EYES

# N

nails see FINGERNAILS
nannies see CARETAKERS
naps see SLEEPING AND
  WAKING
navel, in newborn 41
neonatal jaundice 523
neonatal urticaria 39
nettle rash 496
night feedings see SLEEPING
  AND WAKING

nightlights 15, 311
nightmares
  older 214–15; toddlers
    311–12, 329, 330; pre-
    school 398–9
night terrors 398–9
night waking see SLEEPING
  AND WAKING
nipples see BREAST-FEEDING;
  FEEDING EQUIPMENT
nits 524
nose
  foreign body in 485
  in newborn 42
nosebleeds 527
nurseries, day 276–7
nursery classes 383, 414
nursery schools 374, 378–82,
  417–23
nursing bras see BREAST-
  FEEDING
nursing sick children 527–9

# O

obesity
  babies 124–5; toddlers
    303–4; pre-school 394
oral contraceptives see BIRTH
  CONTROL PILLS
otitis see EARS
overfeeding see BREAST-
  FEEDING; BOTTLE-FEEDING;
  OBESITY
oxytocin see BREAST-FEEDING

# P

pacifiers 91, 150–1, 209
  and exploring by mouth
    159
  and sleep 309, 311
  and tooth decay 327
papular urticaria 496
parasites
  from animals 476
  lice 524
  worms 536

## A Note About the Author

Penelope Leach was educated at Cambridge University and the London School of Economics, where she received her Ph.D. in psychology (for a study of the effects of different kinds of upbringing and discipline on personality development) and lectured on psychology and child development. For four years she ran a study, under the auspices of Britain's Medical Research Council, of the effects of babies on their parents. She has researched juvenile crime, pre-school education, and many aspects of adolescence. She is a Fellow of the British Psychological Society, works in various capacities for parents' organizations, and is the author of *The First Six Months, Your Growing Child,* and *Babyhood.* She is married to an energy specialist, and they have two children. "Your Baby & Child with Penelope Leach" is broadcast on Lifetime Television.